DATE DUE

HUMAN DEVELOPMENT AND LEARNING
SECOND EDITION

HUMAN DEVELOPMENT AND LEARNING
SECOND EDITION

Hugh V. Perkins

Institute for Child Study
University of Maryland

Wadsworth Publishing Company, Inc.
Belmont, California

To Cynthia

Education and Psychology Editor: Dick Greenberg
Copy Editor: Grace Holloway
Designer: Russ Leong

ISBN 0–534–00345–1
L. C. Cat. Card No. 73–89878
Printed in the United States of America

1 2 3 4 5 6 7 8 9 10—78 77 76 75 74

Preface to the Second Edition

This second edition extends the thrust of the first edition—synthesizing in one volume the diverse but interrelated principles of human growth, development, adjustment, and learning. Often psychologists, teachers, and researchers study the development of the child separately from the child as learner, but this book views human development and learning simultaneously. While the book is designed as a text in teacher education courses, it also speaks to a wider audience of parents, counselors, community workers, and others who seek deeper understanding of human development and learning.

The new material in this edition reflects breakthroughs in theory and research findings in the behavioral sciences. In this edition the need to understand ourselves along with others has been emphasized, since both kinds of understanding contribute vitally to helping children and youth realize full potential. The material on development in this text now encompasses the total life span. A new chapter on infancy and early childhood describes some important gains in our knowledge of these early stages of development. Another new chapter describes the needs of adults for further development and self-fulfillment. This edition gives greater attention to children from various social class, ethnic, racial, and religious groups and how they adjust to larger American culture. Special attention is given to the needs and education of the disadvantaged. A major feature of this edition is the increased discussion of how scientific principles facilitate development and learning in school settings. As before, numerous case studies help clarify concepts and principles.

The format and organization of the first edition have been retained. While sections about developmental stages have been enlarged and strengthened, the emphasis on processes of development and learning—physical, affectional, cultural, peer group, self-developmental, and self-adjustive—remains a unique and continuing feature.

The text is organized into five parts. Part One focuses on the need to understand ourselves if we are to understand others and discusses principles of motivation. Procedures for collecting and analyzing student case records are described and illustrated.

Part Two presents in separate chapters each process that shapes development and learning. The chapters identify the concepts of human growth and development necessary for understanding human beings. New material has been added on the effects of drugs on behavior and adjustment, on sex role and sex stereotyping, on self-concepts, and on the socialization of Appalachian, Black, Italian-American, Jewish, Mexican-American, and American-Indian children.

Part Three examines the emerging individual in relation to developmental tasks he encounters at successive stages of maturity. Material on Piaget's theory of intellectual and cognitive development has been expanded in a new chapter on infancy and early childhood and in the chapters on middle and late childhood and adolescence. A new chapter about adulthood continues the focus on development throughout the life span.

Part Four focuses on learning and education. A largely new chapter on the nature and theories of learning presents the principles of conditioning and cognitive field learning, specifically describing how applications of these principles facilitate classroom learning. The chapter on readiness for learning includes a discussion of Jensen's hypothesis of social class and racial differences in IQ heritability. Subsequent chapters describe and illustrate the major outcomes of learning—cognitive, psychomotor, and affective.

Part Five takes a further look at how the teacher can apply his knowledge of human behavior to facilitate student development and learning—how to organize the classroom for learning, select instructional methods and patterns of organization, and evaluate development and learning. Included in this section are new materials on the culturally disadvantaged, discipline and classroom management, Head Start, open education, career education, mastery learning, and accountability.

The book concludes with a model of effective teaching that reiterates the need for a teacher to know, understand, and accept himself as well as his students.

I wish to pay tribute to the memory of Dr. Daniel A. Prescott, first director of the Institute for Child Study, University of Maryland, who introduced me to the study of children and youth and contributed in important ways to my own development and learning. I am indebted also to Dr. H. Gerthon Morgan, Director of the Institute for Child Study, and to my colleagues, the staff of the Institute, for the contributions each has made to my knowledge of human development and learning. Though their influence has been considerable, the responsibility for the specific content of the book is, of course, my own.

Finally, I wish to express my appreciation to Thomas L. Good of the University of Missouri, Frank Costin of the University of Illinois, John J. Hays of Indiana University, Pennsylvania, Maxwell G. Bilsky, Madison College, and Laura L. Dittmann of the University of Maryland for their many helpful suggestions in their critiques of the manuscript. Special thanks are extended to the editors of Wadsworth, Dick Greenberg and Grace Holloway, for their contributions in the development and editing of this second edition.

I gratefully acknowledge the permission granted by the following persons to reproduce material from unpublished case records: Sharon P. Burcham, Virginia Creed, Dorothy H. Denick, Mollie Joyce, Orva Leta Ledbetter, Madelaine Mershon, Lucile S. Mooney, Dorothy V. Nichols, Evelyn P.

Preface to the Second Edition

Reed, Hannah Sessions, Herbert R. Stolz, Martha E. Thompson, Sue Vinkovich, and L. Idella Watts.

The poem "Outwitted," by Edwin Markham, is quoted by permission of Vergil Markham.

Hugh V. Perkins

Contents

Contents

Contents

Contents

Part One

Understanding Human Behavior

Understanding Ourselves and Others

1

If you wish to know yourself, observe how others act. If you wish to understand others, look into your own heart.

Friedrich Schiller

Every human being wants to understand the events and people in his world so that he can respond to them appropriately and meaningfully. However, because each person is unique and because the forces that shape his behavior are complex, people are often the most difficult part of our world to understand. This book describes the forces that contribute to an individual's growth, development, learning, and becoming. With an understanding of these forces, parents, educators, and other concerned adults can better understand human behavior and thus can make decisions that will enhance the development and learning of the child and the adolescent.

In no area is the need for understanding human behavior greater than in the education of children and youth. Much of the disenchantment of students with school and much of the failure of some to progress academically can be traced to a lack of understanding of students' needs, motives, and concerns by parents and educators.

The idea that teachers must better understand their students as both persons and learners has gained considerable support in recent years. The once popular stereotype that a teacher does little more than assign work, listen to recitations, and give and grade a few tests is no longer viable, nor can it be assumed that anyone who knows his subject can teach it. If telling or showing were all there is to education, we would not need teachers; we would simply give students books and equipment and let them learn by themselves. However, specific subject matter and skills are important only to the degree that they contribute to the primary goal of education, the realization of an individual's potential in all aspects of his development. The role of the teacher is to help him realize it.

The teacher is most successful in this role when he offers resources and understanding in a helping relationship with each student, for, as we shall find when we discuss the nature and processes of learning in later chapters, *teaching is primarily a matter of relating to people.* Thus, the effectiveness of the teacher's helping relationship with his students depends in great measure upon his knowledge of the general characteristics of growth and development at his students' maturity level. It also depends upon his understanding each student as an individual.

Understanding others is facilitated by a better understanding of oneself. When one is aware of his own motives, beliefs, and values, he can view others and their behavior more objectively. Accepting these traits, both positive and negative, increases self-understanding, for they are what makes him unique.

How can the teacher increase his understanding of himself and others, and how can he gain the general knowledge of human behavior and development that is so important in understanding a particular student? The following descriptions by two young teachers of themselves and their initial teaching experiences provide partial answers to the first part of the question. Materials in later chapters provide help with the second part.

Barbara Taylor

I've wanted to be an elementary school teacher ever since I was in the first grade. I had a happy childhood growing up in a fairly conservative, small town in the Midwest, where my father owned a successful hardware store. I enjoyed school, worked hard, and got good grades. I remember especially well Miss Arnold, my third grade teacher, who held us to high standards in schoolwork but seemed very much interested in each of us as persons. She really believed that each of us could do well in school if we tried hard enough. In high school I was active in school and church activities, taught a Sunday School class, had a few close girl friends, and dated occasionally but had no steady boy friends.

After graduating from high school, I entered the state university, where I enrolled in a program preparing elementary school teachers. University life broadened my horizons. I met and became friends with people from backgrounds and cultures quite different from my own. I enjoyed most of my courses and did well in them. I gained a lot from my student teaching experience with Mrs. Berry and her first grade class in a public school near the university. She allowed me to try out my own ideas. The children responded well and seemed to progress during the time I worked with them. After graduation I accepted a job teaching an ungraded, primary level group in an inner-city elementary school with a majority of black and Spanish-speaking children. I knew this might be a difficult year, but it seemed preferable to teaching in a small rural school in another part of the state. Besides, here I am near Frank, my steady since last spring, who is attending law school.

September 5.   I wondered whether I would ever get through this first day of school! I arrived at school before eight so I would be fully prepared for the day when the children arrived shortly be-

fore nine. The children came in noisily, smiled, and ducked their heads in response to my greeting. I felt a bit nervous but determined as I stood before 28 black and seven white faces staring expectantly up at me. After preliminary matters were taken care of, I planned to start the day off by getting acquainted. I told them a little about myself and then asked for volunteers who would stand and tell us something they did this past summer. No hands were raised. The children looked at one another and then began giggling, squirming, and whispering. I coaxed, but only two girls were able to complete their accounts before bedlam broke out in the classroom. A boy named Robert seemed to take the lead in getting the other boys to misbehave. In desperation I passed out paper and asked them to draw a picture of something they did this summer. Most of the children proceeded with their pictures, but Robert and those around him began to scribble and waste paper. None of the other things I tried today went very well except the games and singing during the afternoon. I am discouraged and exhausted, and I dread tomorrow.

October 8.　　During the past month most of the children have settled down and are beginning to work, but Robert still bugs me. He is nine and big for his age. His father does not live at home, his mother works late, and after school he is usually out on the streets and unsupervised. I have tried every way I know to get through to him but with little success. He sneers, swears, once called me a "honky bitch," and seems to be waiting for me to send him out of the room or otherwise punish him. What is so exasperating is that he really isn't dumb. He just won't complete written assignments. During class discussion he frequently blurts out the answer or whispers it to one of his classmates. I am really baffled over why he disrupts the class and wastes his time and abilities.

October 15.　　This week marked a turning point in my relationship with Robert. On Monday Mr. Davis, our principal, asked me to select three students from my room to send to another classroom so that the enrollment in primary level classes would be equal. I chose two boys and a girl whose academic levels would enable them to fit into the other class. Robert gave me a quizzical look when his name was not called. Later that day he said to me, "This is the first time in this school someone didn't try to get rid of me."

I smiled and said, "Robert, you are a member of this class. We want you to stay."

On Thursday I learned that Robert's mother had been taken to the hospital suddenly. Because Robert and his younger brother had no one to care for them until an aunt arrived from out of state, I offered to take Robert and his brother home for the weekend. With my friend Frank we took the boys to the zoo, saw a movie, and went on a picnic. Robert is a changed boy. I actually find myself liking him—something I never expected to be able to do before last week.

During the first month of school, Barbara discovered a kindred spirit in Mary Jenkins, whose classroom was down the hall. Mary had been teaching for five years and had a knack for relating easily to young and old and to people from a different social background. After school Barbara often talked of her trouble in dealing with Robert. Mary listened with interest and empathy, and her occasional question or comment enabled Barbara to examine her own motives, perceptions, and attitudes.

Barbara came to see that the rigidity of some of her thinking about curriculum and children's behavior handicapped her in working with and trying to help a minority group child like Robert. She noted, for example, that some children made greater progress in reading and language skills in informal experiences of dictating and reading stories of their experiences than they did using basal readers and workbooks. She also recognized that children with ability may not progress academically in school if they see no purpose and relevance in what they are learning or if they feel alienated from the school and the larger culture. Finally, Barbara came to see that nearly every child can be reached, although reaching some requires of the teacher a great deal of patience, understanding, and forbearance. She learned, however, that helping a child become happier and more productive can be one of the teacher's greatest satisfactions.

During this first year of teaching, Barbara's self-knowledge and positive feelings about herself grew. In trying to understand Robert, Barbara learned that she was not nearly as tolerant of other life styles and personality types as she had thought. She noted with satisfaction that she was strongly motivated toward teaching and that she did have skills and resources for adapting to and working through difficult problems. Finally, she felt good about herself. She discovered that she really was not the cold, unresponsive person some of her classmates had thought, that she could relate to people, especially children, with deep concern and compassion.

Mike Anderson

I grew up in an upper-middle-class suburb of a large city on the East Coast. My father is a corporation lawyer, and my mother is active in school and community affairs. I had a fairly normal childhood and adolescence. My parents had rather definite expectations of me, my older brother, and my younger sister, but Mom and Dad seemed to be so busy with their own affairs that they seldom spent much time with us. In high school I made good grades without much effort. My main interest, however, was sports, and during my last two years I got letters in both basketball and baseball. I was always rather shy around girls and preferred to be with boys who also had a strong interest in sports.

It seemed natural to enter after graduation the same Ivy League college my father had attended. He urged me to prepare for a career in law or business, but I had no clear idea of what I wanted to do. During my freshman year I went out briefly for sports but did not find the satisfaction in sports here that I had in high school. I drifted through my first two years of college, still with no clear idea of where I was going. I met a lot of different people, experimented with drugs, and found myself participating in protest marches and demonstrations. My parents became very upset when they learned that I had been arrested and jailed briefly after a confrontation with the police. For more than a year my parents and I had become increasingly estranged. When I went home, they criticized my long hair, my clothes, my friends, and my tirades against the establishment. Increasingly, my parents and I have not had much to say to each other.

I suppose I might have continued to drift and remain mixed up in my own feelings if it had not been for Kathie, whom I met near the end of my sophomore year. Kathie was working in a neighborhood youth center, and I was there as a volunteer worker three nights a week. She had real feeling and empathy for those kids, and I learned a great deal from her. We saw a lot of each other away from the center and fell very much in love. For the first time I began thinking seriously about marriage—but how would I earn a living? As a result of my work at the center, I decided that I really wanted to work with kids. I liked English and had always done well in it, so that becoming a high school English teacher seemed like a possibility. At the beginning of my junior year, I switched to teacher education.

Now I have just finished student teaching, and graduation is in two weeks. My student teaching experience was a mixed bag, so I am still somewhat uncertain about my future. The negative part was the conservatism of the high school and of Mr. Simpson, the regular teacher under whom I taught. The rules of the school affecting teachers as well as those for students were absolutely stifling. Mr. Simpson wanted me to follow the eleventh grade curriculm guide to the letter. He was visibly annoyed with me when he returned to the classroom and found that I had taught a lesson on the literature of folk music.

One of the most satisfying aspects of my student teaching experience was my relationships with students. One student I became quite attached to is Pete, who seemed to have a lot of the hangups that I had had in high school. I discovered that he has a consuming interest in short stories. He wrote two as class assignments that I thought were so good I urged him to submit them to the school literary magazine. I had many long conversations with Pete after school in a local coffee house. He seemed to have many of the same problems in dealing with authority figures and in finding out who he is that I have experienced. He had repeatedly been suspended for infractions of school rules, and I wondered whether he might be on drugs. During the two months' contact with Pete, he seemed to me to become more relaxed and to feel more positively about himself and about life in general. It was a shock to learn last week of his withdrawal from school after being busted in a drug raid. I thought my talks with him were helping, but his problems are obviously more serious than I realized.

Now that I am about to graduate, where to? Jobs are really scarce. I need a job so that Kathie and I can get married, but I would be miserable teaching in a school like this last one. There must be someplace where I can fit in!

This account shows that Mike's understanding and acceptance of himself have grown. Throughout high school and his first two years of college, he had no clear idea of who he was or where he was going. His relationship with Kathie, however, brought a sense of self-identity and of direction and purpose, as well as being evidence of growth in heterosexual relationships. His struggles with the problem of dealing with authority figures is a continuing one, but even in this he is making some progress. Finally, students responded warmly to Mike, and, because of his encouragement, some became freer in expressing themselves in creative writing. These experiences did much to increase Mike's self-esteem.

Barbara's and Mike's accounts reveal some of the ways in which people who want to work with children and youth can go about the task of understanding both themselves and those they wish to help. The accounts also indicate two reasons that teachers are often unable to help students like Robert and Pete: (1) The teachers are not sufficiently aware of their own motivations and attitudes, so they are likely to be less sensitive to and less understanding of others' behavior. Thus, for example, teachers are sometimes unable to interpret certain acts as signals of a need for help, or they may not be aware that they need more information before they can diagnose a behavior problem correctly. (2) Teachers who lack this understanding of self and others are likely to take inappropriate action or no action at all.

The Nature of Human Nature

Before one can learn to understand himself and others, he must have a conception of what human beings are like. And, he will soon discover, there is no single generally accepted concept of human nature but instead a great many different conceptions. Some compare the newborn infant to a blank slate; his growth and development, his learning and becoming, is a life story recorded on this slate. Human development, in this view of human nature, is a process of unfolding. Freud's dynamic psychology, however, presents quite a different conception of human nature: Man is a composite of sometimes conflicting internal and external forces, which he seeks to reconcile as he adjusts to his environment. Still others conceive of the human being as a series of relatively discrete age or maturity levels, with specific norms and behavior associated with each age or maturity level.

Any conception of human nature we choose will determine what we expect from children and the approaches we employ in helping them to develop and to learn. In this book we view the human being as a dynamic, evolving complex of three interrelated and interacting forces: *organism,* *culture,* and *self.* Only the most fundamental aspects of this conception of human nature are discussed here, since subsequent chapters examine each of these forces in greater detail. Although we will consider these three aspects separately, they do not, of course, function separately; *the human being functions and responds as a whole.*

The Human Being as a Physical Organism

Man as a physical being has a particular place in the biological ordering of animal life. As a member of the Chordata phylum he shares with other animals of that group a highly complex tissue and organ differentiation and highly developed bilateral symmetry. As a vertebrate he possesses a jointed backbone. As a mammal he provides special care of his young before birth, maintains a high level of activity, maintains stability and flexibility of the skeleton during growth, and utilizes food efficiently. His differentiated brain, large in relation to body size, marks him as a primate. Finally, his advanced brain and nervous system enable him to develop qualities of intelligence, flexibility, and sociableness to a much higher degree than other animal forms can. These characteristics identify man as the only member of the classification *Homo sapiens.*

Man is highly sensitive to changes in his environment. This sensitivity is manifested in tissue irritability, which increases when the organism is stimulated by internal or external changes. The body seems to require and to seek stimulation of various kinds in order to reduce its irritability and disequilibrium. A child can hardly be expected to sit still in school for any extended period, since maintaining arms, legs, and trunk in the same position creates tensions which soon become painful. On the other hand, the child whose arms and legs ache from the fatigue of hard play seeks a change of stimulation that is provided in reading, resting, listening to a story, listening to music, or working on a puzzle. This tendency to seek stimulation seems to relate to another human quality, curiosity—whether it is the urge to wade in a creek or to travel into space.

The organism, then, seeks change—imbalance and discontentment; at the same time, it seeks stability—balance and contentment. This condition is a fundamental paradox of organic life. The child seeks contentment and rest after an exciting game or movie. Too much contentment or inactivity produces discontentment, which activates a drive for new or added stimulation. Stimulation, change, and some imbalance are needed if the individual is to reach out and to achieve progressive steps in development. As a new development level is reached, adjustment processes serve to return the individual to equilibrium; but soon further stimulation and change signal a movement toward further development. The alternating contentments and discontentments are the reflection of the alternating tides of human activity: development and adjustment. In short, the human being can gain satisfaction only if he has previously experienced dissatisfaction.

Tissue irritability and the tendencies to seek stimulation and at the same time to achieve a degree of internal stability are physical characteristics that have far-reaching implications for human development and learning. Knowledge of these processes provides us with a partial understanding of the physical basis for *motivation*—why people behave as they do.

The Human Being as a Social Organism

Man's existence has no meaning apart from his interactions and relationships with other men. The human infant is more helpless and matures more slowly than any other animal. The young child is dependent on other persons for love, care, and nurturance. In maturing, the child not only grows and develops physically in response to his genetic endowment; he also comes to behave and to develop like those human beings with whom he lives and associates. These significant other persons serve as models for the child's patterning of his own feeling, thinking, and behaving.

Man has a lifelong need to belong—to be loved, wanted, and accepted. When these needs are in large measure satisfied, the individual has a secure underpinning that enables him to move toward development and greater independence. Maturing is accompanied by growth away from dependency on others toward greater independence. A maturing adolescent becomes less dependent when his parents refrain from telling him what he should wear, whom he should have as friends, and what time he should be home. In this sense he is less dependent on his family, but he will never be completely independent of the need for people who will care for and love him. Every human being needs the love and support of family and friends, especially in times of stress.

The Human Being as a Psychological Organism

Man's large, well-differentiated brain provides him with the possibilities for developing an intelligence far exceeding that of any other living thing. Man is extremely complex at all levels, physical and psychological, but the complexity is most startling and impressive on the psychological level. Man's brain and nervous system have frequently been compared to electronic computers; and, indeed, computer models have been developed for the study of the functioning of the brain and nervous system. When we learn that in a matter of seconds high-speed computers compute answers to complex mathematical problems which would take a human mathematician months or years to compute, we may be tempted to conclude that a large computer is more complex than the human brain. Admittedly, the computer can transmit information more rapidly and does have a larger memory-storage capacity, but it lacks the capacities for growth, self-repair, and reproduction that are characteristic of man. Therefore, in spite of the computer's superiority over man in the computation of difficult problems, it remains a very crude mechanism when compared with the human brain.

The brain and the nervous system, consisting of roughly 10 billion neurons, form a fantastically complicated system. As many as 10,000 neurons connect with a single nerve cell, and the branches of one neuron may connect with thousands of others. The total number of nerve circuits that could be activated in the human nervous system is vastly greater than the number of particles in the universe. Even the smallest elements of the nervous system are so complex that something like an eighth-order differential equation would be needed to describe one neuron's behavior.

The marvelous coordination of this system makes possible an almost limitless number and variety of human responses. Because of this potentiality for variation of response, the human organism is better equipped than other organisms to adjust both to its present environment and to the unknown and unpredictable environment of the future. That is, man is endowed with flexibility—which enables him, more than any other living thing, not only to survive but also to develop and flourish in a wide variety of environments.

The complex psychological qualities of human behavior are most dramatically revealed in the human being's potentialities for symbolizing the meanings of his experience through the use of language. With this symbolization of meanings, the possibilities for variability of response are enormously increased. Symbols can be stored in memory, they can be used to communicate meanings to others, and they can be manipulated so as to capture higher-level meanings through the cognitive processes of thinking, reasoning, and problem solving.

Basic Assumptions Underlying the Study of Human Behavior

The preceding discussion makes it abundantly clear that the task of understanding human behavior is awesome. However, it is certainly not hopeless. Understanding human behavior is not something we need to leave completely to the "head shrinkers." In fact, for more than 30 years teachers participating in in-service child study programs have revealed in their teaching increased scientific knowledge of children's behavior and development, warmer and more accepting attitudes toward children, and changes in their own classroom behavior toward use of more positive ways of handling children.[1]

[1] Richard M. Brandt and Hugh V. Perkins, "Research Evaluating a Child Study Program," *Monographs of the Society for Research in Child Development*, 21 (1956), 62.

Each of us has both the need and the ability to better understand ourselves and those with whom we live and work. Before we begin this dual task, let us examine some basic assumptions underlying our study of human behavior.[2]

1. Every human being is inherently valuable.   The assumption that every human being has worth and dignity is of first importance. Without it, there is real danger that skills in human understanding might be used to exploit or even to destroy human beings. In benign but exploitive ways, for example, some advertisers use a shrewd understanding of human behavior to entice the unwary consumer into purchasing products that he does not need and cannot use, and that may even be harmful. Thus, this assumption of human worth cannot be naively taken for granted. It must be continuously reiterated in word and deed by those who seek to understand and to help others.

Accepting every human being as valuable is a very high ideal that most persons find difficult to live up to. We find it especially difficult to accept those whom we do not like or trust or those who reject us. Barbara Taylor tried to accept all her students, but the negative feelings that Robert expressed toward her made it difficult for Barbara to accept him. This assumption of human worth, however, does not deny us the right to choose our friends, to dislike some people, or to hold some persons in higher esteem than others. It simply means that we grant everyone the right to and the opportunity for human realization.

Our task in living up to this assumption is to strive genuinely and consciously to be more accepting in all our human associations. Mike Anderson responded to this task by striving to accept the high school principal and Mr. Simpson as persons. Although he strongly disapproved of Pete's turning to drugs, Mike accepted Pete as a person who was striving to overcome his problems. This distinction between the person and his behavior is a crucial one. The person has value and is worthy of acceptance because of his potentialities for fulfillment as a human being. A person's sometimes irrational behavior is merely a symptom and a reaction to the stresses involved in growing up. If this were not so, how would we explain the many unlovely adolescents who grow up into fine human beings?

2. Every individual is unique.   The assumption that each person is unique is well documented by scientific evidence. Geneticists have demonstrated each individual's unique genetic inheritance; in addition, each individual has developed his own pattern of thinking and behaving as a result of his own unique experiences. However, although this assumption of the uniqueness of each individual is generally accepted intellectually, a great many people still act as if everyone were pretty much alike. Parents expect their child to be just as athletic, just as popular, or just as smart as the kid

---

[2] These assumptions are adapted from Daniel A. Prescott, *The Child in the Educative Process* (New York: McGraw-Hill Book Co., 1957), pp. 26–50. Used by permission.

down the street. Teachers seem to expect all students to be much the same in intelligence, readiness, and motivation for learning and are unable to deal with the student who deviates from the norm—in either direction. Our commitment to mass education has made it difficult for teachers to be truly responsive to human differences or to treat students as unique individuals.

Failure to realize the uniqueness of the human individual frequently leads to grave errors in interpretations of behavior. A person may or may not play golf just because others of his group play; he may play because he is challenged by the demands and pleasures of the game itself. Thus, we cannot automatically assume that two persons with the same behavioral symptoms behave that way for the same reason. Mike Anderson thought he saw in Pete's behavior some of his own earlier alienation and lack of self-identity. As Mike learned more about him he found that Pete's problems were quite different from those he himself had experienced. Because each person is different, we must seek to understand each individual by analyzing what we know about him (from case records or other data), using those principles of human behavior, development, and learning which apply to his situation.

If we are to facilitate the optimum development and learning of each person, we must respond to him as a unique individual. Too often, uniqueness and creativity are crushed by demands for conformity. School programs which encourage growth, openness, and expression of individuality must be developed and expanded if our needs for imaginative, divergent, and creative individuals are to be met.

3. *Behavior is caused. The causes are multiple, complex, and interrelated.* This assumption, an application of the principle of causal relationships to the behavioral and social sciences, has strong scientific support in the physical and biological sciences from which it is taken. Just as there is a cause-effect relationship between heating a liquid and producing a gas, so there is a causal relationship between the stimuli people receive and their responses to those stimuli. However, the task of the behavioral scientist in achieving an understanding of human behavior is more difficult than the natural scientist's search for an understanding of physical phenomena because the causes of human behavior are infinitely more complex. Psychological variables, such as motivation, perception, and cognition, are not open to direct observation and hence are difficult to measure with precision. Our knowledge of another person's motivations, perceptions, and cognitions, therefore, is dependent upon the inferences we make from our observations of his behavior—a process which involves subjective error, thus requiring continuous verification and correction.

Once the individual fully accepts and acts upon the assumption that behavior is caused, life will never be quite the same. A teacher who accepts and acts on this premise will see the student and his behavior quite differently. At first, when Robert spoke disrespectfully to Barbara Taylor she was inclined to mete out automatic, swift punishment. This way of handling Robert made his behavior worse; he remained in a sullen, angry mood all day and refused to do any work. As Barbara came to accept the principle that behavior has many complex and interrelated causes, her hypotheses concerning the causes of Robert's behavior became sharper and more accurate, for they were based upon what she actually knew about him. She found, for example, that when Robert came into the room in the morning in a surly mood, he seemed to have had a fight with his mother at home or with peers on the playground. On these days she gave him extra time to settle down before encouraging him to begin his work and was quick to respond to a request for help.

Finally, this assumption enables us to approach with optimism the task of understanding human behavior. As we strive to understand another person, we cannot help gaining increased respect and awe for the order, intricate design, flexibility, and marvelous complexity of the human being which this process reveals.

4. The human being is an indivisible unity. He can be understood only as each part is related to the other parts and to the total person.   The tendency to divide the human being into parts so that he can be better understood has a long history. The ancient Greeks thought of man as possessing several faculties: a rational faculty, a spiritual faculty, and an appetite faculty. More recently, it has been popular to view man as a body-mind dualism or as the product of a heredity-environment dualism. It is often useful and even necessary to examine separate aspects of the human being. Misinterpretations arise, however, if we think of the two parts of these dualisms as separate entities rather than as parts of an interrelated, integrated whole person. Kelly emphasizes this concept of the whole person when he says, "If we want to produce whole men, we will have to abandon our efforts to train or educate them in parts. . . . When a man meets a problem he meets it with all he has—foot, ear, fist, purpose, value."[3]

5. The scientific method provides the most valid basis for interpreting human behavior.   Because man is complex and his behavior often seems mysterious, over a period of several thousand years sorcery, the workings of supernatural beings, mythology, folklore, qualities and characteristics presumably within man himself, and empirical observations have all been used to explain the behavior of human beings.

The scientific method—that is, the search for knowledge through the testing of alternative explanations or solutions by empirical, objective evidence—has been the keystone of research in the physical and biological sciences since the Renaissance. Only during the present century, however, has the scientific method of experimentation been applied to social and behavioral phenomena.

The application of the scientific method to problems of understanding human behavior and development requires that one develop both a self-discipline in collecting and analyzing objective data and a healthy

---

[3] Earl C. Kelley, *Education for What Is Real* (New York: Harper & Row, 1947), p. 65.

skepticism toward the conclusions which emerge from these analyses. Valid interpretations of behavior depend on (1) a broad range of objective data and (2) initial assumptions that are tentative and subject to modification in the light of additional evidence.

The use of the scientific method is no less important in the human sphere than it has been in the physical world, where scientists on many frontiers are probing the universe. As in other sciences, the validity of the scientific method in the study of human behavior rests upon the *accurate predictions* the scientific method generates in predicting future events. Validation of the hypothesis that schoolwork is unrelated to Robert's major interests enables us to predict Robert's behavior in school next term—given no appreciable change in Robert or the school situation.

What It Means to Understand

Understanding implies more than knowledge and comprehension of what has been observed. In seeking to understand another person, one looks for pertinent data in present and past situations; he also searches for relationships between seemingly isolated facts. More specifically, if one is to acquire something more than a superficial understanding of another person, he must have the following information and skills:

1. Functional knowledge of human development and learning principles. A knowledge of human development and learning principles is functional when it enables the teacher or observer to see the significance in behavioral data and to offer fertile, tentative hypotheses for explaining the behavior. Historians, poets, storytellers, philosophers, and religious leaders have for centuries recorded and interpreted men's motives and actions. However, not until the latter part of the nineteenth century, with the work of Wilhelm Wundt in Germany, did there emerge a separate scientific discipline focusing on the study of behavior—the science of psychology. During the twentieth century a great many other disciplines have contributed to increased human understanding. These disciplines (*anatomy, physiology, endocrinology, genetics, pediatrics, morphology, anthropology, sociology, child* and *adolescent psychology, educational psychology, learning theory, psychology of personality, psychoanalysis and psychiatry*) are referred to collectively as *the behavioral sciences.*

An interdisciplinary field of knowledge called *human development* brings together and synthesizes data and principles of human behavior from the several behavioral sciences, and organizes these principles into a coherent body of knowledge about human behavior, development, learning, and adjustment.

2. Valid and complete information about the person whom one seeks to understand. When one lacks information that is needed to answer a question or to solve a problem, he is likely to look for a good book on the subject. Books, lectures, and talks with experts frequently provide useful clues and insights into a youngster's behavior, but these resources alone will seldom explain why a particular Robert Harris does not complete his classwork. Something more than general principles and descriptions are needed if we are to understand and help Robert.

In addition to the principles of human development and learning which can be gained from books and lectures, one needs a factual descriptive picture (a case record) of the child in various situations. What is he like? What does he do and say? How does he seem to feel about his various experiences? How do others respond to him? In short, one must discover and record a broad range of data about the child, his environment, and the significant people in his life.

3. Acceptance and application of the scientific method.   The steps and general method which scientists use in seeking a cure for cancer or in studying the behavior of high energy particles are also those used by behavioral scientists. Since the steps of the scientific method are in general the same as those used in the solution of any problem, they can be understood and applied by the teacher, parent, and nonscientist as well as by the scientist. The scientific method consists of a series of steps or operations which begin with identification, clarification, and statement of the problem. This is followed by data gathering, suggesting hypotheses, hypothesis testing, drawing conclusions, and applying the new concept or principle.

Acceptance and use of the scientific method as a tool in the study of human behavior necessarily implies a commitment to specific values and standards, especially with respect to the kinds of evidence which the scientist accepts as valid and the steps and safeguards which he uses in drawing inferences or conclusions from evidence. The specific steps which implement these values and standards have been established by convention and custom. In the next chapter, we will consider their application to the study of human behavior.

Summary

Human understanding is a goal of people everywhere, but in no area is the need for human understanding greater than in the education of children and youth. The efforts of parents, teachers, and others to help children and youth realize their full potentialities are greatly influenced by two kinds of understanding, understanding oneself and understanding others. Self-acceptance facilitates self-understanding. When one is aware of his own motives, biases, beliefs, and values, he can understand others better because he is able to view other people and their behavior more objectively.

One's understanding of people is based upon his conception of what human beings are like. The human being is a dynamic, evolving complex of three principal interrelated and interacting processes: physical, social, and psychological. Physically, man is a highly organized and dynamic energy system. His greater differentiation and complexity mark him as distinct from all other living things. Tissue irritability produced by physiological imbalance is characteristic of the human organism at its many levels of activity. At times this tissue irritability signals a need for stimulation; at other times it signals a need for release from stimulation. These alternating contentments and discontentments are a reflection of the alternating tides of human activity: development and adjustment. Man becomes a social being through interaction and association with other human beings. Through these relationships he seeks to fulfill his need to belong—to be loved, wanted, and accepted. Man's uniqueness is demonstrated most clearly in his psychological development—his highly differentiated brain and nervous system, which promote flexibility, adaptability, and symbolization of meaning.

Our study of the human being is guided by the following assumptions:

1. *Every human being is inherently valuable.*

2. *Every individual is unique.*

3. *Behavior is caused. The causes are multiple, complex, and interrelated.*

4. *The individual is an indivisible unity.*

5. *The scientific method provides the most valid basis for interpreting human behavior.*

Finally, if we are to increase our understanding of another person, we must acquire (1) a knowledge of the important concepts and principles which assist in explaining behavior, (2) as much information as possible about the person whom we wish to understand, and (3) the ability to use the steps and safeguards that the scientific method offers for checking and rechecking our facts, interpretations, and conclusions.

Study Questions

1. Imagine yourself in Barbara Taylor's situation trying to help Robert —except that her opportunity to keep him in her class, take him home, and get through to him has never presented itself to you. Devise a plan of action aimed at effecting positive change in Robert's attitudes and behavior.

2. Examine your present feelings toward the students you expect to teach. Do you expect to direct their learning, or should they be free to develop and learn in their own ways?

3.   Describe the teacher you most admire. What are the qualities that were most important in making this person a successful teacher?

4.   Can one understand others if he does not first understand himself? Discuss.

5.   Does acceptance of another person necessarily imply approval of his behavior? Discuss.

Suggested Readings

Good, Thomas L., and Jere Brophy. *Looking in Classrooms.* New York: Harper & Row, 1972. Taking as its central theme the need for teachers to become more aware of their classroom behavior, this book surveys educational research and gives detailed advice about effective teaching. Among the subjects covered are teachers' attitudes and expectations, the teacher as a behavioral model, classroom organization and management, ability grouping, cooperative learning and peer tutoring, and strategies for framing questions and conducting discussions. Strategies for motivating and controlling students are discussed, and a variety of observation schedules and rating scales are included.

Gregory, Thomas B. *Encounters with Teaching: A Microteaching Manual.* Englewood Cliffs, N. J.: Prentice-Hall, 1972. A manual that describes how microteaching can be used to help one gain insight into and understanding of his role as a teacher. The manual presents a series of tasks or activities through which a beginning teacher can have an early encounter with himself as a teacher. They are also designed to provide the beginning teacher with a set of process and affective skills that will enable him to adapt to the new curricula he will be using in his teaching.

Rogers, Carl R. *On Becoming a Person.* Boston: Houghton Mifflin Co., 1961. Chapter 1 presents a brief autobiographical sketch followed by a candid and lucid analysis of the experiences that contributed to the development of Rogers' own personal beliefs and values. The reader is afforded considerable insight into Rogers' development as a person, psychotherapist, and teacher.

Smith, B. Othanel. *Teachers for the Real World.* Washington, D. C.: American Association of Colleges for Teacher Education, 1969. A report of the Task Force of the National Institute for Advanced Study in Teaching Disadvantaged Youth which outlines a program of teacher education designed to prepare teachers for all children, regardless of their cultural backgrounds or social origins. The report suggests that the central task of teacher education is using what is known about teaching and learning to develop instructional materials and training teachers to use them. A plan for helping teachers identify their own attitudes and personality problems is described in Chapter 7.

Films

Incident on Wilson Street, 16 mm, sound, black and white. Part 1, 24 min.; Part 2, 27 min. Syracuse, N. Y.: Film Library, Syracuse University, 1455 E. Colvin St. This film shows individual and group reactions to an in-school "incident" in which a young student suddenly strikes out at her teacher. A 10-year-old child is revealed as a person frustrated by her surroundings, a father is enraged by what he believes classmates are doing to his child, and a young teacher feels she cannot keep the child in her class. Classmates express a surprising amount of concern and understanding. As it reveals the responses of teachers, pupils, and parent, *Incident on Wilson Street* points to the need for human understanding by all persons concerned.

The Scientific Study of
Human Behavior

2

We now know, from the scientific point of view, that we cannot neglect little children and expect them to grow into fine adults.

Howard A. Lane

Scientists in all disciplines use the same general method in their search for and application of knowledge. Essentially, this method involves a series of seven steps[1] toward the solution of a problem. (These steps are summarized in Table 2.1, p. 25.)

1. Location and definition of a problem. The first step in the solution of any problem is to recognize that a problem exists. Often, the existence of a problem is experienced as a perplexity, a felt need, or a recognized difficulty. The problem that requires a solution may be as mundane as getting a car started or deciding which brand of toothpaste is the best buy. On the other hand, the problem may be one of profound importance, such as the large-scale desalinization of sea water or a cure for cancer. One has located and defined his problem when he can state it in a way that clearly communicates what he wishes to find out.

Educators who seek to facilitate their pupils' development and learning face one general problem: to discover how and why children and youth behave and develop as they do. Since each individual is different, this general problem becomes further defined and limited to discovering the causes for the behavior of a specific student. Scotty's teacher has noticed that Scotty sometimes does not complete his art classwork. An example of this behavior is described in the teacher's case record entry for November 6:

---

[1] These steps parallel those in statements found in Bruce W. Tuckman, *Conducting Educational Research* (New York: Harcourt Brace Jovanovich, 1972), pp. 12–15. They also follow in general the steps of reflective thinking presented in John Dewey, *How We Think* (New York: D. C. Heath & Co., 1910), pp. 68–78.

> *In art class today Scotty sketched a fantastic but lovely imagi-*
> *native bird. He started to paint it with water colors and, when he*
> *was about half finished, brought it up to show me. I complimented*
> *him on his work, and he smiled and said, "I think it looks nice too.*
> *I'll go finish it."*
>
> *About five minutes later I noticed him sitting idly, his arm*
> *resting on the back of his seat, his head propped on his hand. I*
> *strolled back to his desk to see if there was any reason for the ap-*
> *parent change in attitude.*
>
> *He had made a small blot on the body of the bird and had de-*
> *cided the picture was ruined. I showed him how to remove the blot,*
> *but he seemed uninterested. Later, I saw the picture in the waste-*
> *basket.*

This recurring behavior pattern intrigues Scotty's teacher, so that in this instance the general problem is limited to the specific question "Why does Scotty not complete his artwork?"

2. Collection and organization of pertinent data.   After one has identi-fied and defined the problem, he surveys what is already known about it. This step is essentially one of gathering data on the problem being investi-gated.

In a study of human behavior, the educator's information about a particular child can be drawn from a variety of sources. The teacher who wants to find out why Scotty did not finish his picture would need to secure a great deal of data about Scotty, including those from the school records, from other persons at school and at home, and from his own direct observa-tions of Scotty in a variety of situations. (Further discussion of these sources of information appears on pp. 29–42.)

3. Formulation of hypotheses or tentative solutions to the problem. The preliminary survey of data in step 2 frequently points to one or more possible solutions to the problem. After the data have been collected, the step of formulating hypotheses begins in earnest. A hypothesis is simply a tentative statement about events or relationships which is provisionally accepted as valid for the purpose of reasoning, experiment, or investigation. The medical researcher hypothesizes about a particular drug or some other type of therapy which he suspects may prove effective in combating a dis-ease or which has already proved effective in tests with animals but has yet to be fully tested with human beings.

In the study of human behavior, hypotheses explaining why a person behaves as he does can be of three types: (1) hypotheses suggested by the particular circumstances under which the behavior occurred, (2) hypotheses suggested by other case record information on the person, and (3) hypothe-ses suggested by scientific concepts and principles of human development and learning. The following hypotheses were suggested by Scotty's teacher as tentative explanations for Scotty's failure to finish his picture of the bird. Other, equally plausible explanations for Scotty's behavior could be added to this list.

1. *Scotty is in competition with another student in the class. (Hence he does not want his work to appear in comparison.)*

2. *Scotty is ambivalent in his attitude toward art.*

3. *Scotty believes that art is sissyish and feminine.*

4. *Other children laugh at and make fun of Scotty's pictures.*

5. *Scotty expresses an interest in sports and games. (This he views as incompatible with an interest in art.)*

6. *Scotty expects high standards of performance from himself.*

7. *Scotty has aspirations inconsistent with his abilities.*

8. *His parents place high expectations on Scotty for achievement and proper deportment.*

9. *Scotty is competing with a sibling.*

10. *Scotty adjusts to unpleasant situations by withdrawing or giving up.*

11. *Scotty's parents believe that art is a waste of time.*

12. *Scotty talks about and identifies with his father and masculine interests.*

13. *Scotty is asserting that he is independent of adult authority. (He showed this by not finishing the picture that the teacher liked.)*

14. *Scotty has a warm, friendly, permissive relationship with the teacher. (He feared that his completed picture might not fulfill her expectations.)*

15. *Scotty lacks confidence in his own abilities.*

16. *Scotty has a short attention span.*

17. *Scotty's interest is in working with art materials but not in completing a project.*

18. *Scotty has a preference for realism rather than for things imaginary.*

19. *Scotty's family has not trained him to complete things that have been started.*

20. *Scotty gains emotional support by depending on others.*

4. Testing of the hypotheses. The researcher cannot know which of his hypotheses are valid until he tests them in the light of the data he has collected. His data therefore become the basis for his confirming or refuting each of the hypotheses he has advanced as tentative solutions to his problem. In an analysis of Scotty's failure to finish his picture, Scotty's teacher found that the evidence in her case record seemed to confirm four of her hypotheses:

13.   *Scotty is asserting that he is independent of adult authority.*

14.   *Scotty has a warm, friendly, permissive relationship with the teacher.*

18.   *Scotty has a preference for realism rather than for things imaginary.*

20.   *Scotty gains emotional support by depending on others.*

Hypothesis 9 (competing with a sibling) and hypothesis 19 (lack of training at home for taking responsibility) were clearly refuted.

5. Collection of additional data.   Sometimes the initial testing of hypotheses fails to confirm or to refute some of the hypotheses. In analyzing the case of Scotty, his teacher found that additional information would be needed before she could adequately test hypothesis 11 (attitude of parents that art is a waste of time) and hypothesis 12 (Scotty identifies with his father).

The collection of additional data permits new hypotheses to be tested and existing hypotheses to be rechecked or verified. This step of gathering additional data is similar to step 2, except that here the researcher's or educator's discrimination in the kinds of data needed has become sharper and more precise as a result of what he has learned in the preceding steps of making and testing hypotheses.

6. Summary of data and drawing of conclusions.   After all the hypotheses in a particular study have been tested and the various analyses have been completed, the data are summarized and conclusions are drawn. That is, in a brief statement or series of statements, the researcher reports the essence of what he has learned from the particular scientific problem-solving activity. In the study of human behavior, the conclusions or summary can take one of two forms: (1) validated explanations (hypotheses) of why the person behaved as he did in the specific situation chosen for analysis or (2) a series of tentative generalizations or conclusions about the person's state of physical health, growth, and energy; the qualities of his interpersonal relationships; his culture; the peer group and his relationships to it; his self-development and self-adjustment; his perceptions and goals, as revealed in the development tasks he is working on; and his concept of self.

Table 2–1.   Steps in the Scientific Method and Their Adaptation for Studying Human Behavior

Step	Scientific Method	Studying Human Behavior
1. Location and definition of a problem		General problem: How can I achieve a deeper understanding of human behavior and development? Specific problem: How can I gain a more complete understanding of this particular student? Why does this student behave this way?
2. a. Survey of what is already known about the problem—gathering data b. Organizing the data		Building an objective, descriptive, complete case record of information on a specific student, using the seven sources of information listed. (1) Identifying and listing recurring patterns *or* (2) Grouping data according to an organizing framework.
3. Formulation of hypotheses or tentative solutions to the problem		(1) Listing tentative multiple hypotheses which may explain a particular behavior *or* (2) Formulating tentative generalizations suggested by the data collected in each process area *or* (3) Making inferences about the child's self-concept.
4. Testing of the hypotheses		Testing the hypotheses, generalizations, or inferences by checking them against the evidence to determine whether case record data support or refute them.
5. Collection of additional data		Obtaining additional case record data, particularly in areas where information about this student is meager.
6. Summary of data and drawing of conclusions		Final analysis and summary of case record may be completed in relation to (1) Developmental tasks and adjustment problems *and/or* (2) Child's concept of self versus world's (e.g., teacher, parent) concept of child.
7. Formulation of new generalizations or principles and of a plan of action for applying what has been learned		Application of increased knowledge and understanding of this student and of human behavior in facilitating this and other students' development and learning. (1) In view of what I have learned about this student, what have I done to help him? (2) In view of my increased understanding of this student, what would I recommend for further helping this student to develop and to learn more effectively?

7. *Formulation of new generalizations or principles and of a plan of action for applying what has been learned.*   The last step in the scientific method of problem solving is the formulation of new generalizations or principles which make a further contribution to man's understanding of the problem being studied. Our ultimate goal in using the scientific method is to learn something that will enable us to do the job better than we could before; the products of scientific study and thinking (new principles, generalizations, inventions, and so on) not only constitute new knowledge but may also be used to improve human life. Principles and generalizations derived from the scientific study of human behavior, therefore, are used to devise a plan of action for facilitating the development and learning of a specific individual or group.

Often this step of applying what has been learned from scientific study begins as early as step 4, the testing of hypotheses. For example, when Scotty's teacher learns that his "asserting that he is independent of adult authority" is a valid hypothesis which explains in part why he does not finish his picture or at times follow the teacher's directions, she responds by reducing expectations and pressures to a minimum and giving him added responsibilities. As her analysis proceeds, the teacher finds in a home visit further evidence of Scotty's asserting independence in his performing household tasks and caring for younger children, tasks which a father might ordinarily do. Validation of the hypothesis that Scotty prefers realism to imaginary things guides the teacher in recommending to Scotty books on sports, first-person accounts of exploration and adventure, and biography.

Evaluation of each of the action steps taken by the teacher to help Scotty provides additional data which lead to a redefinition of the problem of understanding Scotty's behavior, suggestions for new hypotheses, the validation of some hypotheses and the discarding of others, new conclusions, new generalizations and principles, and new plans of action. Thus, the scientific method of problem solving does not end with the completion of these seven steps; problem solving is a never-ending process. New data being fed into the process at each step may change the initial problem or permit the formulation of a more complex problem. Hence, this never-ending cycle of investigation enables man continuously to extend his field of knowledge and understanding.

Selecting a Student for Study

We noted earlier that depth of understanding is best achieved through an intensive case study of one individual. The initial step in applying the scientific method to the study of human behavior is to select a student to study. Which student of a classroom of 30 or 40 should the in-service teacher or the student teacher choose to study? What guidelines should he follow in making a choice? Since the educator will be focusing on the dynamics of human behavior common to all persons at that maturity level, the selection of a student from the broad normal range of behavior and development would probably best satisfy the professional objectives of the study experience. The educator should select from that range a student in whom he is really interested, for then he is much more likely to become absorbed in finding out what makes the youngster tick and thus will find the task of collecting information less burdensome. Finally, since the teacher's success and satisfaction depend upon the amount and variety of information he can obtain about this student, he should select a fairly active student with whom he has frequent contacts.

The following are brief statements which teachers or observers wrote in explaining why they selected a particular student for study.

> *I'm not sure whether it's lack of inhibition, unpredictable sense of humor, or something more subtle which attracts me to Heidi.*

> *I chose [Pedro] because my observations, his records, his activities, and the responsibilities that he shares at home all point to greater potentialities in both mental and physical abilities than he usually displays in his classroom learning activities.*

> *My decision in choosing V. Jones, a 12-year-old seventh grader, is based on the conversation I had with her mother during the summer. She remarked, "I do hope you are her teacher. I believe you can make her happy. She is broken-hearted because she has to go to Edison. She wants to go to Lee, where all her little friends will be going."*

> *I have chosen Teena as my object for study because I was much attracted by her large brown eyes set in a small dark face.*

Frequently a teacher will want to choose a so-called problem student for his first case study. Understandably, the teacher wants especially to understand this kind of student so that he can help him to adjust and thus perhaps can alleviate some difficult classroom situations. Such a choice has, however, often proved unwise. First, studying a student who deviates considerably from the norm makes it more difficult for the teacher to understand the dynamics of normal behavior. Second, the causes of deviant behavior may be so imbedded in the student's past that the educator cannot gain the information necessary for understanding the case. An outcome of the teacher's growing understanding of human behavior is his increased skill in discriminating between normal but *disturbing* behavior (such as occasional poking, pushing, talking, or failing to follow directons) and deviant, *disturbed* behavior (such as chronic lying, fighting, stealing, or daydreaming). As the teacher learns to discriminate between these two types of behavior, he is able to make appropriate referrals to pupil personnel or psychological services. Early identification of these students needing such services makes it possible for them to receive specialized help sooner.

One final point: Neither the student nor anyone else except professional personnel involved in the study experience should be informed that the student is being studied. A person who knows he is being observed is unlikely to act spontaneously and naturally.

Gathering Information

Ethics of Information Gathering

From our discussion thus far, it is apparent that an educator's understanding of human behavior depends to a considerable degree upon the depth and amount of information about the student he is able to obtain. The numerous sources and broad scope of information about a student indicate clearly the need for a professional attitude and code of ethics for guiding educators and others in their study of human behavior. Consistent with our belief in the value of every human being is the need to protect the student and his family by keeping all information about them completely confidential. Safeguarding information which one obtains and uses in serving patients, clients, or students is a fundamental principle in the ethical codes of all professions that serve people.

The general ethical principle of safeguarding information about a student and protecting his identity has been translated by educators who study behavior into the following specific codes of conduct:

1. *One does not reveal the identity of the student or his family to anyone not involved in studying students. Giving the pupil a fictitious name in writing the case record helps to protect his identity.*

2. *The educator keeps the information he acquires about a child in strict confidence. He does not gossip about what he has learned, and he especially refrains from discussing his case study where he may be overheard by others.*

3. *Information about a student should be written in a hard bound stitched notebook. This case record should be safeguarded at all times.*

4. *The educator keeps his information as objective as possible. Differences in points of view should not alter his fundamental acceptance of the student as an individual.*

Seven Sources of Information

The educator begins his study of human behavior by collecting and writing up in a case record as much information as he can obtain about the particular student he has selected for study. Since interpretation and understanding of human behavior depend upon the validity and completeness of the information, the teacher should draw upon a variety of sources of information. Seven sources of information can be used in developing a case study record. Information from these seven sources enables the educator to view the student from different perspectives and in relation to different areas of his life; it also enables him to verify information obtained from different sources. In the following pages each of the seven sources will be discussed and illustrated by excerpts from the case of Scotty.

1. Direct observation and objective description. The first source of information, the teacher's own observation and description of the student, is immediately and continuously available to the teacher. Each situation that the teacher describes is called an *anecdote*. A case record contains a great many anecdotes about the child's behavior, his interactions with others, and the specific details of a wide variety of situations that the teacher has observed. Anecdotes may include descriptions of the child in class, in the hallway or the cafeteria or on the playground, after school in the shopping center, or in almost any other conceivable place.

At the beginning, teachers often wonder, "What shall I write about?" and "How shall I begin?" The absence of a set pattern permits teachers to begin their records in a variety of ways. Some begin by describing what they already know about the student. Others begin by watching a student and writing a description of the behavior and events which first brought him to their attention. Scotty's teacher began her record by writing a physical description of her student:

> *Scotty is a tall, slender boy, 13 years old. He is freckle-faced and brown-eyed and has two dimples when he smiles. His teeth are white and even. His clothes are clean, but his hands are usually dirty.*

As the teacher observes and records what he sees and hears day after day, he learns to select events that illuminate important characteristics of the student and events that present a new or different side of his life or his behavior. However, although the teacher cannot help being *selective*, he must always be *objective*. Some teachers find it difficult to refrain from including opinions, generalizations, and interpretations in their descriptions because they have habitually used generalized interpretative words in communicating ideas to others. Teachers become increasingly objective when they describe as completely as possible exactly what took place, what each person did or said, what the reactions of others were, what facial expressions and gestures were used, and any other details observed. The goal is to describe behavior and situation vividly, objectively, and completely, so that the people and the situation come alive to the person reading or listening to the anecdote.

Anecdotes that are not objective reflect the evaluations, interpretations, or generalizatons of the observer. The teacher's entry for October 5 is an example of an *evaluative anecdote:*

> *Scotty is reading, and reading well, on the fifth grade level. His arithmetic work is very good, and he is an average speller. He seems uninterested in social studies but is very interested in art, in which he does beautiful work.*

This anecdote could have been written more objectively if data on learning performance, test scores, and projects were included in place of the subjective evaluations. What reader or outside reading is he reading? What kinds of arithmetic problems can he solve? What contributions does he make in science and social studies?

The teacher's background description of Scotty is an example of an *interpretative description:*

> *Scotty is quiet-spoken and seems to have a sulky look on his face. He becomes glum and resentful when corrected, but if the correction is made with a smile, one is rewarded with a quick grin and a flash of dimples.*

Again, this statement would have been more objective if the teacher had included a specific description of Scotty's face (knitted brows, turned-down mouth, drooping jaw) in a specific situation. What did Scotty actually do that gave rise to the interpretation "sulky"? If specific details are included, they provide us with a far clearer, more precise picture than interpretations do.

An example of a *generalized description* has also been taken from the background statement:

> *His hair is nicely combed [evaluation] when he arrives at both morning and afternoon sessions [generalization], but as soon as it dries from the combing it receives, it hangs down in his eyes [generalization]. He tosses his head back frequently to try to clear his view, but the hair continues to hang in front of his eyes [generalization].*

The writer of this record could have avoided generalizations and achieved objectivity if she had described completely what occurred on each of several different occasions. If "hair hanging down in front of his eyes" is included in several anecdotes, we have what later will be called a recurring pattern.

Finally, we include an anecdote which is predominantly specific and objective:

> November 1.   *Scotty punched Dick today, and Dick told me about it. I hadn't seen Scotty do it, but Dick said, "Every time he goes by my desk he punches me." I called Scotty up to the desk and asked him about it.*
>
> *"Sure, I punched him," said Scotty. "Every time he goes by my desk he says, 'wise guy!' under his breath, so I just let him have it. If he stops calling me a wise guy I'll stop punching him, but he's not going to call me names and get away with it!"*
>
> *I looked at Dick. Dick said, "Yeah, I call him 'wise guy' because he thinks he is one. He acts like a big shot."*
>
> *Scotty said, "Who acts like a big shot? Me or you? What did I ever do to you?"*
>
> *Dick hung his head and mumbled, "Nothing, but I think you act like a big shot."*
>
> *Scotty looked at me and smiled. "See? I don't know why he calls me a wise guy and I don't think he knows either, but every time he says it I'm going to punch him."*
>
> *I talked to them both and then told them to return to their seats. As Dick sat down he looked at Scotty and said, "Wise guy!" Scotty punched him.*
>
> *Dick looked at me and I said, "You asked for it." He said no more.*

Although there is no one correct way of describing an incident, we can note several criteria which characterize good anecdotal recording:

1.   *The description begins with the date, time, and place and includes a statement or explanation of the background situation or setting in which the event occurred.*

2.   *The* action—*what happened, who did what or said what, and how it was done—is described as objectively and completely as possible.*

3.   Interactions *of the student with classmates and teacher are included in the description, together with* reactions *of each of these persons during each phase of the episode.*

4.   *Verbal interaction is reported as much as possible in* direct quotes. *With practice the observer will markedly increase his ability to recall the words and phrases used in conversations.*

5.   *Posture, facial expressions, gestures, and voice qualities are described without interpretation:* "His eyes flashed, he frowned, his body became rigid, and his fist was clenched" *instead of the interpretative* "He became angry."

6.   *The recording of the anecdote continues until all aspects, interactions, and reactions of the episode have been fully described, until the scene or activity shifts or terminates. The teacher avoids leaving the description up in the air like a continued magazine serial. Instead, he includes final or follow-up actions and conversations to give a sense of closure and completeness.*

2. School records.   A second source of information, school records contain a wide variety of data about the student's development and learning:

Family data: *parents' names and education, father's occupation, home address, number and ages of siblings.*

Health data: *records of physical examinations, disease, immunizations, physical defects, physical growth measurements, school attendance.*

Results of standardized tests: *intelligence, achievement in academic skill areas, aptitude and interest inventories.*

Records of academic progress: *school marks, promotions, reports of teacher-parent conferences, teacher evaluations.*

Teachers' evaluations of the child: *brief generalized evaluations or impressions of the child by teachers at successive grade levels; teacher ratings of the child's relationships with his peers, his interests, his hobbies, and his characteristic adjustment patterns.*

Written communications: *between the home and school.*

Data from the school records should be recorded verbatim in the case record book. No attempt should be made at this point to interpret these data. Interpretations of them may be made later, when they are shared with a psychologist, a guidance worker, or a professional group studying behavior. Material from Scotty's school cumulative record, copied by Scotty's teacher into her case record book, is reproduced in Figure 2–1.

3. Information from other people.   Facts and anecdotes about a student or his family are frequently obtainable from the student's teachers and friends and acquaintances and from the school's principal and guidance counselor. As much as possible, the teacher should try to secure facts as well as opinions. If another teacher reports, "Scotty was sneaky and deceitful," the teacher studying Scotty might ask, "Can you describe what Scotty did in one or two specific situations last year in which he revealed this type of behavior?" Thus, one can record many specific, objective facts describing Scotty's behavior in these situations, as well as other people's feelings and opinions about Scotty. However, any material based upon opinion, hearsay, or general impressions should be verified with other data.

Miss Sawyer, Scotty's teacher, learned things about Scotty from another teacher and also from a neighbor, as the following entries reveal.

December 11.   *I was talking to Scotty's fifth grade teacher today, and she commented on how Scotty has grown in the past two years. Among the other remarks she made in a desultory conversation was this one: "You know, don't you, that Mr. Martin isn't Scotty's real father?"*

I blinked and said, "No, how do you know?" I received the following story.

During Scotty's year in the fifth grade, we had been asked to check vital information preparatory to the adopting of a new type of cumulative record card. All children were asked to bring in their birth certificates. Scotty's didn't appear and the teacher kept after him about it. His excuse was that his mother wouldn't let him have it. Finally, the teacher sent a note home and Scotty's mother brought it to school herself.

She explained to the teacher that Scotty didn't know Mr. Martin wasn't his father and she never wanted him to find out.

The secret was so well guarded that the fact is not on the record card.

February 5.   *I got a bit of information from a neighbor over the weekend about Mr. Martin, Scotty's stepfather.*

Said the neighbor, "I know that guy. He and I were in high school together and a nicer fellow you'd never meet. He was one of our football stars and was very popular and well liked. What's he call himself Martin for? That's not his name. He's 'Lefty' Logan."

I tried to take this knowledge unblinkingly and assured the neighbor I didn't know the reason for the change in name, but when he mentioned "Logan" it certainly rang a bell!

About two years ago there was a lurid divorce court trial described in the paper with "Lefty" as the defendant and the grounds as adultery. The then Mrs. Logan accused her husband of living with another woman and having a son by her. The divorce was granted.

The above information, furnished by another teacher and a person outside the school, provides clues helpful in understanding Scotty's home situation. It emphasizes, too, the extreme care which those who study

Figure 2–1.   A Cumulative Record

Name: Walter Scott Martin   Three previous addresses
Date of birth: July 23, 1950   are shown on the
Place of birth: Orion, Michigan   cumulative record card.
                                   The fourth and latest
                                   is: 316 Beechwood
                                   Avenue.

Father's name: Edward   Mother's name: Helen
Father's education:12th grade h.s. Mother's education: 11th grade h.s.
Father's occupation: cab driver,   Mother's occupation: housewife
                Yellow Cab Co.

Siblings: Frank, age 7 (attending 2nd grade in this school)
          Eddie, age 17 months

The following standardized test scores have been recorded:

ACHIEVEMENT TESTS

Date	Grade	Test	CA	Total Grade Equiv.	Expected Grade Equiv.
5-6-57	1	Metropolitan	6-10	1.2	1.8
5-8-59	3	Metropolitan	7-10	2.5	3.8
10-2-59	3	Iowa Test of Basic Skills	8-2	2.7	3.2
4-10-62	5	Stanford Achievement Total	11-9	4.8(composite)	5.7

Reading Vocab.	4.5
Reading Compr.	4.2
Arith Reasoning	5.6
Arith Fund.	5.8
English Mechanics	4.9
English Spelling	4.0

INTELLIGENCE TESTS

Date	Grade	Test	CA	Verbal	Nonverbal	Total IQ
10-2-60	4	Lorge Thorndike	10-2	81	92	86
4-5-62	5	Calif. Test of Mental Mat.	11-9	87	96	92

HEALTH RECORD

Height and Weight

Date	Age	Grade	Height	Weight
11-56	6-4	1	47	48
5-57	6-10	1	48½	50
11-57	7-4	2	49½	55
5-58	7-10	2	51	60
11-58	8-4	3	52¼	65
5-59	8-10	3	53	69½
11-59	9-4	3 (Re-tained)	55¼	75
5-60	9-10	3	57	82
10-60	10-3	4	58	82
4-61	10-9	4	59¼	88½
10-61	11-3	5	60	100
5-62	11-10	5	61½	101½
10-62	12-3	6	62	107

TEACHERS' COMMENTS

First Grade (1956-57)

Scotty is a large boy, active, and well coordinated. Progress in reading was very slow. Was still in a pre-primer at the end of the year. Showed interest in our social studies and science projects.

F. Schultz

Second Grade (1957-58)

Scotty is still very slow in his reading. Likes science. Mother very cooperative. Enjoys games and people. Takes active part in group discussions.

C. Brown

Third Grade (1958-59)

No interest, a poor student, needs motivation. Retained.

T. Bowles

Third Grade (1959-60)

Scotty is a large, active boy. Became a leader among boys on playground. Seems to dislike reading and spelling.

H. Fairfax

Fourth Grade (1960-61)

Not willing to work hard enough to achieve. Mother attended spring conference. She is interested in Scotty's progress, but said she is unable to help him at home.

E. Abel

Fifth Grade (1961-62)

Scotty was new to our school this year. He is a large, well-coordinated boy, and quickly became a leader among boys, especially in games. Has shown an interest in art, but many times will not finish a picture. Scotty spent two days a week with a remedial-reading teacher, and he made considerable progress in his reading. Conference with mother revealed Scotty is very helpful at home. Scotty seems to have real potential, if we could only help him to improve his skills in reading and language.

E. Downing

READING BOOKS COMPLETED

First Grade (56-57)
Ride Away
Tip and Mitten
The Big Show
Come with Us

Second Grade (57-58)
Guess Who
Fun with Dick and Jane
Up and Away
Our New Friends
Open the Gate

Third Grade (58-59)
Come Along
On We Go
Around the Corner

Third Grade (59-60)
Over a City Bridge.
Just for Fun
Neighbors on the Hill
Looking Ahead

Fourth Grade (60-61)
Neighbors Far and
Near
If I Were Going

Fifth Grade (61-62)
High Road
Times and Places

children must take in keeping confidential the information they have about a student. Adherence to a professional code of ethics is essential.

Studies of students made by persons training to become teachers will in most cases be limited to the three sources of information already described: direct observation and objective description, school records, and information from other people. Limitations imposed by their unofficial status as observers and their brief visits to the classroom preclude their utilizing four additional sources of information available to the child's teacher and other professional personnel in the school.

4. Home visits and parent conferences.   Unfortunately, many parents initially feel apprehensive when a teacher asks to visit the home. Their previous experiences with a representative of the school coming to the house may have been with a truant officer or someone who has complained about the student's behavior. However, teachers who have studied children say that home visits, when they are carefully planned in advance and when the primary purpose is to establish friendly relationships between the school and the home, result in greater teacher-parent rapport and communication.

From the first the teacher seeks to establish warm, friendly relationships by placing the parent at ease and by being gracious and accepting. To accomplish this, the teacher refrains from making notes of any kind during the visit. He is alert and pays full attention to objects, people, and events in the home. Later, he writes up in narrative form what was observed and what he and the parents talked about.

The teacher's description of a home visit includes what he observes while driving through the neighborhood—the street, the houses, the yards, the general appearance and state of upkeep, and other details. The teacher may also wish to include a description of the student's home—furnishings, magazines, books, TV, appliances, and number and size of rooms. He will also include descriptions of the family—their speech and gestures and facial expressions. Asking the mother to describe Jimmy when he was a baby or inquiring about his interests and hobbies outside of school is often effective in putting the mother at ease and encouraging her to talk. The teacher can describe the projects the class is working on at school and Jimmy's role and participation in them. The ideal home visit is characterized by a free-flowing, easy interchange of ideas and information by persons who have a mutual interest in and concern for the student. In such a climate, the major purpose of the home visit, the establishment of rapport and friendly relations between home and school, has in large measure been fulfilled.

Parent-teacher conferences also provide opportunities for teachers and parents to share information about the child. Conferences are more frequent than home visits and often are more formal, since they are usually held at school and are often used in the elementary grades as a method of reporting the student's progress. Although parent-teacher conferences are held for the specific purpose of obtaining or communicating information about the child, the suggestions made for home visits apply also to parent-teacher conferences.

Miss Sawyer had many opportunities to become acquainted with Scotty and his family in their home, as the following excerpts from the record reveal.

November 13.   *The house in which I live has an apartment on the first floor (one step above street level) which was recently vacated.*

Today Scotty and his family moved into it. The apartment has a living room, two bedrooms, a kitchen, and a bath. One bedroom is very small, just large enough for a single bed. This is to be Frank's room. The parents have the large bedroom with a crib in it for Eddie, the 17-month-old boy. Scotty is to sleep on the studio couch in the living room.

The puppy, too, is still a member of the family.

November 27.   *On Saturday we had a severe storm with the ocean moving into our street. The water began rising shortly before 7 A.M. and by 9 A.M. had reached a depth of 11 inches in the Martins' apartment. They were forced to make a hasty exit through the rear window, and Mrs. Martin and Frank (the seven-year-old child) came up to my quarters. She wanted to know if we would take the children in with us. . . .*

Scotty was in the living room watching the rising water; and when he saw that it apparently wasn't going to recede, he began to move the furniture about and roll up the rug. He then went to the kitchen to get his mother's help. Mrs. Martin says that Scotty said, "Which is more important, for you to get your coffee or help me get things off the floor so the water won't hurt them?" . . .

When we had them all corralled, Scotty announced that he was hungry. None of them had had breakfast. The electricity had failed, so we fed them by the light of an oil lamp, which Scotty examined carefully. After the table was cleared, Scotty started to wash the dishes. I tried to chase him from the job, but he said he always did them. . . . When the dishes were done, Scotty was told to mind his brothers. Mr. Martin went for several more walks, and Mrs. Martin went down to their apartment to try to salvage some of their food from low cupboard shelves.

Scotty rocked Eddie until he went to sleep. Then he carefully placed him on the couch and covered him up. He played with Frank for a while and then gave him some magazines to look at.

The pup was next on his list of chores. He went downstairs and got the jar containing the pup's formula, brought it upstairs, heated it, and tried to feed the squirming and very hungry dog. I volunteered my services as puppy holder, and Scotty held the bottle. In the excitement the puppy's breakfast had been forgotten, and she was ravenous, gulping her food much too fast.

As soon as the bottle was empty, what had been in the dog was out of the dog all over my slacks. Scotty let out a horrified "Oh!" and his face turned crimson. I couldn't move but told him to get me a rag. He got a rag and began to mop me off. I said I'd do it but he said no, that his dog had done it and he'd clean me up. He kept apologizing as he wiped me off and said he'd get my slacks cleaned for me. After much talking he got over his embarrassment and was able to laugh about it. . . .

When Scotty came to school this morning, he looked at me and grinned and said, "Wasn't Saturday some day? But we had fun, didn't we?"

December 25.   *Mrs. Martin visited us today to see our gifts and seemed embarrassed at Scotty's contribution of soap. It seems that Scotty had asked her to get something nice for him to give me, so Mrs. Martin bought a very pretty pair of nylon panties. She showed them to Scotty, and he agreed that they were nice, but he said, "Mom, I can't give my teacher pants!"*

There ensued a discussion, and Scotty reluctantly agreed to present me with the panties. Mrs. Martin wrapped them up and gave Scotty the package to deliver. She said he walked slowly to the door, stopped, looked at the package, and said, "Mom, I just can't! I'll run downtown and buy something else for Miss Sawyer." He went, but all the stores were closed except the Sun Ray Drug Store. So Scotty bought soap. Mrs. Martin said that Scotty said, "When we go back to school after vacation, the kids are going to ask me what I gave Miss Sawyer. I can't tell them I gave her pants!" "So," said Mrs. Martin, "I have a pair of fancy nylon panties now!"

Through these home contacts, Miss Sawyer learned things about Scotty and his family that she could not have obtained in any other way: the quality of the relationships between Scotty and other members of the family, including the puppy; his taking on responsibilities at home—in sharp contrast to his failure to take responsibility for his work at school.

5. *Life space.* The environment in which the child lives is another important source of information because it contains clues to the kinds of experiences he may be having. Since the nature of the school environment is gleaned from other sources of information, the term *life space* generally refers to the student's out-of-school environment. Life space is that part of the world with which the child comes into direct contact. It includes the child's physical environment: the houses, yards, stores, factories, churches, railroad yards, wharves, woods, open fields, and streams; the people with whom he interacts; and the attitudes, feelings, and folkways of the region.

The teacher may obtain important life space data by driving or walking through the neighborhood around the child's home and by writing up fully what he sees, hears, smells, and feels. Many teachers ask the child to write about what he sees as he plays in his neighborhood or on his way to school, and they include the child's impressions in the record. A teacher then can contrast the child's perceptions to his own perceptions of the child's life space.

Life space information helps to complete the descriptive picture of the child and his world; in addition, it reveals the kinds and qualities of the child's sensory experience (which, as we will note in a later chapter, is of crucial importance in a child's learning). Since the child at birth knows nothing of the world, what he learns and knows depends upon what he has experienced—everything he sees, smells, hears, touches, manipulates, explores, reads about, and talks about. Life space, then, is the setting for all experiences, and experiencing is fundamental to all learning.

The following is a description of Scotty's life space prior to his family's moving into the apartment in the same building where Miss Sawyer lived.

October 10.   *This afternoon after school I decided I would drive through the district where Scotty lives. The street where Scotty lives is about three blocks from school in Southtown, an area of small one-story homes which adjoins an industrial area. Most of the fathers of children who attend our school are employed as semiskilled workers in the nearby plants. I approached Southtown by way of Fulton Avenue, which is a busy street with stores, service stations, and a variety of business establishments including a real estate office, beauty parlor, bar, dry cleaner, launderette, and pool hall.*

Two blocks beyond Madison I turned right, went one block, and turned left on Beechwood, the street on which Scotty lives. This street is in a development of small two-bedroom clapboard houses built by a developer 20 years ago to sell for $8,500. All the houses have the same floor plan. They are mainly distinguishable from one another by the color of the exterior paint. Scotty's house is white and occupies a good part of the 60-by-90-foot lot. Paint is peeling off the house, there are several bare spots in the front lawn, and only in the living room did I see curtains. I noticed a baseball bat and glove on the steps, a '66 Chevrolet sedan in the driveway, and an old bicycle in the front yard.

As I passed down the street, I saw many mothers outdoors with small children, sitting with neighbors on their steps or pushing babies in strollers. The street seemed to be crawling with children. I spotted Scotty and some of the older boys playing football in the street. I smiled and waved to them as I drove by. On the next corner I saw a small Christian church with a gas station nearby. Two blocks to the west there is a small electronics plant and a warehouse. Three blocks east is a three-acre wooded area and ravine which Scotty has often mentioned.

I noticed in my drive back that several houses were vacant. I then recalled that the new freeway is to be built through here, and several houses have been condemned to make way for it. I expect Scotty and his family will be looking for another home before long.

December 3.   *Scotty took a Sunday morning stroll to the local dump and returned with the skull of a dog. When my doorbell rang, there stood Scotty with a handful of teeth.*

"Look at these, Miss Sawyer," he said. "I found them on the dump."

"Ye gods, Scotty," I exclaimed, "how did you find so many teeth? Weren't they fastened to some kind of bone? They look like dog's teeth to me."

He laughed heartily and said, "They are dog's teeth. I found the whole skull and brought it home. Then I pulled the teeth out. The skull's downstairs. It don't smell, though; there's nothing but bone left of it. I thought the Science Club might like to see it."

So I told him to bring it to Science Club next Thursday!

6. Samples of work and evidences of creativity.   Samples of a student's work and products of his creative expression are a sixth source of information. This information is helpful in two ways. First, a child's drawings, paintings, models, stories, and autobiographical sketches provide important information about the child himself—his feelings, fears, concerns, interests, goals, and values. These are not revealed directly in the student's products but may be inferred when these data appear to be consistent with other facts in the record. The teacher must take care not to project his own ideas and feelings into the creative product he is interpreting. It is best to include the picture, painting, or essay in the case record, together with the student's comments about it and the teacher's and other children's comments and evaluations of it.

Second, samples of work and creative products are evidences of a student's development and learning. An arithmetic paper may reveal evidence of the student's computation and reasoning skills. A language paper may show the level of the student's physical maturation and development of motor coordination as reflected in his handwriting, his mastery of spelling and punctuation skills, and his mastery of skills for organizing ideas and expressing himself in writing. Drawings and paintings provide evidence of the student's development of artistic skills, motor coordination, and aesthetic sense. Samples of work and creative products are included in the case record, and these can be accompanied by evaluation comments of the student, the teacher, the art consultant, and other teachers and children.

Further evidence of Scotty's creativity and his feelings about his creative products are described in the following anecdote.

> November 20.   *In art class we designed Thanksgiving cards. Scotty worked carefully and painstakingly on a pencil sketch of a Pilgrim man, gun on shoulder and a wild turkey lying at his feet.*
>
> *The other children were doing theirs in water color. Scotty asked if he had to paint his, saying he always made a mess with paint. I told him I thought his type of drawing would look nice if it were done in India ink. "India ink?" asked Scotty. "What's that?" "I'll show you," I replied, and got the ink and a pen for him, showing him how to use it. He returned to his seat and worked very carefully, finishing the card. He came up to the desk with the finished product, laid it down in front of me, and queried, "How does it look?" "Scotty," I exclaimed, "that's lovely. You did a beautiful job. Aren't you pleased with it?" "Yeah," he replied, "I think it looks nice. Would it be all right if I made another one like it? Then I'd have one for both my mother and my father." "By all means," I replied. "Go ahead." The second card lacked the exactness and precision of the first, but it too was well done.*

7. Teacher-student conversations.   If the teacher has been successful in establishing a warm, friendly relationship with the student and has his confidence, conversations which take place between them (before school, on the playground, at noon, after school, or at any other appropriate time) will constitute yet another valuable source of information. If there is rapport between teacher and pupil, these conversations often take place spontaneously and are almost always informal. The teacher avoids probing for information but appears interested in listening to whatever the student wants to talk about.

If a warm, friendly, trusting relationship is established, significant information can emerge from these conversations. Again, as with descriptions of behavioral episodes in anecdotes, these conversations are most vivid and meaningful when they are reported in direct quotes and when they include descriptions of posture, facial expressions, gestures and other evidences of feeling and emotion.

The warm, friendly, valuing relationship which developed between Scotty and his teacher enabled Miss Sawyer to make effective use of informal conversations as a source of information, as shown in the following entries.

November 7.   Scotty came up to me today and told me he had acquired a two-day-old boxer puppy. I said, "Two days old? That puppy's too young to leave its mother. How do you care for it?" Scotty replied, "Its mother died, so the man had to get rid of all the puppies. There were seven of them, and he gave me one. I make a formula for it like you do for a baby, and I feed it with a medicine dropper. I keep it in a box wrapped in a woolen blanket. It'll be all right if I take care of it."

February 8.   Scotty has developed the habit of punching girls in their upper arms whenever he passes them. He is indiscriminate in his choice of arms, showing no particular preference for the arm of any one girl.

That's a painful wallop to receive, and I've spoken to him about it. His reply was, "Aw, they just like to complain. It really doesn't hurt."

I said, "It does hurt. I've had it happen to me, and I want you to stop it." Scotty replied, "Girls are just a lot of sissies anyway."

I laughed and said, "But you think some of them are pretty nice sissies, don't you?" Scotty shrugged and answered, "They're all right, I guess."

March 15.   Scotty told me that his dog, Chubby, is sick. He looked worried when he talked to me about it and said that she doesn't eat. He said, "I went over to the store and bought some liver for her. I cooked it and mashed some vegetables in it, but she wouldn't even eat it."

I suggested that he give Chubby some mineral oil, and he said he'd get some for her.

Analyzing the Case Record

The case record that the teacher or observer compiles will, hopefully, utilize extensively the sources of information that have been described. The purpose of writing this case record has been to collect information about the student's life story, so that accurate, objective analyses of his behavior, development, and learning can be made from these data. The teacher may acquire some hunches and a partial understanding of a student in the process of gathering information and building a case record, but a more complete understanding follows the observer's utilization of the final steps in the scientific method of problem solving described earlier in the chapter.

Although some insights are gained from observing and from building a case record, a formal analysis of the record should be delayed until a considerable body of data has been gathered and recorded. This delay reduces the likelihood that incorrect interpretations will be made because of insufficient information. Also essential to the observer's understanding of a student are the knowledge and application of principles of development and learning. Thus, although steps and processes in analyzing a case record are briefly described here, analyses of the case record should be deferred until a considerable body of facts about the student has been collected and some understanding of important principles and concepts in the later chapters has been acquired.

Analysis with Multiple Hypotheses

Whenever the case record information yields a fairly complete and valid picture of this student and his life situation, a *multiple hypothesis analysis* can be made—that is, an analysis in which a number of tentative hypotheses are advanced to explain a subject's recurring behavior patterns.

The multiple hypothesis analysis follows explicitly the steps of the scientific method of problem solving described earlier in the chapter. The reader will recall that the recurring behavior of Scotty which Miss Sawyer selected was "Why does Scotty not complete his artwork?" She had collected a great deal of information about Scotty over a two-month period before beginning her multiple hypothesis analysis. In our earlier discussion 20 tentative hypotheses were suggested as possible explanations of this behavior. Miss Sawyer found that the facts of her case record strongly supported four of her hypotheses, refuted two others, and neither confirmed nor refuted the remaining 14 (suggesting the need for collecting additional data).

Final Analysis and Summary of Case Record

A further opportunity for enlarging one's understanding of behavior and development is afforded by the completion of a final analysis and summary of the case record near the end of the period of studying a student. The final analysis and summary of a case record can take any one of several forms.

One approach involves organizing the data into a list of *recurring patterns*. A recurring pattern is any behavior, event, or situation which has occurred two or more times. The following are illustrative of the recurring patterns to be found in the complete case of Scotty:

1.   *Scotty fails to complete his picture.*

2.   *Scotty argues or fights with another boy.*

3.   *Scotty punches girls on the arm.*

4.   *Scotty talks to the teacher about his dog.*

5.   *Scotty helps his mother, teacher, and others in the community.*

In studying the list of recurring patterns that emerged from the case of Scotty, Miss Sawyer noted that the patterns could be grouped according to the forces or critical activities or events in Scotty's life. She found clusters of recurring patterns which related to Scotty's physical coordination and abilities, his relationships with others, his acceptance of responsibility, his progress in specific school subjects, his aesthetic sense, and his values. Miss Sawyer's final analysis and summary of Scotty's case record consisted of tentative answers to the following guide questions:

1.   *What developmental tasks is this student working on?*

2.   *What adjustment problems does he face?*

3.   *What assets does he have?*

4.   *What have the school and the teacher done to help this student develop and learn more effectively?*

5.   *What more can the teacher and the school do to help this student develop and learn more effectively?*

By reexamining the case record data presented in this chapter, the reader may wish to test his skill and understanding by developing tentative answers to these summarizing questions, either now or after he has gained an understanding of the principles presented in later chapters.

Summary

The steps in the scientific method of problem solving are (1) location and definition of a problem; (2) collection and organization of data; (3) formulation of hypotheses or possible solutions; (4) testing of the hypotheses; (5) collection of additional data; (6) summary of data and drawing of conclusions; and (7) formulation of new generalizations, principles, or laws and of a plan of action for applying them to the solution of further problems.

In his study of a student, the teacher is guided by an explicit code of professional ethics, which ensures the safeguarding of information about a student and which protects the student's identity.

In studying a student, the educator builds a case record by utilizing seven sources of information: (1) direct observation and objective anecdotal description, (2) school records, (3) information from other people, (4) home visits and parent conferences, (5) life space, (6) samples of work and evidences of creativity, and (7) teacher-student conversations.

Attaining a depth of understanding of human behavior depends upon analyses of case record data, using the steps of the scientific method of problem solving. A tentative *multiple hypothesis analysis* is available to teachers or observers during their initial experiences in studying behavior. Later, in final analysis and case record summary, the teacher or observer interprets the recurring patterns and total case record data and forms tentative answers to guide questions.

Study Questions

1. This chapter describes the procedures that can be used in the teacher's intensive study of one student. How would you respond to the teacher who says, "I have thirty students in my class, and it isn't fair for me to give most of my time and attention to one student and neglect the other twenty-nine"?

2. What differences do you see in the application of the scientific method in the study of human behavior and its application in the solution of problems in the natural sciences?

3. Objectivity of data is a fundamental requirement of research activity in a science. Since much of the data which a teacher gathers about a student consists of statements made by him or by others talking about him, how can the teacher ascertain that what is said is factual and objective?

4. Apply the steps in the scientific method to your own major field of interest. What problems in your own field are amenable to scientific

investigation? How might the steps of the scientific method be employed in the solution of these problems?

Suggested Readings

Brandt, Richard M. *Studying Behavior in Natural Settings.* New York: Holt, Rinehart and Winston, 1972. Describes and illustrates a wide range of methods and procedures for studying human behavior in nonlaboratory settings. Chapter 4 discusses procedures that can be used in obtaining and recording narrative anecdotal descriptions of behavior.

Commission on Teacher Education. *Helping Teachers Understand Children.* Washington, D. C.: American Council on Education, 1945. Describes and illustrates the steps and procedures used by teachers in a child study program in observing and studying a student through time. Chapter 2 contains examples of adequate and inadequate anecdotes; other chapters describe the analysis and interpretation of case records through the use of actual case illustrations.

Gordon, Ira J. *Studying the Child in the School.* New York: John Wiley, 1966. Emphasizes the teacher's need to understand the transactional nature of learning. Describes techniques and tools which the teacher can use in assessing children's intellectual, cognitive, personality, and social development.

Lane, Howard, and Mary Beauchamp. *Understanding Human Development.* Englewood Cliffs, N. J.: Prentice-Hall, 1959. Chapter 15 describes sources of information and procedures that teachers can use in child and adolescent study. Included are discussions of school and anecdotal records, home visits, parent conferences, free play, creativity, role playing, and sociometric techniques.

Prescott, Daniel A. *The Child in the Educative Process.* New York: McGraw-Hill Book Co., 1957. Describes with numerous case illustrations the steps and procedures by which a teacher obtains, organizes, and analyzes case record data on a student.

Films

Helping Teachers Understand Children, 16 mm, sound, black and white. Part 1, 21 min.; Part 2, 25 min. Bloomington: Audiovisual Center, Indiana University. Part 1 presents a case study of one child and illustrates sources of information a teacher can use in writing a case record. Part 2 shows a summer workshop in child study in which educators and others study the processes which influence and shape the child's behavior, development, and learning.

Learning to Understand Children (Part 1—*A Diagnostic Approach;* Part 2—*A Remedial Program*), 16 mm, sound, black and white. Part 1, 22 min.; Part 2, 25 min. Bloomington: Audiovisual Center, Indiana University. Part 1 presents the case of Ada Adams, an emotionally and socially maladjusted girl of 15. Her teacher diagnoses her difficulties by observation of her behavior, study of her previous record, personal interviews, and home visits, and formulates a hypothesis for remedial measures. Part 2 continues the case study. An interest in art improves her self-confidence and interest in schoolwork, although some of her problems remain unsolved.

The Direction of Human Behavior

3

Childhood may do without a grand purpose, but manhood cannot.

J. G. Holland

Probably no problem is more puzzling, intriguing, and crucial in the study of human development and learning than the one posed in the question "What is this person trying to accomplish and why?" Before we can enlarge our understanding of behavior, development, and learning, we must extend our understanding of what is meant by the term *motivation*.

The need to discover and to understand what makes people behave as they do is shared by all human beings, young and old, in all cultures at all ages; for an individual can respond appropriately and effectively in life's varying situations only if he assesses accurately other people's motives. The district attorney, in developing a case for the prosecution, seeks to establish the defendant's motives for committing the crime. The advertiser promotes a product most successfully when he discovers, responds to, and influences the desires and preferences of millions of consumers. The parent must understand his children's motives if he is to guide and socialize them in accordance with their own expressed needs and goals. The teacher must understand his students' interests and needs if he is to plan effectively for their learning.

Psychologically unsophisticated persons explain behavior in terms of simple motives. One may overhear a parent or a teacher say, "Freddie does not do his homework because he is lazy." Behavior, however, is never a simple, separate, or isolated phenomenon. Rather, it is related to the conditions, forces, and events which precede and accompany it. Perhaps this is just another way of stating that behavior has many interrelated causes.

If behavior does not occur as an isolated, spontaneous response, it must be instigated by something. This something, a bodily state or condition which impels one to respond, is called *motivation*. As we shall note presently, human motives have their sources in social and psychological needs as well as physiological needs. Regardless of its source, however, motivation is an internal state that mobilizes and directs an individual's energy toward some object or part of the environment. After the individual achieves the goal toward which he is motivated, his energy expenditure decreases and his effectiveness in coping with his environment increases.

Motivation, as it can be inferred from observations of animal and human behavior, involves three interrelated processes. McDonald has included in his definition of motivation all three processes: "Motivation, an energy change within the person, is characterized by affective arousal and anticipatory goal reactions."[1]

The first of these processes is an internal *energy change*—usually the result of some kind of imbalance. The individual gets hungry, or too warm or too cold, or his best friend does not speak to him, or he faces an arithmetic test on material he does not understand, or the coach urges him to try out for the varsity football team. In each case the student undergoes a change from a more or less quiescent state to an activated state. Such a change, impelling him to restore balance, is sometimes called a *drive*.

As a result of this internal energy change, the motivated individual usually experiences some emotional arousal (or, in McDonald's words, "affective arousal"). For most persons, the physical discomfort of hunger, heat, or cold, or the experience of being misunderstood by friends, or the prospect of a test for which one is not prepared is unpleasant. Being asked by the coach to try out for the team may be pleasant if the student considers himself a pretty good player. If, however, he loathes football, or fears contact sports, or feels he is a poor player, his placidity prior to the coach's invitation may give way afterward to apprehension and anxiety—evidence of strong affective arousal.

Affective arousal prepares one for the third aspect of motivation: appropriate action in dealing with the situation ("anticipatory goal reactions"). Appropriate action in the above examples may be buying and eating a candy bar (if hungry), turning off the radiator or opening a window (if one is too hot), turning up the thermostat (if one is too cold), writing a conciliatory note to the estranged friend, and asking the teacher or a classmate for help with difficult arithmetic problems. Appropriate action by the student invited to try out for the team may involve performing enthusiastically the exercises needed to get in top physical condition and putting forth maximum effort in blocking and tackling (if the coach's invitation reinforces his own aspirations and feelings of competence in playing football). If the student dislikes football or believes he is a mediocre or poor player, appropriate action in response to the coach's invitation may be getting an after-school job, becoming involved in other extracurricular activities, or pleading to be excused from trying out for the team because of the pressure of studies. In each case the appropriate action is directed toward reducing the imbalance created by the initial energy change. In the process, affective arousal diminishes and a state of relative quiescence is restored.

One's internal basis for responding in a learning situation is greatly influenced by present and past events and future aspirations, as the following anecdote reveals.

[1] Frederick J. McDonald, *Educational Psychology*, 2nd ed. (Belmont, Calif.: Wadsworth Publishing Co., 1965), p. 112.

As Hazel Brown watched her eleventh grade English class taking a test, she observed a wide variety of behaviors among her students. Some were busily at work—reading, thinking about the questions, jotting down the answers. Others were biting their pencils, erasing, and staring at the ceiling in hopes that correct answers would somehow come to them. A few were staring out the window, looking around, playing with objects on their desks—apparently making no effort to complete the examination.

That some students were strongly motivated toward academic achievement while others were much less motivated in this direction was quickly discernible to Hazel. She did not expect to find, however, a variety of motivations among her top students. She had assumed that her best students were motivated by a desire for personal achievement and for remaining in the college prep section, but her conferences with students revealed an astonishing variety of individual motives. Ronnie Wilson wanted most of all to beat out his arch rival, Bill James. Shirley Weston sought to maintain her parents' approval, which high grades earned for her. Ted Jenkins frankly admitted he had to make the grades to be admitted to engineering school. It seemed clear that Bob Hammond was compensating in academic areas for his lack of skill in sports. Barbara, Jean, and Tim were mainly interested in staying on the honor roll no matter what, while quiet Margaret Hanson, seemingly oblivious to grades, was more interested in analyzing the plot and characters of Macbeth. *The statements of several students revealed not one but two or three such motives.*

This anecdote illustrates several principles which are important to our understanding of motivation. First of all, each student's behavior during the test was in response to some internal state or bodily condition. *Motivation is a process within the individual.* It is not something that the teacher does or gives to the student.

Second, we cannot observe motives directly. Behavior can be observed directly, but *motives can only be inferred.* When his group is called to the reading circle, Andy frequently reports that he has misplaced his book. After test papers have been handed back, Evie brings her paper to the teacher to complain that the teacher's scoring of her paper was not fair. In each case we observe the situation and the child's response in that situation, but we have no direct evidence of the coordinated activities of receptors, nervous system, muscles, and glands which presumably intervened and influenced the observed behavior. Since motives are inferred, they are tentative and must be checked and revised in the light of additional evidence. Hazel Brown's initial inferences about her top students, based on her observations of them as they took the test, proved to be oversimplified and only partially correct. As Hazel observes these and other students over a period of several months in a variety of situations, the consistencies she observes in their behavior will enable her to make successively more accurate inferences of their motives.

Finally, an individual's behavior is not the result of just one motive or one need but *is influenced by many different and complex motives, some of which may be unconscious.* Hazel Brown was surprised to learn not only that she had to cope with different levels and kinds of motivation within a single classroom but also that students who behave in a similar manner often respond in this way for quite different reasons. How can a teacher organize a learning environment which will be meaningful to persons with such widely varying motive patterns? It is on this problem that the present chapter focuses.

Motivation in Historical Perspective

Free Will

Philosophers from the time of Plato and Aristotle have conceived of man as a rational being who uses his human capacities to achieve his conscious desires. According to this view, man's behavior is explained by what he has willed; and through the faculty of will, man can control the base and evil side of his nature in the interests of virtue and salvation.

Psychologists have not found free will satisfactory for explaining why a person has acquired his particular set of wants and desires—why one man, for instance, steals money, while another gives it away in philanthropic enterprises. One must perforce look beyond each man's will for a more adequate explanation of his behavior.

Hedonism

Everyday experience suggests that individuals respond to stimuli or events in ways that bring pleasure and avoid pain. This "seeking-pleasure–avoiding-pain" conception of motivation is called *hedonism.* Hedonism as a theory of motivation has had a long history, extending back to the ancient Greek philosophers; but it gained its greatest prominence in the eighteenth and nineteenth centuries—probably achieving its fullest development and advocacy in the words of Jeremy Bentham (1748–1832), who argued that man's conduct of practical affairs must be in accord with what is good, *good* being defined as pleasure or happiness.

Psychologists have criticized hedonism as a theory of motivation because of its dependence on the subject's self-reports of his own internal, private affective state. How can we really know the degree of pleasure or pain that another person feels, and does the presence of unconscious factors permit the person to give an objective account of his own feelings? The problem is further complicated by evidence that some persons do things and seek out experiences that bring pain, while others avoid doing things that would bring pleasure. Climbing mountains, hunting wild animals, and fighting in wars are activities in which pain, discomfort, and the possibilities of death are very great. Yet men and women choose dangerous occupations or volunteer for dangerous missions in preference to the comforts and pleasures they would have at home in a more sedentary occupation. To explain this apparent paradox by suggesting that some people gain pleasure from the rigors and dangers of mountain climbing is circular.

A second limitation of hedonistic theories of motivation is that they explain a person's motivation only after the behavior has occurred. Florence worked uninterruptedly at her desk until she completed the assignment. When she handed in her paper, the teacher smiled and said, "Well done!" Frank refused to join his friends who skipped school yesterday and were sent to the office this morning. If the observer must wait until after the behavior occurred to infer that Florence in completing her work sought pleasure and that Frank in refusing his peers wished to avoid punishment, it is evident that hedonistic theories of motivation offer little help for predicting a subject's future behavior. The limitations of hedonism in explaining motivation are succinctly summarized by Allport: "Happiness is at best a byproduct of otherwise-motivated activity. One who aims at happiness has no aim at all."[2]

In spite of its limitations as an overall theory, many current psychological theories incorporate elements of hedonism. Freud's pleasure principle, for example, hypothesizes that the id functions to discharge tension and to restore balance. In learning theory, Thorndike's initial statement of his law of effect proposed that stimulus-response (S-R) connections are strengthened or weakened if they are followed, respectively, by a satisfying or annoying state of affairs. More recently, two researchers have suggested that the arousal, maintenance, and direction of behavior depend upon the degree of positive or negative feelings associated with the activity or goal. Young,[3] for example, found that well-fed, healthy animals responded more vigorously in running a maze when sugar was the reward than when casein (protein in milk), a less palatable food, was the reward. McClelland[4] suggests that when a variety of stimuli or cues are associated with a pleasant situation, any one or several of these stimuli or cues, on subsequent occasions, may reactivate the pleasant feeling. Thus, if the pleasures of a very special date are linked with a particular food, song, or perfume, the individual on subsequent occasions is likely to prepare the food, select the

[2] Gordon W. Allport, *Pattern and Growth in Personality* (New York: Holt, Rinehart and Winston, 1961), p. 200.

[3] P. T. Young, "Food-Seeking Drive, Affective Process, and Learning," *Psychological Review*, 56 (March 1949), 98–121. See also P. T. Young, *Motivation and Emotion* (New York: John Wiley, 1961).

[4] David C. McClelland, *Personality* (New York: William Sloane Associates, 1951).

song, or use the perfume in seeking to reexperience the pleasures initially associated with these stimuli.

Instincts

Darwin's theory of evolution provided an impetus for the development of more objective and scientific theories of motivation. Darwin observed that many responses of lower animals to specific environmental stimuli are apparently unlearned. The homing tendencies of pigeons and salmon are examples of such innate behavior patterns, called instincts. An *instinct* has been defined as an inherited and specific stereotyped pattern of behavior common to all members of a species which is elicited by particular environmental stimuli. Higher animals possess fewer of these innate behavior patterns. Most of their behaviors are learned and reflect the advantage of a highly developed brain and nervous system.

During the latter half of the nineteenth century, considerable progress was made in identifying specific innate behavioral tendencies of birds, ants, wasps, spiders, and various mammals. In the early part of the twentieth century, McDougall[5] developed a theory that instincts and their associated emotions are the most important determiners of conduct. According to McDougall, instincts are not mere reflexes or mechanical blind strivings; rather, they are purposive, inherited, goal-seeking tendencies which serve as mainsprings for action. The major instincts postulated by McDougall are those for flight, repulsion, curiosity, pugnacity, self-abasement, self-assertion, and parenthood. Freud gave a prominent place to instincts in his theory of psychoanalysis, but since his instincts of sex, self-preservation, and death are more like drives, they are discussed in the section on drive theories.

By 1920, instinct theories, when used to explain human motivation, had come under increasing attack. The list of instincts grew so long that little difference remained between the naming of an instinct and the listing of the behavior it was trying to explain. This loss of meaning of the term was shown by Bernard, who listed nearly 6,000 instincts—including "the instinct to avoid eating apples that grow in one's own orchard."[6]

Since the term *instinct* as it was being used no longer fitted its definition of "inherited stereotyped behavior which is common to all members of a species," use of the term by psychologists to explain human motivation has generally been abandoned. However, the concept is related to studies of animal motivation—most notably in studies of *imprinting*. Imprinting is the process whereby an animal such as a baby duck becomes attached to

[5] William McDougall, *An Introduction to Social Psychology* (London: Methuen, 1908), pp. 39–76.

[6] Luther L. Bernard, *Instinct: A Study in Social Psychology* (New York: Holt, Rinehart and Winston, 1924), p. 212.

and follows any stimulus object that appears during a critical period of a few days after it has hatched from the egg. Although the attachment is usually made to the mother duck, it can be made to a hen, a decoy, or a quacking human experimenter. Once this attachment is made, the duckling will thenceforth continue to follow that object. The response pattern to the "imprinted" stimulus becomes fixed. After the critical period, the duckling does not change to follow a different object.

Through imprinting, animals acquire unlearned, fixed motivation and behavior patterns, each of which is peculiar to a given species. Imprinting and the older, more general term *instinct* now refer to the specific, built-in, automatic motives and responses of lower animals, who possess limited capacities for learning. Learning, on the other hand, plays a central role in the development of human motives. Drives and needs, most of which are learned, have proved more useful for understanding human motivation.

Drives

About 1925, the term *drive* gained prominence as an explanatory concept in motivation and learning theory. Woodworth introduced the concept of drive in 1918 to describe energy which impels the organism to action in response to tissue needs arising from hunger, thirst, sex, or bodily inactivity. Soon the term *drive* became associated with specific drives instead of the general supply of energy to which Woodworth had initially referred. In this manner the term gradually supplanted the term *instinct*.

Psychologists generally have preferred a theory of motivation based on drives because the concept of drive has proved more amenable to scientific investigation. In a typical experimental study, a single drive is selected and defined operationally in measurable terms. The effects of drive, expressed in terms of a specific number of hours of food or water deprivation or level of intensity of an electric shock, can then be studied in relation to various behavior and learning outcomes. These experiments have used animals as subjects and thus appear to have few implications for classroom learning; however, they have made important contributions to the development of a general theory of behavior.

Drive, as a motivational concept, has a central role in Hull's reinforcement learning theory. Reinforcement theory postulates that a response is strengthened by events that result in a reduction of drive or by events that increase the probability of a response being emitted. Hull[7] described two kinds of drive, primary and secondary. A *primary drive* is an arousal state produced by deprivation of food, water, or other physiological requirement. A *secondary drive* (also called an acquired drive) is a stimulus present at the time a primary drive is activated. When a child touches a hot

[7] Clark E. Hull, *Principles of Behavior* (New York: Appleton-Century-Crofts, 1943).

stove, the pain (primary drive) is followed by a withdrawal of the hand, while fear of being burned (secondary drive) leads to an avoidance of stoves. In Hull's theory, responses which are associated with a reduction of drive (primary or secondary) are said to be reinforced; reinforced behaviors tend to be repeated and to become habits, and indicate that learning has occurred.

Further support for a drive theory of motivation was provided by Cannon's[8] concept of *homeostasis*—numerous complex physiological processes which maintain most of the steady states in the organism. Any physiological imbalance arising from extremes in temperature or from changes in the water, salt, sugar, protein, fat, or calcium content of the blood triggers certain physiological mechanisms; these mechanisms effect a return of the organism to a stable state. For example, loss of body fluids in hot weather activates compensatory neural and chemical changes (involving principally the sympathetic portion of the autonomic nervous system) which divert fluid from the lymph system and tissues into the blood stream. Increasing one's salt intake during hot weather assists the organism's homeostatic response of effecting a retention of water in the body.

Cannon points out that hunger and thirst produce instabilities which require behavioral intervention to restore homeostatic balance. When an organic imbalance (such as hunger, thirst, or pain) requires behavioral intervention to restore equilibrium, the state of arousal, manifested in heightened sensitivity and tense muscles, is called drive.

Some psychologists[9] have extended the concept of homeostasis and have used it to explain psychological phenomena. One's perceptions, habits, beliefs, and values thus are regarded as higher-level (psychological) responses which function to maintain personality organization. Critics of this position,[10] however, object to the use of a physiological concept to explain a psychological problem. Furthermore, the critics contend, this position fails to account for spontaneous, altruistic, creative behaviors—unique characteristics of human beings.

Needs

The term *needs* refers to general and specific conditions of lack or deficiency within the organism. In seeking to explain motivation by a concept of needs, psychologists and educators suggest that it is more meaningful and useful to identify the specific deficiencies and their causes than to focus upon the drive state which these deficiencies arouse. The existence of

---

[8] Walter B. Cannon, *Wisdom of the Body* (New York: W. W. Norton & Co., 1939).

[9] J. M. Fletcher, "Homeostasis as an Explanatory Principle in Psychology," *Psychological Review*, 49 (1942), 80–87; R. Stagner, "Homeostasis as a Unifying Concept in Personality Theory," *Psychological Review*, 58 (1951), 5–17.

[10] See H. H. Toch and A. H. Hastorf, "Homeostasis in Psychology," *Psychiatry*, 18 (1955), 81–92.

a need provides an impetus for goal-seeking behavior directed toward reducing the lack or deficiency. Subjectively, the reduction of the lack or deficiency is often associated with satisfaction. Thus, needs describe the general sources of people's motives. By observing an individual over a period of time, we may make inferences about his motives and the needs he is attempting to satisfy. If we observe that a particular student, Virginia, makes frequent contributions to class discussions, carefully prepares assignments and gets high test marks, tries out for the school's academic quiz team, and expresses concern over maintaining a high scholastic average and getting into a good college, we can infer that she has needs for achievement and self-esteem.

The term *needs* is popular with educators because it points to the goals toward which students are striving and thus can lead to effective curriculum planning. In inferring needs from observations of a student's behavior, however, some teachers unfortunately use the term normatively —that is, they use the term to refer to what the student *should* need, do, or accomplish. In contrast to *normative needs, psychological needs* are the actual states of deficiency or tension in a particular individual—states that are inferred from his goal-directed behaviors. A chief distinction between the two kinds of needs is that psychological needs are linked to motives and specific behavior, whereas normative needs represent what ought to occur. The two meanings reflect a confusion as to whose needs and goals are being described—the adult's or the child's.

A number of schemes for classifying psychological needs have been developed. Three of these systems (Murray's, Maslow's, and Raths and Burrell's) are presented in Table 3–1, Figure 3–1, and Table 3–2.

Murray,[11] through a series of individual interviews, tests, and experiments with 50 men of college age, sought to discover some of the principles that govern human behavior. He attempted to correlate observed directions of behavior with subjective reports of intention (wish, desire, aim, or purpose) and to infer the operation of one or more drives or needs. By analyzing the responses of his subjects to certain contrived situations, he identified 12 viscerogenic (physical) needs and 28 psychogenic needs. Later these were reduced in number to the list of 20 needs shown in Table 3–1. Murray's system of needs has been widely used in personality and motivation research. Both the Thematic Apperception Test (TAT) and McClelland's need-for-achievement research (discussed later in the chapter) are based on Murray's need theory.

Maslow[12] proposed a hierarchical set of six needs: (1) physiological, (2) safety, (3) love and belonging, (4) self-esteem, (5) self-actualization, and (6) desire to know and to understand (see Figure 3–1). According to Maslow, the lower physiological and safety needs (which he calls deficiency, or D, needs) must be satisfied before one can satisfy the higher needs for

[11] Henry A. Murray, *Explorations in Personality* (New York: Oxford University Press, 1938), pp. 142–242.

[12] Abraham H. Maslow, *Motivation and Personality*, 2nd ed. (New York: Harper & Row, 1970), pp. 35–50.

Table 3–1. Murray's List of Needs

Abasement. To submit passively to external force. To accept injury, blame, criticism. To admit inferiority.

Achievement. To accomplish something difficult. To master or manipulate. To excel oneself. To rival and surpass others.

Affiliation. To please and win affection of a valued object. To adhere and remain loyal to a friend.

Aggression. To overcome opposition forcefully. To fight. To revenge an injury. To attack, injure, or kill.

Autonomy. To get free. To resist coercion and restriction. To be independent and free to act according to impulse. To defy conventions.

Counteraction. To master or make up for failure by restriving. To overcome weakness, to repress fear.

Defendance. To defend the self against assault, criticism, and blame. To vindicate the ego.

Deference. To admire and support a superior. To praise, honor, or eulogize. To conform to custom.

Dominance. To control one's human environment. To influence or direct the behavior of others.

Exhibition. To make an impression. To be seen and heard. To excite, amaze, fascinate, entertain, shock, amuse, or entice others.

Harmavoidance. To avoid pain, physical injury, illness, and death. To escape from a dangerous situation. To take precautionary measures.

Infavoidance. To avoid humiliation. To refrain from action because of the fear of failure.

Nurturance. To give sympathy to and gratify needs of a helpless other. To feed, help, support, console, protect, nurse, heal.

Order. To put things in order. To achieve cleanliness, arrangement, organization, balance, neatness, and precision.

Play. To act for "fun" without further purpose. To laugh and make jokes. To participate in games, sports, dancing, parties.

Rejection. To exclude, abandon, expel, or remain indifferent to someone who is inferior.

Sentience. To seek and enjoy sensuous impressions.

Sex. To form and further an erotic relationship.

Succorance. To have one's needs gratified by the sympathetic aid of an allied other. To be nursed, supported, sustained, protected, loved, guided, forgiven, consoled.

Understanding. To ask or answer general questions. To speculate, formulate, analyze, and generalize.

Source: Adapted from Henry A. Murray, *Explorations in Personality.* Copyright © 1938 by Oxford University Press, Inc., renewed 1966 by Henry A. Murray. Used by permission.

self-actualization and knowledge. Thus, two types of motivation are identified by Maslow: (1) *deficiency* (or *D*) *motivation*, which centers on the gratification of lower needs; and (2) *growth motivation* (represented by *B* for *being*), which focuses upon the satisfaction of higher needs. While all of us at one time or another must respond to deficiency needs, greater human fulfillment and satisfaction seem to result from the stimulation of growth motivation. Psychologically healthy persons, Maslow suggests, are characteristically aroused by growth motivation, wherein they extend their being through spontaneous exploring, experiencing, choosing, and enjoying.[13]

[13] Abraham H. Maslow, *Toward a Psychology of Being,* 2nd ed. (Princeton, N. J.: D. Van Nostrand Co., 1968).

Figure 3–1.   Maslow's Hierarchy of Needs

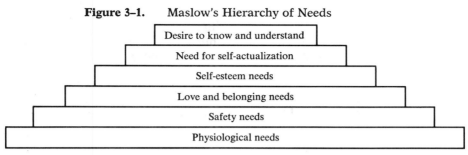

Source: Adapted from Abraham H. Maslow, *Motivation and Personality*, 2nd ed. (New York: Harper & Row, 1970), pp. 35–50.

Table 3–2.   Raths and Burrell's List of Needs

Belonging is manifested by a child who feels unwanted or neglected. He may ask why he is not desired by group, club, or age mates.

Achievement is shown when a child expresses a desire for more attention and praise. He may wish to "do more" or "do something better."

Economic security is seen when a child worries about his father's job, the cost of things, or why he cannot have some of the things he wants.

Freedom from fear is shown when a child evidences anxiety concerning persons in authority, sickness, death, or certain animals. Fear of being in a minority group.

Love and affection is shown when a child asks his teacher if he can sit beside her, and if she likes him. May shower affection on others.

Freedom from intense feelings of guilt is revealed when a child expresses guilt concerning relationships with people. May blame self and internalize guilt.

Sharing and self-respect is shown when a child indicates he wishes people had more faith in his judgment or that he might have more of a part in group activities.

Understanding is evidenced when a child seems bewildered by his surroundings and the demands upon him. May ask questions, insist on anwers to his questions, or express doubt about things he is told.

Source: Adapted from Louis E. Raths and Anna P. Burrell, *Understanding the Problem Child* (West Orange, N. J.: Economics Press, 1963), pp. 7–20. Used by permission.

As shown in Table 3–2, Raths and Burrell[14] have identified eight needs (emotional needs for belonging, for achievement, for economic security, for freedom from fear, for love and affection, for freedom from intense feelings of guilt, for self-respect, and for understanding). Raths and Burrell provide suggestions designed to help teachers identify these needs as they are expressed in students' behavior. In addition, they discuss approaches

---

[14] Louis E. Raths and Anna P. Burrell, *Understanding the Problem Child.*

which teachers can use in helping school children to gain increased satisfaction of these needs.

Thus, needs identify motives that arouse and direct the organism's behavior toward remedying specific lacks or deficiencies (such as food, affiliation, or self-esteem). A classification of needs provides a framework for the study of human behavior. Although they will not be identified as such, human needs which emerge from the interplay of physical, cultural, and psychological forces will be a central focus of the next six chapters.

Innate versus Acquired Motives

Some of the motives we have discussed (such as those arising from hunger, thirst, and nonactivity) have a direct bearing on man's existence as a physical organism. These motives are said to be basic because they relate to the satisfaction of needs that are essential to the preservation of the life and health of the individual. Motives which relate to the social and pyschological development of man, however, seem to be of a different order. They are acquired and appear to bear little relationship to physiological needs. An *acquired motive* is an arousal state within the organism which has been learned.

Evidence that much of human motivation is acquired comes from anthropologists' studies of other cultures. Some societies (such as the Zuñi and Hopi Indian cultures of Arizona and New Mexico and the Arapesh of New Guinea) attach little importance to acquisitiveness and competitiveness—motives that are prominent in many parts of Western culture. Studies of social class differences, reported in Chapter 6, show that motives for academic achievement and self-esteem are more strongly manifested among middle class persons, whereas motives reflecting strong loyalty to and support of family, friends, and community are commonly observed among lower class persons and groups.

A frequently observed example of an acquired motive is fear—a learned response to stimuli associated with pain or discomfort (stimuli such as a hot stove or being left alone). Fears may be specific, objective, and real; or they may be imaginary, irrational, and generalized. A persistent fear of the latter type is often called *anxiety*. The anxieties people reveal concerning an examination, their job, their families, or their sense of adequacy indicate that anxiety, too, is a powerful motive for shaping human behavior.

Several theories have been advanced to explain how acquired motives are derived from physiological motives. One such theory is Freud's explanation of sublimation. According to Freud, the instincts, impulses, and energies of the id become redirected by the ego away from socially disapproved objects and toward socially approved ones by a process called *displacement*. When the substitute object represents a higher or more socially approved cultural goal, the displacement is called *sublimation*. In the process of sublimation, new motives are acquired as energies are rechanneled into intellectual, humanitarian, cultural, or artistic pursuits. Boys may sublimate their aggressive impulses by participating in contact sports such as football, boxing, and hockey. Adolescent girls may channel and sublimate their sex and nurturing drives by serving as a nurse's aid or by caring for young children. In this manner new motives (in the form of arousals toward substitute goals and activities) are formed as energies are expended and tensions are reduced through sublimation.

Allport,[15] in his theory of the functional autonomy of motives, offers another explanation for the emergence of acquired motives. He contends that a motivation based solely on instincts (as suggested by McDougall) or on sublimation of sexual and aggressive impulses (as put forth by Freud) is inadequate for explaining the uniqueness, the spontaneity, and the forward-looking, concrete character of adult motivation. *Functional autonomy* describes the process through which the child's early physiological and social drives, expressed in his dependence on parents, are replaced by self-sustaining contemporary goals, which often bear little relationship to earlier antecedents. A successful businessman in a large city may purchase a farm so that he can savor on weekends some of the experiences he had as a boy growing up on a farm. He no longer has the need to identify with his father, to prove himself able to do a man's work, or to feel needed by his family. His desire to reexperience the joys of country living is functionally autonomous. Similarly, the desire to attend school persists in a few "perpetual students" long after they have earned the academic degrees for entrance into their vocation or profession. They long to remain students even though this role no longer earns them parental approval or social recognition. Do some people become teachers to satisfy curiosity and learning motives, experienced initially as a student, which have since become functionally autonomous?

It is frequently difficult to discern whether certain motives are innate or acquired. Since the needs for affiliation with and love of another human being do not appear to be expressed in the newborn infant's behavior, one might conclude that motives reflecting these needs are acquired. However, human infants who have been denied tactual experience and "mothering" by a human mother or her substitute suffer disabling effects—which seems to suggest that there is an innate component in the motives for affiliation and love.

A strong desire on the part of human beings for environmental stimulation is shown by Heron's[16] studies of *sensory deprivation*, in which male college students were paid 20 dollars a day to be enclosed in a lighted cubicle and do nothing. They wore translucent plastic visors which transmitted diffuse light but prevented patterned vision. Cotton gloves and card-

[15] Allport, pp. 226–253.

[16] Woodburn Heron, "The Pathology of Boredom," *Scientific American*, 196 (January 1957), 52–56.

board cuffs extending beyond the fingertips prevented feeling by touch. Auditory perception was limited by a U-shaped foam rubber pillow and the continuous hum of an air conditioner. Most of the subjects had planned to use their time in the sensation-free cubicle reviewing their studies, planning a term paper, or organizing a lecture. During perceptual isolation their thoughts changed from thinking about studies to reminiscing about past incidents and friends. Eventually it took too much effort to concentrate, and they let their minds drift. The most striking effects were the subjects' reports of hallucinations over which they felt they had little control. One subject could not stop "seeing" dogs, while another could see nothing but eyeglasses. The childish emotional responses, disturbed visual perception, and hallucinations suggest that the human being requires continuous sensory stimulation; for, without it, the brain ceases to function adequately, and behavioral abnormalities appear.

Organic motives for food, water, and activity are dominant when the life of the organism is threatened. For most human beings, however, learned (acquired) motives, such as those expressed in needs for affiliation, achievement, and self-esteem, exert the greatest influence on behavior. The origin of these motives is not certain. They might be derived from basic physiological motives (such as a child's learning to love the person who feeds him), or they may be functionally autonomous (an achievement drive becoming autonomous as it replaces an earlier need for love or self-esteem), or they may be evidences of intrinsically motivated behavior (a boy takes apart an old clock to learn how it works).

Intrinsic Motives

Intrinsic motives are energy arousals which involve behavior that is satisfying in and for itself. A student is intrinsically motivated when he works on puzzles for the satisfaction he gains in finding a solution. In studying for an examination, he is likely to be responding to an extrinsic source of motivation—a high grade which he hopes his studying will earn for him. The intrinsic motives discussed in this section cannot be traced to a specific homeostatic imbalance, nor are they derived from a physiological drive.

Exploratory and Curiosity Drives

Organisms appear to seek not just any kind of environmental stimulation but some degree of novelty and change in what they see, hear, feel, and touch. Novel stimuli arouse curiosity in animals, children, and adults. An individual manifests curiosity when he avoids familiar aspects of the environment; seeks new experiences; approaches and investigates new, ambiguous, or incongruous aspects of the environment; or asks for information from other people.[17] Children show curiosity when they examine and manipulate toys, puzzles, or mechanical gadgets, when they explore woods, dumps, caves, or beaches, or when they ask questions about events or ideas that appear to be incomplete or incongruous.

The observation that young children appear to be curious is supported by a number of researches. Mendel[18] showed 60 nursery school children, aged three to five, first one array of eight small toys (either 0 or 100 percent in novelty) and then four other arrays. The five arrays of toys were graduated in degree of novelty as follows: 0, 25, 50, 75, and 100 percent. Most of the children chose the novel arrays of toys in preference to more familiar toys.

Young children who are curious and engage in exploratory behavior tend to maintain these characteristics through time and to reveal greater development and learning than children who are less curious and less exploring. Minuchin,[19] in a follow-up study of 18 disadvantaged inner-city black children who had been observed at age four in their first year of a Head Start program and two years later after finishing first grade, found consistent, internalized differences in curiosity and exploratory behavior among these children. Children who were most curious and exploring at age four were among the most vigorous, searching, and adaptive at age six. Moreover, the more exploring and vigorous children at age six tended to be more confident of the support and effectiveness of adults, more differentiated in their self-image, and more inclined to have a stronger sense of their own effectiveness. Finally, Minuchin's study found that methods of teaching and curricula used with these children in the first grade did not provide them with opportunities to question and to explore. Indeed, there was some evidence that these activities, so important in learning, were actively discouraged.

The powerful effects of curiosity in motivating children in school is strikingly shown in Minuchin's study. The teacher who uses bulletin boards, walls, tables, and various parts of the room to show pictures, posters, books, magazines, exhibits, experiments, puzzles, mechanical toys, animals, and artifacts arouses the curiosity of students, with the result that many will want to find out more about these issues and objects. Field trips and films also serve to arouse curiosity. The teacher's understanding of the interests, developmental needs, and backgrounds of students will enable him to select items for display which have high arousal value for these students. If the curiosity of students is to be maintained, it is clear that exhibits and displays should be changed frequently.

Other studies have investigated the motivational basis of curiosity.

[17] Daniel E. Berlyne, *Conflict, Arousal, and Curiosity* (New York: McGraw-Hill Book Co., 1960), pp. 79–162.

[18] Gisela Mendel, "Children's Preferences for Differing Degrees of Novelty," *Child Development*, 36 (June 1965), 453–465.

[19] Patricia P. Minuchin, "Curiosity and Exploratory Behavior in Disadvantaged Children: A Follow-Up Study," ERIC (1971), ED 056 747.

Smock and Holt[20] sought to ascertain children's responses to a series of quite different pictures—some of them ambiguous and incongruous, others relatively familiar. The subjects, 44 first grade children (22 boys and 22 girls), were shown pictures projected on the screen of a mock TV set. Each child sat in front of the set and was instructed to press a "repeat" button to request a repetition of the same picture. He was also shown a lever which he could press to signal a "change" to a different picture. Results of the study showed that novel stimuli (ambiguous and incongruous pictures) elicited significantly more "repetition" responses and hence greater curiosity than did nonnovel pictures. Smock and Holt also found that children who were perceptually rigid (reluctant to change their interpretations of a picture in response to change in cues) were less responsive to the incongruous pictures. In general, however, the results of this study suggest that curiosity is aroused in response to a mismatch between one's mental set and his perception of environmental events.

In a study involving fifth grade children, Maw and Maw[21] found that children with high curiosity (those so identified by teachers, peers, and themselves) chose unbalanced and unusual pictures, in preference to balanced and usual ones, more frequently than did children identified as having low curiosity. Maw and Maw conclude that curiosity level may be more important than IQ for determining the teaching materials and procedures that should be used with a given classroom group. Children with similar IQs may desire different degrees of uncertainty in a learning situation.

Activity and Manipulatory Motives

Children may be observed to persist in physical movements and manipulatory activities over fairly extended periods. Swinging, running, climbing the jungle gym, riding a tricycle, and punching the keys on a toy cash register or typewriter are activities which children appear to continue for their own sake. Few studies have investigated manipulatory drives in children, but Piaget's[22] observations of his infant son, Laurent, tells us something about how these drives develop. Piaget observed that Laurent accidentally shook the rattle that was placed in his hand and then continued shaking it for 15 minutes, during which time he emitted peals of laughter. Later, giving Laurent a notebook, a beaded purse, and a wooden parrot, Piaget noted four stages of response: (1) visual exploration, passing the object from hand to hand; (2) tactile exploration, passing his hand over

[20] Charles D. Smock and Bess G. Holt, "Children's Reactions to Novelty: An Experimental Study of 'Curiosity Motivation,'" *Child Development*, 33 (September 1962), 631–642.

[21] Wallace H. Maw and Ethel W. Maw, "Selection of Unbalanced and Unusual Designs by Children High in Curiosity," *Child Development*, 33 (December 1962), 917–922.

[22] Jean Piaget, *The Origins of Intelligence in Children*, trans. by M. Cook (New York: International University Press, 1952), pp. 162, 255.

the object; (3) moving the object slowly in space; and (4) shaking the object, then striking it, then rubbing it against his bassinet, then sucking it. In each instance Laurent seemed to study the effect of his activity.

Cognitive Motives

Other intrinsic motives are those in which the individual uses mental processes and cognitive functioning. Children become fascinated with making up limericks and solving puzzles and riddles; adults read murder stories, play chess, or work crossword puzzles—apparently for the intrinsic satisfactions that these cognitive activities provide. Indeed, the doctor who tries to save the life of a patient, the businessman who works to stay ahead of the competition, and the teacher who helps a nonreader learn to read are motivated by something beyond the remuneration they receive. In each case the use of cognitive processes and intellectual abilities is intrinsically satisfying, even though these processes and abilities are directed toward external goals.

Another aspect of cognitive motivation is one's motivation to make his behavior consistent with his ways of viewing, evaluating, and thinking about this behavior. Inconsistency between one's behavior and his cognitive responses toward the behavior creates what Festinger[23] calls *cognitive dissonance*. According to Festinger, if a discrepancy exists between one's behavior and his evaluation of that behavior, the individual will justify and rationalize his behavior so as to reduce the discrepancy. The motive to reduce dissonance is comparable to achieving a kind of "cognitive homeostasis." John, for instance, perceives himself as an able student and yet does poorly on an examination. He may try to reduce the resulting cognitive dissonance by intellectualizing that grades do not measure the most important outcomes of a college education, that the most successful people are not always those who received the highest grades, that the instructor has a reputation for being unfair, or that he is a good student in every subject except this one. John's intellectualization has enabled him to reduce cognitive dissonance by devaluing the importance of grades and modifying his self-concept.

Concept of Competence

Curiosity, exploratory activity, and manipulative behavior, according to White,[24] all play important roles in the attainment of *competence*. Competence, or *effectance*, is not acquired through behavior instigated by drives

---

[23] Leon Festinger, *A Theory of Cognitive Dissonance* (Stanford, Calif.: Stanford University Press, 1957).

[24] Robert W. White, "Motivation Reconsidered: The Concept of Competence," *Psychological Review*, 66 (September 1959), 297–333.

based on physiological deficits. Rather, it is a process through which animals and human beings actively seek environmental stimulation. Monkeys manipulate objects placed in the cage, infants shake rattles, and children and adults explore caves. Exploration and manipulation increase one's level of competence and are motives in their own right.

Earlier, Harlow[25] took a similar position. He found no evidence that intensity of drive state and the correlated amount of drive reduction are positively related to learning efficiency in primates. In fact, rather than being influenced by food deprivation, monkeys seemed to learn more efficiently if they were given food before testing. Harlow concludes that a drive reduction theory of learning is untenable and that curiosity is a first-order motive, not a derived drive.

External Rewards versus Intrinsic Motivation

We have noted that one is said to be intrinsically motivated to perform an activity when he receives no apparent reward other than engaging in the activity itself. If a boy who enjoys playing the violin begins to receive payment for practicing on his instrument, what will happen to his intrinsic motivation for performing this activity? Deci[26] conducted a series of experiments in which college students placed in experimental and control groups participated during three separate sessions in an intrinsically motivating activity (forming configurations using 27 one-inch cubes and writing headlines for stories appearing in a college newspaper). In two of the experiments, the members of the experimental groups were given money during the second session for each configuration or each headline completed. In the third experiment the experimental group during the second session was given verbal praise for each configuration completed. The difference in time spent on the task by experimental groups in session 3 (when no monetary or verbal reward was given) and time spent on the task in session 2 (when external reward was provided) was an indication of the influence of external reward on the performance of the presumably intrinsically motivating task. Control groups were given no external rewards during the three sessions they were engaged in the same task.

Results of the first two experiments revealed that, when money was used as an external reward for engaging in an activity which the subjects had found to be intrinsically motivating, the time spent on this activity decreased when the reward was discontinued. In the third experiment, however, when verbal reinforcement and positive feedback were used as external rewards, the subjects' intrinsic motivation, evidenced by time spent engaged in the activity, seemed to increase in comparison to that of non-

[25] Harry F. Harlow, "Mice, Monkeys, Men, and Motives," *Psychological Review*, 6 (1953), 23–32.

[26] Edward L. Deci, "Effects of Externally Mediated Rewards on Intrinsic Motivation," *Journal of Personality and Social Psychology*, 18 (1971), 105–115.

rewarded subjects. Table 3–3 presents the experimental design and results of the three experiments.

It would appear that money—possibly because of its connotation and use in our culture—may act as a stimulus which leads a person to a cognitive reevaluation of the activity from one which is intrinsically worthwhile to one which is worthwhile primarily because it is associated with financial reward. It may be that as the feeling of personal causation shifts to an external source, the individual feels he has become a pawn of external

Table 3–3. Experimental Design and Results of Three Experiments Studying Effects of Externally Mediated Rewards of Intrinsic Motivation

Experiment and Group	Session 1	Session 2	Session 3	Difference (Session 3—Session 1)
Experiment 1 (Task: making configurations using one-inch cubes)				
Experimental group $N = 12$	No reward 248.2*	$1.00 for each correct configuration 313.7	No reward 198.5	 −49.7
Control group $N = 12$	No reward 213.9*	No reward 205.7	No reward 241.8	 27.9
Experiment 2 (Task: writing headlines for school newspaper)				
Experimental group $N = 4$	No reward 22.39†	$.50 for each headline 20.34	No reward 21.35	 −1.04
Control group $N = 2$	No reward 22.19†	No reward 20.97	No reward 12.60	 −9.59
Experiment 3 (Task: making configurations using one-inch cubes)				
Experimental group $N = 12$	No reward 134.0*	Verbal praise for each correct configuration 146.7	No reward 129.3	 −4.7
Control group $N = 12$	No reward 246.8*	No reward 146.1	No reward 64.7	1 −182.1

* Mean number of seconds spent working on the puzzle during the eight-minute free choice periods. The higher the score, the higher the motivation.

† Mean number of minutes spent in writing each headline. The lower the score, the higher the motivation.

authority. His behavior is then motivated by external reward rather than interest.

On the other hand, rewards such as social approval do not seem to influence a person's self-perceptions in the same way. He will continue to be intrinsically motivated because he is less likely to think of affection or verbal approval as a control mechanism. These findings are a reminder that reinforcements, if used indiscriminantly, are likely to be counterproductive and thus impede learning. Reinforcement is most effective when it is appropriate to the situation and is used for strengthening desired behavior.

Motivation and School Learning

The previous section makes clear that a number of intrinsic motives (such as curiosity, exploration, and manipulation) significantly influence learning. Certain other intrinsic motives, however, play a particularly important role in school learning.

Social and Affiliative Motives

Pupils desire acceptance, approval, and recognition by parents, teachers, and peers. The social and affiliation motives are very effective in stimulating participation in learning activities. The first grader who has mastered his first reader often appears to experience as much satisfaction from demonstrating to his parents that he can read as he does from an inner sense of accomplishment.

The influence of social and affiliative motives on learning is revealed in several studies. Bandura and Huston[27] studied the effect of various adult-child relationships on the child's subsequent learning. Nursery school children who experienced consistently warm and rewarding interactions with the adult model imitated this model to a greater extent than did children who had not experienced this nurturing relationship. Sears,[28] in a study of learning conditions and children's behavior in fifth and sixth grade classrooms, found that the children who score high on creativity have usually received a great deal of personal attention and praise from their teachers. The satisfying of social and affiliative motives appears to facilitate learning among older students as well. High school students produce a greater number of original poems and artwork for teachers whom they view as warm

---

[27] Albert Bandura and Aletha C. Huston, "Identification as a Process of Incidental Learning," *Journal of Abnormal and Social Psychology*, 63 (1961), 311–318.

[28] Pauline S. Sears, *The Effect of Classroom Conditions on the Strength of Achievement Motive and Work Output on Elementary Children*, Cooperative Research Project No. 873 (Washington, D. C.: Office of Education, U.S. Department of Health, Education, and Welfare, 1963).

and considerate than they do for teachers whom they perceive as less warm.[29] Teachers who communicate personal warmth in their relationships with others also tend to make increased use of intrinsic motives and to promote pupils' interest in science.[30]

There is some evidence, however, that continuous nurturance on the part of teachers may be less effective than intermittent nurturance and nurturance withdrawal. Hartup[31] compared two groups of four-year-old children who were asked to learn a simple concept and a memory task. One group received consistent support and affection from a female experimenter during a 10-minute period of interaction. The other group received five minutes of such nurturant interaction followed by five minutes of nurturance withdrawal, in which the experimenter ceased to interact with the child and responded to his supplications by saying she was busy. Hartup found that children in the nurturance withdrawal group needed fewer trials and made fewer errors in learning. These results suggest that nurturance withdrawal produces greater motivation than consistent nurturance. After a child has experienced warm interaction with an adult, withdrawal of nurturance arouses him to take action toward restoring the warm relationship.

Teachers facilitate student learning through responding to both affiliative needs and cognitive needs. By arousing students' interests, offering help and support, and responding to their bids for attention, teachers help to satisfy pupils' needs for affiliation. The teacher may arouse cognitive motives in students by using materials or procedures which make the task more understandable, relating the new learning to tasks or concepts encountered previously, breaking the task down into component parts, or identifying a sequence of steps needed to solve a problem. Clifford[32] has developed a theoretical model which predicts that a teacher's arousal of students' affective (affiliative) motives increases their performance on a noncomplex task, such as learning vocabulary, whereas the stimulation of students' cognitive motives facilitates their learning a complex task, such as obtaining the volume of a pyramid. Clifford's investigation of the performance of 2,256 fifth grade children in a vocabulary-learning task supports in part the proposition that affective motivation encourages noncomplex learning as much as cognitive motivation does. Comparisons were made between group types of competition, one in which high-scoring students on the vocabulary test were given candy (affective motivation) and the other in which high-scoring students were given an advantage in a follow-up scoring game (cognitive motivation). As measured by perform-

[29] Morris L. Cogan, "The Behavior of Teachers and the Productive Behavior of Their Pupils," *Journal of Experimental Education,* 27 (December 1958), 89–124.

[30] Horace B. Reed, "Implications for Science Education of Teacher Competence Research," *Science Education,* 46 (December 1962), 473–486.

[31] Willard W. Hartup, "Nurturance and Nurturance Withdrawal in Relation to the Dependency Behavior in Preschool Children," *Child Development,* 29 (June 1958), 191–201.

[32] Margaret Clifford, "Goals and Motivational Effects in the Elementary School," ERIC (1971), ED 056 355.

ance, interest, and retention, both competitive situations were equally effective.

Achievement Motives

The importance of achievement motives in school learning is self-evident. The need-for-achievement motive, often shortened to *nAch*, has been studied extensively by McClelland and his co-workers.[33] Their *nAch* measure consists of four TAT ambiguous-picture cards; the cards are projected on a screen, and the subjects are asked to write stories about the pictures. Children whose stories contain many achievement-related themes score high in *nAch*, the high score being interpreted as evidence of a strong need to achieve. McClelland found that persons high in achievement imagery (high *nAch* scores) complete more tasks when told that such tasks are measures of intellectual ability, solve more simple arithmetic problems in a timed test, get better grades, recall more uncompleted tasks, and have a higher level of aspiration.

Since the need-for-achievement motive is learned by the child as part of his socialization, the strength of this motive must depend on the parents' expectations and values and on the strength of the child's identification with parents and teachers. Winterbottom[34] found that the children of relatively demanding mothers scored higher in need for achievement than did children whose mothers made few demands on them. For example, mothers of off-spring scoring high in *nAch* were more likely to expect their children, even before age eight, to know their way around the city, to try new things for themselves, to do well in competition, and to make their own friends. In a later study of middle class mothers and sons, Winterbottom[35] found the strongest achievement motivation among boys whose mothers expected them to be self-reliant at a fairly early age.

Since parents who have attained high-ranking occupational levels usually attended college and had a certain amount of academic success, they might be more likely to expect their children to attend college than would parents at lower occupational levels. A study by Kahl[36] supports this assumption to a certain extent. In Kahl's study the percentage of high school

[33] David C. McClelland et al., *The Achievement Motive* (New York: Appleton-Century-Crofts, 1953).

[34] Miriam R. Winterbottom, "The Relation of Childhood Training in Independence to Achievement Motivation" (unpublished doctor's dissertation, University of Michigan, 1953).

[35] Miriam R. Winterbottom, "The Relation of Need for Achievement to Learning Experiences in Independence and Mastery," in John W. Atkinson, ed., *Motives in Fantasy Action and Society* (Princeton, N. J.: D. Van Nostrand Co., 1958), pp. 453–478. See also Bernard C. Rosen and Roy D'Andrade, "The Psychosocial Origins of Achievement Motivation," *Sociometry*, 22 (1959), 185–195, 215–218.

[36] Joseph A. Kahl, *The American Class Structure* (New York: Holt, Rinehart and Winston, 1957).

boys who expected to go to college was progressively higher for those whose fathers were at successively higher occupational levels.

Motivation and the Self-Concept

Achievement motivation is also revealed in a person's striving to act in ways that are consistent with his view of himself (self-concept). Students who receive average or low marks often develop negative self-images which may lessen motivation for school achievement. Some children who experience failure in school seem to be influenced by a negative self-image when they continue to set unrealistic academic goals that are markedly above their past achievement. By holding to unrealistically high aspirations, these children unconsciously seem to want once again to confirm to themselves and others that they are failures. Other "failure" students, on the other hand, persistently set academic goals so low that they confirm their self-images as low achievers. In contrast, successful students reflect a positive self-concept in setting academic goals slightly above their past performance. Their past success contributes to a positive self-image that translates into increased motivation and higher aspiration to surpass their past performance.[37]

The findings of other studies investigating self-concept and achievement, however, have been inconsistent, especially in studies of the relationships between self-concept and achievement of disadvantaged youth, most of whom are black. Kerensky[38] found that the achievement of 452 elementary children in 13 inner-city schools declined from third grade to sixth grade, although the measured self-concepts of these children did not differ significantly from those of other populations. These children expressed a high need for achievement and recognition which was not related to their actual performance. Coleman,[39] in his nation-wide study of equality of educational opportunity, found that blacks and whites made similar responses in reporting self-perceptions of their academic abilities. This similarity of responses is puzzling because many black children report experiences which lower self-esteem.

On the other hand, Gay[40] found that the relationships between the self-concepts of 207 black eighth graders and their intelligence and academic

[37] Pauline S. Sears, "Levels of Aspiration in Academically Successful and Unsuccessful Children," *Journal of Abnormal and Social Psychology*, 35 (October 1940), 498–536.

[38] Vasil M. Kerensky, "Reported Self-Concept versus Relation to Academic Achievement in an Inner-City Setting," *Dissertation Abstracts*, 27 (1967), 2,325-A.

[39] James Coleman et al., *Equality of Educational Opportunity* (Washington, D. C.: U. S. Government Printing Office, 1966), pp. 218 ff.

[40] Cleveland J. Gay, "Academic Achievement and Intelligence among Negro Eighth Grade Students as a Function of the Self-Concept," *Dissertation Abstracts*, 27 (1966), 112-A.

achievement were significant for both sexes. His finding that the teacher's estimate of the student's self-concept was the best predictor of his achievement suggests that the self-concept is probably a greater motivational factor in achievement than intelligence. Henderson,[41] however, found that aspirational level, as a partial indicator of self-concept, is especially inaccurate with certain low-income blacks who aspire to different societal conditions that are based on white standards. Similarly, setting very high or very low goals seems to be characteristic of children who have experienced failure (see Sears' study cited above), as well as of those who have strong feelings of self-rejection.[42]

Studies which have investigated the effect of compensatory education programs on the self-concepts of disadvantaged youth also report mixed results. Geisler[43] found that high school students from low income families who participated in an Upward Bound summer program had significantly more positive self-concepts and higher grade point averages after participating in the program than before. Hershovitz,[44] however, reported that a compensatory program combining educational and vocational elements resulted in negative changes in the self-concepts of 58 Negro high school youths who were potential dropouts. The results were attributed to the shortness of the program and an overemphasis on work adjustment in the vocational part of the project.

Finally, there is evidence that a large perceived discrepancy between actual self and ideal self may be motivating for some individuals. Self-concept is the image of oneself, the person one presently sees himself as being, while the ideal self is the individual's image of the person he would like to be. Martire[45] found that persons with high need-for-achievement scores exhibited a greater discrepancy between ideal and actual self-concepts under both neutral and achievement-motivating conditions. This discrepancy suggests that these persons had developed an unrealistically high achievement motivation. Dissatisfaction in such highly motivated people, possibly caused by low intelligence or lack of opportunity, appears to be reflected in a discrepant self-ideal self-concept. The low aspirations expressed by persons who have strong generalized achievement motivation but who are also anxious about failure suggests that, for these individuals, fear of failure is stronger than the desire to achieve.

[41] George Henderson, "Aspiration and Social Class," *Dissertation Abstracts,* 26 (1965), 5,586.

[42] I. D. Cohen, "Level of Aspiration, Behavior, and Feeling of Adequacy and Self-Acceptance," *Journal of Abnormal and Social Psychology,* 49 (1954), 84–86.

[43] John S. Geisler, "The Effects of a Compensatory Education Program on the Self-Concept and Academic Achievement of High-School-Age Youth from Low Income Families," *Dissertation Abstracts,* 29 (1968, 2,520-A.

[44] Frieda S. Hershovitz, "The Effects of an Educational-Vocational Rehabilitation Program upon the Self-Concepts of Disadvantaged Youth," *Dissertation Abstracts,* 30 (1969), 2,801-A.

[45] John G. Martire, "Relationships between the Self-Concept and Differences in the Strength and Generality of Achievement Motivation," *Journal of Personality,* 14 (June 1956), 364–375.

Similarly, Friedman[46] reported that self–ideal self discrepancy increased as ability of middle- and high-achieving ninth graders increased, while the discrepancy decreased for low achievers. These findings suggest that discrepancies between a student's actual self and his ideal self serve as a spur to school achievement.

The Teacher's Influence on Students' Motives

Results of studies already cited, as well as common observation, attest to the central importance of motivation in learning. Thus, in seeking to guide and to promote the learning of students, the teacher is concerned with discovering ways through which they can be aroused to respond actively in learning situations. In general, the way in which one person influences the arousal state of another person is through the use of incentives. An *incentive* is a reward or source of satisfaction which a person *may* obtain. A merchandiser may offer price reductions, service, convenience, or trading stamps as incentives to consumers to induce them to purchase a certain product. A teacher frequently gives praise and high grades to students who perform well in school, the aim of these rewards being to encourage continuous strivings in the recipients and in the other pupils. Anxiety growing out of a fear of failure may also serve as an incentive in arousing the person to expend effort in seeking to avoid failure. Intrinsic motives, such as curiosity, need for achievement, and need for self-enhancement, may also serve as incentives.

Teachers, then, have a wide choice of incentives: externally controlled incentives, such as rewards and punishments; intrinsic incentives, such as the student's own need for achievement and self-enhancement; or some combination of extrinsic and intrinsic incentives. Although externally controlled incentives (rewards and punishments) are relatively easy to establish and administer and thus are widely used—by parents in rearing children, by courts and law enforcement officers, by captains of business and industry, as well as by teachers—such incentives are most effective when they are linked to intrinsic incentives. Thistlethwaite[47] analyzed the effects of praise (in the form of favorable publicity) given to two groups of talented students who took the National Merit Scholarship Test. As a result of this praise (which bolstered their intrinsic need for achievement), a greater number of these students decided to work toward advanced degrees in college.

---

[46] Joel R. Friedman, "The Relationship of Self-Ideal Self-Concept to Intellectual Ability and Academic Achievement in Ninth Grade Boys and Girls," *Dissertation Abstracts*, 30 (1969), 3,783–84–A.

[47] Donald L. Thistlethwaite, "Effects of Social Recognition upon the Educational Motivation of Talented Youth," *Journal of Educational Psychology*, 50 (June 1959), 111–116.

With few exceptions, studies show that reward in the form of praise, support, and encouragement significantly promotes learning. Page[48] investigated the motivational effects of teachers' comments on test papers. Seventy-four randomly selected high school teachers administered to their 2,139 students an objective test appropriate to the usual course of instruction. After the tests were scored, the papers were randomly assigned to one of three treatment groups: (1) the *no comment* group, which received no marks beyond those for grading; (2) the *free comment* group, which received whatever comments the teachers felt were appropriate; and (3) the *specified comment* group, which received uniform, generally encouraging comments designated by the experimenter for each letter grade—for example, *A:* "Excellent! Keep it up!" *C:* "Perhaps try to do still better?" *F:* "Let's raise this grade!" On the next objective test, students in the free comment group made slightly higher grades than those in the specific comment group. However, those who had previously received a specified comment performed significantly better than students who had received no comment.

Learning Content and Cognitive Structure

A teacher who wishes to make effective use of students' motives in encouraging learning should find out as much as he can about each student's cognitive structure—what the student knows, believes, wants, expects, and values. Findings of earlier cited studies investigating curiosity motives suggest that motivation for school learning is highest when there is a slight to moderate mismatch or dissonance between the learning content and the student's cognitive structure.[49] A moderate mismatch inducing an arousal in the student may be the result of noting the intriguing title of a story, analyzing a science experiment which went awry, or being presented a mathematics problem the teacher believes no one in the class can solve. If there is nearly a perfect match between the learning content and the student's cognitive structure, as when the teacher states an obvious truth or presents material already well known to the student, then the student is likely to be bored and minimally aroused. In situations where learning content and the student's cognitive structure are incongruent, the mismatch is likely to create anxiety, which impedes learning. In cases of serious mismatch, the learning content may be completely unfamiliar or appear irrelevant or inconsequential to the learner. Or the mismatch may be caused by the inability of the learner to process large amounts of data in a short time.

The degree of motivation that is likely to produce the most learning

[48] Ellis B. Page, "Teacher Comments and Student Performance: A 74 Classroom Experiment in School Motivation," *Journal of Educational Psychology*, 49 (August 1958), 173–181.

[49] Walter B. Waetjen, "The Teacher and Motivation," *Theory into Practice*, 9 (February 1970), 10–15.

depends, in part, on the relationship of arousal level to the level (or clarity) of *behavioral cues* offered by a particular stimulus, as shown in Figure 3–2. Thus, for example, a biology class in which a student uses familiar equipment and procedures in finding the *ph* (acid base) value of a soil sample from his backyard contains elements of medium to high cue and moderate arousal, which characterize optimal learning. Low cue and low arousal ex-

Figure 3–2.   The Amount of Behavioral Cue Offered by a Given Stimulus at Different Levels of Arousal

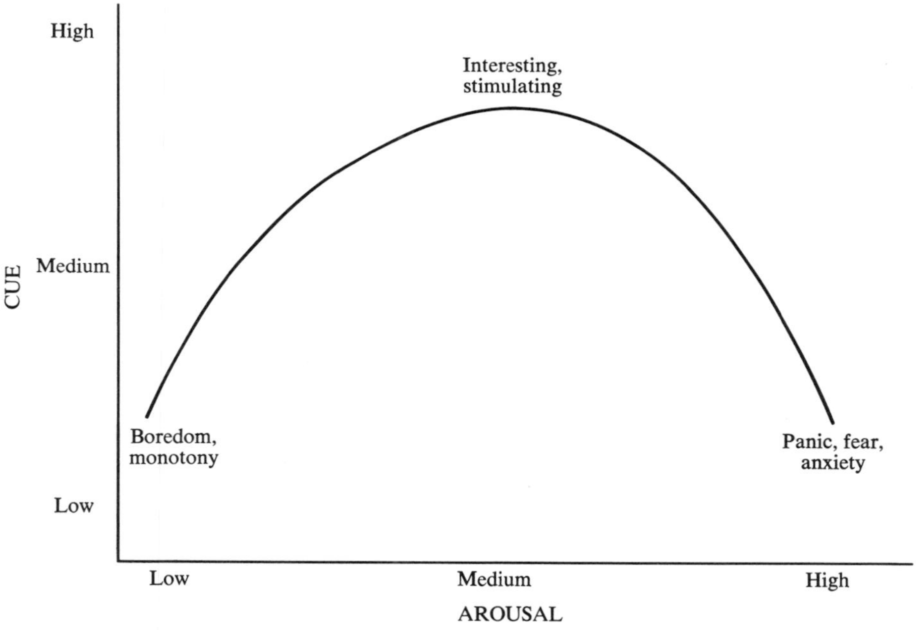

Source: Ronald C. Johnson and Gene R. Medinnus, *Child Psychology: Behavior and Development* (New York: John Wiley, 1965), p. 110. Reproduced by permission.

perienced by subjects in experiments of sensory deprivation or by persons listening to a lecture delivered in a monotone are usually associated with boredom and monotony. When arousal is high and cue level is low, as in driving at night on an icy road or trying to answer unfamiliar questions on an important examination, the learner's affective response is likely to be panic or anxiety. Results of animal studies[50] as well as observations of human learning suggest that if the task involves easy discriminations or

---

[50] Jerome S. Bruner, Jean Matter, and Miriam L. Papanek, "Breadth of Learning as a Function of Drive Level and Mechanization," *Psychological Review*, 62 (1955), 1–10.

responding to a minimum number of cues, then high arousal can produce fast learning and high achievement. If, however, low cue level involves responding to many cues or making difficult discriminations among several cues, then optimal learning will likely occur only under medium to low levels of arousal. Being required to perform a difficult task under high arousal can be expected to produce panic and anxiety.

By defining and structuring the learning task in ways that are appropriate to the learner's cognitive structure and level of arousal, the teacher is able to increase the learning potential of each student. Kersh[51] studied the influence of teaching strategies on students' subsequent behavior and performance. In his study each subject in each of three groups of college students was asked to learn the *odd numbers* and the *constant difference* rules of addition:

> The odd numbers rule. *The sum of any series of consecutive odd numbers, beginning with 1, is equal to the square of the number of figures in the series. (For example, 1, 3, 5, 7 is such a series; there are four numbers, so 4 times 4 is 16, the sum.)*

> The constant difference rule. *The sum of any series of numbers in which the difference between the numbers is constant is equal to one half the product of the number of figures and the sum of the first and last numbers. (For example, 2, 3, 4, 5, is such a series; 2 and 5 are 7; there are four figures, so 4 times 7 is 28; half of 28 is 14, which is the sum.)*

The first group, called the *no help* group, was required to discover the rules for working the problem without any help from the experimenter. The second group, called the *directed reference* group, was given some direction in the form of perceptual aids. The third group, called the *rule given* group, was told the rules directly and was given practice in applying them without any reference to the arithmetical or geometrical relationships. Thus, the teaching strategies used with the first two groups involved two approaches to discovery learning, while for the third group the teaching strategy involved the use of rote or mechanical learning.

The results of this study showed that students under the directed reference (some help) treatment scored highest on measures of retention and on transfer tasks involving use of the two rules. The no help group scored higher than the rule given group. Of particular interest in this study were the varied effects of teaching strategies on students' motivations in carrying out and extending the learning task. Subjects in the no help group who failed to discover the rule during the practice session told of their

---

[51] Bert Y. Kersh, "The Adequacy of 'Meaning' as an Explanation for the Superiority of Learning by Independent Discovery," *Journal of Educational Psychology*, 49 (1958), 282–292.

efforts to learn the rule, even going so far as to look up the algebraic formula in the library. On the other hand, one subject in the rule given group complained that the experimenter had not instructed him to remember the rules, so he promptly forgot them.

An important part of the teacher's task, then, is selecting and implementing strategies that will promote effective learning. Some of the ways which a teacher and the learning experiences she plans can relate to a student's motives are revealed in these excerpts from the case of Heidi, an eight-year-old girl in the third grade. Heidi's school records list straight *A* marks for the first and second grades.

October 6.   *The first part of our afternoon story hour is used for contributions (literary) from both the class and the teacher. On certain days a child is allowed to read or tell a favorite story or poem. Yesterday I devoted the period to poetry reading, so today Heidi arrived with a shabby copy of* A Child's Garden of Verses *and asked if she could read two poems to the class. After telling the class that the book had belonged to her great-grandmother, she read "The Land of Counterpane" and "Windy Nights." Before I could compliment her choice of poetry and choose another reader, she continued, "And here's another favorite, 'My Shadow,'" and "I just love this one." She monopolized the 15-minute period reading her favorites. After each reading she would give an introduction to the next poem: "My mommy read this to me when I was two," or "I've known this ever since I could talk." Heidi's expression was so good and her animation so infectious that the entire class seemed to enjoy the entertainment.*

October 8.   *Today I was reading* Bambi *to the class when Heidi arrived late. She was again clasping her volume to her as she clumped noisily to her seat. As soon as she sat down, she opened her book and, with one hand keeping the place in the book, raised her hand as high as she could reach and kept it up during the entire story period.*

November 4.   *Heidi and Jerry are team captains for our subtraction and addition contests for the month of November, and until today Heidi's team has been scoring ahead. Today, however, Jerry's team won by three points, and Heidi made her first mistake at the board. Immediately after the mistake, Heidi complained of a headache, so I had her put her head on her desk. She kept her head down until noon recess, then left the room without glancing left or right.*

November 8.   *Heidi's and Jerry's teams had another contest involving subtraction facts. Each child did five problems at the blackboard when his name was called. I noticed one little fellow*

*glancing at his left hand, which rested on the chalk tray, and in-
vestigation revealed he had the answers to the combinations on a
slip of paper in his hand.*

*When I questioned the class, three admitted they had cheated
in the same way, and another boy said that Heidi had cheated. He
said she had looked at answers written on a slip of paper on her
desk. (Because she was the leader of her team, her desk was near
the board.) Heidi admitted her guilt but said, "I only looked at
two answers. I knew the rest." (She turned red, hung her head, and
fingered the folds of her skirt.) I stopped the contest and had everyone return to his regular place in the classroom to do the arithmetic
test on paper.*

Particularly evident in these excerpts are the ways in which some motives
(such as need for achievement and self-enhancement) are strengthened and
become dominant, with the result that they may endanger the gratification
of other motives—in Heidi's case, the need for acceptance and belonging.

Summary

Motivation is a process within the organism that mobilizes and
directs energy toward some object or part of the environment. Although behavior can be observed directly, motives can only be inferred. Behavior is
not the result of a single motive but is influenced by many different and
complex motives, some of them unconscious.

Motivation has been defined as an internal energy change that results
in affective arousal and anticipatory goal reactions.

Many theories have been advanced to explain motivation. One of
these theories, free will, is compatible with many philosophical and theo-
logical doctrines but is not useful to psychologists in their attempts to explain the motives underlying behavior because it appears to beg the question. Another theory, hedonism, has had many adherents but fails to explain
many things—for instance, why some persons seem to court danger and
eschew the easy life.

Instinct theories conceive of motivation as innate and identify specific
behavioral tendencies at various levels of animal life; by 1920, however, the
instinct theory began to lose adherents because it proved inadequate for
explaining the wide range of behavior that could not be classified as instinctual in the usual meaning of the term. *Drive theories* of motivation then
attained prominence. A useful model for a drive theory of motivation is
Cannon's concept of *homeostasis*—complex physiological processes that
maintain most of the steady states in the organism. Various *need theories*,
emphasizing specific lacks or deficiencies within the organism, are popular
with educators because they point to goals toward which students are

striving and provide data useful in curriculum planning. A distinction has been made between *normative needs,* needs that adults believe students *should* have, and *psychological needs,* needs that students actually do have.

Acquired motives (such as fear, anxiety, need for sensory stimulation) play important roles in human motivation. Various theories have been advanced to explain how acquired motives are learned. They may be derived from basic physiological motives (as suggested by Freud's concept of sublimation); they may be functionally autonomous; or they may be evidence of intrinsically motivated behavior.

Intrinsic motives are energy arousals which involve behavior that is satisfying in and for itself. Various intrinsic motives are exploratory and curiosity motives, activity and manipulatory motives, and cognitive motives. Animals as well as human beings who express curiosity and engage in exploratory and manipulative behavior evidence the seeking of environmental stimulation and the attaining of *competence* through coping effectively with the environment.

Intrinsic motives important in promoting school learning are social and affiliative motives, achievement motives, and motives which serve to maintain and enhance the self-concept. The influence of self-enhancement motives in learning is revealed in studies of levels of aspiration and achievement. In general, students who have experienced failure have unrealistically high or unrealistically low aspirations for academic success, while those who have experienced success are more realistic and consistent in estimating their subsequent performance. Findings of some studies reveal that the development of more positive self-concepts, especially among disadvantaged students, is accompanied by an improvement in academic achievement, but in other studies there was no parallel improvement of self-concept and school achievement.

Teachers who seek to arouse in students positive, active responses toward learning have a wide choice of *incentives* available. Reward incentives appear to be most effective in ecouraging learning when they are linked to such intrinsic motives as need for affiliation, achievement, and self-enhancement. Research findings support the teacher's use of praise and encouragement in improving pupil performance. Also effective are teacher strategies which adapt specific kinds and levels of motivation in the student to the requirements of the learning task and teacher strategies which encourage students to find out things for themselves.

Study Questions

1. Helen, a junior in high school, has made average to poor grades during most of her years in school. She seldom completes a homework assignment and barely scrapes by in her academic subjects. She is an attractive girl, wears expensive clothes to school, and spends much time primping. Her major interests seem to be fashion magazines, a career in modeling, and her boy friend.

Ted, a high school senior, has an IQ of 130 but has never done well in school. He views himself as something of a rebel and a revolutionary and continually baits his teachers. He has a broad fund of knowledge which he uses to put down teachers and students he does not like. He reads extensively in history and philosophy and is believed to be the editor of an underground newspaper that appears periodically.

Edna, a high school sophomore, seldom joins in school activities with her classmates. She spends most evenings studying. Although her IQ is 121, she has the highest grade point average in the sophomore class. Neither her parents nor her older siblings have gone to college.
What additional information would you need about each of these students to plan educational strategies for facilitating their development and learning? What specific strategies would you use with each student?

2. Some children who begin kindergarten and first grade eager, enthusiastic, and curious are observed in later grades to be apathetic or uninterested. What facts or principles concerning motivation might explain these changes in their behavior?

3. "You can lead a horse to water, but you can't make him drink" is a proverb that might characterize the belief that teachers cannot motivate students directly. What can a teacher do to influence a student's motivation so as to effect a change in his behavior?

4. At the moment of its onset, an individual's behavior is already predetermined. Do you agree or disagree with this proposition? Discuss.

Suggested Readings

Cofer, C. N., and M. H. Appley. *Motivation: Theory and Research*. New York: John Wiley, 1964. Presents a comprehensive discussion of the several trends in motivation and research and analyzes the contribution each makes toward a unified theory of motivation.

Maslow, Abraham. *Motivation and Personality*. Second Edition. New York: Harper & Row, 1970. Brings together the author's varied writings on the role of motivation in personality development. Of particular interest is Maslow's statement of a theory of motivation in Chapter 5 and his discussion of the qualities and characteristics of self-actualizing people in Chapters 12 and 13.

McClelland, David C., et al. *The Achievement Motive*. New York: Appleton-Century-Crofts, 1955. Summarizes a five-year study of the achievement motive. Of special interest is the description of the development, scoring, and interpretation of a projective test for measuring the achievement motive. Chapter 2 presents a statement of the authors' theory of motivation.

McDonald, Frederick J. *Educational Psychology*. Second Edition. Belmont, Calif.: Wadsworth Publishing Co., 1965. Chapter 4 draws distinctions between motives, needs, and incentives. How motives and needs are learned, the effects of school experiences on goal setting, and the relationship of motivation and teaching strategies are discussed.

Murray, Edward J. *Motivation and Emotion.* Englewood Cliffs, N. J.: Prentice-Hall, 1964. Integrates various theoretical viewpoints and research studies on motivation. Discusses the origin, nature, and characteristics of homeostatic, sexual, and emotional motives, intrinsically motivated behavior, and derived social motives for achievement and affiliation.

Sears, Pauline S., and Ernest R. Hilgard. "The Teacher's Role in the Motivation of the Learner," in Ernest R. Hilgard, ed., *Theories of Learning and Instruction.* Sixty-Third Yearbook of the National Society for the Study of Education, Part 1. Chicago: University of Chicago Press, 1964, pp. 182–209. Reviews studies which describe the range of motives in students that a teacher can arouse and utilize in facilitating students' learning. Important student motives which teachers can use include the social motives of warmth and nurturance, the achievement motive, and curiosity. Effective use of motivation in school learning is based on a recognition that the teacher is both a model and a reinforcer of learning as well as a releaser of intrinsic motives.

White, Robert W. "Motivation Reconsidered: The Concept of Competence." *Psychological Review,* 66 (September 1959), 297–333. Discusses the widespread discontent with theories of motivation built upon primary drives. Advances the concept of competence as an explanation for the apparent tendency of people to explore their environment and interact effectively with it.

Films

Focus on Behavior: The Need to Achieve, 16 mm, sound, black and white, 30 min. Bloomington: Audiovisual Center, Indiana University. In this film Dr. David McClelland demonstrates the tests with which he seeks to verify his psychological theory—that the economic growth or decline of nations is dependent to a large extent upon their entrepreneurs. The need to achieve is one of a variety of phenomena studied in motivation research.

Focus on Behavior: The Social Animal, 16 mm, sound, black and white, 29 min. Bloomington: Audiovisual Center, Indiana University. This film portrays some of the ways in which man is influenced and changed by his society. The effect of group pressure to conform is demonstrated through the experimental work of Dr. Stanley Schachter. The consequences of publicly stating ideas contrary to one's private belief illustrates Dr. Leon Festinger's theory of cognitive dissonance. The influence of motives of competition and cooperation in the bargaining process is explored by Dr. Morton Deutsch.

Part Two

**Forces That Shape Development
and Learning**

The Physical Organism and Its Growth

In complexity of organization, in structural intricacy, in harmony and balance of pattern, living things are in a separate category from the non-living.

Ralph W. Gerard

In beginning a study of the human organism, we might do well to relate what we know about organic life in general to what we know about the universe. Our universe appears to be governed by natural laws of order, organization, unity, evolution, and change. Some of these natural laws are expressed in the physical sciences by the first and second laws of thermodynamics. The first of these laws relates to the conservation of energy: Energy can neither be created nor destroyed; it can only be changed. Since life, including human life, is a part of the universe, life is a manifestation of unique organizations of energy.

The second law of thermodynamics states that energy is becoming less organized, less available, and more random. The tendency toward the degradation of energy implied by this second law is called *entropy*. An example of the degradation of energy is the operation of machines in which 30 to 50 percent of the fuel energy is converted into work and the remainder is degraded as friction and heat. The life impulse manifested in growth and development at the beginning of life and in adulthood constitutes a major countertendency to this second law of thermodynamics. However, with the increasing rate of catabolism (the breakdown of tissues and decrease in body efficiency) beginning in middle age and the consequent diminishing of vigor, life increasingly fulfills this second law.

Our knowledge of life in general and of human life in particular is increasing rapidly, but much remains unknown. Biologists became convinced a long time ago that it is not particularly useful to try to define life. Quite marvelous mechanical kidneys, hearts, and brains have been constructed, which—although they fit some of the definitions of life—are clearly not alive. Someone has said that the problem of defining life is a lot like trying to define your wife. You recognize her and you can describe her many features, characteristics, and habits—but just try defining her.

Characteristics of Life

We frequently find it useful to study life in relation to the qualities and characteristics shared by all living organisms. Both the amoeba and man metabolize, grow, reproduce, and adapt to their respective environments; and both possess a dynamic organization. Man differs from other living things only in that he is infinitely more complex. We now turn to an examination of five major characteristics of life, with special focus upon the ways each of these is manifested in man. These five major characteristics of life are metabolism, growth, dynamic organization, reproduction, and adaptation to the environment.

Metabolism

Some may wonder why, in enumerating the characteristics of living things, we begin with metabolism. We do so because of a basic law of life: Function precedes structure. The processes of metabolism and growth determine the emergent physical structure—not vice versa. The structure of the body, then, is a response to fundamental processes of metabolism and growth.

Living things take in materials from their environments, change them chemically, and convert them into new products. All of the changes which take place within cells and within the total organism in the synthesis of new materials are subsumed under the general term *metabolism*.

The process of human metabolism may become clearer if we relate it to the carbon cycle of plants and animals. Figure 4–1 shows that through the process of *photosynthesis* green plants take carbon dioxide from the air, take water from the soil, and in the presence of sunlight manufacture carbohydrates and give off oxygen. In animals this process is reversed: Carbohydrates and oxygen are taken in and carbon dioxide and water are given off. In this process, metabolic energy is released. Figure 4–1 thus shows the interdependence of plants and animals. The carbohydrates produced and the oxygen given off by plants are sources of food and oxygen necessary to the life of animals. In turn, the carbon dioxide and water given off by animals are essential to the existence and growth of plants.

The chief product of animal metabolism is freed energy, which is used to satisfy the body's energy requirements for maintenance, growth, tissue repair, and movement. Man has a particularly elaborate, highly differentiated mechanism for obtaining energy from the oxidation of sugar. Digestive enzymes break down complex food molecules into glucose, which is then assimilated into the blood stream and carried to each of the billions of cells of the body. The energy freed by the oxidation of glucose in the cell is transformed into phosphate bonds of the adenosine triphosphate (ATP)

Figure 4–1. The carbon energy cycle. The ultimate source of energy is the sun, some of whose energy is trapped by photosynthesis and formed into carbohydrates and other organic molecules. In animals, organic molecules are broken down by respiration, resulting in metabolic energy.

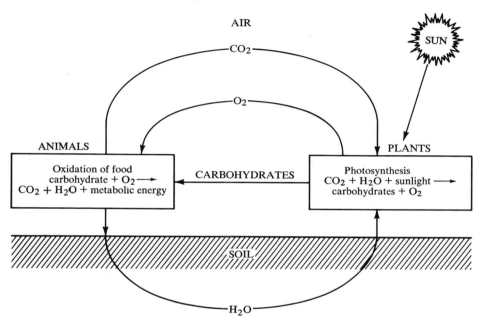

Source: Adapted from Paul B. Weisz, *The Science of Biology* (New York: McGraw-Hill Book Co., 1963), p. 396. Used by permission.

molecule. This ATP molecule is involved in all of the energy-expending processes of the cell. ATP molecules are formed by two processes. In the first process, called *glycolysis,* a single glucose molecule is broken down into two molecules of lactic acid through a series of at least 11 chemical changes. In the second process the two lactic acid molecules are changed chemically, in a series of steps known as the *Krebs citric acid cycle,* to produce 36 energy-charged ATP molecules and the by-products carbon dioxide and water. These ATP molecules are sources of energy available to the cell for carrying on life processes.

We should not conclude this discussion of metabolism without giving special emphasis to the key role which enzymes play in all life processes. The key to many of the secrets and complexities of life lies in the number and specificity of enzymes, proteinlike agents which act as catalysts in an enormous number of chemical changes at every level and in every system of the body. Enzymes play such a dominant role in the chemistry of life that it is exceedingly difficult to imagine the synthesis of living material without their help.

Growth

One of the important functions of metabolism is the synthesis of new cells and tissues. By this process the organism increases in size and complexity in accordance with an overall pattern of growth and development. The growth impulse is closely identified with the life impulse itself: Life is assured only when the anabolic building-up processes greatly exceed the catabolic tearing-down processes in the organism. Although this inherent metabolic urge to grow and to develop is very strong in young children, it may be blunted by many factors (malnutrition, various acute and chronic infections, endocrine disturbances, and congenital anomalies and malformations).

The different aspects of growth and development are contained in Krogman's statement "We grow, we grow up; we grow older."[1] The child increases in size, he changes in proportions, and he progresses toward maturity. The changes in size of the body or of any of its parts is known as *physical growth*. It is measured in inches or centimeters (height) and pounds or kilograms (weight). But increase in size, however important, is only one kind of growth. One also grows up. At the same time that he is increasing in size, he is experiencing changes in proportion, differentiation, and complexity in his body as a whole and in one or more of its parts. A child's growing up is a developmental aspect of the growth process. *Development* refers to the increasing skills and complexity of function which result from increased tissue specialization. Progressive changes in nervous system, muscles, bones, and tissues, for instance, are manifested in motor development, while progressive changes in body physique, sex glands, and associated tissues are manifested in sexual development.

The peak of the anabolic phase of growth is reached soon after attainment of physical maturity, but changes within cells, tissues, and the body as a whole continue to occur. Thus begins the catabolic phase, the slow but inexorable decline of body efficiency brought about by aging of organs and tissues. A wound or bruise in a young child heals quickly; in an adult, the wound heals more slowly; in a very elderly person, it takes a long time to heal and sometimes does not heal at all. The loss of physiological efficiency brought on by the processes of aging is particularly evident in the world of sports. Most professional baseball and football players are beyond their peak by the age of 30; the boxer's legs have begun to slow him up long before he is 30. We grow, we grow up, we grow old.

---

[1] Wilton M. Krogman, "Physical Growth as a Factor in the Behavioral Development of the Child," in Walter B. Waetjen, ed., *New Dimensions in Learning: A Multidisciplinary Approach* (Washington, D. C.: Association for Supervision and Curriculum Development, N.E.A., 1962), p. 9.

Dynamic Organization

The processes of metabolism and growth do not occur in haphazard fashion; they are coordinated processes within a dynamic living system. Dynamic organization—whereby living things maintain internal order while changing, growing, developing, and learning—is one of the foremost characteristics of the life process. Movements and changes within cells, tissues, and the body as a whole are governed by principles of dynamic organization which allow the organism to maintain equilibrium while performing its functions of respiration, digestion, circulation, and elimination and while adapting to lowered caloric intake, growth, infection or disease, or psychological stress.

The maintenance of dynamic organization in organic life is best exemplified by Cannon's concept of *homeostasis*,[2] a term for the coordinated physiological processes that maintain most of the steady states in the organism. One homeostatic process maintains even body temperature by causing heat-producing muscle contractions (shivering) and constriction of blood vessels in cold weather. In hot weather this process causes dilation of blood vessels, permitting body heat to be brought to skin surfaces where it can be released through evaporation of perspiration. In comparable ways, homeostasis of the sugar, water, salts, calcium, and acid base levels is maintained within established limits through the action of blood, heart, vascular system, lungs, liver, kidneys, spleen, brain, and nervous system. The advantage which homeostasis offers man is that of relegating to lower brain centers the mundane but vital tasks of maintaining the dynamic organization of life processes. This frees higher brain centers to coordinate the more complex activities involved in development, cognition, and learning.

Reproduction

At the moment of conception, the pattern of organic propensities for functioning, growth, and structure is established by the hereditary contributions of each parent. The extent to which the potentialities represented by this pattern will be realized depends upon the environment. We are able to understand more clearly the difficulties of assigning causes of behavior exclusively to heredity or exclusively to environment when we realize that the internal environment of the mother's body begins to influence the fertilized egg immediately after conception.

Within the nucleus of the fertilized egg are 46 *chromosomes*, which

---

[2] Walter B. Cannon, *Wisdom of the Body* (New York: W. W. Norton & Co., 1939).

comprise the heredity of the individual—including his potentialities for development. These 46 chromosomes consist of 23 pairs, which differ in size and shape. One set of 23 chromosomes is contributed by the father, and the other set is furnished by the mother. One pair, the sex chromosomes, is homologous in the female (XX) and nonhomologous in the male (XY). Since the sex chromosome of the mother is always X, the sex chromosome of the father determines the sex of the child (X from the father making XX = girl, Y from the father making XY = boy.)

In each of the 23 pairs of chromosomes are smaller substances (called *genes*) arranged in linear sequence along the length of the chromosome. The genes, the carriers of heredity, consist of molecules of desoxyribonucleic acid (DNA). DNA is present in the nuclei of all cells in the human body and in all other forms of life.

Genes do not act independently; rather, they interact with one another and with the environment in the formation of specific hereditary traits. Each body characteristic, such as eye color or body physique, is the result of the action of many different enzymes—each formed according to the genetic instructions contained in a pair of genes. A gene that has a greater capability for producing its own effect over that of its paired gene is called *dominant*, while the one with lesser capability is called *recessive*. The appearance of a specific physical trait in offspring will favor the dominant gene by the familiar 3-to-1 ratio first observed and reported by Mendel. Gene-linked abnormalities may be reproduced by a dominant gene, as in sickle cell anemia; a recessive gene, as in diabetes mellitus; or a sex-linked gene, in which the gene causing an affliction such as hemophilia or color blindness is carried by the mother but appears only in male offspring. The genetic makeup of the individual is called *genotype*, while the term for the characteristics of appearance or body form produced by genes is *phenotype*.

Sexual reproduction in higher animals makes possible a mixing of genes which ensures the uniqueness of each member of the species. The number of gene combinations possible makes it highly unlikely that any two persons (other than identical twins) will ever have the same constellation of genes.

Adaptation to the Environment

The survival of an individual and a species is dependent upon their ability to adapt to the environment. The adaptation of each species to its environment involves evolutionary changes extending over countless generations.

The flexibility provided by man's highly developed brain and nervous system gives him an incomparable advantage in his efforts to cope with his environment. Contrast the Eskimo's igloo, kayak, sealskin clothing, and ingenious ways of obtaining food in Arctic climates to the herdsman's tent, loose-fitting clothing, and continuous movement in search of food and water in desert climates. As individuals change in adapting to changes in weather, climate, geology, and ecology, their adaptive behaviors are marks of increased maturity, development, and learning.

Energy and Behavior

Every part of the body plays an essential role in maintaining the flow of energy into and through the body. The human energy system ingests, transforms, and transports energy to every cell in the body. Within the cells energy is utilized in carrying out three major activities of life: maintenance of organization, growth, and physical activity.

Most of the energy available to the organism is utilized for maintenance of organization. Approximately half of the average person's caloric intake each day is expended in basal metabolism. *Basal metabolism* is the irreducible amount of energy required by the body for circulation, respiration, secretion, and the maintenance of the metabolism of all cells during sound sleep or during rest several hours after the intake of food. The concepts of body maintenance and basal metabolism remind us that it takes energy just to stay alive.

Approximately 6 percent of the body's energy intake is accounted for by the increase in metabolic rate following a meal (*specific dynamic action*), and 10 percent of the energy value of foods is lost through excreta. For the remaining 84 percent of the body's energy intake, the proportions utilized for basal requirements (maintenance), growth, and physical activity vary with age and sex. Prior to pubescence, the 84 percent is divided approximately as follows for both sexes: maintenance, 45 percent; growth, 10 percent; and physical activity, 29 percent. For the average 14-year-old boy, these proportions change to 40 percent for maintenance, 15 percent for growth, and 29 percent for physical activity. This is in marked contrast with the percentages for the average 16-year-old girl, who uses 55 percent of her caloric intake for maintenance, 5 percent for growth, and 24 percent for physical activity.[3]

The amount of energy expended in muscular activity depends upon the type of work in which the individual is engaged, his size, and the energy needs required for growth at his stage of development. If an individual's muscular activity is at a low level compared to his intake of food energy, his body will store the unused calories as fat. If, on the other hand, his muscular activity requires more than 33 percent of his total energy intake, he will register a loss in body weight.

In mental activity, the amount of energy expended by the brain is believed to be quite small. The fatigue that accompanies extended mental

[3] Ernest H. Watson and George H. Lowrey, *Growth and Development of Children* (Chicago: Year Book Publishers, 1951), pp. 219–224.

activity appears to be caused by expense of energy in tension in muscles and nervous system.

We turn next to an examination of the factors which influence the energy levels, and hence the behavior, of children and youth. These are nutrition, health, physical defects, emotional factors, and drugs.

Nutrition

Although the amount, quality, and kinds of food taken into the body vitally affect the growth, behavior, and learning of the human being at any age, some of the most deleterious effects of malnutrition may be observed in the early stages of life. The last months of intrauterine life are a critical period in the growth and development of the brain and central nervous system. At this time brain and body growth and tissue differentiation are particularly rapid; and if the kinds and amounts of the mother's food intake are only marginally appropriate, the nutritional requirements of the fetus may outstrip maternal supplies.

The development of the brain continues to be vulnerable to the effects of malnutrition during the first six to nine months of postnatal life. During this period measuring the infant's head circumference provides an accurate measure of the increase in number of brain cells. Winich[4] found that the reduced head circumference of malnourished children during the first six months of life accurately reflects the reduced number of cells present in the brain. Indeed, Monckeberg[5] demonstrated that the brain of a severely malnourished child may be even smaller than the head circumference would indicate. This and other studies[6] found that malnourished children with reduced head circumference had lower IQs than did adequately nourished children in control groups even after long-term follow-up. Still other studies[7] report significantly lower performance by malnourished children compared with adequately nourished control group children on cognitive tasks involving speed of perception, information processing, short-term memory, and sorting objects for size, color, texture, form, and complexity.

In addition to these relatively direct effects of malnutrition on learning are the effects of poor nutrition on motivation and personality in child-

---

[4] M. Winich, "Malnutrition and Brain Development," *Journal of Pediatrics*, 39 (May 1969), 667; M. Winich and P. Rosso, "Head Circumference and Cellular Growth of the Brain in Normal and Marasmic Children," *Journal of Pediatrics*, 39 (May 1969), 774.

[5] F. Monckeberg, "Nutrition and Mental Development," paper presented at the Conference on Nutrition and Human Development, East Lansing, Michigan, March 1969.

[6] M. B. Stock and S. M. Smythe, "Undernutrition during Infancy and Subsequent Brain Growth and Intellectual Development," in N. S. Scrumshaw and E. Gordon, eds., *Learning and Behavior* (Cambridge, Mass.: MIT Press, 1968).

[7] R. E. Klein and O. Gilbert, "Malnutrition and Intellectual Development," paper presented at the Eleventh Inter-American Congress of Psychology, Mexico City, 1967; L. M. Brockman and H. N. Ricciuti, "Severe Protein-Calorie Malnutrition and Cognitive Development in Infancy and Early Childhood," *Developmental Psychology*, 4 (May 1971), 312–319.

hood. Malnourished children have been observed to be apathetic and irritable and to have a short attention span.[8] As the child's apathy increases, the adult becomes less responsive, and this reduced adult-child interaction is likely to have adverse effects on maturation, interpersonal relationships, and performance on later, more complex learning tasks.[9]

During adolescence the effects of poor nutrition may extend to other areas of development. Of particular concern are the diets of teenagers, who, at this critical stage of development, are often malnourished because of poor choice of foods and irregular eating habits. One study of adolescent girls[10] found that those who scored relatively low on the Minnesota Counseling Inventory Scales in family relationships, emotional stability, conformity, and adjustment to reality had poorer diets and missed more meals than girls with higher scores. Other studies[11] show that adolescents with poorer psychological adjustment have aversions to a greater number of foods. Children with nutritive deficiencies lasting three years or longer show a substantial lag in height and weight. There is evidence, too, that these lags in height and weight increase progressively for boys throughout early adolescence. Girls show a progressive lag in weight but not in height.

The effects of starvation on the behavior of young adults are clearly shown in the findings of the Minnesota Study of Human Starvation.[12] During 24 weeks of semistarvation, a group of mentally and physically healthy young men experienced lowered circulation, moderate anemia, reduced sex drive, loss of strength and endurance, and some loss of coordination involving the entire body. More marked, however, were the psychological changes. Men who initially were even tempered, humorous, tolerant, and enthusiastic became irritable, apathetic, tired, uninterested in their personal appearance, more concerned with themselves than with others, and unsociable to the point that they stopped going out on dates. Their hunger was so great that all they could think about and dream about was food. Only after 33 weeks of adequate nutrition were the men back to normal in all respects.

Health

The effects of extended illness and such chronic diseases as rheumatic fever, polio, tuberculosis, and diabetes in limiting learning are visible and very real. (In more fortunate situations many such afflicted students are

[8] R. Bakan, "Malnutrition and Learning," ERIC (1971), ED 051 321.

[9] J. Cravioto, E. R. DeLecardie, and H. G. Birch, "Nutrition, Growth, and Neurointegrative Development: An Experimental and Ecologic Study," *Pediatrics Supplement*, Vol. 38, No. 2, Part 2 (1966), 319.

[10] M. A. Hinton et al., "Influences of Girls' Eating Behavior," *Journal of Home Economics*, 54 (December 1962), 842–846.

[11] T. D. Spies et al., "Skeletal Maturational Progress of Children with Chronic Nutritive Failure," *American Journal of Diseases of Children*, 85 (1953), 1–12.

[12] A. Keys et al., *The Biology of Human Starvation*, Vols. 1 and 2 (Minneapolis: University of Minnesota Press, 1950).

able to continue their education with the help of visiting teachers and home study.) Of still greater concern to educators, however, are disorders that often go undetected—such as anemia, endocrine disorders, poor teeth, and chronic infections. Undetected physical ailments can rob a student of enough energy to be a chief cause of mediocre or poor academic performance.

The effects of chronic and severe illness in retarding growth and development are dramatically shown in successive X-ray measurements of skeletal growth. Some children, after a severe illness, will show bone scars indicating an interruption of normal growth; and transverse lines which appear on X rays of certain long bones—for example, along the shaft of the diaphysis—are frequently related to past illness.

The importance of good physical and mental health for the development of children and youth is reflected in the increased emphasis which schools have placed on expanding health services and health education.

Physical Defects

Many kinds of physical defects may affect a child's development and learning. Often, children who seem unable to respond appropriately in the learning situation are labeled "dumb" when poor eyesight or hearing is actually the major cause of their poor performance. Even mild physical anomalies, such as a high mouth palate or unusual-looking eyes, ears, hands, or feet, may exert a strong influence on behavior. Waldrop and Goering,[13] for example, found a higher incidence of hyperactivity (continuous movement, fidgeting, and scuffling) among elementary school boys having mild physical anomalies than among male classmates having fewer of these anomalies.

In other cases poor performance may be attributable to neurological impairments. Injury, either through accident or disease, may result in a permanent disability (such as cerebral palsy or organic epilepsy) to a brain that was previously normal.

Still other children may suffer from neurological nonalignment. In their neurological organization normal persons tend to have *unilateral dominance.* If they are right-eyed, right-handed, and right-footed, the dominant right side of the body is controlled by the left hemisphere of the brain. Conversely, if the left side of the body is dominant, it is controlled by the right hemisphere of the brain. A person whose dominant eye, say, is controlled by the right cerebral hemisphere, but whose dominant hand is controlled by the left hemisphere, is referred to as *crossed dominant. Mixed dominance* exists when the individual does not show a consistent preference for one eye, hand, or foot. *Directional confusion* is demonstrated by the

---

[13] M. F. Waldrop and J. D. Goering, "Hyperactivity and Minor Physical Anomalies in Elementary School Children," *American Journal of Orthopsychiatry,* **14** (July 1971), 602–607.

person who is uncertain and confused when asked to indicate his right hand or his left eye.

Children who are crossed dominant or mixed dominant or show evidence of directional confusion frequently experience difficulties in learning that seem to be perceptual in origin. Some poor readers, for example, are unable to differentiate and integrate such letter sequences as *was* and *saw* and *were* and *where*. Research studies, however, offer few consistent findings of a direct relationship between laterality and reading performance. Some of the inconsistent findings are revealed in a study by Cohen,[14] who examined the relationship between laterality and reading performance in 60 first grade and 60 fourth grade children in a suburban school system. Reading performance was determined by the grade the student received in reading on his report card. The results of this study showed that good readers in the first grade were more likely to have a dominant hand and to know their right from their left, whereas poor readers were more likely to have mixed hand dominance and to exhibit confusion about left and right. Among fourth graders, however, reading ability was not significantly related to hand dominance or knowledge of left and right. Although left-handed and mixed-dominant children in the total population were more likely to be hesitant or confused in their knowledge of left and right, no significant relationships were found between crossed dominance and reading performance in the total population.

The findings of this and other studies[15] suggest that atypical patterns of laterality associated with poor reading are most frequently to be found in students who are mixed dominant (show no consistent eye, hand, or foot preference). Some studies show a significant relationship between poor reading or school achievement and crossed dominance (left eye, right hand), while other studies fail to show any significant differences between these variables.[16] The finding of significant differences in Cohen's study between laterality and reading performance for first graders but not for fourth graders or the total population suggests that the achievement of lateral dominance and control may, for many students, be largely a function of maturation. Some children may experience a developmental lag in their ability to discriminate direction important in reading, while other children may be subject to emotional blocks and confusion. These findings suggest that the teacher should be alert to the child whose behavior and

[14] A. Cohen, "Relationship between Factors of Dominance and Reading Ability," in G. D. Spache, ed., *Reading Disability and Perception*, Vol. 13, Part 3 (Newark, Del.: Proceedings of the Thirteenth Annual Convention of the International Reading Association, 1969), 38–45.

[15] See B. Blai, "Learning Conflict among Mixed Dominance Left-Handed Individuals," ERIC (1971), Ed 052 474.

[16] See S. R. Forness and M. C. Weil, "Laterality in Retarded Readers with Brain Dysfunction," *Exceptional Children*, 36 (May 1970), 684–685; Angus McDonald, Jr., "Differences between High Ability Underachieving Students and High-Achieving Students in Relation to Self-Concept, Anxiety, and Lateral Dominance" (unpublished doctor's dissertation, University of Maryland, 1964); and J. R. Kershner, "Children's Spatial Representation of Directional Movement and Figure Orientations along Horizontal and Vertical Dimensions," *Perceptual and Motor Skills*, 31 (1970), 641–642.

learning difficulties do not seem to be explained by commonly known causes. Such a child can be recommended for a neurological examination. He may also benefit from efforts in the field of special education, a rapidly expanding discipline seeking to understand and to educate the many kinds of atypical children and youth in our communities.

Emotional Factors

There can be little doubt that emotions and trauma produced by threat, conflict, and frustration do affect in unique ways the body's patterns of energy expenditure and the development and learning of people. A further discussion of the physical-psychological factors involved in the individual's response to emotional situations is to be found in Chapter 9.

Drugs

We are a drug-using culture. Increasing numbers of youths as well as adults use drugs to alleviate a variety of physiological and psychological discomforts. The specific effects of well-known drugs upon the body and upon behavior are presented in Table 4–1. The psychological implications of drug use in adjusting to threat or anxiety are discussed in Chapter 9.

As we note the characteristics and effects of various drugs listed in Table 4–1, we should keep in mind that no two individuals can be expected to respond in the same way to equal amounts of the same drug. Varying responses to a drug are related to the length of time the drug has been used, the expectations of the user, the circumstances or setting in which the drug is taken, and the meaning of drug use to the individual. Even the same individual taking the same dose of a drug on two different occasions may have two completely different reactions. The moods of the people around him and the setting, for example, can markedly alter the drug's effects.

Many of these drugs, administered in medically prescribed doses, have beneficial effects; they assist the body in fighting disease and alleviating discomforts. In larger doses these same drugs and other, nonmedical drugs are frequently harmful and may prove lethal.

The following terms and their definitions will provide assistance in interpreting the data in Table 4–1. *Drug abuse* is the use of any drug, usually by self-administration, in a manner that deviates from approved medical or social patterns within a given culture.[17] *Drug dependence*—physi-

---

[17] Jerome H. Jaffe, "Drug Addiction and Drug Abuse," in Louis S. Goodman and Alfred Gilman, eds., *The Pharmocological Basis of Therapeutics*, 4th ed. (New York: Macmillan Co., 1970), p. 276.

cal or psychological—is a condition which results from chronic, periodic, or continuous use of various chemicals. The type of dependence varies according to the type of drug used. *Habituation*, exemplified in the heavy smoker's need for tobacco, is the psychological desire to repeat the use of a drug intermittently or continuously because of emotional needs. *Addiction* is physical dependence on a drug, and its definition includes the development of tolerance and withdrawal. As a person develops *tolerance*, he requires larger and larger amounts of the drug to achieve the same effects. *Withdrawal* occurs when the use of an addicting drug is stopped abruptly, and it is characterized by a wide range of distressing symptoms, such as diarrhea, vomiting, and cramps. Many drug users develop a compulsion to continue taking a drug to avoid the withdrawal symptoms.[18]

Rest and Activity

Fatigue is a common bodily condition of persons of all ages; as the normal result of vigorous physical exercise or mental activity, it is harmless. Chronic fatigue, however, is a more dangerous condition; it reduces the body's capacity for work, causes damage to tissues, and reduces the body's resistance to infection. The health and efficiency of every human being's dynamic energy system depend on the avoidance of chronic fatigue through a balance between rest and activity. The energies of most schoolchildren seem irrepressible. The task of the teacher is to plan a program of activity—adapted to the individual energy needs of each student—which provides for changes of pace, changes of activity, and opportunities for pursuing restful and relaxing activities after periods of intense physical or mental activity. Such an individually tailored, balanced program will help to improve the student's respiration and circulation, stimulate his appetite, and improve his muscle tone. These in turn lead to better posture, normal elimination, reduced tension, and increased body strength, endurance, and coordination. The maintenance of all of these physical conditions is vital to the efficiency of learning and development.

Levels of Energy Output

Knowing something about the level at which a particular child expends energy is extremely useful to teachers and parents as they seek to help children and youth develop and learn. The following excerpts make abundantly clear the need of teachers to understand the energy needs of their students.

[18] *Drug Abuse: Some Questions and Answers*, Publication No. (HSM) 71–9065 (Washington, D.C.: U.S. Government Printing Office, 1971).

Table 4-1. Some Substances Used for Nonprescribed Drugging Effects

Substance	Slang Name	Source	How Taken	Usual Form of Product	Effects Sought	Possible Long-Term Effects	Physical Dependence Potential	Psychological Dependence Potential
Tobacco	Fag, coffin nail	Natural	Smoked, sniffed, chewed	Snuff, pipe-cut particles, cigarettes	Relaxation	Loss of appetite, habituation	Possible	Yes
Amphetamines	Bennies, dexies, hearts, pep pills, speed, lid proppers, wake-ups	Synthetic	Swallowed or injected	Tablets, capsules, liquid, powder (white)	Alertness, activeness	Loss of appetite, delusions, hallucinations, toxic psychosis	Possible	Yes
Cocaine	Corrine, coke, flake, snow, gold dust, star dust, Bernice	Natural (from coca leaf)	Snuffed, injected, or swallowed	Powder (white), liquid	Excitation	Depression, convulsions	No	Yes
Alcohol	Booze, juice, sauce	Natural (from grapes, grains)	Swallowed or applied topically	Liquid	Sense alteration, anxiety reduction	Toxic psychosis, addiction, neurologic damage	Yes	Yes
Barbiturates	Barbs, red devils, yellow jackets, phennies, peanuts, blue heavens, candy	Synthetic	Swallowed or injected	Tablets, capsules	Anxiety reduction, euphoria	Severe withdrawal symptoms, possible convulsions, toxic psychosis	Yes	Yes

				Intoxication			
Glue		Synthetic	Inhaled	Plastic cement		Impaired perception, coordination, judgment	No	Yes
Morphine	White stuff, M	Natural (from opium)	Swallowed or injected	Powder (white), tablet, liquid	Euphoria; prevent withdrawal discomfort	Addiction, constipation, loss of appetite	Yes	Yes
Heroin	H, horse, scat, junk, smack, scag, stuff, Harry	Semisynthetic (from morphine)	Injected or sniffed	Powder (white, gray, brown)	Euphoria; prevent withdrawal discomfort	Addiction, constipation, loss of appetite	Yes	Yes
Codeine	Schoolboy	Natural (from opium); semisynthetic (from morphine)	Swallowed	Tablet, liquid (in cough syrup)	Euphoria; prevent withdrawal discomfort	Addiction, constipation, loss of appetite	Yes	Yes
Marijuana	Pot, grass, tea	Cannabis Sativa	Smoked or swallowed	Plant particles (dark green or brown)	Euphoria, relaxation, increased perception	Usually none; bronchitis, conjunctivitis, psychosis possible	No	Probable
Hashish	Hash	Cannabis Sativa	Smoked or swallowed	Solid, brown to black, resin	Relaxation, euphoria, increased perception	Usually none; conjunctivitis, psychosis possible	No	Probable
LSD	Acid, Big D, sugar, trips, cubes	Semisynthetic (from ergot alkaloids)	Swallowed	Tablets, capsules, liquid	Insight, distortion of senses, exhilaration	May intensify existing psychosis; panic reactions	No	Possible

Source: Abridged from "Some Substances Used for nonprescribed Drugging Effects" (Washington, D. C.: Pharmaceutical Manufacturers Association, 1973). Used by permission.

Jimmy burst into the room at 8:45 this morning and seemed to be in perpetual motion until I called the class to order to begin the day's work. During the arithmetic lesson Jimmy kept popping in and out of his seat like a jumping jack. First he popped out to sharpen his pencil, then he asked me which page we were working on, and frequently he made trips over to Ted's desk to borrow his eraser. Twice I escorted Jimmy to his desk, but as soon as my back was turned, he was up and away again. Each time his row was excused to line up for recess, lunch, and at the end of the day, Jimmy shot out of his desk in an attempt to be the first of his row in line.

Phil clumped into class today at 9:10, late for the second time this week. He moved slowly to his desk and took another five minutes to find his book, paper, and pencil. Most of the class finished the 10 fraction problems in about 20 minutes, while Phil had only finished four problems after 30 minutes; but all of his were correct. Phil is usually the last one out of the room for recess and lunch. In games on the playground, his running is labored and awkward. Phil is big for his age, he is above average in intelligence, and he eats a good lunch at school each day. In response to nicknames of "Pokey" and "Speed," Phil smiles and responds good-naturedly, "I'm trying to hurry."

Teachers frequently wonder what to do about their Jimmys and Phils. In flights of fancy, some teachers may wish that the school health services would provide long-lasting shots of adrenalin for such as Phil and tranquilizers for such as Jimmy. However, both Jimmy and Phil may be well within the normal range of energy output for their 10-year-old age group.

Normal children of the same age may vary greatly in their rates of energy output. Some of these wide variations may be due to differences in nutrition, health, patterns of rest, physical defects, and emotional factors that were described earlier in the chapter. For instance, some children from families where emotional tension is high and great demands are made upon them become accustomed to responding quickly and vigorously in a wide variety of situations. The sluggish responses of a Phil and the hyperactivity of a Jimmy may be due, respectively, to an underactive and an overactive thyroid gland. Frequently, both medical tests and observational data are needed to ascertain the reasons for a child's marked overactivity or underactivity.

After all environmental factors and all the physical factors so far mentioned have been considered, however, teachers will still have children in their classes who differ markedly in rates and levels of energy output. These differences are likely to be related to three factors: age, expectancies of normal distribution, and sex.

Age.   Figure 4–2 reveals that the basal energy production of infants and young children, per unit of weight, is one and a half to two times

Figure 4–2. Rate of Basal Heat Production per Unit of Weight (Metabolism) from Birth to Age 26

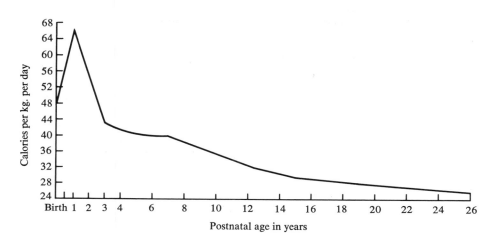

Source: Norman C. Wetzel, "On the Motion of Growth, xvii. Clinical Aspects of Human Growth and Metabolism with Special Reference to Infancy and Pre-School," *Journal of Pediatrics*, 4 (1934), 465–493. Reproduced by permission of The C. V. Mosby Company, St. Louis, Missouri.

greater than that of older children, adolescents, and young adults. These data merely confirm observations, common to mothers and teachers, that the energy levels and energy expenditures of most young children are high and that these levels and rates decrease as individuals mature.

Differences in energy output in middle and late childhood were dramatically revealed in a visit by this writer to an elementary school. First, he visited a sixth grade class which was busily engaged in working on a large mural. Activity was evident in the painting, drawing, measuring, and group work in which all class members participated. Later he moved on to a fifth grade classroom. Although these fifth graders were engaged in work at their desks, an increased tempo of activity—twisting, turning around, and talking—was evident. Finally the writer looked in on a fourth grade classroom. Here the surge of energy was irresistible. Arms, legs, and bodies seemed to be in continuous movement as the teacher tried valiantly to lead a discussion, for the benefit of the visitor, on the class project for beautifying the school grounds.

The energy levels of adolescents as a group are variable and thus are difficult to characterize. Some adolescents' energy levels are fluctuating and erratic. At times they show great bursts of energy, some of which may be sustained. At other times they appear to be practically immobilized. Physical changes associated with the adolescent growth spurt make great demands on the adolescent's energy. Added to these requirements is the energy needed for active participation in games and activities and the energy required for doing homework and household chores. Trying to keep up with so many demands, many adolescents are literally exhausted.

Expectancies of normal distribution.   People who are the same age or
at the same maturity level also differ markedly in their rates of expending
energy. This was clearly evident in the behavioral descriptions of Jimmy
and Phil. One of the fundamental facts concerning individual differences in
rate of energy output is that the scores of individuals in a randomly selected population will, with respect to a given trait, approximate a *normal
curve of distribution.* The concept of the normal curve is best illustrated
in relation to intelligence, where the IQs of 68 percent of the general
population fall between 85 and 115. Each slope of the curve tapers, so that

Figure 4–3.   Normal Curve of Distribution Showing Standard Deviations from the Mean, Percentage of Population in Each Area of
the Normal Curve, and Corresponding IQs and Levels of Energy
Output

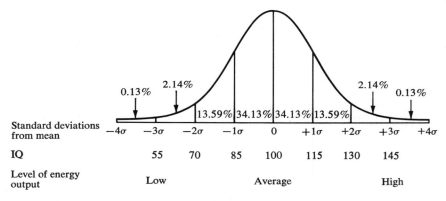

about 2 percent of the population is expected to measure above 130 and a
like percentage below 70.
        In similar fashion, an unselected group of students of approximately
the same age and maturity will vary in the rates with which they expend
energy. Jimmy's high rate of energy output places him near one end of the
distribution, while Phil's low rate of energy output places him near the
other extreme. Since both are within the normal range, albeit at the extremes, we should not be surprised to find Jimmys and Phils in most classrooms. Most of their classmates can be expected to expend energy at rates
somewhere between Jimmy and Phil. (See Figure 4–3.)

Sex.   From observations of both sexes we might conclude that boys
expend energy at generally higher rates than do girls. Research appears to
support this conclusion. Lewis and his associates[19] found that boys have a
higher rate of oxygen consumption under basal conditions than do girls.

[19] R. C. Lewis et al., "Standards for Basal Metabolism of Children from 2 to 15
Years of Age Exclusive," *Journal of Pediatrics,* 23 (1943), 1–18.

These differences in rate of oxygen consumption were found to be so marked as to require separate norms for boys and girls beginning at age seven. The question of whether sex differences in metabolic rate may be due to boys' larger body mass interested Garn and Clark.[20] They found that at all age levels boys consume more oxygen than girls. Girls between ages six and 17 increased their oxygen consumption 30 percent, while boys increased their oxygen consumption 60 percent during the same period. Garn and Clark concluded that sex differences in metabolic activity are not due to differences in size or internal composition, but that the male's increase in oxygen consumption begins early and persists through adult life. In a later study[21] they found a close relationship between ketosteroid hormone and higher oxygen consumption in boys, a relationship not found in girls. It appears, then, that males possess an energy-stimulating hormone associated with sex, which may account in part for their seemingly greater physical activity.

The evidence appears to provide ample support for the generalization that individuals vary in rates of energy output on the bases of maturity level, normal variation within the same general age group, and sex. Since differences in energy levels can be expected in every classroom, the resourceful teacher will seek to develop activities and programs that utilize the different energy levels of children in the group. To expect some students to slow down and others to speed up in order to conform to some norm would be a denial of individual differences.

Treatment of the hyperactive child. There frequently are a few children in the classroom who are continuously hyperactive and seem unable to settle down and adjust to the school program. Typically, the hyperactive child, usually a boy, cannot sit still, will not stick to any task, and is disobedient and moody. Misbehavior and underachievement are frequently reported from the first grade on. The continuously hyperactive child often has a history of slow language and motor development; he was slow in learning to button his clothes and tie his shoes, he often appears clumsy, he may have a minor speech problem, and his handwriting is illegible.

This hyperkinetic syndrome, marked by inattention, disruptive behavior, distractability, and impulsiveness is found in between 5 and 10 percent of the elementary school population. Although it may involve a neurological as well as a general physical examination, the diagnosis is usually based upon medical and developmental history and a symptom profile rather than upon tests and examinations. Eisenberg[22] reports that doctors as yet simply do not know the cause of the hyperkinetic behavior syndrome. It may run in families, and it sometimes follows complications of the

[20] S. Garn and L. Clark, "The Sex Differences in the Basal Metabolic Rates," *Child Development*, 24 (1953), 216–222.

[21] S. Garn and L. Clark, "Relationship between Ketosteroid Secretion and Basal Oxygen Consumption in Children," *Journal of Applied Psychology*, 6 (1954), 546.

[22] Leon Eisenberg, "The Clinical Use of Stimulant Drugs in Children," *Pediatrics*, 49 (May 1972), 709–715.

mother's pregnancy. Although these symptoms may be a reflection of brain damage, it accounts for only a minority of hyperkinetic behavior cases.

The most effective treatment is the use of a stimulant drug—detroamphetamine or methylphenidate (trade name Ritalin). The effect of these drugs on the hyperactive child is to suppress overactivity and impulsivity and to lengthen attention span. They have produced excellent results with minimal side effects over the short run, but since the hyperkinetic syndrome tends to occur in elementary school children, the long-term effects of the drugs are unknown. Prescribing these drugs for hyperactive children, however, has aroused controversy among educators as well as physicians. Use of the drug is usually justified if the cause of the hyperactivity appears to be physiological. If the child's hyperactivity is due to family stress or a rigid educational program, other types of therapy, such as counseling and behavior modification, should be used instead.

In the preceding discussion, only the physiological bases for differences in energy expenditure have been considered. For a more complete understanding of any individual's behavior, the physiological bases of behavior must be related to cultural and psychological factors. These will be considered in subsequent chapters.

Physical Growth

For our present considerable knowledge of physical growth and development we are indebted to numerous researchers working in the past 50 years. The findings of these researchers substantiate the following generalizations[23] concerning the nature and processes of human growth.

1. Growth is a continuous process, but it does not proceed at a uniform rate. The individual is growing all of the time, from conception to maturity and beyond into adult life. Though few would question the continuity of the growth process, many adults seem to forget this fact when they work with children and youth. We are well aware of the process of growth when we observe the enormous changes that occur in babies or early adolescents during the period of a few weeks; but when changes are less obvious, we tend to forget that growth is still going on.

Like the rate of growth of the body as a whole, the rates of growth of particular parts of the body vary at different periods in an individual's life. One evidence of this variation comes from the observation that the infant is not a miniature adult. His head appears oversized, while his body and legs appear undersized. As he grows older, these body parts become better proportioned. These changes in the rates of growth of head, body,

[23] Adapted from Marian E. Breckenridge and E. Lee Vincent, *Child Development,* 4th ed. (Philadelphia: W. B. Saunders, 1960), pp. 1–15. Used with permission.

and limbs parallel changes in rates of growth of the primary body systems.

The four curves in Figure 4–4 show the progress of growth toward maturity of four systems of the body: the lymphatic system, the brain and nervous system, the general system (skeleton, muscles, and internal organs), and the genital system. Following the neural curve in Figure 4–4, we note that the brain and nervous system grow faster and mature earlier than other parts of the body and appear to be 90 percent complete by the age of six. The growth of the skeleton, muscles, and most internal organs is relatively slow until pubescence, when it begins to accelerate. The lymph masses appear to be proportionately nearly twice as large during ages 10 to 13 than at maturity. (Between the ages of seven and 20, the thymus gland is larger than its adult size.) The sexual system is almost dormant prior to the pubescent period. After this, genital growth accelerates sharply.

Figure 4–4. The Major Types of Postnatal Growth of Various Parts and Organs of the Body

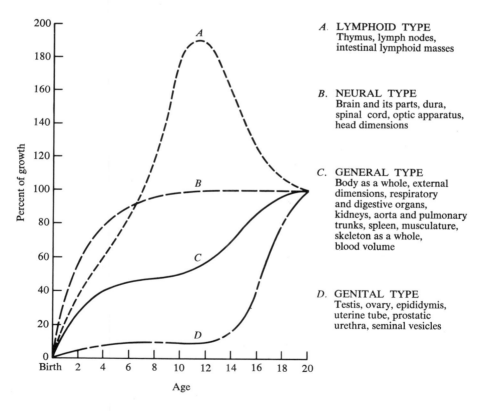

A. **LYMPHOID TYPE**
Thymus, lymph nodes, intestinal lymphoid masses

B. **NEURAL TYPE**
Brain and its parts, dura, spinal cord, optic apparatus, head dimensions

C. **GENERAL TYPE**
Body as a whole, external dimensions, respiratory and digestive organs, kidneys, aorta and pulmonary trunks, spleen, musculature, skeleton as a whole, blood volume

D. **GENITAL TYPE**
Testis, ovary, epididymis, uterine tube, prostatic urethra, seminal vesicles

Source: R. E. Scrammon, in J. A. Harris et al., *Measurement of Man* (Minneapolis: University of Minnesota Press, 1930). Used with permission.

Human growth can be compared to a huge engine that runs continuously. In the process of building up to peak performance, different parts of the engine work at different rates of speed, some idling at five miles per hour while others are racing at 80 miles an hour.

2. There is a general growth pattern for human beings.   Numerous studies of physical growth show that human beings follow a general pattern: a sequence of decelerated, accelerated, and steady periods in growth. These sequential changes are best represented by a curve showing the velocity of growth (see Figure 4–5). We note that the highest velocity of increase in height per six-month period is about 17 percent and occurs at birth. Though the infant increases 50 percent in length during his first postnatal year, his increases in height during each successive six-month period are progressively smaller, so that the period from birth to age three is one of sharp deceleration. From age three to about age 11 in girls and age 13

Figure 4–5.   Velocity of Average Increase in Height Each Six Months for Boys and Girls, Birth to Age 20

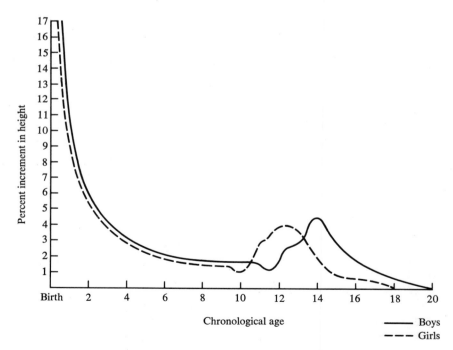

Source: The curve for boys is adapted from Lois H. Meek et al., *The Personal Social Development of Boys and Girls with Implications for Secondary Education* (New York: Progressive Education Association, 1940), p. 34. Reproduced by permission.

in boys, there is a relatively steady 2 to 4 percent increase in height every six months. Girls at about age 11 and boys at about 13 enter their pubertal growth spurt. Prior to pubescence there is usually a marked period of accelerated growth lasting for one to three years, followed by a long period of gradual deceleration. Menarche in girls and the comparable point of sexual maturation in boys usually occur at or just beyond the peak of the pubertal growth spurt.

3. *Each person has an individual growth cycle which only roughly approximates the general pattern of human growth.* 　　　Measures of growth for a large number of persons in a given population will be distributed in accordance with the bell-shaped normal curve (see Figure 4–3). In other words, the "normal" growth pattern is a generalization based on a range of widely varying individual growth patterns. Each individual's pattern is the result of his own body's progressively changing balance of forces. These forces include heredity, characteristics of sex, endocrine factors, and other factors peculiar to each growth dimension.[24] It is characteristic of the delicacy of this balance of forces to produce in the population a broad continuum of growth patterns, including at one end the pattern of the "early maturer" or "fast grower," and at the other end the pattern of the "late maturer" or "slow grower" (see Figure 4–6).

Late-maturing youth do not grow quite as fast as the early maturing, but their growth is continued over a much longer period. Rather marked differences can be noted in physique between early-maturing and late-maturing adolescents. Early-maturing boys tend to have relatively broad hips and narrow shoulders, while late-maturing boys tend to be very long legged and to have slender hips and broad shoulders. Early-maturing girls tend to have narrower shoulders than late-maturing girls. From these data it appears that early-maturing boys and late-maturing girls tend to deviate slightly in body proportions from the norms of their own sex group toward those of the opposite sex.[25]

Wide differences in physical growth patterns are particularly evident in the junior high school population, where boys and girls of all sizes, shapes, and degrees of physical maturity can be observed. At this age in particular, differences in size and maturity are felt keenly, and those who deviate most from the group norms often suffer acutely. Early maturers tend to feel self-conscious among classmates who are less mature, while late maturers often worry about whether they are normal and whether they will ever grow up. Adults who recognize and accept the fact that most growth deviations are perfectly normal can provide much-needed reassurance and support to students whose growth patterns deviate from the

---

[24] Frank K. Shuttleworth, "The Physical and Mental Growth of Girls and Boys Age Six to 19 in Relation to Age at Maximum Growth," *Monographs of the Society for Research in Child Development*, 4 (1939), 216–221.

[25] Nancy Bayley and Read D. Tuddenham, "Adolescent Changes in Body Build," in Nelson B. Henry, ed., *Forty-Third Yearbook, Adolescence, Part I*. National Society for the Study of Education (Chicago: University of Chicago Press, 1944), pp. 33–55.

Figure 4–6.   Velocity of Increase in Height of Early-Maturing and Late-Maturing Boys and Girls

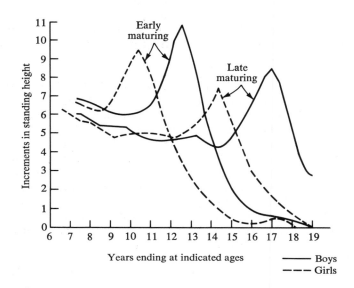

Source: Frank K. Shuttleworth, "The Physical and Mental Growth of Girls and Boys Age Six to 19 in Relation to Age at Maximum Growth," *Monographs of the Society for Research in Child Development,* 4 (1939), 216–221. Reproduced by permission of the copyright owner, The Society for Research in Child Development, Inc.

norm. Adult understanding and affection can do much to help adolescents accept their physical selves and their own particular patterns of growth.

4.   Girls on the average are more advanced in physical maturity than are boys at all stages of growth.   The greater physical maturity of girls over boys of the same chronological age is an empirical fact widely recognized and accepted long before its scientific confirmation. Skeletal growth, the rate at which cartilage ossifies in becoming bone, is more advanced in girls at all stages of development. X rays of the wrist, for example, show that the average six-year-old girl has almost the same skeletal growth as the average seven-year-old boy. By age 12, the average girl may be as much as two years ahead of the boy in skeletal growth.

Sex differences in the timing of the onset of the pubertal cycle of growth are shown in Figure 4–6. Early-maturing girls achieve their peak velocity of growth about two years before early-maturing boys, and a similar difference is shown between late-maturing girls and boys. Figure 4–6 also shows that not all girls mature ahead of all boys: The early-maturing boys mature about the same time as the average-maturing girls and ahead of the late-maturing girls.

5. In general, all aspects of growth are interrelated.   The concepts of unity and dynamic organization of the organism, which were presented earlier in the chapter, are particularly relevant to an understanding of the processes of growth. For example, when the arm or leg grows longer, the increase in bone length is accompanied by proportionate growth in nerves, blood vessels, muscles, connective tissue, and skin covering. During pubescence, physical growth is interrelated with sexual maturation; the hormones secreted by the maturing gonads exert a slowing effect on the growth of the long bones. Studies have shown that boys and girls who are further advanced toward sexual maturity than are others of the same age and sex may be as much as 20 pounds heavier and more than four inches taller than those who are maturing more slowly.[26]

The question has frequently been raised as to whether changes in a child's mental development parallel changes in physical growth. Olson and his associates[27] have studied large numbers of children from ages eight to 13 in an effort to ascertain the interrelationships between various kinds of development. In these studies the following physical and mental measures were used: height age, weight age, dental age, calcification (skeletal) age, grip age, reading age, and mental age. A diversity of growth patterns emerged from the data for children at any given age. When the researchers examined the data from the standpoint of the child as a whole, however, they discovered an underlying unity in structures, functions, and achievement. Lorusso,[28] on the other hand, studying an elementary school population (grades one to eight), found that physical and mental maturity, frequency of being chosen by classmates, and interest measures are not adequate predictors of achievement or athletic performance. In individual classrooms children generally maintained their relative positions in school achievement, classroom status, and verbal interest measures, but this was not true for the total sample. Lorusso suggests that too strong a reliance on the principle "all aspects of growth are interrelated" may oversimplify processes and events that are in reality quite complex.

Growth, Development, and Learning

Earlier in the chapter we stated that any factor influencing the status or operation of the human energy system will have an effect on development and learning. In this section selected studies of the interrelationships

---

[26] H. S. Dimock, "A Research in Adolescence. I. Pubescence and Physical Growth," *Child Development*, 6 (1935), 176–195; Herman G. Richey, "The Relation of Accelerated, Normal, and Retarded Puberty to the Height and Weight of Schoolchildren," *Monographs of the Society for Research in Child Development*, 2 (1937).

[27] Willard C. Olson, *Child Development*, 2nd ed. (Boston: D. C. Heath & Co., 1959).

[28] Rocco E. Lorusso, "A Study of the Interrelationships of Selected Variables in Child Development in an Elementary School" (unpublished doctor's dissertation, University of Maryland, 1960).

of physical maturity and various aspects of learning are reviewed to show the reciprocal influences of each set of forces on the other.

Of particular interest to elementary school personnel are studies that show positive relationships between selected physical maturity indexes and academic success. Zeller,[29] a German physician, suggested in a study of first grade children that school readiness is related to body configuration. Zeller identified two types of body configuration observable in children from ages five to seven. In the first of these types, the early childhood figure, prominent characteristics are a head and trunk dominating the extremities; a relatively large, rounded, prominent forehead; a short, stocky neck that merges with a sloping shoulder line; a trunk that is sacklike, with no apparent waist; a protruding abdomen; narrow shoulders; and a lateral body outline formed by adipose tissue rather than by muscles and joints. In the second type of figure, a more mature body configuration, called the middle childhood figure, head, trunk, and forehead are better proportioned, neck is longer, trunk is cone-shaped, shoulders are broad, hips are narrow, abdomen is flat, waist is clearly indicated, muscles and joints of arms and legs are clearly visible, adipose tissue has decreased, and linear body is clearly evident. Figures that cannot be classified as either type because they have mixed characteristics were termed *intermediate figures* by Zeller. The contrasting early childhood and middle childhood figures are shown in Figure 4–7. So strongly did Zeller associate the early childhood figure with a lack of school readiness that he urged parents not to enter these children in school.

Simon[30] used Zeller's procedure in a further test of relationships between body configuration and school success. She selected 50 highly successful and 50 failing first grade American Caucasian students ranging in age from six years, four months, to seven years, six months. These students were drawn from five metropolitan public schools and represented all socioeconomic groups. A battery of standard body measures indicated that failing students were less mature than successful students. When failing students were matched by age and IQ with successful students, the failing students still showed up as physically less mature. Simon found that of the measures studied, the ratios of head circumference to leg length and waist circumference to leg length were the most sensitive indicators of school readiness.

A study of the relationship between physical maturity and behavior of adolescent boys was made by Jones and Bayley.[31] They used assessments of skeletal age to identify two groups of adolescent boys—a group of early maturers and a group of late maturers. These two groups were studied and contrasted in relation to social behavior and reputation among classmates.

---

[29] W. Zeller, *Der erste Gestaltwandel des Kindes* (Leipzig: Barth, 1936).

[30] Maria D. Simon, "Body Configuration and School Readiness," *Child Development,* 30 (December 1959), 493–512.

[31] Mary C. Jones and Nancy Bayley, "Physical Maturing among Boys as Related to Behavior," *Journal of Educational Psychology,* 41 (1950), 129–148.

Figure 4–7.   Contrasting Body Configurations of Children Five to Seven Years of Age

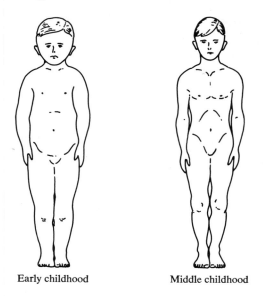

Early childhood   Middle childhood

Source: Maria D. Simon, "Body Configuration and School Readiness," *Child Development*, 30 (December 1959), 496. Reproduced by permission of the copyright owner, The Society for Research in Child Development, Inc.

The early-maturing adolescent boys were rated by others as significantly more attractive physically, better groomed, and more unaffected and relaxed. Early-maturing boys were accepted and treated by adults and peers as mature; although several became student leaders in high school, they appeared to have little need to strive for status. The late-maturing adolescent boys, on the other hand, tended to be more active and attention seeking and thus were treated by adults and others more like the little boys they seemed to be.

In another study Mussen and Jones[32] investigated the self-conceptions and motivations of adolescent boys who differed in physical maturity. A group of 16 adolescent boys who were accelerated in physical growth and a group of 17 adolescent boys who were retarded in growth made up stories in response to Thematic Apperception Test picture cards. Analyses of these stories revealed that the generally unfavorable sociopsychological environments of the late maturers did appear to have adverse effects on their personality development. Late-maturing boys more frequently revealed

[32] Paul H. Mussen and Mary C. Jones, "Self-Conceptions, Motivations, and Interpersonal Attitudes of Late- and Early-Maturing Boys," *Child Development*, 28 (June 1957), 243–256.

negative self-conceptions, feelings of inadequacy, strong feelings of being rejected and dominated, prolonged dependency needs, and rebellious attitudes toward parents. The early maturers, on the other hand, presented a more favorable psychological picture. They appeared to be more self-confident, independent, and capable of playing an adult role in interpersonal relationships. Relatively few seemed to feel inadequate, rejected, dominated, or rebellious toward their families.

These findings were generally corroborated in a later study by Mussen and Jones[33] of the behavior-inferred motivations of late-maturing and early-maturing boys. Strong aggression drives and drives for social acceptance were found to be more characteristic of the physically retarded than the physically accelerated adolescent boy. In interpreting their findings, Mussen and Jones suggest that the late maturer's strong social drives may stem from feelings of insecurity and dependence, which are frequently manifested in childish, affected, attention-getting social techniques. Highly aggressive drives among late maturers also tend to be associated with social behavior and personality characteristics indicative of social and emotional maladjustment.

The differences in social and personality variables between early-maturing and late-maturing girls are less marked than those for boys. Though late-maturing girls appear to enjoy greater popularity than early-maturing girls,[34] early-maturing girls reveal in general a more favorable psychological adjustment. Early-maturing girls tend to evince a more positive self-conception, while late-maturing girls tend to reveal a greater need for recognition.[35] A study by Tryon[36] using a self-report inventory also reported higher scores for early-maturing girls on total adjustment, family adjustment, and personal adequacy.

More[37] studied the relationships between puberty and the emotional and social development of both boys and girls. His data show that the American girl at puberty appears to go through a period of abrupt changes in her emotional life and in the patterns of her social behavior. Girls generally are able to handle these new emotions and social patterns, but they seem to do it through considerable repression of sexual feelings. More's data reveal that a socially successful girl is one who acts *as if* she were sophisticated and sexually mature but at the same time does not allow herself to feel the emotions she acts out.

---

[33] Paul H. Mussen and Mary C. Jones, "The Behavior-Inferred Motivations of Late- and Early-Maturing Boys," *Child Development*, 29 (March 1958), 61–67.

[34] Robert Ames, "A Longitudinal Study of Social Participation" (unpublished doctor's dissertation, University of California, 1956).

[35] Mary C. Jones and Paul H. Mussen, "Self-Conceptions, Motivations, and Interpersonal Attitudes of Early- and Late-Maturing Girls," *Child Development*, 29 (December 1958), 491–501.

[36] Caroline M. Tryon, *Adjustment Inventory I: Social and Emotional Adjustment* (Berkeley: University of California Press, 1939).

[37] Douglas M. More, "Developmental Concordance and Discordance during Puberty and Early Adolescence," *Monographs of the Society for Research in Child Development*, 18 (1953).

More's study indicated that, for boys, puberty appears to be a more gradual affair. That is, the impulses experienced by adolescent boys may be as strong as or stronger than those of girls, but these impulses apparently develop more slowly and gradually. In addition, the sexual impulses of adolescent boys are not as repressed as they generally are in adolescent girls. For these reasons the adolescent boy is perhaps better able to adjust to sexual changes when they appear.

These several studies seem to show that physical growth changes do exert a pervasive influence on the behavior, development, and learning of children and youth. The powerfulness of that influence can be seen in the following excerpts from the case records of a late-maturing boy and an early-maturing girl.

A Late-Maturing Boy

Shorty was a dark-haired, chunky boy with a rather large head, legs rather short in proportion to his trunk, and muscular strength markedly above average for his years. He rated well above average in IQ tests in spite of careless answers, and his motor coordination was rated superior. He was aggressive and mischievous in his relations with other boys and adults, but no more so than some of the other boys of his sixth grade class.

Shorty was a leader of sorts. When a social situation was unorganized, he talked the most and the loudest and made more than his share of suggestions of things to do. But when the group organized for a game, Shorty's pseudo-leadership vanished, and he resorted to clowning as his chief contribution. His teachers in elementary school described him as restless, talkative, and easily distracted from the task before him.

At first Shorty found junior high school exhilarating, but his enthusiasm waned as the gap between his goals and his achievement in social significance grew wider and more evident. His attention-seeking and clowning techniques, which had previously given him status, were less acceptable in junior high school. It was during his second year in junior high school that he started talking about his height. Each time he was measured, he stretched himself as far as he could but was always disappointed by the answer to his question "How much have I grown?" The growth situation was hard to accept. Shorty was not only distinctly short but in his overall development was about a year behind his classmates. He took to hanging on bars and rings every day to "stretch himself," and he asked the examining physician what medicine he could take to make himself grow. His concern over his lack of appropriate male characteristics was reflected in wisecracks and comments he made about these changes in other boys.

In informal social experiences with classmates, Shorty in-

dulged in childish horseplay. The physically more mature girls and boys criticized and rebuffed him. He withdrew to a group of less mature boys, who expressed their frustration by engaging in exaggerated little-boy antics.

In senior high school Shorty was most interested in shop and began working on an old car in an effort to make it run. The days when the "heap" actually ran were few, and the process of repair and replacement went on continuously for months. One day toward the end of this year, Shorty was caught stealing auto parts from a junkyard; and during his brief detention by the police, Shorty seemed to go berserk. After he was released to his mother's custody, the symptoms of acute mental disturbance subsided, and he returned to school.

With wise understanding and help, Shorty built a new, more realistic pattern of self-expression. He was appointed an assistant football manager, and he was helped in getting a part-time job after school. After graduation he got a full-time job and was going steady with a very nice girl.

With the wise, sympathetic understanding of interested adults, Shorty Doyle finally came to terms with himself and his world.

An Early-Maturing Girl

Betty, 14 years old and in the ninth grade, was referred to the guidance office for doing unsatisfactory work in class. She was described by her teachers as an extremely lively girl who seemed proud of the "tough" things she did.

[Results of tests administered by the guidance department showed that Betty had an IQ of 129; her superb performance on a reading test carried her beyond the point where achievement can be reliably measured. Nothing in these test results gave a clue to Betty's educational maladjustment.]

Prior to the testing, Betty asked Miss M., the guidance counselor, "How tall are you?" Betty measured herself against Miss M. and then said, "I am taller than you are, but I don't believe I look any taller. I quit letting them measure me when I got to be five feet eight, so I don't know exactly how tall I am, and I don't want to know." Betty continued, "Will this work show whether or not I'm nuts? They think I am nuts around here, but honestly sometimes I think I will go crazy with all those little kids all day. There are a couple of girls who have some sense, but do you know what we do in gym now? We dance sometimes with the ninth grade boys. Can you imagine me dancing with those little squirts of boys? No, I don't dance at all. Quote. Dancing is a trapdoor to hell. Quote. That's my father speaking, and he ought to know—he was a sailor!"

Betty was asked if she went to movies with other junior high school boys and girls, and she replied, "Those infants? No! My boy friends are out of high school, and that's another thing I have trouble over at home. The other day I wanted to go someplace, and Mother said, 'Betty, you aren't old enough to do those things. You are just a little girl. You are only fourteen and you ought to be playing with dolls.' Imagine me playing with dolls! I always hated dolls! Me, five feet eight and just a little girl. I feel eighteen or nineteen. I can't stand this kid stuff. I want action!"

The nurse came into the guidance office very much excited because Betty had offered to bring some marijuana for a project on tobacco and intoxicants. The nurse wanted to have Betty questioned by state narcotics agents. Betty seemed to take special delight in doing things that would cause the nurse to "flip."

The guidance counselor reported that Betty staged a crying jag in the office which lasted for an hour and a half, during which time she went on a tirade against her home, her parents, her brother, and everything in general. Her parents are from the mountains and are very religious; they believe that almost all recreation is sinful and that anyone who attends movies will go to hell. Betty has evidently made up her mind that if she is going to hell anyway, she might as well go all of the way.

Assessing Growth

Our understanding of an individual's growth and its relation to his behavior and learning is facilitated by our acceptance of the principle that individuals mature at different times and at different rates in accordance with their own patterns of growth. Given these differences in growth and maturity, the educator or parent may ask, "How can one know whether a particular child or adolescent is growing and maturing as he should?" "How can needed information about a student's growth be obtained and analyzed in order to forestall or alleviate some of the problems faced by Shorty Doyle and Betty Burroughs?"

A number of available growth grids permit an assessment of a child's growth in relation to his own growth pattern. One of the best instruments for assessing growth is the *Grid for Evaluating Physical Fitness,* developed by Wetzel.[38] The effectiveness of this grid depends upon the use of standard procedures of measurement (with accurate instruments and under similar measurement conditions) of height and weight at six-month intervals. A Wetzel Grid is shown in Figure 4–8. On it have been plotted growth curves from the physical growth data for Betty Burroughs and Shorty Doyle. The grid at the left enables one to ascertain direction, level, and speed of

---

[38] Norman C. Wetzel, *The Wetzel Grid for Evaluating Physical Fitness* (Cleveland: NEA Service, 1940).

Figure 4–8.   Growth Curves Plotted on Wetzel Grid from Physical Growth Data for Betty Burroughs and Shorty Doyle

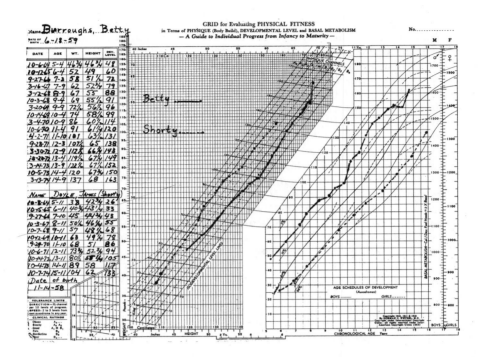

Source: Norman C. Wetzel, *The Wetzel Grid for Evaluating Physical Fitness* (Cleveland: NEA Service, 1940). Copyright 1940, 1941, 1948 by Dr. Norman C. Wetzel. Reproduced by permission of Dr. Wetzel and Newspaper Enterprise Association.

growth. Height (horizontal scale) is plotted against weight (vertical scale), with each pair of coordinates marked by a dot. Successive coordinates are plotted for successive measurements of height and weight. The coordinates are expected to move up the physique channel that corresponds to the child's body type. Successive parallel lines across the physique channels designate *isodevelopmental levels*, which are used as a standard measure of growth rate. Through much of school life, the normal speed of moving up a physique channel is one developmental level per month, or 12 per year. Figure 4–8 shows that Shorty Doyle's rate of growth falls short of this norm during the early and late parts of elementary school, while Betty Burroughs' rate of growth approximates or exceeds the norm during most of her growing years.

The right grid measures the comparative level of development according to age. The measure of isodevelopmental level is carried over from the left grid and is plotted against chronological age. The individual's curve on the right grid can be compared with the nearest *auxodrome*, which indicates the percentage of persons at any given chronological age who are physically more mature than persons whose coordinates are at or below that auxodrome. Figure 4–8 shows that Betty is among the most mature 15 percent of her age group, while Shorty is consistently among the least mature 10 to 20 percent of his age group.

The Wetzel Grid is but one of several instruments available for evaluating the status and quality of the individual's growth. Information obtained from such an instrument is especially useful when it is related to other kinds of data from school—anecdotal records, sociometric choices, parent conferences, and records of home visits.

Summary

Human development and learning are profoundly influenced by the physical processes consonant with life itself—the processes of metabolism, growth, dynamic organization, reproduction, and adaptation to environment.

Physiologically, the human being is an open, complex, dynamic energy system. Energy is used by the body for maintenance of organization, growth and tissue repair, and physical and mental activity. Any process or event which influences the status or operation of the human dynamic energy system affects development and learning. Variables which most frequently influence energy and behavior are nutrition, health, physical defects, drugs, the balance of rest and activity, and emotional factors. Individuals vary widely in rates of energy output. Differences in energy levels not directly due to physical causes may be related to differences in maturity, the normal population, and/or sex.

Physical changes of profound significance in the development and learning of children and youth are those associated with physical growth

and maturation. Numerous studies of physical growth support the following generalizations regarding physical growth:

1.   *Growth is continuous but does not proceed at a uniform rate.*

2.   *There is a general growth pattern for human beings.*

3.   *Each person has his own unique growth pattern.*

4.   *Girls on the average are more advanced in physical maturity
      than are boys.*

5.   *In general, all aspects of growth are interrelated.*

Studies of differential physical maturation and early school performance show that physically less mature students usually perform less
adequately in academic tasks. Early-maturing adolescent boys are more
advanced in social and emotional development and reveal better personal
adjustment than their late-maturing peers. While a number of personal and
social problems are posed for early-maturing adolescent girls, the effects of
differences in maturity on behavior are less evident for girls than they are
for boys. In general, the adolescent boy accepts and expresses the impulses
which result from physical and sexual maturation, while the adolescent girl
represses these impulses.

Excerpts from the case records of a late-maturing boy and an early-
maturing girl show the impact of physical growth and maturity on adolescent development, behavior, and learning. The Wetzel Grid, an instrument
for assessing the status and quality of physical growth, can be used to
evaluate the physical growth and maturation patterns and to record the
growth changes of such students as Shorty and Betty.

Study Questions

1.   In November Mrs. Atkins noticed a marked change in Keith Roberts,
      an able student in her tenth grade biology class. In September Keith
      had been vivacious, talkative, and outgoing. Now he was listless and
      apathetic, and he occasionally fell asleep in class. Whenever Mrs.
      Atkins commented to Keith about his behavior, Keith merely
      shrugged and said nothing. She suspected that Keith might be on
      drugs, but neither she, the counselor, nor other teachers could learn
      anything that might explain his behavior. As his teacher, what steps
      would you take to try to help Keith?

2.   Mary Tompkins has five boys in her first grade class who are short
      and chubby with round faces and prominent foreheads. All of these
      children have a short attention span, tend to be hyperactive, and have
      difficulty expressing themselves in front of the class. What do these
      facts suggest about the timing and the kinds of learning experiences
      which may be appropriate for these boys?

3.   The term *maturity* is frequently used and misused. The concept of physical maturity refers to the appearance of certain physiological and growth changes in body function and structure. What meaning does the term have in reference to an individual's social, emotional, or intellectual development? Does it have a meaning comparable with physical maturity in these other areas of development? Discuss.

4.   You are helping a student committee plan a party for members of your eighth grade homeroom class. With your knowledge of the wide variations in physical growth and maturity observable in a class of eighth grade students, what suggestions would you offer the committee regarding the types of activities and recreation they might plan for this party?

5.   At what point should Shorty have been given help in understanding the realities of his own physical growth? What might a teacher do to help Shorty with his problems?

6.   As one of Betty Burroughs' teachers, what would you have done to help Betty adjust to ninth grade in this junior high school?

Suggested Readings

Breckenridge, Marian E., and E. Lee Vincent. *Child Development*. Fourth Edition. Philadelphia: W. B. Saunders, 1960. Chapters 1 and 2 present and discuss basic generalizations relating to physical growth and the relationships between physical growth and other aspects of development. Chapters 7 and 8 report research findings on growth of the body and motor development.

Eichorn, Dorothy H. "Biological Correlates of Behavior," in Harold W. Stevenson, ed., *Child Psychology*. Sixty-Second Yearbook of the National Society for the Study of Education. Chicago: University of Chicago Press, 1963, pp. 4–61. Reviews research on human genetics, vision, and rate of maturing relating to human behavior and development.

Hardin, Garrett J. *Nature and Man's Fate*. New York: New American Library, 1959. Explores the crucial social, political, and ethical problems of man in terms of evolution and heredity. Presents a history of evolutionary thought and explains the biological laws of man, his composition, and future possibilities.

Louria, Donald B. *The Drug Scene*. New York: Bantam Books, 1968. Examines each of the drugs subject to drug abuse and describes simply and clearly the biological and psychological effects of each. Surveys recent trends in drug abuse prevention and suggests approaches and predictions for the present and future in dealing with the problem.

Watson, Ernest H., and George H. Lowrey. *Growth and Development of Children*. Fifth Edition. Chicago: Year Book Medical Publishers, 1967. Presents factual information on several phases of physical growth and development. Includes discussions of fetal development and methods of assessing growth as evidenced by behavior, organ development, and bone development. Included are discussions of the roles of endocrines, metabolism, and nutrition in growth and development.

Films

Drugs and the Nervous System, 16 mm, sound, color, 16 min. Los Angeles 90069: Churchill Films, 662 N. Robinson Blvd. Demonstrates the effects of drugs on body organs and the serious disruption of the nervous system caused by airplane glue, stimulants, depressants, and hallucinogens.

Human Growth, 16 mm, sound, color, 19 min. Bloomington: Audiovisual Center, Indiana University. Pictures changes which take place in the human growth cycle from fertilization of the egg through adulthood. Special emphasis is placed on body changes that occur during adolescence.

Physical Aspects of Puberty, 16 mm, sound, black and white, 18 min. Bloomington: Audiovisual Center, Indiana University. Describes, with the help of diagrams of the human body, the physical changes in a girl and a boy from the age of 10 to puberty. Explains the functions of the endocrine system and its effects on the development of primary and secondary sex characteristics. Discusses the effects of rapid physical growth on emotional, social, and mental development.

The Interpersonal Environment

5

He drew a circle that shut me out—Heretic, rebel, a thing to flout.
But Love and I had the wit to win: We drew a circle that took him in!

Edwin Markham

Man's most significant learning and development take place in a context of social interaction with other human beings. The infant's fumbling efforts to grasp a ball, to feed himself, or to take his first tottering steps are made in response to the friendly encouragement of parents, siblings, and others. The 10-year-old who practices long hours alone in throwing and catching a ball has before him the goal of showing his teammates in the next game how well he can play. The adolescent and the adult learn facts and concepts at least partly in order to deal more effectively with people and their concerns. Most important, the individual's beliefs, attitudes, values, and self-concept are all developed predominantly in social interaction.

Personal observation and clinical studies clearly reveal that man's mental and physical health are profoundly affected by the quality of his relationships with others. Abandonment, rejection, or deprivation of human contact pose the greatest threats to self and to man's will to live; over an extended period such threats lead first to insanity and eventually to death.[1]

Why is contact with others so important to man? Erich Fromm[2] gives one answer. According to Fromm, man is constantly searching for meaning and purpose in his existence. In this search he is confronted with the anomaly of his own existence. He is a part of nature, subject to the processes of growth, aging, disease, and death, as are all other living things. Yet the complexity of the brain, nervous system, and total organism endows him with qualities that enable him to transcend the rest of nature. He possesses capacities to remember, to visualize future events, to symbolize his experience, to conceptualize, to reason, and to use imagination. The realization that no other human can fully share the thoughts, feelings, doubts, and

---

[1] Rollo May, *Man's Search for Himself* (New York: W. W. Norton & Co., 1953), pp. 13–45, 146–148.

[2] Erich Fromm, *Man for Himself* (New York: Holt, Rinehart and Winston, 1947); *The Art of Loving* (New York: Harper & Row, 1956).

perplexities of his own inner, private world causes him to feel a "separateness," which he may translate as "aloneness." This threat of aloneness, and the uncertainty it creates, is most fully assuaged by the bonds of human relatedness that join each individual to the rest of mankind.

As the human being grows and develops, the dependence of his early life gives way to a relatively high degree of independence in adulthood. Man, however, is never completely independent; he continues to share an interdependence with other persons, other living things, and the resources of his environment. He is dependent upon other human beings to assuage his "core of aloneness" in the same way that he is dependent upon the other resources of his environment for materials that sustain life and promote growth and development. The needs for independence and dependence are not antagonistic but complementary. Each individual achieves independence as he gains a greater understanding of and control over his environment. At the same time, he remains dependent upon other human beings for sustenance and support and for love and security.

Concepts of Love and Security

Love (or, as we shall call it, *affection*) connotes valuing, fondness, and a feeling of strong personal attachment. Its specific and subtle meanings vary for different cultures and different relationships. Although the search has frustrated philosophers and writers throughout the ages, men still seek to discover and to describe the meaning of love. Fromm speaks of love as the active concern for the life and growth of another. Productive love, according to Fromm,[3] embodies four qualities: care, responsibility, respect, and knowledge. Prescott[4] identifies eight qualities of the love relationship, including empathy with the loved one, concern for his welfare, happiness, and development, and expression of this concern through an offer of personal resources by the lover to the loved one. Love may include sexual components, but it is not dependent upon them. Symonds[5] views sex as one form of sharing and joint activity—the most complete union of which a man and a woman are capable. But sex in which partners do not esteem and value each other as separate personalities is not a component of love.

Love or *affection*, then, refers to those acts, feelings, and responses in a human relationship which are perceived as connoting personal valuing and acceptance. For any affectional relationship to be fully satisfying, how-

[3] Fromm, *The Art of Loving*, p. 26.

[4] Daniel A. Prescott, "Role of Love in Human Development," *Journal of Home Economics*, 44 (1952). 173–176.

[5] Percival M. Symonds, *The Dynamics of Human Adjustment* (New York: Appleton-Century-Crofts, 1946), pp. 548–549.

ever, one must develop and respond to an *urge to love* as well as experiencing the feeling of *being loved*. Fromm emphasizes the distinction between complementary processes of loving and being loved when he writes: "Most people see the problem of love primarily as that of *being loved*, rather than that of *loving*, one's capacity to love."[6] Loving and being loved are experienced in close, intimate relationships between two persons in which the feelings and responses of each are focused on the other. Thus, the young child who is praised, patted on the head, and hugged reciprocates by reaching up to embrace his mother. The older child manifests these twin urges to love and be loved by developing a strong affectional bond with a peer. Many of the frustrations of adolescence seem to stem from an inability to give appropriate expression to the need to love. The "love in" practiced by some contemporary adolescents and young adults, for example, appears to be a response to reciprocal needs to love and be loved, not primarily a response to a need to relieve sexual tensions. It has been suggested, too, that the antagonism and violence of many young people toward contemporary institutions (notably government, church, university, and society in general) may reflect youth's frustration in wanting to love something or somebody that no longer seems to be lovable.[7] Government policies which favor special interests and deny the rights and interests of other people alienate many young people and make them disdain expressing love for their country. Similarly, many are less inclined to speak with affection and loyalty of their schools, for they have become increasingly impersonal and bureaucratic, responding to the students as though they were merely Social Security numbers. The impersonal quality of our technological, computer-run society may have made us all a little less loving.

The feeling that one is valued and accepted by others leads one to value and accept himself. A sense of personal value and self-worth comes to be reflected, often covertly, in an individual's responses to life situations. The term *security* has become associated with this sense of self-worth. A conviction of self-value gives one, in the psychological sense, a feeling of safety and freedom from fear and anxiety which the word *security* connotes.

Sensations of security begin in infancy. Pleasant feelings which accompany the satisfaction of physiological drives tend to become associated with the kinds and quality of human relationships existing between the child or adolescent and the significant persons in his life. Thus, a feeling of security may be experienced initially in the strong affectional bond which develops between a mother and her child as she nurses and cares for him. Qualities of valuing and support expressed in other ways will also characterize the relationships which the child has with his teachers or friends. The need to feel secure is a need which continues throughout life.

The term *security* has become associated with various behavioral symptoms which reflect the individual's responses to feelings of safety and

[6] Fromm, *The Art of Loving*, p. 1.

[7] Irene M. Josselyn, "The Capacity to Love: A Possible Reformulation," *Journal of the American Academy of Child Psychiatry*. 10 (January 1971), 6–22.

certainty. The secure individual, sure of his own value, is free in his relationships with others. Indeed, studies of persons undergoing counseling reveal that those who have positive feelings about themselves also tend to respond positively to others.[8] Children who feel secure are outgoing, confident, curious, accepting, and self-assured. This positive orientation toward life also facilitates an individual's development and learning.

Insecurity can also manifest itself in a variety of ways. Commonly, the insecure child is outwardly aggressive, physically or verbally, toward others or toward himself. His dependence upon others or his preoccupation with the uncertainty of his self-worth is manifested in attention seeking, bragging, demanding, dominating, or exploiting others, or in other selfish and self-centered behavior. When faced with unfamiliar situations, tasks which are too hard, or situations involving competition, the insecure child often becomes panicky, gives up easily, or runs away.[9]

Some children who feel insecure withdraw from contact with other persons. A child whose valuing and acceptance of himself has been damaged by lack of affectional relationships seeks, by withdrawing, to avoid further emotional pain. The insecurity behind this behavior may not be easily detected by adults because the withdrawn child causes no trouble in the group. Undetected, however, withdrawal, through increasing loss of contact with reality, often leads to mental illness.

The specific behavior patterns and roles that one learns in interaction with others are those which he judges will be most effective in fully satisfying his need to feel secure. Each child learns highly individual ways of dealing with this important need, and probably no learning in the individual's life is so crucial to his overall development and adjustment as is the learning which enables him to achieve a feeling of security.

Affectional Needs in Infancy

Emergence of Relatedness Needs

During the first several weeks of life, the human infant is wholly dependent upon others for the satisfaction of physiological needs. These needs provide his first interpersonal experience. His success or lack of success in satisfying his hunger through nursing, for example, is expressed

---

[8] Elizabeth Sheerer, "An Analysis of the Relationship between Acceptance of Self and Acceptance and Respect for Others," *Journal of Consulting Psychology*, 13 (June 1949), 169–175; Dorothy Stock, "An Investigation into the Interrelations between the Self-Concept and Feelings toward Other Persons and Groups," *Journal of Consulting Psychology*, 13 (June 1949), 176–180.

[9] James S. Plant, *Personality and the Cultural Pattern* (New York: Commonwealth Fund, 1937), p. 101.

in reactions of satisfaction and contentment or of dissatisfaction and pain. These pleasant or unpleasant feelings and responses become associated with and directed toward the person (usually the mother) most responsible for them.[10]

The infant's ability to register and associate sensory impressions from personal contacts with his mother extends to other experiences as well. So closely related are a child's physical and psychological needs that anything that makes him more comfortable physically (such as nursing, changing diapers, or picking him up) also improves his psychological well-being. Particularly important to his psychological well-being, in Ribble's view,[11] are closeness, warmth, support, and acts of mothering, such as fondling, caressing, rocking, and singing or speaking to the baby while caring for his physical needs.

Studies of Maternal Deprivation

Evidence of the crucial importance of relatedness and security needs to the growth and development of young children comes from many sources. One important source is controlled experiments investigating the effects of maternal deprivation in animals.

In a study cited by Bowlby,[12] a pair of goat kids lived with and were fed by the mother except during a daily 40-minute experimental period when one kid was separated from the mother. During the experimental period, the lights were periodically extinguished, a situation which is known to create anxiety in goats. This treatment produced very different behavior in the twins. The one with its mother appeared at ease and moved about freely, while the isolated one cowered in a corner.

A number of experiments investigating the development of affectional responses of neonatal and infant monkeys to an artificial inanimate mother have been reported by Harlow.[13] Two different surrogate mother figures were constructed. One was made from a block of wood covered with sponge rubber and sheathed in tan terry cloth, with a light bulb in its back radiating heat. The second mother surrogate was made of wire mesh and was warmed by radiant heat; it differed from the cloth mother surrogate mainly in the quality of contact comfort which it could supply.

[10] The critical importance of nursing experiences to the child's later personality development is emphasized in Harry Stack Sullivan, *The Interpersonal Theory of Psychiatry* (New York: W. W. Norton & Co., 1953), pp. 75–91.

[11] Margaret A. Ribble, *The Rights of Infants* (New York: Columbia University Press, 1943), p. 9.

[12] John Bowlby, *Child Care and the Growth of Love* (Baltimore: Penguin Books, 1965), p. 22.

[13] Harry F. Harlow, "The Nature of Love," *American Psychologist*, 13 (December 1958), 673–685.

In the initial experiment a cloth mother and a wire mother were placed in different cubicles attached to the infant monkey's cage. For four newborn monkeys the cloth mother lactated and the wire mother did not; for another four the condition was reversed. In both cases the infant received all its milk through the mother surrogate as soon as it was able to. The infants had access to both mothers, and the time spent with each was automatically recorded. The infants fed by the cloth mother spent 15 to 20 times as much time with her as with the wire mother; and those fed by the wire mother spent five to eight times as much time with their nonlactating cloth mother as with the wire mother. These findings clearly show that contact comfort is of fundamental importance—greater importance even than nursing—in the experiencing of affection. Indeed, Harlow suggests that "the primary function of nursing as an affectional variable is that of ensuring frequent and intimate body contact of infant with mother."[14]

In other experiments Harlow studied the role of the mother or mother surrogate in providing infants with a source of security, especially in strange situations. When placed experimentally in a strange environment, infant monkeys always rushed to the mother surrogate when she was present, clutched her, rubbed their bodies against hers, and frequently manipulated her body and face. A little later, the infants began to use the mother surrogate as a source of security and a base of operations to which they would return from explorations of their new world. When the mother was absent from the room, however, most of the infants would freeze in a crouched position, frantically clutch their bodies, and begin crying, rocking, or sucking. A few monkeys would rush to the center of the room, where the mother was customarily placed, and then run rapidly from object, to object, screaming and crying all the while.

The effects of maternal deprivation on human beings have been observed mainly in individuals growing up in institutions. The literature is replete with cases reporting the effects of maternal deprivation on human growth, development, and mental health. Ribble[15] cites the case of an infant left by the mother in an understaffed hospital. Lack of mothering was accompanied by an inability to retain and assimilate food, a continuing loss of weight, a suspension of growth development, and a slipping backward in physiological functioning that threatened the child's life. Although subsequent mothering and attention did restore normal body and growth processes, development was retarded and the child's emotional life was severely damaged. Bowlby[16] cites numerous reports of British children separated from parents for long periods during World War II. These children developed numerous symptoms of emotional maladjustment: inability to love or to form lasting relationships or to care for others; avoidance and rejection of those who sought to help; lack of normal emotional responses; deceit, evasion, stealing, and lack of concentration at school.

[14] Harlow, p. 679.
[15] Ribble, pp. 4–7.
[16] Bowlby, pp. 18–49.

Spitz[17] found a dramatic contrast between children reared under conditions of adequate social stimulation and contact and those reared in a socially impoverished environment. One group, consisting primarily of children whose mothers were unable to support them, lived in a foundling home; a second group lived in a nursery attached to a women's prison. In both institutions the children were admitted shortly after birth, and in both they were given excellent physical and medical care. The two groups differed markedly in the amount of human association they experienced. Babies in the foundling home were kept in cribs where they could see only walls, ceiling, and corridors. These children were raised from the third month by overworked nursing personnel, who fed and washed them but had no time to play with them. Mothers of babies in the prison nursery, however, were available to spend a few hours each day with their babies, so that these children had more social experiences than those in the foundling home. Spitz's findings revealed that in an infant personality test the foundling home babies registered a precipitous decline in their monthly developmental quotient from 130 in the third month to 70 at the end of the first year and 45 at the end of the second year. The developmental quotient of children in the prison nursery, on the other hand, averaged 95 to 110 each month during the first year.

A more serious condition associated with maternal deprivation in the foundling home is *anaclitic depression*, which Spitz observed in 19 of 23 foundling home infants. The principal behavior symptoms included mourning, withdrawal, inability to act, and loss of appetite, sleep, and weight. The children eventually became extremely lethargic and withdrawn and showed a general physical deterioration. This condition Spitz called *hospitalism*. Associated with this general decline was a high mortality rate among the foundling home children. During a two-year period 37 percent of these children died, whereas none of the nursery infants did.

Later writers[18] have been critical of the research methodologies and the interpretations of Spitz and Ribble. When all is said, however, the evidence does suggest that lack of maternal contact and love—although it does not produce invariable effects in all individuals—can cause marked retardation in development and severe damage to physical and mental health.

---

[17] Rene A. Spitz, "Hospitalism: An Inquiry into the Genesis of Psychiatric Conditions in Early Childhood," *The Psychoanalytic Study of the Child*, Vol. 1 (New York: International University Press, 1945), pp. 53–74; Rene A. Spitz and K. M. Wolfe, "Anaclitic Depression: An Inquiry into the Genesis of Psychiatric Conditions in Early Childhood," *The Psychoanalytic Study of the Child*, Vol. 2 (New York: International University Press, 1946), pp. 313–342.

[18] S. M. Pinneau, "A Critique of the Articles by Margaret Ribble," *Child Development*, 21 (December 1950), 203–228; "The Infantile Disorders of Hospitalism and Anaclitic Depression," *Psychological Bulletin*, 52 (September 1955), 429–452; and H. Orlansky, "Infant Care and Personality," *Psychological Bulletin*, 46 (January 1949), 1–48.

Affection and Socialization

Since the child learns the ways of his culture primarily in interaction with others, his socialization experiences will influence and be influenced by affectional ties with significant persons in his life. In many cultures, including our own, it is these significant persons—members of the family, the kinship group, the peer group, and neighbors—who fulfill the dual and inseparable functions of teaching the customs and mores of the culture to the child and at the same time of giving him affection and helping him to feel secure. This dual role often creates conflict and confusion for child and elder alike. The affection the child seeks and needs should be unconditional—a valuing of the individual for himself alone, regardless of his particular qualities or characteristics. But sometimes the affection seems to be contingent on good behavior—so that lapses in acceptable toilet habits, aggression toward a sibling, or a violation of any of the middle class mores brings about disapproval, censure, or punishment by the elder. The child often interprets such acts as personal rejection or the withdrawal of love. On the other hand, the overindulgent elder, who avoids correcting or curbing a child's antisocial behavior for fear that such action will cause the child to feel unloved, can contribute to an increase in a child's self-centeredness and lack of respect for elders. On the whole, however, children who early and continuously experience love and a feeling of being valued are usually able, with increased maturation and experience, to distinguish between the two functions of adults. The secure child or adolescent has the support necessary to accept correction and can work toward meeting and accepting the ways imposed by the culture.

Affection and Patterns of Child Training

Two major approaches to child training, the behaviorist and the psychoanalytic, differ substantially in the emphasis they place on the child's feelings and need for affection. Dominating the scene during the second and third decades of this century was J. B. Watson's behavioristic view that nearly all human behavior and development are the result of *conditioning*. The theory of conditioning describes learning as a series of events in which a stimulus (such as a loud noise) becomes associated with and evokes a response (such as a startled or fear reaction). Under behaviorism, the environment is controlled in so far as possible by parents and other socializing agents, who introduce stimuli designed to evoke desired behaviors in the young. Behaviorism gives little attention to events that intervene between stimulus and response, and it excludes from consideration consciousness, feelings, cognitions, and introspection.

In applying behaviorism to problems of child rearing, mothers were instructed to feed the infant on a strict schedule, to refrain from picking up a fussy child, and to place him on the toilet at regular times after meals—so that in each case the appropriate stimulus-response associations would be formed. Child training under behaviorism is little concerned with a child's feelings, his relationships with others, or his psychological needs. Focusing on these is equivalent to "spoiling" the child; effective development and learning depend wholly upon the child's forming appropriate stimulus-response patterns.

The principles of psychoanalysis began to be disseminated more widely and to exert increasing influence on psychological thought in the United States beginning about 1930. Freud, and later psychoanalytic theorists, placed great emphasis upon the quality of the early interpersonal relationships of the child because of the influence of these relationships on later personality development. The damaging effects of early emotional deprivation—neuroses, maladjustment, and mental illness—were shown in studies of maternal deprivation, such as those cited earlier. Ribble and Sullivan,[19] therefore, advised mothers to satisfy fully the emotional needs of their children by cuddling, mothering, rocking, and playing with them. These writers also indicated that the parent's own feelings toward the child are extremely important; that is, the parent's acceptance or rejection of the child may be communicated to him through psychomotor tensions. For instance, if the parent holds his child firmly, the child has comfortable, pleasant feelings associated with security; if the child is held loosely or carelessly, he feels fearful and insecure. According to these writers, satisfying the child's physical needs contributes to relieving his tension and to making him feel more comfortable and secure.

Psychoanalytic writings have tended to make parents more aware of and concerned about the affectional needs of children. Thus, psychoanalysis has made a major contribution to an understanding of human development, even though many of its claims have not as yet been fully substantiated by research.

Characteristic Emotional Climates

Children may experience any one of four general types of emotional climates: affection, rejection, inconsistency, or overprotection. Since the description of each climate is rather general, the emotional climate in the home of any particular child is likely to vary somewhat from the description of the type.

Climate of affection.   In a home that provides a climate of affection, family members express toward one another the fundamental qualities of acceptance and valuing. A child who grows up in such a climate feels wanted and valued. His relationships with others, especially his parents, are

[19] See notes 10 and 11.

pleasurable and satisfying; he learns that he can depend upon others for support and help. Such a child gains a certainty of his own worth and thus is freed from anxiety. He is able to express affection for others and to progress toward growth and maturity. In short, his interactions with others confirm and reinforce his conception of his own value, thereby providing him with a firm feeling of security.

Climate of rejection.   Some children live in homes in which family relationships are cold, indifferent, hostile, or rejecting. In such a climate the child feels uncertain of his own worth and, consequently, feels threatened, anxious, and in constant conflict. Burdened by these emotions, he cannot make optimum progress in learning and development, and often behaves aggressively. Thus, the child who tries intentionally to hurt others or himself or to behave in ways sure to result in punishment is really grasping for crumbs of attention as a substitute for the affection and acceptance he has been unable to secure. Such a child is emotionally crippled; he has simply not learned that he can gain love and acceptance by socially acceptable behavior.

Climate of inconsistency.   In some families the relationship between child and parents is variable and inconsistent. On some days the parent may be overindulgent, generous, and affectionate toward the child; at other times, for no apparent reason, the parent may be critical, punishing, hostile, or rejecting. This inconsistency deprives the child of adequate perceptual cues to the behavior desired of him. Not knowing for sure how his parent will respond to his behavior in any given situation, he becomes anxious and immobile. Although he is loved and valued at times, the overall inconsistency of the treatment he receives from his parents creates within the child an uncertainty and a fear of taking chances—qualities that are inimical to learning and the development of a well-integrated personality.

   Whether the climate is affection, rejection, or inconsistency is revealed in the mother-infant relationship and the infant's response to an unfamiliar environment and to strangers.[20] Mothers who successfully establish a climate of affection are accessible, cooperative, accepting, and sensitive to the child's signals of distress. At home their children engage in spontaneous play and tend not to be disturbed by minor everyday separations. In a strange situation these infants use their mothers as a secure base from which to explore. Under the stresses of successive strange situations, however, these children reduce their exploratory play, increasingly seek out their mothers, and show signs of increasing distress during periods of separation. This pattern of mother-infant interaction and maternal sensitivity reflects the normal healthy pattern of infant responses to people and environment toward the end of the first year of life.

   At the other end of the continuum in Ainsworth's study was a group of mothers whose insensitive responses to their children showed a climate

---

[20] Mary D. S. Ainsworth et al., "Individual Differences in Strange Situational Behavior of One-Year-Olds," ERIC (1969), ED 056 742.

of rejection. The insecurity of the children was reflected in inconsistent behavior. In successive strange situations they increasingly sought their mothers in a manifestation of separation anxiety. On the other hand, the pain of rejection experienced in interaction with the mother seemed to lead to defensive responses and independent play. Apparently, absorption in play allayed insecurity somewhat and blocked proximity-seeking behavior, which had frequently been associated with rejection.

In between these two extreme groups are the mothers who create a climate of inconsistency by being erratic in their sensitivity and responsiveness to their babies' distress signals. Ainsworth found that the responses of these infants are quite different from those of infants who live in a climate of acceptance or rejection. In strange situations they may at first use their mothers as a secure base from which to explore, but they show less attachment behavior in reunions with their mothers and maintain exploration at a fairly high level. The independence of these infants appears to be used as a defense against stresses in strange situations.

Climate of overprotection.   Some children are smothered with love. Their parents overindulge them, establish no firm or realistic limits for their behavior, or accede to their every whim. As a result, they become overdependent and self-centered and gain a distorted view of their own importance.

The indulgent and overprotective adult often has emotional problems of his own. Overprotection may be evidence of irrational fears about the safety and health of an only child or a handicapped child, or it may serve as compensation for emotional needs left unfulfilled by the marriage. Robert's mother, in the following case record, manifests both the irrational fears and the unfulfilled needs.

Robert's mother had had several miscarriages before Robert's difficult birth, and she was past 40 when Robert was born. Robert's father spent most of his time working at his office, thereby continuing the distant relationship with his wife which had existed since early in the marriage. During Robert's growing years, his mother scarcely let him out of her sight. She nursed him until he was two, boiled his bottles until he was four, and would not let him play with other children for fear he would catch some dread disease. Both shared the same bed until Robert was eight.

Early, Robert sought to feed and dress himself, to build with blocks and to color pictures, but he soon gave up when his mother insisted on their doing things together. As time went on, Robert learned that he could get what he wanted from his mother by screaming his demands or by lying on the floor and kicking. His social adjustment to kindergarten and first grade was difficult. He demanded the teacher's total attention, grabbed toys and materials from other children, and generally failed to conform to school expectations. During the whole of first grade, Robert's mother brought him to school and came each afternoon to take him home in the car. In response to the teacher's note about Robert's messy desk, his mother appeared at school one afternoon and proceeded to clean out his desk while Robert chased other boys around the room.

This case illustrates the characteristics of overprotection noted by Levy:[21] excessive contact between mother and child, infantilization of both mother's and child's behavior, and prevention of independent behavior on the part of the child. For Robert, overprotection blocked healthy emotional relationships with others, frustrated growth toward the independence, and severely limited development and learning. Overprotection distorts a child's perceptions of himself and the world, thereby creating adjustment problems which must be overcome if learning and development are to proceed.

The Development of Affectional Relationships

The feeling of security that emerges from shared affectional relationships is not gained at once but is developed gradually. The child changes and matures in his way of giving and receiving affection just as he changes and matures in physical size and complexity. The development of the child's affectional life has three aspects: (1) psychosexual development, as shown in a change from self-love and self-centeredness toward increased acceptance and valuing of others; (2) social development, as the child broadens his base of affectional relationships from the family to an ever widening circle of friends and associates in adolescence and adulthood; and (3) individual development—the change from a state of complete helplessness and dependence upon others to a state of relative independence, which enables the child to help and to share with others.

Psychosexual Development of the Child

The first aspect of the development of the affectional life of the child is described by Freud's theory of psychosexual development.[22] Freud's description of development was selected for discussion because of its relevance to the development of affectional relationships and its relationship to the psychoanalytic theory of personality theory, of which it is a part.

---

[21] David M. Levy, *Maternal Overprotection* (New York: Columbia University Press, 1943).

[22] A critical analysis of Freud's psychoanalytic theory of personality, including psychosexual development, is presented in Chapter 8.

The account that follows is confined to those parts of Freud's theory which assist in explaining the changes in the child's feelings toward self and his relationships with others. A summary of the stages of psychosexual development, the approximate age when each appears, and the characteristics of each stage is presented in Table 5–1.

Table 5–1.   Stages of Psychosexual Development

Stage	Age Range When Stage Appears	Characteristic Behavior Patterns
Oral	Birth to 2 years	Infant seeks pleasure and gratification through stimulation of mouth and lips in sucking, biting, and putting things in mouth. Sucks nipple, pacifier, and other objects.
Anal	1½ years to 3 years	Focus of pleasure and gratification is lower digestive tract and anus and in control of sphincter muscles. Pleasure experienced in holding in and expelling bowel movements. Often period of parent-child conflict over toilet training.
Phallic Oedipus (boys)	2 to 6 years	Boy's love of mother manifested in jealous rivalry with father. Boy's fear of castration viewed as punishment for masturbation.
Electra (girls)	2 to 6 years	Girl blames mother for female anatomical deficiency (manifested in penis envy) and expresses love for father.
Latency	5 to 14 years	Child represses incestuous love for parent of opposite sex. Represses all sexual cravings. Period of quiescent sexuality.
Genital	10 years to adulthood	Period of physical and sexual maturation, heterosexual relationships, courting, marriage, procreation, and raising family.

Freud names the initial stages of the infant's psychosexual development for regions or parts of the body whose stimulation bring pleasure. The period of the first few months of life—when the infant gains pleasure from nursing, putting things in his mouth, and biting—is called the *oral phase*. The later months of the second year—when the child's attention comes to be directed to the anus—is called the *anal phase*. Tensions arising in the anal region as a result of the accumulation of fecal material are pleasurably released with the expelling of this material. These physical pleasures produce in the child a fondness for his own body, a fondness manifested in feelings of self-love which Freud calls *narcissism*. Initially, the young child is literally in love with himself. He is wholly self-interested, self-willed, and selfish. Later, as he learns to respond to others, he tends to choose as love objects persons who accede to his wishes and persons who appear to be as fond of him as he is of himself. Thus, his fondness for love objects during this secondary stage of self-love is contingent upon what they can contribute to his comforts and satisfactions. The period of narcissism, in which the child exercises his self-will in manipulating the people and objects of his environment for his own purposes, has been aptly called *the age of infantile omnipotence*.

For most children the age of infantile omnipotence comes to an end during the preschool years, when parents stop acceding to the demands of the child and instead place demands upon him. He is not permitted to eat, sleep, defecate, or strike at others according to his wishes but must seek satisfaction of these needs in ways approved by his parents. At about two or three years of age, the centering of the child's attention on pleasures associated with his stroking and manipulating his sex organs marks the *phallic stage* of psychosexual development. For a boy, affection for his parents was expressed through close emotional ties with his mother and respect for and emulation of his father. With the onset of the phallic stage, however, the young boy experiences a rivalry with his father as he seeks the exclusive love and possession of his mother. In interpreting this behavior, Freud theorized that the boy's love for his mother becomes incestuous, and, as a result, the boy becomes jealous of his father. Freud called this psychological phenomenon the *Oedipus complex*. Strong incest taboos and fear of the father generally lead to the boy's repressing both his incestuous love for his mother and his rivalry with his father, with the result that the Oedipus complex gradually disappears.

During the phallic stage, parallel but quite different changes in relationships between a girl and her parents occur. The girl's perception of male dominance leads her to express love for her father and to feel jealous of and to reject her mother. This shift in feelings and relationships is called the *Electra complex*. If the daughter experiences a warm, affectionate relationship with each parent, and if both encourage her to develop her femininity, the Electra complex is gradually replaced by a strengthened identification with the mother. This enables the daughter to maintain and to develop warm affectional ties with both parents.

A major step toward achieving mature affectional ties with others occurs when relationships reflecting narcissistic self-love and Oedipus or Electra complexes are no longer satisfying or appropriate to the maturing child. When the child has reached five or six years of age, the cultural forces of home, neighborhood, and school openly disapprove of and discourage his selfish, self-willed ways. Recognizing that he has fallen short of the standards that parents and teachers have set for him, he tends to feel inadequate and dissatisfied with himself. He seeks to relieve these feelings of inadequacy and dissatisfaction by accepting and identifying with the standards of his parents and teachers and by centering affection on another person. By freeing himself from the persistent demands of self-love, the child becomes able to give himself fully in relationships with others. He expresses concern for others and a willingness to help not only parents and siblings but persons outside his family as well. This increasing capacity for love, and a sense of fulfillment in loving another person without guilt or anxiety, are the characteristic marks of mature affectional relationships. One cannot freely love another, however, unless he first feels loved and valued. Thus, the acceptance and value that one feels beginning in early life are crucial variables that determine his capacity for achieving mature affectional relationships later.

Between the age of five and the beginning of pubescence (for girls, between the ages of eight and 14; for boys, between the ages of 10 and 16) is a period of relative quiescence in sexual development which Freud calls the *latency period*. It is a period of vigorous physical activity and development during which the child moves beyond the home to form affectional ties primarily with a group of peers and secondarily with selected adults in the school and community.

Puberty, marking the beginning of sexual maturing, signals the beginning of the *genital stage*, the last phase of psychosexual development. This psychological development, and the physical growth changes which mark entrance into adulthood, exert a profound influence on the formation of affectional ties during adolescence. The young person is faced with the problem of sublimating his awakening sex drives, the direct expression of which is blocked by the culture. Initially, the adolescent achieves this sublimation by establishing friendships with persons of his own sex and age. Boys may spend long hours together hunting, fishing, bowling, playing tennis, or working on bicycles or an old car. Girl chums frequently spend long hours talking about boys, other girls, favorite movie or singing stars, clothes, grooming, teachers, and parents, doing homework together, and tying up the family telephone.

These close attachments with others of the same sex fail, however, to provide complete satisfaction. The beginning of physical and sexual maturity in adolescence, together with mounting cultural pressures, results in the young person's seeking strong affectional ties with one or more members of the opposite sex. One such attachment with a particular man or woman becomes regarded as permanent and is formalized by marriage. With the centering of the most intense expressions of affection in one's relationship with one's mate and children, the cycle of the development of affectional relationships reaches fulfillment. This maturing of affectional relationships is related only in a very general way to chronological age. Many adults remain dependent and self-centered throughout life, while many children and youth reveal considerable maturity in achieving mutually shared affectional relationships.

Broadening of Affectional Ties

The rather marked changes in one's interpersonal behavior from birth to maturity are paralleled and facilitated by a broadening of one's base of affectional relationships. Strengthening of the child's feeling of security is dependent not only upon the personal acceptance and valuing he experiences with his mother, his father, or a nurse, but also upon the continuing formation of additional one-to-one relationships with significant others, together with other affectional relationships of a less intense nature.

The first and primary relationship with the mother or nurse grows out of the nurturance and care which she provides in satisfying the infant's physiological and dependency needs. As his ability to differentiate objects in his environment and to make social responses increases, the infant establishes relationships with father, siblings, and in many cases with grandparents, aunts, and uncles. These are personal relationships of varying intensities and meanings. Relationships with siblings, as will be noted later, are likely to be mercurial—reflecting contrasting feelings of love and envy, fear, or hate.

In early childhood, after the child has learned to walk and to talk, the base of affectional relationships broadens to persons beyond the family. Characteristically, the young child seeks out a neighbor child of approximately the same age. Playing near each other, each engrossed in his own play activities, the children experience acceptance. The importance of these early childhood relationships is shown in the strong identifications revealed in children's language, dress, interests, and shared activities. A two-year-old girl, for example, may not give her mother a moment's peace until she has a coat with a fur collar like the one her little friend has.

Adults outside the family are often important sources of a child's security throughout childhood and adolescence. Among the most prominent of these are the succession of teachers whom he has in his years at school. School is a significant experience for every child regardless of the particular personal meaning each gains from it. A special bond of affection usually forms between the kindergarten and first grade teacher and the children. The teacher becomes a kind of second mother to her children, and many will forget and call her "mother." The warmth and support the kindergarten or first grade teacher gives the child influences to a considerable degree his adjustment and progress in school. In subsequent school experiences, as the teacher-pupil relationship becomes less close and more formal, the student still looks to the teacher for acceptance and understanding.

As the child grows into late childhood and early adolescence, his base of affectional relationships broadens to include ties with other children and adults in many different groups and situations. The peer group becomes an important influence in the life and development of the student during this period (see Chapter 7). His participation as an accepted member of the peer group not only gives him a feeling of belongingness but also contributes to his feelings of value and self-worth. At this time, as we have noted, the child often shares a special chum relationship with a same-sexed member of the peer group. For many, this relationship remains a strong affectional tie even into adult life.

Identifications with older persons of the same sex provide a further broadening of affectional ties. Often the older person is a favorite teacher, a scout leader, a baseball or football coach, or an older brother or sister or aunt or uncle whom the child or adolescent greatly admires and emulates. Children and youth also experience a feeling of oneness in make-believe relationships with movie, TV, or athletic stars or fictional heroes.

Affectional ties with members of the opposite sex, leading to the selection of a mate in courtship and marriage, mark a shift toward a new base for one's affectional life. For those who do not marry, a new base of affectional relationships will include the close, lasting friendships they establish with members of both sexes. Each person's affectional base continues to broaden throughout life, as friendships and associations with others are built with members of community, civic, and church groups and with associates on the job. Thus, one develops through the years a widening circle of relationships in which valuing and concern are mutually experienced. This circle of friends and associates changes in membership from time to time, but it continues to serve as an important source of personal valuing and support throughout one's adult life.

Varying kinds of relationships and activities may contribute to one's feeling of security. Some will seek to satisfy their affectional needs through dedicating their energies and lives to an organization, movement, party, or cause, while many others will experience acceptance and a sense of security through a personal relationship with God. Children, and many adults, often experience a special kind of acceptance and affection in their relationships with a pet. These take on added significance when human relationships fail to provide for full satisfaction of this need.

The importance of a broad base of affectional relationships cannot be overemphasized. The individual needs to feel secure not only with his family and close friends but also in the other areas and activities of his life. One's feeling accepted, valued, and supported enables him to respond freely and creatively in all of life's situations. Failure to maintain or to extend a circle of affectional ties results in a narrow affectional base which the changes wrought by time will slowly erode away. For human development and learning to proceed at optimal levels, there must be a broad and expanding base of affectional ties.

Growth toward Independence

We noted earlier that progress in human development is evidenced in change from dependence upon others toward relative independence in functioning. The individual's growth toward independence is also evident in mature affectional relationships that are manifested in his concern for others and in giving as well as receiving love. His feeling of security, his sense of self-worth and certainty that he is loved, enables him to be less dependent upon others for continuous or frequent expressions of affection. Feeling secure frees him to act independently and to respond rationally and objectively in problem-solving and decision-making situations. Yet our independence is never complete, for each of us needs the support and valuing of other human beings.

Threats to Security

Parental Rejection

The first and most devastating threat to a child's security is the threat of being unwanted or rejected, particularly by his parents. Parents—one or both of them—may reject a child for a number of reasons: The mother may have feared pregnancy; the birth may have been difficult; the child may add to an already unbearable financial strain; the child may not have been planned; there may be some real or imagined defect in the child himself; the child may interfere with the parents' own pleasures or goals; or the parents may have no real interest in or desire for children. Parental affection that is inconsistent also threatens the child's security by making him unsure of whether or not he really is loved. In a different way over-protective love threatens a child's security by making him too dependent upon others and by limiting his learning and development.

Parental rejection of a child can be manifested in a variety of ways. Often the parents constantly criticize the child and set unreasonably high expectations for him. Or they may avoid any show of care and responsibility, leaving him to be cared for by others and having as little contact and association with him as possible. Many times overprotection is a mask for parental rejection; a parent who overindulges his child may be trying to convince others and himself that he or she is a good parent. The child quickly senses, however, the lack of acceptance and valuing which is communicated in the relationship with the parent. The effects of parental rejection can be seen in the case of Louise:

> Louise, age nine and in the fourth grade, had many unhappy experiences with other children at school. They called her dumb and made biting remarks about her appearance and dress. Yet the teacher noted that she was attractive, her dresses were similar to those worn by the other girls, and she was above average in her schoolwork.
>
> Louise tried very hard to please the other children by sharing her bicycle and other possessions, by giving in to their wishes, and by inviting a few children to her home to play. Their play would be harmonious for a while, and then one or more would start to call Louise names and would refuse to play with her.
>
> In looking into Louise's home background, the teacher learned that Louise was born when her mother was 46 and that her only sister was 17 years older than Louise. The mother was quite upset at becoming pregnant when she had looked forward to freedom from child rearing. During Louise's childhood her mother was very critical of her, and Louise finally gave up trying to please her.

An analysis of this case revealed that Louise had felt unwanted from an early age. She tried very hard to gain acceptance, especially from her agemates. Somehow her peers sensed and exploited her lack of a feeling of self-worth, and their cruel treatment added further to her feelings of rejection. Since rejection is something that the child or adolescent is unable to prevent or to understand, he does not know how to cope with it or to acquire the love and acceptance that others have denied him. There is considerable evidence that mental illness, delinquency, and failures in many areas of development and learning are often caused by the feelings of insecurity that follow rejection. A major responsibility falls to the school and other agencies of the community to undergird the home in providing security—giving acceptance and affection to all children, especially those whose homes fail them in this important need.

Sibling Rivalry

Sibling rivalry—the envy, dislike, or even hate of a child for a brother or sister who appears to usurp the parents' love—is a frequent phenomenon in American culture. Its manifestations are varied and well known. Aggressive feelings and actions of the older child, directed toward the sibling and toward the parent, and regressive behavior toward more infantile patterns—wanting to be treated like a baby, resuming bottle feeding, and sometimes failing to control defecation—are quite normal and found in most families. The older child of two, three, or four years of age is egocentric and narcissistic. Having had his parents all to himself since birth, he is baffled and hurt at being displaced by the newcomer who seems to take most of his parents' time and attention. Later, at school, the teacher may unwittingly rekindle feelings of animosity and rivalry in a child toward his sibling by such invidious comparisons as "Why can't you be like your little brother?"

The negative effects of sibling rivalry upon a child's feeling of security and relationships within the family can be minimized if the parents set aside particular occasions when each child individually can have the parent completely to himself—in reading a story, in helping and working together in the kitchen or the yard, or in going shopping. Resolving conflicts brought on by the arrival of a sibling results in positive growth. As each child finds his place in the family and feels more secure, he grows in feelings of brotherly love for the sibling—a love which later becomes generalized in feelings of concern and compassion for all men.

Ordinal Position and Size of Family

Birth order and size of family also influence a child's feeling of security. The only child has the undivided attention of his parents; but, contrary to popular opinion, he may not necessarily be overindulged. In a study of 46 pairs of children whose mothers had been rated on the Fels Parent Behavior Rating Scales, Lasko[23] found that parent behavior toward first children is on the average less warm and more restrictive and coercive than behavior toward second children. She also found that parent behavior toward second children does not tend to change markedly as the child grows older. Shifts do occur, however, in the parents' treatment of first children as they grow older, mainly in the direction of less approval and affection.

In a study of the relationship of ordinal position and school achievement in two-child families, Blustein[24] found that although first-born and second-born children did not differ in scholastic aptitude, first-born children made higher grade point averages and higher achievement test scores than their second-born siblings. In addition, first-borns were perceived by their teachers as working harder or more effectively; and first-born boys were rated as more conforming to classroom standards of behavior than second-born boys. In spite of differences in school achievement, first- and second-born boys and girls did not differ in self-ratings of school ability. Oldest children generally reveal higher levels of achievement motivation.[25]

More recent studies,[26] however, reveal almost no reliable evidence that birth order affects behavior and achievement among men living in the United States in the mid-1960s. There is only a marginal increase in these relationships when restrictions of time, place, and sex are removed. Kohn and Schooler,[27] for example, found that neither middle class nor working class mothers of 10-year-old children were significantly affected by their children's birth order in child-rearing values or reactions to misbehavior. Even the frequently reported finding of greater intellectual attainment or occupational achievement among first-borns does not seem to hold up. Kohn and Schooler found no significant differences in level of occupational attainment between first-borns and their siblings.

In many ways the middle child may be the "forgotten child" in the family. He has neither the privileges nor the prestige of being the oldest, nor is he likely to get the attention the youngest child enjoys. Moreover, in many families the middle child finds himself the recipient of hand-me-down clothes and toys and thus may feel less valued by his parents since they

[23] Joan K. Lasko, "Parent Behavior toward First and Second Children," *Genetic Psychology Monographs*, 49 (1954), 97–137.

[24] Esther S. Blustein, "The Relationship of Sibling Position in the Family Constellation to School Behavior Variables in Elementary School Children from Two-Child Families" (unpublished doctor's dissertation, University of Maryland, 1967).

[25] James V. Pierce, "The Educational Motivation Patterns of Superior Students Who Do Not Achieve in High School" (Quincy, Ill.: Youth Development Project, 1960). Mimeographed.

[26] Carmi Schooler, "Birth Order Effects: Not Here, Not Now!" *Psychological Bulletin*, 78 (September 1972), 161–175.

[27] Melvin L. Kohn and Carmi Schooler, "Class, Occupation, and Orientation," *American Sociological Review*, 34 (1969), 659–678.

seldom buy new clothes or toys just for him. The case of Lavonne illustrates the feelings of a middle child in this regard:

> *Lavonne is 10 years old and in the fifth grade. She has one older sister and one younger sister. One morning at school she called the teacher's attention to a dress she was wearing. She said, "Of course, it isn't new. I always have to take Alice's old clothes. I'll certainly be glad if I can ever have a new dress. I bet when I grow up I'll get a job and buy all kinds of pretty clothes." Two weeks later the teacher tested Lavonne's eyes. Afterward Lavonne wanted to know if her eyes were all right. The teacher assured her everything was fine. Lavonne said, "I wouldn't care if I did have to buy glasses. If I had to wear glasses, at least they certainly would have to be new!"*

Lavonne's parents probably valued her as much as they did her sisters, and passing on Alice's outgrown clothes enabled the family to make full use of its limited financial resources. To Lavonne, however, this meant that she did not stand as high in her parents' affection.

Failure to Live Up to Cultural Expectations

Every society expects its young to learn the behaviors, customs, and values that are of central importance in that culture. By internalizing the ways of his culture, the child gains approval, acceptance, and a feeling of belonging to and identification with his social group. Since acceptance and approval are rewards for learning one's culture, the kinds of socialization experiences which children and youth have will clearly be an important factor influencing their feelings of security. Many children experience a threat of loss of parental love and approval because of their failure to conform to expected standards of behavior.

Many children and adolescents feel less secure because of the disapproval and punishment they receive from parents for failure to master a developmental task. This threat of loss of love often weighs most heavily upon the middle class child, whose culture expects fast and early achievement. Davis and Havighurst[28] note that the middle class child often suffers parental disapproval when he has setbacks in learning toilet training and fails to take proper care of personal property. Similarly, they point out that the lower class child also experiences disapproval from family or gang for avoiding a fight or for being too submissive and secretive.

[28] Allison Davis and Robert J. Havighurst, *Father of the Man* (Boston: Houghton Mifflin Co., 1947).

Perhaps the most common threat to the middle class child's feeling of being loved by his parents is his failure or inability to fulfill the image his parents hold of the kind of person they want him to become. The child who fails to make the honor roll, to be elected homecoming queen, or to follow in his father's footsteps by becoming a doctor or lawyer is likely to interpret the disappointment and dissatisfaction expressed by his parents as meaning that he is less worthy or less lovable. Acceptance and love must be unconditional and must not be dependent upon how handsome, popular, intelligent, or well-behaved a child is. Parents and teachers should recognize that every individual needs to feel valued for himself alone, and that his security should not depend upon the system of approval and rewards used in teaching the culture.

Absentee Fathers

The demands made upon fathers by their corporations, businesses, or the armed services cause them to be frequently separated from their families, thus limiting the opportunities for contacts and the formation of affectional relationships between them and their sons and daughters. Middle class suburban fathers often become so preoccupied with their jobs or with civic responsibilities that they come to be seen by their families as weekend guests. Similarly, many working class fathers are away from home on construction jobs or driving trucks or buses. Other fathers are in the armed forces and assigned to sea duty or to overseas posts.

The love of both parents increases the young person's feeling of security, since the affection of each parent reinforces and complements that of the other. Affectional relationships with a father are crucial in the learning of the appropriate sex role by both son and daughter. If a boy loses his father (by death, divorce, separation, or desertion) after age five, the masculinity of his self-concept does not seem to be affected. If, however, the father's absence occurs before the boy is age five, he is likely to have greater difficulty in achieving an appropriate masculine identification. In such a situation, the critical factor influencing the boy's sex role development is his relationship with his mother. If the mother encourages aggressive behavior in her son, he is more likely to have a masculine self-concept.[29]

The father also significantly influences his daughter's feminine identification and social adjustment. If the father plays an active, competent role in the family, his daughter is more likely to imitate his non-sex-typed positive attributes and be more adaptable and less narrow in her behavior repertoire than if he is unmasculine, aloof, or both. Although the importance of this relationship between father and daughter is not dependent on cul-

[29] Henry B. Biller and R. M. Bahm, "Father Absence, Perceived Maternal Behavior, and Masculinity of Self-Concept among Junior High School Boys," *Developmental Psychology*, 4 (March 1971), 178–181.

ture or race, it is critical in relationships between black adolescent girls and their fathers. Biller and Weiss[30] found that the social adjustment of black girls (as well as of black boys) is severely affected by the father's absence. In lower class black families where the father is absent or ineffectual, the daughter is likely to develop negative attitudes toward black males and to view them as inadequate in economic and social areas. These negative attitudes seem to contribute to the lower class black female's difficulties in relating to male relatives, boy friends, husband, and male children. Ideally, irrespective of culture or race, the daughter in her relationship with her father learns appropriate patterns of giving and receiving affection in her relationship with a man; in addition, her relationship with her father contributes to a feeling of security which will find more complete fulfillment later, in her relationship with her husband.

Working Mothers

Since World War II increasing numbers of women have entered the work force. In 1972 there were 12 million mothers in the labor force, more than eight times as many as in 1940. More than half of these 12 million mothers had children between the ages of six and 17, and one third of all the mothers with children under age six were working.[31] No longer is the woman's role soley that of mother and homemaker. Women not only seek greater self-realization and fulfillment for themselves in a career in addition to homemaking, but they want these opportunities to be available for their daughters and other women as well. Their opposition to women's being restricted to the traditional roles of homemaking, teaching, nursing, and office work is reflected in movements directed toward removing discrimination in employment and pay based upon sex.

Working outside the home would seem to reduce the opportunities for mother-child interaction and hence contribute to children's insecurity. The evidence, however, is inconclusive. The many studies of the effects on children of mothers' working have produced conflicting results. Few broad generalizations emerge; the effects on the child appear to be influenced by his age at the time his mother takes a job, by provisions made for child care, and by the unique dynamics and relationships within the particular family. The increase in the number of working mothers underscores the need for a large-scale national program of child care which would provide not only custodial care but also permit children's affectional and developmental needs to be met by trained, sympathetic teachers. The need for

[30] Henry B. Biller and S. D. Weiss, "The Father-Daughter Relationship and the Personality Development of the Female," *Journal of Genetic Psychology*, 116 (March 1970), 79–93.

[31] Mary B. Keyserling, *Windows on Day Care* (New York: National Council of Jewish Women, 1972).

public-supported child care is most acute for children of one-parent families in which the one parent, usually the mother, must work.

In an extensive review of the literature, Stolz[32] found no differences between the cases of working and nonworking mothers in (1) incidence of delinquency among children (only mothers who worked sporadically had more delinquent sons), (2) incidence of psychosomatic symptoms and quality of adjustment of adolescent sons and daughters, (3) incidence of dependency behavior shown by elementary school children, (4) sons' achievement test scores and sons' and daughters' school marks for grades nine through 12, and (5) expressions of dependent and independent behavior among preschool children.

In an earlier study of adolescent-parent adjustment, Nye[33] found that adolescents whose mothers worked part-time revealed better adolescent-parent adjustment than did those whose mothers worked full-time or were not employed at all. In a later study Nye found no differences in adolescent-parent affection for mothers who worked and those who did not.[34] A more recent study by Nelson[35] suggests that the mother's working has a more favorable influence on the personality adjustment of adolescent boys than it has on the personality adjustment of adolescent girls. In Nelson's study ninth grade boys whose mothers worked full-time scored higher on a personality adjustment inventory than did ninth grade girls whose mothers were employed full-time. Moreover, girls with nonworking mothers had better adjustment scores than girls whose mothers worked full-time or part-time.

Broken Homes

The home broken by divorce, separation, or desertion has been pictured generally as a tragic situation, damaging to the family members' affectional relationships and feelings of security. Similar though less devastating are the effects on families broken by the death of a parent.

Studies of the adjustment of children and youth from broken homes appear to substantiate the proposition that a break in the family will have different effects on different children, different families, and in different

[32] Lois M. Stolz, "Effects of Maternal Employment on Children: Evidence from Research," *Child Development*, 31 (December 1960), 749–782.

[33] Ivan Nye, "Adolescent-Parent Adjustment: Age, Sex, Sibling Number, Broken Homes, and Employed Mothers as Variables," *Marriage and Family Living*, 14 (1952), 327–332.

[34] Ivan Nye, "Employment Status of Mothers and Adjustment of Adolescent Children," *Marriage and Family Living*, 6 (1959), 260–267.

[35] Deane D. Nelson, "A Study of Personality Adjustment among Adolescent Children with Working and Nonworking Mothers," *Journal of Educational Research*, 64 (March 1971), 328–330.

situations. In general, children and adolescents from broken homes tend to have poorer adjustment than children and youth from unbroken homes.[36] Other studies,[37] however, have found that there is less juvenile delinquency among adolescents from broken homes than among adolescents from unbroken but quarrelsome and neglectful homes. Although parental death may play a part in the maladjustment of some adolescents, delinquency is primarily associated with breaks that follow parental discord rather than with the loss of the parent as such. The longer the parental disharmony lasts, the greater is the risk to the children. A good relationship between the child and one parent helps to reduce the damaging effects of marital discord, but it does not counteract them completely. In addition, the child whose main affectional ties are with persons outside the family is likely to be less threatened by a break within the home. Finally, when divorce or separation resolves a long-standing conflict in the home, the break may actually lead to more stable affectional ties with the remaining family members and thereby help the child to feel more secure.

Lack of Teacher Sensitivity and Understanding

Students bring to school with them the feelings and anxieties they have acquired in their homes and in their previous school experience. As learning and classroom activities proceed, the perceptive teacher comes to know and to respond to the perceptions and feelings of his students. Frequently, the teacher's attention is drawn to a child who appears to be having considerable difficulty in adjusting to the school experience. The child may continuously call attention to himself by calling out, demanding help, refusing to conform to classroom rules, failing to complete his work, showing disrespect toward the teacher, or being aggressive toward others. Often a teacher responds as if he believes such behavior is caused by the child's not having learned acceptable ways of acting. He is puzzled and bewildered when the usual punishments fail to change the undesirable behavior. If the teacher does not recognize the need for accepting and helping the child over an extended period, the emotional scars the child already bears will not heal and his feelings of insecurity will continue to increase. The amount of time required to help him and the degree of success of efforts to help him will depend upon the unique dynamics and the severity of his particular case.

---

[36] N. Clancy and Faith Smitter, "A Study of Emotionally Disturbed Children in Santa Barbara County Schools," *California Journal of Educational Research*, 4 (1953), 209–218; H. Reyburn, "Guidance Needs of Students from Broken Homes," *California Journal of Educational Research*, 2 (1951), 22–25; Nye, "Adolescent-Parent Adjustment."

[37] William McCord and Joan McCord, *Origins of Crime: A New Evaluation of the Cambridge Somerville Youth Study* (New York: Columbia University Press, 1959); Michael Rutter, "Parent-Child Separation: Psychological Effects on the Children," *Journal of Child Psychology and Psychiatry*, 12 (December 1971), 233–260.

Lack of Peer Belongingness

A major threat to a child's sense of security in school is lack of acceptance by his peers. Children and adolescents who have had difficulties in gaining acceptance in their families frequently are handicapped in relating to peers. These children are less able to give themselves unreservedly to group purposes because the question of their own self-value has not been resolved. The insecure child often insists on having the most desired role in the game, interprets the rules of the game to his or his team's advantage, and acts more in his own self-interest than in the group's interest. Children whose behavior is contrary to the group's interests experience disapproval and rejection.

Poor Academic Performance

High among the values of most teachers is their perception of themselves as adequate and competent teachers. Students who perform well academically confirm these teachers' perceptions of themselves. Not only do such students receive high grades, but they frequently earn the personal recognition, interest, and approval of their teachers. This contributes much to the student's feeling of security. On the other hand, children of lesser abilities and lower achievement motivation are likely to receive less recognition and approval from the teacher. Poor academic performance, therefore, may constitute a threat to a student's security, because he is less likely to win the teacher's approval.

When the teacher centers his attention and interest upon the individual student and his learning and development, poor academic performance is less likely to pose a threat to these students' feelings of security. In fact, as Burrell[38] found, students' performance may actually improve. In Burrell's study, when teachers focused on meeting children's individual emotional needs, the children made significant gains in achievement test and IQ scores. Moreover, the effectiveness of their work increased, their social relationships improved, deviant behavior decreased, interest in school increased, and truancy declined. The teachers, in giving attention to the emotional needs of a few students, found that they also learned more about how they might meet the needs of their other students.

---

[38] Anna P. Burrell, "Facilitating Learning through Emphasis on Meeting Children's Basic Emotional Needs: An In-Service Program," *Journal of Educational Sociology*, 24 (1951), 381–393.

Teachers' Conceptions of Their Role

A further block to a student's achievement of a feeling of security in school is a teacher's limited conception of his role and of his opportunities for helping students to feel more secure. Too often the teacher's role is viewed only in relation to instruction, to guiding and evaluating learning activities. Many teachers are influenced by traditional stereotypes and believe they should remain aloof from their students. They fear that becoming friendly with and close to a student will result in poor discipline or will give the appearance of partiality. Moreover, in the minds of many teachers, the giving of affection is viewed only in terms of those overt, demonstrative evidences of affection which one uses in greeting members of one's family or close friends.

The conception of teaching presented in this book is one of an open, sympathetic, supportive, helping, facilitative relationship between teacher and pupil, a relationship that focuses on activities that promote individual learning and development. The facilitative effect on learning of a social-emotional climate characterized by warm, accepting, supportive teacher-pupil relationships has been amply demonstrated by research.

Lewin, Lippitt, and White,[39] in their study of three experimentally created social climates, found that under democratic leadership boys more freely praised one another's work, while under an autocratic leader the only way to receive praise was to get it from an adult. As competition for the leader's approval increased in autocratic groups, the boys became less inclined to approve the work of fellow members. Under democratic leadership, recognition was more readily gained from both leader and peers; as a result, the greater incidence of cooperative behavior benefited the individual as well as the total group.

Anderson and his associates,[40] in their studies of teachers' classroom personalities, found that dominating teachers usually produced antagonistic and aggressive behavior in children, while flexible teachers more frequently elicited facilitative, cooperative, and self-directive responses from their students. A study by this writer[41] of social-emotional climate and group learning revealed that teachers in groups where the leader used a high proportion of accepting, clarifying, and problem-centered statements indicated a greater understanding of students' behavior than did teachers whose group

[39] Kurt Lewin, Ronald Lippitt, and Ralph K. White, "Patterns of Aggressive Behavior in Experimentally Created 'Social Climates,'" *Journal of Social Psychology*, 10 (1939), 271–299.

[40] Harold H. Anderson, Joseph E. Brewer, and Mary F. Reed, "Studies of Teachers' Classroom Personalities, III. Follow-Up Studies of the Effects of Dominative and Integrative Contacts on Children's Behavior," *Applied Psychology Monograph No. 11* (Stanford, Calif.: Stanford University Press, 1946).

[41] Hugh V. Perkins, "The Effects of Climate and Curriculum on Group Learning," *Journal of Educational Research*, 44 (1950), 269–286.

leaders used higher proportions of information-giving, directive, and critical statements. (This study and the study by Lewin, Lippitt, and White are reported in greater detail in Chapter 17.)

Human beings communicate an acceptance and a valuing of each other not by overt and demonstrative displays of affection but by the concern, interest, support, and valuing expressed in relationships. The manner of communicating this valuing of another person will vary according to the roles of the persons involved, the culture, and each person's own conception of the appropriate response in a particular situation. A teacher's expression of affection for his students need not be limited to a pat on the head, a hug, or holding of hands, which often means so much to preschool and primary school children. The teacher communicates his interest, concern, and valuing of a student of any age through his ready smile, warm greeting, responsiveness to the student's interests and concerns, and willingness to listen and to help the student. The true measure of a teacher's affection for a student is his full acceptance of the student as a person regardless of his ability, IQ, achievement, or behavior. For many students, approval and praise by the teacher are stronger incentives for learning than are grades, honors, or prizes.

Insecurity: An Example

An indication of the specific ways a child's feeling of insecurity influences his learning is revealed in the case of Jane:

> *Jane is 10 years old and in the fifth grade. The teacher describes Jane as a rather nice-looking girl with brown hair and eyes, well dressed, and neat. She wears glasses and has crowded teeth. Often in class she sits chewing her fingernails or a strand of her hair. Her score on the California Test of Mental Maturity in the fourth grade yielded an IQ of 117. Jane's father is a college graduate and works as a chemist. Her mother had two years of college. There is a sister, Marcia, age seven, who is in the second grade at the same school.*
>
> *Several times during the early part of the school year Jane came to the teacher and stated that the other girls did not like her and were mean to her. Later the teacher noticed Jane talking to Lee, Prue, and Audrey. Later in a conference the teacher commented to Jane that she was glad Jane was having a good time with the other girls. Jane's reply was "Oh, I wasn't having a good time. They weren't nice ιo me. They didn't want to talk to me."*
>
> October 24.   *Today the class was illustrating poems and Jane was the first one to hand hers in. The teacher noticed that the title was written and suggested that it would look nicer if it were printed.*

Jane reddened, grabbed the picture from the teacher's desk, took it to her seat, and tore it into tiny pieces.

After school the teacher talked to Jane about her picture and Jane said, "Oh, I was so mad I tore it up and then I told Gwen. I always do things like that. I get awfully mad, especially at home at my little sister." She frowned, screwed up her face, and said, "She is the meanest, horridest little brat. I just hate her. She won't do a thing I want."

October 29. *Yesterday the class had planned to make maps of an imaginary land to show such geographical terms as* capes, bays, *and* isthmuses. *Jane and Weldon each came in today with maps they had made at home. The teacher praised both maps and showed them to the class. Jane seemed pleased when the class showed interest but frowned when they offered some criticism. As the class started to work, Jane sat and looked at hers, grumbling, "It isn't fair. They had more help than I had. They got to look at the maps in the room." The teacher went to her and said, "Yours is fine, but some of the formations are not shown. Wouldn't you like to make a perfect one now?" Jane continued to grumble. Finally, she walked across the room to the teacher with her map in her hands. Her face was red. She said defiantly, "I'm going to tear mine up." The teacher looked at her and smiled and said, "Why, Jane, it's your paper." Jane went back to her seat, stood there a minute, tore the paper in shreds, and sat down. The teacher didn't look at her. The children smiled at the teacher, shrugged their shoulders, some shook their heads, and then went on with their work. Jane sat with her head in her hands the rest of the period. Later the teacher said quietly to Jane, "I'm not sure you belong with us today. You have not been helping." In a few minutes Jane came up to the teacher and said she would like to stay after school and help. The teacher smiled and said she was sorry but that she had a meeting at 3 o'clock.*

November 12. *Today Jane couldn't get one of her examples in arithmetic. She came to the teacher, but the teacher could not help her because she was with another group. Jane returned to her seat, grumbling. Soon she began tearing her paper in pieces and stuffing them in her desk. No one paid any attention to her. After school Mrs. S., the teacher, detained Jane for a moment and said firmly, "Jane, there is one thing we are through with and that is tearing up papers. Tearing up papers is only something a very small child would do, and you are much too big for that. I don't want to see any more of tearing up papers." Then the teacher walked away without giving Jane a chance to talk about it.*

In late January the teacher had a conference with Jane's mother at the mother's request. In the conference Jane's mother expressed concern over Jane's social relationships. She reported that

*Jane had never had any friends and had never been able to get along
with children. The only ones Jane plays with are younger children
whom she can dominate. She also plays with a rejected sixth grade
girl. Mrs. J feels that Jane is learning to handle adults but that she
has no idea how to get along with children. The mother is sure that
Marcia, the little sister, is back of a great deal of Jane's trouble.
"Marcia is friendly and liked by everyone, adults and children. Marcia
often brings home friends and is always having a good time. This
makes Jane extremely jealous and she treats her sister mean, and
openly says she hates her."*

*The mother believes that Jane's difficulty is also largely caused
by the fact that she and her husband tried too hard to be model
parents. "We read all of the books on child rearing at the time and
tried from her birth to follow every schedule to the letter. The books
at that time were poor, I am convinced, and I am afraid that kind of
training has harmed Jane. We expected to have a model child, perfect in every way. We stressed perfection so much that I am afraid
we made Jane feel inadequate."*

The reader may wish to study these excerpts from the case of Jane as
they relate to the concepts of affection and security presented in this chapter. The questions listed at the end of the chapter will aid in the analysis
and discussion of the case of Jane in relation to these concepts.

Summary

Man's most significant learning and development take place in a
context of social interaction with other human beings. He becomes human
only as he relates himself to other human beings. Through his relationships
with others he assuages his feelings of aloneness and separateness and discovers meaning and purpose for his life.

The meaning of human relatedness is communicated in the personal
valuing and self-worth one feels in one-to-one relationships with others. In a
human relationship, acts, feelings, and responses that are accepting and
valuing define the term *affection. Security* has the deeper meaning to the
self of feeling personal value, self-acceptance, and self-worth. So pervasive
is a feeling of relative security or insecurity that it is reflected in the individual's general behavior and in his responses to life situations.

The human need for affection begins in infancy as pleasant feelings
accompanying the satisfaction of the child's physical needs become associated with mother, nurse, and others who care for and nurture the child. A
warm mothering relationship in early life exerts a positive and vital influence on all aspects of the child's development and learning. Some differentiation should be made by parents and teachers between socialization

roles and security-giving roles, so that disapproval and punishments related to child training are not interpreted by the child as a loss of love. Children grow up in social-emotional climates of affection, rejection, inconsistency, or overprotection. Each emotional climate will communicate different meanings to the child in relation to his personal value and self-worth, and these unique meanings will be reflected in his behavior.

The development of the child's affectional life can be viewed in three dimensions: (1) the psychosexual development of the child from a stage of self-love to an acceptance and valuing of others in mutually shared relationships, (2) the broadening of the base of affectional relationships to include a widening circle of persons with whom he shares affectional ties, and (3) the change from strong dependence on others to a considerable degree of independence, in which relationships with others are characterized by mutual acceptance and valuing.

A child's security may be threatened by events and dynamic relationships at home and in the school. Major threats to his security related to his home and family are parental rejection, sibling rivalry, difficulties associated with ordinal position and size of family, failure to live up to cultural expectations, absentee fathers, working mothers, and broken homes. Some children may find their security at school threatened by an adjustment problem that hinders their acceptance by others, by a lack of peer belongingness, by poor academic performance, or by the teacher's limited understanding and conception of his role in giving affection and providing emotional support to his students.

Study Questions

1. Betty Jean, 10 years old, attractive, and a good student, seeks to be close to Miss Thompson, her fifth grade teacher. Betty Jean frequently engages Miss Thompson in conversations about books, people, and places, she sits beside her teacher at lunch, and she takes the teacher's hand in walking to and from the classroom. Miss Thompson feels a special fondness for Betty Jean and hopes to have a daughter like her someday. What explanations can you suggest for Betty Jean's seeking a closeness to her teacher? How should Miss Thompson handle the situation?

2. Sam Phillips, aged 25, is in his second year of teaching social studies at Roosevelt Junior High School. He believes that getting close to his eighth grade students and "rapping" with them about their personal problems will create a favorable climate for learning. As the semester progresses, a few students monopolize the time during the rap sessions while the majority remain silent, with some expressing increasing hostility toward the teacher. What explanations would you offer for the students' reactions to Sam's efforts to relate to the class? How should Sam handle the situation?

3. Bobby, aged seven, bites, hits, and pushes other children, often for no apparent reason. The mother reports that the father beats Bobby for

misbehavior, and she states that she is unable to control Bobby. The teacher has tried a variety of approaches, including giving Bobby extra attention, but none has produced any marked change in Bobby's classroom behavior. What explanations can you offer for Bobby's behavior? What recommendations would you make for dealing with the situation?

4.   Joe Engel, single and aged 23, is in his first year of teaching biology at Lake Forest High School. Debbie, an intelligent, pretty 17-year-old, is a student in Joe's advanced biology class. Joe noted that Debbie seems to have few friends in her peer group. Joe welcomed Debbie's assistance in helping him set up the lab, but lately she has been spending more and more time with him after school in the lab. Joe is aware of the dangers in getting involved with a student. He is afraid, however, that if he tries to discourage her hanging around, she may spread gossip about him which would endanger his job. How should Joe handle this situation?

Suggested Readings

Bettelheim, Bruno. *The Children of the Dream.* New York: Macmillan Co., 1969. Intimate first-hand study of child rearing in the kibbutz. Aspects of communal living, education, and interpersonal relations are discussed and evaluated with sensitivity and insight.

Bowlby, John. *Maternal Care and Mental Health.* Second Edition. New York: Schoken Books, 1966. A report to the World Health Organization which discusses the adverse effects of maternal deprivation on mental health and suggests a number of ways to prevent or ameliorate them.

Fromm, Erich. *The Art of Loving.* New York: Harper & Row, 1956. Points to the separateness of man's existence and to his need for developing his capacity to love. Discusses and contrasts brotherly love, mother love, erotic love, self-love, and love of God.

Ginott, Haim G. *Between Parent and Child.* New York: Macmillan Co., 1965. Offers concrete suggestions of more effective ways a parent can relate to the child in situations involving praise and criticism, expressions of anger, achievement of independence, and assumption of responsibility. Presents realistic dialogues that illustrate how a parent might respond when a child misbehaves, including words and phrases which exemplify better communication between parent and child.

Harlow, Harry F. *Learning to Love.* San Francisco: Albion Publishing Co., 1971. An eminent research psychologist describes five forms of love: maternal love, infant love, peer love, heterosexual love, and paternal love. All have been identified and investigated in numerous experiments with primates. Fear, anger, and social behavior are also examined.

Hetherington, E. Mavis. "Girls without Fathers." *Psychology Today*, 6 (February 1973), 47–52. A study of the social behavior of two groups of adolescent girls aged 13 to 17 who had grown up without fathers. All these girls repeatedly displayed inappropriate patterns of behavior in relating to males. Girls whose fathers had died exhibited severe sexual anxiety, shyness, and discomfort around males. Girls whose fathers were absent because of divorce exhibited tension and inappropriately assertive, seductive, or sometimes promiscuous behavior with male peers and adults. Neither group had difficulty relating to female peers.

Films

Jamie: The Story of a Sibling, 16 mm, sound, black and white, 28 min. New York: McGraw-Hill Textfilms, 330 W. 42nd St. Describes the problem of sibling rivalries in the family by telling about a 10-year-old boy whose resentment of his older sister and his little brother finds an outlet in aggressive behavior toward other children.

Mother Love, 16 mm, sound, black and white, 26 min. Bloomington: Audiovisual Center, Indiana University. Presents the experiments of Harry Harlow, who studied the responses of newborn rhesus monkeys to two inanimate substitute mothers, one made of wire and the other of cloth. These experiments demonstrate that the single most important factor in an infant's love for its mother is body contact. Deprivation of contact can cause deep emotional disturbances and even death.

Rockabye Baby, 16 mm, sound, color, 28 min. New York: Time-Life Films, 43 W. 16th St. Stresses the importance of and possible irreversible effects of early experiences in development, highlighted in part by discussions of the work of Spitz, Bowlby, Harlow, Heath, and Fraiberg. Shown are effects of maternal deprivation on institutionalized children and isolated motherless monkeys. Other topics include appearance of early stress reactions, stereotypic behavior, work with premature infants, various aspects of mothering, and attempts to ameliorate developmental problems. The emphasis is upon stimulation provided by touch and movement.

The Cultural Environment

6

Tis education forms the common mind: Just as the twig is bent the tree's inclined.

Alexander Pope

Children the world over are at birth much more alike than they are different. A Chinese infant exchanged at birth with an American infant would start on equal footing with native-born sons and daughters in learning the language, customs, and ways of his adopted country. Children become increasingly different as their hereditary potentials interact with their environment to produce varying patterns of development. By far the most important differences between people are those resulting from differences between environments—the ways of feeling, thinking, and behaving each has internalized from his society as the result of growing up in that society.

The influence of the immediate environment and its people on the language and behavior of individuals, irrespective of national origins, is described by Laurence Wylie:[1]

From our house we could hear the children down in the school yard, and it sounded as though our ruse had worked. We lived in a village I will call Peyrane, a few miles east of Avignon, for two months, and our children had not learned French as fast as children are rumored to pick up a foreign language. On that Sunday morning we had suggested that the two boys take their soccer ball down to the school where they might attract some French friends to play with them.

To see what was up I walked down and looked around the corner of the building. The situation was not what I had expected. An exciting soccer game was in progress—but Jonathan and David were not learning French phrases. On the contrary, all the children

[1] Laurence Wylie, "Bringing up Children—French Way, Our Way," *New York Times Magazine* (June 30, 1957). Copyright 1957 by the New York Times Company. Reprinted by permission.

in the neighborhood were shouting at the top of their lungs: "Keek eet to me!!! Keek eet to me!!!"

In spite of their American aggressiveness the boys did learn French before the village children learned English. Within five months both of them could express themselves effectively, if not grammatically, in the language. Little by little they came to prefer French to English and French customs to American ones. We tried to cling to some parental tenets from home—no eating between meals, getting to bed by 8 o'clock. As our children rejected these sacred institutions, they began to reject us, too. We were immigrants.

Perhaps if we had stayed in France longer, our family unit would have become French enough, that is, a sufficiently tight unit, to withstand this attack, but we were not put to the ultimate test. After almost a year in Peyrane, our leave was up and we left for home. When we stopped in Paris, our two children, so obviously American in appearance but with the most exaggerated of southern French accents, were a delight to French friends and to the liftiers of the Hotel Lutetia. The wonder grew to amazement among relatives back in this country at these two little boys who politely shook hands with everyone and who spoke French when playing together.

But this Gallic behavior did not last long. First went the handshake which had caused American adults to laugh and make coy remarks. Then it became apparent that the French language could not resist the corrosive influence of different surroundings. Day by day chunks of it dropped out and were replaced by English.

This excerpt raises an age-old question: Which exerts the greatest influence in shaping human behavior—heredity or environment? Though human heredity and the processes of growth and development give the child a body that is human in appearance and structure, the behavioral qualities that mark him as distinctly human are acquired as he grows up in the company of other human beings. The few accounts of lost or abandoned children who have somehow survived and grown up without human care, presumably having lived with animals, report that their behavior is more like that of animals in their natural environment than of human beings. These children are described as ferocious; they bit their captors, crawled on all fours, ate raw flesh, and seldom if ever were able to use or understand a human language.[2] Thus, man becomes human only as he internalizes his culture's way of thinking, behaving, and feeling—as taught to him by parents, siblings, teachers, and others.

[2] Wayne Dennis, "A Further Analysis of Reports of Wild Children," *Child Development*, 22 (March 1951), 153–158.

Concept of Culture

In the preceding chapter we noted that an individual's affectional relationships with significant people in his life are important because of the much-needed feeling of security they provide. Interactions with others, however, are important also because through them children learn a great deal about behavior in society.

The set of feelings, behaviors, and ways of perceiving, thinking, and valuing which one is taught by his social group is what is meant by the term *culture*. In the anthropological sense, the term refers to much more than architecture, art, music, dance, drama, and literature. It comprises everything that contributes to a total way of life: communication, food and housing, sex, marriage, child rearing, various interpersonal relationships, transportation, economic organization, social organization, government, and dealings with the supernatural. National and racial cultures differ from one another mainly in the ways they have learned to cope with such problems of life as these. They differ to the degree that their responses to these problems are different. Within a culture these responses are handed down from one generation to the next in the process of socialization. In this way, one comes to have built into him the patterns of thinking, feeling, and behaving that characterize his culture. In its broadest sense, then, culture can be defined as *those customs, beliefs, ways of behaving, and values which evolve from cumulative group experience and which are passed from generation to generation as the best or the most acceptable solutions to problems of living.*

Cultural Institutions

Every society has established formal and informal agencies or institutions charged with preserving the status quo and communicating the ways of the culture to each oncoming generation. Although simpler cultures may employ fewer institutions to carry out these tasks, Western, industrialized culture has six major cultural institutions: (1) the family, (2) the church, (3) the school, (4) the peer group, (5) the community, and (6) the mass media. These cultural institutions contribute to the socialization of each individual in the culture.

The Family

Some type of family organization is found in every culture. The helplessness of the child at birth, his dependence on others for sustenance and life, makes it nearly inevitable that much of the child's early socialization will take place in the family setting. It is within the family that most children gain their first perceptions of what the world is like.

The cultural behaviors and values taught by the family relate to every phase of human living, including the infant disciplines of weaning and toilet training, the acceptance and learning of one's sex role, language, courtesies governing interpersonal relationships within and outside the family group, religious observances and rituals, and vocational preferences reflected in children's play. Family influences also are conveyed through the choice of a neighborhood, the formal and informal clubs and associations which the parents join and those they permit their children to join, and the kinds of TV programs which parents allow their children to watch. Many of the behavior patterns and values that the child learns are consistent with and reflect the larger culture; others are characteristic of the particular family; still others, as we shall note in a later chapter, are unique to the individual himself.

The family can also be viewed as a group bound together by reciprocal ties manifested in culturally determined roles and patterns of interaction. Each role carries a status which defines the ways in which the individual will respond and relate to other people. The father's role in child rearing may require him to warn the adolescent against experimenting with drugs and sex. The father expects his son to comply with his wishes. The culture may also expect the son to comply. Whether the son does comply, however, will depend in part upon the role he believes his culture expects him to play. Many of the roles which the individual is taught by the culture at different stages from infancy to adulthood are contradictory to one another, and the adolescent may be caught between two of them. For example, as Benedict[3] points out, children are expected to be dependent and compliant, whereas adults are considered immature and not quite grown up if they do not exhibit independence and self-reliance. By recognizing and responding to the discontinuities within our culture, we are better able to understand the atypical and immature behavior of some youth and adults in our society.

The Church

The church can be viewed as a separate institution apart from the community, or it can be seen as one of the forces within the community. Whether and to what extent the church influences the socialization of children and youth seems to depend upon the religious beliefs and commitments of family members, especially the mother and father. When parents participate actively in the church, the child, through his identification with

---

[3] Ruth Benedict, "Continuities and Discontinuities in Cultural Conditioning," *Psychiatry*, 1 (1938), 161–167.

his parents, also is likely to become involved. In families that lack an affiliation with a church, the influence of the church in the socialization of the child is likely to be limited or nonexistent.

The problem of ascertaining what children learn from experiences with religious education is extremely complex. Since one's religion is an individual and personal matter, what one learns from religious experience can also be presumed to be unique and personal. In a study of a midwestern community, Havighurst and Taba[4] found that church affiliation seemed to influence one's reputation in the community, but they could not determine whether an individual's character was changed because of his affiliation with a church. The study showed that the stricter the codes of conduct of a denomination, the higher the character reputations of persons affiliated with that denomination. Hartshorne and May,[5] in a study of honesty in children, developed ingenious tests that could be passed only if one cheated, and gave these tests to one group of students who attended Sunday School and to another group who did not go to Sunday School. Both groups attended the same public school. Hartshorne and May found that the percentage of children who cheated on these tests was about the same for both groups (approximately 30 to 40 percent). Neither the length of time children were enrolled in Sunday School nor the regularity of their attendance was found to be associated with their tendency to cheat.

What concepts of their religion and their church do children acquire? Elkind[6] found, in studies of children, ages six to 14, of all three major denominations that these children's concepts of (1) what it means to be a Protestant, Catholic, or Jew, (2) the features of one's sect, and (3) how membership in the sect is attained all appear to develop according to Piaget's three age-related stages of intellectual development.[7] In stage one, at about age six, children had only a vague, confused awareness of what being a Protestant, a Catholic, or a Jew really meant. At stage two, usually between ages seven and 10, the child understood the word *Protestant*, *Catholic*, or *Jew* to be the name of a group of people with characteristic ways of behaving ("A Catholic goes to mass and goes to Catholic school"). Finally, at stage three, about age 11 or 12, children have developed an abstract conception of their denomination. Being a Protestant, Catholic, or Jew meant believing in the teachings of one's church ("A Protestant is a faithful believer in God and doesn't believe in the Pope").

While church affiliation provides the individual with a sense of group

[4] Robert J. Havighurst and Hilda Taba, *Adolescent Character and Personality* (New York: John Wiley, 1949).

[5] Hugh Hartshorne and Mark A. May, *Studies in the Nature of Character, Studies in Deceit I* (New York: Macmillan Co., 1928).

[6] David Elkind, "The Child's Conception of His Religious Denomination: I. The Jewish Child," *Journal of Genetic Psychology*, 99 (1961), 209–225; "The Child's Conception of His Religious Denomination: II. The Catholic Child," *Journal of Genetic Psychology*, 101 (1962), 185–193; "The Child's Conception of His Religious Denomination: III. The Protestant Child," *Journal of Genetic Psychology*, 103 (1963), 291–304.

[7] Jean Piaget, *The Child's Conception of the World* (London: Kegan Paul, 1951).

identity, there is little scientific evidence as to what beliefs and values he acquires from religious experience and denominational life. Part of the difficulty is that the specific influence of the church in the socialization of children and youth cannot always be separated from the influence of family and community. In some communities, such as those of the Amish of the Pennsylvania Dutch country, religious beliefs are dominant in guiding the lives of the people. The Amish's ways and values—his plain black clothes, his thrift and hard work, and his eschewing of the use of the automobile—all are based on religious beliefs and church teachings. To assist in inculcating these teachings and values in their young, the Amish developed a system of parochial schools. Several states, however, sought to enforce compulsory school attendance laws in requiring Amish children to attend public schools. In May 1972 the United States Supreme Court (in *Wisconsin* vs. *Yoder*) narrowly upheld the right of the Amish to educate their children in their own schools. This ruling upholds a group's individual freedom to maintain their own schools and own way of life. For most Americans, however, the church's influence, if any, in inculcating beliefs and values is likely not to be consistent across the board of church teaching but to be very personal, highly variable, and difficult to measure.

Complicating attempts to measure the church's influence in communicating beliefs and values is the tendency in America to minimize the differences between religious sects. Evidence of this is revealed in the ecumenical movement toward Christian unity that is being urged and worked for by many denominations. Increasingly, America is pictured as a pluralistic society in which Protestants, Catholics, Jews, and secularists live side by side as citizens. Religious affiliation has been rejected as a test both for citizenship and for holding public office. The United States Supreme Court's decisions against mandatory prayer and Bible reading in the public schools reflect the trend toward strengthening the concept of pluralism in our society.

The School

As technology and rising standards of living induce more women to work outside the home, the school has been called upon to assume increased responsibilities for the socialization of children and youth. Greater numbers of nursery schools and day care centers are being organized for young children, and more and more teen clubs and extracurricular clubs are being formed for older students. The following broad purposes of education, initially stated more than a generation ago, emphasize socialization functions which our schools seek to achieve:

1. *To provide a basis of communication and a common core of traditions and values.*

2. *To teach children to work and live together.*

3.   *To help people find ways of realizing their social ideals.*

4.   *To teach skills for carrying on the economic life of society.*

5.   *To select and train children for upward mobility.*[8]

The school tends to mirror the culture of the power group that controls it. In most communities the power controls over schools are centered in persons of middle class status. As a consequence, in what the school teaches, in the standards it enforces, and in relation to the group it is best adapted to serve, the typical American school has often been labeled a middle class institution. School administrators and teachers, as members of the middle class, generally support middle class aspirations, values, and mores. In schools where middle class behavior, language, dress, and high academic achievement patterns are the norm, children from lower class groups often become alienated because of their different motivational patterns and vocational aspirations. Only as recent social revolution and war on poverty programs have brought these discrepancies in cultural background to the attention of the American people have steps been taken to make the school programs in depressed areas more responsive to the needs of the cultural groups they serve.[9]

The Peer Group

Children learn much from one another. Skills and knowledge required in sports and hobbies as well as attitudes and values of fair play, trust, and loyalty are most frequently acquired through interaction with one's peers. During adolescence the fads of hair style, hit songs, dancing, dress, language, and social behavior are among the most obvious ways in which peer group codes and customs shape the responses of individual group members. The peer group is a force of sufficient importance in human development and learning that we shall devote the next chapter to a discussion of its influence in childhood and adolescence.

The Community

The community consists of many organizations and agencies, both visible and invisible, which exert influence, both direct and indirect, on the socialization of children and youth. The immediate social and physical en-

---

[8] W. Lloyd Warner, Robert J. Havighurst, and Martin B. Loeb, *Who Shall Be Educated?* (New York: Harper & Row, 1944), pp. 54–57.

[9] A. Harry Passow, ed., *Education in Depressed Areas* (New York: Teachers College Press, Columbia University, 1963).

vironment of the community, mediated in part by family, peer group, and
school, provides the child with an initial, often lasting view of the world.
The child and his family tend to be influenced by the behavior and attitudes
of other children and adults who reflect the prevailing mores of the community. A stranger can quickly determine a community's attitudes toward
race relations, religion, jobs, economic growth, welfare, politics, zoning,
community planning, and a host of other problems simply by a visit to the
local barbershop or beauty salon.

The community also plays a role in the socialization of children and
youth through its cub scouts, girl scouts, boys' clubs, Little League baseball
teams, teen clubs, and other youth organizations. This is revealed in Barker
and Wright's investigation of the everyday behavior and the social participation of the children and youth of a midwestern town.[10] The focus of this
ecological study was on the *behavior setting*—the place, event, or occasion
(Kane's grocery, 4H Club picnic, Thanksgiving Day) where or when social
interaction among members of a community occurs. Barker and Wright
found that children in the town they studied participated in a large proportion of the behavior settings available to them, including food sales, pa-
rades, paper routes, funeral services, club meetings, town elections, restau-
rants, and school classes. By participating in a large number of activities,
many of them essentially adult activities, children learned the ways and
mores of the community.

Mass Media

One of the concomitants of a technological culture is an increase in
the kinds and uses of media of mass communication. Indeed, the growth of
the economy depends upon the wide dissemination of information through
newspapers, magazines, comic books, movies, radio, and television, so as to
promote popular consumption of products created by the technology. The
newspaper editorial, the mass-circulation magazine article, and the TV program are written and produced for a mass heterogeneous audience. Although the individual can, of course, decide whether he will read the editorial or the article or watch the TV program, the family and the peer group
exert considerable influence in popularizing and in some cases influencing
the content of magazine articles, radio, and TV programs.

Because of their impersonal nature and the diversity of their offer-
ings, the impact of mass media on the socialization of children and youth is
difficult to assess. Television, movies, and comics teach many of the ways of
society as portrayed by the sheriff, policeman, private investigator, defense
attorney, judge, doctor, nurse, sergeant, colonel, nightclub hostess, business
tycoon, secretary, and gangster. Idealized portrayals of these roles and of

---

[10] Roger G. Barker and Herbert F. Wright, *Midwest and Its Children: The Psychological Ecology of an American Town* (New York: Harper & Row, 1954).

the courts, hospital, industrial corporation, city hall, armed forces, however, frequently communicate to children and youth inaccurate pictures of the culture. Because of the strong fantasy and comedy content of many TV programs, movies, and comic strips, children can be expected to respond to these for their entertainment rather than their educational value. For some children, knowledge of TV, movie, and comic strip characters and plots assists them in gaining or maintaining acceptance and status in the peer group. Thus, in spite of the wide exposure of children and youth to mass media, what is learned from this exposure is likely to vary from child to child and, consequently, will be difficult to measure.

Exposure of children to mass media may have undesirable effects. Commercial television, for instance, is criticized for its portrayal of sex, crime, and violence. However, the impact of this portrayal on children's personalities and development is not consistent. A study by Himmelweit, Oppenheim, and Vince,[11] conducted in England, concluded that the effect of television on a child varies not only with the programs and the time spent viewing TV but also with the personality of the child and the context in which the viewing takes place. These findings are corroborated by a review of subsequent research on the effects of televised violence in the United States that is contained in the report of the Surgeon General's Scientific Advisory Committee on Television and Social Behavior.[12] The committee found that the sequence of viewing television violence followed by aggressive behavior is most likely applicable only to a small group of children who are predisposed in that direction. Among children aged four to six, for example, those most responsive to television violence are those who are highly aggressive to start with—who are prone to engage in spontaneous aggressive actions toward their playmates and, in the case of boys, who display pleasure in viewing violence inflicted upon others. A second general conclusion cited in this report is that the way children respond to violent film material is affected by the context in which it is presented. Parental explanations, the favorable or unfavorable outcomes of violence, and whether it is seen as fantasy or reality all seem to make a difference in the response the child makes to the portrayal of violence.

On the positive side, television can implant information, stimulate interests, improve tastes, and widen the range of the child's experience, so that he is able to gain a better understanding of issues and people different from those with whom he customarily associates. The potential of television as an instructional medium has been amply demonstrated by *Sesame Street*, *The Electric Company*, and similar programs. *Sesame Street* has used novelty, variety, animated cartoons, puppetry, and comments from friendly children and adults to captivate the attention and stimulate the respon-

[11] Hilde T. Himmelweit, A. M. Oppenheim, and Pamela Vince, *Television and the Child* (London: Oxford University Press, 1958).

[12] Surgeon General's Scientific Advisory Committee on Television and Social Behavior, *Television and Growing Up: The Impact of Televised Violence* (Washington, D. C.: U. S. Government Printing Office, 1972); see also Leonard D. Eron et al., "Does Television Violence Cause Aggression?" *American Psychologist*, 27 (April 1972), 253–263.

siveness of preschoolers. It is estimated that between 5 and 6 million preschoolers have watched this program daily. Evaluations of *Sesame Street*
reveal that preschoolers from all socioeconomic levels and all parts of the
United States learned a wide variety of educational skills, not merely counting and the alphabet, but classification, sorting, geometric forms, and even
problem solving. The more children watched, the more they benefited.
Ghetto children who watched five days a week learned more than did middle cass children who saw the program less frequently. Three-year-old regular viewers learned more than did four- and five-year-old occasional viewers.[13] While this and similar programs have clearly demonstrated their
potential for teaching cognitive skills, no TV program, no matter how successful, can minimize the importance of the teacher who facilitates learning
as she responds to the affective needs of the child. A further value of television is that it provides children with a way of satisfying their hunger for
fantasy.

On the negative side, however, the child who accepts the fantasies of
TV as real may come to believe that the one who is the most clever, decep-
tive, or the best fighter is the one who is sure to survive or win. To guard
against these misconceptions, parents should communicate and interpret
events to children so that they are able to develop a sense of reality and an
acceptance of everyday life, including joy and sorrow, triumph and despair.
Watching television may have negative effects for both children and adults
if it serves as a frequent escape from the frustrations or dreariness of one's
present situation or as a way of combating boredom. While this type of adjustment may seem to make one's problems manageable, it frequently post-
pones or avoids the confrontation with one's problems that could lead to
their solution. Finally, television viewing which is habitual and reflects a
lack of discrimination in choice of programs can lead to lessened acquisition of knowledge by limiting one's participation in other developmental
activities, such as reading, outdoor play or sports, and peer activities.

Cultural Diversities

More than 200 million people live in the United States. These 200 million people, although bound together in a common culture, nevertheless represent many diverse cultural subgroups. The diversities of these groups
would soon become apparent if a cross-section of Americans were to try to
reach agreement on a set of values representative of American society. Cultural diversities characteristic of subgroups highlight differences between
people which relate to (1) sex roles, (2) geographical region, (3) urban-
suburban-rural background, (4) social class, (5) ethnic, religious, and racial
differences, and (6) age and maturity.

[13] Samuel Ball and G. A. Borgatz, *The First Year of Sesame Street: An Evaluation*
(Princeton, N. J.: Educational Testing Service, 1970).

Sex Roles

Differences between males and females in patterns of feeling, thinking, and behaving go far beyond the physical differences related to sex. The
culture into which each boy and girl is born defines for each the norms of
sex-appropriate behavior which the boy or girl is expected to internalize.
Failure to act in accordance with sex-appropriate modes of response frequently brings social disapproval and leads to social and personal maladjustment.

At an early age, each child is expected to accept his sex role and to
behave appropriately as a boy or a girl. Generally, this has meant for boys
that being active, aggressive, and engaging in rough play is not only tolerated but subtly encouraged. Girls, on the other hand, have been expected
to be quiet, sedate, nurturant, and dependent. As we will presently note,
however, these stereotyped sex roles are undergoing marked changes in our
culture.

Girls in our culture are presumed to experience less difficulty than
boys in learning sex-appropriate behavior. Girls are surrounded from an
early age with female models with whom they can identify. Mother, older
sister, and grandmother and a succession of woman teachers all communicate and reinforce the feminine ways and mores of the culture. The daughter's acceptance of her feminine role, however, is facilitated not only by the
presence of a highly adequate mother as a feminine model but also by the
presence of a father who is aware of the behavior expected of young girls
and who encourages his daughter to act in feminine ways and to participate
in feminine activities.[14]

The influence of the father on the sex role development of his son is
important, but often it is not as pervasive as the influence of the mother
who serves as a feminine model for the daughter. During the preschool
years the young son reveals on numerous occasions that he is identifying
with his father and is taking on some of his masculine ways. Much of the
time during the preschool and elementary school years, however, the boy is
being socialized by his mother and a succession of female teachers. In their
socialization of the boy, mother and teachers expect him to behave in accordance with a culturally defined, somewhat stereotyped masculine model
which they hold up to him through their expectations and admonitions.
Thus, in early and middle childhood, girls learn their sex role behavior
through identifying with their mothers, while boys at these maturity levels
are increasingly influenced in their sex role behavior by a culturally defined,
stereotyped masculine role.[15] Although parents continue to influence the sex
role behavior of their children throughout late childhood and adolescence,

---

[14] Paul H. Mussen and Eldred Rutherford, "Parent-Child Relations and Parental
Personality in Relation to Young Children's Sex Role Preferences," *Child Development*,
34 (September 1963), 589–607.

[15] David B. Lynn, "Sex Role and Parental Identification," *Child Development*, 33
(September 1962), 555–564.

same-sex peers and older siblings, TV, and sports and entertainment figures become increasingly important as models for appropriate sex role behavior. This trend can be observed in the hair styles, dress, and values adopted by youth which diverge from those of the parents.

In contemporary Western culture, behavior and roles appropriate to each sex are becoming blurred and less distinct. Many persons of both sexes wear their hair long and dress in jeans or shorts, jackets, and low-heeled shoes or sandals. This shift away from stereotyped sex roles has occurred during a period when increasing numbers of women, both individuals and groups, have challenged the status quo and restrictions which have hampered their fulfillment as human beings. The maintenance of practices, policies, attitudes, and values which reflect a bias favoring males and restrict the roles and opportunities of women have come to be labeled sexism.

The recent questioning of traditional definitions of sex roles by women's liberation groups and others has increased our awareness of the sex role stereotyping which pervades our culture. Placing people into narrowly defined roles because of their sex is communicated subtly and early to the child. A study of 154 picture books for preschoolers revealed that women were portrayed either as primarily a housewife or mother doing essentially dull tasks or as a semiprofessional engaged in a typically female occupation, such as nurse, teacher, or secretary.[16] Similar findings emerged from a study of school readers which showed that the ratio of boy stories to girl stories favored boys 5 to 2. In the stories boys generally were portrayed as creative, strong, and brave, while girls were shown as passive, dependent, and fearful.[17]

Children's conceptions of appropriate sex role behavior appear to be most stereotyped during the ages of 10 to 12. Both sexes during this period see men as bosses, taxi drivers, mayors, factory workers, and lawyers; women are nurses or housekeepers. Both sexes at these ages see boys as fighting more and girls as kinder. Career goals of boys in the fifth grade are to be a craftsman, engineer, scientist, doctor, lawyer, sportsman, or pilot. Girls' career choices in the fifth grade are more varied, but they seem to be unable to translate their aspirations into the realities of their own lives. In their themes they picture themselves in the future as performing traditional female work.[18] Teachers often unwittingly reinforce stereotyped sex role behavior. For girls, the school's expectations for achievement and appropriate sex role behavior provide a double-barreled message reinforcing the girl's obedience, docility, and dependence. For boys, the school's expectations for achievement conflict with traditional male sex role expectations. The confusing double message for boys is: Be aggressive, active,

[16] John Stewig and Margaret Higgs, "Girls Grow Up to Be Mommies: A Study of Sexism in Children's Literature," *School Library Journal*, 19 (January 1973), 44–49.

[17] Carol Jacobs and Cynthia Eaton, "Sexism in the Elementary School," *Today's Education*, 61 (December 1972), 20–22.

[18] Lynne B. Iglitzin, "A Child's View of Sex Roles," *Today's Education*, 61 (December 1972), 23–25.

achieving, and independent (be masculine), but also be passive, quiet, and conforming (be a good pupil).[19]

As the above studies suggest, much more can be done in the school and the home to reduce sex role stereotyping. First, the adult needs to reexamine and possibly change his conception of appropriate behavior and roles for each sex. He should encourage in himself and others a wider range of roles, interests, and talents, irrespective of sex. Open the shop to girls and the home economics labs and kitchens to boys. Finally, instead of focusing on one type of discrimination, it is probably better to work for the elimination of all the inequalities which schools maintain and perpetuate. In this sense, working to eliminate rigid grouping based upon academic ability is more important than getting a few more girls into the honors group.[20]

The movement toward more flexibility and variation in expressing one's sex role can be liberating for men as well as for women. Men could then pursue interests in the arts, literature, music, cooking, interior decorating, and child care without feeling that they are unmasculine or that other people think they are.

Geographical Region

The culture an American child learns reflects in some degree the language and ways of the part of the United States in which he grows up. Most Americans are aware of the differences in speech, attitudes, and social behavior of persons who live in different regions of the country. A major difficulty one faces in analyzing regional differences is the tendency to be blinded by stereotypes. It must be kept in mind that all Texans, for instance, are not tall, slender men wearing cowboy boots and ten-gallon hats, and that all New Englanders are not reserved, serious, and aloof.

People do, of course, reflect the speech, dress, customs, and behavior patterns generally characteristic of the region where they grew up. However, the amount of regional culture a child internalizes varies and can be ascertained only by careful observation and study of that individual. Many children do not assimilate some of the regional culture patterns of their area because of the influence of parents who grew up in another area. Moreover, due to the high geographical mobility of American families, a child may be exposed to a series of different regional cultures as his family moves from place to place and could assimilate elements of each of these cultures. In short, while differences in regional culture are very real, these differences do not appear to have a predictable effect on any particular individual.

[19] Betty Levy, "Do Teachers Sell Girls Short?" *Today's Education*, 61 (December 1972), 27–29.

[20] Levy, pp. 27–29.

Urban-Suburban-Rural Background

Not only the region but the type of community a child lives in—urban, suburban, or rural—influences what he will learn in the process of socialization. Farm children early assume responsibilities for the care and feeding of animals, for the cultivation and harvesting of crops, and for the preparation of food, all of which contribute to the farm family's health and economic well-being. Because of their chores, these children find it more difficult to participate actively in programs for youth sponsored by the school, community, or peer group. Much of the socialization of farm youth centers in learning the skills and attitudes related to making a success at farming. Rural youth will spend more of their free time by themselves, with siblings, or perhaps with one or two children from neighboring farms. With improvement of roads, increased use of automobiles, and rural electrification, however, some of the cultural differences between rural and urban youth have tended to disappear.

The urban child is usually less of an economic asset to his family than is the rural child. The urban child tends to spend considerable time in his and other children's homes playing games familiar to his age and peer group. If he lives in an apartment house or slum dwelling, he will be in physical proximity to dozens, perhaps hundreds of other human beings, but he will probably be able to relate himself emotionally only to a very few. The socialization task for the urban child is to achieve personal meaning and integration in a complex milieu of smells, sounds, and visual images and a melange of nationalities, races, languages, and religions.

Both the social and the geographical mobility of Americans is reflected in the flight of middle class families to suburbia. In 1970 over one third of the population of the United States lived in the suburbs surrounding large and medium sized metropolitan areas.[21] Although there are industrial and working class suburbs adjoining nearly every city, most suburbs are predominantly middle class. A nice home in the suburbs is a cherished goal of upwardly mobile families who aspire to respectable middle class status. When asked why they prefer the suburbs, their rationalizations may be that in the suburbs there is more room for the children to play, more privacy, better schools, nicer people, or less traffic and noise.

Suburban culture appears to center around the family, the home, and the activities of the children. Neighborliness among mothers of young children is promoted through morning kaffee klatsches in one another's homes. Suburbanites tend to participate actively in community organizations, with mother serving as PTA chairman and den mother, while father is coach of the Little League team; both are active in church work and civic associations.

[21] Table 34, PC 1-A1, *Number of Inhabitants: United States Summary. 1970 Census of Population* (Washington, D. C.: U. S. Government Printing Office, 1971).

Suburban culture tends to be characterized by trends toward conformity and a limited degree of tolerance. While people who differ in religious and ethnic background are generally tolerated, the suburban response to racial integration has been mixed. Some suburban residents have welcomed black families into their communities, and a few have sold their homes to blacks. Other suburban residents, however, have expressed strong opposition to integration, busing, and civil rights.

Generally, then, the socialization of the suburban child takes place in a sheltered, homogeneous setting. He grows up with other children who are very much like himself. In his socialization he tends to take over the suburban, middle class ways of his parents and in time becomes indistinguishable from thousands of other suburbanites.

Social Class

Even though equality is a professed national value, American communities exhibit a hierarchical status system of socially ranked classes or groups. Various studies have identified these classes and estimated the proportion of a town's population belonging to each class. Warner and Lunt,[22] in an early study of a New England town, developed an Index of Participation, which assessed social class status in terms of the status of persons in the community with whom the person being rated was linked in intimate social interaction. An Index of Social Characteristics was developed which permitted a more direct estimate of a person's social status in one of six social classes (upper-upper, lower-upper, upper-middle, lower-middle, upper-lower, and lower-lower). This index used four criteria in assessing a person's social status: source of income, occupation, house type, and dwelling area. Other indexes for assessing social status use similar criteria, some including educational level as well.

The distribution of persons in upper, middle, and lower classes varies widely from community to community. Some communities are quite homogeneous, made up almost entirely of one social status group. In a heterogeneous community, such as a town or a small city, the two upper classes tend to include relatively few individuals (less than 5 percent), while the proportion of persons in the middle and lower classes is likely to vary between 40 and 60 percent.

The middle class child.   The ways of life of the middle class and the lower class, each having a prominent identity in American culture, have frequently been analyzed and compared. The socialization of the middle class child, in contrast to that of the lower class child, has been described as

[22] W. Lloyd Warner and Paul S. Lunt, *The Social Life of a Modern Community* (New Haven, Conn.: Yale University Press, 1940).

"conscious, rational, deliberate, and demanding."[23] Middle class parents tend to have a very clear idea of what they want their child to become. They are constantly checking the child's developmental progress and academic achievement in relation to age-graded norms, and their anxieties concerning his progress are communicated to the child.

The middle class child tends to be oriented to the future. He is urged to observe accepted moral values, to work hard and to achieve in school, and to delay marriage until he has completed the education which will assure him a middle class job and status. Self-discipline and sacrifice are virtues which the middle class child is expected to emulate. His parents willingly make financial sacrifices to provide him with toys, books, music lessons, clothes, social advantages, and a college education. They evaluate and exert close supervision over his choice of friends. Middle class parents teach their children to respect and value property, order, cleanliness, punctuality, and thrift, and to recognize the dignity of work and the value of money. The parent cooperates fully and stands shoulder to shoulder with the school, the church, and other agencies that have a part to play in instilling middle class mores and values.

The middle class child is strongly motivated to conform to his parents' expectations. Love and approval by parents are his reward for achievement and "right living." Failure or fear of failure is always in the picture, so that he is seldom free from the anxieties that lie just below the surface of his consciousness. In short, the middle class child is given early, rigorous, and long-term training in learning the skills, social graces, and habits that will enable him to perform successfully in a highly competitive society.

Middle class parents, in reflecting upon their own successes, often see themselves as living confirmation of the values that made these successes possible. Such parents are likely to bring to bear on their children pressures for achievement based on the parents' own "proven" values. These pressures—particularly those applied to academic performance—can become quite intense, as these excerpts from the case of Skippy reveal:

> *Skippy is a tall, dark, curly-haired, brown-eyed boy in my fifth grade class at Broadmoor Hill School. He dresses casually but neatly. He is 10 years, two months of age and was born in Midwest City of Jewish parents who were also born in Midwest City. His father is a part owner of a winery in Kentucky. The father is Skippy's favorite because he spends some time with his children every evening helping with homework and in boxing sessions. In Skippy's language his mother is "just like anyone else's mother," but his dad is "better than anyone else's." He has one brother, age 14, for whom school success has always been quite easy. The brother is in grade nine at Winchester Hill, a college preparatory high school. Skippy also has a*

---

[23] Albert K. Cohen, *Delinquent Boys: The Culture of the Gang* (New York: Free Press, 1955), p. 98.

cousin in the A section of grade five in Broadmoor Hill School. Skippy's school achievement records through the first four grades reveal average or below average grades, and he has always had some difficulty with reading. His IQ, according to the Kuhlman-Anderson test given in grade four, is 110.

September 12. An agitated well-dressed woman interrupted my classes at 2 o'clock and introduced herself as Skippy's mother. She wished to know how Skippy was doing, if he was prepared for grade five, if he had passed the test I gave, and if he would fail this year. It took me some time to identify Skippy as I was not yet acquainted with the 70 children who came to me. But as Skippy's mother was most insistent, I finally managed to identify him by the vivid coloring of a shirt she described him as wearing. I attempted to explain that inasmuch as I didn't know who the child was, I was in no position to judge his work so soon and I didn't know to what test she referred. I had given several small written exercises but no full-scale tests.

I quote Skippy's mother: "But Miss Denham, that test made Skippy ill. He is positive he didn't pass it. He wouldn't eat his dinner last evening and cried practically all night. I considered it important enough to break a dental appointment to come up and see you, and you know how hard they are to get."

I asked her to send Skippy to me and promised to do everything I could to relieve his worry and suggested that she treat the matter lightly.

In the background of this episode is the familiar pattern of parental pressures on a middle class child for high academic performance. The acuteness of the mother's concern for Skippy's progress in school is revealed in her anxiety and agitation.

A child who fails to live up to his parents' expectations for academic success may react to parental pressures in a variety of ways. Some may rebel, give up, and become labeled as "underachievers," a designation that refers to a variety of types of students whose academic performance is below their expected or measured ability. Fink[24] found that underachieving boys were among the most inadequate and immature groups he studied. They feel alienated from society and family and do not accept the ideals and goals of the culture. Often such students become tense, frustrated, and hostile, and may develop various symptoms of maladjustment. Bright male underachievers have been found to express more hostility than bright male achievers,[25] and conferences with junior high school underachievers re-

[24] Martin B. Fink, "Objectification of Data Used in Underachievement Self-Concept Study," *California Journal of Educational Research,* 13 (1962), 105–112.

[25] Merville C. Shaw and J. Grubb, "Hostility and Able High School Underachievers," *Journal of Counseling Psychology,* 5 (1958), 263–266.

vealed that in general they complain more than achievers and express more dissatisfaction and self-pity. They also feel a strong urge to escape from situations which place pressures on them to achieve.[26] Skippy's anxieties and doubts concerning his abilities and adequacy as a student are revealed in the following anecdote.

> December 23.   *Skippy remained after school to help arrange the room for the Colonial Christmas Ball. During the day the children had left many gifts on my table for me. As I was preparing to leave, I gathered them up and remarked to Skippy that I was afraid Broadmoor Hill children felt a necessity to give teachers Christmas gifts.*
>
> Skippy, *with an alluring twinkle: We give 'em to the ones who give us important grades.*
>
> Teacher, *returning the twinkle: So that's it, is it? I've often wondered why you didn't work for them.*
>
> Skippy: *Now, Miss Denham, I've worked and you know it. My dad says this is the first year I've really worked since I've been in school.*
>
> Teacher: *Well, it's better than worrying, isn't it? I've often wondered why you got so upset the first week of school and sent your mother up here. What was it all about?*
>
> Skippy: *Well, kids talk, and the guys that had you last year said a guy had to learn to read in your room and I couldn't read and I didn't believe you when you said that reading test wasn't important. I knew it meant the lowest reading group for me, and Dad was getting sore again.*
>
> Teacher: *But there isn't a lowest reading group.*
>
> Skippy: *Yeah, but I didn't know that then. There always had been, and I always was in it. Being in a low comprehension group was different. You told us things to do about that, and I tried to do them. Before I just read and hated it.*
>
> Teacher: *Do you like to read now?*
>
> Skippy: *Some books I do. I don't like fairy tales.*

[26] B. B. Williams et al., "Identifying Factors Related to Success in School" (Rochester, N. Y.: West Irondequoit Central School, April 20, 1962). Mimeographed.

Teacher: *Well, Skippy, you should be proud of your success this year. Both Mrs. Andrews and I think you are doing as well as the children in 5A.*

Skippy (*in tears, overcome with joy*): *Gee, do you mean it?*

Teacher: *If it means that much to you, I can see about having you transferred after the holidays, but there are drawbacks to it.*

Skippy: *What do you mean?*

Teacher: *Those children read better than you do, so you'd still have the same problem, although I'm sure you can keep up with them. But you would be at the bottom of that group while you are at the top of this one.*

Skippy: *I like the kids in this group, too.*

Teacher: *You'd like them, too.*

Skippy: *I don't care about being there if you just tell my dad I'm good enough.*

Teacher: *I'll be happy to do that, but I think you are more interested in the grades you are getting than what you are learning. Why?*

Skippy: *Because a guy has to get ahead in school and that's grades, isn't it? Gee, I even get test colds.*

Teacher: *What?*

Skippy: *Yeah, I get a cold just thinking about a test.*

This anecdote reveals vividly the effects of pressures for achievement on one middle class child. Note that while the primary pressures on Skippy for academic performance are being exerted by his parents, Miss Denham and the school are reinforcing these pressures by the emphasis they give to academic skills and by their offer to place Skippy in the A section of the fifth grade. Skippy has clearly internalized the importance and value of high scholastic achievement. This is reflected in his concern about grades. His anxieties, his doubts about his own adequacy, and his uncertainties regarding his own abilities to do satisfactory schoolwork are deeply felt. Skippy reveals a measure of self-insight when he relates his feelings of inadequacy over schoolwork to physical ailments, such as catching a cold.

The case of Skippy illustrates that too often parental and teacher pressures and expectations for school success take little account of a child's abilities, background, and developmental needs. Many of the methods of socialization employed by the adult culture serve to constrict the student's responses rather than to free him to use his capacities and abilities.

The lower class child.   The socialization of the lower class child is more informal and less exacting. The child of the slum is oriented to the present. The memories of the past may be too painful to dwell upon, and the future appears too remote and uncertain. What the lower class child does and learns is frequently governed by his own inclinations, his parents' convenience and impulses, and the needs of the family. The lower class child is less closely supervised and thus spends many hours with peers in group-initiated activities. He fails to learn the value of self-discipline and postponement of pleasure because such behaviors are seldom rewarded or seen as important.

Physical strength and toughness as a fighter have special significance for the lower class child. Fighting occurs in both middle and lower class cultures, but it is more likely to be recognized as an acceptable way of settling disputes in lower class culture. Whereas the middle class child is anxious about whether he is achieving in school as well as he should, the lower class child's anxieties grow out of the uncertainty of whether others consider him a good and fearless fighter. Physical punishment or the threat of punishment is more frequently employed in the socialization of lower class children and youth, while fear of loss of love or approval by parents acts as a powerful motivating force in the socialization of the middle class individual. Thus, the affectional ties of the middle class child are primarily with his parents, while those of the lower class child are mainly with his peers.

The reader should be cautioned against accepting these generalized descriptions of middle and lower class socialization patterns as characteristic of all members of these groups. In reality, each person and each family is unique, so that each family will express its own unique variations of these patterns. One may observe some middle class persons, for example, who frequently appear disheveled and unkempt, and others whose indifferent care of house or car expresses a lack of valuing of personal property. Some children from lower class homes, on the other hand, may be observed to have attractive clothes, good grooming, polite manners, and good work habits. Such children are often erroneously judged by their teachers to be from middle class homes.

Case examples of lower class children are presented in the next section, which describes ethnic, religious, and racial cultural differences.

Ethnic, Religious, and Racial Differences

The American people are the product of fusions of many races, nationalities, cultures, and religious groups. Immigrants to this country have usually settled in areas inhabited by others of similar language, national origin, religion, and racial background. As a result, Old World patterns persist in these ethnic communities, and assimilation into the mainstream of American life is delayed. In ethnic groups where assimilation has lagged, the second or third generation child frequently finds that he has a dual status and a dual identity. In his family and community Mario is an Italian, but at school and in the world beyond the ethnic community Mario wishes to be identified and accepted as an American like everyone else. Having to learn the ways of both the ethnic culture of his family and the American culture of his teacher and peers often places the ethnic child in conflict. If he accepts the language, manners of dress, food preferences, patterns of dating and courtship, and religious observances characteristic of his ethnic culture, he is set apart as "different" by the larger nonethnic peer group. On the other hand, if he abandons these ethnic patterns, he has difficulty maintaining his self-identity and his emotional ties with his family. Although the competing cultures frequently pose conflicts for the ethnic child, these conflicts tend to decrease as successive generations become more completely assimilated into the American way of life.

For many Americans, differences in religious affiliation, practices, and beliefs are yet another cultural difference. While people of different denominations do learn different dogmas, rituals, responses, and symbols, the traditions of religious freedom and tolerance in the United States tend to make religious group identities less distinct and less subject to stereotyping.

Differences in physical appearance, culture, and economic and social status have tended to keep racial groups separated from one another, often in segregated communities. In a segregated society the learned behaviors and attitudes governing social interaction between two racial groups are clearly defined by each group. The cultural differences between blacks and whites in the United States, for example, are in part the result of the limited participation of Negroes in American life, the lack of real communication between the races, and the long subordination of the Negro group. In geographical areas where white and Negro groups have moved toward integration, many of the cultural differences between the two groups have begun to disappear. Davis and Havighurst[27] found that in patterns of child training Negro middle class families are much more like white middle class families than they are like Negro lower class families. Similarities were also found between white and Negro lower class families.

Thus, children and youth in the United States grow up in distinctive cultural milieus that relate to social class, ethnic, religious, and racial differences. An examination of the cultural milieus of representative subcultures in our society will show how each influences the development and learning of children and youth in that subculture. In reading the case record excerpts of Appalachian, Italian-American, black, American Indian, Jewish, and Mexican-American children and youth which follow, the reader is cautioned against assuming that the behaviors of a given individual are characteristic of other members or families in that subculture. Making such

[27] Allison Davis and Robert J. Havighurst, "Social Class and Color Differences in Child Rearing," *American Sociological Review*, 11 (1946), 698–710.

unwarranted assumptions is called *stereotyping*—denying the uniqueness of the individual by ascribing to him generalized characteristics of some members of his religious, ethnic, or racial group. Stereotypes such as "Scandanavians are tall and blond" and "Latins are short and emotional" lack validity because differences within a group with respect to a given trait are often as great as the differences between cultural groups for that trait.

Children of Appalachia.   Appalachia, the original American frontier, extends from southern Pennsylvania to northern Alabama and contains land rich in timber, sandstone, natural gas, water, and some of the most magnificent scenery on the continent. The people of Appalachia are largely of Scotch-Irish stock, descendants of the early pioneers who settled this region beginning in the late eighteenth century. Today the impoverished whites of Appalachia constitute a third welfare generation in which the average adult has a sixth grade education and the dropout rate from public school is 75 percent.[28] In the half-abandoned coal-mining camps that adjoin the sulfur-polluted creeks, in the streets of the hollows and little towns, the poverty of the people stands in brutal contrast to the wealth of the land. From the case record excerpts which follow, we gain a partial view of the cultural milieu of Appalachia that is shaping the life of Eddie Franklin.

> *Eddie, aged 12 and in the fifth grade, lives with his mother, father, and three sisters in a dilapidated frame house near an abandoned coal mine in Jackson's Hollow, Kentucky. The family has been on relief since Eddie's father lost his job when the mine closed two years ago. Eddie has been absent frequently from school because of respiratory infections. He has been retained in grade twice and is presently reading two years below grade level.*
>
> *Eddie walks in a slouchy, bent-over manner, and his bodily movements are awkward. His shoes are big and clumsy. He always wears the same pair of soiled jeans, which are much too tight and too short. Eddie's bright red hair, which is seldom combed or cut, stands straight up like the bristles of a hair brush. He talks and sings in a high nasal tone.*
>
> *The Franklin's house is much too small for a family of six. Because his parents and his sisters have the two bedrooms, Eddie must sleep on a couch in the living room. His mother cooks on a wood stove, so Eddie is kept busy carrying in wood and water. Eddie speaks of helping his father make repairs on their 10-year-old car.*
>
> *Eddie attends a consolidated school in Plainsville which serves the children of that city and children from five outlying communities who are bused in. Many of the children in Eddie's classroom are*

[28] Joe L. Frost and Glenn R. Hawks, *The Disadvantaged Child: Issues and Innovations,* 2nd ed. (Boston: Houghton Mifflin Co., 1970), pp. 4, 47–55.

*from families whose fathers are unemployed or work only sporadi-
cally. Jerry Steel, Frank Beall, and Jim Phillips are also in Eddie's
class. Jerry's father owns three movie theaters in Plainsville and
neighboring towns. Frank's father is the largest landowner in Logan
County, and Jim's father is the best-known and busiest physician in
Plainsville. All three families live in large modern new homes on the
hill outside Plainsville. In the spring Jerry, Frank, and Jim talk of
their visits to horse shows in Lexington and the Derby in Louisville
—places far beyond Eddie's life space.*

*One day in early November, Eddie and Harry S. skipped
school so they could collect pop bottles and get money for turning
them in. The next day Mr. Franklin came to school. In a conference
with the teacher, he insisted that she "whip hell out of Eddie." He
said, "Since we have moved down to the hollow Eddie thinks he can
do what he wants to do. I let him come down to the movies one
night and told him to come right home after the show. Instead of
coming home he ran all over the country until twelve o'clock that
night with Harry S. Now I won't let him go to the movies. That
Harry S. is a bad one! I hear Harry's father gives Harry whiskey to
drink and he himself gets drunk. I don't give Eddie whiskey to drink,
but I share my beer with him. But he doesn't get enough to get
drunk."*

*Mr. Franklin said he didn't like his wife to beat Eddie because
when she had one of her tantrums she went crazy. "But someone is
going to have to take Eddie in hand," he continued. "I guess I was
a mean little devil when I went to school. I want you to see that he
behaves himself. If he doesn't, thrash him! Eddie is the only boy I
have. I am going to give him every chance I can. I want him to at
least go through high school. My hopes are centered on him. His
mother yells and nags at him because he has always been so slow in
school, but he is just like me. I never could learn much."*

As Eddie and his classmates finish or drop out of high school, they
will probably leave home because there are few opportunities for employment in Logan County. Some will join the army or the Marines, while others
will migrate north to Cincinnati, Indianapolis, Chicago, and Detroit in
search of work in steel mills, automobile assembly lines, and other factories. They will be faced with adjusting to big-city urban culture, with its
increasing concentrations of blacks, ethnics, and other displaced persons
from Appalachia. Once or twice a year some will return to Logan County
for holidays and reunions with family and friends of their childhood and
youth.

The Italian-American.   By 1900, the flow of Italian immigrants to the
Western Hemisphere had shifted from Argentina, Brazil, and Uruguay to
the United States. The great mass of Italians who emigrated to the United
States between 1900 and 1920 came from southern Italy and Sicily. They

were different in culture and outlook from their countrymen from northern and central Italy who had settled in this country earlier. A large number of the southern Italians coming to the United States during the early part of the twentieth century, unskilled and illiterate, at first worked as common laborers on railroad and construction projects throughout the Northeast. Persons of Italian descent can be found in all parts of the country, but they tend to be concentrated in New York, Boston, Philadelphia, Baltimore, and other urban centers of the Northeast.

The cultural milieu of Italians in America is shaped by the Italian neighborhood and the Italian family. In contrast to those of other ethnic groups, the Italian neighborhoods remain very stable. Italians continue to live in their old established communities even though adjoining areas change as Negroes, Puerto Ricans, and other ethnics move in. The stability of the Italian neighborhoods is further strengthened as married sons and daughters remain in the community close to their parents.

The central value in the Italian family is loyalty to one's family. Life revolves around the family. A son or daughter is expected to remain close to home and to advance the fortunes and well-being of the family through helping in the family business or caring for younger children. One is taught to eschew personal advancement in favor of advancement of family. Even in the case of Italian gangsters and racketeers, there is a high degree of family stability and concern for children, brothers, sisters, and other relatives.[29] The pervasive influence of family and community in shaping the life of a third generation Italian in America is revealed in the following excerpts from the case of Angela Cassini.

Angela is 14 and is in the ninth grade of Howard Junior High School in east Baltimore. She is the fourth of six children and lives with her mother, father, older brother, and two younger brothers in a row house with marble steps. Her two married sisters live nearby. Angela's grandparents, who came to this country from southern Italy, also live close by. Angela's father owns a neighborhood fruit and vegetable market, and the whole family helps out in the market after school and on Saturdays.

Angela's father works long hours at the market and is seldom home, but he still is the strong head of the family. Mr. Cassini is known to have a terrible temper, and he often explodes if one of his children disobeys or displeases him. Maria, one of Angela's older sisters, has a beautiful coloratura soprano voice. In her late teens and early twenties, Maria received wide acclaim throughout the city for her singing as a soloist and for her roles in operas and operettas. Once she sang with the Baltimore Symphony. Maria's singing coach wanted her to go to New York for professional study and make a

[29] Nathan Glazer and Daniel Patrick Moynihan, *Beyond the Melting Pot* (Cambridge, Mass.: MIT Press, 1963), p. 196.

career of singing. Her father forbade it. Grandfather Cassini, too, disapproved of her going and reminded Maria's father of the southern Italian proverb "Do not make your child better than you are." Maria bowed to the family's wishes, got a job at Hutzler's, and soon after married a boy in the neighborhood. Michael, Angela's 17-year-old brother, is still at home and is in constant conflict with the father. He has dropped out of school, has threatened to leave home, and works sporadically as a tile setter. His father is openly contemptuous of Michael's male friends, whom he calls a bunch of hoodlums.

Angela's mother is devoted to her family, remaining in the home to cook, clean, and care for them. Angela and her mother are the only members of the family who attend Mass regularly. The Cassinis would have liked to have sent their children to a Catholic school but have been unable to afford it. Angela has done well academically in public schools. There are blacks and Irish in the junior high school Angela attends, but most of her friends are girls from Italian families in the neighborhood. Angela occasionally goes shopping with her mother, but she does not know other parts of the city very well, for she seldom ventures forth from the Italian community.

Angela looks forward to family weddings, which are always festive occasions. Last year, for Lisa's wedding, aunts, uncles, cousins, and friends descended upon them from as far away as New York and Boston. Such food, wine, dancing, and pretty clothes! The singing and dancing went on for hours.

Angela is curious about the world beyond her immediate life space, but then there is her father! He was terribly upset when she accepted a date with a boy from a nice Irish family, and he made her break it. When she mentioned to the family her wish to go to college and become a nurse, her father frowned and her mother showed no change of expression. Angela yearns to see what the rest of the world is like, but it is hard to break away from family and friends.

The black child.   Although migration of blacks out of the Deep South has continued since the days of Reconstruction, the largest influx of blacks into California and northern cities occurred during World War II. Blacks went to Los Angeles, Pittsburgh, Washington, Chicago, and New York, where the men found work as laborers in steel mills, aircraft factories, and shipyards while the women usually worked as domestics. The result of this migration is that today over 65 percent of American blacks live in urban areas.

Most of the blacks who had moved to the North were crowded into the slums of the cities. Discrimination and low economic status placed blacks at a severe disadvantage compared to other urban groups in their efforts to obtain decent housing, decent jobs, and an adequate education. Many blacks have been forced to live in dilapidated, often substandard housing. They have been forced to accept menial jobs, have been systematically barred from many unions, and have been especially vulnerable to loss of job during economic recessions. Ghetto schools are often overcrowded and the poorest staffed and equipped. The milieu of the black child growing up in the urban ghetto of Chicago is described in these excerpts from the case of Roy Jones.

Roy Jones is a small light-skinned Negro, nine years old, with a flashing smile, handsome features, and deep brown eyes. He comes to school each day well dressed in new-looking wool trousers and knit shirt. He is clean, his hair is combed, and his shoes are shined. He lives with his mother, older brother, and two sisters in a small four-room apartment in Woodlawn, a predominantly Negro community on the south side of Chicago. Roy is in the third grade in Woodlawn Elementary School, and his sister Barbara is in the sixth grade there. Ninety-five percent of the children in the school are black, half of the children are from homes in which only one parent, usually the mother, is present in the home, and about one third of the families are on welfare. The school is an ugly 60-year-old brick building with high ceilings. Additions to the building have so reduced the play area that physical education and play periods have been sharply curtailed.

Mrs. Jones works long hours as a maid in a downtown hotel. She and her husband moved to Chicago from Alabama 10 years ago. Two years later, when Roy was a baby, Mr. Jones deserted the family. He has provided no child support for the past five years. George Thompson, Mrs. Jones' boy friend, visits from time to time, and he is the father of Janice, Roy's three-year-old half sister. Because of the unhappiness involving her first husband, Mrs. Jones says she has no wish to marry again.

Although Roy's mother comes home exhausted each night, she is still vitally concerned about her children. A neighbor cares for Janice during the day and tries to watch out for the older children after they get home from school. Most of Mrs. Jones' satisfactions come from relationships with her daughters. Eleven-year-old Barbara is popular in the neighborhood, receives high grades in school, and is a great help at home in cooking, cleaning, and caring for Roy and Janice. Janice is a healthy, happy youngster who is petted by everyone.

Mrs. Jones' major worries are her sons. Sixteen-year-old Edgar had always had a poor relationship with his father. Edgar had been in continuous trouble at school. He had failed twice, and he dropped out of ninth grade earlier this year. Mrs. Jones berates Edgar for the bad gang he goes around with. She was especially humiliated when she had to appear in court after Edgar was arrested on a drug charge. He is presently on probation, but Mrs. Jones is afraid that Edgar and his companions may be involved in thefts and other illegal activities.

In school Roy received a score of 88 on the full WISC intelligence scale, but the guidance counselor believes his real IQ may be higher than that. Much of the time in the classroom Roy is hyperactive, wiggles, and moves around the room. At other times he sits slouched in his chair and stares into space. Mrs. Turner, Roy's third grade teacher, is black. She urges Roy to concentrate and work hard, but she gives him little individual attention. In the first and second grades Roy had a succession of teachers and substitutes. He is retarded in reading, and schoolwork is difficult for him. In talking to another teacher about Roy, Mrs. Turner was heard to remark, "He's one of those from the project. There's no use spending too much time with them and neglect those who can and want to learn."

Mrs. Jones is particularly distressed by the reports of Roy's daydreaming and misbehavior. The last time she received a bad report on Roy, she sat him down in a chair and shouted: "Why can't you pay attention in class and get your lessons? I work hard all day so you can get an education and be somebody. I don't want you to turn out like that no-good brother of yours. Now, boy, you get down and study hard. Don't you give me more trouble, you hear?" Mrs. Jones has tried at other times to sit down and help Roy with his homework, but Roy's slowness in catching on to the work and her own fatigue and impatience make her give up early in the sessions. At school Roy looks enviously at black classmates from a nearby new apartment building who have bicycles and expensive toys and whose fathers come home each night to wife and children. After seeing these children, Roy comes home and has been heard to ask his mother plaintively, "Where's my daddy?"

The American Indian.   The oldest ethnic group in the United States is the American Indian. Some 600,000 Indians live in the United States today, and of these one in every five is a Navaho, most of whom live on reservations in Arizona and New Mexico. American Indians are not a single cultural entity but many peoples, each with its unique culture. In the northeastern, southern, and midwestern sections of the country, except for small enclaves of Indian families, Indians have long been assimilated into the American culture. Keeping Indians on reservations in the north central and southwestern regions of the country, however, has retarded their assimilation into the larger American culture. Thus, Indians are a distinct cultural group in the Dakotas and in the Southwest, areas where a great proportion of them live. In this discussion we shall focus primarily on the Indians of the Southwest.

The dilemma facing all Indians growing up on or near the reservations is whether to continue the essentially agrarian and herding way of life of their Indian forebears or become more completely Americanized by leaving their Indian community, enrolling in public school, adopting the white man's ways, and settling down to live like a white man in the Anglo community. It is difficult for any group to abandon a rich cultural heritage that is central to their social and personal identity. For many Indians, however, life on the reservation is hard, primitive, and impoverished. Food and water are scarce, housing, sanitation, and health care are poor, infant mortality is high, and few opportunities for employment are available. Yet for many, leaving family and reservation does not necessarily guarantee a better life. Not only do Indians suffer a wrench in giving up their tribal ways, but caught between two cultures, they are discriminated against in housing and jobs, as are other racial and ethnic minorities. Some of those who have drifted to the cities have been unable to adapt to urban life and have become costly additions to the welfare roles.

The Indian is first exposed to the white man's culture in government schools on the reservations. He learns to speak, read, and write English and studies the white man's history, mathematics, and science. Until recently these schools were staffed mostly by Anglo teachers, many of whom lacked an adequate understanding of the Indian culture. Thus, attendance at government schools for Indians intensifies for many youth the dilemma over whether to remain or to leave the reservation. This dilemma is reflected in excerpts from the case of Roger Lightfoot, a 16-year-old Hopi Indian boy. The Hopi Indians in northern Arizona and their neighbors, the Navahos and the Zuñi, are Pueblo Indians.

> *The earliest experiences that Roger can remember are being with his father and brother all day long, planting and weeding crops, caring for the sheep, and building traps to catch predatory animals. His father, a big, warm, friendly man, taught Roger many things about the desert and seldom scolded him. The days he was left back in the village with his mother and older sister were far less fun, for he had to spend much of the day hauling wood and water for his mother. When he slipped away to play with friends, his mother would find him and threaten to have the kachinas [Indian spirits represented by male relatives dressed in costumes and wearing masks] beat him so that he would become a good Hopi. The family attended all the ceremonial dances, and Roger's father dresses up in costume and participates in the Snake Dance each year it is held in their village. Roger was initiated into the secret society of the kachinas when he was 12, and shortly after that he was enrolled in the government boarding school at Tuba City, some distance away.*
>
> *During the first year at the boarding school, Miss Thompson, a white woman, was Roger's teacher. She introduced Roger and the other Indian children to the white man's ways, and many of these he found very strange. Roger was particularly perplexed by the white man's notion of wanting to be the best, striving to get ahead of others, and crowding so many things into one hour or one day. Roger was a good student, but this also caused him problems. He remembered how embarrassed he was when Miss Thompson praised him in front of the class for a good paper. He was sure the other boys would tease him. He recalled, too, how angry Mr. Wilson, the track coach,*

*was during a track meet when Roger looked back at his slower op-
ponents in the race and waited until they caught up so they could all
finish together.*

*Next week Roger is to begin his junior year in high school. He
must decide whether to include in his program chemistry and mathematics, which he needs if he is to go to the university, or whether
to take the general curriculum, which Hopi youth take if they expect
to remain on the reservation. Roger would like very much to help
his people. He could return to his village and work through the tribal
council to win from the federal government greater concessions for
determining the use of their lands and control over Indian affairs. But
he is also curious about the world beyond the reservation. His interests in books and in his people make him want to become a teacher
and return to the reservation to teach. His family is split on the question and gives him little help with the decision—but he must make a
choice, and soon.*

The Jewish child. Jews are a distinctive cultural group that cannot be
readily compared to any other ethnic group in the United States. The proportion of Jews among those in America who have achieved preeminence
in the professions, arts, science, business, finance, and the entertainment
fields far exceeds the proportion of Jews to the total population. American
Jews have moved upward faster and further than any comparable group. In
the face of these accomplishments, however, Jews have borne the brunt of
prejudice and discrimination—as indeed they have for 2,000 years. Restrictions against Jews seeking housing in better neighborhoods, acceptance
into colleges and professional schools, and membership in private clubs
have only recently been removed. Nonetheless, many barriers still remain,
perpetuated in subtle ways in the covert traditions of institutions.

Instilled into almost every Jewish school child is the importance of
getting a good education. Among Jews the college-educated group is proportionately three times as large as it is in the rest of the population.[30] This
high level of educational achievement by Jews accounts in large measure
for the disproportionately high number of Jews who are prominent in the
intellectual and business life of the community, especially in large urban
centers and the suburbs surrounding them.

Jews have a deep-seated concern for maintaining a Jewish identity.
This need to maintain a group identity is strong in every ethnic group, but
some subcultures are more quickly, easily, and completely assimilated into
the majority culture than are others. Jews seek to maintain their cultural
identity through trying to live in neighborhoods where a sizable number of
Jews already live, discouraging intermarriage between Jews and non-Jews,
observing Jewish holidays, and enrolling their children in synagogue schools
which teach Hebrew language, history, and culture. A more complete pic-

[30] Glazer and Moynihan, pp. 143–185; Marshall Sklare, *Jewish Identity on the
Suburban Frontier* (New York: Basic Books, 1967).

ture of the cultural milieu that influences the development and learning of the Jewish child is revealed in these excerpts from the case of Sheila Cohen.

> *Sheila, age 10, is a tall, slender, pretty girl with long dark hair and dark eyes. She lives with her father, mother, and two older brothers in a predominantly Jewish neighborhood in an affluent east side suburb of Cleveland. Sheila's grandparents on both sides emigrated to the United States from Poland more than 50 years ago. Her father is the chief accountant for a steel company in Cleveland, and both parents have graduated from college.*
>
> *For Sheila, almost every day is fully scheduled, leaving little time for play. Once a week after school her mother takes Sheila for a ballet lesson, and on another day she goes for a piano lesson. On the other week days she must practice her ballet exercises and piano in addition to doing her homework. Mr. and Mrs. Cohen have urged all their children to work hard in school, and Sheila and her brothers have consistently been on the honor roll.*
>
> *Abraham and Rose Cohen are members of the Shalom Temple, a Reformed congregation. The family attends temple services on High Holidays but seldom participates in the weekly social events or religious services. Sheila's parents explain that their minimal involvement in temple life is a reaction to the strict observances imposed upon them as children by their Orthodox parents. "Besides," Abe Cohen remarked, "if Judaism is to be a vital, dynamic force in the modern world, it must cast off the outmoded Orthodox rituals and beliefs. But it is important for a Jew to know who he is. He must know and understand his Jewish heritage and traditions. That is essential if he is to accept and take pride in his Jewishness." Sheila attends Hebrew School on Saturday mornings, and she is already preparing for confirmation, to occur at age 13. She remembers well the excitement and the fun she had at the Bar Mitzvahs of both of her older brothers.*
>
> *Most of Sheila's friends are Jewish girls from families similar to her own. Her father works with both Jews and Gentiles on the community Human Relations Council as does her mother, who serves with the League of Women Voters. The Cohens' closest friends are other Jews living in the immediate neighborhood, members of the temple, and some friends from their childhood and youth. Sheila has noted that her mother does not seem quite as friendly toward some of the Gentile girls whom she brings home as toward her Jewish girl friends who visit the house. She well remembers her parents' distress when Richie, one of her older brothers, dated and spent a great deal of time during his senior year in high school with Barbara, a pretty blonde whose family is Unitarian.*
>
> *Richie, now a sophomore at the University of Wisconsin, still worries his parents. He is a political activist who has demonstrated for a wide range of liberal causes and reforms. Richie was in the forefront of the demonstrations for an immediate end to the war*

and continues to demonstrate for the legalization of marijuana and an increase in enrollment of minority group students at Wisconsin. Rose and Abe quietly admire Richie's commitment and idealism, which reflect the liberalism they themselves have espoused all their lives. But they do wish Richie would be more careful. They live in fear of his getting hurt, getting arrested, or getting expelled from school.

Already Sheila is absorbing much of this liberal influence, but she is pretty sure she won't go as far as Richie. Sheila feels good about herself and about life. Her family loves her, she has friends, she makes high grades, and she enjoys music and dancing. The next few years are well planned. She is sure she is going to college, and she wants to be a teacher. All in all, it is a good life.

Mexican-Americans. In 1970 over 5 million persons in the United States were of Mexican descent. This is not many people in a nation of more than 200 million, but because they are mainly concentrated in five states of the Southwest (California, Texas, New Mexico, Arizona, and Colorado), Mexican-Americans are a minority group of significant importance. Immigrant Mexicans and their descendants now form the largest concentration of people of Latin American descent outside Latin America.[31] Most Mexican-Americans live in California and Texas, and within those states they tend to be concentrated in particular areas (Los Angeles and nearby cities of southern California and the lower Rio Grande valley and border cities of Texas). The Mexican-American population is growing faster than the Anglo population in these states (between 1960 and 1970, the number of Mexican-Americans increased by 51 percent, the number of Anglos by 37 percent). Because of the widespread use of *braceros* as farm laborers prior to 1960 (when immigration was curtailed), the number of Mexican-American males is disproportionately higher than the number of females. Mexican-Americans are a predominantly young population with a high birth rate and a median age of 19.6 years compared to 28.0 years for Anglos.

Large numbers of Mexican-Americans still live in rural areas, but their migration to the *barrios* (ethnic enclaves) of the cities is accelerating as the introduction of more sophisticated farm machinery eliminates the jobs traditionally held by Mexican farm laborers. Except for the relatively small Indian group, no population in the Southwest is so pinched economically. The Mexican head of a family, in comparison with his Anglo counterpart, must stretch his lower income to cover a larger family. About 35 percent of the Spanish surname families have incomes below the poverty line although they comprise only about 10 percent of the families of the Southwest. Many live in overcrowded, dilapidated houses, and their poverty makes them more susceptible to acute illnesses.

Education thus far offers little hope for helping Mexican-Americans

[31] J. W. Moore, *Mexican-Americans* (Englewood Cliffs, N. J.: Prentice-Hall, 1970), p. 52.

escape from their poverty. Schools serving Mexican-Americans have tended to be segregated because of neighborhood housing patterns. As in the case of segregation of blacks, schools enrolling predominantly Mexican-American children have tended to be inferior to those enrolling predominantly Anglo children. A major handicap in the education of the Mexican-American child is a language problem which impedes his learning in a school that requires a high level of fluency in English. The Mexican-American child is said to be bilingual, but Spanish is used almost exclusively in the home and barrio, so he begins school ill-prepared to profit from instruction conducted in English. The following excerpt from the case of Maria Sanchez helps us better to understand the life and problems of Mexican-American youth.

Maria is 18, the second oldest of five children, and she lives with her family in the Mexican barrio of Los Angeles. Until three years ago Maria's family lived in Delano, in the San Joaquin Valley, where they were among the thousands of Mexican farm families who followed the crops. After the grapes were picked, the melons would be ready. During the harvest season both parents and the three older children worked in the fields, and some weeks their earnings totaled 200 dollars. A good part of this money had to be saved so that they could live through the winter months when there were no crops to pick. Life was different during those years. The family lived in a two-room shack with no running water and no indoor plumbing, and they subsisted on a steady diet of beans and rice. Any illness presented a crisis, since the doctor had to be paid out of the grocery money.

During the years the family worked as migrant farm laborers, Maria attended school during the winter months. In school Maria was introverted and shy. She did improve in her ability to speak English, but during successive years she dropped further behind in reading because she forgot over the summer what she had learned at school the year before. Maria did enjoy going to school; she liked being with the other children, and the schoolroom was much prettier and warmer than her home.

Maria and her family well remember the year Cesar Chavez created the United Farm Workers Organizing Committee in Delano in an effort to win better wages and working conditions for farm workers. A national boycott of grapes was later followed by a lettuce boycott. It was a time of great hope, but this hope was short-lived. After the strike and the boycott, many of the growers began buying machinery to harvest their crops. Unable to find employment, the Sanchez family three years ago moved to Los Angeles. Maria's father is unemployed, but Maria and her mother now have jobs as maids in a hotel.

Maria's older brother, George, embraced Cesar Chavez's movement with enthusiasm. George was bitter at the intransigence of the farm operators and for the past year has been active in the Chicano movement. George, who had always done better in school than Maria, is now an active leader of the Chicanos at Los Angeles State. They exhort Mexican-Americans to be proud of their Spanish heritage, and they have demanded better jobs and better schools. George and his fellow Chicanos are demanding of the college administration that a program of Chicano studies be offered next year. The movement marks an awakening and a growing cultural identity of increasing numbers of Mexican-American youth.

These descriptions of six representative subcultures reflect differences in cultural milieu and socialization which American children and youth experience in growing up. Experiences within a unique family setting and a distinctive cultural milieu provide the child with a self-identity and perspective of the world that exerts a pervasive influence on subsequent development and learning.

Age and Maturity

A further cultural diversity is based upon differences in age and maturity. One learns to behave in ways that are appropriate to one's age and level of maturity as well as in ways that are appropriate to one's sex and to one's geographical, social class, ethnic, religious, and racial background. Since differences in the learned behaviors of persons of different age and maturity are in part a function of development, these differences will be discussed in later chapters on childhood and adolescence.

Methods of Socialization

The case record excerpts presented in the preceding sections reveal that children and youth are socialized through (1) parental control, (2) imitation, (3) identification, and (4) group membership. We shall next consider each of these in turn.

Parental Control

Parents' own socialization experiences in early life influence their attitudes toward child rearing.[32] In addition, the personalities of the parents influence their patterns of child rearing and the adjustment of their chil-

---

[32] Percival M. Symonds, *The Dynamics of Parent-Child Relationships* (New York: Appleton-Century-Crofts, 1949); Wanda C. Bronson, Edith S. Kalten, and N. Livson, "Patterns of Authority and Affection in Two Generations," *Journal of Abnormal and Social Psychology*, 58 (1958), 143–152; I. D. Harris, *Normal Children and Mothers* (New York: Free Press, 1959).

dren. In a study of 25 Jewish, urban, lower-middle-class mothers and their first child of preschool age, Behrens[33] found that the quality of the child's adjustment (measured by judgments of his responses to feeding, weaning, and toilet training) is more dependent upon his total interaction with his mother than upon whatever specific methods of child training she uses. That is, the kind of person the mother is seems to be more important in promoting favorable adjustment of the child than are her specific techniques of child training.

For most parents, socialization of the child involves the use of rewards and punishment. As we shall note later in Chapter 15, reward (or reinforcement) is a powerful tool for shaping and guiding another's behavior. Rewards have proved effective in socializing young children to rid themselves of a fear or to stay dry. They have also proved effective in shaping the responses of hyperactive, emotionally disturbed, and mentally retarded children toward more acceptable behavior.[34]

The types of punishment an adult uses, and the manner and frequency of their use, are variables which relate to strict and permissive discipline. The relative effects on children's personalities of strict and permissive discipline were studied by Watson.[35] Forty-four children brought up in good, loving, but strictly disciplined homes were compared with 34 children in the same community who were reared in good, loving, but extremely permissive homes. In general, the children from permissive homes showed more initiative and independence, except in school tasks; better socialization and cooperation; less inner hostility and more friendly feelings toward others; and a higher level of spontaneity, originality, and creativity. Both Peterson and Hoffman[36] conclude that, although parental firmness is necessary for older children, younger children primarily require kindness. Hoffman also points out that whereas the socialization of the young child is more a matter of unquestioning conformity to specific do's and don'ts, the standards of the older child tend to be generalizations from many previous experiences.

Thus far, our discussion of parental control has assumed that the child is a member of a nuclear family, usually with two parents but sometimes only one. In this age of alternative life styles, what are the socialization experiences of a child growing up in a commune with several "parents"? We lack definitive answers to this question, but the account[37]

[33] Marjorie L. Behrens, "Child Rearing and the Character Structure of the Mother," *Child Development*, 25 (September 1954), 225–238.

[34] See Roger W. McIntire, *For Love of Children: Behavioral Psychology for Parents* (Del Mar, Calif.: CRM Books, 1970); Teodoro Ayllon and Nathan H. Azrin, *The Token Economy* (New York: Appleton-Century-Crofts, 1968).

[35] Goodwin Watson, "Some Personality Differences in Children Related to Strict or Permissive Parental Discipline," *Journal of Psychology*, 44 (1957), 227–249.

[36] Donald R. Peterson et al., "Child Behavior Problems and Parental Attitudes," *Child Development*, 32 (March 1961), 151–162; Martin L. Hoffman, "Child-Rearing Practices and Moral Development," *Child Development*, 34 (June 1963), 295–318.

[37] John Poppy, "Child of the Commune," *Saturday Review* (February 5, 1972), pp. 34–39.

of one nine-year-old boy's year in a commune with his mother and sister revealed that he gained many skills (including glass blowing) and a deep sense of responsibility in performing duties expected of adults in the commune. Doubtless formal studies of child rearing under alternative life styles will eventually appear which will give us a clearer picture of children in these cultural settings.

Imitation

Imitation is a less formal and more subtle method of socialization than is parental control. One imitates by modeling his behavior on that of another person. When pretending to feed her dolly, the three-year-old girl holds it and talks to it in the same way her mother does with baby brother. Jim, a 10-year-old boy new in the class, watches the behavior of Joe and Mike, the leaders of the other boys. Jim laughs at the things Joe and Mike laugh at and asks his mother to get him the same kind of jeans as Joe and Mike wear. During the following weeks Jim's teacher observes that Jim seems to strut like Joe and Mike. Similarly, the tenth grader and the college freshman look to and imitate the ways of upperclassmen in learning what a person in that school should be like.

Rosenblith,[38] in a study of learning by imitation, found that kindergarten children made greater improvement in copying a maze when they imitated an adult model than when they were only given additional turns without a model. Hartup[39] studied the imitative behavior of kindergarten children in forced two-choice situations in which the two potential models were always a mother and a father doll. The experimenter manipulated the mother and father dolls so that they appeared to act; the child manipulated a child doll in imitation of one of the parent dolls. Both boys and girls imitated the like-sex parent more frequently than the opposite-sex parent. Girls who imitated their mothers were rated higher in femininity. Masculine behavior of kindergarten boys, however, is less influenced by their imitation of their father than it is by their contacts with older brothers and male peers.

Identification

One of the most important and most effective ways one learns his culture is through identification. Identification is the process through which the individual incorporates into his own feeling, doing, and thinking the

---

[38] Judy F. Rosenblith, "Learning by Imitation in Kindergarten Children," *Child Development*, 30 (March 1959), 69–80.

[39] Willard W. Hartup, "Some Correlates of Parental Imitation in Young Children," *Child Development*, 33 (March 1962), 85–96.

behavior, attitudes, and characteristics of another person whom he wishes to be like. It involves more than imitation, although the tendency of the child or adolescent to model himself after another is a frequently observed characteristic of identification. Identification appears to be largely an unconscious process in which one comes to feel like and to perceive the world like the model with whom he identifies.

The child identifies with those whom he fears as well as those whom he loves. He will usually identify with the parent who is most dominant in dispensing rewards and punishments. However, as Mussen and Distler[40] suggest, young boys are more likely to identify strongly with their fathers—and thus acquire appropriately sex-typed responses—if their relationships with their fathers are rewarding, warm, and affectionate.

The child not only identifies with the model's way of behaving, but he also accepts the model's definition of what he, the child, should be. In the process of growing up, he learns to change his picture of himself so that it conforms more closely to what others expect of him at successive age levels. The child, by becoming more skillful, more knowledgeable, and more socially responsible in ways expected by the model, is also learning his culture, though he may not be conscious of being socialized.

Early in the child's life at school, he identifies with the teacher and other adults who play important roles in his life. During middle childhood, the child's identification is often with real life and storybook heroes. During early adolescence, the young person frequently admires an attractive young adult whom he knows personally. Coaches, teachers, scout leaders, youth leaders, and athletes are some of the people whom adolescents wish to be like. Identification in late adolescence frequently involves forming an integrated picture of what one wishes to be like from the many people he has known and admired.[41]

Identification plays a crucial role in all areas and levels of socialization. People learn the ways of their culture more quickly, effectively, and completely through the process of identification than through the external controls of reward and punishment. The critical lessons in the development of self are more readily learned through identification than through the exhortations of parents and teachers.

Group Membership

The ways of the culture are also learned as one conforms to the expectations of the social group of which he is a member. Identification, imitation, and reward and punishment all play a part in ensuring conformity

[40] Paul H. Mussen and Luther Distler, "Child-Rearing Antecedents of Masculine Identification in Kindergarten Boys," *Child Development*, 31 (March 1960), 89–100.

[41] Robert F. Peck, "The Child Patterns Himself after His Favorite Models," in Caroline M. Tryon, ed., *Fostering Mental Health in Our Schools* (Washington, D. C.: Association for Supervision and Curriculum Development, N.E.A., 1950), pp. 146–157.

of members to the group's codes and standards. The culture of the group is a configuration of patterned ways and values abstracted from the culture at large. Socialization thus may be facilitated by learning the organized patterns and values of the group in place of the piecemeal learning to which the individual would have to resort if he were not a member of a group. The advantages of group membership in learning one's culture will receive further elaboration in the discussion of the peer group in the next chapter.

The Culture of Change

Rapidity of change is a reality of contemporary culture that stuns and bewilders modern man. Evidence of this accelerating change can be observed on all sides. It has been fueled by explosions of knowledge and breakthroughs in science and technology which have made obsolete firmly rooted ideas, principles, theories, methods, products, occupations, and institutions. Within their own lifetime, millions now living have witnessed the change from a preautomobile horse-and-buggy era to an age of supersonic jets, moon rockets, and spacecraft. Many Americans barely complete their education and become established in a career before they must return to school for updating their knowledge or retraining for a new career. Accelerating cultural changes affect in profound but differing ways persons of all ages, in all cultures, and in all parts of the world.

The real meaning of this rapid change is that socialization experiences are no longer confined primarily to childhood and adolescence. Instead of adapting in our early years to a relatively stable culture, most of us must continuously adapt to changing ways, patterns, and life styles in a lifelong process of acculturation. Toffler[42] has coined the term *future shock* to describe the shattering stress and disorientation that we induce in individuals by subjecting them to too much change in too short a time. Today's children, whose total experience has been in a world of rapid change, may be better able to adapt to change and the unknown future than many adults. Yet the reality of rapid change clearly demonstrates the need for all to understand the dynamics of change and to discover ways of coping effectively with future shock.

One way that an individual can deal with change is periodically to tune out the external environment so that he can evaluate his inner bodily and psychological reactions to change. Another way is to reduce stimulation and change by consciously maintaining longer-term relationships with people and contacts with the physical environment. Persons who are encountering or who are about to encounter an abrupt transition in their lives may be helped by an Alcoholics Anonymous type of group experience which would provide members with mutual help and support in facing and adapting to change. Crisis counselors and halfway houses are resources a

---

[42] Alvin Toffler, *Future Shock* (New York: Bantam Books, 1970).

community might provide to help persons work through problems created by rapid change. Education also has a role to play in helping people prepare for and adapt to an unknown future. Curricula that prepare students for change would emphasize the skills of learning how to learn, unlearn, and relearn, relating quickly and meaningfully to others in a highly transient world, and evaluating and choosing among alternatives. The student needs these skills if he is to evolve a system of personal values that is viable and relevant in a world of accelerating change.

Summary

The processes of internalizing the ways of the world are learned. The feelings, behaviors, and the ways of perceiving, thinking, and valuing which an individual learns in conformity to society constitute his *culture*. In its broadest sense, culture evolves from cumulative group experience; it arises from solutions passed on from generation to generation as the best or most acceptable solutions to problems of living. The term *socialization* refers to the processes and experiences through which one internalizes his culture.

Every society has established formal and informal institutions which are charged with preserving the culture and communicating it to each oncoming generation. The family has a primary role in meeting the child's dependency needs, in inculcating a set of fundamental beliefs and values, and in defining the roles, status, and expected behavior of each person within the family group. Church affiliation tends to influence one's character reputation, but the church's overall influence on children and youth appears to depend upon the religious commitment of parents and family. The school, as a cultural institution which affects the lives of nearly all children, tends to communicate predominantly middle class values and thus is not always responsive to the needs of children from lower class and ethnic cultures. The peer group and the community provide experiences through which children and youth develop and modify their understanding of the social world and their relations to it. Mass media, especially television, influence the child's socialization through communicating information, stimulating interests, improving tastes, and widening the range of the child's experiences. However, television viewing, which is habitual and reflects a lack of discrimination in selection of programs may limit the child's participation in other developmental activities, such as reading, outdoor play, and peer activities. The effect of television violence in stimulating aggression seems to be limited to a small group of children who are predisposed in that direction.

American culture can be divided into subcultures on the basis of differences in (1) sex, (2) region, (3) rural-urban-suburban residence, (4) social class, (5) ethnic background, (6) race, (7) religion, and (8) age. The culture defines for each sex the norms of sex-appropriate behavior each is expected to internalize, but in contemporary Western culture behavior and roles deemed appropriate to each sex are becoming blurred and less distinct. Recent questioning of traditional definitions of sex roles has increased our awareness of sex role stereotyping, which is prevalent in our culture. The influence of cultural differences on the development and learning of children and youth is evident in representative social class, ethnic, religious, and racial subcultures present in America: Appalachian, Italian-American, black, American Indian, Jewish, and Mexican-American.

The parents' own socialization experiences in early life tend to influence the methods of socialization they use with their own children. Reward and punishment is frequently used by parents in socializing their children. Permissive methods of discipline appear to be more fruitful and to have more favorable effects on children's personalities than do strict methods of child rearing. Other means of socialization are imitation, identification, and group membership.

Socialization does not, however, end in young adulthood. Our culture is changing so rapidly that most of us must continuously adapt to change in a lifelong process of acculturation.

Study Questions

1. You are teaching a class in which 60 percent of the students are Anglo-American and 40 percent are black (or Mexican-American or some other minority group). There are some friendships across cultural lines, but for the most part social interaction of students is restricted to their own group. What would you do to increase accepting and understanding by each culture of the other? How would you involve the parents and community?

2. Suppose that you are appointed to a faculty committee to draw up a plan for helping new students feel accepted in high school to which a sizable number of black students are being bused in order to achieve integration. What guidelines would you recommend regarding the grouping of pupils, and what would you recommend to assure equal opportunity of all students to participate and hold office in school clubs and activities?

3. You teach in a relatively affluent middle class suburban school. In your class are one or two students like Skippy (see pp. 170–172) who are frequently overanxious about grades and progress in school. How would you work with these students to alleviate the pressures for achievement and reduce feelings of self-doubt?

4. In your class is a student named Ronald who is intelligent and creative. Yet he does not conform to many of the rules and expectations of the school. Ronald fails to complete class assignments, and he skips classes to work on a project, a wall mural, a student petition, a novel he is writing, or whatever he is interested in at the moment. If he does not complete assignments in required subjects, Ronald will not be able to graduate. Should Ronald's creativity be encouraged, or

should he be expected to meet the same requirements as the other students? How would you deal with this situation?

Suggested Readings

Charnofsky, Stanley. *Educating the Powerless*. Belmont, Calif.: Wadsworth Publishing Co., 1971. Points out that much of American education is geared toward a traditional middle class education that is irrelevant to large numbers of children and youth in our schools. The powerlessness of most dark-skinned minority groups in our country limits their success in the educational system and perpetuates their feelings of powerlessness. Special attention is given to the problems of the urban black, the Puerto Rican, the Mexican-American, the American Indian, and the rural poor.

Glazer, Nathan, and Daniel Patrick Moynihan. *Beyond the Melting Pot*. Cambridge, Mass.: MIT Press, 1963. Describes the roles of black, Puerto Ricans, Jews, Italians, and Irish in the life, business, and politics of New York City. Shows how each group has maintained a distinct, if changing, identity and how cultural inhibitions and reinforcements have affected school performance, choice of career, recreation patterns, choice of neighborhood, political action, and attitudes toward other ethnic groups.

McNeil, Elton B. *Human Socialization*. Belmont, Calif.: Brooks/Cole Publishing Co., 1969. Examines the processes of socialization and the forces which influence it. Emphasizes the broad sweep of socialization as it is shaped by physical variations, motivation, learning, family influence, social class, intelligence, education, and emotional and behavioral problems. Major attention is given to socialization in youth and adults.

Neill, A. S. *Summerhill: A Radical Approach to Child Rearing*. New York: Hart Publishing Co., 1960. Describes a small private school in England founded upon a philosophy that accords students freedom coupled with responsibility for their own growth, development, and learning. The school atmosphere is characterized by love, trust, responsibility, egalitarian relationships between teachers and pupils and an absence of adult-imposed authority, obedience, assignments, examinations, punishment, and discipline.

Toffler, Alvin. *Future Shock*. New York: Bantam Books, 1970. Describes the shattering stress and disorientation induced in individuals by a rapidly changing world which subjects them to too much change in too short a time. Suggests ways in which one can come to terms with the future and deal with personal and social change.

Films

Four Families, 16 mm, sound, black and white, 59 min. Bloomington: Audiovisual Center, Indiana University. Explores the generalization that the care a child receives during his early years has an effect upon the continuation of the national character of a people. Shows a day in the life of a rural, middle class family in India, France, Japan, and Canada. Cultural patterns emphasized include infant dress, differing roles of family members, eating patterns, means of discipline, modes of bathing the baby, and the special place of the child in the family.

The High Wall, 16 mm, sound, black and white, 30 min. Bloomington: Audiovisual Center, Indiana University. Shows that social forces, especially within the home and school, can create conflict between races and cultural groups. When an outbreak between two teenage gangs sends the two leaders to the hospital, a psychiatrist, with the help of a social case worker, reconstructs the backgrounds of the two boys and their families. He finds that fear, frustration, and deep-seated prejudice have been communicated subtly and directly in the boys' home life, at school, and in the adult club of the parents.

Portrait of the Inner City, 16 mm, sound, black and white, 17 min. Bloomington: Audiovisual Center, Indiana University. Shows the streets, the schools, and the living quarters in the inner city of a large urban community in the United States. Shown are the inhabitants who serve as models for young Tommy Knight: the shoeshine man, the porter, the carwash man, and the junkman. In contrast is shown the more positive model of Tommy's older brother, who works as a salesman in a store after school. Some of the techniques of communication between school and inner city community are portrayed.

The Environment and Culture of the Peer Group

7

Just children on their way to school again?
Nay, it is ours to watch a greater thing.
These are the World's Rebuilders!

Theodosia Garrison

Few goals or aspirations so fully engage the attention and energies of children and youth during their years at school as gaining acceptance in their peer group. Knocking in the winning run, being invited to the party of a popular classmate, or being asked by a small clique to join in building a secret clubhouse may be a more important event in a child's self-development than anything he learns at school that week. A young person frequently will work day and night for weeks and months to achieve a place in the peer group. Many children will not hesitate to break the rules established by adults if it enables them to gain a place in the group.

The term *peer group* refers to a number of persons (of about the same age) who are linked together in some kind of group structure involving reciprocal relationships among group members and probably some hierarchical ordering of roles within the group.[1] A child or adolescent may be a *peer* (an equal) without being accepted as a member of a peer group. We also speak of the *peer society*—a set of children or adolescents who share certain common characteristics—and the *peer culture*—the beliefs, feelings, thought, behavior, language, dress, activities, interests, codes, and values of a specific peer group. An entity within the peer group is the *clique*, an exclusive and relatively stable subgroup composed of only a few individuals.

A person may belong to many different peer groups at the same time—his class at school, the neighborhood clique, Little League, a Sunday school class, scouts, and summer camp. His status may be different in each group, but the mere fact of membership in some such groups is vitally important in his socialization and his self-development.

---

[1] Although the term *peer* is also used with reference to adults, as in a "jury of one's peers," the terms *peer* and *peer group* here refer only to preschool and school-age children, adolescents, or young adults.

Emergence of the Peer Group

The child's first meaningful interactions with peers begin during the second year of life, after he has made progress in walking and talking, has achieved some independence, and has had experiences interacting with persons outside his immediate family. During early childhood the young child is usually immersed in his own play; increasingly, however, he indicates a preference for playing in close proximity to a peer, though he may not wish actually to play in collaboration with the other child. The two children play near each other, but each builds his own tower of blocks or digs his own tunnel in the sand. Such children are engaging in *parallel play*, a characteristic of early childhood. The young child continues to carry on self-initiated independent activities as he grows and develops increased strength and motor coordination and learns to run, jump, climb, ride a tricycle, and perform many other skills appropriate to his age and level of maturity.

Between the ages of three and five, children begin to engage in collaborative play. This marks the onset of an age of *peer relationships*. During this period, children are limited in the number of peer relationships they can handle in a play situation. Two preschoolers of approximately the same age will often play together quite peacefully in the play corner; but should a third child enter the play situation, a conflict frequently arises as two become allied against one over whose turn it is to play with the toy bulldozer. Early childhood is also a period of experimentation with different roles. In a single play session four- and five-year-old boys may play at being, in turn, Superman, G-man, the Lone Ranger, and astronaut; girls at this age may shift during a play session from mother to teacher to nurse to cowgirl. *Fantasy*, exemplified in this experimentation with roles, is another characteristic of early childhood.

When children enter kindergarten and first grade, they begin to have greater and more varied opportunities for forming peer relationships and broadening their social horizons. The child at this age is adult oriented. His most important relationship in school is with the teacher, who serves as a mother substitute in providing help, understanding, and support. For most children in first grade, the friendship and support of the teacher is even more important than the relationship with peers. Tryon[2] suggests that the teacher in kindergarten, first grade, or second grade, by her standards and values and by her assigning or withholding of roles, can influence children's responses in ways that affect their relationships with peers in later grades.

The second grade is a period of change in children's groups. During

[2] Caroline Tryon, "Youngsters Learn Social Roles," *Educational Leadership*, 3 (April 1946), 325–28.

their second year at school, as they increase their physical coordination, strength, and control, children learn new skills and assume new roles. Organized games of jump rope, tag, tetherball, and hopscotch require children to collaborate in coordinated group effort and to learn the rules of the game that are essential for continued team effort in competition with opponents. Children at this age often invent games, making up rules for these games and seeing that others observe the rules.

At this time also, children begin to be more independent of adults. They are more adept at dressing themselves, organizing their own play, and solving their own problems. At the same time many have learned that adults are fallible and do not always carry out their promises.

Friendship choices become more stable during second grade, and cliques begin to form that may persist for several months. Toward the end of second grade there emerges a true peer society, characterized by common goals and purposes and sustained collaborative group activity. The following anecdotes show the increase in group feeling that was observed in one second grade classroom.

October 29.   *Davy was swinging as high as he could and as fast as he could, singing "Let It Bleed." Before this, Davy had asked the teacher, "Do you like Mick Jagger?"*

The teacher said, "I do not like that kind of singing. Do you?"

Davy said, "Of course I like him." (He giggled.) "My big brother likes him too. Mom just has a fit sometimes. She says, 'Turn that thing off, or I'll throw out the stereo!' She means it too."

October 30.   *Billy sat across from Davy at lunch. Davy said to Billy, "Say, do you want to hear a good joke? You know my big brother's boy friend likes my jokes. Well, Bill, here it is. Knock, knock." Bill frowned and looked up. Davy said, "Ask who's there." Billy finally said, "Who's there?" Davy said, "Red. Now ask Red who?" Billy said, "Red who?" Davy said, "Red Pepper, that's a hot one." At that he laughed. Others at the table laughed. Billy finally smiled and said, "Oh, you!"*

Davy said, "Oh, I have another one. Knock, knock." Bill said, "Who's there?" Davy said, "Boo." Billy said, "Boo who?" Davy said, "Well, don't cry about it." They laughed. Both proceeded to eat lunch.

November 8.   *At lunch Davy said, "Oh say, gee whiz, I sure have a lot to tell you about our playhouse or clubhouse we made. Sometimes we call it 'the shack.' We sure have fun there."*

Teacher: "I'd love to have you tell me about your clubhouse."

Davy: "You see there's a creek and a steep bank, and you cross the log to get over to the shack. There's water in the creek too. One boy's father put a light in it. You know we get demerits if we don't behave. If we get twenty-four, we get kicked out. Then Mike, he's another boy, he goes out on the log. You can guess what happens." He haw-hawed. "Yes, he fell into the water. You see, we got a bucket to bring up water. So he lost our bucket. We haven't figured how to get the bucket yet. I went down all the way to the bank of the creek in my wagon. We sure have fun in that place."

Teacher: "It sounds very interesting. Perhaps I can see it sometime."

Davy giggled and nodded, his eyes danced, and he said, "Well, yes, I guess we can have visitors."

The peer group, with its emerging codes and culture, is a going concern by the time children reach the intermediate grades of elementary school. The boys' interest and increased skills in football and baseball are evident in the long hours spent on the playing field. Girls engage in games of their own—jump rope, four-square—or in just walking and talking in pairs or groups. In most fifth grades, a definite sex cleavage can be observed. Boys avoid talking to girls at this stage for fear of being called a sissy by the other boys. Girls look on disdainfully as boys strut around in the role of rough, tough, rugged he-men who wouldn't be caught dead talking to a girl.[3]

Peer interactions characteristic of the fifth and sixth grades are illustrated in these excerpts from the cases of Skippy and Andy:

November 22.   I was invited to the boys' football game after school. The game progressed smoothly until Skippy was downed and an argument arose between him and a player of the opposite team as to where the ball should be put into play.

His opponent: I got you here. You're cheating.

Skippy: I'm not. You touched me but didn't down me until I got here (indicating a line about 12 feet distant).

Opponent: You're a liar! I downed you here.

Skippy: Well, ask the other guys. (General opinion was that Skippy was correct.)

Opponent: You're a liar!

---

[3] For data on a variation in this pattern of sex cleavage, see Lawrence E. Kanous, Robert A. Daugherty, and Thomas S. Cohn, "Relation between Heterosexual Friendship Choices and Socioeconomic Level," *Child Development*, 33 (March 1962), 251–255.

Conversation stopped at this point and Skippy landed a good left which started his opponent's nose bleeding. His opponent started to cry, and the game went on with the ball where Skippy had placed it. The two boys went home together (apparently the best of friends).

December 10.   *Ellen H. returned at lunchtime and came into the room laughing. "Guess what I saw at lunchtime," she said, "Andy sitting out in the road smoking a big cigar." About this time Andy came into the room and saw Ellen standing near me and laughing. "Go on, horse-mouth," he said, "tell her." I asked him what he meant. He answered, "A horse has a big mouth, and so does she."*

The crescendoing of peer group activity and influence during adolescence is a phenomenon with which nearly all adults are familiar. Early adolescents, in adjusting to new feelings associated with the change that puberty is making in their bodies, frequently find greater understanding and support among their age mates than among parents and teachers. Most early adolescents at first are still engrossed in activities and relationships within their own sex group. Twelve- and 13-year-old boys are active and aggressive and prefer to be with other boys, playing or watching sports, working on their hobbies, going to movies, or wandering uptown to see what is happening. Girls prefer to be with girls as they play records, go shopping, or talk about boys. Many students maintain a strong chum relationship with an age mate of the same sex during these years of early adolescence.

In later adolescence, interactions between the sexes become freer and more frequent as dating and other heterosexual activities come to predominate over activities limited to one's own sex group. Now status depends upon one's acceptance by the other sex as well as by his own sex, and acceptance by the other sex depends on how well one learns a whole new repertoire of social skills—dating, dancing, carrying on a conversation with the opposite sex and knowing how to act in a heterosexual setting.

Kuhlen and Lee[4] noted a striking increase in heterosexual relationships as age increased in their study of 700 boys and girls in grades six, nine, and 12. Students were asked to indicate first and second choices of companions in their grade for each of eight activities (such as going for a walk, playing outdoor games, or studying). At the sixth grade level, 45 percent of the boys and 39 percent of the girls chose members of the opposite sex; by the twelfth grade, 75 percent of the boys and 63 percent of the girls chose persons of the opposite sex. The general picture, then, is one of association with the opposite sex in early childhood, gradual withdrawal of opposite-sex contacts in late childhood, and reestablishment of heterosexual relationships as development proceeds into adolescence. (See Figure 7–1.)

---

[4] Raymond G. Kuhlen and Beatrice J. Lee, "Personality Characteristics and Social Acceptability in Adolescence," *Journal of Educational Psychology*, 34 (1943), 331–340.

Figure 7–1.   Hypothetical Curve Showing Changes in Proportion of Same-Sex and Opposite-Sex Friendship Choices at Various Grade Levels

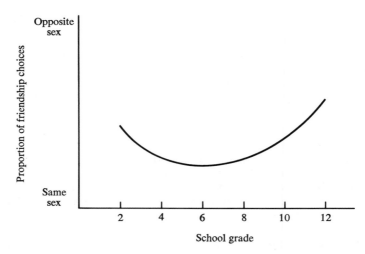

Source: Lawrence E. Kanous, Robert A. Daugherty, and Thomas S. Cohn, "Relation between Heterosexual Friendship Choices and Socioeconomic Level," *Child Development*, 33 (March 1962), 251–255, with extrapolations made from data from Raymond G. Kuhlen and Beatrice J. Lee, "Personality Characteristics and Social Acceptability in Adolescence," *Journal of Educational Psychology*, 34 (1943), 321–340.
Reproduced by permission of the copyright owner, The Society for Research in Child Development, Inc.

As age increases, boys show greater activity and greater daring than girls and begin to take over domination of the adolescent social scene. At the sixth grade level, girls are more frequently mentioned than boys as being popular; at the twelfth grade level, boys are mentioned more often than girls. The highly accepted persons of both sexes and at all ages are those who are judged to be popular with others, those who appear to be cheerful, happy, enthusiastic, and friendly, those who enjoy jokes, and those who initiate games and activities. Descriptions such as "talkative," "seeking attention," and "bossing others" do not differentiate between the highly accepted and those not accepted at the sixth grade level, but these traits do differentiate between the two groups at the twelfth grade level.

As adolescence continues, the peer culture becomes exceedingly elaborate, developing definite codes of dress, grooming, and behavior, a language which is continually changing, and a set of attitudes and values which defines who and what is "cool," "hoody," or "square." Most children and youth seek to avoid becoming the object of negative references by peers by carefully conforming to the moral codes, standards, and values of the peer culture.

Other changes can be noted as young people move from early adolescence to late adolescence and early adulthood. The early adolescent, for instance, appears to be concerned mainly about his status with the larger peer group of the classroom or school, whereas the late adolescent and young adult seem to be more interested in being identified and gaining status with a smaller group, such as the high school clique or the college fraternity or sorority. All young people moving toward adulthood, however, individually and as a group, explore, sift, and test appropriate standards, values, roles, and skills needed for building a philosophy of life, getting started in a vocation, and choosing a desirable mate. The following anecdotes document some of these explorations as well as some of the changes we have described in the peer group.

September 12.   The bell had rung for classes to reconvene after the lunch hour. Three of the high school girls, Alice, Janet, and Nora, were ascending the steps. Dennis, a ninth grader, was following, and I followed Dennis. I did not hear one sound from any of the group; but, as I watched, Dennis proceeded to slap Alice across the posterior.

Immediately Alice yelled, "Dennis, don't ever let me see you do that again, or I'll slap your face until it blisters!"

Dennis laughingly replied, "Oh! What did I do? Don't tell me you haven't had that happen before!"

After the girls were in their room, I called to Dennis, "Somehow I feel that a public display of this type is not in order."

Dennis did not answer. He merely smiled and went into his room.

November 8.   Tonight was our Homecoming Game. It was really a hot contest because it was being played between us and the neighboring school. We were behind 13 to 0.

I noticed a long, lanky fellow jump from the wall around the stands to the bench of cheerleaders. It was Dennis. He grabbed the megaphone and yelled, "Give the old fight yell, and yell it!"

Dennis kept the megaphone to his mouth and used his right arm in a beating-time motion as he spelled, "F-I-G-H-T, F-I-G-H-T, F-I-G-H-T, Fight, Fight, Fight!" At the end of the last "fight!" he gave forth with a big scream. From here Dennis left for the concession stand, where I lost him in the crowd.

November 17.   Dennis appeared in class today with a radio. He brought it to my desk and said, "This is what I've been working on for months." I asked, "Did you do all the construction yourself?"

"I certainly did," he said.

"Do you want to tell the class about it?" I asked.

Dennis shook his head and said, "They wouldn't understand!"

I was afraid someone would resent the statement and Becky

spoke: "Don't measure my corn in your half bushel!" The class laughed.

October 9.   *Although this is only the fifth week of school, I have noticed that Suzy, age 17, is one of the more spirited talkers in my senior social problems class. Today we were discussing how students should dress tomorrow for individual visits to industry. Some boys felt that the girls should wear dresses, not pants. Suzy protested, saying, "We are high school students, not fashion models." She added, "Besides, if we have to wear dresses, you boys ought to wear jackets and ties." The class finally decided to leave the jeans at home and strike a reasonable balance between informal and dress-up clothes.*

October 14.   *Overheard on the field trip:*

Helen (*to Susan, looking at Susan's left shoulder*): *No pin?*

Susan: *No, I gave it back to him.*

Helen: *Did you have a fight?*

Susan: *Oh, no. By mutual agreement. We still see each other.*

October 26.   *In class today, Suzy challenged the validity of a question I had used on a quiz. Many of the other students also felt it was not a fair question. There was a good deal of discussion, and finally I showed the class that it was taken almost word for word from the textbook. Suzy then said that she thought the students did not understand one of the words used in the text and in my question. In reply I said that the text was written for high school students and that I had often told the class to look up new words or to ask me. Then I said to the whole class, "I never saw a group so intent on raising one quiz grade by three points." Suzy quickly replied, "Oh, I'm not. I got the question right." At this point we all laughed very heartily and I said, "That's too much!" and we moved on to another subject.*

The preceding discussion and case illustrations reveal that peer relationships and peer culture at successive maturity levels mirror the changes that occur as children and youth grow and develop. For example, the motor development of boys during late childhood and early adolescence facilitates and in turn is enhanced by peer group interest and participation in sports and games. Similarly, physical and sexual maturation is manifested in increased sex role behavior and heterosexual relationships and activities during adolescence. Thus, the study of the peer group affords us opportunities to increase our understanding of the individual as well as the group.

Functions of the Peer Group

Provision of Emotional Support

One's relationships with peers is a source of emotional support. The extent to which the child gains emotional support from relationships with peers and with the group will depend, as in all human relationships, on the qualities of human acceptance, interest, and concern which are manifested in these peer relationships. A child or adolescent who wins a place in the peer group gains from these experiences increased feelings of value, self-worth, and self-esteem. Acceptance by the peer group enables the student to broaden his base of affectional relationships beyond his family and the world of adults to include a much more discriminating group—his peers.

Another important kind of support is that which the peer group gives any of its members who have been treated unfairly by an adult. The teacher may find that the way he responds to one student markedly influences his relationship and rapport with the whole group. Frequently, the group may show its support of a peer against a teacher by responding with criticism, hostility, or general restlessness and resistance to the teacher and the learning activity.

Identification with Peers

In the last chapter we discussed the process by which the individual learns the ways of his culture through his identifications with a variety of cultural groups—family, church, school, community, social class, ethnic group, and race. One's identification with his peers and peer group during childhood and adolescence is a further important influence in his cultural development. In one's identification with peers, their ways, goals, purposes, and values become internalized into his own patterns of feeling, thinking, and behaving.

Unlike his identifications with many other cultural groups, the young person's identification with peers is an identification with equals, with persons who share a commonality of interests, goals, attitudes, and points of view. As one teenager put it:

Our crowd is made up of kids who are about my age, who like the same TV programs and games I like, who have about the same feelings toward the teacher, principal, and school that I have, and they are the kids I'd like to spend most of my time with.

The group's ways and values are perceived to have greater meaning and relevance for the young person because they are the ways and values of persons just like himself, rather than of some more distant authority figure. This kinship with equals is, as we shall see, a powerful influence in the development and learning of the individual.

A Setting for Important Learning

As a member of the peer group, the young person learns skills, concepts, attitudes, and values which are vital to his own development as a person. It is probably no coincidence that the peer group develops as a significant social force during the intermediate years of elementary school— the time when children are making great strides in motor development and in skill at games. The individual activities of the primary years, running, jumping, swinging, and climbing, give way in elementary school to jump rope, hopscotch, tetherball, four-square, kickball, baseball, and other group and team sports. The rules of these games provide an important learning experience for the individual, and differences in interpreting the rules serve as a test of the group's cohesiveness and skill in resolving conflicts.

The peer group is also the setting for important socialization experiences. Many of the things which the child or adolescent learns from his peer group fulfill the needs and objectives of the larger adult culture. The family, church, school, and community give strong approval to the motor and game skills, the social skills, the skills of dating and courtship, and the skills and attitudes involved in teamwork, cooperation, and loyalty, which are learned and reinforced in group interaction. Adults frequently attempt to teach these attitudes and skills through exhortation and advice, but children and youth learn them most quickly and effectively by participating as equals in the activities of the group.

Peer groups in the United States enjoy a considerable degree of autonomy in identifying goals and carrying out activities which promote group purposes. In previous generations these peer group goals and activities tended for the most part to conform to limits acceptable to adults. Peer group experience served as a training ground for participation in the larger culture. More recently, however, peer groups in the United States and other Western countries have become a catalyst for cultural change. Youth, singly and in association with their peers, have registered dissent against an unpopular war, penalties for possession of marijuana, laws prohibiting abortion, traditional sexual mores, environmental pollution, irrelevant content and methods of education, and conventional styles of dress and grooming.

These very different roles of the peer group in reinforcing existing mores on the one hand and serving as a catalyst for change on the other are also evident in comparisons of widely different national cultures.

Bronfenbrenner[5] conducted a comprehensive study of children's reactions to pressure from peers versus their reactions to pressure from adults. The subjects participating in this study were 12-year-old children in six classrooms in the United States and six classrooms in the Soviet Union. The children were asked to respond to series of conflict situations under each of three different conditions: (1) a *neutral* condition, in which the children were told that no one but the investigators would see their responses; (2) an *adult* condition, in which the children were told that the responses of everyone in the class would be posted on a chart and shown to teachers and parents; and (3) a *peer* condition, in which the children were told that a chart would be prepared containing their responses and would be shown a week later to the class itself. For one of the 10 conflict situations, the child was asked what he would do if he and his friends found a paper which contained questions and answers of a forthcoming test. Would he refuse to go along with his friends and tell the teacher, or would he go along with his friends and conceal the information? The child was asked to respond on a six-point scale ranging from "absolutely certain" he would refuse to go along with his peers to "absolutely certain" he would go along with his peers. Possible total scores ranged from −25 to +25, with negative scores indicating going along with peers and positive scores indicating siding with adults.

The results of this study are presented in Table 7–1. These data show

[5] Urie Bronfenbrenner, "Response to Pressure from Peers versus Adults among Soviet and American School Children," *International Journal of Psychiatry*, 2 (1967), 199–207.

Table 7–1. Mean Scores Obtained by Boys and Girls in the United States and the USSR under Three Experimental Conditions

Subjects	Neutral	Adult	Peer	Mean across Conditions
Boys				
Soviet	12.54	14.21	13.18	13.30
American	1.02	1.57	.16	.92
Difference	11.52	12.64	13.02	12.39
Girls				
Soviet	15.13	17.02	16.90	16.35
American	3.83	4.35	2.38	3.52
Difference	11.30	12.67	14.52	12.83
Both sexes				
Soviet	13.84	15.62	15.04	14.83
American	2.43	2.96	1.27	2.22

Source: Urie Bronfenbrenner, "Response to pressure from Peers versus Adults among Soviet and American School Children," *International Journal of Psychology*, 2 (1967), 202. Used by permission.

that while the scores of Russian boys and girls clearly reflect values on the adult side of the continuum, those of American children are barely above the dividing line—indicating that American boys and girls are almost as ready to follow the prompting of peers toward deviant behavior as to adhere to adult-approved standards of conduct. It is clear, too, that in both the USSR and the United States, boys are more inclined than girls to engage in socially undesirable behavior. Finally, in both countries children give more socially approved responses when told that their answers will be seen by adults than they do when informed that their responses will be shown to their classmates.

The results of this study suggest that social pressure has very different effects on children in differing social systems and that these effects can vary significantly as a function of the social context. Where the peer group is largely autonomous, as it often is in the United States, it can and does exert influence in opposition to values held by the adult society. In social systems such as the USSR, the peer group, through its power to influence the attitudes and actions of its members, may be used as an instrument of adult society to further its own values and objectives.

The peer group also influences the learning of children and youth within the subcultures of a given society. In the United States, for example, the knowledge, skills, and values which middle class children and youth learn as members of peer groups differ from those which lower class children and youth learn in their peer groups. In middle class culture, the peer group provides children and youth with opportunities for assuming a variety of group roles and responsibilities and for learning cooperative group action in achieving goals. The importance of these group skills is communicated to the middle class child through his observing that many of the goals and achievements of his parents have been gained through their active participation in business, professional, social, civic, and community associations and groups. The middle class adolescent gains from the group understanding and support and acquires new attitudes and skills when, singly and in cooperation with others, he resists and rebels against the mounting pressures and expectations of his culture. The group in these instances not only acts as a safety valve for reducing individual and group tensions but provides youth with valuable experiences which they can later use as citizens to influence the changes that are necessary to keep democracy strong and viable.

Since the lower class culture tends to be more permissive, more informal, and in many ways less exacting, the lower class child is more often thrown upon his own resources or the resources of an autonomous group of peers. Even more than the middle class child, the lower class child becomes emotionally dependent upon his peers, and much of what he does and learns in the group centers in having fun or solving immediate practical problems. For many lower class youths, the emotional relationships, satisfactions, and rewards of the peer group frequently outweigh those of the family.

Ways of Achieving Peer Acceptance

Identification with Group Goals

Children and youth, as well as adults, come together to achieve individual and group goals. Frequently, a child will fail to gain acceptance in the group because his personal goals differ from those of others in the group. Because of this potential conflict between individual and group, much of the interaction and activity in every group focuses upon achieving compatible individual and group goals.

Group goals are more frequently implicit than explicit. Clues to the group's goals are revealed in answers to the question "What does the group do?" From a group's activities one may infer its goals and purposes. The delinquent gang, for example, seeks to enhance its own and its members' self-esteem by defying authority, stealing, destroying property, or by physical violence. A middle class clique achieves a measure of self-esteem by pledging the same fraternity, becoming active in school politics, or by organizing teams and competing with other groups in bowling, baseball, or basketball. In each case, the activities reflect the group's purposes.

Participation in Group Activities

To become a part of the group, the individual must participate to some degree in its *preferred activities* (those activities that are most significant in relation to the group's goals). Individuals who contribute knowledge and skills needed by the group gain added opportunities to participate in group activities and to gain group acceptance. The kinds of knowledge and skills which the group values and needs will again depend upon the activities and goals of the group and on the maturity levels of its members.

The skills needed for acceptance and participation in the group are clearly evident in the efforts of a new child to be admitted to the group. Among six- or seven-year-olds, the new child may attempt to get into the group by doing things another member has done, but only after the leader or some other group member has initiated the activity. If the new child moves in too early to initiate, direct, or influence the group's activities himself, he is likely to be rebuffed or ignored. By following the lead of the group, the new child becomes included in the group activity, and later the group responds readily as the new child initiates or influences group activity.[6] Among older children and adolescents, induction of new members

---

[6] E. Lakin Phillips, Shirley Shenker, and Paula Revitz, "The Assimilation of the New Child into the Group," *Psychiatry*, 14 (August 1951), 319–325.

into the peer group follows a similar pattern except that acceptance into the group is more dependent upon the personal qualities possessed by the new member and on the skills and knowledge he may contribute to the group.

Participation in group activities is particularly important in achieving acceptance among older groups of children. Bud was an awkward, poorly dressed 13-year-old who attended school in a mining community. The difficulties Bud faced in achieving a place in the peer group stemmed in part from his lack of participation in the group's activities, as the following anecdote reveals.

April 8.   *Today we were planning what each group was going to do during recreation period. I remarked to the boys that I had not noticed Bud taking part in playing ball. Lynn said, "We asked him to play with us, but all he wants to do is to swing or just sit around." Sometimes he plays marbles with Gary. (Gary is about eight years of age.)*

Bud seems to lack energy. He takes very little part in active games. The children coax him to play with them, but he refuses. He looks tired and haggard.

Lynn said, "We would like for Bud to play with us because we need him to make two teams. He could learn to play ball if he would practice, even if he is left-handed. He can bat right-handed."

The preferred activities of delinquent gangs often appear to be nonutilitarian, malicious, and negativistic. Stealing, for example, is nonutilitarian when gangs neither need nor use the things they steal. In spite of the effort expended and the danger incurred in stealing, stolen goods are often discarded, destroyed, or casually given away. Malice is expressed in hostility toward nongang peers as well as adults, in engaging in gang wars, and in taking keen delight in terrorizing "good" children by driving them from playgrounds and gyms for which the gang may have little use.

Two other characteristics of delinquent gangs, as well as of peer groups in general, are *short-run hedonism* and *group autonomy*. Delinquent gangs tend to be impatient, impetuous, and out for fun, paying little attention to the less obvious gains or costs to themselves or others. Gangs display an intolerance for restraints except for those arising from the informal pressures within the group itself. Their autonomy is shown in their active resistance to the home, school, and other agencies which seek to influence or regulate the gang's activities or to compete with the gang for the time or other resources of its members.[7]

---

[7] Albert K. Cohen, *Delinquent Boys: The Culture of the Gang* (New York: Free Press, 1955), pp. 24–32.

Peer Values

Peer values of children's and adolescents' groups have been studied by a number of investigators. Among elementary school children friendliness and sociability are qualities possessed by the most popular age mates, while hostility, withdrawal, and negative attitudes are associated with peer rejection. Intelligence and creativity, if they are not too far above the level of the group, are also characteristics of the most frequently chosen peers. Elementary school boys value athletic ability, muscular strength, and coordination in themselves and in others and continue to value these qualities in junior and senior high school.

An early study by Tryon[8] which investigated the peer values of early adolescents in junior high school found that the peer values most admired in boys shifted from being daring, aggressive, and boisterous in the seventh grade to being poised, likable, and personable in the ninth grade. As noted above, skill in sports and physical strength were valued at both levels. Among junior high school girls, the shift in peer values was from being docile, prim, and ladylike in the seventh grade to being a good sport, popular, friendly, enthusiastic, happy, daring, and having a good sense of humor in the ninth grade. Observations of present-day junior high school students reflect a similar shift of peer values for each sex between seventh grade and ninth grade. Tryon's study, as well as others, emphasizes the dynamic quality of peer group culture by showing that values important at one maturity level frequently fade and are replaced by other values as the group becomes older.

A large-scale study of adolescent values in 10 midwestern high schools carried out by Coleman[9] during the late 1950s found that higher value was attached by boys to being a star athlete and by girls to being an activities leader than by either group to being a brilliant student. At the time of this study, in order to get into the top crowd in high school, a girl needed to have a nice personality, good looks, nice clothes, and a good reputation. For boys in the schools studied, athletic ability and having a car were important for being accepted into the top status group. Good grades counted for something with one's own sex group, but cars and clothes counted for more in popularity with the opposite sex.

Among contemporary high school students, some of these adolescent values of more than a decade ago have been maintained while others have been abandoned. The valuing of athletic ability still prevails among most high school boys, but skill in sports appears to be less valued in college, where, for many, career plans or personal interests loom as more important. The value of having a car has probably increased over the past decade for

---

[8] Caroline M. Tryon, "Evaluations of Adolescent Personality by Adolescents," *Monographs of the Society for Research in Child Development*, 4 (1939).

[9] James S. Coleman, *The Adolescent Society* (New York: Free Press, 1961).

both sexes, since high teenage employment during these years and the increased affluence of American society have placed cars within the reach of more teenagers. For increasing numbers of adolescents, nice clothes and careful grooming are no longer valued as they were by adolescents in Coleman's study. Influenced by the casual dress and hair styles of many college youth, today's high school students have opted for jeans, shorts, T-shirts, sandals, and surplus army clothing. Girls almost universally wear their hair long and straight, while their male contemporaries often outdo their brothers in college in the length of their sideburns or of beard and hair. The movement toward more informal dress has been abetted by some of the younger teachers who come to school in contemporary dress and hair styles. These changes have resulted in many high schools with a conservative tradition giving up a losing battle to maintain a dress code which no longer could be enforced.

There also appears to be a marked shift in the personal and social values of today's adolescent youth. Who you are is less important than what you are. For increasing numbers of young people, it is more important to be real and true to oneself than to be virile or glamorous. Being human is the highest value, and this means being open to all of one's sensations and "telling it like it is." Students' reluctance to allow anything to interfere with or to distort their perceptions may explain in part the trends among many to experiment with drugs and sex. Thus, the valuing of authenticity and openness and the avoidance of pretense are manifested by candor in interpersonal relationships and a disdain for styles of dress and grooming which youth label as "phony."

In our examination of peer values, however, we should not overstate the importance of any one characteristic, such as athletic skill, in gaining acceptance and status in peer groups. Harrison and his associates[10] found, for example, that 278 six- to 11-year-old children frequently chosen by peers as leaders were significantly healthier, more active, more aggressive, more intelligent, higher achievers, more gifted, more likely to be Caucasian, more socially adept, and better adjusted than were 416 of their peers who were rarely chosen as leaders. The individual leader excelled in at least one of the areas of physical, mental, and social development, but not necessarily in all three. Similarly, an early study[11] of culture, roles, and status among lower class Italian young-adult peer groups of Boston found that the leader need not be the best baseball player, bowler, or fighter, but must have some skill in whatever activities are of particular interest to the group. The leader's ability to influence the group depends in considerable part upon his competent performance in those activities, and he is likely to promote activities in which he excels and to discourage those in which he is not skillful.

---

[10] C. W. Harrison, J. R. Rawls, and D. J. Rawls, "Differences between Leaders and Nonleaders in Six- to 11-Year-Old Children," *Journal of Social Psychology*, 84 (August 1971), 269–272.

[11] William F. Whyte, *Streetcorner Society* (Chicago: University of Chicago Press, 1943), p. 259.

A poignant example of a girl who utilized her skill in art to gain some measure of group recognition is that of Ada Adams in the film *Learning to Understand Children* (see pp. 46–47). Ada, a lower class girl in shabby clothes, won peer recognition by her sketches of the characters of Shakespeare's *Twelfth Night*, which the class had been studying. Her work on the costume committee in the class's presentation of the play led to closer association with and acceptance by some of the popular middle class girls in the class. In addition to gains in peer acceptance, Ada's changed hair style and improved grooming seemed to be accompaniments to a more adequate self-concept.

Personal Qualities

The personal qualities which elicit positive responses from others are frequently those associated with good mental health. Persons quickly and warmly welcomed into the group are likely to be those who have achieved some measure of personal security and self-esteem, who have developed effective ways for dealing with psychological threats, and who are emotionally independent. Emotional dependence on adults has been found to be related rather consistently to low status among peers.[12]

There is also evidence that high popularity with peers is enjoyed by young people who are able to play a nurturant role in satisfying the dependency needs of others. Among underprivileged adolescent girls in a state training school, for instance, the qualities of self of the most widely accepted girls included being concerned and helping others to develop, to improve their skills, and to achieve goals; expressing impartial fairness and a strong adherence to personal values; and being able to establish rapport quickly and effectively with a wide range of personalities.[13]

Adherence to Group Codes

Some children and adolescents appear to have the knack of melding their personal interests and goals with those of the group; others lack finesse to such an extent that they quickly antagonize other group members

---

[12] H. R. Marshall and Boyd R. McCandless, "Relationships between Dependence on Adults and Social Acceptance by Peers," *Child Development*, 28 (September 1957), 413–419; Boyd R. McCandless, Carolyn B. Bilous, and Hannah Lou Bennett, "Peer Popularity and Dependence on Adults in Preschool-Age Socialization," *Child Development*, 32 (September 1961), 511–518; Shirley Moore and Ruth Updegraff, "Sociometric Status of Preschool Children Related to Age, Sex, Nurturance Giving and Dependency," *Child Development*, 35 (June 1964), 519–524.

[13] Helen H. Jennings, "Leadership and Sociometric Choice," in Theodore M. Newcomb and Eugene L. Hartley, eds., *Readings in Social Psychology* (New York: Holt, Rinehart and Winston, 1947), p. 410.

and create dissension in the group. To maintain unity and harmony, the group develops a set of group codes, standards, and values and enforces group members' adherence to them.

The group's codes, standards, and values often conflict with the expectations of adults, and this poses a severe dilemma for those children and adolescents who wish to maintain the acceptance and good will of both adults and peers. Frank[14] counsels parents to remain flexible and to work toward compromise in their differences with their adolescent offspring. He cautions that the young person does not actually want total freedom; he simply wishes to be released from parental control enough to comply with the often more exacting expectations of his own age and sex group.

The codes, standards, and values of the peer group may be implicit or explicit; at times they may be expressed only covertly and unconsciously. Frequently, group codes or values can be identified in a group's response to an individual's behavior. This is particularly evident in this anecdote from the case of Billy:

> March 20.   *During the morning recess, Billy, age nine, jumped on Bradley's back, threw him down on the concrete, and hurt him pretty badly. The children came rushing in ahead of Billy to tell me about it. Finally, Bradley came in, limping and crying. Billy came in white-faced and shaky and told me, "Mrs. R., I didn't aim to hurt Bradley. I was just playing." Again, I had to remind him that he played too rough. About 15 minutes passed and Bradley became worse. I was afraid his leg was broken, so I had two boys make a hand saddle and carry him downstairs to the cot. Miss B. called his mother to come for him. Billy made several trips to ask how I thought Bradley was. I promised I would call his home at noon and find out. He was really sorry and very upset over it.*
>
> *At noon he came in to see me. Miss B. called me in from the lounge, and there stood Billy with a grin on his face. He very matter-of-factly told me that the boys had run him through the belt line for hurting Bradley. Bradley is their favorite. He is a good-natured and even-tempered child. He was in my room last year, and due to illness and loss of time at school he didn't pass.*
>
> *After lunch I had a long talk with the boys about the belt line affair and told them that they would have to be punished for it because it is strictly against school regulations to have such a thing happen. They took their punishment nicely, but were surely off Billy for several days. Bradley was out of school two days. It proved to be a bad bruise, no broken bones or sprains.*

[14] Lawrence K. Frank, "The Adolescent and the Family," in Nelson B. Henry, *Forty-Third Yearbook, Part I, Adolescence,* National Society for the Study of Education (Chicago: University of Chicago Press, 1944), pp. 240–245.

Roles of Status in Groups

Roles

Certain expected behaviors, tasks, and jobs must be performed by group members in order for the group to carry on its activities and to achieve its purposes. The pattern of expected behavior which an individual performs in relation to another person or group of persons is known as his *role*. In order for each individual in a group to perform his role effectively and in harmony with others in the group, he must know the roles of every member of the group. Just as the quarterback is unlikely to complete a pass unless he anticipates and responds to the moves of his blocking linemen and his pass receivers, the group member's efforts to achieve individual and group goals are likely to be frustrated unless he can anticipate the response of other members of the group.

When observing children and youth, adults frequently dichotomize peer group roles simply in terms of leaders and followers. An analysis of students' social behavior, however, reveals many far more subtle differentiations of role. Caldwell,[15] in an analysis of over 4,000 case records written by teachers, identified 18 social roles of children in kindergarten and grades two, four, and eight. Three are active roles: the *director*, the take-charge person who directs and dominates the activities of others; the *bully*, who secures compliance by threatening and intimidating others; and the *initiator*, who has ideas and frequently suggests what ought to be done. Roles that facilitate group processes, group harmony, and group cohesion are those of the *clarifier, morale builder, mediator, catalyzer,* and *nurturer*. The *sustainer* is a child who sticks up for and identifies with the leader, while the *attendant* is one who follows constructively and cooperatively the dictates of the leader and may also enjoy the confidence and share the secrets of the leader. The *clown,* the well-known wit or jokester, is expected to provide humor. The *imitator* is seen as lacking in initiative but is capable of persistent effort and sacrifice. The *subverter* is one who manipulates people or situations to serve his own self-interest. The remaining five roles identified by Caldwell reflect status in the group: *rejectee, fringer, isolate, scapegoat,* and *dependent*.

A distinction should be made between the roles a person desires to play and the roles the group permits him to play. These may be quite different, as the following anecdote from the case of Horace reveals.

[15] Charles G. Caldwell, "The Social Behavior of Children: Studies in a Child Study Program" (unpublished doctoral dissertation, University of Chicago, 1951).

Horace, age 11 and in the fifth grade, has on several occasions displayed a quick temper, which has led to altercations with children on the playground.

November 21.   Our softball had been missing for two days until Horace found it behind some boxes in our supply closet. In finding it Horace announced gleefully, "I'm going to be pitcher for our team at recess." Several boys in the room disagreed. At recess Horace failed in four pitches to get the ball over the plate. Jimmy walked over and told him to stand aside and he would pitch for him. Horace said, "No," and Jimmy pushed him away while the other boys yelled, "Get out of the way, Horace." Horace frowned deeply, put his hands in his pockets, shrugged, and walked to a position in the outfield.

In the contrasting setting of an East Side New York delinquent gang, Bloch and Niederhoffer[16] observed that roles of leadership and influence were shared by four individuals, each of whom operated with autonomy in his own sphere of interest. Paulie masterminded some of the gang's most impressive burglaries and had the final say in all important decisions. Lulu's knack for working with tools and electricity made him a natural for taking care of the technical details connected with a burglary job. Solly was public relations expert and spokesman in encounters with the police. Blackie was preeminent in matters relating to girls. This differentiation of leadership roles was accompanied by a division of power that allowed different personality types to function efficiently in the spheres of interest allotted to them. In this way a clash of rivals was avoided because each had enough autonomy to satisfy him.

Status

Each role carries with it a certain status or prestige, the amount of which depends on the importance of that role for the group. Roles which require greater knowledge and skills or entail greater responsibilities are generally accorded higher status and prestige because they are more valued and needed by the group for the achievement of its purposes. An individual's status in the group can be ascertained by observing the effects of his actions on the rest of the group, the responses of the group toward him, and the roles the group permits him to play.

A number of studies have investigated the characteristics, abilities,

[16] Herbert A. Bloch and Arthur Niederhoffer, *The Gang: A Study in Adolescent Behavior* (New York: Philosophical Library, 1958), pp. 193–219.

and personality traits associated with peer status at various maturity levels. Bonney[17] found that status in the second grade is concentrated among a few individuals and that as children in the second grade become recognized as good readers, their status increases. At the sixth grade level, play activities provide a better medium than academic activities for establishing close interpersonal relationships. Children chosen as playmates are accorded greater acceptance than those chosen as partners on a quiz-kid program.[18] Laughlin[19] found that favorable personality traits are a more important determiner of peer status at the sixth grade level than is mental ability. Children who are well liked tend to be described as friendly, enthusiastic, good-looking, and cheerful, while those who are not well accepted are described as talkative, restless, and attention seeking.

Other researchers have studied the relationships of academic achievement, IQ, socioeconomic status, and occupational status of father to a child's peer status. In a study of peer status in classrooms of grades five through eight, Morgan[20] found that children whose fathers have higher occupational prestige are preferred in social activities over children whose fathers have lower occupational status. Morgan also found that children who score high in achievement are preferred over children who have lower achievement test scores. In a study of 37,000 boys and girls in grades three to six, Roff and Sells[21] found that the most frequently chosen children had IQs 15 to 20 points higher than children of the same sex and socioeconomic group who were less frequently chosen.

The accuracy of an adolescent's self-perceptions also appears to influence his peer acceptance. Goslin[22] found that adolescents who perceive themselves differently than they are perceived by the group or who are unable to predict how others will rate them are likely to be accorded a low degree of acceptance by others. Occupying a relatively uncertain place in the larger group, these rejected adolescents frequently encounter considerable inconsistency in the behavior of their peers. This, in turn, causes those who are rejected to have still less accurate perceptions of themselves and others.

---

[17] Merl E. Bonney, "A Study of Social Status on the Second Grade Level," *Journal of Genetic Psychology*, 60 (1942), 271–305.

[18] Merl E. Bonney, "A Study of the Sociometric Process among Sixth Grade Children," *Journal of Educational Psychology*, 37 (September 1946), 359–372.

[19] Frances Laughlin, *Peer Status of Sixth and Seventh Grade Children* (New York: Teachers College Press, Columbia University, 1954).

[20] H. Gerthon Morgan, "Social Relationships of Children in a War-Boom Community," *Journal of Educational Research*, 40 (December 1946), 271–286.

[21] Merrill Roff and S. B. Sells, "Relations between Intelligence and Sociometric Status in Groups Differing in Sex and Socioeconomic Background," *Psychological Reports*, 16 (1965), 511–516.

[22] David A. Goslin, "Accuracy of Self-Perception and Self-Acceptance," *Sociometry*, 25 (September 1962), 283–296.

Sociometric Testing

Adults frequently make judgments concerning a student's status in the peer group based upon observations of the roles he plays and the behaviors and feelings revealed in his interactions with peers. Judgments based on these observations, however, are subject to error. Children and youth often mask their true feelings toward peers, making it more difficult for adults to learn about the actual relationships within the peer group. Adults are most likely to be inaccurate in judging the peer status of older students. Moreno[23] found that teachers' judgments of children's status in kindergarten and first grade are 65 percent accurate, but that at the seventh grade level they are only 25 percent accurate.

Sociometric testing offers educators and social scientists an objective means of ascertaining the status and relationships of members in a group. A *sociometric test* is a technique for obtaining from each group member his choices of persons in the group with whom he would like to interact or with whom he would like to develop or to maintain a relationship. A *sociogram* is a graphic representation of actual or desired relationships within a group. The information presented in a sociogram is based upon data obtained from a sociometric test.

The teacher who desires to obtain data on students' choices first selects a criterion for choosing appropriate to the classroom situation. Generally, students choose with less hesitancy when they see that the reason for choosing is to enable the teacher and class to organize for play or instruction. Teachers, then, might ask students whom they would like to sit beside, whom they would choose to work with on a committee, or whom they would choose as a work or play partner. It is important that the teacher use the students' choices for the purpose for which they were requested; that is, in the assignment of trip partners, the arrangement of seating, or the organization of committee work.

Collecting the choices of each member of the class is facilitated by the preparation of a duplicated form which explains briefly the use the teacher will make of student choices. One form that can be used or adapted is shown in Figure 7–2. Some teachers prefer not to solicit choices of rejectees. If these choices are desired in order to gain a clearer picture of relationships within the group, the request for last choices in the second paragraph of the form shown in Figure 7–2 is the kind of approach likely to elicit information.

When sociometric choices have been obtained, they are recorded on a Sociometric Matrix Summary Sheet (a form for recording each student's

[23] J. L. Moreno, *Who Shall Survive?* (Washington, D. C.: Nervous and Mental Disease Publishing Co., 1934).

Figure 7–2.   A Form for Eliciting Classmate Choices

Your name_____

Date_____

Boys and girls:

Next week we will take our trip to Washington D.C.
In order for us to stay together and avoid getting lost,
it will be necessary for each of us to have a partner for
this trip. Please write the names of three classmates,
any of whom you would like to have as a partner on the
trip.

(1)_____

(2)_____

(3)_____

Many of the persons whom we do not choose will be
chosen by other members of the class. In order that I
may place persons closest to classmates whom they would
like to be near on the bus, please indicate whom you
would choose last as a partner on this trip.

(1)_____

(2)_____

(3)_____

sociometric choices).[24] Next, the teacher selects the type of sociogram that will display the relationships within the group most clearly and effectively. Symbols representing children who have chosen each other or have both chosen the same child are placed near each other on a piece of paper as a first step in constructing a sociogram. In successive steps, the symbols for other children are positioned on the graph near symbols for persons whom each chooses or persons who choose him. Another way of portraying the choices and the position of each student in the group is to use a target

[24] For further details on procedures of sociometric testing, see Mary L. Northway and Lindsey Weld, *Sociometric Testing: A Guide for Teachers* (Toronto: University of Toronto Press, 1957); and Norman E. Gronlund, *Sociometry in the Classroom* (New York: Harper & Row, 1959).

sociogram, in which symbols for persons receiving the most choices are placed in or near the bull's-eye, with those receiving fewer choices being positioned in areas between the bull's-eye and the periphery of the target in accordance with the number of choices received. Those with fewest or no choices are placed at the periphery of the target sociogram.

Another sociometric instrument is the Classroom Social Distance Scale developed by Cunningham and her associates.[25] Each student in a class is asked to place every other student in that class in one of five categories from (1) "Would like to have him as one of my best friends" to (5) "Wish he weren't in our room." Using this scale, one is able to obtain information on the social group as a whole and to ascertain the degree to which individuals and subgroups accept the larger group and the extent to which the larger group accepts them.

Sociometric procedures enable teachers and adult group leaders to acquire useful information concerning interpersonal relationships within a group. These procedures are most useful, however, when they supplement the knowledge of peer relationships which the teacher has acquired from direct observations of group members in daily interaction with one another. The following anecdotes reveal how Miss T. used these sources of information to understand and to help Horace. Horace, it will be recalled, is the fifth grader who wanted to be the pitcher but was sent to the outfield instead.

November 26.   *Horace came back from lunch early today and was waiting when the boys and girls came out of the building. He had the bat in his hand and declared he was going to be a batter. Two other boys and one girl demanded the position because they had been up at recess and the game was a continuing one. Horace protested by saying, "No, it isn't fair. I was here first." All the other children yelled to him to give up his place and become pitcher. He finally took the bat and walked to the pitcher's mound while Jane stood in the batter's box with her back turned toward him. When he reached the mound, he turned around and threw the bat high in the air toward home plate. It came down and struck Jane in the back of the head. She cried a while but finally took her turn at bat. After five more minutes of playing, however, she suddenly began to lose her sight. She was taken to the hospital by her mother about an hour later. When Horace went back to the room he had tears in his eyes, his mouth was drawn down at the corners, he kept his head down, looked at the floor, and scuffed along.*

December 1.   *Horace was standing on the walk outside the building surrounded by five boys smaller than himself. Every now*

<hr>

[25] Ruth Cunningham et al., *Understanding Group Behavior of Boys and Girls* (New York: Teachers College Press, Columbia University, 1951), pp. 401–406.

and then one of the boys would run up and shove him or hit him and he would shove them or hit them back. One of the boys kept saying, "You big stiff, I'll beat you up." Another said, "I'll bash you." One of the boys hit him, and Horace chased him around the corner of the building.

December 17.   *In physical education today, Horace was playing center on his basketball team. The girl who was playing opposite him could outjump him when the ball was tossed up for the tip off. He became very disturbed about this. Each time he would grit his teeth, grunt, and jump as high as he could, but he was never able to beat the girl.*

After the fourth or fifth attempt, instead of trying to hit the ball, he batted the girl on the arm. This caused his team to have a foul called against them. The other members of the team all growled and fussed at him for it. He walked around looking at the floor for a short time and remarked, "I couldn't help it." I noticed that the next time he jumped for the ball it was against a shorter opponent and he slammed the ball clear out of the court.

January 5.   *The children in the room were telling about interesting things they had seen and done over the holidays. Horace sat and read a book through the whole series of reports.*

On December 10, Miss T. asked the class members to write the names of up to three classmates whom they would like to work with on committees to plan the Christmas party. The choices of the boys in the class were used to construct the sociogram in Figure 7–3. Not only was Horace not chosen by any child in his room, but he was rejected by eight boys (as well as by two girls, who were not recorded on the sociogram). Horace did not choose anybody and handed in a blank piece of paper. When Miss T. asked him about this later, he said, "There isn't anybody I particularly want to work with on a committee."

February 15.   *During the past three or four weeks, Horace's behavior and attitude have changed markedly. He appears happier and more at ease, and conflicts with his classmates appear to be fewer. During the morning, we planned our newspaper collection for the week. One of the girls needed help to bring a wagonload of papers up the Fourth Street hill, which is very steep. Horace quickly offered to help her and made the necessary arrangements.*

During our game period today, Horace did not try to catch the ball himself all of the time. Several times he actually gave his teammates the ball so that they might throw it.

The whole day Horace has really worked with the group. I

Figure 7–3.   Sociogram Showing Choices Made by Children in Miss T.'s Fifth Grade Classroom on December 10 in Response to the Question "With Whom Would You Like to Work on a Committee?"

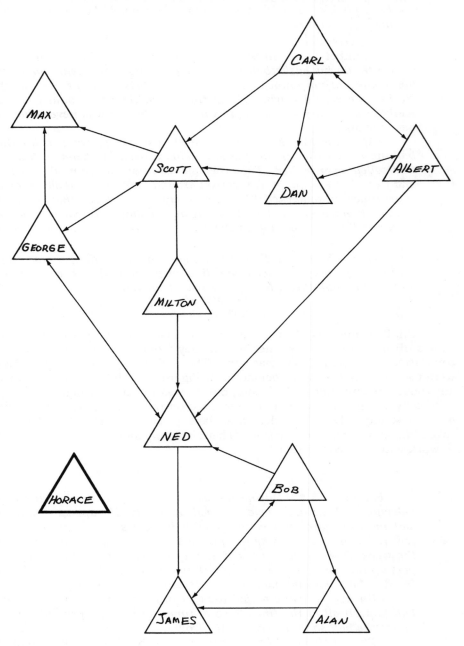

asked the children if they had noticed how much Horace had helped us. One boy replied, "He certainly is full of energy today."

February 20.   *Today Horace was chosen by the class as one of the fifth grade representatives on the safety patrol. He grinned broadly when the results of the election were announced. I congratulated Horace on his being elected.*

"Whew," he said. "I didn't think I would ever make the patrol."

"The class must think you'll make a good patrolman or they wouldn't have voted for you," I said.

"This is the first time I have ever been chosen for anything by my class."

March 12.   *Horace has been performing his patrol duty unsatisfactorily for the past week. He hasn't worn his belt, has been late, and has talked while on his corner. Several times I have talked with him about his patrol work. It seems that he just can't do everything right. If he has his belt and is on time, he talks to the girls on the other corners. Today I talked with him again, and he said that he would try not to talk while on duty.*

April 8.   *A group of about 50 boys and girls were gathered around Horace on the playground. He had drawn a line on the ground and started a broad-jumping contest. He had a tape measure and was measuring each jump. He lined the boys and girls up so each would have a chance to jump in turn. After each jump, he would measure it and shout out the distance jumped, then call for the next jumper. He was in complete control. The children who were watching were lined up on each side of the jumpers' path, and Horace kept waving his arms and yelling to them to stand back and give the jumpers room. This went on until the bell rang, at which time Horace declared Joe the winner with a jump of 13½ feet.*

On March 24, Miss T. obtained choices from the children which enabled her to construct a second sociogram. The responses of boys (and one girl) in the room to the question "Who would you like to sit beside?" are shown in Figure 7–4. This time Horace was chosen by two boys and was rejected by only four classmates.

These few brief anecdotes cannot give us the full flavor of the case of Horace, but they do reveal some of the ways Miss T. tried to help him in his efforts to relate to the peer group.

Figure 7–4.   Sociogram Showing Choices Made by Children in Miss T.'s Fifth Grade Classroom on March 24 in Response to the Question "Which Children in This Class Would You Like to Sit Beside?"

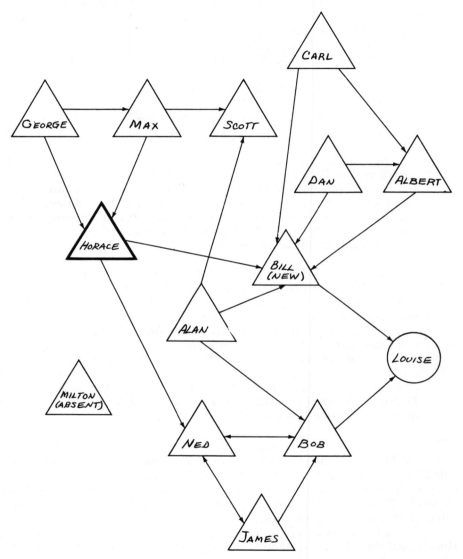

The Teacher's Role

When we consider the ways in which a student can be helped to achieve a place in the peer group, one thing seems clear: The adult cannot win group acceptance for a student who is ignored or rejected; group acceptance is something that must be achieved by the pupil himself. Even when the adult is highly regarded by the group, his efforts to persuade the group to accept a rejected pupil are usually ineffectual. Most peer groups are quick to see through the adult's subtle efforts to maneuver, manipulate, or control the group. Often, group resentment toward the adult is directed toward the child the adult is sponsoring, thereby making it even more difficult for the child to win group acceptance.

Elliott[26] has suggested three ways in which a teacher may assist a student who is seeking a place in the group: (1) by providing opportunities for development of friendly relations, (2) by helping the student to improve his social skills, and (3) by helping him to build a sense of accomplishment and adequacy. Providing opportunities for pupils to become better acquainted may be accomplished by seating arrangements, by forming committees, and by a variety of other ways. Jane's teacher, in the case introduced in Chapter 5, suggested Jane's name to a mother who was planning a birthday party for her daughter, a popular girl in the class. The teacher's suggestion was readily accepted.

Helping a student improve his social skills is sometimes a bit more difficult, because adult exhortations to a student to be kind, courteous, and considerate seldom change his behavior. For students who strongly desire to improve their status in the group, individual and group counseling frequently can help them to become more sensitive and perceptive of the feelings of others in the group. Quite often, the child's improvement of social skills is dependent upon his having available appropriate models in the persons of peers, older children, or the teacher.

Helping the student to experience an increased sense of adequacy and competency is one of the most effective ways of helping him to improve his position in the group. Ada's teacher, in the film cited earlier, increased Ada's feeling of adequacy and brought her favorable group recognition by showing the class Ada's sketches of the characters of *Twelfth Night*, which the class had been studying. Bud's teacher encouraged him to demonstrate before the class his hobby of taking apart and repairing old clocks. Another teacher, who was reassigned after the beginning of school to a combination grade, kept with her eight students who were less frequently chosen on a friendship chart. These children, older and more mature than the children

---

[26] Merle H. Elliott, "Patterns of Friendship in the Classroom," *Progressive Education*, 19 (November 1941), 383–390.

coming from the lower grade, were given responsibilities in the new class which helped them to feel more adequate and secure.

Probably the most important thing a teacher can do is to accept the child who is ignored or rejected by the group. A teacher who genuinely accepts and values children earns their respect and affection. A teacher who has gained the group's esteem is often able to influence the feelings of the group toward persons whom the teacher accepts and values.

It is doubtful that the teacher can change or influence the peer group to any great extent by direct manipulation. Rather, the teacher should be genuinely accepting of the group and should work with it as it seeks to evolve and mature. At times the peer group may appear to be engaged in activities and to be moving toward goals that are opposed by the adult culture. The best way for adults to influence the group is not to interfere with it but to conduct adult society in a manner and toward goals that the peer group will emulate and move toward.

The teacher's acceptance of each student and of the group as a whole is the basis for the mutual trust and respect essential for cooperative, democratic group living. In the classroom, the teacher is free to focus on the broad aspects of the learning experience and to leave to the group the planning of details, activities, and ideas, which the students are eager to contribute. This increased involvement of students in the learning experience facilitates their development by making them active partners in the educative process.

The Peer Group and Conformity

The peer group can help each individual member gain skills, emotional support, and a sense of self-identity; it can also, however, dull his individuality and compel his adherence to group standards so rigidly that he may become an unquestioning conformist.

As our society has become more highly industrialized and complex, warnings against the dangers of conformity have become more insistent. Riesman[27] describes a trend in the national character away from the inner-directed self-made man of prior generations to an *other-directed* man, whose source of direction and guidance is the group. Reisman sees this dependence upon the group's views and mores as leading to behavioral conformity and an attendant depersonalization and loss of individual autonomy. Whyte[28] documents the erosion of autonomy—in education, business, science, suburbia, personnel practices, and the cultures of the large corporations—as the

[27] David Riesman, *The Lonely Crowd* (New Haven, Conn.: Yale University Press, 1950).

[28] William H. Whyte, *The Organization Man* (New York: Siimon and Schuster, 1956).

Protestant ethic is replaced by the social ethic and conformity to the group.

The tendency of persons to conform to group norms is supported by research. Asch[29] conducted an experiment in which each person in a group of eight was asked to give aloud his perceptual judgment as to which of three lines matched the length of a standard line. One member of the group was informed of the true nature of the experiment and was instructed by the experimenter to give as his best judgment an answer which was at variance with his private judgment. Answers of subjects reporting after the "confederate" had reported tended to conform to the "confederate's" judgment, thereby creating and lending support to a "group norm." The judgments of the seven naive subjects conformed to this false "group norm" about 30 percent of the time. Asch's experiment demonstrates the power of social pressure to promote conformity to the group norm, even to encourage rejection of accurate personal perceptions of reality.

The peer group, like the other social forces to which it is related, can either ennoble or enslave. Group experiences are essential to the optimum development of every human being, but when the person surrenders his individuality and freedom in blind conformity to the group, human development and learning are likely to become blighted and stunted.

Summary

Interaction and identification with a group of peers are of vital importance in the socialization and self-development of each child and adolescent. One's *peers* are those persons of approximately the same age with whom one interacts or with whom one is associated over a period of time. The *peer group* consists of persons (of about the same age) who are linked together in some kind of group structure. The *peer culture* comprises the patterns of belief, feeling, thinking, behaving, language, dress, activities, interests, codes, and values that characterize a specific peer group.

During the preschool years, peer relationships are formed as the young child interacts and plays with age mates in the neighborhood and at nursery school. The second grade has been identified as a period of change in children's groups. Children during this period show marked gains in physical coordination and independence. During the second grade, *cliques* begin to form that may persist over several months. Toward the end of second grade, there emerges a true *peer society*, in which common goals and purposes are recognized and collaborative activity can persist over a long period. Peer group activity in the intermediate years of elementary school is focused on sports and organized games. A cleavage of the two sexes is characteristic of the peer group during this period.

---

[29] Solomon E. Asch, "Studies of Independence and Conformity: I. A Minority of One against a Unanimous Majority," *Psychological Monographs*, 70 (1956).

Early adolescents are engrossed in activities and relationships within their own sex group. As adolescents move toward heterosexual relationships and emotional independence of adults, marked changes occur within the peer group. Interactions between the sexes become freer and more frequent as dating and heterosexual activities come to predominate over activities limited to a single sex.

The peer group has a variety of functions in the development of children and youth. As young people make their way in the world beyond the family, the peer group provides needed emotional support and is a social entity with which young people can strongly identify. The peer group also becomes a setting for important learnings and a significant factor in the process of socialization.

Winning the acceptance and esteem of the peer group is an achievement of great importance for nearly all children and youth. Their success or failure in these endeavors appears to be influenced by the compatibility of the individual with group purposes and goals, by the readiness and the extent of the individual's participation in and contributions of needed knowledge and skills to the group, and by certain subtle personal qualities that influence positively or negatively acceptance by the group. The extent to which the individual accepts and adheres to group codes, standards, and values also is an important variable influencing the group's acceptance of him. Adult social pressures have different effects on children's peer groups in different societies. In the United States, where the peer group is largely autonomous, the group often exerts influence in opposition to values held by adult society, whereas in the Soviet Union, children's groups may be used as an instrument of adult society to further its own values and objectives.

The child's or adolescent's acceptance in the peer group is reflected in the roles and status accorded him by the group. Sociometric techniques have enabled teachers and social scientists to study the relationships of members in a group and the structure of that group. Excerpts and sociograms from the case of Horace reveal how his teacher used sociometric data to help Horace improve his position in the group.

Peer acceptance is an achievement that the child or adolescent must win for himself. Adults, however, can help the student by accepting and working with the peer group instead of trying to control it. Adults can also assist a student in gaining peer acceptance by helping him to develop skills and competencies that bring group recognition. Group acceptance requires that one conform to group customs, standards, and values. However, if the almost overwhelming forces and pressures for conformity in our contemporary culture are not resisted, they may inhibit rather than enhance the development and learning of individuals and groups.

Study Questions

1. Observe a group of teenagers in a snack bar, coffee house, or other teenage hangout. Note their dress, topics of conversation, vocabulary, and the interactions and reactions within the group. What do they talk about? What are the different ways you see individual teenagers relating to this group? What estimates would you make concerning the status of each member of the group?

2. Try to recall one or more of the codes, customs, or fads that were introduced into your child or adolescent peer group. Describe the process through which this fad caught on. Why was this fad accepted while other similar innovations were not adopted by the group?

3. Miss Edgerton has noticed that Effie, one of her fourth grade students, is shunned by her age mates and is left out of their games. The teacher is baffled by the students' reactions to Effie, for Effie dresses like the other girls, is pleasant to everyone, and is a good student. What hypotheses would you offer to explain the class's behavior toward Effie? What can Miss Edgerton do in helping Effie with her peer relations?

4. You are developing a new seating arrangement for your social studies class. During the first six weeks you have noted several friendships and cliques among students in your classroom. Should you arrange the seats on the basis of friendship choices, or should you keep friends and clique members separated? Defend your position.

5. Edison High School was desegregated two years ago, and since then the blacks, who make up 20 percent of the school enrollment, have complained that they have been frozen out of important clubs and school activities. During tryouts for the school's academic quiz team, Corrine Davis, a highly intelligent black girl, performs as well as any of the white candidates. Sue Egloff, faculty sponsor, knows that Elsie Hamilton, a senior who is already a member of the team, is likely to use her influence with other members of the student selection committee to prevent Corrine Davis from being selected for the team. If that happens, the blacks will feel even more alienated from the school. What action, if any, should Sue Egloff, the faculty sponsor, take in this situation?

Suggested Readings

Golding, William. *Lord of the Flies.* New York: Capricorn Books, 1954. Novel depicting the adventures of boys on a tropical island. The moral of the story is that the shape of a society must depend on the ethical nature of the individual and not on any political system, however logical or respectable. The book is symbolic except for the rescue at the end, where adult life appears enmeshed in the same evil as the symbolic life of the children on the island.

Northway, Mary L. *A Primer of Sociometry.* Second Edition. Toronto: University of Toronto Press, 1967. Presents a comprehensive review of the research literature related to sociometry and its meaning for education. Describes in detail procedures for obtaining and analyzing sociometric data.

Opie, Iona, and Peter Opie. *The Lore and Language of School Children.* London: Oxford University Press, 1959. Report of a study containing contributions of 5,000 children of Great Britain who furnished investigators with descriptions of their games, chants, humor, rhymes, riddles, nicknames, pastimes, and pranks which children pass on to succeeding generations of children.

Riesman, David. *The Lonely Crowd.* New Haven, Conn.: Yale University Press, 1950. Presents the thesis that social character is related to patterns of population growth. Chapter 3 discusses the change from an inner-directed society, which focuses on production, to an other-directed society, in which consumption, peer group approval, and popularity are major goals.

Smith, Henry Clay. *Sensitivity Training: The Scientific Understanding of Individuals.* New York: McGraw-Hill Book Co., 1973. Describes a program for developing the ability to understand people through training. The book is concerned with improving sensitivity through an examination of theories, methods, laboratory and field findings, and clinical training. Tests and scales for assessing growth in sensitivity are included.

Solomon, Lawrence N., and Betty Berzon, eds. *New Perspectives on Encounter Groups.* San Francisco: Jossey-Bass, 1972. A series of essays which analyze the encounter experience in terms of issues, technologies, and applications. Topics discussed include screening and selection of participants, standards for group leadership, the value of encounter, the use of non-verbal exercises and physical contact, Gestalt therapy, psychodrama and role training, and applications in school, college, and industry and for married couples and single-sex groups.

Films

Six-, Seven-, and Eight-Year-Olds—Society of Children, 16 mm, sound, black and white, 27 min. (A Long Time to Grow Series, No. 3.) New York 10003: New York University Film Library, 26 Washington Place. Presents experiences contributing to the social growth and development of the six-, seven-, and eight-year-old child as he moves into a bigger world seeking the support of his own age group, through which traditional activities, games, magic, and customs are learned and handed down to succeeding children's groups.

Social Acceptability, 16 mm, sound, black and white, 20 min. Bloomington: Audiovisual Center, Indiana University. Portrays a high school girl who fails to be accepted by a popular school clique and indicates the importance of social acceptability for successful adjustment and happiness. Shows also how adults can help the adolescent gain social skills.

Social Development, 16 mm, sound, black and white, 6 min. Bloomington: Audiovisual Center, Indiana University. Analyzes social behavior at various age levels, showing how behavior patterns change as the child grows, and depicting the reasons for these changes.

The Self: Integration and Development

To gain in knowledge of self, one must have the courage to seek it and the humility to accept what one may find.

Arthur T. Jersild

The preceding chapters have presented a number of scientific concepts that help to explain how various physiological and environmental forces—the child's level of energy output, his pattern of physical growth, the quality of his affectional relationships, the learnings passed on to him from the adult culture and the peer group—influence human development and learning. Yet this picture is not complete. From even a casual observation of children and youth, we can see that persons with equally high energy levels do not behave in the same ways and that persons who experience a similar lack of affection respond differently. They respond differently because each of them perceives, interprets, and organizes experience in a unique way.

Thus, each individual's unique organization of the personal meanings arising from his experience emerges as a force in its own right—a force we refer to as *self*. Self is a third set of forces emerging from the interaction of the first two, the organism and the environment. Self is a construct, a useful and convenient abstraction not open to direct observation and analysis. The use of this construct enables us to make inferences about the deeper motives of human behavior.

In the discussion that follows, we shall need to distinguish between the global term *self* (which we are defining and using as roughly equivalent to the term *personality*) and the more restricted term *self-concept*. We define *self* as the individual's unique, dynamic organization of personal meanings (emerging from the interaction of organism and environment) that determines his characteristic behavior, feelings, and thought. Thus, the term *self* encompasses the totality of meanings of one's personal existence (including those at physiological and unconscious levels) which directs and influences his behavior. The self-concept, on the other hand, includes only those meanings or facts which the individual in some degree consciously recognizes as part or aspects of himself. The *self-concept*, then, consists of the most highly differentiated perceptions, beliefs, feelings, attitudes, and values which the individual holds of or about himself. The following illustration may clarify the distinction between self and self-concept. The self-percept "I am a cautious person" describes an aspect of one's self-concept, but his self includes not only this percept but also the repressed fears of failure which lie beyond his awareness.

Characteristics of the Self

Self as an emergent process.   The human infant does not possess a self at birth but does have the capacities for developing a self. Newborn infants differ in temperament and sensitivity to stimuli, but each infant's development of an organization of personal meanings takes place gradually as receptors, muscles, brain, and nervous system mature. As these structures mature, enabling the child to distinguish between an increasing array of stimuli, self emerges as a dominant process shaping development and learning.

Uniqueness of self.   Individuality and uniqueness of self are revealed in the very different ways each person views and responds to the world. Each of us is different, and this makes the understanding of self both an enigma and a challenge. In responding to this challenge, man's study of self centers in a search for understanding how and why each individual is different.

Maintenance of organization.   The word *organization,* connoting order and stability, is probably the most meaningful and descriptive term in any definition of self. In discussing the concept of homeostasis in Chapters 3 and 4, we noted that maintenance of physiological stability is a characteristic of living things. On the physiological level, an individual perceives minimal changes toward imbalance, such as hunger pangs, as cues for action. Similarly, as Stagner[1] points out, changes in the social environment may function as signals for organic disequilibrium, thereby increasing tension, energy mobilization, and action toward restoration of a social environment constancy. Thus, behavior that reduces tension and restores homeostatic balance exemplifies the maintenance of self-organization.

Dynamic process.   Maintenance of organization does not imply a static quality, nor does it refer to the restoration of some prior equilibrium. Both the term *homeostasis* and our reference to maintenance of organization connote the continuous activity of adjusting and readjusting to changing conditions.

---

[1] Ross Stagner, "Homeostasis as a Unifying Concept in Personality Theory," *Psychological Review,* 58 (January 1951), 5–17.

Stability and change, then, are pervasive qualities of both the physical organism and the self. Although these characteristics seem to refer to opposite or conflicting processes, in the context of the living organism and of human behavior they are complementary and interdependent. The child changes in size and structure as he grows taller and as his tissues and body parts become more differentiated; but he is an organized system at all times—before, during, and after these changes in physical growth and development. Change in self is revealed in the changes in the ways one sees himself and sees the world as he acquires knowledge, skills, and roles and experiences shifts in beliefs, goals, attitudes, and values.

Consciousness and self.   Consciousness is in some degree a characteristic of the self, since the term *self-concept* implies a measure of self-awareness. The nature and origins of consciousness are still very much of an enigma to psychologists, but the term generally refers to a level of subjective awareness.
         Freudian psychology distinguishes between conscious, preconscious, and unconscious levels and processes. While self is largely formed by the individual's organizing of personal meanings at a conscious level, some meanings of critical importance to self are present in the psychological structure below the level of consciousness.

Self as an inferred process.   Since self is an abstraction, it is neither tangible nor visible. Subjectively, I experience self as my ways of thinking, feeling, and behaving, which relate to the way I perceive the objects and events in my life space. An outside observer's perception of another's self is limited to inferences concerning the kind of unique organization of personal meanings the subject is likely to have in order to have responded the way he did to a given stimulus or situation. Since these inferences are at best only hypotheses, they should be checked against all other data available on the subject.

Representative Theories of Self

Freud and Psychoanalysis

Freud conceived of man as a dynamic system of energies. Self, said Freud, is comprised of three major systems: the id, the ego, and the superego. These three psychological systems continuously interact to produce the individual's behavior. The *id*, the original system from which the ego and the superego gradually evolve, is the source of all psychic energy (*libido*). This energy is expressed as *instincts*, inner excitations that drive the organism. Instincts arise out of the inherited biological nature of the organism and are of two kinds: life instincts, which are concerned with survival and are expressed as tensions related to thirst, hunger, sex, or inactivity; and death instincts, which are expressed as destructive impulses and take the form of aggression. When increases of energy produce uncomfortable states of tension, the id serves to discharge the tension so that the organism moves toward equilibrium at a lower energy level. The principle by which the id operates to reduce tension is called the *pleasure principle:* the avoidance of pain and the pursuit of pleasure.

The *ego* emerges as the organism, seeking to satisfy the impulses of the id, comes to grips with the forces and realities of the external world. The ego is a system of forces which redirects id impulses toward gratifications appropriate to the specific environment or situation. The principle by which the ego prevents discharge of tension until appropriate objects for gratification are available is called the *reality principle:* the adjustment of behavior to the demands of the outside world. The principal role of the ego is to mediate between the instinctual impulses of the organism and the limitations imposed by the surrounding environment. It serves as the executive of the self, deciding which instincts will be satisfied and the manner in which they will be satisfied. Its primary objective is to maintain the life of the individual and to ensure the survival of the species.

When the individual attempts to express and to satisfy id impulses by direct action, he tends to be blocked or restrained by the customs, rules, and values of society. As these rules and values are adopted and internalized by the child, they form the *superego*. The superego is a moral arbiter of conduct; it functions to restrain or to inhibit those basic impulses, especially sex and aggression, which society regards as dangerous. In time, the superego becomes the conscience of the child; internalized controls replace those of parents and society in guiding behavior. A well-developed superego enables the individual to maintain adequate control over id impulses.

When the immediate or direct expressions of libidinal energies are blocked, the resulting frustrations, conflicts, and anxieties are reduced through processes such as identification and displacement. In *identification*, as we noted in Chapter 6, the individual incorporates into his own self features of another person. He learns to reduce tension by modeling his behavior after someone else. In *displacement*, id instincts are redirected toward substitute means or objects of satisfaction, as a child directs anger with his parents toward a sibling or a toy. These and other ways of reducing anxieties, often referred to as *defense mechanisms* or *adjustment patterns*, are described in the next chapter.

Freud and his theory of psychoanalysis have made a significant contribution to our understanding of human behavior. The affection which preschool children extend to the parent of the opposite sex is a normal development which Freud identified and described by the terms *Oedipus complex* and *Electra complex*. In everyday experiences residual effects of Oedipal tendencies are revealed in one's behavior toward mother surrogates or father surrogates. Each of us may recall countless examples of behavior which reflects ambivalent feelings toward parents, children, and spouses, symbolisms which emerge from dreams and fantasies, and the uses of repression, identification, and sublimation in defense of the ego.

Freudian theory, however, also has serious limitations and shortcomings. First, it offers much better explanations of pathological behavior than it does of normal behavior. Second, in emphasizing id impulses, libido, life instincts, and death wishes, Freud gave disproportionate weight in explaining behavior to biological facts of heredity, maturation, and drive and insufficient weight to culture, socialization, personal experiences, and the life style of the individual. Third, Freud's view of motivation is much too narrow and inadequate for explaining the range and diversity of human behavior. Children and adults in the latter half of the twentieth century do not appear to be intent on immediate gratification of hunger, activity, and sex drives. Rather, they often appear cheerful, curious, explorative, oriented toward mastery of skills and objects, and affectionate without discernible evidence of lustful desire. Finally, it is impossible to make an adequate verification of Freudian theory because Freud's observations of his patients were made under uncontrolled conditions. Moreover, the lack of quantification of his empirical data has made it impossible to ascertain the statistical significance and reliability of his observations.

Social Theories of Self

With the emergence in the early twentieth century of sociology, anthropology, and social psychology as independent disciplines, man began to be viewed as a product of the culture or society in which he lives. Some social theories of self are based on psychoanalytic concepts, but in general they emphasize the role of social forces rather than biological drives in the development of self.

The ideas of George Herbert Mead[2] laid the foundation for the later development of a theory of the self-concept, a way of thinking about and analyzing personality which has become popular with both psychologists and educators. Mead describes self as an object of which one gradually becomes aware as he interacts with others. The child is born with no awareness of self, but as other people respond to him he develops an awareness of self by taking over their responses toward him and responding in like manner toward himself. Mead suggests that each individual has multiple selves, varying according to the situation and the role expectations of different social groups. Mead's ideas about the development of self-awareness and self-image have provided the basis for the organismic-existential theories of Rogers, Maslow, and Combs which emphasize the self-concept. These theories are discussed later in this chapter.

For Karen Horney,[3] anxiety, the feeling of being isolated and helpless in a potentially hostile world, is a primary concept. This anxiety is produced

[2] George Herbert Mead, *Mind, Self, and Society* (Chicago: University of Chicago Press, 1934).

[3] Karen Horney, *Neurosis and Human Growth* (New York: W. W. Norton & Co., 1950).

by unwholesome early relationships. As the child attempts to cope with his anxiety, he develops irrational patterns of adjustment—"neurotic needs" for such goals as affection, power, exploitation, prestige, achievement, and independence.

According to Erich Fromm,[4] the basic conditions of man's existence pose a fundamental contradiction and a dilemma. Man is both a part of nature and separate from it; he is both an animal and a human being. He has specific needs (relatedness, transcendence, rootedness, identity, and orientation) which define his human condition apart from society. Societal demands that are inconsistent with his nature tend to alienate man from both his human condition and society and to thwart the satisfaction of his needs. Man can rid himself of feelings of alienation either by uniting himself in productive love and shared work with others or by submitting to authority and conforming to society. By selecting the first alternative, however, man helps to create a society that is better adapted for assisting all persons to become fully human.

According to the theory of Harry Stack Sullivan,[5] the individual does not exist apart from his relations with other people; though heredity and maturation do play a part in shaping the individual, all that is distinctly human about him is the product of social interactions. The study of self, then, is a study not of the individual but of the interpersonal situation.

In an interpersonal self theory such as Sullivan's, the images one develops of himself and of other people are called *personifications*. Initially, the infant who is nursed and given solicitous, tender care develops a personification of the "good mother" (or mothering person). On the other hand, if the mothering person withholds tenderness and does not care for the infant's needs, the infant develops a personification of the "bad mother." Sullivan believes that the mothering person who is anxious and unsure of her feelings toward the child communicates her anxiety to the child in the way she handles and cares for him. Thus, the mother's anxiety is contagious and may infect the child. By a nonverbal type of communication called empathy, the mother may transmit her anxiety to the child before the child is able, through his own awareness, to sense or perceive what is transpiring between himself and the mothering one. By communicating tenderness the "good mother" relieves the child's tensions and provides him with a sense of security. As one grows older, a multitude of other personifications are formed and labeled the good or bad father, brother, sister, friend, teacher, student, boss, employee, husband, wife, son, daughter, and so on.

These images or personifications which the individual forms and carries around in his head are subjective and thus are often inaccurate descriptions of the persons to whom they refer. They are formed initially for dealing with specific persons in specific situations, but once formed they

---

[4] Erich Fromm, *Man for Himself* (New York: Holt, Rinehart and Winston, 1947); *The Sane Society* (New York: Holt, Rinehart, and Winston, 1955).

[5] Harry Stack Sullivan, *The Interpersonal Theory of Psychiatry* (New York: W. W. Norton & Co., 1953).

usually persist and influence the individual's attitudes toward other people. A person, for example, who has an image of his father as cold and domineering may project it onto other older men he encounters, such as teachers, coaches, employers, or policemen. If the child's principal mode of reducing anxiety in confrontations with his father is to submit to his wishes and placate him, the child may continue this pattern of behavior in adulthood in interactions with father figures even though these figures may be warm, sympathetic, and understanding. Thus, personifications which were associated with anxiety in early life may interfere with interpersonal relationships in later life. Personifications of the self, such as the "good me" and the "bad me," follow the same principles as personifications of others. The good-me personification results from interpersonal experiences which increase one's sense of security, esteem, and enhancement, while the bad-me personification follows threatening, frustrating, rejecting, anxiety-producing situations. Like personifications of other people, self-personifications tend to hinder objective self-evaluation.

Sullivan's interpersonal theory of personality provides us with valuable insights into human behavior, but it leaves several questions unanswered. Sullivan does not clarify, for example, the differences between individual anxiety, which may be mild or acute, and that anxiety which is universal and inherent in human existence. Although he emphasizes the importance of interpersonal relationships, he does not make clear the child's role at the beginning of this relationship. Finally, like Freud, Sullivan did not conduct empirical studies that would permit a verification of his theoretical postulates.

A Transactional View of Self

Freud's psychoanalytic theory and Sullivan's interpersonal theory of personality have provided the theoretical basis for the development of a method for studying personality called *transactional analysis.* Psychiatrists Berne[6] and Harris[7] note that a person may change his behavior and role and become somebody quite different from the person he was a moment before. In the classroom the teacher who has been criticized by parent or principal may react emotionally, like a small child dominated by his feelings. A little later, in correcting a student's misbehavior, the teacher may act the part of a self-righteous parent; in the next instant, in helping a student with his reading, he may be seen as a reasoning, logical, mature, nurturant adult. These changes in behavior and role are obviously related to the influence of persons with whom the individual becomes involved in social interaction. Transactional analysis is a method of examining a social transaction ("I do something to you and you do something back") and determining which part

[6] Eric Berne, *Games People Play* (New York: Grove Press, 1964).
[7] Thomas A. Harris, *I'm OK—You're OK* (New York: Harper & Row, 1967).

of the multiple-person (parent, child, or adult) individual is dominant in the given situation.

According to Berne and Harris, the parent, the child, and the adult are the three active elements in each person's makeup. The *parent* personifies the admonitions—the "do's" and "don'ts"—implanted in one's psyche in his earliest years that communicate what is true and the way things are. The *child* represents the internal subjective events of "seeing and hearing and feeling and understanding" which he has experienced since he was a small child. The *adult* is the rational, cognitive aspects of the person and serves as a data-processing computer that grinds out decisions based upon the data derived from experience. The goal of transactional analysis is to strengthen and emancipate the adult from the archaic recordings in the parent and child. If the adult part of the person is dominant, he can make better choices in coping with life situations than he can if the parent or child prevails.

Harris states that there are four life positions underlying people's behavior. They are (1) "I'm not OK—you're OK" (the anxious dependency of the immature); (2) "I'm not OK—you're not OK" (the give up or despair position); (3) "I'm OK—you're not OK" (the criminal position); and (4) "I'm OK—you're OK" (the response of the mature adult at peace with himself and others). Most persons still unconsciously operate from the "I'm not OK—you're OK" position. Transactional analysis permits one to view human behavior as reflecting predominantly either the parent, adult, or child and as expressing one of the four life positions. Effective living and good mental health calls for the adult in the person to become dominant and make most of the decisions and for the "I'm OK—you're OK" to become the prevailing life position. The advantage of using transactional analysis in seeking an understanding of self is that most of us are familiar with the personified roles of parent, adult, and child and that we have subjectively felt good or bad about ourselves and others. A disadvantage of the system is that the dynamics of personality as presented through transactional analysis are often oversimplified. In addition, the system provides only limited help for explaining the deeper causes of behavior—for example, why a person characteristically responds in the role of a child when dealing with authority figures or in the role of a parent in situations involving frustration.

Organismic-Existential Self Theories

A third perspective on the self, offered as an alternative to both Freudian psychoanalytic theory and S-R behaviorist learning theory, is the organismic-existentialist view, represented in the theories of Maslow,[8]

---

[8] Abraham H. Maslow, *Motivation and Personality*, rev. ed. (New York: Harper & Row, 1970).

Rogers,[9] and Combs.[10] All three postulate that human beings move toward a unity of selfhood (variously referred to as *self-actualization*, the *fully functioning person*, or the *adequate self*). Maslow believes that personality develops as the individual achieves adequate modes of satisfying successive levels of needs that form a hierarchy from basic physiological needs to self-actualization, the highest level of need. (See Chapter 3 for a discussion of Maslow's hierarchy of needs.)

Every individual, according to Rogers and Combs, is in continuous interaction with a changing world of experience and responds as a whole to his perceptual field. A portion of the perceptual field becomes differentiated as the self. A knowledge of the individual's perceptual field, especially his self-concept, affords the best vantage point for understanding his behavior. The individual behaves in a manner consistent with his self-concept. Perceptions inconsistent with one's self-concept may be perceived as threatening to the self and hence be denied awareness or symbolization or be given distorted symbolization. Psychological adjustment occurs when the individual can assimilate at a symbolic level all experience into a consistent relationship with his concept of self. The well-adjusted individual becomes more understanding and more accepting of others, and he tends to replace his existing, static value system with a continuing evolution of values.[11]

Processes of Self-Development and Change

In describing the characteristics of self, we noted that it is a dynamic process. We are constantly being bombarded by stimuli, new information is being fed into and processed by our perceptual, affective, and cognitive systems, and, as a result, each of us is not the same person at this moment that he was a moment, a day, or a week before. If we are to understand ourselves and others better, we need a clearer understanding of how the self develops and changes. *Self processes* refers to the organized sequence of activities or operations that contribute to the development, change, and maintenance of self. In this section we shall examine the self processes of development, motivation, perception, and language; in Chapter 9 the processes of emotion and adjustment will be described.

[9] Carl R. Rogers, *Client-Centered Therapy: Its Current Practice, Implications, and Theory* (Boston: Houghton Mifflin Co., 1951).

[10] Arthur W. Combs and Donald Snygg, *Individual Behavior*, rev. ed. (New York: Harper & Row, 1959).

[11] Rogers, *Client-Centered Therapy*.

Stages of Development

Important to an understanding of self and behavior is a conception of the processes through which the self emerges and changes. The psychoanalytic theorists, beginning with Freud, have given considerable attention to this problem. According to Freud, the self develops in specific stages.[12] The first is the *oral stage*. This stage predominates during the first year of life, when the infant gains erogenous satisfactions from sucking. In the *anal stage* of the second and third years, the child seeks gratification through anal activity and experiences anxieties growing out of taboos associated with toilet training and anal eroticism. In the *phallic stage*, the child's interest is in the sex organs and the pleasures associated with their manipulation. At this stage also, the *Oedipus* and *Electra* complexes appear as the child develops erotic feelings toward the parent of the opposite sex. The phallic stage is followed by a *latency period* in late childhood, wherein impulses tend to be repressed. Puberty ushers in the *genital stage*, during which the individual's interests are centered in other people and objects. This stage marks the emergence of heterosexual relationships and the trend toward the more mature interests and activities of approaching adulthood.

Sullivan[13] identifies six stages of personality in the period from birth to maturity. During the first stage the infant moves from a prototaxic to a parataxic mode of cognition, develops personifications in relation to a good or bad mother, begins to develop a rudimentary self system (the psychological mechanism, organized out of interpersonal experience, for coping with anxiety), differentiates between parts of his own body, and learns to coordinate eye-hand movements. Childhood witnesses the emergence of language, the need for playmates, and further integration of the self system (including the identification of one's sex role, dramatic play, anxiety-producing experiences with people, and the use of sublimation for reducing tension). During the juvenile stage, the child becomes social, learns to accept subordination to authority figures outside the family, and gains an orientation to living through interpersonal relationships that enable him to satisfy his physical, social, and psychological needs. The preadolescent stage marks the beginning of genuine relationships with other people. In the early adolescent stage, heterosexual patterns of activity develop. The late adolescent stage is a period of initiation into the satisfactions and responsibilities associated with mature social living. During successive periods of development, interpersonal relationships are formed with many different persons, language becomes increasingly important as a mode of communication, and the self system becomes stabilized as one develops more effective ways of coping with anxiety and maintaining security.

[12] Sigmund Freud, *Collected Papers*, Vol. 2 (London: Hogarth Press and the Institute of Psycho-Analysis, 1924), pp. 36–75, 244–49, 269–76.

[13] Sullivan, *The Interpersonal Theory of Psychiatry*.

Erikson's[14] theory of psychosocial development distinguishes eight stages in the life cycle of man. At each stage, according to Erikson, a particular issue or problem is most important.

1. Infancy—*trust versus mistrust (of self and environment).*

2. Early childhood—*autonomy versus shame and doubt (seeking autonomy in controlling the environment or having to subordinate one's autonomy to the will of others).*

3. Play age—*initiative versus guilt (activity, curiosity, and imagination in play may be inconsistent with adult expectations, thereby creating guilt in the child).*

4. School age—*industry versus inferiority (success or failure in school learning accompanied, respectively, by feelings of adequacy or inadequacy).*

5. Adolescence—*identity versus role diffusion (achieving or failing to achieve a sense of self-identity).*

6. Young adulthood—*intimacy versus isolation (achieving or failing to achieve close, security-giving relationships with spouse, children, or friends).*

7. Adulthood—*generativity versus stagnation (expansion of ego expressed in service of guiding the young or regression toward more self-centered activities which limit development).*

8. Maturity—*integrity versus disgust, despair (achieving in one's life and work a self-integrity or experiencing despair and disgust in failing to achieve it).*

Allport[15] identifies seven aspects of an evolving sense of self. The first aspect, beginning in infancy, is a *bodily sense of self*. Throughout life our bodily sense of self is the concrete evidence of our continuing existence as persons. Continuity of selfhood is also achieved by a growing sense of *self-identity*, beginning in the second year of life. A year or two later the child's increased control over his environment is accompanied by an increased feeling of *self-esteem* and a need for autonomy. There follows from his contacts in the community and school *an extension of self*, which includes the objects, people, institutions, ideas, beliefs, and values with which he is identified. These and the reflected appraisals of the significant people in his life form a *self-image*. The striving of the child for the mastery of physical and

[14] Erik H. Erikson, *Childhood and Society* (New York: W. W. Norton & Co., 1950).

[15] Gordon W. Allport, *Pattern and Growth of Personality* (New York: Holt, Rinehart and Winston, 1961), pp. 110–138.

intellectual skills is the hallmark of *self as a rational coper.* Like Erikson, Allport sees adolescence as a search for self-identity, but in addition, for Allport, the adolescent's pursuit of long-range goals constitutes another dimension in the growing sense of selfhood, a dimension that Allport calls *propriate striving.*

A further examination of the development of self during childhood and adolescence will be found in the discussion of developmental tasks in Chapters 10–13.

Motivation

Motivational processes are of central importance in the development of self. That part of another person's self that we can observe is expressed in his consistent patterned responses to various life situations. Motivation, as we noted in Chapter 3, is an internal energy change which arouses and directs behavior toward goals. The relationships of motivational concepts and self are shown in Figure 8–1.

Motivation begins with (1) a *stimulus,* a pattern of energy discharge from inside or outside the organism which strikes receptor organs, causing a change in energy relationships. This energy change is transmitted from receptors along sensory nerves to higher nerve and brain centers and to the rest of the body. The body condition that triggers this increased activity is experienced as (2) *need,* a disequilibrium or imbalance registered as tension in organs, muscles, neural or cortical tissue, and the organism as a whole. Forces within the organism associated with restoration of balance and maintenance of organization bring about a mobilization of energy that is generally referred to as (3) *drive.*

As the individual searches for, tests, and evaluates possible alternative ways to respond to a drive, he engages in activities which can be subsumed under the general term (4) *learning.* These activities, like all behavior cycle activities of the brain, the nervous system, and the total organism, are directed toward an appropriate (5) *goal response,* a behavior, decision, or solution which effects a restoration of balance and a reduction of tension. The goal response activates appropriate (6) *neuromuscular patterns,* which translate the goal response into (7) *behavior* to meet the situation.

Self, as the individual's unique dynamic organization of personal meanings, develops and is changed by need, drive, learning, and goal response data. Evaluations of these data as being consistent or inconsistent with one's present organization of personal meanings are expressed as *affect* (feelings and emotions). If these data are consistent with and reinforce one's present organization of personal meanings, the affect experienced is pleasant; if these data are inconsistent (that is, threaten self), the affect experienced is unpleasant. On the basis of these evaluations of incoming data, information from the highest centers of control (self) are *fed back* to maintain or modify need, drive, learning, and goal response activities. Feedback

Figure 8–1. The Human Behavior Cycle

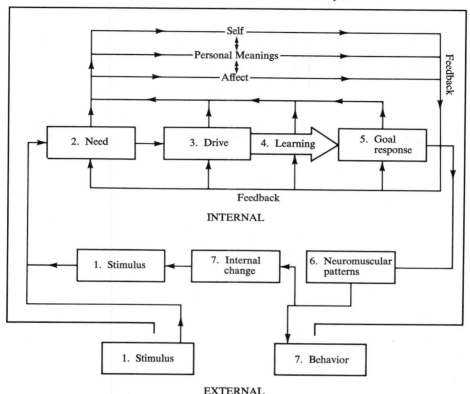

Source: Adapted from an earlier model developed by Glenn C. Dildine. Used by permission.

from self, for example, will determine the receptor thresholds for various stimuli and hence the degree and intensity of need and resulting drive generated toward a goal response which will restore balance. Similarly, feedback will maintain or modify learning activities of seeking, testing out, evaluating possible alternative goal responses, and selecting the goal response most consistent with self. We should caution the reader that any graphical representation of psychological processes whose descriptions are based largely on inference is at best an approximation of the events that take place and is an oversimplification of the dynamics involved.

The possible uses of this model can be shown in its application to a specific case:

Jim Barnes, a 16-year-old high school junior, was a star athlete who made average grades and was popular with his classmates.

Jim's father, a prominent physician, had dreams of Jim's entering medicine and joining him in a clinic he had founded. Jim had barely scraped through biology and was presently failing in chemistry and algebra—not only because he lacked aptitude in these subjects but also because he spent most of his time with athletics and in tinkering with things mechanical, especially cars and motor scooters.

The critical blow came when Jim failed his chemistry final at the end of the semester. Mr Jones, the chemistry instructor, was willing for him to go into second semester chemistry conditionally; but if Jim failed at the end of the year, he would be ineligible for football next fall. The coach, other boys, and the whole school were counting on his playing.

With the help of the high school counselor, Jim saw his alternatives as (1) being tutored in chemistry and algebra to try to pass even though his heart wasn't in the work, (2) dropping his college preparatory subjects over his father's objections and taking shop and mechanical drawing, or (3) following his father's suggestion of transferring to Brookville Prep School, where it was hoped he would be able to improve his scholastic record.

Jim's motivation is reflected in a variety of interrelated needs: his need for self-esteem and recognition as a person and a football player; his need for acceptance by others, including father, coaches, teachers, students, and friends; his need for autonomy and independence; and his need for a sense of achievement. Jim's self reflected the unique organization of personal meanings formed over a lifetime in his relationship with a strong-willed, dominating father, in satisfactions with peers in athletics and work with machines, and in school experiences which provided only a limited sense of achievement. Self not only determined the intensity of each need but also influenced the selection of the most appropriate goal response. Of the three alternatives, Jim finally realized that the substitution of shop courses for academic courses would best fit his needs. This Jim did, even though challenging his father's authority was disquieting.

Perception

Perceptual processes play a central role in the development and adjustment of the self, for it is through perception that meanings are acquired and interaction and intercommunication between organism and environment occur. The term *perception* connotes both a process and a product. It refers to the process of giving structure to stimulation; that is, of ascribing meaning to experience. It also refers to the configuration or pattern of elements produced by the stimulation-structuring process. Like his motivation and self, a person's perceptions can be identified only through inferences drawn from his behavior. We can observe our own percepts, but we cannot know those of another person except by putting ourselves in his place and inferring what he must see, hear, or feel in order to behave in the way he does.

The individual's private world.   A study of perception begins with a recognition that each individual lives in a private world of experience. Our perceptions come from us, not from the environment. This idea conflicts with the popular notion that perception is merely the organism's passive, uncritical registering of images formed by environmental stimuli. By now, there appears to be ample evidence, both experimental and empirical, to indicate that the organism is not passive but actively contributes to its own perceptions.

Perception in the objective sense consists of *transactions* between concrete individuals and concrete events.[16] No perception exists independent of a perceiver, and people and objects exist for us only insofar as we perceive them. Nonetheless, we look at people and objects around us with the assumption that they are existing in their own right; and this commonsense view is necessary if we are to communicate with others and carry on our daily activities.

The process by which the things we see, hear, or feel are experienced as outside of ourselves is called *externalization.* Much of our experience has an external orientation, therefore, even though the perceptions of these phenomena occur within the individual. The individual, as we will note, always behaves in accordance with his perceptions, not in accordance with some objective reality that may exist in the external world.

The uniqueness of one's perceptual world, though readily accepted intellectually, is frequently forgotten or ignored in day-to-day encounters. Often, we act as if others all had the same perceptions we do about an object or experience. We feel, for example, that every child wants to work hard in school, or we feel that other nations naturally want our kind of freedom and democracy. We are baffled when we learn that many children see school as a waste of time or that other peoples express disdain for a democracy whose stresses and demands for conformity produce a high incidence of mental illness.

Our perceptions vary in part, then, because of each person's own unique position in space and time and because of his own combination of experiences, needs, and values. Differences in physiological functioning and structure, however, also account for some differences in perception; physiological factors determine the thresholds at which various receptors will be stimulated. For example, while the taste of a weak solution of a chemical substance known as phenylthiocarbamide (PTC) is perceived as intensely bitter by about 70 percent of Americans, the other 30 percent perceive almost no taste at all in the solution.[17]

Culture influences to a considerable degree the meanings we attach to certain stimuli. Responses to Rorschach inkblot card 3 reveal that, typically,

---

[16] W. H. Ittelson and Hadley Cantril, *Perception: A Transactional Approach* (Garden City, N. Y.: Doubleday and Co., 1954).

[17] L. C. Dunn and T. Dobzansky, *Heredity, Race, and Society* (New York: Mentor Books, 1946), p. 8.

Europeans perceive two women quarreling, while Moroccans perceive a line of Arab riflemen facing a row of Christian soldiers.[18] Samoans, on the other hand, give a large number of "whole" responses to inkblot cards, seeing entire blots as maps or animals and seeing the white portions as objects rather than space.[19]

Perceptions are selective.   It is evident, then, that there is no standard, objective world shared by all persons. At any one moment our receptors are being bombarded with many kinds of stimuli. After first responding to the total configuration of these stimuli, we begin to separate out and respond to individual elements of the configuration, a process called *differentiation*. Different people, however, differentiate in different ways. If the same pattern is presented to a number of people, some will focus on one part of it (perceive that part as *figure*, the remaining part as *ground*), and some will focus on a different part. Perceptions, therefore, are selective. We perceive whatever is most meaningful and important to us and ignore or give less attention to the less meaningful. Sometimes, however, we may ignore (repress) some elements that are too meaningful—so meaningful that they seem painful and threatening.

The defensive aspect of selective perception is shown in a study by Postman, Bruner, and McGinnies.[20] Twenty-five college students were given the Allport-Vernon Scale of Values and then were shown 36 value words, presented singly by a tachistoscope at exposures beginning with .01 second. Exposures for each word were increased in steps of .01 second until that value word was correctly recognized. Results of this study showed that high-value words were recognized at shorter time exposures than were low-value words. A subject who scored high in the theoretical-values section of the scale recognized such words as *logical* and *analysis* in .03 second, whereas it might take him .11 second or longer to recognize a word like *reverent*, which is associated with religious values. These findings indicate that people erect barriers against percepts that do not fit or in some way threaten their values and self-concepts.

Perceptions direct behavior.   Each of us behaves in ways consistent with his own perceptions of reality, as illustrated by the following anecdote.

A few years ago Maria, a six-year-old refugee from Eastern Europe, was enrolled in an elementary school in the United States. As the class filed out to board the school bus at the end of her first

---

[18] M. Bleuer and R. Bleuer, "Rorschach's Inkblot Tests and Racial Psychology," *Character and Personality*, 4 (1953).

[19] T. H. Cook, "The Application of the Rorschach Test to a Samoan Group," *Rorschach Research Exchange*, 6 (1942), 51–60.

[20] Leo Postman, Jerome S. Bruner, and Elliott McGinnies, "Personal Values as Selective Factors in Perception," *Journal of Abnormal and Social Psychology*, 43 (1948), 142–154.

day at school, Maria suddenly screamed and frantically clutched the teacher. The teacher had difficulty in quieting Maria, but eventually learned that Maria was deathly afraid of the yellow bus. It seems that the secret police in her native country had taken her parents away in a yellow bus. Changing Maria's behavior depended upon changing Maria's perception of a yellow bus. Eventually, as she saw the same yellow bus bring her friends and classmates to school each morning, her fear subsided.

Similarly, as a member of a minority group perceives that he is accepted, trusted, and valued, he begins to act more openly and naturally rather than defensively or apprehensively. The recognition that people do behave in a manner consistent with their perceptions gives us a new insight into the nature of human development and learning—the insight that there are processes through which people can be helped to modify self-damaging perceptions of reality.[21]

Perception and the adequate personality. Recently, there has been considerable interest in identifying the qualities of self-development, personal adjustment, and mental health which characterize the adequate personality. A distinguishing characteristic of the adequate personality is the greater clarity, accuracy, and objectivity of his perceptions, in contrast to those of the less adequate person. The adequate personality views himself and others positively. He is able to assess accurately and realistically his strengths and weaknesses and to incorporate these evaluations into his self-picture. The adequate person is also objective and accurate in his perceptions of others. Maslow[22] found that adequate persons, whom he describes as self-actualizing (becoming fully what they are capable of being), were far more likely to perceive people and issues objectively instead of reading into events their own wishes, hopes, fears, anxieties, theories, and beliefs, or those of their cultural group.

The adequate personality is further described as more open to experience than the less adequate person. That is, he is able to accept into awareness a broad range of facts and sense impressions without distorting or rejecting those that are threatening.[23] The adequate person who must drop out of school temporarily, for example, perceives this not as a personal catastrophe, but as an opportunity for clarifying through work experience his vocational and personal goals.

The adequate personality is also less defensive. He accepts failure and disappointment without rationalizing and blaming others. Taylor and

---

[21] Arthur W. Combs, "Personality Theory and Its Implications for Curriculum Development," in Alexander Frazier, ed., *Learning More about Learning* (Washington, D. C.: Association for Supervision and Curriculum Development, N.E.A., 1959), pp. 5–20.

[22] Maslow, *Motivation and Personality.*

[23] Carl R. Rogers, *On Becoming a Person* (Boston: Houghton Mifflin Co., 1961), pp. 187–188.

Combs,[24] for instance, found that better-adjusted sixth grade children accepted many more derogatory and unflattering statements as true of themselves than did less well-adjusted children.

Language

The development of self is facilitated by the cognitive processes of remembering, thinking, generalizing, reasoning, imagining, and evaluating. Language is an essential tool in the development of each of these processes. Language enables one to simplify, to abstract, and to generalize from a series of events. This, in turn, enables him to form concepts. By distinguishing between different levels or qualities of performance in solving arithmetic problems, for example, one can develop a concept designating a particular quality of performance and represent that concept by the word *success*. This concept can be further generalized to connote a quality of performance (individually defined) in such dissimilar activities as playing golf, rearing children, cooking, and speaking French.

In the process of abstracting common features from a series of concrete events, the unique character of a specific event is lost. The term *success*, for example, does not convey information about the difficulty of the task or about how much effort the individual put forth in his successful performance. Abstracting these features would require the forming of additional concepts. The limitations of language for conveying precise, all-inclusive, and universal concepts result in the formation of incomplete or distorted meanings which hamper the development of self. For the slum dweller, the word *policeman* stands for a man to be feared, a man who may arrest you; for the middle class person, on the other hand, *policeman* stands for someone you can call on for help, someone who protects your property. Differences in meanings of words will result in the learning of very different behavior patterns and very different ways of viewing self and the world.

Self emerges and changes as the individual selects and responds to certain stimuli from among the many stimuli that impinge upon his receptor organs. There is considerable evidence suggesting that the selection of stimuli and the organization of behavior patterns bear a close relationship to the structure of the language and the linguistic habits that an individual employs. Bernstein[25] hypothesizes that it is through language structure, even more than content, that values, attitudes, and prejudices are learned. He found that communication in lower class families leans heavily on the language of bodily contact, gesture, facial expression, and intonation rather than on a complex verbal structure. One characteristic pattern is for the lower class parent to issue arbitrary commands to the child without

---

[24] Charles Taylor and Arthur W. Combs, "Self-Acceptance and Adjustment," *Journal of Consulting Psychology*, 16 (1952), 89–91.

[25] Basil Bernstein, "Social Class and Linguistic Development: A Theory of Social Learning," in A. H. Halsey, Jean Floud, and C. Arnold Anderson, eds. *Education, Economy, and Society* (New York: Free Press, 1961), pp. 288–314.

giving any reason or explanation. Hess and Shipman[26] cite a hypothetical example of a small child playing noisily among pots and pans on the kitchen floor when the phone rings. The lower class mother is likely to say simply and imperatively, "Shut up!" while the middle class mother is more likely to say, "Would you please keep quiet while I answer the phone?" The lower class child is asked to respond to a simple command, to make a conditioned response. The middle class child is given the reason that he should make a response (refrain from making noise) and the length of the response. In ways like this, different cultural experiences and patterns of socialization each are linked with a language structure that emphasizes the learning of quite different behavior patterns.

Aspects of the Emergent Self-Structure

Self-structure—the framework or configuration of a particular individual's complex of motives, perceptions, cognitions, feelings, and values—is the product of self-developmental processes. Self-structure is revealed in behavior. One reveals in his behavior the knowledge, skills, and interests he has acquired, the goals he is seeking, the beliefs, values, and attitudes he has adopted, the roles he has learned, and the self-concept he has formed. By interpreting and evaluating the individual's behavior in various life situations, one can describe and assess the status of this person's self-development in relation to each of the aspects of self-structure listed above. Since many of these components of the emergent self-structure, such as concepts, knowledge, skills, attitudes, and values, are described in later chapters on learning, we shall not discuss them here. An aspect of self-structure, however, which is particularly relevant to this chapter is the self-concept. We turn now to a discussion of this important dynamic.

The Self-Concept

Among the most relevant and significant perceptions that an individual acquires are his perceptions of himself in various life situations. As we noted earlier, the *self-concept* is comprised of highly differentiated perceptions, beliefs, feelings, attitudes, and values that the individual views as part or characteristic of himself. The self-concept is formed as one identifies those aspects, qualities, ideas, and things that he regards as "me" or "mine."

Basically, the self-concept is made up of a large number of *percepts*,

---

[26] Robert D. Hess and Virginia Shipman, "Early Blocks to Children's Learning," *Children*, 12 (September-October 1965), 189–194.

each of which contains one or more qualities that one ascribes to himself. For example, one may ascribe to himself such qualities as "I am tall, but I am awkward in games" or "I am pretty, but my feet are too big." Similarly, one may include in his self-concept percepts of his loving and being loved by family and friends or his membership in or identification with a culture, subculture, peer group, or other social group. As we are using these terms, *self-percept* refers to sense impressions of a quality or trait one ascribes to himself, while *self-concept* consists of the totality of one's self-percepts organized in some sort of hierarchical order.

Since each of the percepts one ascribes to himself may have a positive, negative, or neutral value, the aggregate of attributes, qualities, and abilities one ascribes to himself constitutes a hierarchy of personal values. As a hierarchy of values, the self-concept serves as a standard for *evaluating* all experience. Since the individual behaves in a manner consistent with his self-concept, the self-concept also exerts a *directing* influence on behavior. In general, we can expect a person's behavior to be determined by his most prized or cherished percept (his highest value). For example, "I am an honest person" is a valued percept in Frank Jones' self-concept. If Frank lies to the teacher to protect a friend, we must conclude that he values more highly self-percepts of "I help my buddies" or "I am not a square" than he does the self-percept "I am an honest person." Behaviors and self-percepts that are inconsistent with the image one holds of himself are threatening and thus are accompanied by emotion and adjustive behavior, topics discussed in the next chapter.

Also included in the self-concept are self-percepts that describe the person as he would like to be. Those qualities, attributes, and roles that the individual does not presently possess, but hopes to achieve, constitute his *ideal self-concept*. Knowledge of the student's ideal self-concept provides one with clues to the direction his behavior is likely to take.

Basic Qualities of the Self-Concept

We have noted that the self-concept provides one with a basic orientation toward self and the world and serves as a directing force in behavior. The basic qualities of the self-concept which influence the individual's gaining satisfaction and coping effectively with his world are (1) the degree of his self-acceptance or self-rejection and (2) the level of his self-esteem.

The central value of the organization of values which comprise the self-concept is the individual's valuation of himself. We noted in Chapter 5 that one gains *self-acceptance* through sharing love and affection with others. The feeling that one is valued and accepted by others leads one to value and to accept himself. Self-acceptance that is manifested in feelings of value and self-worth is a fundamental quality of the self-concept which exerts a pervasive influence on the individual's response to life situations. The absence of shared love relationships leads to *self-rejection*, a quality that is frequently associated with perceptual distortions, personality disorders, and less effective responses in coping with problems of living.

Self-esteem refers to the evaluation which the individual makes and customarily maintains with regard to himself. It expresses an attitude of approval or disapproval and indicates the extent to which the individual believes himself to be capable, significant, successful, and worthy. The person who can attribute at least part of the failures and deficiencies he encounters to the external world rather than to his own limitations is able to maintain a higher view of his own self-worth. High-esteem, therefore, is in itself a defense giving the individual confidence in his own judgment and abilities and hence increasing the likelihood that he will feel capable of dealing with adversity.

Coopersmith[27] found that persons with high, medium, and low self-esteem have different expectations of the future, different affective reactions, and different basic styles in adapting to environmental demands. Persons with high self-esteem approach tasks and persons with the expectation that they will be well received and successful. They have confidence in their perceptions and judgments and believe that they can bring problems to a favorable resolution. Trust in self enables persons with high self-esteem to follow their own judgment when encountering a difference of opinion, to consider novel ideas, and to express greater social independence and creativity. They tend to exhibit a lack of self-consciousness and a lack of preoccupation with personal problems. These qualities enable them to be candid in expressing their views and objective in examining all sides of an issue.

Persons who are low in self-esteem are apprehensive about expressing unpopular or unusual ideas. This lack of trust in themselves makes them self-conscious, preoccupied with inner problems, and vulnerable to the anger and slights of others. They often feel powerless to cope effectively with a situation and are more likely to blame external factors such as fate or chance for their adversities. The disinclination of the lower class Negro child with low self-esteem to assume personal responsibility for his failures may be an asset as well as a liability. On the negative side, experiences of failure may prevent the child's using negative feedback to modify his behavior in a more realistic fashion. On the positive side, this inability to assume personal responsibility may serve a defensive function in enabling the child to maintain some sense of personal integrity and self-esteem.[28] The greatest handicap of persons with low self-esteem, however, is that preoccupation with their own problems prevents them from relating to other people and issues and thus decreases the chances of their forming friendly, supportive relationships.

In the larger American culture, self-esteem appears to be unrelated to height or physical attractiveness, two widely respected attributes in

---

[27] Stanley Coopersmith, *The Antecedents of Self-Esteem* (San Francisco: W. H. Freeman Co., 1967).

[28] R. Epstein and S. S. Komorita, "Self-Esteem, Success-Failure, and Locus of Control in Negro Children," *Developmental Psychology,* 4 (January 1971), 2–8.

middle class society. Moreover, self-esteem is related only to a limited extent to social status and academic performance. Although material wealth, education, and achievement are among the major focuses and motives of American life, these, too, are not the major determinants of favorable self-appraisals. Rather, it is the person's actions and relative position in the intimate social circle of the family, community, and work that exert the greatest influence on his viewing himself as a success or a failure. For children 10 to 12 years of age, acceptance by peers and competence in school and sports appear to be the most important determinants of self-esteem.[29]

What kinds of experiences contribute to the building of self-esteem? Coopersmith reports that self-esteem is enhanced when children have (1) total or nearly total acceptance by their parents, (2) clearly defined and enforced limits, and (3) opportunities and latitude for individual action within defined limits. The enforcement of limits gives the child a sense that norms are real and are not capricious and arbitrarily imposed. Parents who have definite values (which the enforcement of limits implies), who regard their own behavior as appropriate, and who are able and willing to present and enforce their beliefs are more likely to rear children who value themselves highly.

The verbal response patterns of mothers have been found to have a significant influence on the self-esteem of their children. Miller,[30] in a study of 203 eighth grade children, found that when the responses of black inner city mothers toward their children in negative situations are evaluative, their children's self-esteem is lower than when the mothers' responses in these situations are descriptive. This finding was not recorded for peripheral city and suburban mothers, suggesting that the impatient, sometimes inappropriate responses of some inner city mothers may reflect in part the stresses of assuming multiple roles as child rearer, disciplinarian, and head of household. In this study the self-esteem of the child was not significantly affected, positively or negatively, by the mother's being evaluative in positive situations—a finding that was consistent for all sociocultural and racial groups.

Gaining Knowledge of Another's Self-Concept

The self-concept cannot be observed or measured directly but must be inferred from behavior. An approximation of the child's self-concept can be obtained by inferring how the child must see himself in order to behave as he does. Often, verbal statements will provide clues to his self-concept, but the teacher must ascertain whether what the child says about himself is consistent with other statements he has made and whether it is con-

[29] Coopersmith, *The Antecedents of Self-Esteem.*

[30] T. W. Miller, "Differential Response Patterns as They Affect the Self-Esteem of the Child," ERIC (1971), ED 046 542.

sistent with his nonverbal behavior in this and similar situations. Henry, for example, frequently says, "I'm dumb in math." If we note that he seldom does his math homework, makes poor grades on math tests, and frequently fails to bring his math book to class, we can infer that his verbal statement probably is an accurate reflection of his self-percept regarding his math ability. Sally, on the other hand, who constantly deprecates her ability by saying, "Lil ole me, I jus' don' count for much 'cause I can't do anything," may really be saying, "I want people to notice how good I really am." Nonverbal behavior, then, provides valuable clues to the person's self-concept. Mike, wearing a big smile after hitting a home run, can be presumed to see himself in terms of "I can really hit that ball" or "I can come through in the clutch" or some other appropriate self-picture.

Unverified statements of what a person says he is might better be labeled *self-reports*, since they often reflect socially desired qualities and those things the individual is ready, willing, or able to say that he is. Many of the Q-sorts, checklists, and scales used in self-concept research are really self-report instruments because they measure only what the individual is willing to admit about himself. Thus, one who seeks knowledge of another's self-concept must evaluate the subject's self-reports in relation to the inferences which the observer and others draw from a broad sampling of the subject's behavior over a considerable period.

Formation and Change in the Self-Concept

The self-concept is formed as the individual internalizes the views, feelings, and evaluations of significant others about him. Parents, teachers, and peers, therefore, strongly influence a young person's self-concept. Many of their views about and responses toward him, including the nicknames they give him, become a part of the child's view of himself—a view that often persists over a lifetime. Thus, a teenager who is looked upon and treated by parents, teachers, and peers as a bully or a good sport, as intelligent or dumb, as attractive or homely, as a nice guy or a bad egg, as cool or square, begins to see himself in the roles ascribed to him by others and to behave accordingly.

Differences in the relative influence of parents and teachers in modifying students' self-concepts may be partly due to differences in culture and race. Among white students in grades 10 and 11, parents' perceptions and evaluations of their children's academic abilities were found to be more closely related to their children's academic self-concepts than were their teachers' perceptions and evaluations of the children's academic abilities.[31]

---

[31] W. B. Brookover, E. L. Erickson, and L. M. Joiner, *Self-Concept of Ability and School Achievement*, Vol. 3 (East Lansing, Mich.: Human Learning Research Institute, 1967); J. Kleinfeld, "The Relative Importance of Teachers and Parents in the Formation of Negro and White Students' Academic Self-Concept," *Journal of Educational Research*, 65 (January 1972), 211–212.

A program of working with white parents to improve parents' perceptions of their children's self-concepts was found to increase the children's self-concepts and achievement in school.[32] For black students in grades nine and 11, however, the teacher's evaluation of the student's academic ability was more closely related to the student's academic self-concept than was the parent's evaluation of his child's academic self-concept. This difference between parents' and teachers' evaluations of children's academic abilities was significant for black females but not for black males.[33] These findings, as well as the following excerpt from the case of Jackie, suggest that teachers' positive comments can indeed increase students' favorable self-images.

> *Jackie is an active, mischievous, 11-year-old boy who frequently tries things out and tests the acceptable limits. One day, just before the bell rang, Bob said, "Hey, Mrs. A., somebody's took my money." Mrs. A. said, "Bobby, look in all your pockets and in your desk. You know we don't take things in this class."*
>
> *Bob looked all around, and several boys helped him. The money was gone. He said, "Mrs. A., you saw me put it in my glasses case." Mrs. A. replied, "Bob, somebody's playing a joke on you. Nobody in the fifth grade steals. Now, whoever is teasing Bob, give him his money. It's time for the bell." Jackie reached into his pocket and drew out 65 cents (Bob had lost 75 cents). "Here it is, Bob. I was just teasin' you."*
>
> *Bob said, "That's only sixty-five cents, Jackie. Where's the rest of it?" Jackie said, "That's all there was. If you don't believe me you can search me." Mrs. A. told Jackie to stay in a minute after school, but she let him go after discussing catfish for a moment because she was puzzled about what to do.*

The issue in this anecdote is not the particular technique used by the teacher in handling the perplexing problem of items reported missing in the classroom. Our interest is rather in the kind and quality of the teacher's response, which showed a deep respect for these children as persons. A different response from Mrs. A. might well have caused these children to see themselves as bad, dishonest, untrustworthy, and thieving. The response Mrs. A. did make in this situation permitted each child to ascribe more positive characteristics to himself and his classmates.

---

[32] W. B. Brookover et al., *Self-Concept of Ability and School Achievement*, Vol. 2 (East Lansing, Mich.: Educational Publishing Services, 1965).

[33] Kleinfeld, pp. 211–212.

Physical Processes and the Self-Concept

Because self-awareness is first manifested in a bodily sense of self, we might hypothesize that physical processes are an important influence in shaping the self-concept. Several studies have found significant relationships between timing of physical maturation, physical disabilities, and body physique and the self-concept. Mussen and Jones[34] found that early-maturing boys, in contrast to their late-maturing peers, saw themselves as mature, independent, and capable of playing an adult role. Early-maturing girls also reported more favorable self-concepts, but the differences in personality for early- and late-maturing girls were generally not as marked as those for boys.[35] As noted in Chapter 4, the late-maturing underdeveloped adolescent boy in our culture is particularly vulnerable to lowered self-esteem as he compares himself against male contemporaries with more masculine qualities and physiques. The late-maturing boy's smaller size and lack of masculine qualities make it difficult for his peers to take him seriously when he strives to compete with more mature boys in sports and in gaining the favorable attention of girls. Delayed physical and sexual maturation may also be accompanied by lowered self-esteem in the adolescent girl. Bodily narcissism pervades our culture. To have achieved menarche, to have breasts of a suitable size, and to have the preferred hip shape and size are the confirmation a girl seeks of knowing she is a woman.[36]

In a study of sex differences and body perception, Fisher[37] found that the female has a more definite and stable concept of her body than does the male. The woman perceives her body as related to the fulfillment of her principal life goals, whereas the man is less likely to associate his body attributes with requirements for achievement and success. Consistent with this is the further finding that women reveal stronger feelings of both satisfaction and dissatisfaction with their bodies.[38]

Those who compete in various intercollegiate sports also differ in the ways they perceive and accept their bodies and accept themselves. Darden,[39]

---

[34] Paul H. Mussen and Mary C. Jones, "Self-Conceptions, Motivations, and Interpersonal Attitudes of Late- and Early-Maturing Boys," *Child Development*, 28 (June 1957), 243–256.

[35] Mary C. Jones and Paul H. Mussen, "Self-Conceptions, Motivations, and Interpersonal Attitudes of Early- and Late-Maturing Girls," *Child Development*, 29 (December 1958), 491–501.

[36] Paul L. Adams, "Late Sexual Maturation in Girls," *Medical Aspects of Human Sexuality*, 6 (March 1972), 68, 73.

[37] Seymour Fisher, "Sex Differences in Body Perception," *Psychological Monographs*, 78 (1944), 14.

[38] Paul Secord and Sidney Jourard, "The Appraisal of Body-Cathexis: Body-Cathexis and the Self," *Journal of Consulting Psychology*, 17 (1953), 343–347.

[39] E. Darden, "A Comparison of Body Image and Self-Concept Variables among Various Sport Groups," *Research Quarterly*, 43 (May 1972), 7–15.

in a study of male athletes at a state university, found that basketball players and weight lifters have the most positive feelings regarding body and self, but they also expressed the most dissatisfaction with their body physique, strength, and skills. Baseball players and gymnasts, on the other hand, had the least positive feelings about body and self but were the most satisfied with their body image and development. The great success of that school's basketball team that year and the infrequent success of their gymnastic team in intercollegiate competition suggest that positive feelings about body and self plus body image dissatisfaction are motivational factors associated with winning in sports. At the other end of the continuum of physical performance, physically handicapped children not only see themselves as less adequate physically but also have fewer friends and are less well adjusted in comparison with a matched group of nonhandicapped children.[40]

Socialization Processes and the Self-Concept

The self-concept is strongly influenced by one's experiences and socialization as well as by the strength of one's identification with and feelings about his culture. A great deal has been written about the deleterious effects that poverty, discrimination, and lack of opportunity have on the self-images of disadvantaged members of minority groups. Some inner city black children, for example, are victims of a "self-fulfilling prophecy" because they perform in accordance with a self-image given them by their teachers that they cannot learn.[41] The Negro male is particularly vulnerable to developing a negative self-concept and low self-esteem. The high incidence of unemployment among Negro males and the resultant inability of the Negro father to support his family cause him to see himself as rejected and inferior. Damage to self-esteem appears to be less severe for Negro girls, since they surpass Negro boys in school achievement and they reveal a greater responsibility in child rearing and a greater capacity for keeping a job.[42]

While poverty and discrimination appear to reinforce negative self-concepts and lowered self-esteem of some individuals in the ghetto, studies which have compared the self-concepts of disadvantaged versus advantaged and black versus white students show that the self-concepts of the disadvantaged and blacks are not significantly different from those of ad-

---

[40] Winifred T. Kinn, "Self-Reports of Physically Handicapped and Nonhandicapped Children" (unpublished doctor's dissertation, University of Maryland, 1962).

[41] Kenneth B. Clark, *Dark Ghetto: Dilemmas of Social Power* (New York: Harper & Row, 1965).

[42] Jean D. Grambs, "The Self-Concept: Basis for Reeducation of Negro Youth," in William C. Kvaraceus, ed., *Negro Self-Concept: Implications for School and Citizenship* (New York: McGraw-Hill Book Co., 1965), pp. 11–51.

vantaged and whites, respectively.[43] A similar lack of significant differences in self-concepts emerged also in comparisons between Spanish-American and Anglo children in Nebraska and California.[44] Coleman,[45] for example, found that Negro and white ninth and twelfth grade students gave similar responses to such items as "How bright do you think you are in comparison with other students in your grade?" "I sometimes feel I just can't learn" and "I would do better in schoolwork if teachers didn't go so fast." Black children also appear to be increasingly valuing physical characteristics associated with their race. In an early study[46] black children showed a preference for white dolls over brown dolls. More recently, a majority of black children aged seven and eight indicated a preference for a black puppet over a white puppet. Black children who chose the black puppet more often had significantly more positive self-concepts than black children who chose the black puppet less often.[47] Soares and Soares[48] found that disadvantaged children of all ages in their sample registered higher self-concepts than did advantaged children. The same study showed, however, that both black and white students in elementary school had more positive self-concepts than did students of both races in high school. This finding suggests that the change from the neighborhood elementary school to the integrated high school, with its greater size, increased depersonalization, and less security for students, may contribute to the lowering of self-concepts for both blacks and whites in high school.

A variety of reasons may account for the lack of significant differences between the self-concepts of disadvantaged and those of advantaged youth. First, for some disadvantaged youth, positive self-concepts and expectations of high grades may be a response to inconsistent patterns of past achievement.[49] Second, the self-concept is formed from the individual's perception of the appraisals of significant others, and we have no reason to believe that ghetto children are any less loved and valued by their families than are middle class children. Third, the low scholastic achievement of a disadvantaged child is not the threat to his self-esteem that it is to the

---

[43] L. Douglas, " 'Negro' Self-Concept: Myth or Reality?" *Integrated Education,* 9 (November–December 1971), 27–29; see also notes 44, 45, 48, and 49.

[44] A. M. Valenzuela, "The Relationship between Self-Concept, Intelligence, Socioeconomic Status, and School Achievement among Spanish-American Children in Omaha," ERIC (1971), ED 056 785; T. P. Carter, "The Negative Self-Concept of Mexican-American Students," *School and Society,* 96 (March 30, 1968), 217–219.

[45] James S. Coleman, *Equality of Educational Opportunity* (Washington, D. C.: U. S. Government Printing Office, 1966), OE 3800, pp. 218–230.

[46] Kenneth B. Clark and Mamie P. Clark, "Racial Identification and Preference in Negro Children," in T. Newcomb and E. Hartley, eds., *Readings in Social Psychology* (New York: Holt, Rinehart and Winston, 1947), pp. 169–178.

[47] Susan Harris and J. P. Brown, "Self-Esteem and Racial Preference in Black Children," ERIC (1971), ED 056 773.

[48] L. M. Soares and A. T. Soares, "Self-Concepts of Disadvantaged and Advantaged Students, ERIC (1970), ED 042 871.

[49] A. T. Soares and L. M. Soares, "Expectancy, Achievement, and Self-Concept Correlated in Disadvantaged and Advantaged Youth," ERIC (1971), ED 056 134.

middle class child, whose family places a high value on scholastic success. Indeed, the feeling of belongingness derived from membership in a gang, physical toughness and daring, and skills in sports contribute far more to the self-esteem of most ghetto youth than does scholastic success. Life in the ghetto has been described as a fight for survival. The skills and ingenuity needed for surviving are themselves important sources of self-esteem for the ghetto child.

Developmental Changes in the Self-Concept

Numerous studies have described changes in the self-concept at successive maturity levels. Ames[50] notes that during the first two years, the child is primarily egocentric; his sense of self is expressed through obtaining and hoarding objects. By age two and a half, the child's sense of self is strengthened in interpersonal relationships, first with the nursery school teacher and later with peers, but the focus is still on the acquisition and protection of objects. By age four, the child's excessive boasting about himself, relatives, and possessions suggests that he is not completely sure of himself and that his sense of self may need strengthening.

In elementary school, the child is striving for a position in his peer group, but he still sees himself as highly dependent upon his parents, particularly for affectional relationships. There is now some growing sense of responsibility and a need to conform to social expectations. At age 10, some interest in the opposite sex is expressed, but few heterosexual relationships are formed.[51]

Other studies[52] have found that fourth and sixth grade girls report greater congruence between self-concept and ideal self-concept and more positive self-images than do boys in these grades. Perkins found, however, that during a six-month period in school the self-concepts and ideal self-concepts of both sexes became increasingly congruent. Bledsoe found that self-concept correlated positively with intelligence and achievement for boys but not for girls. This finding suggests that boys perceive traits measured by intelligence and achievement tests as more important to their self-esteem than do girls.

Adolescence is marked by an increased stability of the self-concept. In a study by Engel,[53] students reporting positive self-concepts in the tenth

---

[50] Louise Bates Ames, "The Sense of Self of Nursery School Children as Manifested by Their Verbal Behavior," *Journal of Genetic Psychology*, 81 (1952), 193–232.

[51] Marjorie B. Creelman, "The C S C Test: Self-Conceptions of Elementary School Children" (unpublished doctor's dissertation, Western Reserve University, 1954).

[52] Hugh V. Perkins, "Factors Influencing Change in Children's Self-Concepts," *Child Development*, 29 (June 1958), 221–230; J. C. Bledsoe, "Self-Concepts of Children and Their Intelligence, Achievement, Interests, and Anxiety," *Childhood Education*, 43 (March 1967), 436, 438.

[53] Mary Engel, "The Stability of the Self-Concept in Adolescence," *Journal of Abnormal and Social Psychology*, 58 (1959), 211–215.

grade viewed themselves even more positively when they were retested in the twelfth grade.

Self-Concept and Learning

Learning that effects a positive change in one's self-concept is, perhaps, the most significant learning any of us acquires. For instance, it is not the ability to recognize word symbols as such but the self-percept "I can read" that is most crucial in influencing a pupil's behavior in subsequent reading situations. As one might expect, academic success has a stronger influence on schoolchildren's seeing themselves as students than does failure or mediocre academic performance. Among high-achieving students, both blacks and whites are equally as likely to see themselves as students, but at lower levels of achievement, whites identify themselves as students more frequently than do blacks.[54]

The teacher bears a major responsibility for helping students develop positive self-concepts. Staines[55] found that children in a classroom where the teacher helps pupils to clarify their self-concepts and to accept themselves as they are report significantly more positive self-pictures than children taught by a teacher who emphasizes correct answers and the passing of examinations. Children with more favorable self-images see their teachers as expressing positive feelings toward them. The more positive are the children's perceptions of their teacher's feelings toward them, the better is their academic achievement and the more desirable is their classroom behavior as rated by the teachers.[56]

Several studies have found positive relationships between self-concept and measures of school achievement. In a study of ninth grade students, Fink[57] found that underachieving girls feel alienated socially, see themselves as victims of circumstances, and are unable either to accept or to perceive the goals and values of others. Underachieving boys appear to be even more inadequate and immature; they seldom achieve their goals and they complain of powerlessness to improve or to change a situation.

Does one's concept of his general ability or his concepts of his specific abilities exert the greater influence on his academic achievement? Brandt[58] asked sixth and eleventh grade students to estimate how well they

---

[54] E. Murray and B. Wellman, "Success and Self-Conception: The Impact of Grades on the Student Role Identities of Black and White Adolescents," ERIC (1971), ED 055 140.

[55] J. W. Staines, "The Self-Picture as a Factor in the Classroom," *British Journal of Educational Psychology*, 28 (1958), 97–111.

[56] Helen H. Davidson and Gerhard Lang, "Children's Perceptions of Their Teachers' Feelings toward Them, Related to Self-Perception, School Achievement, and Behavior," *Journal of Experimental Education*, 29 (1960), 107–118.

[57] Martin B. Fink, "Objectification of Data Used in the Underachievement Self-Concept Study," *California Journal of Educational Research*, 13 (May 1962), 105–112.

[58] Richard M. Brandt, "The Accuracy of Self Estimate: A Measure of Self-Concept Reality," *Genetic Psychology Monographs*, 58 (1958), 55–99.

expected to do, compared to each of their classmates, on each of several academic and physical tasks. The students were then asked to perform these tasks and their estimates were compared with their actual perform-ances. In general, each student's accuracy of self-estimate showed little variation for the different tasks. Brandt therefore concluded that perform-ance is influenced more by one's generalized view of his abilities than by his percepts of his specific abilities. Brookover, Thomas, and Paterson[59] found among seventh grade students, however, that the specific self-concept relative to a given ability is significantly more accurate than the generalized self-concept of ability in predicting the grade point average of boys in mathematics, social studies, and science. This finding did not hold for girls, except in social studies.

Looking beyond the research evidence, it seems that the self-concept influences a child's learning in at least two ways. First, in order for a child to learn successfully, he must see himself as a learner, as being able to learn. Second, one's self-structure—his organization of personal meanings—determines what ideas and facts are relevant for him and hence influences what he will learn. In elaborating the first point, it can be said that one's perception of himself as a learner is probably far more important in in-fluencing his learning performance than is his intelligence, aptitude, or the level of difficulty of the learning material. For many children, early criti-cisms of their school performance and low grades do much in shaping self-concepts that reflect inadequacy and defeat. They say of themselves, "I never was any good in arithmetic" or "I hate reading." If any of these students is told that he performed well on an intelligence or aptitude test, he may well respond, "There must be some mistake, I never do well on those kinds of tests."

This influence of the self-concept on learning is revealed in an experi-ence reported by Lecky[60] in which he found that a group of children always made about the same number of spelling mistakes per page of writing, re-gardless of the difficulty of the material. Since all would be expected to make more errors when given the harder material, the finding that on suc-cessive tests each made approximately the same number of errors irrespec-tive of difficulty suggested that each child performed as if he were expected to make a certain number of errors (corresponding to his usual perform-ance) no matter how easy or hard the task was. Lecky wondered whether their test behavior in spelling reflected their perceptions of themselves as spellers and not their actual skill level in spelling. This proved to be the case, for after discussions with a counselor in which feelings about them-selves were explored, these children registered a marked increase in their spelling performance even though they had no further work in spelling.

If one is more likely to learn those concepts and skills that are most relevant to his organization of personal meanings, as our second point sug-

---

[59] Wilbur B. Brookover, Shailer Thomas, and Ann Paterson, "Self-Concept of Ability and School Achievement," *Sociology of Education*, 37 (Spring 1964), 271–278.

[60] Prescott Lecky, *Self-Consistency* (New York: Island Press, 1945).

gests, this means that how one views himself determines to a considerable extent whether he will learn, what he will learn, and how well he will learn it. Reminding students that Chaucer, quadratic equations, or the history of Greece and Rome are part of our cultural heritage and therefore are important things to be learned may not be enough. These experiences, and others in the school curriculum, should be planned and organized so that each student can gain some personal meaning in studying them. Thus, a further knowledge of Greek drama may be enhancing to one student, a study of Greek or Roman architecture to another, and Greek mythology to another; and perhaps a study of the origin and history of the Olympic Games will be enhancing to a star athlete.

The influence of the pupil's self-concept on his learning performance is revealed in these excerpts from the case of Becky:

> *Becky is older than any of the other girls in a combination fourth and fifth grade class and is one of the larger girls physically. Becky lives in an apartment with mother, sister, and stepfather. The family is Jewish. After kindergarten, Becky spent one semester in a nonreading group. She was retained in the second grade, and during these two years Becky changed schools twice because of moves by the family. After she had finished the third grade, she was sent to summer school for strengthening, but she was under the impression that she was making up a grade. It was nearly the end of the next semester before she and her family understood her placement. The following June she wanted to go to summer school again. When the teacher explained that she could not send her to a new grade in summer school, Becky lost interest and did not ask any more.*

> *September 17.   The class was organized into three reading groups today. Becky was put into the middle group. When the books were given out, the children spent time looking at them and getting acquainted with them. Becky came up to me and said, "This is a fifth grade book, isn't it?" I replied, "Yes it is, Becky. Doesn't it look interesting? All the stories have been selected to appeal to fifth grade boys and girls." She relaxed as I talked and said, "I didn't want any fourth grade book." She returned to her seat smiling and hugging the book.*

> *September 20.   On the basis of the previous week's work, the class was divided into two spelling groups, one an independent spelling group and the other a supervised study group. Becky was put into the latter. As I worked with the group, Becky was sulking. She kept her head down and doodled on her notebook. When I explained that in this group we would learn how to study and to use new words so that we could attack them independently, she sat up quickly and said, "If anyone in this group gets perfect on Friday, can they be put in the other group?" I suggested that it might be wise to work in the group for a steady period to get the full benefit. Getting perfect*

*would mean real progress, but other things would have to be con-
sidered. She dropped her head and returned to her doodling.*

*April 28.   We had a very comprehensive test on possessives
last Friday. This is a new experience for these children, and they reviewed like mad to get ready for it. At the children's request I
marked the papers in percentages, as in junior high school. Becky
made 88 percent, fifth highest in the class. I read the top five names
and marks before returning the papers. Becky fairly beamed. She is
so proud of her success. The highest mark was 92 percent.*

Some of Becky's strongly motivated goals and characteristic adjustment patterns are clearly revealed in these few descriptions of her classroom behavior. She seems to be saying, "I am a fifth grader," "I want to
make up the grade I had to repeat," "I want to be a good student." Being
reassured that she has a fifth grade book and receiving one of the highest
test grades in the room resulted in personal meanings consistent with and
enhancing of her self-concept. Her behavior reveals a desire for further
learning and achievement, but incidents inconsistent with her self-concept
result in apathy, loss of motivation, and little progress in the skills and
subjects involved in the incident.

Summary

An understanding of human behavior depends not only upon a knowledge of physical and environmental forces but also upon an understanding
of the self, the unique way each person perceives, interprets, and organizes
experience. *Self* is defined as a person's unique dynamic organization of the
personal meanings arising from his experience.

Self is an emergent process and is unique and personal. It is a process in which change takes place while, at the same time, organization is
maintained. Much, though not all, of one's knowledge of the activities of
the self consists of the inferences one makes about another person's
organization of personal meanings. The development of self is facilitated
by warm, supportive human relationships with the significant others in
one's life.

A brief examination of representative self theories further reveals the
abstract and complex nature of the self and makes it evident that self can
be viewed from many different vantage points. Freudian theory, which
emphasizes the ego's control and redirection of id impulses toward gratifications appropriate to the environment or situation, contrasts with the
ideas of social-self theorists such as Sullivan, the transactional analysis of
Berne and Harris, and organismic-existentialist theorists such as Maslow,
Rogers, and Combs.

The various theories of self-development emphasize the importance of warm interpersonal relationships, the extension of self as the child moves into the broader world, the search for a new sense of self-identity in adolescence, and the seeking of fulfillment in adulthood. The role of motivation in the development of self is shown in the steps of the human behavior cycle. An energy change producing a *stimulus* creates a *need* which activates *drive*. Drive leads to *goal responses* directed toward reducing the drive and satisfying the need.

Perception plays a central role in the development and adjustment of self, for it is through perception that meanings are acquired and interaction between organism and environment occurs. Since each individual lives in a private world of experience, perceptions arise from within the individual and are selective. The *self-concept* emerges as the individual identifies those aspects of his perceptual field that he perceives to be part or characteristic of himself. Selectivity of perception may operate in the defense of self. Adequate personalities, however, are those whose perceptions are more accurate, objective, and realistic and who are more accepting of self and others. Language is the symbolization of meanings, and is thus a fundamental process through which self develops. Language makes possible the development of the processes of reasoning, thinking, and imagining.

From the interaction of self-processes there emerges a *self-structure* —the configuration of a specific individual's complex of motives, perceptions, cognitions, feelings, and values at any given time. The self-structure is revealed in behavior and includes a person's knowledge, skills, interests, goals, beliefs, values, attitudes, and roles.

The *self-concept* is the highest integrative level of the self-structure and is defined as those most highly differentiated perceptions, beliefs, feelings, attitudes, and values which the individual views as part or characteristic of himself. Behavior tends to be consistent with the self-concept and reflects the individual's effort to maintain and enhance the self-concept. The student's self-concept appears to be the most important single factor influencing learning performance—more important than intelligence, aptitude, or difficulty of the material to be learned. Since the self-concept is such a major factor influencing development and learning, the school must assume a prominent role in helping children and youth to develop more adequate self-concepts.

Study Questions

1. Put yourself inside the skin of the student you are studying or of someone else you know well. In the first person singular, write a paragraph describing the self-concept of this person. How would you check the validity of the statements you have made?

2. Try to recall your self-picture at ages five, 10, and 15 and contrast these with your present self-image. In what ways has your self-

concept changed? Is your present self-concept similar or dissimilar to your ideal self-concept of a few years ago? In what ways?

3.   Bill Rodgers has been a top student for as long as his teachers and classmates can remember. Yet, prior to every important test, Bill becomes anxious and says he is afraid he will not do well on the exam. He is tense until his test is returned. Upon seeing the high grade on his paper, he exclaims, "Whew, I sure was lucky!" How would you account for the seeming inconsistency between Bill's self-concept and his success on examinations? How might Bill's teachers, parents, and friends help him to modify his concept of his abilities?

4.   You have written a full objective case record on Esther, one of your sixth grade students. In writing this record, you learn that at age three Esther's mother and father were divorced and that Esther has not seen her father since. You recall that last year Esther frequently grabbed the hand of the young unmarried man who was her teacher, asked him to sit beside her at lunch, and demanded much of his attention. Flattered by Esther's interest in him, the teacher did little to discourage this relationship. Esther acts with self-assurance and seems to be very competitive in her interactions with boys.

In analyzing your case record of Esther, you might seek to explain Esther's behavior in terms of Freud's psychoanalytic theory, which tends to explain a person's behavior in terms of past experiences and interactions of inner and outer forces. Or you might choose to analyze Esther's behavior in terms of the perceptual-existentialist self theories of Maslow, Rogers, and Combs, which emphasize the importance of the person's perceptions, self-concept, and need for self-actualization. What are the advantages and disadvantages of each approach in understanding behavior? Which would prove more helpful in your understanding of Esther? Why?

Suggested Readings

Combs, Arthur W. *Perceiving, Behaving, Becoming.* Washington, D. C.: Association for Supervision and Curriculum Development, N.E.A., 1962. The contributions of four phenomenological-existentialist self theorists, Earl Kelley, Carl Rogers, A. H. Maslow, and Arthur Combs, are presented and the implications of their ideas for teaching and learning are explored. The characteristics of the adequate person and the process of becoming are given special emphasis.

Hall, Calvin S., and Gardner Lindzey. *Theories of Personality.* Second Edition. New York: John Wiley, 1970. Presents a brief survey and discussion of major psychological personality theories and developments from Freud to existentialism. The last chapter contrasts and synthesizes major ideas from the several theories.

Hamachek, Don E., ed. *The Self in Growth, Teaching, and Learning.* Englewood Cliffs, N. J.: Prentice-Hall, 1965. A collection of readings contributed by contemporary self theorists and researchers. The papers are grouped in relation to self theory, perceptual processes, formation and development of self, growth processes, teaching, learning, and self-understanding. Particular emphasis is placed upon phenomenological self theory, and a broad range of studies investigating various correlates of the self-concept is reported.

Harris, Thomas A. *I'm OK—You're OK: A Practical Guide to Transactional Analysis.* New York: Harper & Row, 1967. Describes a method of studying personality called transactional analysis in which one can analyze his own and others' behavior as reflecting predominantly either the parent, adult, or child and expressing one of four life positions centering in variations of my being OK or not OK and your being OK or not OK.

LaBenne, Wallace D., and Bert I. Greene. *Educational Implications of Self-Concept Theory.* Pacific Palisades, Calif.: Goodyear Publishing Co., 1969. Describes the nature of the self-concept, its historical roots, and its development. Discusses how teachers can use knowledge of students' self-concepts to improve the testing, grouping, promotional practices, grading practices, and classroom discipline of pupils.

Films

Action Self and the Idealized Self, 16 mm, sound, black and white, 29 min. Minneapolis: Audiovisual Educational Services, Westbrook Hall, University of Minnesota. Describes the development of the action self from the standpoint of the various proprioceptive and kinesthetic activities. Emphasizes self from an environmental point of view.

Eye of the Beholder, 16 mm, sound, black and white, 25 min. Bloomington: Audiovisual Center, Indiana University. Shows that no two people see the same thing or situation in the same way. Demonstrates this concept by showing how, through a progression of events, a number of people come to view an artist, Michael Gerard, in quite different ways. The episode culminates with a beautiful girl lying on the studio couch with a red-stained knife at her side. Film shows how people react differently to the artist in terms of how they have been conditioned to view his actions.

Focus on Behavior, 1. *The Conscience of a Child,* 16 mm, sound, black and white, 29 min. Bloomington: Audiovisual Center, Indiana University. In the laboratory, Dr. Robert Sears shows some of the ways in which psychologists study the growth and development of personality and emotional behavior in children. Focuses on the interaction between parental behavior and attitudes and the emotional development of children.

The Self: Emotion and Adjustment

> *Emotions, then, are among the most basic, deeply rooted, and biologically useful forms of behavior. They are the modes of physiological integration through which we meet relatively critical situations.*

Daniel A. Prescott

As the individual develops and changes, he also seeks to achieve and to maintain a stable self. Stability of self is manifested in a consistency in one's behavior in response to similar stimuli or situations, in a stability through time of one's self-concept, interests, goals, attitudes, and values, and in a tendency to perceive and to distort events in ways consistent with one's self-concept and views of the world.

Although the process of achieving and maintaining a stable self (self-adjustment) is discussed in a separate chapter, self-adjustment and self-development are in reality complementary processes. Since self-development involves the organizing and reorganizing of personal meanings, a stable self is both a prerequisite to and an outcome of increased self-development. As we noted in the preceding chapter, a student must see himself as able to read if he is to progress in reading. Increased reading achievement, in turn, reinforces and increases the stability of the self-percept "I can read."

One's evaluation of the personal meaning of an event or experience is manifested in feelings and emotions. The psychological term *affect* will be used to refer to feeling states aroused by internal and external events. In perceiving and responding to events and situations, the individual evaluates each in terms of its relevance to or its consistency or inconsistency with his view of himself and the world. Events that have little relevance for self arouse little feeling. Events that are consistent with one's self-concept and view of the world evoke pleasant affect (relaxed musculature, minimum tension, and so on). Events that are inconsistent with one's perceptions of self and the world evoke unpleasant affect (discomfort, tension, fear, or anxiety). In this chapter the term *affect* will be used interchangeably with the term *emotion*. Although emotion is a more familiar term, its several meanings makes it less precise for describing the kinds of feeling responses people reveal in evaluating the meaning of events for the maintenance and enhancement of their self-concept and views of the world.

Events that are inconsistent with one's view of self and the world threaten the maintenance of a stable self. Threat to self, however, not only produces tension and anxiety but also prompts the individual to seek to resolve the conflict between self and the world, and so to reduce the threat. *Adjustive behavior* is behavior whose purpose is to reduce threat. Reducing threat, in turn, facilitates the maintenance of a stable self. Emotion and adjustive behavior together constitute the *self-adjustive processes*, which operate to restore and to maintain self-stability and self-consistency. In this chapter, we shall examine these interrelated processes, emotion and adjustment, in greater detail.

Physiology and Affective Experience

Physiological Basis of Emotion

Emotion or *affect* can be defined as the physiological changes which occur in response to the psychological meaning of an event or situation. These physiological changes are initiated by the autonomic nervous system. Under conditions of threat, the thoracolumbar (sympathetic) segment of the autonomic nervous system stimulates marked physiological changes in receptors, blood, muscles, and viscera. These changes include an increase in respiration rate, an increase in pulse rate, a rise in blood pressure, the secretion of adrenalin and release of additional sugar into the bloodstream, the release of additional red blood cells into circulation by contraction of the spleen, and an increase in the tension of striped muscles. Other physiological changes occurring at the same time include the dilation of pupils, an increase in perspiration, and a decrease in gastrointestinal activity. These internal changes are reflected in such external reactions as a flushed face, a tense body, and a trembling hand.

The physiological changes associated with heightened affect follow the principle of homeostasis introduced in Chapter 4. The temporary imbalances produced by these physiological changes serve to prepare the organism for actions directed toward restoring and maintaining stability of organism and self. They prepare the organism for "fight or flight,"[1] for the mobilization of body energy resources required to meet the perceived threat. Although this energy mobilization facilitates the organism's making a maximum response in situations which endanger physical life, there is often less opportunity for expending this mobilized energy in vigorous physical movements when psychological threats such as loss of self-esteem or loss of security are involved. The constraints the situation may place upon active responses of skeletal muscles are experienced as tension. As

---

[1] Walter B. Cannon, *Bodily Changes in Pain, Hunger, Fear, and Rage* (New York: Appleton-Century-Crofts, 1929).

noted earlier, the individual seeks to reduce tension by various modes of adjustment.

Affect can be experienced at any one of four levels of intensity: (1) feeling, (2) mild emotion, (3) strong emotion, and (4) disintegrative emotion.[2] The intensity of affect depends upon the degree of threat involved. Feeling and mild emotion, in general, create a state of motivation which facilitates learning and the optimum functioning of the organism. Strong emotion is manifested in the marked physiological changes described above and the mobilization of energy to meet the threat. Disintegrative emotion is manifested in hysteria, shock, and loss of control of body functions—responses evoked in crises involving great danger or destruction, such as fire, flood, vehicle collision, or war.

Affect may be either pleasant or unpleasant, but in both cases the physiological changes produced are similar. The changes associated with pleasant emotion, however, are usually of shorter duration, since pleasant events (which are perceived as need fulfilling and consistent with self-concept) are followed by tension reduction and the restoration of physiological and psychological stability. Since the present chapter focuses upon emotions and adjustive behavior evoked in response to threat, the discussion which follows will examine various manifestations of unpleasant affect and the events and situations that arouse them.

Disabling Effects of Stress

The debilitating and disabling effects on the organism of strong, unpleasant emotion continued over long periods are well known to clinicians and to those who have studied the effects on animal behavior of experimentally created neuroses. While the gap between animal and human behavior is very wide, the bodily changes occurring in animals and humans under stress are similar. Experiments with animals in stressful situations have, therefore, increased our understanding of the effects of stress on human behavior and adjustment.

Masserman[3] describes the behavior of cats who were subjected repeatedly to a physically harmless but "psychically traumatic" stimulus consisting of a mild air blast across the snout or a pulsating shock through the paw. Eventually, the cats developed aberrant responses very much like those manifested in human neuroses. They became "irrationally" fearful of harmless lights, sounds, closed spaces, air currents, and vibrations. In addition to manifesting the physiological changes characteristic of strong emotion, these animals developed gastrointestinal disorders, recurrent

[2] Daniel A. Prescott, *Emotion and the Educative Process* (Washington, D. C.: American Council on Education, 1938), pp. 10–48.

[3] Jules H. Masserman, "Experimental Neuroses," *Scientific American*, 182 (March 1950), 38–43.

asthma, persistent salivation, and sexual impotence. The epileptic-type seizures and muscular rigidities of some of the animals resembled the hysteria and catatonia of humans. These physiological and behavioral responses tended to decrease only after the animals were given a three to 12 months' rest in a favorable environment and were exposed to other types of "therapeutic" treatment.

Other experiments with animals have produced evidence relating emotional stress to increased secretion of stomach acid and the appearance of ulcers. Many people believe that the hard-driving "executive type" person is particularly susceptible to ulcers because of the stress of decision making and the other pressures of his job. Brady,[4] in a series of experiments with monkeys, sought to ascertain whether emotional stress of the type that executives experience does, indeed, produce ulcers. In these experiments, two monkeys, yoked together in restraining chairs, received periodic electric shocks. One monkey, the "executive" monkey, could prevent shocks to himself and his partner by pressing a lever 15 to 20 times a minute. It was found that long strenuous periods when the animal was in danger of being shocked did not produce ulcers. Rather, it was a schedule of six hours of shock (which could be prevented by continuously pressing the lever) followed by six hours of no shock (shock apparatus turned off) that produced ulcers in the executive monkey. The significant increase in stomach acidity began when the shocking apparatus was turned off, and it increased to a peak several hours later, when the animal presumably was resting. Thus, sustained periods of great stress are not as likely to produce ulcers as an alternation of periods of imminent threat and periods of potential threat, in which the individual remains tense in anticipation of possible danger.

In another study of the physiological effects of stress, Selye[5] identified distinct physiological changes (which he calls "alarm reactions") that occur when the body is exposed to tissue injury or psychological threat. In studies of animals subjected to stress, he found three characteristic alarm reactions: (1) enlargement of the adrenal cortex, (2) shrinking of the thymus, spleen, and all lymphatic structures, and (3) formation of deep ulcers in the lining of the stomach and duodenum. But these alarm reactions are only the first stage of the body's struggle against stress. If stress continues, a second stage, called the "stage of resistance," follows. In this stage, body organs and functions should return to normal as the body adapts to the stressful situation. If the body's responses fail to effect an adaptation to stress in the second stage, a third stage, called the "stage of exhaustion," begins. Here, a repetition of the initial alarm reactions signals a critical weakening of body defenses which, if not arrested, foreshadows collapse and eventual death. Selye calls this three-phase struggle of the body against stress the *general adaptation syndrome* (GAS).

[4] Joseph V. Brady, "Ulcers in Executive Monkeys," *Scientific American*, 199 (October 1958), 3–6.

[5] Hans Selye, *The Stress of Life* (New York: McGraw-Hill Book Co., 1956).

The studies of Masserman, Brady, and Selye show that emotion serves as an efficient alarm system warning the organism of actual or impending danger or threat. If, however, the alarm continues to ring for too long, it produces organic damage to the system it is supposed to protect.

Stress may produce many kinds of organic damage. Psychosomatic medicine has found links between stress and cases of allergies, asthma, gastrointestinal disturbances, hypertension, heart disease, eczema, sexual impotency, infertility, diabetes, and tuberculosis. Certain types of emotional responses and patterns of adjustment appear to be linked to particular types of diseases or disabilities. A competitive, aggressive person suffers from hypertension, migraine headaches, heart trouble, or arthritis more frequently than a person who is not competitive or aggressive. Persons who bottle up their feelings and do not relate easily to others have higher incidences of ulcers, diarrhea, colitis, chronic fatigue, and asthma.[6] Knowledge of such general relationships may be useful in helping some patients, but the uniqueness of each person's organism and psyche usually requires that a detailed study and analysis be made of the patient's life. Only in this way can the sources of stress be identified and the manifestations of stress be treated.

Some Kinds and Qualities of Affective Experience

Fear and Anxiety

Fear and anxiety are feelings of apprehension, pain, or tension that one experiences in facing a real or imagined threat. Although the physiological and behavioral manifestations of fear and anxiety are often quite similar, the feelings themselves differ in ways related to the meaning, source, and duration of the particular threatening experience.

Fear is an affective state produced by threats that are specific, observable, objective, rational, and localized. Examples of fear reactions are the nonswimmer's apprehension of deep water, the marginal worker's worry when he learns of a cutback in production, and the sense of panic aroused in anyone when a fire, flood, tornado, menacing gunman, or careening car poses a threat to life and limb. Fear is a strong emotion produced by threats that are viewed as real and legitimate by the objective observer as well as by the person experiencing the threat.

Anxiety is a more diffuse feeling of apprehension concerning objects or events that are less specific and less easily identified. Anxiety is often subjective and irrational and is more likely to involve unconscious factors.

---

[6] Franz Alexander, *Psychosomatic Medicine* (New York: W. W. Norton & Co., 1950), pp. 54–80.

Anxiety generally arises out of interpersonal relationships. We become anxious when we are uncertain whether we really are loved or accepted or when we are uncertain whether we will perform adequately in a difficult situation. Because of their nonspecific, diffuse nature, anxieties are generally more chronic, pervasive, and persistent than fears.

A basic form of anxiety is that which is aroused in persons who are uncertain of their own self-worth. As noted in Chapter 5, such persons may remain aloof from others, or they may be cold and hostile. However, anxiety reflecting a sense of unworthiness or rejection may also manifest itself in oversolicitousness and possessiveness, as the rejected one seeks to establish an exclusive friendship tie with another.

The anxious person is more likely than the less anxious person to see unlikely and remote dangers or catastrophes as real and imminent. A mother becomes anxious when her child does not return home at the expected hour and imagines that the worst has befallen him. Some good students become unrealistically anxious prior to every examination. A high mark relieves their anxieties only until the next examination is announced.

One should not conclude, however, that anxiety is synonymous with abnormality or mental illness. On the contrary, anxiety is experienced by everyone in some degree and thus is a part of normal behavior. That is, it is normal to feel anxious when a threat is real, and anxious behavior is normal when it is appropriate to the degree of threat present. Thus, a mother's concern for the welfare of a critically ill child is a normal anxiety, but a hypochondriac's long list of pains and complaints reflects a neurotic anxiety.

A further distinction between normal and neurotic anxiety is that normal anxiety is generally relieved when the threat is removed. Neurotic anxiety, on the other hand, tends to persist in spite of the removal of the threat. The mother's anxiety is relieved when her child recovers, but the person with imagined ills continues to complain about his pains no matter how many doctors treat him or how many operations he has.

Frustration

Frustration is an unpleasant affect or an internal tension state aroused by prolonged blocking or thwarting of satisfaction of a need or of achievement of a goal. The tension associated with frustration is more disturbing and painful than the initial tension of an unsatisfied need, because continued failure to overcome the barrier tends to intensify the initial tension. These differences in tension states are important, since behavior that follows continued blocking is different from behavior that follows the initial blocking of a need. The anger and resentment of a member of a minority group who, though qualified, has time and again been refused employment is quite different from the disappointment of another man, not a member of a minority group, who has failed to be appointed to a position of higher pay and responsibility.

Dollard and his associates[7] hypothesized that frustration is characteristically followed by aggressive behavior. Support for this frustration-aggression hypothesis comes from studies of children's responses to frustration in the classroom and at home. Preschool children who experienced eight consecutive repetitions of a mildly frustrating situation responded with increased aggressiveness between the first four and the last four experiences of the situation.[8] Children and adolescents become frustrated and respond aggressively when they experience rejection or restrictive and autocratic patterns of child training by one or both parents.[9]

People differ considerably in their capacities for tolerating frustration, and these differences reflect differences in self. Differences in student responses to varying degrees of frustration were revealed in a study by Maier.[10] A group of college students was asked to choose between two cards and to indicate their choice by turning a knob to open the door on which the card was mounted. If the subject chose incorrectly, the door would not open and he received a slight electric shock. Subjects were instructed to try to find a basis for choosing between the cards. By prearranging the punishment, varying degrees of frustration were introduced into the experiment, so that different students failed in the task 75, 50, or 25 percent of the time. Results of this study revealed that people do differ in the degree to which they become frustrated by the same event, that they respond differently to frustration, and that these responses are related to other personality characteristics. The more frustrating was the situation, the greater was the proportion of students who used stereotyped behavior and the greater was their difficulty in learning later discrimination tasks.

A common source of frustration is the blocking that frequently occurs during the course of almost any learning experience. Where the problem or skill to be mastered is appropriate to the individual's capacities, the frustration experienced is often short-lived. Frustration diminishes as the student gains fresh insight with the help of a teacher or peer or from his own further study or analysis of the problem. Mild, temporary frustration, then, often motivates a student to expend further efforts toward achieving success.

With continued failure, however, the picture becomes quite different. When failure follows failure, frustration persists and deepens. Such experiences of continued failure inevitably lead to a modification of the learner's self-concept; he begins to express through his behavior a self-image of "I am dumb" or "I am no good." After a change in self-concept

[7] John Dollard et al., *Frustration and Aggression* (New Haven, Conn.: Yale University Press, 1939).

[8] Nancy B. Otis and Boyd R. McCandless, "Responses to Repeated Frustrations of Young Children Differentiated According to Need Area," *Journal of Abnormal and Social Psychology*, 50 (1955), 349–353.

[9] W. McCord, Joan McCord, and A. Howard, "Familial Correlates of Aggression in Nondelinquent Male Children," *Journal of Abnormal and Social Psychology*, 62 (1961), 79–93; A. Bandura and R. H. Walters, *Adolescent Aggression* (New York: Ronald Press, 1959).

[10] N. R. F. Maier, *Frustration: The Study of Behavior without a Goal* (New York: McGraw-Hill Book Co., 1949), pp. 77–122.

from "adequate" to "inadequate," new experiences of failure prove less threatening and are less frustrating because they are more nearly consistent with the student's revised opinion of himself. In terms of the learning process, however, a downward revision of self-concept is not completely satisfactory, since seeing himself as inadequate constitutes a further block to a student's learning.

Depression

The term *depression* describes a state of inactivity, a feeling of being drained of emotion, and a sense of powerlessness to influence the situation. It is generally believed that depression is associated with the grief and despair felt when one has lost a family member or close friend or when he has witnessed a great tragedy or catastrophe. Many persons go into depression, however, who have experienced no recent stress. This suggests that depression is a reaction different from the deep sorrow associated with bereavement. The person in a depression appears to undergo a complete personality change. He often views his situation as hopeless, reveals a lowered self-esteem, and engages in self-pity and self-deprecation. Often there is a pronounced social withdrawal from friends and associates, and he may become disinterested in and careless about his personal appearance. Depression is associated with physical changes as well. The depressed person has little energy, and he may feel too exhausted to get out of bed. He may experience insomnia, loss of appetite, weight loss, constipation, and loss of sexual appetite, and he may complain of aches and pains. Scientists are uncertain of the cause of depression, but some believe that the cause may be due to a change in body chemistry. Some suspect, too, that there exists a depression-prone personality, the most vulnerable persons being those who cannot compete in a competitive situation, those who cannot get rid of their anger, and those who take on more work than they can handle. Antidepressant or mood-elevating drugs appear to be the most effective treatment, although frequent contact with and the active concern of family and friends are especially important for preventing the patient from sinking into deeper depression and for the support needed in his ultimate recovery.

Fear, anxiety, frustration, and depression are characteristic types of unpleasant affective experience. If we are to understand the individual, however, we must become sensitive to the characteristic ways he expresses his feelings and emotions. It is this topic to which we now turn.

Patterns of Emotional Response

Observing the specific ways one expresses unpleasant feelings and emotions provides us with important clues for understanding his behavior and adjustment. Since the term *emotion* refers to the physiological changes that occur in response to threat or frustration, each person's mode of expressing his emotions will be influenced by differences in sensory and neural thresholds and by differences in experience, maturation, and learning. While each person's modes of emotional response are unique, we can identify general patterns of affective behavior which people reveal in coping with threat and frustration.

Physiological changes marking the arousal of emotion frequently affect the face, mouth, eyes, and neck. The flushing of face and neck, the prominence of large veins, and the curling and quivering of lips are all evidences of strong unpleasant emotion. Other evidences of emotional stress are the set jaw, the clenched fist, and the stiffening of muscles of the face and body. As noted earlier, frequent or prolonged "emergency" responses—heightened pulse rate, blood pressure, or stomach secretion of acid—may result in psychosomatic ailments, such as hypertension or ulcers. When the threat or frustration is diminished, the reduction of tension is reflected in a relaxation of muscles that may be expressed in smiling, laughing, greater expressiveness, and freer body movement.

It is especially important for the observer to describe in specific objective terms the emotional responses of the person he is studying. The following description of Craig's behavior provides us with a picture of some of the characteristic ways this 16-year-old boy responds to threat.

> *Craig sat slumped in his seat with his feet sprawled out in front of him. As Miss Thomas conducted the review for the grammar test, Craig idly tapped his pencil and gazed out of the window with no change in facial expression. A messenger from the office brought a note which Miss Thomas handed to Craig. As he read the note, Craig flushed deeply, turned quickly, and looked directly at Larry with flashing eyes, lips firmly pressed together, and his fist clenched. When Miss Thomas suggested that Craig better go see what the office wanted, Craig struggled to his feet and walked unsteadily and trembling toward the door. His brows were knit, his face was very red, and as he left the room he glowered at Larry and muttered, "You! You! I'll get even with you if it's the last thing I do."*

This description tells us Craig's way of expressing strong unpleasant emotion, but gives no clear picture of the events that precipitated his change in affective behavior. If we are to understand Craig, we must relate his mode of expressing his emotions with the situations or events that aroused those emotions. In the next section, we shall describe characteristic types of situations that evoke unpleasant affect and threaten self.

Situations That Threaten Self

Since one's perceptions are always somewhat different from those of other people who witness the same event, the particular situations that threaten self (and hence are emotion producing) and the degree of threat inherent in such situations are unique for each individual. We might expect that events involving physical danger, such as fire, flood, or war, would be equally threatening to all persons exposed to the danger. However, even in the face of such clear-cut dangers, the intensity of the threat and the affect it arouses are likely to be different for each individual involved. Some will become hysterical; others will remain calm. Since the sources of threat are different for each person, it is not possible to catalog all of the situations that may threaten self. Instead, we shall identify general situations that pose a threat to most people.

The situations most likely to pose a threat to most people are those where physical flight is impossible, where there is a strong anticipation of punishment, where there is no opportunity to make a rewarding response, or where there is actual or imminent loss of emotional support.[11]

Threats to personal safety where physical flight is impossible are experienced by combat units in warfare and by persons in a burning building or a sinking ship. The anxiety of the student caught stealing or cheating may also reflect the futility of "escape." Persons who commit indiscretions or violate laws or mores often experience continuing anxiety caused by the threat of punishment, whether in the form of imprisonment or in the form of loss of acceptance, power, prestige, influence, or esteem. Indeed, this anxiety may become so great that the embezzler, adulterer, thief, or murderer may surrender or confess in order to gain relief. Anxiety arising from a lack of opportunity to make a rewarding response occurs when a student is torn between withholding or fabricating information to protect a peer and losing by this action the acceptance and good will of an adult whose respect he values. This example is also illustrative of the fourth type of emotion-producing situation, the actual or imminent loss of emotional support.

Our understanding of emotional behavior can be increased by identifying the sources of threat faced by children and youth at successive maturity levels.

Sources of Threat in Infancy and Early Childhood

The needs and developmental tasks of the infant are related to growth, physiological functioning, and a sense of security. Situations that produce distress for the infant include hunger, digestive discomfort, fatigue, illness, restriction of physical activities, and deprivation of human contacts and affectional relationships. Beginning at 18 months, the child experiences increased socialization pressures, and these confront him with many new situations having the potential to produce unpleasant affect. Chief among these situations are learning to use language, to control eliminative func-

---

[11] N. Cameron and A. Margaret, *Behavior Pathology* (Boston: Houghton Mifflin Co., 1951).

tions, to walk and to master other motor skills, and to accept and satisfy a broad range of cultural expectations. Failure, difficulty, or other unpleasant experiences arising from the attempt to master these developmental tasks can transform them into situations of threat.

Since young children are very self-centered, conflicts arising between self and cultural expectations are likely to be particularly threatening for them. The kindergarten and primary grade child is expected to relate and adjust to persons, groups, and institutions outside the family. Having to conform to the school's rules and expectations thwarts his desires for activity and independence. The six-year-old playing on the jungle gym expresses annoyance when the bell sounds as a signal to return to the classroom. The eight-year-old becomes upset when his peers exclude him from their game because of his refusal to give others a turn.

As children continue through school, they face the growing expectations of parents and teachers regarding the mastery of a succession of school learning tasks. Failure of the student in any area of school learning is a potential threat and may arouse unpleasant emotion. But emotion evoked in learning situations is not necessarily undesirable. Emotion may have a facilitating effect on development and learning. Mild emotion, or strong emotion of limited duration, often impels the individual to make an optimal effort to perform the task at hand. Emotion of this type is manifested in the physiological imbalance, drive, and arousal that constitute motivation. Such an imbalance or mild tension state is experienced by a student who, for instance, perceives that he cannot do arithmetic or play ball as well as his peers, but believes that it is important for him to strive to equal his peers in these areas and is confident that he can equal his peers.

Stronger emotion of longer duration, however, can jeopardize learning. If, for example, a lack of success in reading is prolonged, the negative feelings aroused in the child can cause emotional disturbances which, in turn, can further interfere with reading performance.[12] Ephron,[13] in treating children and young adults who had reading problems, found that emotional problems, rather than poor reading skills and habits, were invariably responsible for the poor reading performance. Frequently, through counseling and psychotherapy, poor readers were able to resolve personal conflicts and to improve reading performance even though they received no special instruction in the skills and mechanics of reading.

Studies of anxiety and school achievement show that children with higher anxiety have lower mental ages and score lower in school achievement.[14] Underachieving boys reveal feelings of inferiority, are less able to

[12] A. F. Grau, "The Emotional World of the Nonachiever," *Journal of the American Optometric Association*, 28 (1957), 523–531.

[13] B. K. Ephron, *Emotional Difficulties in Reading* (New York: Julian Press, 1953).

[14] Boyd R. McCandless and A. Casteneda, "Anxiety in Children, School Achievement, and Intelligence," *Child Development*, 27 (1956), 379–382; Seymour B. Sarason et al., *Anxiety in Elementary School Children* (New York: John Wiley, 1960).

express negative feelings, and are more anxious about expressing physical aggression than are achieving boys.[15] Shaw and Grubb,[16] however, found that bright male underachievers expressed considerably more hostility toward others than did male achievers.

Anxiety among elementary school children has been studied intensively by Sarason and his associates.[17] Their investigations show that the testing situation—an almost universal experience in our culture—begins to induce anxiety in students long before they reach high school or college. Sarason and his coworkers developed a Test Anxiety Questionnaire and a General Anxiety Questionnaire and used them to obtain indirect measures of children's anxieties. The Test Anxiety Questionnaire asked children to answer "Yes" or "No" to such questions as "Do you worry when the teacher says that she is going to ask you questions to find out how much you know?" and "Do you worry more about school than other children?"

The General Anxiety Questionnaire asked such questions as "When you are away from home, do you worry about what might be happening at home?" and "Do you sometimes get the feeling that something bad is going to happen to you?"

Sarason found that most elementary school children of high intelligence and high achievement have low test anxiety. He also found that from grade two to grade five, teachers' ratings of a child's anxiety become increasingly *less* accurate in predicting the child's performance on IQ and achievement tests, while the child's own self-estimate of his anxiety becomes increasingly *more* accurate in predicting his performance. Highly anxious boys appear academically less adequate, respond less well to the task at hand, and show greater insecurity in relationships with the teacher than do less anxious boys. The similarities in the behavior of low-anxious and high-anxious girls in Sarason's studies suggest that in our culture it may be more difficult for boys than for girls to admit that they are sometimes anxious. Sarason's findings consistently favor the low-anxious child. The child with low anxiety is more effective in his school performance, has fewer and less intense conflicts, and is better prepared and better able to cope with problems of emotional development.

Sources of Threat in Adolescence and Adulthood

Any situation that the adolescent perceives as a threat to his feelings of security and adequacy, his acceptance by his own sex, his attractiveness to the opposite sex, or his chances for future vocational success is likely to

---

[15] Barbara Kimball, "Case Studies in Educational Failure during Adolescence," *American Journal of Orthopsychiatry*, 23 (1953), 406–415.

[16] M. C. Shaw and J. Grubb, "Hostility and Able High School Underachievers," *Counseling Psychology*, 5 (1958), 263–266.

[17] Sarason et al., *Anxiety in Elementary School Children*.

arouse unpleasant emotion. Situations that are particularly disturbing are those in which the young person sees himself as possessing an inappropriate physique, appearance, or pattern of growth; a lack of game or social skills; inadequate finances; or a lack of close friends and supportive adults. Restrictions on the adolescent's independence also produce feelings of threat. Lack of success in dating, choosing a life mate, or preparing for and becoming established in a vocation are still further sources of threat for adolescents and young adults.

Situations that arouse unpleasant emotion in adults are those that frustrate the satisfaction of one or more of the human needs described earlier. Situations that most frequently evoke strong, unpleasant affect are those that threaten one's view of the world or his view of himself, including his hopes and aspirations for the future. Experiencing disappointment in love, failing in one's vocational goal, becoming estranged from family or friends, identifying oneself with the failures or problems of family or friends, failing in one's responsibilities as a parent, being unable to provide adequately for one's family, or failing to hold a steady job or to progress in one's vocation are all sources of potential threat for most adults. Similarly, the person who values peace, human brotherhood, and compassion for and tolerance of others will feel anxious and threatened in a world that appears hostile, cruel, cynical, or rejecting. In short, perceptions that are inconsistent with one's views of himself or his views of the world are sources of threat and arouse unpleasant emotion.

The affective state brought on by threat or frustration is manifested in heightened tension or drive which impels the individual to take action toward reducing the tension and restoring equilibrium. As noted earlier, responses made in an effort to reduce tension are called *adjustive behaviors*. It is this important topic to which we now turn.

Adjusting to Threat

One generally uses adjustive behaviors that have in the past proven effective in reducing tension and restoring equilibrium. Thus, the learning of adjustive behaviors conforms to reinforcement theory, which states that behaviors that persist and become habits are those associated with a reduction of drive or tension.

To understand other people's adjustive behavior, we must be able to make accurate inferences concerning the ways they see themselves and the world. Adjustive behaviors, for example, which appear to us to be self-defeating, irrational, or incomprehensible are often seen by the person himself as the only appropriate way he can behave in the situation. Thus, while we can identify general patterns of adjustive behavior, we must remember that each person's adjustive behavior is likely to be a unique variation of a general adjustment pattern. In the following pages we shall describe briefly characteristic types of adjustive behavior.

Adjustment Patterns

Aggression.   The purpose of an aggressive act is to remove, control, injure, or destroy a source of frustration or threat. The child's earliest efforts to deal with frustration and threat usually involve direct physical action. The infant who is frustrated by an empty bottle or by being put to bed will often cry and flail his arms in anger. The slightly older child, left at home while his mother goes shopping, may run after his mother or lie down, kick, and cry. Young children learn that grabbing, pushing, hitting, or biting are ways of gaining or retaining a treasured toy. Later, as they develop language skills and a growing vocabulary, children turn to verbal types of aggression, such as name calling, tattling, and teasing. In school, a child may respond aggressively to the teacher's demands by refusing to obey, making faces, or using disrespectful language.

The term *aggression*, however, refers not only to acts of hostility or destruction, but also to efforts to dominate, manipulate, or gain possession of a person, group, or object. The leader who manipulates or controls his followers, party, or organization and the parent who dominates or coerces his child are both using forms of aggression to satisfy their needs and attain their ends. Organized groups such as labor unions, political parties, corporations, or governments may also attempt to manipulate or control the actions of individuals or other groups.

Aggression may be directed toward its source or toward a substitute for that source. Aggression directed toward a substitute, a person or thing totally unrelated to the frustrating event itself, is called *displacement*. This pattern of displaced hostility is frequently used by a child or adult who perceives that an attack on the authority responsible for his frustration is too dangerous. In displacement, aggression is directed toward an innocent victim, as the following anecdote reveals.

> *Phil returned from the office after lunch today with knitted brows and a downcast face. Bobby, a small boy who is popular with all the children, was standing at the window watching the construction men working on the new wing of the school. As he went to his seat, Phil gave Bobby a shove and sent him sprawling to the floor. Phil said angrily, "Why don't you get out of the way?"*
> *When I tried to interest Phil in our social studies assignment, he turned his back on me and said, "No, I won't do it." Later I learned that Mr. Jenkins, the principal, had removed Phil from the safety patrol because of his involvement in a fight that had taken place after school.*

Repression.   A familiar way of dealing with unpleasant thoughts or feelings is to remove them from consciousness by making oneself believe they do not exist. This adjustive behavior is called *repression*. Repression, a key concept in Freudian psychology, is the act of submerging into one's unconscious certain painful, disquieting, or dangerous thoughts, desires, or conflicts. The adolescent, in response to the warnings of adults, tries to put out of mind disturbing feelings and thoughts about sex. When the conversation turns to recent attacks on women in the neighborhood, Mary says angrily, "Let's talk about something more pleasant." As a war crisis deepens, people go on about their daily activities, not daring to talk or think about events that could disrupt their lives.

All of us repress certain thoughts because not thinking about them reduces our anxieties. But when repression is used by an individual to deal with a deep-seated unresolved conflict, he creates for himself a serious emotional problem, a problem reflected in slips of the tongue which reveal that repression is not complete, in disproportionate effort required to maintain the repression, and in behavior distortions which hamper social relationships and the satisfaction of other needs.[18]

Use of repression is revealed in the following report of a series of counseling interviews with Karen.

> In the initial interview, Karen reiterated how fond she was of her mother. She recounted experiences of their going shopping, attending concerts and plays, and taking a trip to Europe together. By the fifth interview, the picture of mother domination of Karen became quite clear. Her mother disapproved of her friends and discouraged her from having dates. In subsequent interviews, Karen's feelings of hostility toward her mother, previously repressed, became increasingly apparent.

Aspects of repression can also be observed in some of the other adjustive behaviors described below, including sublimation, rationalization, and fantasy.

Substitution. When goals are blocked and needs remain unsatisfied, the individual frequently varies his behavior or alters his goals. Adjustment by *substitution* occurs when the individual finds a new behavior or goal to be equally or more satisfying than the original behavior or goal. Thus, the boy whose ambition to become a star athlete is blocked by poor coordination or small size works hard and becomes sports editor of the school newspaper. Through this substitute activity, he satisfies his need for self-esteem and for identification with sports by writing stories of games, interviewing players, and reporting sports activities. A student whose goal of social success has eluded him may substitute the goal of academic success.

---

[18] N. A. Cameron, *Personality Development and Psychopathology* (Boston: Houghton Mifflin Co., 1963).

A special type of substitution is *sublimation*, an adjustment pattern in which behavior approved of by society is substituted for behavior which society would disapprove of. Frequently, sublimation tactics are employed to control expressions of sexual or aggressive drives. Many women sublimate their sex drives through church or community activities or in vocations which emphasize service to others, such as nursing, teaching, and social work. Many men sublimate their aggressive drives through participation in contact sports, such as football, boxing, hockey, and wrestling.

Whether a new goal is an adequate substitute for the initial goal depends on the individual's self-organization (his patterns of needs, motives, and values). One coed vying for selection as homecoming queen may easily accept as a substitute being no more than a member of the queen's court, while another coed may accept nothing less than being selected as the queen herself. In general, substitute goals are seldom as satisfying to achieve as the original goal. This lack of complete satisfaction is revealed in the tension one feels and expresses even after substitution has been accomplished.

Projection.   A common adjustment pattern used by many individuals, especially young children, is projection. In *projection*, one attributes to other persons or groups one's own feelings, attitudes, or motives as a way of disowning them in himself. Usually, therefore, it is one's socially disapproved or forbidden behaviors or motives that are attributed to others. Freddie, who says Jimmie doesn't play fair and cheats, may be ascribing to others characteristics he wishes to disown in himself. Tommy, who was severely chastised for playing in the creek, later told his parents about a bad little boy he saw playing in the creek.

Projection is a common adjustive pattern used by all of us and is not likely to cause difficulty unless it involves a critical aspect of the self-concept.[19] Seeing others as worthy but oneself as unworthy would be one example of self-damaging projection. One minimizes the damaging effects of projection when his responses reflect not only his own perceptions but also the perceptions of others.

Rationalization.   An adjustment pattern common in our culture is rationalization. *Rationalization* is giving to oneself and others socially acceptable explanations in place of the real reasons for one's behavior. This pattern is one a child begins to learn at an early age. Giving adequate explanations for one's behavior is expected in our culture, and the child soon learns that he may escape punishment if the motives he reveals in explaining his behavior are acceptable ones.

It takes time, however, for children to learn what constitutes a so-

---

[19] Roger W. Heyns, *The Psychology of Personal Adjustment* (New York: Holt, Rinehart and Winston, 1958), pp. 62–63.

cially acceptable explanation for their behavior. Thus, three-year-old Susan's explanation that the prized figurine lying in pieces at her feet "slid off the mantel" may bring an inward smile to the disinterested observer, but as a rationalization it is unlikely to be convincing either to the observer or to Susan's mother. As they mature, children become more discriminating in selecting explanations for their behavior.

In rationalization, the individual, consciously or unconsciously, selects from among two or more plausible alternatives the explanation which is most consistent with his self-concept. There must be a valid basis for the explanation in order for the rationalization to be believed and accepted. Of a different nature is *prevarication*, the use of deception and falsehood when no objectively valid basis for the individual's explanation exists. Strong cultural disapproval of prevarication is communicated to children at an early age. Because of this strong disapproval and the penalties associated with prevarication, most persons use it sparingly, and, when they use it, they justify its use as the lesser evil in the situation.

The use of rationalization is usually not harmful, since accurate, valid accounts of one's behavior are usually unnecessary and since rationalization often does help a person to maintain his self-esteem. However, when one uses rationalization almost exclusively as an adjustment pattern, or when his rationalizations are inconsistent or lack validity, then the delusions created interfere with adjustment.

Withdrawal.　　Withdrawal is an adjustment pattern that may manifest itself in a variety of ways. There is physical withdrawal, the running away from a problem or threatening situation, which may be observed in adults as well as in children. The child refuses to continue playing the game when he can't get his own way; the adolescent drops out of school or leaves home if conflicts with teachers or parents continue unresolved; the adult resigns his job or withdraws from a club, association, or church as a protest against policies or conditions he cannot accept.

Another type of withdrawal is *insulation*, in which the individual makes himself inaccessible to others. This type of adjustment can be observed in the student who says nothing and does not participate in class activities. Some adults insulate themselves by having telephones with unlisted numbers. All of us feel the need at times to insulate ourselves from too much stimulation so that we can have some privacy and time alone to think. However, too much insulation cuts the individual off from interaction with others, and interaction is important for personal development and adjustment.

Still another manifestation of withdrawal is *noncommunication*. This type of adjustment is being used by a student whose response to the teacher's question is to answer, "I don't know," or to look at the floor and say nothing. It is also being used by political leaders who respond to reporters' questions with "No comment" and by witnesses before Congressional committees who invoke the Fifth Amendment. The following anecdote illustrates the use of aggression and noncommunication by Harold, age seven.

December 9.   *As the teacher came into the room after 2 o'clock recess she was greeted by an uproar in the cloakroom. Mid-afternoon recess was just over, and the children were hanging up their hats and coats in the cloakroom and coming into the room. Most of the children were already inside, but Harold stood in the middle of the cloakroom surrounded by three children, who were shouting, "You did so!" "Where is my hat?" "Get it down, Harold!" Harold had taken the hats of these children and had thrown them on top of a very high locker. The teacher was greeted with "Harold threw our hats up!" "We can't get them." The three children were asked to go inside.*

When the teacher and Harold were alone, the teacher said, "Well, Harold, what are you going to do about it? You have started something now. How are you going to finish it?" There was no answer from Harold. He stood still and looked down. After a little wait the teacher said, "Hadn't you better think of a way to get them down?" Harold tried first with a small chair. Then he got the teacher's chair. Still he couldn't reach the hats. After a few minutes the teacher said, "What can you do now?" No answer from Harold. "Perhaps the other boys and girls can help you to decide." Without a word, Harold got the window stick. He climbed up on the chair and with the stick got the hats down and gave them to the children. The teacher said, "Do you think it was worth all that trouble?"

Harold said softly, "I don't know," and looked at the floor.

Fantasy.   Another type of withdrawal is *fantasy,* in which the individual seeks to reduce tensions by daydreaming, by creating in his imagination a situation which is less threatening and more comforting than real life. The young child pretends he is a horse or a dog; the homely girl dreams of parties where she is the most beautiful of all the beautiful women present; the boy with few athletic skills dreams of becoming a hero by scoring the winning touchdown against his school's bitterest rival. Fantasy expressed in telling tall tales or in make-believe dramatic play is engaged in by most young children and is quite normal. But fantasy may become a harmful adjustment pattern when a person at any age uses it to avoid or to insulate himself from a threatening situation rather than to face the situation and deal with it openly and objectively.

Use of drugs.   Drugs for centuries have been used by man to adjust to pain, threat, anxiety, boredom, and frustration. Although drugs have always had many beneficial medical and therapeutic uses, the upsurge and frequency of use of unprescribed drugs in America and other Western countries, especially by adolescents and young adults, is a more recent phenomenon.

It is often difficult to know why a given individual turns to drugs instead of using some other adjustment pattern in coping with his problems. Since the problems each of us faces are quite different and since our responses to these problems vary, we can expect a wide range of reasons to lie behind the taking of drugs.

At one end of the continuum is a sizable group of "experimenters" who, because of curiosity and peer group pressure, try a drug, most likely marijuana, for kicks, to overcome their shyness with others, to relieve boredom and frustration, to protest, or to increase their sense of feeling and awareness in a search for truth and meaning. The effects of specific drugs on the body and on behavior were reviewed in Chapter 4. Most persons who have used drugs are in the "experimenter" group. Since their experience with drugs is limited to an occasional social exposure, drugs never become very important in the lives of these individuals. As they move on to other interests, their use of drugs decreases, and in time most "experimenters" give them up completely. The use of alcohol to relieve tension and frustration, however, is far more widespread among youth (as well as adults) thar the use of hard drugs and hence offers more frequent opportunities for abuse. Excessive use of alcohol not only is linked to brain damage, liver damage, heart disease, and ulcers, but its interference with motor coordination, mental functioning, decision making, and sound judgment seriously handicaps the person in his efforts to work through his emotional problems.

At the other end of the continuum are the hardcore addicts for whom drugs are a main prop used in dealing with emotional problems which vary widely in kind, scope, and complexity. Initially, some adolescents, faced with a loosening of family ties, a decrease in parental authority, an increase in responsibility, and sexual maturity, turn to drugs in seeking to overcome their anxiety, frustration, fear of failure, and inner conflicts and doubts. Many adolescents who become addicts seem unable to form meaningful interpersonal relationships, while others may have suffered in childhood from deprivation of love or from overprotection. The addict is frequently described as having one or more of the following traits: immature, passive, dependent, unreliable, unable to postpone gratification, depressed, poor sexual identity (in males), low self-esteem, and poor relationships with others. Although addicts are only a small proportion of all drug users, their dependence on drugs—both physical and psychological—is mainly responsible for the disturbing incidence of drug abuse. An account of how one adolescent sought to adjust to his problems first through trying drugs and later through drug abuse and addiction is revealed in the case of Ronnie:

When he was in junior high school, Ronnie Andrews was quiet, shy, and introverted and had always had difficulty in making friends. When he was in elementary school Ronnie had been chubby, and he was hurt and resentful when age mates called him "Fatty." He avoided active play and sports, preferring instead the companionship of pets and a retreat to books.

A sharp change in Ronnie occurred at the beginning of the tenth grade. He had always earned above-average grades; now he was failing in most of his subjects. He frequently appeared to be in a stupor, drowsy and bleary-eyed. At times his hands shook, his speech was slurred, and he stumbled over things. He avoided meals, complaining of no appetite. Ronnie decorated his room at home with grotesque drawings of demons with huge heads and bulging eyes.

He had never had many friends, but now he seemed to have friends of a sort—boys as bleary-eyed and lethargic as he. His parents noticed that Ronnie began getting increasing numbers of telephone calls, many of them late at night. His parents tried talking to him, punishing him by withdrawing privileges, reasoning with him, pleading with him, and offering him rewards, all to no avail. One day when he was out of the house, they searched his room and found a bottle of different colored pills, an empty vial, and some rolled cigarettes. When confronted with this evidence, Ronnie denied using drugs, demanded that his parents never enter his room again, and proceeded to lock himself in his room. His parents alternately threatened and pleaded, and even promised him a car if he would get off drugs and stay off. They sought help from ministers, clinics, and psychotherapists, but Ronnie seldom kept the appointments.

During his junior year in high school, things went from bad to worse. Ronnie continued to receive failing grades in school, he was frequently suspended, and the relationship between Ronnie and his parents became so strained that they seldom spoke to each other. In April of that year, Ronnie disappeared after having withdrawn from the bank all of his savings. Mr. and Mrs. Andrews reported his disappearance to the police, but the police were unable to trace him.

By this time his parents were frantic with worry. They asked each other again and again why they had been unable to get through to Ronnie. The odyssey ended a month later with a telephone call from the New York City police informing the parents that Ronnie had been found dead that morning in an abandoned tenement from an overdose of barbiturates.

One should not conclude from the case of Ronnie that all youth experiencing Ronnie's insecurities and anxieties will turn to drugs or that those who seek a solution to their problems by taking drugs will reach a tragic end. Only a very small percentage of drug users die of an overdose, but the potential danger of a drug abuser's achieving a permanent solution to his problems through death by overdose should not be minimized.

In general, as an adjustment pattern, taking drugs has the same limitations in effecting a satisfying resolution to problems as do withdrawal and fantasy. Drugs may enable one to escape from his problems temporarily, but the problems are likely to be still there when the effects of the drugs wear off.

Regression.   When a habitual method of solving a problem proves ineffective, one frequently turns to another method proven effective in the past in solving a similar problem. *Regression* is a pattern of adjustment in which the individual responds to frustration or threat in ways that were appropriate or effective at an earlier stage of his development. Regression in young children responding to threat may take the form of thumb sucking, temper tantrums, clinging to mother, rebelliousness, or aggressiveness. The use of regression by adolescents may manifest itself in sulking or having temper tantrums in response to disagreements with adults, in prolonged dependence upon parents for difficult personal decisions, or in the use of various forms of physical or verbal aggression in conflicts with peers. Examples of regressive behavior in adults are the young wife's return to mother after a marital quarrel and the blaming of others for one's own shortcomings and faults.

When the usual adjustive patterns prove ineffective, regression to earlier behaviors is normal and inevitable. Less mature forms of adjustments, however, are seldom as effective or as satisfying as adjustive patterns that have been acquired at a later stage of development. One who makes extensive use of regression is often perceived and treated by others as immature.

Identification. In earlier chapters, we discussed the importance of identification in the establishment of affectional ties and the internalization of cultural patterns and values. Identification, however, is also a process of adjustment. In adjustment through *identification*, the individual reduces tension by attributing to himself "the achievements, characteristics, status, and possessions of other persons or groups."[20] Identifying with a person or group more powerful or successful than oneself is an effective way of coping with threat. The five-year-old is using identification when he says to his tormentor, "My daddy can beat up your daddy." A teenager in conflict with his parents is using identification when he turns to his peers for comfort and support.

One can also adjust to threat or conflict through negative identification with the oppressors or the majority group. A few inmates in concentration camps under Hitler adjusted to torture and incarceration by treating fellow inmates as brutally as did their guards. Members of a minority group adopt the same standards or bases (such as color, mores, or habits) by which they are discriminated against when they, in turn, discriminate against other minority groups. Identification is a pattern of adjustment extensively used by persons in weak or subordinate positions, and sometimes its use is to the detriment of others.

Modifying self-concept. Another way of adjusting to threat is to change one's perceptions of self and the world so that they are more consistent with the reality one has experienced. The high-achieving high school student who does less well in college, the popular student who loses a school election, or the healthy person who suddenly develops a chronic physical impairment may all reduce the tension evoked by the disturbing event by modifying their self-concepts. However, since self is a stable, consistent organization of personal meanings, it is not always feasible or satisfactory to modify one's perceptions of self and the world. Maintenance of self requires a measure of self-consistency. We must be ourselves; we

[20] Cameron, p. 156.

cannot be all things to all people or all things in every situation. Thus, while modifying one's self-concept in response to some threats is an effective adjustive behavior, it is a behavior that cannot be used as a response to every threat.

We noted earlier that the perceptions of psychologically healthy, adequate people are more objective, realistic, and accurate, and that compared to those of less healthy people, psychologically healthy people are more "open" to experience (that is, they are less likely to distort what they perceive). Such individuals are best equipped to adjust to threat by modifying their perceptions of self and the world. They are able to reduce their anxieties by admitting their guilt and atoning for their deeds. This is shown in the following ancedote from the case of Cheryl, age nine.

October 3.   *As the hostess for the week prepared to dismiss the room at 3:15, I took my post at the door of our room. I noticed Sue was crying as she came toward the door. I asked her what the matter was. Sue said, "All the kids are making fun of me. I missed jumping the rope last period and had to take an end. They said I cheated in holding the rope for others to jump as I was mad because I had missed in jumping the rope." I asked, "Who said you cheated, Sue?" She replied through her tears, "Cheryl."*

Since Cheryl hadn't been dismissed, I asked her to stay a few minutes after school along with Sue. Cheryl burst into tears and said, "I'm just plain guilty, Mrs. M. I said things I didn't mean. I don't know why I did." I thanked Cheryl for admitting her guilt and assured her that sometimes everyone says things that they are sorry for later. I said, "Let's just forget all about it. Always try to remember that everyone has feelings, and let's not forget it." After I dismissed the girls, I glanced out of the window and saw the two girls going down the sidewalk with their arms around each other talking and laughing.

Criteria for Evaluating Adjustment Patterns

Most individuals have a variety of adjustment patterns available for reducing tension and maintaining self-organization. Our daily experience reveals, however, that some adjustive behaviors are more appropriate or more effective than others for coping with threat in a given situation. The effectiveness of a specific adjustment pattern in a given situation can be evaluated in relation to the following criteria:

1.   Does the individual's use of this adjustment pattern result in a reduction of tension?

2. *Is the pattern employed appropriate to the situation and to the individual's age, sex, and culture?*

3. *Does this individual have a variety of adjustment patterns that he can use?*

4. *Do the adjustment patterns he uses enable him to maintain contact with reality?*

Obviously, if the function of an adjustment pattern is to defend the self against threat and anxiety, its effectiveness will be judged initially in terms of how well it performs that function. We have noted, for example, that such adjustive behaviors as withdrawal, fantasy, and insulation are likely to be relatively ineffective, because these patterns tend not to cope with threat or anxiety but to postpone coping with them until a later time. Any adjustment pattern is ineffective to the degree that it leaves conflicts unresolved and thus capable of creating further tension in a later situation.

Adjustive behaviors that are not appropriate to the situation or to one's age, sex, or culture are ineffective because their use is accompanied by social disapproval, which produces further anxiety and tension. Thus, overt aggression is generally a less effective adjustment pattern for persons of middle class culture than for members of other culture groups; it is also less effective for adults than for young children and less effective for women than for men. Use of humor to reduce tension may be clearly inappropriate, and therefore ineffective, in situations requiring dignity and reverence. Prevarication is an inappropriate adjustment pattern in most situations.

If, to be effective, adjustive behavior must be appropriate to the situation, it is apparent that one must develop a large repertoire of adjustment patterns. This repertoire can be thought of as a "defense in depth." If the first line of defense is breached, there are other lines of defense to fall back on.

Finally, since behavior and development have meaning only in the context of a reality that is shared by other people, one's mode of adjustment should also assist one in maintaining contact with that reality. Living in a fantasy world, regressing toward a less mature adjustment pattern, and repressing or distorting sensory data all tend to disassociate an individual from reality. Exclusive use of these patterns is symptomatic of deepening maladjustment and poor mental health.

The School's Role in Minimizing Threat

Accepting Emotion

The emotion one experiences and the modes of adjustment he has available to respond to threat are vital resources which assist him in maintaining his self-organization. Emotion and adjustment, therefore, should be viewed as assets rather than liabilities. This positive view contrasts with the contemporary attitude that expressing emotions is dangerous or is a sign of weakness. The general public tends to admire the individual who appears cool and unperturbed under fire, who reveals no evidence of strong emotions in physically or psychologically threatening situations. It is possible, however, that such an individual is doing himself damage. There is considerable evidence that people who repress, deny, or distort their feelings hamper their own self-adjustment.

If the school accepts the idea that it is both normal and necessary for children and youth to express emotion and to adjust to threat, then principals and teachers will be better able to help students to understand and to cope with their own emotions and adjustive behavior and those of other people. Recognizing that forbidding a child to express anger or hostility may cause him to repress those feelings or to resort to more damaging or less satisfactory modes of adjustment, the understanding teacher will accept the student's feelings and encourage him to express them in ways appropriate to the situation and to the student's age, culture, and self-concept. The child's progress in development and learning depends as much or more upon the teacher's skill in helping him to learn satisfying and appropriate ways of coping with threat as it does upon the teacher's skill in teaching him reading or arithmetic.

Establishing a Climate of Psychological Safety

The teacher who accepts students and their feelings has taken an important step toward creating a psychologically safe climate conducive to learning. As Rogers[21] points out, conditions of psychological safety and freedom encourage creative behavior. Rogers describes a climate of psychological safety as one in which the individual is accepted as a person of unconditional worth, external evaluation is avoided, and empathic understanding is promoted.

In a climate in which one is accepted as a person of unconditional worth, he knows that whether he feels angry, sad, happy, or indignant, his feelings will be accepted. In such a climate, both teacher and students are free to be themselves.

In a climate in which external evaluation is absent, teachers and students are free to make mistakes without feeling threatened or defensive and without fearing punishment or loss of prestige. Students come to accept their mistakes as a normal and inevitable part of learning; the teacher comes to feel safe in answering "I don't know" to questions for which he lacks information or competence to answer. When the learning climate does

---

[21] Carl R. Rogers, "Toward a Theory of Creativity," in Harold H. Anderson, ed., *Creativity and Its Cultivation* (New York: Harper & Row, 1959), pp. 69–82.

not provide psychological safety, students do not take chances; they hold back and do not explore ideas for fear their statements will cause them to appear less intelligent or less able than their classmates. The importance of a psychologically safe climate for facilitating learning is emphasized by Haggard: "The best way to produce 'clear thinkers' is to help children develop into anxiety-free, emotionally healthy individuals who also are trained to master a variety of intellectual tasks."[22]

In a climate of psychological safety, the relationships between teacher and children and among the children themselves are characterized by empathy and understanding. Teacher and pupils learn to accept each other's foibles, shortcomings, irritating habits, and ill-tempered outbursts and grow in their sensitivity to each other's acts of thoughtfulness, interest, and concern. Each will accept and respond appropriately to the other's retort, "I've got problems today. Don't bug me!"

Discipline

The term *discipline* is derived from the word *disciple*, one who follows a leader. The idea of the leader who exerts control "by enforcing obedience and order" is one of the traditional meanings of the word *discipline*. Other meanings of the term include "training which corrects, molds, strengthens, and perfects"; "punishment"; and "a system of rules affecting conduct and action." These traditional views of discipline are based upon the concept that the human being and his development and learning must be carefully guided, supervised, and controlled. This conception further implies that without this guidance, supervision, and control the young person is unlikely to learn the rules of conduct and action essential to his becoming a mature, effective adult.

Traditional views of discipline applied to the classroom imply that teacher control of student behavior is necessary and desirable for promoting learning. Unless firm control by the teacher is established and is continuously enforced, it is assumed that students are likely to be unruly, disrespectful, mischievous, or obstinate. Failure of the teacher and pupils to maintain discipline results in control of the classroom becoming a contest (and sometimes a battle) between teacher and students. Such a contest is inimical to effective learning, for this type of control creates a restricting, threatening, and uncertain psychological climate which discourages and inhibits free, open, and thoughtful exploration and expression of ideas.

Our discussion of the teacher's role in creating a psychologically safe classroom climate emphasizes a very different view of the human being and a correspondingly different view of discipline. This view of the human being

[22] Ernest A. Haggard, "Socialization, Personality, and Achievement in Gifted Children," *School Review* (Winter 1957), p. 409.

postulates that all of us have inner potentialities, capabilities, and motives for developing, learning, and becoming productive, thoughtful, sensitive, and compassionate human beings. We do not have to be coerced, controlled, or forced into a mold that reflects someone else's conception of what each of us should be like. Rather, each of us is capable of moving in positive directions toward growing and becoming. Positive growing and becoming is most likely to be achieved in a psychologically safe climate characterized by mutual, genuine, empathic acceptance, which affords opportunities for free, open, and thoughtful expression. Thus, discipline, as redefined, is the task of helping students to utilize their abilities, energies, and talents in ways that promote their development and learning.

Continued evidences of tension and unresolved conflicts in the classroom are inimical to the development of a psychologically safe climate and a growth-oriented discipline. Students need help in clarifying and accepting the feelings aroused by disappointments, threats, and frustrations. The sensitive, empathic teacher is accepting of the student and his feelings. This teacher will not dismiss the feelings of concern of the bright but anxious student with the comment "You have nothing to worry about." Rather, he will help the student examine his feelings and the factors that may contribute to his anxiety, thereby assisting him to gain new insights and increased self-understanding.

If the teacher is successful in communicating a genuine, empathic acceptance of the student and his feelings, the student senses, "Here is someone who is concerned and understands how anxious I feel about tests and not being able to satisfy my parents." When the student senses that someone really does care and understand how he feels, his anxieties subside and his negative feelings tend to be replaced by more positive ones. As the student is encouraged to express his feelings, they become clarified. He understands why he feels this way, and his self-acceptance increases as the teacher communicates to him that it is all right to feel this way. Once the student has accepted and clarified his feelings, his anxieties diminish, and he is ready to plan and to take effective action in dealing with the sources of the anxieties.

The qualities of a psychologically safe climate reflect this newer conception of discipline. As students accept and clarify their feelings, they become free to pursue goals that promote the development, learning, and self-enhancement of themselves and others. Through these cooperative endeavors, students grow in self-discipline, a quality that characterizes the mature human being. Persons guided by an increasing sense of *self-discipline* assume increased personal responsibility and self-direction for engaging in activities and acting in ways that enhance the development and learning of themselves and others.

This newer view of discipline is exemplified in one teacher's response to Tom, a seventh grader:

September 11.   *I was giving a diagnostic test in arithmetic. While helping a boy at the next table I heard a commotion and* looked over to see Tom bang his desk with both hands until his knuckles were red, tear up his paper, and dash over to the window saying, "I just won't do it."

His face was very red. I waited a few moments for him to cool down, went over to him, and asked him quietly if I could help him. "Nobody can" was his reply. I went over to his table with him, sat down, and got him to work several problems. Most of them were not correct. We went over them to find the cause of the mistakes. When I asked if he knew his tables, he started to cry. "It's just no use," he said. "I want to do it, but I can't." I told him if he wanted to we could lick the "can't" together.

September 12.   I made a multiplication chart for Tom before school, using very large numbers with red numbers for a guide. He seemed quite pleased and thanked me. Later in the day, after we had been working on arithmetic problems for about 15 minutes I noticed Tom was getting upset, so I asked him if he would help me out by making charts like his for several others having difficulty. He worked on them for the rest of the period and handed me 12 neat copies as he was leaving for P.E. He came back and said, "You know, that was fun."

A teacher holding a traditional view of classroom discipline would probably have silenced or punished Tom for disturbing the class with his outbursts. Such a response would have aggravated a situation that had already produced strong unpleasant emotion for Tom. Tom's teacher, identifying with Tom's goal of increasing his skill in arithmetic ("If you want to, we can lick the 'can't' together") utilized a more positive approach. Each time Tom's anxiety was aroused by difficulties in solving an arithmetic problem, the teacher wisely suggested a meaningful alternative activity. This reduced Tom's anxiety, yet was a step toward the goal of improving his arithmetic skills.

Summary

As the individual develops and changes, he seeks to achieve and to maintain a stable self. Stability of self is manifested in a consistency of behavior, a stability of self-concept, and a tendency to perceive and to distort events in ways consistent with self-concept and view of the world.

Emotion or *affect* is defined as the complex of physiological changes that occur in response to the meaning of an event or situation for the maintenance and enhancement of self. The effect of these physiological changes is to mobilize the body's energy resources to meet the perceived threat. Physiological manifestations of tension and stress serve as an alarm, warning the organism of actual or impending danger or threat. In humans, certain emotional responses and patterns of adjustment have been linked to particular diseases and disabilities. Although knowledge of these relationships may be useful in helping a patient, the uniqueness of each person's organism and psyche requires that a detailed study be made of the individual's life.

Fear is a strong emotion related to sources of threat that are viewed as real or legitimate, while *anxiety* tends to be a more diffuse feeling of apprehension, a less specific and less easily identified feeling. *Frustration* is an unpleasant affect or an internal tension state aroused by prolonged blocking or thwarting of a need or of achievement of a goal. There is considerable evidence to support the hypothesis that frustration is characteristically followed by aggressive behavior. A common source of frustration is the blocking that occurs during most learning experiences, especially those involving the learning of a complex skill or the solving of a complex problem. *Depression* is a less frequently encountered emotional experience in which one feels drained of emotion and powerless to influence the situation. Observing the specific ways one expresses unpleasant feelings and emotions provides us with important clues for understanding his behavior and adjustment.

Since one's perceptions are always somewhat different from those of other people who witness the same event, the situations that threaten self will also be different for each individual. As understanding of emotional behavior can be increased by identifying the sources of threat faced by children and youth at successive maturity levels. Although emotion evoked in learning situations is not necessarily undesirable, learning difficulties can cause emotional disturbances, and these disturbances can interfere with learning performance.

Responses made in an effort to reduce tension are called *adjustive behaviors*. One generally uses adjustive behaviors that have in the past proven effective in reducing tension and restoring equilibrium. Although general patterns of adjustive behavior can be identified, the particular adjustive behavior one uses is likely to be a unique variation of a general adjustment pattern. Principal types of adjustive behavior include *aggression, repression, substitution, sublimation, projection, rationalization, withdrawal, fantasy, use of drugs, regression, identification,* and *modification of one's self-concept.* The effectiveness of an adjustment pattern can be evaluated in terms of its success in defending the self by reducing threat and anxiety, in terms of its appropriateness to one's level of maturity, sex, culture, and situation, and in terms of its compatibility with reality.

Since emotion and adjustment are vital resources that assist one in maintaining and preserving self-organization, they should be viewed as assets rather than as liabilities. The understanding teacher accepts the student and his need to express his feelings, though he may not condone adjustive behavior that is clearly inappropriate to a particular situation. The teacher who accepts students and their feelings has taken an important step toward creating a psychologically safe climate, the climate most conducive to students' learning. Rogers describes a psychologically safe climate as one in which the individual is accepted as a person of unconditional worth, external evaluation is avoided, and empathic understanding is promoted.

The qualities of a psychologically safe classroom climate reflect a new view of the human being and a new view of discipline. In this view of discipline, all persons are seen as having potentialities, capabilities, and motives for developing, learning, and becoming productive, thoughtful, sensitive, and compassionate human beings. *Discipline*, therefore, as redefined, is the task of helping students to utilize their abilities, energies, and talents in ways that promote their development and learning. As children and youth assume increased personal responsibility and self-direction, they manifest an increasing sense of *self-discipline*, a quality that characterizes the mature human being.

Study Questions

1. Barbara, age seven, is particularly sensitive to any minor slights or correction, and, as a consequence, she bursts into tears two or three times a day. Teacher and classmates apologize and try to console her, but this has little effect on her pattern of emotional response. After some of these episodes, Barbara's mother comes to school quite upset. How would you go about trying to find the causes of Barbara's emotional difficulties? As her teacher, what would you do in trying to help Barbara?

2. Ed Barrett, who is a good student, became greatly agitated and upset when, for the first time, he was caught cheating on an examination. Later, in a conference with the counselor, Ed admitted that he had cheated on other occasions but had not been caught. Does Ed and do each of us have at least two self-images, one of the person we want others to see us as being and another of the person that deep down we really are? If so, which self-image determines our behavior? Why?

3. Ted, age 17, is a high school junior and is from a prominent, affluent family. He appears to be loved by his family and to have had many advantages favorable for his development. In the past he has had many friends and until last year had done well in school. Lately, however, he has been a different person and seems to be apathetic toward school and life in general. He is suspected of being on drugs and at times appears to be "high" while at school. Thus far, Ted has failed to respond to the entreaties, threats, and punishments meted out by his parents or to the efforts of sympathetic teachers and the school counselor to communicate with Ted and help him. What would you hypothesize may be the source of Ted's emotional problems? How would you check your hypotheses, and how would you try to help Ted?

4. Sarah Davis and Eleanor Hutchins both teach eighth grade English in Marshall Junior High School, but their methods of discipline and classroom control are quite different. Sarah is friendly but firm, her

classes are interesting, and the class activities are well planned. Sarah is quick to correct anyone who gets out of line, and everyone in Sarah's class knows exactly what is expected of him. Eleanor, on the other hand, is more easygoing. There is greater informality, noise, and moving about in Eleanor's class, and some of the class discussions get a little loud and somewhat heated. Eleanor spends a great deal of time listening to and counseling students about their schoolwork and their personal problems. Both teachers are regarded by students and faculty as excellent teachers. Which teacher do you feel has the most effective classroom discipline? Which classroom is likely to be more conducive to the development and learning of students? Why?

Suggested Readings

Axline, Virginia M. *Dibs: In Search of Self*. Boston: Houghton Mifflin Co., 1964. A case history of a troubled boy whose early experiences did not permit him to build a positive self-image. This account describes how Dibs, a disturbed but intelligent preschooler, was able, with the help of an empathic, supportive therapist, to take important steps toward improved mental health.

Grimes, William H., and Price M. Cobbs. *Black Rage*. New York: Bantam Books, 1968. Analyzes the causes of blacks' hatred of themselves and of whites. Presents an angry indictment of white society for the injustices and denial of human dignity that it has accorded black Americans. Case studies provide illuminating insights into the psyches of black men and women.

Rogers, Carl R. *On Becoming a Person*. Boston: Houghton Mifflin Co., 1961. A collection of papers presenting and interpreting the conditions and goals of client-centered therapy. The task of helping each person to become less defensive and more open to all sensory experience is a central theme of the book.

Sarason, Seymour S., et al. *Anxiety in Elementary School Children*. New York: John Wiley, 1960. Describes the development of test anxiety and general anxiety scales for children and reports the findings of long-term research investigating the relationships to anxiety of achievement, behavior, and other correlates.

Films

Angry Boy, 16 mm, sound, black and white, 32 min. Bloomington: Audiovisual Center, Indiana University. Presents the story of Tommy Randall, who has been caught stealing at school and is sent to a child guidance clinic for treatment. The clinic staff identifies Tommy's emotional problem, and, through interviews with his mother, traces the problem to family relationships of mother, grandmother, and father. Tommy's mother learns to understand him, and Tommy does become better adjusted through the help of the clinic.

Fears of Children, 16 mm, sound, black and white, 29 min. Bloomington: Audio-visual Center, Indiana University. Portrays a parent-child situation in which the mother of five-year-old Paul tends to overprotect him, while the father advocates sterner discipline and encourages him to do things for himself. The resulting conflict confuses Paul and arouses his fears. A friend of Paul's mother points out that it is normal for children to become angry with their parents. Paul's parents make a greater effort to understand the situation and the problem is resolved.

Feeling of Hostility, 16 mm, sound, black and white, 31 min. Bloomington: Audio-visual Center, Indiana University. Presents the case history of Clare, who develops a feeling of hostility because of a lack of affection and under-standing from her family. She compensates by achieving academic success, often at the expense of others. She improves with the help of an under-standing teacher, but her capacity for love and friendship is permanently impaired.

Part Three

The Emerging Individual

Developmental Tasks

In order to achieve integration, and at the same time to function acceptably in the society of which he is a part, the individual must adjust successfully to key experiences which arise as part of development in our society.

Caroline M. Tryon

Each individual, as he progresses toward maturity, encounters along the way specific *developmental tasks*—"those major common tasks that face all individuals within a given society or subculture of society."[1] The successful accomplishment of these tasks—at the time they are encountered—is crucial to the individual's subsequent development: "A developmental task is a task which arises at or about a certain period in the life of the individual, successful achievement of which leads to happiness and to success with later tasks, while failure leads to unhappiness in the individual, disapproval by society, and difficulty with later tasks."[2] Thus, a developmental task involves two interacting forces: the *maturing organism* and the *expectations of the culture.*

The physiological maturity of an individual sets general limits for the responses which can be expected of that individual. Lack of adequate strength and motor development makes it impossible for a child to walk much before 10 or 12 months of age. Thus, a specific developmental task becomes a necessary learning only when the individual has the physiological ability to learn it.

Since individuals vary widely in their rates and patterns of physical growth, developmental tasks cannot be grouped neatly and precisely by chronological age. Instead, these tasks are commonly grouped according to the individual's *maturity level* (for instance, early childhood)—each level encompassing three or more years rather than a single year. This division of the developmental span from birth to maturity includes the following maturity levels (shown graphically in Figure 10–1).

---

[1] Caroline M. Tryon and Jesse W. Lilienthal, "Developmental Tasks: I. The Concept and Its Importance," in Caroline M. Tryon, ed., *Fostering Mental Health in Our Schools* (Washington, D.C.: Association for Supervision and Curriculum Development, N.E.A., 1950), p. 77.

[2] Robert J. Havighurst, *Human Development and Education* (New York: David McKay Co., 1954), p. 2.

Figure 10–1.   Stages of Development and Changes in Velocity of Growth

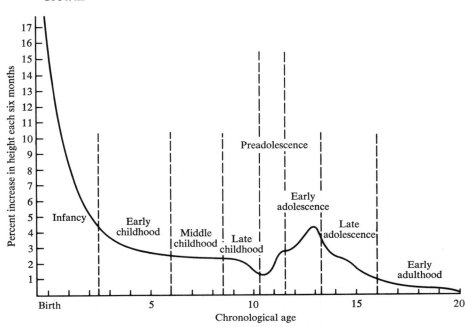

Source: Lois H. Meek, *The Personal-Social Development of Boys and Girls with Implications for Secondary Education* (New York: Progressive Education Association, 1940), p. 34. Used by permission.

Infancy.   Birth to age two or three. Period marks the change from complete helplessness to some degree of independence accompanied by rapid growth and increased stability of physiological processes.

Early childhood.   Age two to three to age five, six, or seven. Period of stable growth; large-muscle activity; role exploration through fantasy and parallel play with age mates; and identification with adults. Period of intense socialization in meeting demands and expectations of a different cultural institution, the school.

Middle childhood.   Age five, six, or seven to eight or nine. Period of slow steady growth; motor development uneven, with large muscles better developed than finer muscles; child becoming more oriented toward and responsive to peers.

Late childhood.   Age eight or nine to beginning of physical changes associated with pubescence (nine to 14 years for girls, 11 to 16 years for boys). Continuation of slow steady growth. Child achieves increased coordination of fine muscles and skill in manipulation; increase in social awareness and identification with peers; wider range of interests relating to understanding of the world in which he lives.

Preadolescence. Age 10 to 13 (covering school grades five to eight). Transition period of one or two years encompassing the latter part of late childhood or the early part of early adolescence. Characterized by hyperactivity, rebelliousness, moodiness, and irritability.

Early adolescence. Beginning at pubescence and extending to puberty. Period of rapid growth, especially of long bones of legs and arms. Some feeling of restiveness or rebellion against adult controls. Strong identification with peers—at first, with peers of the same sex; later, with members of the opposite sex.

Late adolescence. Puberty to early maturity. Deceleration in rate of growth. Individual more and more looks and acts like an adult, expects to be treated as an adult, but lacks an adult's experience.

Early adulthood. Onset of physical maturity to time of marriage and beginning of child rearing or establishment of oneself in a vocation. Period of additional schooling and preparation for a vocation. Induction into world of work. Courtship, marriage, beginning a family.

The second major force in the setting of developmental tasks for children and youth is the culture, which specifies the kinds of learning and development that are expected of its members at successive maturity levels. This means that Jimmy Brown's development in early childhood or early adolescence can appropriately be analyzed only in relation to the developmental tasks of the culture or subculture of which Jimmy is a part. Certain expected developmental learnings (weaning, toilet training, learning to talk, relating to others) are a part of nearly every culture; but differences in the timing and in the manner whereby each is to be learned makes each of these developmental tasks a unique learning in every culture.

In addition to maturation and societal expectations, certain self processes influence the individual's accomplishment of his developmental tasks. For instance, unless Frank sees the task of relating to his peer group as an important step in his own development, he probably will not work at this task even though he has the physiological maturity for it and even though the culture expects it to be learned. If, on the other hand, he perceives this task as important, he will work at it and probably master it to some extent—thereby progressing a step further in his development of self.

Each developmental task functions as part of a series of graded, progressive, and interrelated tasks. Consequently, a failure to learn one task often hampers the achievement of related developmental tasks. The child who has not achieved a feeling of security with his family or friends, for example, frequently is unsuccessful in winning the acceptance of others. Similarly, if an individual fails to accomplish a developmental task during the expected period, this failure may cause adjustment problems at a later period of his development. If, for instance, he does not achieve emotional independence from his family during his adolescence, he may be unable to develop a stable marital relationship when he becomes an adult.

Conversely, the successful achievement of a developmental task leads to the achievement of related or more complex tasks. As the physical organism matures and new capacities and potentialities emerge, the individual develops a readiness for working on and accomplishing tasks at the next higher stage of development. A child's learning to walk is followed by his learning to run, skip, hop, and jump. In addition, the same task may require increasingly complex behavior as the individual reaches successively higher levels of maturity. The preschooler, for example, works at the task of "achieving independence" by playing with other children in the neighborhood unsupervised by his mother; the early adolescent works at this same task by disregarding the advice of adults on a great many matters; the late adolescent gets a job, thus making himself financially less dependent on his parents. The preadolescent works at the task of "establishing heterosexual relationships" by teasing or by professing dislike of the opposite sex. In adolescence, the same task (or, more accurately, a task with the same label—"establishing heterosexual relationships") calls forth quite different behavior—dating, going steady, courting. Because the specific behaviors that must be learned at each maturity level in achieving such tasks are markedly different, the task itself is virtually a different task at each different level.

Tryon and Lilienthal[3] have identified 10 broad categories of developmental tasks:

1. *Achieving an appropriate dependence-independence pattern.*
2. *Achieving an appropriate giving-receiving pattern of affection.*
3. *Relating to changing social groups.*
4. *Developing a conscience.*
5. *Learning one's psycho-socio-biological sex role.*
6. *Accepting and adjusting to a changing body.*
7. *Managing a changing body and learning new motor patterns.*
8. *Learning to understand and control the physical world.*
9. *Developing an appropriate symbol system and conceptual abilities.*
10. *Relating one's self to the cosmos.*

Each of these tasks calls for the learning of different behaviors at successive maturity levels. Through an analysis of the specific behaviors

[3] Tryon and Lilienthal, pp. 84–87.

required for each category of developmental tasks at successive maturity levels, we can gain a clearer perspective of the continuity of human development and learning during childhood and adolescence.

We should note also that each child or youth works on a given developmental task in a unique way. A great many boys in late childhood and adolescence seek peer acceptance by developing athletic skills, but boys who lack athletic skills will strive to gain acceptance of peers in other ways. Tim, a small, underdeveloped 12-year-old boy, is accepted by his peers in part because he brings his football to school for them to play with. Alex, a studious 14-year-old, is accepted because of his skill at leading sing-ins. Thus, although all individuals in a given culture face similar developmental tasks, Tim's or Alex's mode of working on a specific task is *a unique expression of a general pattern of development.*

In the next two chapters we shall present case records describing children and adolescents at successive maturity levels. These behavioral descriptions will be analyzed in relation to the developmental tasks which individuals at each maturity level are striving to achieve.

Summary

The concept of *developmental tasks* (tasks that all individuals within a given society encounter as they progress from infancy to adulthood) enables us to analyze each person's uniqueness in relation to the common patterns of development associated with each maturity level. The maturity levels include *infancy; early, middle, and late childhood; preadolescence; early* and *late adolescence;* and *early adulthood.*

The accomplishment of developmental tasks is influenced by the maturing organism, the expectations of the culture, and various self processes (specifically, the processes of perception and motivation).

Developmental tasks are viewed as a series of interrelated, interdependent learnings. Developmental tasks identified by the same verbal labels are encountered at successive maturity levels. Although they might appear to be repetitions of a task first encountered at an earlier maturity level, each is a distinctly different task requiring different behaviors for its achievement at a given maturity level.

Study Questions

1. In the previous chapter, "turning on" with drugs was described as an adjustive behavior. Might the use of drugs also be evidence of one or more developmental tasks which some adolescents and young adults

are working on? What developmental tasks might the young person be striving to achieve through the use of drugs?

2.   Jennie, only marginally accepted by her peer group, has a strong interest in dramatics and the theater. She has considerable talent, but until now was never given a lead in school plays, only bit parts. She has been given the part of Anne Frank in *Diary of Anne Frank* instead of Terry, a popular girl in the class who had her heart set on playing the role. Now the other girls are avoiding Jennie. Although she is thought to be the best person for the part, she comes to you saying she wants to withdraw from the cast and the production. How would you respond to Jennie in this situation?

3.   We have presented in this and recent chapters two integrative concepts in human development, the self-concept and developmental tasks. Which concept permits the gathering of more reliable and useful data? Which concept do you feel is more useful in analyzing the behavior and development of children and youth? Defend the positions you have taken.

Suggested Readings

Havighurst, Robert J. *Human Development and Education.* Third Edition. New York: David McKay Co., 1972. Discusses the concept of developmental tasks and identifies the major developmental tasks commonly observed in American culture from infancy to old age. Notes the biological, psychological, and social forces that influence each task and indicates the educational implications of each task.

Tryon, Caroline M. and Jesse W. Lilienthal. "Developmental Tasks: I. The Concept and Its Importance" (Chapter 6) and "Developmental Tasks: II. Discussion of Specific Tasks and Implications" (Chapter 7), in Caroline M. Tryon, ed., *Fostering Mental Health in Our Schools.* Washington, D.C.: Association for Supervision and Curriculum Development, N.E.A., 1950. Identifies and discusses 10 major developmental tasks and learnings which appear in modified form at successive maturity levels. Chapter 7 takes up each major task or area of learning and defines the specific learning behavior at successive maturity levels from infancy to late adolescence.

Infancy and Early Childhood

So runs my dream; but what am I?
An infant crying in the night;
An infant crying for the light,
And with no language but a cry.

Alfred, Lord Tennyson

Before we describe the emerging individual and his growth and development during successive maturity levels, it may be useful to examine briefly the cultural milieu into which children are born and in which they grow up at the beginning of this last quarter of the twentieth century. The preceding chapters make abundantly clear that the kind of person one becomes is strongly influenced by his interpersonal, cultural, and peer environments. What, then, are some of the contemporary realities and trends likely to have a significant influence on the lives of children, youth, and adults during the immediate years ahead?

A fact of far reaching significance is the sharp drop in the birth rate in the United States in recent years, which, if the trend continues, will produce a leveling off and stabilizing of population growth in this country several decades earlier than was expected. The 1972 projection of family size was 2.08 children per family, which is less than the 2.1 children per family average needed to achieve "zero population growth," or a balance between births and deaths in the population. Projections of the population in the United States by the year 2000 have been revised sharply downward from 300 million (if the birth rate produced 2.8 children per family) to 264 million (if the birth rate produces an average of 2.1 children per family).[1] The reasons for the declining birth rate appear to go beyond the improvement and increased use of contraceptives. More young women are not marrying, some are marrying later, others are marrying and delaying having children, and still others are marrying and deciding to have no children at all. Although this lower fertility rate may be a temporary phenomenon, all current trends point to a period of slower population growth. Included in these trends are the increase in the proportion of women who work and

---

[1] "Leveling Off," *Scientific American*, 228 (February 1973), 46.

the expressed intention of women at all economic and educational levels to have smaller families, an objective that will be easier to attain because of increased efficacy of contraceptive techniques and increased availability of legal abortion.

A lower birth rate should make possible an improvement in the quality of life, since the resources available can be concentrated on fewer people than would be possible with a higher birth rate and a larger population. A stable population growth should make it possible for young children at all socioeconomic levels to receive better health care and have access to quality nursery schools and day care centers. Smaller families mean that for most wives and mothers, homemaking and child rearing will not be their primary adult role, as was true in former generations. Instead, most women will spend their adult lives in careers outside the home, interrupting them from time to time to bear and raise children.

We can expect, too, some changes in the American family in the years ahead. Some social scientists have predicted the decline of the nuclear family in Western culture due to the stresses on parents and children which grow out of the intensity of parent-child relationships, role conflicts, and isolation from close relatives. Yorburg,[2] however, predicts that the nuclear family will not only persist into the twenty-first century but will become stronger than ever. She predicts that the current dissatisfactions with the nuclear family will not lead to its abandonment but to its strengthening. At the same time, other life styles—homosexual marriage, group marriage, single-parent households, and communes—will become more prevalent as tolerance increases, but they will not pose a serious threat to the nuclear family as the predominant life style. Optimal emotional gratification requires a stable one-to-one relationship between human beings at all ages. Marriage and the nuclear family, at times imperfect and inefficient, are expected to continue as basic institutions, since nothing else appears to be more workable in providing for the basic emotional needs of human beings, both young and old.

This prediction suggests that in the years ahead relationships within the nuclear family will become even more important. Parent-child relationships in the future can be expected to be warmer, more permissive, and oriented primarily toward mutual psychological gratification. The extreme permissiveness which has led to overprotection and overpermissiveness is likely to be tempered by more defined limits and strictness in child rearing. The intensity of the parent-child relationship that is found in many nuclear families is likely to diminish with the spread of universal government-subsidized day care centers. Conflicts between middle-aged parents and their adolescent offspring can be expected to decline with the diminishing of sexual repression in our society.[3]

With this crystal ball view of Western society in the decades just

[2] Betty Yorburg, *The Changing Family* (New York: Columbia University Press, 1973).

[3] Yorburg, *The Changing Family*. Summary of selected points taken from pages 187–204 of this reference used by permission.

ahead, we turn now to an examination of what the individual in our society is like at successive stages in the life span. We start with the beginning of life.

Life Begins

Human life begins when a spermatozoon, the male germ cell, penetrates and fertilizes an ovum while it is in the Fallopian tube on its way from the ovary to the uterus. The sperm swim upstream by lashing their tails back and forth, and they move at a rate of three inches per hour across the cervix, through the uterus, and up the Fallopian tube to meet the egg. There are more than 200 million sperm in this race, but only one will fertilize the egg. The egg, which carries all the food and energy, is about 90,000 times larger than a sperm, but egg and sperm contribute exactly half of the new individual's hereditary material.

The chromosomes of the sperm and the egg combine during the first half hour after fertilization in the nucleus of the new cell. These threadlike chromosomes carry the genes, genetic information in molecular form, which regulate successive steps in the development of the organism. Since the individual is a product of cell divisions from the fertilized egg, every cell of an organism contains exactly the same genetic information. Thus, the genetic code not only shapes prenatal development but is a major influence throughout the life span. Specific genes in interaction with other genes and with the environment determine the hereditary characteristics of the child; eye and hair color, physique, physical and mental aptitudes, and susceptibility or resistance to various common diseases and disorders (including diabetes, heart trouble, and high blood pressure). The units of the genetic code, like words in a sentence, change meaning as they are used in different ways by different cells at different periods of development in the life span.

It takes about three days for the fertilized egg, or *zygote*, to pass through the Fallopian tube to the uterus and another four or five days for it to become implanted in the uterine wall. Cell division and multiplication begin shortly after fertilization; by the time the fertilized egg reaches the uterus, it is a hollow cluster of more than 100 cells. The cluster of cells resulting from cell division is known as a *blastocyst*. As the number of cells of the blastocyst increases, three layers of cells are formed, from which further cell differentiations into specialized tissues, organs, and body parts take place. The outer layer, called the *ectoderm*, is the point of origin for the skin, sense organs, and nervous system. From the inner layer of cells, called the *endoderm*, are formed the glands of internal secretion and the alimentary canal. The middle layer of cells, the *mesoderm*, is the point of origin for the muscular, circulatory, and skeletal systems.

During the embryonic period, which extends from the second week to the beginning of the third lunar month, the initial phases of development of the main systems and body organs take place. Organs and organ systems emerge in a fixed sequence, each with its allotted time for appearance and development in conformity to an overall timetable of growth. If an organ system does not develop normally during its assigned time, or *critical period*, it does not have a second chance, for the focus of growth shifts to successive systems. During the first month the embryo has the beginning of eyes, spinal cord, nervous system, thyroid gland, lungs, stomach, liver, kidneys, and intestines. Its primitive heart has already begun to beat, and bulges on the embryo show that buds of arms and legs are beginning to form. By the end of the first month, the embryo is about one-quarter to one-half inch long. The development of the body from 18 days to four months of prenatal life is shown in Figure 11–1, with the differentiations and formation of internal organs and structures at four weeks shown in the insert.

At the beginning of the second month, it is almost impossible to distinguish the human embryo from any other mammalian embryo. It is a critical time, for each organ and organ system is most vulnerable to the effects of deleterious agents during its period of most rapid growth and development. During the fifth and sixth weeks of prenatal life, the arms and legs may be deformed by thalidomide. The brain, too, is susceptible to damage. During the second and third months, the embryo is most susceptible to the ravages of German measles, or rubella virus; should the mother contract the disease at this time, the child may develop heart malformation, cataracts, deafness, or brain damage.

Ordinarily, the embryo is protected against the hazards of viruses and drugs by the placenta, a spongy organ that is attached to the developing embryo by the umbilical cord. The placenta acts as a liver and kidney in removing poisonous wastes; and it serves as a lung for the fetus in the interchange of oxygen and carbon dioxide, which are transported to and from the placenta by the mother's bloodstream. The mother's blood and the child's blood do not mix. The placenta acts as a barrier between the two bloodstreams, allowing nutrients to reach the child in the proper amounts and keeping out most noxious substances. The placenta sometimes fails to prevent the passage of some noxious substances, as in the cases of thalidomide and rubella.

The fetal period extends from the beginning of the third lunar month to the end of gestation. At 11 weeks the fetus, now more than two and a half inches long, floats buoyantly in the amniotic fluid along with the umbilical cord. Although it is totally immersed, the fetus inhales and exhales just enough to send the salty fluid into and out of its lungs. It does not drown because it gets oxygen—not from the air but from the blood brought in by the umbilical cord. By this time all of the body systems are working. Nerves and muscles have become synchronized with the young bones, so that arms and legs can make their first movements.

Beginning at 18 weeks some fetuses have been known to suck their thumbs, a practice which prepares the child for learning to suck and nurse after birth. At 28 weeks the fetus is more than 10 inches long and weighs two and a quarter pounds. In place of earlier generalized patterns of responses, many separate reflexes are beginning to appear. During the last

Figure 11–1. Development of the Body from 18 Days to Four Months of Prenatal Life

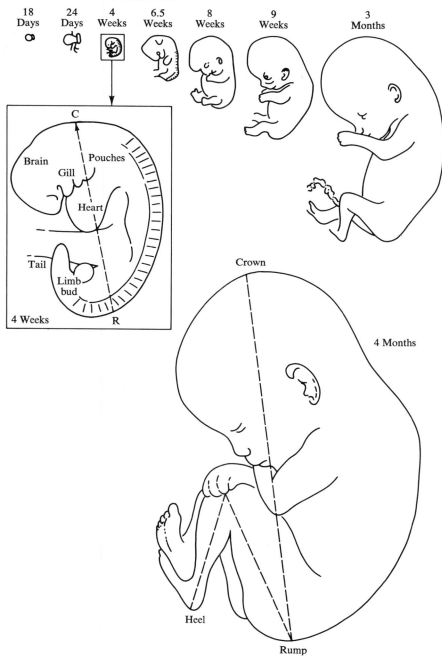

Source: P. C. Martin and E. L. Vincent, *Human Biological Development* (New York: Ronald Press, © 1960), p. 247. Used by permission.

two months of fetal life, deposits of subcutaneous fat cause the fetus to become rounded. Fingernails reach the fingertips, toenails lengthen, and the lower extremities grow rapidly.

The Neonate

Birth at full term occurs after 266 to 280 days, when the baby is shoved out of the mother's womb by a 100-pound propulsive force. Birth is a traumatic experience, since the vital systems must begin to function if the child is to maintain life in the outside world. The newborn infant is called a *neonate*, and the period from birth to approximately four weeks of age—a period which marks the transition from fetal to postnatal ways of living—is called the *neonatal period*. At birth the child must use his own apparatus to obtain oxygen from the air. If breathing does not occur spontaneously, it can be instigated by a sharp spank by nurse or doctor. The infant's loud cry enables his first breaths to be strong enough to inflate the tiny air sacs in the lungs and get rid of the mucus that has accumulated there. The most dramatic adjustment of all at birth must be made by the heart and circulatory system. At birth the pulmonary circulation is activated, and the blood entering the right auricle is pumped by the right ventricle to the lungs, where it is aerated. In addition, beginning at birth all waste matter must be filtered and excreted by the infant's own organs. During the first six months of postnatal life, the infant is afforded protection from many infections by the immunities obtained from the mother through the placenta.

Physiological Stability

The neonate's first developmental task, then, is to *achieve stability in physiological functioning*. To assist him in achieving physiological stability the infant has, at birth, *reflexes*, unlearned and involuntary responses to specific stimulation. The respiratory reflex includes a carbon dioxide reflex, which automatically controls the amount of air the infant breathes. No less important for survival are the nursing reflexes, including the hunger cry, active movements in search of food, and suckling and swallowing activities. A characteristic postural reflex, often observed during the sleep of newborn babies, is the tonic neck reflex. When the baby's face is turned to the right, the arm automatically straightens out, while the left arm is bent up so that his clenched fist is against the back of his head. The Moro, or startle, reflex is a defense reaction in response to a sudden loss of equilibrium or a loud noise; the infant's body becomes rigid and his arms extend upward and outward in an arc while his face takes on an agonized expression accompanied by wild shrieks.[4] A related startle pattern may also occur; this response begins with an eye blink and is followed by a thrusting forward of the head and neck and a flexion of other parts of the body.

Responsiveness to Stimulation

The achievement of physiological stability and the activation of receptors and effectors enable the newborn to become increasingly *responsive to environmental stimulation*. Characteristically, neonates at first make rather generalized responses to the total sensory input in a given situation. Emotional responses to hunger, pain, heat, or cold often are intense and may be manifested in crying, thrashing, and turning red all over. If a crying infant is picked up, he ordinarily quiets down, at least for a time, thereby indicating his responsiveness to sensations that go with being held, cuddled, and rocked. In their responses to contentment as well as to discomfort, neonates vary widely. One infant who is contented after feeding may actively flail about, while another infant may lie passively in his crib with a smile on his face.

Within the first two or three days of life newborns can focus their eyes on a rattle or a bright-colored ball, but they reveal marked individual differences in their responsiveness to stimulation. One difference is in the amount of time their eyes fixate on an object. Infants who fixate visually on an object most frequently and for the longest period, however, show the most visual pursuit when the object is moved. Ordinarily, the visual fixation of neonates exposed to a small checkerboard or similar object will wane rather quickly, a process called *habituation*. Older newborns (mean age of 78 hours) show greater habituation (less visual fixation per unit of time) than do younger newborns (mean age of 38 hours). This finding suggests that the increased habituation of older neonates may reflect a developmental process in which their greater maturation enables them to become familiar with the stimulus more quickly than younger newborns and hence visually turn away more quickly after repeated exposures to the stimulus.[5]

Not only do some newborns turn to look in the direction of sounds and track fairly well a moving object with their eyes, but they also are able to discriminate between patterns. Moreover, the newborn appears to structure what he perceives into some kind of pattern; he focuses significantly more attention on a crude approximation of a human face than he does on

---

[4] C. Anderson Aldrich and Mary M. Aldrich, *Babies Are Human Beings* (New York: Macmillan Co., 1947), pp. 8–10.

[5] Steven Friedman and Genevieve C. Carpenter, "Visual Response Decrement as a Function of Age of Human Newborn," *Child Development*, 42 (December 1971), 1967–1973.

a random arrangement of the same features.[6] The newborn's responsiveness to auditory input has been ascertained by measurements of the infant's heartbeat or respiration before and after stimuli are introduced. Increase in the neonate's heartbeat varies directly (within limits) with increases in sound, yielding a curve of auditory response that is very similar to that found in adults.[7] The neonate's sensitivity and thresholds of response to other stimuli are in some cases similar to and in other cases quite different from those of adults. Tactual cues are important in guiding the baby's rooting movements in searching for the nipple. Like the adult, he reacts with some distress to the smell of ammonia and the taste of quinine.

Learning

By the end of the first month of life, human infants have learned where milk comes from, as evidenced by their rooting movements and opening their mouths in turning toward the breast or bottle. Learning to associate mother's voice or footsteps with food (as in classical conditioning)[8] occurs later, since the infant must first develop cognitive systems for differentiating between the two types of stimuli (mother's voice and the nipple) before he can integrate the two and make the conditioned response of rooting movements and sucking. It takes about three weeks for cognitive systems for perceiving distance to develop, after which the infant begins to coordinate his various perceptual systems with other sensorimotor responses such as sucking and head turning.[9]

There are, however, limitations on the learning and response capabilities of the newborn infant. The only vocal sounds he makes are crying and the noises that accompany digestive processes. With rare exceptions he cannot raise his head, roll over, or move his thumb and finger separately. He does not reach out with his hands for things at a distance. Although he begins almost from birth to look at human faces, he cannot distinguish one face from another. He does not know that he has feet. He has nothing to remember, and he remembers nothing. His life is governed largely by the rhythms of his digestive tract and other physiological processes and by the routines of feeding, bathing, holding, carrying, dressing, and undressing imposed by those who care for him.[10]

[6] Robert L. Fantz, "Pattern Vision in Newborn Infants," *Science*, 140 (1963), 296–297.

[7] A. K. Bartoshuk, "Human Neonatal Cardiac Responses to Sound: A Power Function," *Psychonomic Science*, 1 (1964), 151–152.

[8] See Chapter 15, pp. 462–465.

[9] Arnold J. Sameroff, "Can Conditioned Responses Be Established in the Newborn Infant: 1971?" *Developmental Psychology*, 5 (July 1971), 1–12.

[10] L. Joseph Stone and Joseph Church, *Childhood and Adolescence: A Psychology of the Growing Person*, 2nd ed. (New York: Random House, 1968), p. 19.

Human Individuality

Adults who have had little exposure to newborn infants often think of them as very much alike, yet they are very different from one another. The uniqueness of each is an expression of his special genetic makeup and his exposure to a particular uterine environment. Newborn infants are different from one another in the tones of their bodies; the vigor or sluggishness with which they react; the speed at which they move their limbs; the zeal with which they attack the nipple; the patterning of bursts of sucking; their sensitivity to light, sound, and touch; their irritability, and their alertness. Newborns also differ in size and shape, in absolute and relative size of body organs, in blood chemistry, and in hormonal balance.[11]

Although newborns differ from one another in anatomical structure, physiological functioning, and temperament, it is not clear what these differences mean for later development. Measurements using various indexes of development taken in early infancy provide some basis for predicting the child's development during the first two or three years, but they cannot predict what the person will be like in later life. In short, though the forces described in Chapters 3 through 9 in large measure determine the kind of a person one becomes, some aspects of individuality are likely to be impervious to developmental change and experience and to persist throughout life. With the newborn now having achieved a measure of physiological independence, we consider next his development and learning during the subsequent months of infancy.

Early Infancy

During the second month of postnatal life, the baby is awake more than he was as a neonate, and he is increasingly responsive to a wide variety of stimuli. The changes in behavior and development which take place beginning at three months of age are revealed in the following excerpts from the case of Peter, which was written by a friend of the family.

Peter weighed eight pounds, nine ounces when he was born on May 8, 19—, in a large suburban hospital near Washington, D. C. He is the first and only child of Harry and Phyllis Baxter. Peter's father

[11] R. J. Williams, "The Biological Approach to the Study of Personality," paper read at the Berkeley Conference on Personality Development in Childhood, 1960.

is a computer systems engineer employed by the federal government. His mother was a teacher for five years before Peter's birth but now is a full-time housewife.

August, age three months.   *Before I ever met Peter, friends had prepared me to encounter a smiling, happy baby of three months. One of those friends, a pediatrician, remarked, "Peter is the most cheerful baby I've ever seen. He never cries." When I finally met Peter in August for the first time, my impression was that I had discovered the Gerber baby in person, complete with rosy cheeks and chubby fingers. His mother reported that he has been breast-fed since birth and just recently has begun to eat solid foods.*

October, age five months.   *Peter is very alert and responsive to people and to changes in his environment. He greets his parents and friends of the family with smiles and gurgles, but strangers are met with a solemn watchful stare. Lying in his crib, Peter hits at the plastic rings, rattles, and colored tassels that are suspended above his head. He also is able to grasp, hold onto, manipulate, and let go of rings and rattles. He uses both hands in a coordinated way to handle things and transfers finger food from hand to mouth by himself. Peter studies and plays with his fingers, and whatever he can grasp he puts into his mouth for tasting. He now sits up in his playpen or crib without support.*

January, age eight months.   *Each night for several weeks Peter cried for an hour before falling asleep, but this has gradually subsided, and now he goes right to sleep. He may awaken once during the night. His mother says, "I let him cry a little while to see if he'll get over it, but usually he won't. So I go in and hold him for a few minutes until he goes back to sleep." He usually takes a nap twice a day. He crawled at seven months, and he now can stand alone for three or four seconds. Peter seems to be working on language skills. He goes "click, click" with his tongue and already is saying "da" and "na."*
Recently a two-year-old came to visit. He shoved Peter and took his toy. Peter appeared to ignore the intrusion, picked up another toy, and continued playing. Often he will play with one toy for several minutes before going on to something new.

February 11, age nine months.   *This morning his mother and I went into Peter's room. He looked at me, screwed up his face, and cried. Spying his mother, he rolled from his back to his tummy and crawled toward her. He pulled himself up on the crib side and reached for her with one hand, his other thumb in his mouth. His mother picked him up and the crying ceased while he nestled his head on her shoulder and sucked his thumb. His mother carried him to the living room and set him on the floor. The crying began again, but he did not move toward her.*

His mother said, "Peter, do you want to play peekaboo?" Again the crying ended, and this time a smile broke out on his face. His mother hid behind a hassock, popping her head up to say, "Peekaboo," which was greeted with laughing from Peter. After the fourth time his mother popped up, Peter crawled around the hassock to her. She hugged him, then went back to her chair as Peter spotted my purse. He reached for it and dragged it toward him. Then he sat down and ran his fingers around the handle and the opening. He looked up at me and laughed and then looked at his mother. After about 10 seconds of looking at the purse, he crawled to a small table and picked up a straw mat. He held it out to me, smiled, and said, "Da." Dropping the mat, he reached for my notebook and riffled the pages. He grabbed my pen, and when I did not release it, he pulled for a few seconds, smiling, then crawled away, sat down, and said, "Click, click."

March 3, age 10 months. *Today I administered the Denver Developmental Screening Test to Peter. This test is often used by hospital pediatric personnel to get a rough idea of a child's developmental level in four areas: personal-social, fine motor, language, and gross motor.*

In the personal-social area, Peter demonstrated that he is shy with strangers, but he does warm up after a time and will smile at and play with the new person. He plays pat-a-cake. In playing ball, Peter will go after the ball when it is rolled toward him and pick it up. He feeds himself crackers, resists my efforts to pull toys away, and plays peekaboo. He will indicate one or two of his wants without crying. For instance, he will reach toward an object he desires and try to attain it. He is not able to drink from a cup.

In the fine motor area, Peter readily banged two cubes together and passed them from hand to hand. He demonstrated pincer grasp with a raisin.

Language development is exemplified by the imitation of several sounds, typically "ba," "da," "oo," and so on. He has not referred specifically to his mother as "Mama" or to his father as "Dada." In fact, he has not used either of these terms at all to my knowledge. His "words" seem to be all monosyllabic.

In the gross motor area, Peter stands alone for several seconds without toppling over or appearing shaky. He stands and walks holding on to furniture and can sit down from this position and pull himself up again. He cannot stoop from an unsupported standing position without falling.

March 5, age 10 months. *This evening Peter played ball with me. I would roll a tennis ball toward him, and he would scramble after it, pick it up, and chew on it. He held it tightly when I tried to retrieve it from him, but he kept smiling as I pried it away and rolled it back to him once again. We had been playing happily together with various toys in the living room for about 10 minutes when I decided to try a little experiment. I thought I would see if Peter would willingly go into another room with me alone and away from his parents. I picked him up, carried him into his bedroom, and closed the door. He contentedly played with his stuffed animals for a couple of minutes and then suddenly seemed to realize that we were alone and his parents were not in sight. He began to cry and could not be distracted or comforted by any of his toys. I held him, and he clung tightly to me, but the crying would not cease. As soon as we returned to the living room, he laughed and smiled. He did not go to either of his parents, however, when I placed him on the floor. Rather, he played alone with a toy, seeming to be content simply in his return to the group.*

May 3, age one year.   I stopped to visit and helped feed Peter his breakfast. He gobbled down a scrambled egg as fast as I could shovel it in. I have never seen a child eat so much and with so little effort.
He walks everywhere now and has not crawled for more than a week. I should say that he runs rather than walks. He laughs and babbles continually, but I still haven't heard him form any recognizable words or refer to his parents as "Mama" and "Dada." He recognizes me and several other adults now and will come to us without hesitation.

Social Development

The basic reality for the human infant is that he is totally dependent upon others for his survival. Not only is he dependent upon the mothering one for satisfying his physiological needs for food, rest, warmth, and relief from discomfort, but he is dependent upon her also for satisfaction of his psychological needs for tactual contact, comforting, and human interaction. Thus, a fundamental developmental task for the young infant is what Erikson[12] describes as *achieving a basic sense of trust that someone will protect, care for, and nurture him.* Here we are referring to the qualities of human relatedness manifested in love and affection that provide the infant with a basic feeling of security. (In Chapter 5 the qualities of interpersonal experiences in early infancy were shown to exert a pervasive influence on the child's development and learning.)

[12] Erik Erikson, *Childhood and Society* (New York: W. W. Norton & Co., 1950), pp. 219–222.

A number of entries from the case of Peter indicate that he has achieved a sense of trust in his mother and father. The entries also indicate that as he grows older this sense of trust is extended to close friends of the family. On February 11, he was startled when he looked up from his crib and saw a stranger, but his sense of trust in his mother was indicated in his stopping crying and nestling his head on her shoulder when she picked him up. On March 5, he showed a sense of trust when he played ball with an adult friend of his mother while his mother sat close by. This feeling of trust was threatened momentarily when he was taken from the room where his parents were, but it was reconfirmed when he was returned to the room. Peter played on the floor rather than going to either parent.

Numerous studies have documented the effects of maternal and social deprivation, institutionalization, hospitalization, and parental abuse, neglect, or indifference upon infant and child development. When an infant is separated from loving, attentive parents, the initial stage of protest, agitation, and distressful crying is followed by depression and withdrawn, autisticlike behavior. Severe motor and mental retardation can develop, as can movement stereotype, such as endless rocking back and forth. Some of these characteristics were observed in the foundling home infants studied by Spitz[13] in a research project cited in Chapter 5. This and other studies show that infants experiencing severe maternal and social deprivation may die even when the physical, nutritional, and medical care of the infant is satisfactory.

Animal studies by Harlow and others[14] indicate that a crucial variable in the relationship between the infant and the mothering one is the quality of tactual sensation experienced by the infant in his contacts with the mother figure. For human infants, optimum physical contact is characterized by warmth, tenderness, closeness, and yielding softness backed by firmness and support—qualities which connote mothering, affection, caring, touching, holding, cuddling, rocking, and body pleasure. Experiencing these bodily sensations is vital to the optimum development of the *somatosensory system*, that part of the nervous system which mediates emotional behavior. Prescott[15] suggests that deprivation of these pleasant bodily sensations during the formative periods of development may lead to structural abnormalities of brain cells—brain damage—in the cerebellar, vestibular, and other brain structures that are believed to regulate body movements, sensory in-

[13] Rene A. Spitz, "Hospitalism: An Inquiry into the Genesis of Psychiatric Conditions in Early Childhood," *The Psychoanalytic Study of the Child*, Vol. 1 (New York: International University Press, 1945), pp. 53–74; Rene A. Spitz and K. M. Wolfe, "Anaclitic Depression: An Inquiry into the Genesis of Psychiatric Conditions in Early Childhood," *The Psychoanalytic Study of the Child*, Vol. 2 (New York: International University Press, 1946), pp. 313–342.

[14] John Bowlby, *Child Care and the Growth of Love* (Baltimore: Penguin Books, 1965), p. 22; Harry F. Harlow, "The Nature of Love," *American Psychologist*, 13 (December 1958), 673–685.

[15] James W. Prescott, "Early Somatosensory Deprivation as an Ontogenetic Process in the Abnormal Development of the Brain and Behavior," *Medical Primatology*, Second Conference of Experimental Medical Surgery of Primates, New York, 1969 (Basel: Karger), pp. 356–375.

put, and social and emotional behaviors. Heath,[16] for example, found abnormal neuroelectrical activity in the cerebellum and other brain structures of parentally and socially deprived monkeys.

Our growing knowledge of the effects of tactual-sensory deprivation on emotional development and mental health may help us to explain in part the alarming incidence of aggression and violence in our culture, including the growing incidence of *child abuse*. Child abuse is associated with the *battered child syndrome*, seen in infants and children who have been brought to a hospital with bruises and broken bones later determined to have been inflicted by an adult who was caring for the child (usually a parent). Frequently, battering parents were themselves battered children. In one study[17] of child abusers, tactual-sensory deprivation was traced back three generations and was found to be the one common characteristic of abusing parents, regardless of socioeconomic status.

The factors which lead to child battering and the ways through which abusing parents can be helped are becoming clearer. It has been suggested that the majority of child abusers—as many as 90 percent—are normal and can be helped.[18] Characteristically, abusing parents tend to be isolated from friends and relatives who might be able to help them resolve their emotional stresses without resorting to violence. Moreover, abusing parents often are woefully ignorant about what is involved in being a responsible parent. Their perceptions and expectations of the child are often totally unrealistic. Parents whose own mothering was poor may look to the tiny child to give them the love and understanding they missed. When a parent responds to a stressful situation with abuse, he may not be aware of his own motivations and often does not realize that he has injured the child. Thus, the abusing parent requires help rather than punishment. Support for the offending parent is important in helping him to change his basic attitudes about himself and the situation. Families Anonymous, a program modeled on Alcoholics Anonymous, seeks to provide help by bringing together former child abusers in group therapy sessions so that they may help themselves and one another. In addition, a growing number of therapists are specializing in working with and helping these parents.

The infant reinforces and extends his sense of trust as he works on the complementary developmental task of *learning to relate emotionally to parents, siblings, and others.* Ainsworth[19] found that a series of signs of at-

---

[16] R. G. Heath, "Maternal-Social Deprivation and Abnormal Brain Development: Disorders of Emotional and Social Behavior," in James W. Prescott, Merrill S. Read, and David B. Coursin, eds., *Neuropsychological Methods for the Assessment of Impaired Brain Function in the Malnourished Child* (Bethesda, Md.: U. S. Department of Health, Education, and Welfare, 1971).

[17] Brandt F. Steele and Carl B. Pollack, "A Psychiatric Study of Parents Who Abuse Infants and Small Children," in Ray E. Helfer and C. Henry Kempe, eds., *The Battered Child* (Chicago: University of Chicago Press, 1968), pp. 103–147.

[18] R. C. Smith, "How to Help Battering Parents," *Today's Health*, 51 (January 1973), 57–62.

[19] Mary D. S. Ainsworth, "The Development of Infant-Mother Interaction among the Ganda," in B. Foss, ed., *Determinants of Infant Behavior*, Vol. 2 (New York: John Wiley, 1963), pp. 67–104.

tachment marks the development of infant-mother interactions during the first year of life. The infant shows his attachment to his mother in a variety of ways. His crying, smiling, and vocalization change when he notices that his mother is gone. Frequently, the infant will cry when his mother leaves him and will scramble toward her, bury his face against her, and cling to her. Upon her return he lifts his arms or claps his hands in greeting. At about eight to 10 weeks, the infant can discriminate between his mother and other adult figures. Infants at this age accept mother substitutes quite readily. During the period from age three months to six months, however, crying occurs when the mother leaves the room. Earlier we noted that, at the age of nine months, Peter did note differences between familiar people and strangers; he cried the first time he saw the observer. By ten months of age Peter related easily to the observer, who by this time had become familiar from frequent visits to his home. He and the observer played with a ball, he handled her purse, and he allowed her to feed him.

As the infant relates to other people he is developing capacities for discriminating, remembering, and responding—aspects of perceptual-cognitive development which we will examine next.

Perceptual-Cognitive Development

The young child's varied responses to the world, as he works on his developmental tasks, depend a great deal upon the messages received through the senses from the outside world. The description of perceptual-cognitive development presented in this and the next two chapters is that formulated by Jean Piaget, a Swiss developmental psychologist.

For Piaget, cognitive development is strongly influenced by maturation. Cognitive growth occurs in successive stages which incorporate and integrate the characteristics of earlier stages into the next stage. The stages are thus sequential, hierarchical, and integrated into a mental structure that develops out of interactions with the environment as these are influenced by the limits set by heredity.

Basic constructs of Piaget's system. Piaget views cognitive development as acts of *organization* of and *adaptation* to the perceived environment, just as biological acts are responses of adaptation to and organization of the physical environment. He believes that cognitive structures called *schemata* (singular, *schema*) are formed in the mind which enable the individual to adapt to and to organize the environment. Schemata can be thought of as concepts or categories which one uses for deciding what something is or what something means. An initial schema of the neonate, for example, utilizes the reflexes he was born with and his developing sense organs. The tactual sensation of the lips around the nipple and the sucking reflex combine to form the schema for "reducing hunger pangs," while being picked up is the schema for "change in activity." The neonate's knowledge of these events is obviously not obtained by means of language, but by developing schemata which involve sensorimotor interactions with the environment.

If the child is to progress in his perceptual-cognitive development, his schemata must continuously change. According to Piaget, schemata can change in two ways, through assimilation and accommodation. *Assimilation* is the cognitive process by which the person integrates new perceptual data or stimulus events into his existing schemata or patterns of behavior. The young infant, for example, has sensorimotor patterns (schemata) which are assimilations representing "mother." Mother is the person who feeds him, bathes him, picks him up, plays with him, puts him to bed, and so forth. Later, the infant will assimilate various mental images (schemata) of the face and figure of his mother. Though he may see his mother on different occasions from a front view, a side view, dressed in a pink dress, a night gown, or a coat, he readily assimilates each of these images into his existing schema for "mother."

Accommodation is the process of forming new schemata or modifying old ones so as to integrate perceptual data or stimulus events that do not fit existing schemata. At nine months of age, Peter assimilated familiar adults who were friends of his parents, if one or both parents were in the same room. But when one of these familiar adults took Peter into the bedroom, out of sight of his parents, Peter began to cry, evidence of his trying to accommodate to the new situation. In a study by Turnure,[20] infants of three months, six months, and nine months each were presented with three tape-recorded versions of his mother's voice: normal voice, voice slightly distorted, and voice grossly distorted. The finding that the six-month-olds cried more than the three-month-olds during all versions of the mother's voice, but especially her normal voice, suggests an accommodation by the six-month-old infants to hearing mother's voice without being able to see her. Their crying also represents their accommodation to an attachment to mother that is stronger than that which existed when the child was three months of age.

Optimum cognitive growth requires that there be a relative balance between assimilation and accommodation. *Equilibrium* is the term Piaget uses in referring to the state of balance between processes of assimilation and processes of accommodation.

Piaget's stages of cognitive growth.   Piaget[21] identifies four stages of cognitive development which the individual passes through between birth and age 15:

1.   The period of sensorimotor intelligence (*birth–two years*). *During this period behavior is primarily motor. The child does not*

[20] Cynthia Turnure, "Responses to Voice of Mother and Stranger by Babies in the First Year," *Developmental Psychology*, 4 (March 1971), 182–190.

[21] Jean Piaget, *The Psychology of Intelligence* (Paterson, N. J.: Littlefield, Adams, 1963).

yet *"think"* conceptually, but *"cognitive"* development can be observed.

2.   The period of preoperational thought (*two–seven years*). *This period is characterized by the development of language and rapid conceptual development.*

3.   The period of concrete operations (*seven–11 years*). *During this period the child develops the ability to apply logical thought to* concrete *problems.*

4.   The period of formal operations (*11–15 years*). *During this period the child's cognitive structures reach their highest level of development, and he becomes able to apply logic to all classes of problems.*

Piaget thinks of cognitive development as cumulative, with each step in development integrated with previous steps. The age span listed for each period is normative and suggests the time during which most children can be expected to exhibit the intellectual behaviors characteristic of the particular period. Piaget contends that all individuals may reach various periods at different ages because of variations in heredity and environment.

The sensorimotor period.   This initial period of cognitive development can be divided into six stages, four appearing during the first year and two during the second year, as shown in Table 11–1. During stage 1, which encompasses the first month after birth, the behavior of the infant is primarily *reflexive.* The basic reflexes that the infant is born with are sucking, grasping, crying, and movement of arms, trunk, and head. His reflex responses to all objects are pretty much the same. He sucks vigorously, whether it is a nipple or a blanket that he finds in his mouth. During this stage the infant makes no distinctions between stimuli. He *assimilates* all responses through his reflex system. Shortly after birth, the infant *accommodates* through rooting, searching movements if his sucking does not bring any nutrition. At birth the infant is unable to differentiate between himself and the environment. He has no awareness of objects and hence no concept of objects. He is unaware of causality, of why things happen. Any object he encounters is something to suck, grasp, or look at—something that evokes an undifferentiated reflexive response.

Stage 2 of the sensorimotor period of cognitive development extends, in most infants, through the second, third, and fourth months of postnatal life. During this stage thumb sucking becomes habitual (hand-mouth coordination), the eyes follow moving objects (eye coordination), and the head moves in the direction of sounds (eye-ear coordination). Not only does the infant reveal that he is aware of objects, but he can perceive differences in size and shape and respond to the novelty of objects as early as the second month of life. Infants two to four months of age, for example, spend more

Table 11–1.   Characteristics of Development during the Sensori-motor Period

Stage	General Development	Object Concept	Space	Causality
1 Reflex, birth–one month	Reflex activity	No differentiation of self from other objects	Egocentric	Egocentric
2 First differentiations, one–four months	Hand-mouth coordination; differentiation via sucking, grasping	No special behavior concerning vanished objects; no differentiation of movement of self and external objects	Changes in perspective seen as changes in objects	No differentiation of movement of self and external objects
3 Reproduction, four–eight months	Eye-hand coordination; reproduction of interesting events	Anticipates positions of moving objects	Space externalized; no spatial relationships of objects	Self seen as cause of all events
4 Coordination of schemata, eight–12 months	Coordination of schemata; application of known means to new problems; anticipation	Object permanence; searches for vanished objects; reverses bottle to get nipple	Perceptual constancy of size and shape of objects	Elementary externalization of causality
5 Experimentation, 12–18 months	Discovery of new means through experimentation	Considers sequential displacements while searching for vanished objects	Aware of relationships between objects in space, between objects and self	Self seen as object among objects and self as object of actions
6 Representation, 18–24 months	Representation; invention of new means via internal combinations	Images of absent objects; representation of displacements	Aware of movements not perceived; representation of spatial relationships	Representative causality; causes and effects inferred

Source: Barry J. Wadsworth, *Piaget's Theory of Cognitive Development* (New York: David McKay Co., 1971), pp. 36–37. Reproduced by permission.

time looking at complex stimulus patterns than at simple patterns.[22] Infants six weeks of age, after two weeks' daily exposure to a novel stimulus (pink plastic flower) and a familiar stimulus (colored tassel), will fixate longer on the familiar object; but at eight weeks of age infants give equal amounts of attention to the familiar and the novel stimulus.[23] At four months of age, infants have indicated by nonnutritive sucking responses that they can discriminate between natural speech versions of *b, p* and *d, t*.[24] These findings suggest that selective attention to differences in and patterns of visual and auditory stimuli represents an early stage of cognitive development—a stage which may facilitate further development by making visual exploration and auditory discrimination more effective learning processes.

Stage 3 (four–eight months) of the sensorimotor period centers in the infant's acquiring the motor development and control needed for *developing eye-hand coordination.* By the time the infant is three or four months of age, the nerve cells of the brain are more efficiently connected with different muscle groups, so that voluntary action is now possible. During this stage the child's behavior becomes increasingly oriented toward objects and events beyond his body. At four months of age, his muscle control enables him to direct his eyes, turn his head, and hold it erect. His fingers have become more agile and active, and he spends much time playing with his fingers. During the next three months the child reaches out to approach, to contact, to grasp, to feel, and to manipulate the objects within reach in his environment. At first he picks up objects like a block or a rattle by closing his fist around them. A little later he learns to bring his thumb and index finger together to pick up a small object. These progressive changes in motor development follow the *law of developmental direction;* that is, development proceeds from head to tail (cephalocaudal) and from trunk to extremity (proximodistal).

Peter, in the case presented earlier, behaved in many of the ways characteristic of stage 3. At five months Peter grasped, held onto, manipulated, and let go of rings and rattles. He used both hands in a coordinated way to handle things and to transfer finger food from his hand to his mouth.

During this stage the infant begins to exhibit *intentional* behavior. He repeats behavior that is interesting. The egocentric quality of his behavior is revealed in responses which suggest that he sees himself as the primary cause of all activity. This characteristic is shown in Peter's behavior at nine months of age: He spotted the observer's purse, reached for it, dragged it toward him, and ran his fingers around the handle and the opening. He looked up at the observer and laughed, then looked at his mother. Shortly afterward, he reached for the observer's notebook, riffled the pages, and

[22] Robert L. Fantz and S. Nevis, "Pattern Preferences and Perceptual-Cognitive Development in Early Infancy," *Merrill-Palmer Quarterly*, 13 (January 1967), 77–108.

[23] Frederic Weizmann, Leslie B. Cohen, and R. Jeanne Pratt, "Novelty, Familiarity, and the Development of Infant Attention," *Developmental Psychology*, 4 (March 1971), 149–154.

[24] Sandra E. Trehaub and M. Sam Rabinovitch, "Auditory-Linguistic Sensitivity in Early Infancy," *Developmental Psychology*, 6 (January 1972), 74–77.

then grabbed her pen. When she would not release the pen, Peter pulled on it for a few seconds, smiled, and then crawled away.

During stage 4 (age eight to 12 months) of the sensorimotor period, behavior patterns emerge which constitute the first clear acts of intelligence. The child begins to anticipate events, and he begins to use means to attain ends. Objects take on a greater degree of permanence; he begins to search for objects that he sees disappear. He also notes that other objects in the environment can affect what happens (causality). At this stage intentional behavior becomes more evident.

Evidence of intentional behavior and means-ends activity was revealed in the responses of 24 11-month-old infants to a situation eliciting separation anxiety. Each infant watched his mother leave the home through an exit that she normally did not use. The greater incidence of crying, staring at, and crawling to the unfamiliar exit showed that each infant intentionally sought his mother. The child's distress suggests that he has a well-articulated mental image (schema) of his mother's location in relation to himself. Her departure is a discrepancy from that schema which the child seeks to reconcile through accommodating to this change in the situation.[25]

At 10 months Peter displayed many of the behaviors characteristic of stage 4. After being taken by the observer away from his parents, Peter played with his stuffed animals for a moment and then began to cry when he saw that his parents were not nearby. For Peter, his parents are permanent aspects of his environment. He looks for his parents in the bedroom, and when he does not see them, he cries, using this as a means to achieve the end of being taken back to where his parents are. On other occasions his mother's playing peekaboo with Peter enables him to perceive her as a permanent object in his environment.

Piaget[26] has observed that an infant at eight to 10 months of age (stage 4), after finding his rattle twice in the toy box (position A), will continue on subsequent trials to search for the rattle in the toy box in spite of seeing it hidden under a blanket (position B). This is called "A not B behavior." Studies[27] of infants aged six to 12 months tend to confirm Piaget's observations, but they also reveal that infants go through distinct phases of cognitive response in overcoming the "A not B" error. At first, in continuing to look for the rattle by reaching into the toy box, even after he has seen it placed under the blanket, the infant's behavior seems to be controlled by the previously reinforced motor response of reaching into the toy box, not by the most recent visual input of seeing it placed under the blanket. After

[25] Ronnie Littenberg, Steven R. Tulkin, and Jerome Kagan, "Cognitive Components of Separation Anxiety," *Developmental Psychology*, 4 (May 1971), 387–388.

[26] Piaget, *The Psychology of Intelligence.*

[27] Gerald Gratch and William F. Landers, "Stage IV of Piaget's Theory of Infants' Object Concept: A Longitudinal Study," *Child Development*, 42 (June 1971), 359–372; William F. Landers, "Effects of Differential Experience in Infants' Performance in a Piagetian Stage IV Object-Concept Task," *Developmental Psychology*, 5 (July 1971), 48–54.

some confusion he finally overcomes the "*A* not *B*" error by coming to rely on the cue of noting where the rattle was hidden.

Being weaned and *learning to eat solid foods* are accommodations which most infants achieve during their first year. These developmental tasks are faced by children in all cultures, although the timing and completion of these tasks vary in different cultures. There probably is no optimum age for weaning, and the age at which it is accomplished varies widely within any particular culture. In American middle class culture, weaning may begin as early as the seventh or eighth month, but frequently the baby clings to his bedtime bottle until 18 months of age. It may be unwise to force the child to give up his bottle before he is emotionally ready to do so, since some children seem to need more sucking than others and more of the comfort and security that the bottle appears to provide. During the latter part of the first year, most babies are able to bite and chew well enough to eat solid foods.

After having witnessed the eventful first year of the infant's growth, we shall examine next the structures and directions of growth that emerge during the second year, the age of the toddler.

The Toddler

The period of infancy extends from birth to about age two and a half years. Behavior and development during the latter half of infancy are so markedly different from those of the first 12 or 15 months as to require a new designation. We have chosen the word *toddler*, a term which is frequently used to describe the child during the second year of life and a few months beyond. At one year the child is no longer a lap baby. He is or soon will be starting to walk. He is likely to be moving about, exploring, manipulating, and at times quite demanding. The powers of locomotion gained by the toddler open up a whole new world, but they also bring him into confrontation with the culture, with its inevitable prohibitions and restrictions. Through these experiences, however, the toddler gains a sense of self-awareness, identity, and autonomy.

Motor Development

Learning to walk is an important landmark in the development of every human being. Before walking can be accomplished, however, many other steps in motor development have been mastered. During the first year of life, the infant acquired motor patterns of holding his head without support, turning over, and sitting without support. The first real crawling occurred when the child was able to lift both his chest and his pelvis off the floor at the same time. Almost from the time he learned to creep he has been able to go up a flight of stairs on all fours. When he turns to go down, however, the stairs drop away from him, and the "visual cliff" effect keeps him fear-stricken at the top of the stairs. (The child exhibits "visual cliff" behavior by stopping short of the edge of a precipice, even when there is a sheet of heavy plate glass to prevent him from falling.) Following the cephalocaudal law, the child passes through a series of stages in gaining the posture required for sitting and later for standing and walking in an erect position. When he is 10 to 15 months of age, the child, through several stages, learns to walk: He pulls himself up from a sitting position and stands with support. With back upright and arms outstretched for balance, he places his feet far apart to widen his base as he stands alone. He steps out with wide spacing of legs and a very uncertain gait. Finally, when he is sure of his balance, he puts one foot in front of the other and acquires accurate control over his equilibrium.

Learning to walk marks the beginning of a period of gross motor activity. Soon the toddler not only walks but trots and then runs. Successively, he learns to hop on two feet, stand on one foot, walk backward, pivot on one foot, and "dance" to music by bobbing up and down in place. He likes to carry, shove, pull, and otherwise set in motion things in the environment. This is the age when the child trots about pulling or pushing a mechanical duck or some other toy that produces sound and movement at the same time. It is also a time when he likes to beat on pots and pans and to explore and manipulate things used by adults, such as books, ashtrays, waste baskets, and boxes of kleenex or detergent.

Toward the latter part of the second year, the toddler is often ready for toys that require a finer degree of motor coordination. This can be developed by providing the child with large building blocks, a wooden hammer for hammering pegs through a pegboard, push and pull toys, large balls, simple jigsaw puzzles with large pieces, sturdy doll furniture, plastic dishes, cars, trucks, wooden trains, soft animals, and large rag dolls.

With an increasing repertoire of motor skills, play assumes an increasingly important role in the toddler's development. Initially, the baby interacts with an adult in social-affective play[28] in which the adult talks or croons to the baby or plays games such as peekaboo and pat-a-cake—activities designed to elicit a positive response from the baby. Quite early the infant observes, touches, manipulates, and explores objects with varying tastes, odors, textures, and consistencies for the sensuous and aesthetic pleasures he receives from these activities. Once the child has learned to reach out, grasp, and manipulate, play activity increasingly involves the use and practice of the child's new-found motor skills. In *skill play* the child will often play by himself, feeding a doll or changing its diapers, loading, delivering, and unloading materials in his toy truck, and building towers and bridges with blocks. It is obvious that skill play provides the child with a sense of pleasure as well as a sense of mastery.

[28] Stone and Church, pp. 250–253.

Social Development

The child hopefully has achieved a basic sense of trust growing out of a caring, loving, nurturing relationship with his mother in early infancy. The primary adult—the mother or her surrogate—is a source of security, which continues to exert a strong influence on the child's development during infancy, early childhood, and the years beyond. It seems to be important for the child to form a continuing relationship with an adult who dresses, feeds, bathes, and cares for him.

A strong affectional tie with the mothering one bolsters the child's feeling of security at a time when his increased locomotion and motor skills bring him into confrontation with cultural prohibitions and restrictions. Early in the second year of life, the toddler begins working on a lifelong developmental task—*accepting and learning the approved patterns of his culture.* The toddler is the recipient of frequent "no's" as he seeks to satisfy his curiosity by moving toward the stairs or stove, exploring the contents of mother's desk drawer or purse, sticking things in his mouth, and scribbling with his crayons on the wall. The toddler soon learns that the world is full of things that should not be touched, pulled, climbed on, or knocked over. The socialization experiences of curbing and redirecting the child's impulses will at times be disturbing and upsetting to him. Progress toward accepting and learning approved cultural patterns is enhanced if the child finds that transgressing the limits and incurring mother's anger does not result in his losing her love. In guiding the child's socialization, the mothering one needs much patience and understanding as she allows the child to demand and get her attention, to test the limits she sets, and to express anger toward her without in any way weakening the affectional tie between her and the child.

A significant event in the socialization experience is mastering the developmental task of *controlling body elimination.* The child encounters this task in his responses to inner-organ sensations. Distention of the bladder and rectum causes an unpleasant feeling. Urinating and moving the bowels are followed by a pleasant feeling. The infant's elimination processes prior to 18 months are involuntary, since sphincter muscle control is usually not achieved until after this age. But learning as well as maturation is involved in toilet training. The learning of this task is often accompanied by emotional conflict involving both parent and child, but this is not inevitable and should be avoided.

Bowel control is usually achieved first and can be effective when movements come on a fairly regular schedule and when there are advance warnings of which the child himself seems aware. By age two the toddler can begin to recognize the significance of certain internal feelings of pressure and discomfort. This recognition enables him to perform the actions of holding in, relaxing, and expelling, so that voluntary control becomes possible. Bladder control comes in two stages, waking control and sleeping control. Urination occurs more frequently than defecation, but the internal sensations are less distinct and the mechanisms of muscular control are more elusive. The toddler's readiness for bladder control, however, is indicated by his staying dry for ever longer periods and his acquiescence to trying after he has not urinated for a while. Waking bladder control is frequently achieved at about age two, but sleeping control may lag months (sometimes years) behind. The child's acceptance of cleanliness in toilet habits signifies a desire to be like his parents and a willingness to give up certain pleasures in order to obtain the approval and love of a cherished adult.

Cognitive Development

As noted earlier, by the age of one year most infants have completed stage 4 of the sensorimotor period in Piaget's formulation of the steps in cognitive development. During stage 4 the infant develops a concept of object permanence; he searches for objects that have disappeared from view. Another important acquisition of this stage is the perception of constancy in the shape and size of an object which heretofore has appeared to differ from one presentation to the next. It is a stage also of using means to attain ends; he does something to make something else happen, such as knocking his rattle or cup to the floor in order to make a noise.

Stage 5 of the sensorimotor period encompasses the normative changes in cognitive development from 12 to 18 months of age. In this stage the child develops new means, such as experimentation (trying new approaches), rather than using previously formed, habitual schemata to achieve desired ends. When faced with a problem that he cannot solve by means of existing schemata, the child will use trial and error to develop new means (schemata). For example, when a barrier of chairs prevented Elaine from getting to the ashtrays, matches, books, and cigarette box on the coffee table in the living room, Elaine tried alternate routes and found that she could get to the living room unimpeded by going through the den. In stage 5 the child enlarges his concept of causality by seeing objects as causing events independent of any action on his part. Connie, for example, had been accustomed to looking out of the window in the evening and watching the street lights come on. Early one afternoon the sky grew dark, signaling an approaching storm. Connie looked out of the window, but the lights did not come on.

During stage 6 the child moves from the sensorimotor level of intelligence to representational intelligence. Instead of solving problems by trial and error as in stage 5, the child appears to solve problems through an internal representation that is manifested in a sudden invention of a solution with an awareness of causality. David, for example, finds that by standing up in his crib and shaking it, the crib will move little by little across the room. David continues to shake the crib until it is in front of the window, allowing him to look out. During stage 6 internal representation enables the child not only to find objects that he sees hidden but also to search for and find objects that he does not see hidden. In addition, his awareness of causality is increased by his new ability to represent objects by mental as well as behavioral schemata. Billy's toy cars, blocks, and other small playthings were kept in a large can with a plastic cover. Billy was unable to remove the plastic cover to get at his toys. He turned the can over and began shaking it. Finally, the cover loosened and the toys tumbled out.

Language Development

A major step in cognitive development is the beginning use of speech at 12 to 15 months of age. We need to remember, however, that for many months the child has been communicating his wants and feelings by crying, grunting, cooing, fidgeting, and grimacing. The child in turn responds appropriately to things people say to him, even though he himself does not talk. A first step in language development is the random vocalizations that may be observed as early as the third month of life. Initially, these vocalizations are part of the total reactive and expressive system in which the child is responding to internal and external stimuli. This is followed by a babbling stage, in which the child repeats various vowel and consonant combinations. Learning to push the air over the vocal cords and to coordinate the tongue, lips, palate, and mouth is a very complex operation for the young child.

Hearing his own voice becomes a stimulus to repeat and to continue these vocal patterns. When he is about a year old, the child tries to imitate the speech of others. We observe him imitating "mama," "dada," and "bye bye." Not only do the child's own sounds become linked to those of others, but the child gains additional practice in speech by interpreting and imitating those sound combinations that persons around him use in conversations. Children between 12 and 18 months of age carry on in play a continual stream of jargon, occasional phrases of which can be distinguished as comprehensible words. True speech arises during the second year, when the child learns to associate objects with their names, to speak words, to obey simple commands, and, finally, to communicate with others—first using single words and then simple sentences. Most children at age two have a speaking vocabulary of approximately 300 words. Though learning to talk is one of the most complex and satisfying of human learnings, one's continued social and psychological development requires the broadening of one's language skills at successive stages of maturity.

Development of a Sense of Self

Initially, the young child's self-concept is manifested in his sense of physical self. In the first year of life, the child acquires an image of his body as he is held, rocked, and caressed and as he sucks his thumb, discovers his hands, plays with his feet, pats his stomach, and touches his genitals. During the second year, the toddler enlarges his sense of self through learning the names of different parts of his body as he is bathed and played with. The child's self-concept is further enhanced through the love and care which the mothering one communicates by her valuing the child and praising him for his appearance, bodily skills, and his productions. The child also gains the sense of being valued when adults talk and read to him, play with him, and actively look for him and express joy in finding him in the game of hide and seek.

In Erikson's view,[29] development of a sense of self during the age of the toddler centers in the achieving of *autonomy*, the wish for and the achieving in a limited way of some measure of independence. Failure to achieve autonomy evokes shame and doubt, manifested in feelings of worthlessness and incompetence. Probably the most striking manifestation of the toddler's demand for autonomy is the intermittent negativism that is expressed in emphatic "no's," going limp all over, running away, and having a tantrum. As he becomes aware of his new abilities, he wants to exercise them for himself, without help or hindrance from anyone else. "I can do it by myself!" is a familiar refrain. Negativism is a normal part of development and, indeed, is essential if the child is to gain a sense of autonomy. If the toddler has ample opportunity to explore and practice things on his own, with adult support and the protection of necessary limits, he will emerge from this stage with a positive sense of self and a readiness to move into the tasks of the next stage of development.

Interventions in Child Development

The modest and often temporary gains made by four- and five-year-old children enrolled in Head Start and similar programs have convinced many that intervention programs which seek to help children make effective use of school experiences must start when these children are infants. Assisting in this task has been the growing body of research investigating infancy and early childhood, areas that have long been neglected in scientific investigation. Research findings emerging from studies of infancy have enabled educators and child development specialists to launch programs that promote the social, motor, and cognitive development of infants beginning shortly after birth. We shall next review representative infant intervention programs, including some which teach disadvantaged mothers procedures for facilitating and stimulating their infants' development.

One approach has been to send a trained tutor into the home to work with the infant directly. Schaeffer and Aronson[30] used this approach in a program that was designed to promote the intellectual development of disadvantaged infants during the second and third years of life. An experi-

[29] Erikson, pp. 222–224.

[30] Earl S. Schaeffer and M. Aronson, "Infant Education Research Project: Implementation and Implications of a Home Tutoring Program," ERIC (1970), ED 054 865.

mental group of 31 black male infants were selected through door-to-door surveys of two lower socioeconomic neighborhoods in Washington, D. C. A tutor visited the home of each infant in the experimental group for an hour a day, five days a week, beginning when the infant was 15 months of age and continuing until he was 36 months old. Participation by the mother was encouraged but not required. The program emphasized helping the child to be aware and learn the names of objects in his environment. Pleasant interpersonal relationships were encouraged, and the tutor made maximum use of teaching procedures utilizing toys, books, music and rhythms, puzzles and games. Many neighborhood walks were taken, and numerous experiences with toys, games, singing, and listening to music were provided.

The results of the study showed that at the end of the tutoring program (children at 36 months of age), the tutored children registered a mean Binet IQ of 106—17 points higher than the comparable mean IQ of the control group. A year after the termination of the tutoring, the IQ difference between the two groups dropped to 10 points, the IQ of the experimental group dropping from 106 to 100. Comparable drops in IQ have been reported in other, similar studies. This study demonstrated that black children from lower socioeconomic families do score above average in IQ if they have had appropriate intellectual stimulation. The results also show that this intellectual stimulation should be introduced before the child is 15 months of age. The results suggest, too, that the quality of maternal care as well as the tutoring exerts a significant influence on the child's intellectual development.

Another approach in seeking to increase the intellectual stimulation of young children in disadvantaged areas involves teaching mothers to teach and provide stimulating experiences for their children. In one study[31] using this approach, the researchers instructed 20 disadvantaged mothers weekly over a 15-month period in the use of educational toys for stimulating the intellectual and language development of their infants. The mean chronological age of the infants whose mothers completed the program was 20 months. The mean Binet IQ of the children whose mothers had worked with them was 16 points above that of the control group children, who had received no intervention. Even more striking was the 28-point, statistically significant difference in mean Binet IQ between six infants in the program and their sibling controls.

A variation on this approach of training disadvantaged mothers to stimulate their infants' intellectual development at home was used by Gordon.[32] He and his co-workers trained disadvantaged women to teach disadvantaged mothers in the home a series of tasks designed to stimulate infants' sensory and intellectual development. A specific curriculum based

[31] M. B. Karnes et al., "Educational Intervention at Homes by Mothers of Disadvantaged Infants," *Child Development*, 41 (December 1970), 925–935.

[32] Ira J. Gordon, *Early Child Stimulation through Parent Education* (Gainesville, Fla.: Institute for Development of Human Resources, February 1967). Contract R-306, Children's Bureau, U. S. Department of Health, Education, and Welfare.

upon Piaget's and Bernstein's[33] concepts of cognition and language development, respectively, was developed and used in the training of 15 parent educators recruited from the ghetto. During weekly home visits the parent educator demonstrated specific tasks emphasizing such concepts as object permanence for the mother to perform with her infant. The mother was encouraged to call the baby by name and to describe objects to him. Magazines were given to the families and were used for identifying and labeling objects. The parent educator taught the parent how to make toys at home with free or inexpensive materials. These toys and other materials were used to provide the infant with auditory, tactual, visual, and kinesthetic stimulation. The results of this study showed that over 30 percent of the infants whose mothers were taught the tasks were able to play certain games when tested at one year of age, whereas control children could not.

These programs demonstrate that intellectual development does not begin in first grade or even in nursery school; it begins at birth. Parents in disadvantaged areas can be taught to use a wide range of tasks and resources to provide intellectual stimulation for their infants. Finally, these programs suggest that the initial handicaps of disadvantaged children in sensorimotor development can be markedly reduced by appropriate intervention.

Early Childhood

The period of early childhood, as we shall use the term, extends from about age two and a half years to age six. Tremendous changes in all aspects of growth and development occur during these years, though the changes during any one year may not appear to be as dramatic as those during each of the first two years of life. Since children vary greatly in their rates of growth and in the timing of the onset and completion of developmental changes and developmental tasks, using a longer span of time (the early childhood years) will afford a more realistic and valid picture of development than if we were to focus on only one year at a time. We shall begin by presenting general descriptions of the child during the third year of life and at age five. This will be followed by a discussion of developmental tasks that appear at successive stages of early childhood.

The period between two and three years of age is transitional. Baby softness and roundness give way to a physique that is larger, sturdier, and more linear. The marked but decelerating increases in height during the first two years of postnatal life are followed by slow steady increases between ages two and six. At age three years, the child has a full set of temporary teeth, and by age six his first permanent teeth begin to arrive.

[33] Basil Bernstein, "Social Class and Linguistic Development: A Theory of Social Learning," in H. H. Halsey, Jean Floud, and C. Arnold Anderson, eds., *Education, Economy, and Society* (New York: Free Press, 1963), pp. 288–314.

At two and a half years, the preschooler displays an active curiosity about his physical environment. He gets into, pulls out, and pulls apart everything within reach. Motor activity during this period often appears undirected and seems to be instigated by the anticipated pleasure the action itself provides. This pleasure is manifested in the seemingly endless energy he expends in physical activities of running, jumping, and rolling that continue until exhaustion. Climbing a jungle gym and operating vehicles (tricycles, wagons) which can be propelled and steered are further evidence of growth in large muscle control. Increased dexterity in using a cup, spoon, pencil, and crayon and in building a tower of blocks that does not fall down is evidence of his development of finer motor skills.

The preschooler's greater mobility, egocentricity, and autonomy frequently bring him into conflict with other people. Thus, the demands on him by others to conform to the expectations of the culture become increasingly insistent. For many children, toilet training is completed during the third year. Much of the socialization of children during this period involves conforming to schedules and routines of feeding, bathing, playing, napping, toileting, and sleeping. These routines prepare the child to anticipate events and provide him with a sense of regularity and stability against which he can measure his own needs and demands. A major step in his socialization is acquiring a concept of ownership—what is "mine" and what is "his" or "yours." The culture's demands on the child for conformity may be met by strong emotion, outbursts of aggression, tantrums, fighting, and destructive behavior. A wise and accepting adult responds in ways that respect the child's individuality while at the same time helping him to reconcile his personal needs and the demands of the culture.

The period beginning at about age two and a half seems to mark a change in the child's relationship with his mother. It is a time when he may be physically able to move away from her to explore and to interact with other parts of the environment. His success in handling temporary separations from his mother seems to depend upon whether he has established a stable, reliable relationship with her that supports a mental image of her when she is out of sight. Success in handling temporary separation seems to depend, too, upon his mother's being available to him upon her return. At this age, separation takes place *with* the mother, not *from* her.[34] He will touch her or sit on her lap only to move away again. He may pick up a toy or another object that catches his fancy and bring it to her. This ability to separate with mother is a very important step, and it seems to be facilitated if the mother remains available close by.

At this time the preschooler is likely to find himself in small play groups with one or two other children. His own interests and activities remain paramount. Each child is engrossed in building his own tower of blocks or constructing his own tunnel in the sandbox—a type of play we

---

[34] Peter B. Neubauer, "The Third Year of Life: The Two-Year-Old," in L. L. Dittmann, ed., *Early Child Care: The New Perspectives* (New York: Atherton Press, 1968), p. 60.

earlier identified as "parallel play."[35] Each's egocentricity precludes a more cooperative, collaborative type of play. Children's egocentricity is also manifested in rivalry and conflict as they vie with each other for a particular toy or for an adult's attention and support. In spite of these potential conflicts, however, this is a period when children show increased interest in being with one another.

The child's perceptions and his mental development during early childhood are heavily influenced by his egocentricity. Initially, the child views his world as inseparable from himself. Gradually, he becomes more objective as he recognizes events outside himself, having their own causality. Growth in vocabulary and in speech skills enables the child to identify and label increasing numbers of objects in the external world—capacities that mark his progress in intellectual development.

From this picture of the child at age two and a half we turn now to see what he is like at age five as reflected in these excerpts from the case of Tommy. He is one of 45 morning kindergarten children. He is a very small child weighing 30 pounds and is 42 inches tall. He is five years old.

October 20.   *10:30* A.M. *When another child passed Tommy a napkin for his cookie, Tommy put the napkin on his head. The teacher said, "Where does your napkin belong?" He answered, "On my head. I want to look like a clown." "Very well." the teacher said. "Everyone likes to laugh at clowns. You may stand up and clown for everyone." After everyone laughed, he ran to his seat. He hasn't done that again. However, others have tried it, and when reminded of Tommy's standing before the class, each one soon puts the napkin on the table.*

11:30. This was a rainy day. There were lots of boots to be put on. Tommy couldn't find his boots. The teacher found them and started him out alone working on them. After five minutes he had managed to get one on, but it was on the wrong foot. The teacher showed him his mistake, but he insisted on leaving it on the wrong foot. The other was put on the wrong foot. Tommy told the teacher this was the first time he'd ever done it by himself.

February 3.   *During free play period the teacher noticed that Tommy was very busy in the corner with a bulldozer. He was alone and making a motor sound with his lips. The teacher inquired, "What are you doing?" He answered, "I'm making tend I'm knocking down trees to build a new road." The teacher asked, "Is that a tractor?" Very disgusted, Tommy answered, "No, that's a bulldozer."*

"Tommy, why do you always go to the front of the line instead of taking your place behind the other boys?" He answered, "I like to be first." The teacher answered, "You'll have to take your place be-

---

[35] See Chapter 7, p. 198.

hind the others if you don't get here first. That's breaking in line when you get at the beginning of the line."

February 9. *The teacher planned for the children to make valentines this week. Everyone was shown how to cut a heart by folding paper and cutting a half heart. Tommy was completely lost. He could not make the scissors go around and turn the paper at the same time. However, Tommy was not the only one who could not do it. The teacher marked on the paper where to cut, but he still couldn't do it.*

February 24. *When Tommy entered the room, he ran to the teacher to show her his thumb, which looked bruised. He said, "See my sore thumb." The teacher asked, "What happened?" He answered, "I caught it in the* door truck." *The teacher answered, "Gee, I'm sorry you mashed it in the truck door. I know that hurt, but it looks like it's getting well already." Then Tommy started taking off his coat.*

There are several word combinations that he reverses, such as awake wide *for* wide awake.

February 25. *Tommy helped the teacher carry books and pictures to her car this afternoon. Tommy said, "My, you have a big car." (The teacher has a three-seater station wagon.) The teacher asked, "Do you like my car?" He answered, "Yes, I wish you'd come see me again." She asked, "Why do you want me to visit you?" Tommy grinned sheepishly and said, "Cause I like you." She answered, "Maybe I'll surprise you sometime and go see you again." Tommy and the teacher walked hand in hand back into the school.*

March 9. *The children take turns being helpers for a week to give out napkins, milk, scissors, crayons, and so on. Today one of the napkin helpers was absent. The teacher allowed the one present to pick anyone else to substitute for this one day. Tommy was chosen to take the place of the absent child. He threw back his shoulders and strutted to the cabinet to get napkins.*

It is seldom that Tommy is picked by his classmates. He seldom is chosen when the class play "Farmer in the Dell." The teacher was pleased to see him receive some recognition from his classmates.

March 16. *When time came for rhythm band, Tommy said he wanted the cymbals. He said he had not had a turn with them. The teacher asked him why he wanted the cymbals. He answered, "They make the most noise." While the group was marching and playing, Tommy gritted his teeth every time he crashed the cymbals. He has not been able to keep time with any instrument. He can't clap or tap to the time of the music. When the children were putting the instruments away, the teacher asked Tommy how he liked playing the cymbals. He answered, "It hurts my ears."*

April 7.   Tommy was sitting on the floor playing with the oddly shaped blocks. The teacher suggested that he build a high tower. It took him several tries before he could get one to stand. He would try to put a big block on top, causing all to tumble. Finally, he chose the biggest one to put down first and built from there.

April 16.   After two weeks on the playground equipment, Tommy uses everything with ease and enjoyment. He was slow to try the new equipment, but after watching the others, he has become used to it and climbs to the top of the jungle gym.

Physical Development

Early childhood is a period of vigorous physical activity. Children at this stage are working on *developing their large muscles and gaining control over their bodies.* They like to run, jump, climb, and try to balance themselves. They eagerly respond to music and engage in rhythmic play. Motor skills, however, may be unevenly developed at these ages. Gesell and Ilg[36] remind us that children may do well at one motor skill and poorly at another. By age five, however, the average child has a fairly mature sense of balance, which is reflected in more self-reliant abandon in his motor behavior.

Several entries in the case of Tommy point to his working on gaining control of large muscles. Tommy is the smallest child in the kindergarten, and his motor development seems more like that of a younger child. Tommy has great difficulty in keeping time to the music, but he participates in rhythms and asked to play the cymbals. At first he would not try the slide or jungle gym, but after two weeks he was climbing to the top of the jungle gym.

Preschoolers generally love to color, cut, paste—activities that require the *learning of fine muscle control.* Children vary in their timing and progress in mastering this developmental task. Tommy had made only limited progress in learning to put on boots and button his coat; and he, along with several others, was unable to cut out hearts for valentines.

The preschooler also *learns to balance periods of strenuous activity with periods of quiet and rest.* Often children in nursery school and kindergarten will withdraw from play or seek a quiet activity. A child's fatigue may be revealed in his irritability and need for a nap. At 10:30 one morning, after a period of vigorous free play, Tommy called out, "Is it time to go home? I'm tired."

---

[36] Arnold Gesell and Frances L. Ilg, *The First Five Years of Life* (New York: Harper & Row, 1940), pp. 65–107.

Social Development

Early childhood is a period of broadening social horizons. The child is deeply attached to mother throughout this period, but father is becoming increasingly important. His relationships with his family greatly influence his ability to relate to other individuals and groups. A child who feels secure in the knowledge that he is loved usually relates to other adults and to peers quickly and easily. A child who is overly dependent or insecure often has more serious difficulties in relating to others.

We noted earlier that preschoolers learn to relate to peers through fantasy and parallel play. Each likes to be near other children as he acts out his own make-believe story. On February 3, Tommy explained to the teacher that his machine was a bulldozer. In an earlier anecdote he pretended that he was a clown.

An important part of the preschooler's social development is *learning and adhering to the rules and expectations of his culture.* In nursery school and kindergarten, the teacher's expectation that he learn to be friendly and considerate of others is an important part of his socialization. Tommy had many things to learn in relations with others in kindergarten. Early in the year he stomped his feet during "grace" before midmorning milk, knocked over a house that other children had built, and put the napkin on his head. He also was unable to put his boots on and button his coat, and the teacher had to speak to him about butting in at the front of the line. These incidents also show that children are *learning concepts of right and wrong.* As the child internalizes standards and mores of the culture, he *develops a conscience.* When reminded by the teacher that people laugh at clowns, Tommy and others refrained from putting their napkins on their heads.

Another important developmental task for youngsters at this maturity level is *learning to relate emotionally with persons outside the family.* Tommy's relating to the teacher is revealed in his responses to her suggestions and corrections and in his helping her carry things to her car, telling her he liked her, and walking back to the class with her. In learning to play and to share with others, Tommy is making progress in relating to a group of peers. He received the recognition of his peers the day he was chosen as a helper to pass the napkins.

By means of play, exploration, interactions with others, visits to the zoo or farm, by looking at pictures and listening to stories, and in countless experiences of daily life, the child *develops* and *modifies his concepts of social and physical reality.* Tommy learned the principle of beginning with larger blocks in building a tower, but his reversal of the order of words and their modifiers is an example of a concept which has not been mastered.

Children at an early age develop an *awareness of sex differences* from watching younger brothers and sisters being bathed and changed and by noting the different attitudes, behavior patterns, and roles of mothers and fathers and men and women. In learning to cover their genital organs, children acquire attitudes and behaviors which are appropriate to the *development of sexual modesty*. The attitudes and responses of parents toward a child's masturbation and his normal interests in the anatomical differences between the sexes are of critical importance in the child's learning this developmental task. Children need to be helped to develop healthy, positive attitudes toward sex rather than being fearful, anxious, ashamed, or guilty about normal sexual processes and functions. The kinds of sexual behavior one learns and the attitudes and feelings he develops about sex in early years often have a lasting effect on his sexuality throughout life.

By the close of early childhood, the youngster has acquired a certain degree of independence, although mother is still a very important person in his life. He is adult oriented and conforms to adult standards. He is beginning to accept responsibility for his own behavior, to clarify concepts of right and wrong, and to develop a conscience. He is on the threshold of an expanding world of school, neighborhood, society, and the world of varied experiences and ideas.

Cognitive Development

Cognitive development during the preschool years is described by Piaget as the *period of preoperational thought*. This second period of Piaget's system of intellectual development describes the normative cognitive behavior of children aged two to seven. Here we will focus only on the changes in cognitive behavior that appear before age six, the point we are designating as the close of early childhood.

The most important development during the preoperational period is the development of language. We have already noted that about the age of two the child begins to use words as symbols to represent objects. Initially, he speaks in one-word sentences, some of which may be fusions of two or more words, such as *awgone, gimme, goodboy*, and *whatdat*. During early childhood, however, language skills increase quickly. By age four, most children use grammatical rules in speaking, and most can understand what is said to them. The rapid development of symbolic representation through use of language facilitates rapid conceptual development during this period.

The first phase of the preoperational period is one in which the child's ways of thinking become increasingly like those of adults. The learning of language provides him with symbols or labels for ever more varied experiences. He learns to match new experiences with already available symbols, to distinguish between different aspects of experience, and to deal with relationships through the use of symbols. Thus, the child's statement "go bye bye in car to see Grandma" reveals an awareness, through use of language, of distinct phases of a fairly complex operation. During this period the child also invents new categories or schemata for storing and classifying information. Through this process, the young child learns not to call all four-legged, furry creatures "kitty" nor all men in a naval uniform "Daddy."

The period from about age four to age seven marks the *intuitive phase* of the preoperational period. In this phase the child begins to modify his thinking so that his view of things corresponds more nearly with outer reality. But the child's thought processes during the preoperational period are limited to *what he perceives.* This characteristic of preoperational thought is particularly evident in the child's responses to problems whose correct solution requires that he has grasped the principle of conservation. A child demonstrates an ability to conserve when he grasps the idea that number, for example, is not changed when a set of objects is partitioned into subgroups and that mass or substance does not change when the shape or appearance of an object is changed.

In a problem involving the conservation of number, if a four- or five-year-old is presented with a row of checkers and asked to construct a row of the same length, he typically constructs a row the same length, but it may have more or fewer checkers in it. When the five- to six-year-old is asked to perform the same task, he is likely to line his checkers up in one-to-one correspondence with the model, so that his row is equal in number and length to the model. If the child, however, sees one row lengthened (transformed) without any change in the number of elements, he is likely to state that they are no longer equivalent.[37] In a problem involving the conservation of mass, the child is shown two plasticine balls of equal size and weight and identical appearance. One of the balls is then rolled into a long thin sausage, and the child is asked, "Which is bigger?" During the intuitive phase children usually perceive change in shape as also being a change in amount or mass. In each of the problems cited above, the child in the preoperational period is unable to conserve because his thought processes are dominated by his perceptions.

Effective Child Care

At the beginning of this chapter, we predicted that in the years ahead trends toward increased emotional gratification and fulfillment of family members will require a marked expansion of day care centers and child care services. Before concluding a chapter on infancy and early childhood, therefore, it seems appropriate that we describe the characteristics and resources of an optimum setting for the development and learning of young children, whether it be a day care center, nursery school, kindergarten, Head Start center or child care by the mother or a substitute in the home.[38]

The general aim of any child care should be to meet the needs of the child for experiences which will foster his development as a human being. Foremost among the young child's needs is his need for security. Child care personnel can minimize the threat to the child of leaving home by helping

---

[37] Piaget, p. 31.
[38] See Urie Bronfenbrenner, "Day Care USA: A Statement of Principles," *Peabody Journal of Education*, 48 (January 1971), 86–95; Stone and Church, pp. 330–350.

his parents prepare him for the new setting. Once he is in the child care setting, each child should have a warm, sensitive adult with whom he can relate on a one-to-one basis. The close relationship between physical health, overall development, and learning suggests that an optimum program of child care must respond to the health and nutritional needs of young children. Preceding discussions of the social, perceptual, and cognitive development of young children suggest a number of criteria for programs of child care. First of all, children need *freedom* to explore, to experiment, to satisfy their curiosity through asking questions and searching for answers. Within a climate of freedom, however, the young child has a *need for structure* that is embodied in a stable, familiar environment and activities to which he can return after experiencing new, explorative types of activities. These contrasting needs as well as the wide individual differences which characterize human development at any age indicate the importance of variety and flexibility in any program of child care.

It is difficult to make an all-inclusive list of learning materials needed for implementing the program described above. Indeed, the inventive child care worker can often compensate for the limitations of physical resources. Ideally, the child care environment would contain play equipment, blocks, plastic materials, cars, trucks, dolls, props for dramatic play, clothes and accessories for dressing up, books, pictures, and charts. Some homes and many nursery schools and day care centers will also have educational playthings, such as puzzles, mosaic design kits, and science materials. In addition, one would expect to find musical equipment, such as a record player and records, drum and drum sticks, and a xylophone, plus such pets as hamsters, rabbits, fish, and birds. The larger environment is also important in the development of the young child. Hopefully, the environment of the preschool child will provide opportunities for the child to interact with other children and adults, space and time to explore and move about freely, and community resources that permit visits to farms, shopping centers, zoos, and parks.

Finally, the teacher or other adult responsible for child care should be a person who genuinely likes children and enjoys working with them. He or she should have a knowledge of children based upon principles of and research in human development as well as that gained from direct experiences with children. This person should be an alert observer, one who can interpret and clarify the child's intellectual and emotional experiences and can capitalize on situations which offer opportunities for learning. It is evident, too, that caring for preschoolers requires stamina, for maintaining a program and keeping up with lively youngsters is strenuous work. Finally, one who works with children during this formative period should be a real person, one who is human, a person who is eager to share experiences and feelings—in short, one who is compassionate and mature.

Summary

An examination ot the cultural milieu into which children are born and in which they grow up helps us to understand the emerging individual as he interacts in and responds to a rapidly changing world. A projected lower birth rate can provide an increase in the quality of life, since available resources would be used by fewer people. The nuclear family is expected to become stronger, and parent-child relationships in the future are expected to be warmer, more permissive, and oriented primarily toward psychological gratification.

What the individual is like as he grows and develops during the weeks and months after birth is a response in part to the prenatal development which preceded it. Birth is a traumatic experience; the vital systems must begin to function to maintain life in the outside world. The neonate's first developmental task is achieving stability in physiological functioning. This and the activation of receptors and effectors enable the newborn infant to become increasingly responsive to environmental stimulation.

During the first year of life, a fundamental developmental task for the young infant is achieving a basic sense of trust in those who care for him. A crucial variable in the relationship between the infant and the mothering one is the quality of tactual sensation in his contacts with the mother figure. Tactual-sensory deprivation in the mother-child relationship appears to account in part for the alarming incidence of aggression and violence in our culture, including the problem of child abuse.

During infancy great strides are made in perceptual-cognitive development. Our understanding of children's cognitive development has been enhanced by the research and writings of Jean Piaget, a Swiss psychologist. Piaget has formulated a theory of intellectual development which describes the nature and characteristics of cognitive growth during four periods of development from birth to adolescence. They are the periods of (1) sensorimotor intelligence (birth–two years), (2) preoperational thought (two–seven years), (3) concrete operations (seven–11 years), and (4) formal operations (11–15 years). Piaget believes that cognitive development takes place as cognitive structures called schemata are formed in the mind and used to organize and adapt to the perceived environment. These schemata change by assimilation, the integrating of new perceptual data into the existing perceptual structure, and by accommodation, the forming of new structures (schemata) to integrate perceptual data that do not fit existing schemata.

Infancy encompasses the period of sensorimotor intelligence, in which cognitive behavior is primarily motor. Cognitive development during the sensorimotor period is manifested in the infant's development of eye-hand coordination. Being weaned and learning to eat solid foods are other developmental tasks which most infants master during their first year.

The term *toddler* has been used to describe the child during the second year of life and a few months beyond. It is a period when he is active, moving about, exploring, manipulating, and at times quite demand-ing. Learning to walk is the developmental task which starts the toddler on his way. This is followed by learning other motor skills—running, hopping, pushing, pulling, and climbing. With this increased repertoire of motor skills, play assumes an increasingly important role in his development. Early in the second year of life, the toddler is confronted with having to accept and learn the approved patterns of his culture. A significant event in these early socialization experiences is learning to control body elimina-tion. A major step in the cognitive development of the toddler is his learn-ing to talk and his growth in use of language for communication and thinking.

Numerous studies have shown that intellectual development does not begin in first grade or even in nursery school, but at birth. These studies further demonstrate that parents in disadvantaged areas can, with instruc-tion, provide intellectual stimulation for their children and that the initial handicaps of these children in sensorimotor development can be signifi-cantly reduced by appropriate intervention.

The beginning of early childhood is marked by greater mobility, egocentricity, and autonomy. It is a period when the demands on the child by others to conform to cultural expectations become increasingly insistent. His increased autonomy is reflected in his being able to handle separations from mother without distress and his becoming involved with peers in parallel play. Children in early childhood are working on developing their large muscles and gaining control over their bodies. In their play with blocks and their use of crayons, they are also learning fine muscle control. About age four or five, children work on these developmental tasks:

1.   *Learning to relate emotionally to persons outside the family.*

2.   *Learning concepts of right and wrong, leading to developing a conscience.*

3.   *Developing and modifying concepts of social and physical reality.*

4.   *Becoming aware of sex differences.*

5.   *Developing sexual modesty.*

Cognitive processes in early childhood encompass much of the period of preoperational thought, in which the child's increased facility in using language provides him with symbols and labels for ever more varied ex-periences. Characteristically, the child in this period is unable to grasp the invariance of number or mass (unable to conserve) because his thought processes are dominated by his perceptions.

Effective child care should meet the needs of the child in ways that will foster his development. The child care worker should genuinely like children, but he or she should also have a sound knowledge of children and their development. An effective program of child care should provide the child with structure within which he is given freedom to explore and to experiment in an environment rich in people, equipment, and resources.

Study Questions

1. What impact is the application of our growing knowledge of infancy and early childhood likely to have on children's later development? Discuss.

2. James Prescott suggests that there is a relationship between the incidence of somatosensory deprivation during infancy and the level of aggression and violence in contemporary society. What evidence can you cite which supports or refutes Prescott's contention?

3. Piaget's research and writings have given us new respect for the intellectual capacities of the young child. Is there a danger that nursery schools and child care centers will emphasize cognitive development to the detriment of the child's affective and social development? Discuss.

4. If you wished to implement some of Piaget's ideas on children's intellectual development, what kinds of activities or experiences would you introduce into your program for four-year-olds who are in a nursery school serving a ghetto neighborhood? How might these differ from those in a program serving four-year-olds in a middle class suburban neighborhood?

Suggested Readings

Dittmann, Laura L., ed. *Early Child Care: The New Perspectives.* New York: Atherton Press, 1968. Contains 14 papers by prominent educators and researchers in areas of infancy and early childhood. These papers, which grew out of four national conferences on early child care, present a new look at the young child and describe contemporary programs and strategies of child care with special emphasis upon programs designed to alleviate culturally induced retardation.

Gordon, Ira J., ed. *Early Childhood Education.* Seventy-first Yearbook of the National Society for the Study of Education, Part 2. Chicago: University of Chicago Press, 1972. Examines the many facets and issues of early childhood, including nutrition, health, language development, early childhood programs, and the implications of early childhood education for subsequent development.

Hartup, W. W., and N. L. Smothergill, eds. *The Young Child: Reviews of Research,* Vols. 1 and 2. Washington, D.C.: National Association for the Education of Young Children, 1967, 1972. Selections which summarize research on preschool children in the areas of learning, cognition, language, sex role, peer group, mother-child attachment and interaction, parents as educators, socialization, anxiety, and aggression.

Spock, Benjamin M. *Baby and Child Care.* Revised Edition. New York: Pocket Books, 1968. An enlarged, revised edition of a long-time best seller written for mothers in simple, direct, conversational language. Provides very specific suggestions on a broad range of problems encountered in infant and child care.

Films

The Growing Mind, Discovery and Experience Series, No. 10, 16 mm, sound, black and white, 30 min. New York 10011: Time-Life Films, 43 W. 16th St. This film helps the teacher understand what kind of teaching situations will foster growth of thinking in children at the successive stages of intellectual development described by Piaget. The film covers the major stages of a child's thinking to show how he absorbs experience in the development of thinking.

Playing Together, Springs of Learning Series, No. 5, 16 mm, sound, black and white, 30 min. New York 10011: Time-Life Films, 43 W. 16th St. Children three and four years old are shown playing in different situations in nursery school. We learn that the child of three is often physically confident and intellectually curious. He needs to be surrounded with materials that will challenge him to develop his notions of shape, size, weight, distance, speed, color, and texture. Playing with other children cooperatively is still a bit difficult.

The Preschool Child, Springs of Learning Series, No. 6., 16 mm, sound, black and white, 30 min. New York 10011: Time-Life Films, 43 W. 16th St. We see the four-year-old beginning to draw and paint and make things. He now plays cooperatively with other children, depends on perceptual judgments, and is easily confused about number and language concepts. He can now concentrate more and undertake responsibility for specific tasks.

The World of Three, 16 mm, sound, black and white, 28 min. New York 10003: New York University Film Library, 26 Washington Place. Portrays a day in the life of a young boy who obviously is disturbed by the presence of a new sibling, a baby sister, and by the affection his mother is giving her. Shows what effects jealousy has on his behavior as he desperately tries to win back the sole love of his parents.

Middle and Late Childhood

12

The childhood shows the man,
As morning shows the day.

John Milton

     Middle and late childhood encompasses the period of life from age six to about age 11 or 12, the years when most children in Western culture attend elementary school. It is a period of development that is known by a number of different labels. Middle and late childhood is known by some as the *middle years*, a period of relative tranquility marked by slow, steady growth. Compared to the impressive changes occurring in infancy and early childhood and the sometimes tumultuous changes in adolescence, growth and development during the middle years may appear unspectacular. Yet such an impression is deceiving, for this period has its own important landmarks of development.

     The slow, steady growth of the middle years enables the child to consolidate and to extend patterns of growth and developmental tasks begun in infancy and early childhood. By age six or seven, most children have achieved a measure of autonomy, and through their socialization experiences they have internalized a great many of the expectations of the culture. Thus, we see children in middle and late childhood reaching out and extending their social development as they relate to teachers and other adults outside the home, and especially as they develop friendships with age mates and form a peer society. The increase in motor coordination and control of their bodies equips them for rapid gains during ensuing years in physical skills, especially those required in games. Since nearly all children during these years are in school, middle and late childhood can also appropriately be called the *school years*. Children at six and seven are curious and are eagerly soaking up knowledge of people, causal events, and the world about them. Maturation of eye muscles and preschool experiences have provided them with a readiness for reading. Growth in reading and language skills during the middle years in turn enables children during middle and late childhood to acquire essential tools for making the great leaps in intellectual development that occur during the elementary school years. Physical growth during the middle years, however, is relatively quiescent—a fact which led Freud to label this period of psychosexual development the *latency period.*[1] This quiescence is followed near the end of late childhood with internal stirrings which signal the changes in physical and sexual maturation to come.

A unique aspect in the development of elementary school children in our culture is the dominant role which mothers and female teachers play in their socialization. In view of this dominance, much interest has centered on the influence which female teachers are presumed to exert on the development of sex role in both boys and girls. The charge has often been made that the American elementary school is feminine in orientation and thus is less suited to boys than to girls. A review of the literature by Brophy and Good,[2] however, reveals that while in general girls outperform boys academically during the elementary school years in classrooms taught by women, these female teachers do not favor girls over boys in their classroom interactions. Comparisons between male and female teachers of elementary school children show that boys perform no better academically under men teachers than under women teachers. Instead of placing more men teachers in the elementary school, Brophy and Good recommend that changes be introduced into the school program to facilitate the sex role development of girls as well as boys. There should be less emphasis on passivity and inactive modes of learning and less differentiation in roles and activities of both sexes. Girls, for example, could be encouraged to assume greater independence and engage more in problem solving, while boys could be encouraged more in school achievement and verbal skills. The expression of sex role as an integral part of the child's individuality is revealed in the descriptions of middle and late childhood which follow.

Middle Childhood

The sixth year in a child's life is an important milestone. His statement "Now I am six and can go to school" signals the taking of a new and important step toward growth in independence. Children in this phase of early childhood make great strides in learning to control their bodies and to direct their energies purposefully; to relate to many different kinds of people, both adults and children; and to use symbols to communicate and to form concepts.

Perhaps we can best obtain a picture of what children in the primary years of elementary school are like by observing two students through the

---

[1] See pp. 133–135.

[2] Jere E. Brophy and Thomas L. Good, "Feminization of American Elementary Schools," *Phi Delta Kappan*, 54 (April 1973), 564–565.

eyes of their teachers. Clare, aged six, is working on many developmental learnings which youngsters face at the beginning of this stage.

October 10.   At the end of the morning recess period, the yard teacher came into the room. "You have a little girl, Clare, who will not listen or obey. She continued to swing after the bell rang. I blew my whistle ten times, and she never paid any attention to me until I walked over to her. I think she ought to sit down for a few recesses until she remembers." When I discussed the matter with the class, several children spoke up and said that they felt Clare should get another chance. When it was put to a vote, the class voted unanimously in favor of Clare's having another chance. "Clare, you see how the class feels, in spite of what the yard teacher said. You have another chance. I hope you will use it wisely."

At recess, many girls from other first grades were jumping rope. Clare was first. She missed. "I get another turn." No comment from the girls. She missed. "I get another turn." No comment. She missed. "I get another turn." Chorus: "You've had enough." Clare went to the side and sat down rather than go to the end of the line. Girls missed and went to the end of the line. Clare stayed seated. Finally she went to the end of the line to get her turn.

November 27.   Clare's class was called to the reading circle. Clare was the last to come. She continued to sit at her seat working. When she finally came, although the circle had been formed, she skirted it and drew her chair in next to the teacher. Her book remained closed, with the marker remaining in front of it. The other children were studying. Teacher: "Clare, would you like to study the page?" "Oh, I can read it." Teacher let her. She read stumblingly, finally asking on one line, "What does that say?" The teacher suggested she study now. Clare vocalized, "OO-di-do-di-owdy." She turned her back to the circle, discovered some sunflower seeds in the chalk tray. "I like to eat sunflower seeds." She was asked to get her place. Mayer helped her; Clare stood, hands on hips and let Mayer find it for her. Mayer said, "You better stop that fooling around."

She got up, walked over to help Dick with a word. Children at their seats were getting noisy. The teacher rang the triangle. Before she could say anything, Clare chimed in: "Mike, put your head down." When the teacher suggested she would take care of it, Clare vocalized, "Do-di-do-di-do." While the next four readers read, she sat comparatively quiet, helping with words, many times before the child needed it. Then wiggles—she turned and looked away. She wiggled her marker. She stretched in her chair. She wiggled. "Is it lunchtime yet? When is it?" When the reading circle was dismissed, she found work.

January 31.   Clare reported to the class. "We took our rabbits to our friend. He says the reason they didn't make any babies was because they were both does."

"What are does?" asked Glen. "Father rabbits," she replied. The teacher interrupted. "Does are mother rabbits. The father rabbits are called bucks."

"If they were mother rabbits why didn't they have babies?" asked Clare.

"They were both mother rabbits. You need a mother rabbit and a father rabbit," explained the teacher.

Clare was not willing to accept the statement, or else she had to think it over. "Well, we didn't have any babies because they were both does," she said and sat down.

March 6.   Clare's reading class is the fastest one in a group of four. This year I am giving the children many easy books before they are introduced into a hardback book. The vocabularies are similar in most of the preprimers. Since we have been introducing the second and third of a series of preprimers Clare has been more interested in reading.

Today as usual she brought her chair up to the circle and placed it next to the teacher. Their new preprimer, My Little Red Storybook, *had been given to this class the day before to study.*

Clare just couldn't get the children into the circle fast enough. "Hurry up, Bunny. Sit here, Sally. Bring your chair over here. Don't sit too close. It's hot. Now, Miss J., everybody is ready. May I read?" She read four pages without a mistake.

Davy is aged seven and a half and in the second grade.

October 22.   Davy came in this morning smiling. He said, "Ya know, I'm sure glad you're back." The teacher had been absent Friday. Continuing, Davy said, "Do you know what happened when you were out?"

The teacher smiled and said, "Davy, what happened?"

Davy said, "Well, you know Miss Smith was here to teach us, and you know, Robbie wouldn't go up to read." Robbie is a small, immature child. Robbie overheard Davy and rushed up to defend himself. "Miss J.," he said, "I didn't belong in that group. That's why."

Davy said, "Oh, yes you did, Robbie. All the other kids in your group went up. You cried. Why did you cry?"

Robbie said, "I don't know."

The teacher patted Robbie on the head, looked at Davy and said, "Well, Davy, Robbie is new to our school and it takes time to get acquainted with everyone and learn how we do things here. He did not know Miss Smith as well as you do. Perhaps the next time I have to be absent, Robbie will go up to his reading group."

Davy said, *"Well, I sure hope so, and Robbie, please, for heaven's sake, don't cry anymore, huh?" He looked Robbie in the eye.*

November 6.   *Davy and June came to the door of the lunchroom and said, "We've got a place for you again."*

Before the teacher could reply, Tina went and sat on the "saved" chair. The teacher went back to the third table and sat down. Davy and June looked daggers at Tina. The teacher looked up to observe Tina sitting next to Davy crying. By this time June came back to the teacher and said, "Miss J., Davy hit Tina because she sat down there." The teacher got up, went over to Tina, and said, "Tina, what is the matter?" Tina said, "Davy hit me because I sat here. He wanted you to." Teacher looked at Davy, put her hand on his head, turned him around, and said, "Davy, why did you hit Tina? Did she do anything to you?"

Davy sat silent for a minute and then looked up and said, "Oh, she cries if you touch her anyway, but she didn't need to sit there."

The teacher said, "Do you think you should have hit her? Do you hit girls?"

Davy said, "No. I'm sorry, Tina." Tina wiped big tears and said, "OK." They started eating. After lunch Davy walked back to the room with the teacher.

December 6.   *Davy, leaning over toward the teacher, said in a loud voice to be heard above the noise in the lunchroom, "Miss J., I just gotta tell you. This is good (giggled, eyes sparkled). You know our clubhouse. We have a couch. Skippy's dad is putting it in. O yes, Jimmy Baker. He is not a member anymore. He sure cusses. So-o-o he was kicked out. We have our rules up in a box. We keep it locked."*

Miss J. said, "Davy, are there any members left?"

Davy said, "Well (pause), three now." He started to eat.

January 6.   *There are four in the group which includes Davy. All are good readers, enjoy reading, read to the class, and do independent reading. They were finishing "Skippy, the Monkey," a story of a mischievous monkey. Davy began chuckling softly, and his eyes sparkled as he read. Then he laughed aloud. Children said, "Where are you reading that makes you laugh?"*

Davy replied, "Hurry up to page twenty-six and you'll see. Wait until you see what Skippy is doing." The rest of the children read as fast as they could. Davy waited for them to catch up. When they reached it, David said, "Ha! Ha-ha! Did you ever see such a monkey? I'd like to have that little devil!"

Beth made big eyes and said, "Oh, oh, Davy! What did you say?" Davy said, "Why, that's nothing to blow your top about. It isn't bad, is it, Miss J.?"

The teacher replied, "I'm sure you could have used a better word than devil.*"*

Davy said, "Well, the truth is he was a devil or at least acted like one."

Beth laughed. Others joined in. Reading proceeded.

February 1.   *The children had two large basketballs. The girls had one and the boys had one. This was the day they could play anything they chose. Davy ran, jumped, wrestled, bounced the basketball, and began shooting at the goal. He made two goals and clapped his hands and danced when he made them. He told the other boys, "Boy, I made two goals!" They smiled and applauded. Then Davy lay down on his stomach and had James, Bobby, and Dick pull him across the floor as though he were a sled. He was laughing loudly and enjoying it immensely. He had them pull him three times across the end of the gym. Then he saw a group of boys lining up for a race. He dashed to get in line for the race. He ran the race, won, and dashed halfway to the teacher, slipped part of the way, and said, "Boy, I sure put on steam, but I won!" His face was very red and he was perspiring.*

February 19.   *After lunch children hurried with their trays so they could be the first in line next to the teacher. Davy was late today, which is unusual. He hurried to the line, not smiling, and looking somewhat angry. Barry, a large boy for his age and largest in the room, said, "O.K., let Davy in line. He is the leader today." Davy smiled at Barry, who said, "See, I stuck up for you, Davy." Davy said, "Thanks, Barry. I'll remember this." Then with a smile he took his place as leader of the line and led it back to the room.*

Physical Development

Physical growth during middle childhood is slow and steady. Children during this period generally increase two or three inches in length and three to six pounds in weight each year; but, as was noted in Chapter 4, there is considerable variation among children at any level in their rates of growth and maturing. The child's face and body are gradually changing shape. The jaw lengthens as baby teeth work themselves loose, come out, and are replaced by permanent teeth. The heart is in a period of rapid growth, but the brain has achieved about 90 percent of its weight. The eyes of the six-year-old have not reached adult size or shape, and because of their relatively shallow depth, the child at this age is often farsighted. As a consequence, many six-year-olds are delayed in beginning to learn to read. By the end of early elementary childhood, the dominance of left or right eye and handedness has been established.

The high activity of the preschool years carries over to the early elementary period. There is a great deal of running, jumping, climbing. As children play on the swings, do stunts on the bars, participate in rhythms, learn to swim and to balance themselves in walking a plank, play circle games, play tag, run relay races, or play simple games with a large rubber ball, they are *gaining increased skill in using and controlling large muscles.* Clare is working on large muscle control, as shown by her doing stunts on the bars, skipping rope, running, and initiating active games. This is the period when tag, jacks, marbles, hide-and-go-seek, ring toss, spinning tops, and flying kites are popular. Some girls begin to take dancing at this age, and a few have fleeting dreams of becoming a famous ballerina.

In time, this active play becomes more organized, as children form teams and compete against one another. Then active play is focused on *learning skills required in organized games and sports,* a developmental learning of considerable importance in middle childhood. Davy is already beginning to work on this task, as revealed by his initial successes with the basketball.

In conformity to the law of developmental direction which was encountered earlier, children are beginning to *gain increased control over their fine muscles.* At first, they are awkward in using their hands, but in time they do quite well in coloring, cutting, pasting, painting, drawing, and using simple tools such as a hammer and saw.

Social Development

The middle childhood period is marked by important changes in children's social development. The child's identification with adults, especially the teacher, which was noted in nursery school and kindergarten, continues into first grade. The child's relationships with his teachers at this stage influence his feelings of security and also shape his whole outlook on life, his feelings of adequacy, and his experiences in relating to peers and other adults.

As young children interact with and respond to their teachers, they are *learning to relate emotionally to adults outside the home.* Davy enjoyed sitting with the teacher and telling her about his gang's clubhouse and activities. At the same time, as children begin to assume responsibilities (dress themselves, go on errands, go to school alone and arrive there on time, and learn to take care of themselves in a new environment), they are taking important steps in *achieving independence of family.* Six-year-old Clare expressed her independence by continuing to swing after the yard teacher blew her whistle and by not working with the teacher and other children in the reading group.

Children's relationships with their peers increase in importance and intensity during the early elementary years. At ages seven, eight, and nine, children spend increasing amounts of time and effort in activities that will enable them to *win acceptance, roles, and prestige in the peer group.* As we noted in Chapter 7, this is the period when gangs and short-lived clubs are formed, complete with secret language and codes. The mania for collecting baseball cards and other objects and paraphernalia begins about this time. As children improve in motor coordination and develop game skills, they begin to play baseball, soccer, basketball, football, and other games involving a group of peers. As children learn the rules of the game and find ways of settling their disagreements over rules, an increase in group cohesiveness can be noted, and peer activities continue over long periods. Further interactions with peers are provided by Brownie and Cub Scout groups.

The child's relationships with his peers during the primary grades are evident in the excerpts from the cases of Clare and Davy. Clare's classmates supported her so that she was not kept in at recess in spite of the yard teacher's recommendation, but they strongly protested her continuing to jump rope after she missed. Another peer warned her against fooling around during the reading period. Clare became more responsive to the reactions of peers as the year progressed. In the excerpts from the case of Davy, the peer group is seen to exert a strong influence in the daily lives of second grade children. The intolerance of primary children for their less able and mature peers is revealed in Davy's asking Robbie not to cry when the substitute teacher was there. Davy on numerous occasions spoke of his gang's clubhouse, but when the teacher asked to visit the clubhouse, Davy was not sure whether she would be permitted to come. Sticking up for a friend and peer was shown in Barry's holding Davy's place in line.

As children relate to one another, many of their behaviors, such as teasing, name calling, and quarreling, are strongly disapproved by adults. Children at this stage, as well as at earlier and later stages, continue to work on *learning and adhering to the expectations of the culture.* Clare gradually learned to give her attention to the reading activity, and Davy was made aware of his wrongdoing in hitting Tina when she took the seat he was saving for the teacher. Conforming to the demands of the culture is facilitated by the *development of a conscience,* which began with the child's identification with his parents during the preschool years. Moreover, as peer activities of boys and girls become more divergent, further progress can be noted in each child's *acceptance of his sex role.* Evidence of Davy's developing a conscience and acceptance of his sex role is shown in the anecdote of Davy hitting Tina. The teacher asked Davy, "Do you hit girls?" and Davy said, "I'm sorry, Tina."

Cognitive Development

When children begin the primary years, they are ready and eager to learn as much as they can of the world about them and to communicate by using the symbols they have observed older siblings and grownups use. *Learning and gaining increased skill in reading* is a key developmental task of children during their early years in school. At the age of six and a half, most children have acquired adequate breadth of interest and sufficient mental maturity and eye development to be ready to read. Reading vocabulary increases rapidly during the primary years, children learn to read silently, and many children are reading independently by the end of this period. They are acquiring skills that are part of the broad developmental task of *learning appropriate symbol systems and the development of conceptual abilities.* Children during this period not only learn to tell time but, through adapting to the routines of home and school, develop a concept of time. They are beginning to have some awareness of the past and reveal an interest in people who lived long ago. They are acquiring concepts of space and distance beyond their own experience. Differences in sizes and shapes fascinate them. They are gaining a better understanding of spatial relationships, and they show this in the greater realism, proportion, and detail in their drawings and paintings. In these and many other ways, children in the primary years are *learning a vast number of physical and social concepts related to their ever widening world.*

The cases of Clare and Davy show that each in his own way was hard at work on the developmental tasks of mastering a symbol system (implied in learning to read) and of developing concepts related to the physical and social world. Clare's teacher reported that she was in the first reading group and was reading well. Her growth in developing concepts was revealed in a comment that a certain story was silly because it told of rabbits and boys being hatched from eggs. Davy's skill and interest in reading can be inferred from his comments about the monkey in the story. His concepts of what it means to belong to a gang and what constitutes cussing are revealed in several of his comments.

It may be recalled from the previous chapter that with respect to cognitive development, most children at the age of six are in the final phase of what Piaget describes as the period of preoperational thought. We noted that during this period the child's thought processes are dominated by his perceptions. Hence, children during the preoperational period typically cannot conserve; that is, they cannot hold one dimension invariant at the same time changes are made in other dimensions. We recall, for example, that when a five- or six-year-old child, when asked whether the first of two identical plasticine balls is bigger than the second ball, which was transformed into a long thin sausage, will usually answer that the sausage is bigger. Between age six and seven, the child has acquired some of the cognitive structures required in conservation. Many children at this age comprehend the invariance of number, irrespective of the arrangement of elements within the set, and a few have acquired the conservation of area and mass.

The period from seven to 11 years of age is the *period of concrete operations.* In this stage the child's thinking becomes more logical and systematic. Although his thinking is no longer limited to his perceptions, it is, nevertheless, based upon what he has experienced. When he encounters situations with which he cannot deal on the basis of direct experiences, he reasons by use of analogy to something he has experienced. Thus, we refer to these logical operations (conservation, reversibility, classification, and so forth) as "concrete" because they are useful to him only in solving problems involving concrete (real, observable) objects and events which he has experienced. In general, the child cannot yet apply this logic to problems that are primarily hypothetical and verbal.

Asking children to work on problems of propositional logic affords opportunities for studying the thought processes children use at successive stages of intellectual development. During the intuitive phase of preoperational thought, when the five- or six-year-old child is asked to predict whether items such as a plank, a needle, a pebble, or an aluminum cover will float or sink in water, it is quickly apparent that the categories available to the child at this stage are inadequate. Categories such as heavy-light and large-small are inadequate for sorting things into categories of floating and non-floating objects. The six-year-old's explanation that some objects float "because they swim on top of the water" while others sink "because they are big or heavy or stay at the bottom" reveals his lack of a satisfactory organizing principle.

Seven- to nine-year-old children strive to overcome this contradiction through the use of concrete operations. The contradiction is overcome by revising one's concept of weight by viewing it in relation to volume. Thus, the heavy-light schema is transformed into a four-fold classification of big-heavy, big-light, little-heavy, and little-light. This step is necessary in order for the child to develop a concept of relative weight. A typical seven- or eight-year-old is likely to classify objects into three categories: (1) those which float because they are light (wood, matches, paper, and aluminum cover); (2) those which sink because they are heavy (large and small keys, pebbles of all sizes, needles, nails); and (3) those that remain suspended at some midway point (fish). The child reveals his use of concrete operations by stating that the needle (or key) "goes down because it's iron," the nail because "It's light but it sinks anyway. It's iron, and iron always goes under."[3]

Support for Piaget's position that intellectual development is relatively independent of cultural background, schooling, and language development appears in a study by Haney.[4] A battery of Piaget-type tasks was administered to 160 children in kindergarten through grade four who had been matched for socioeconomic status and verbal ability at each grade level. Performance on these tasks was more closely related to verbal ability than to social class background, but most differences in performance between the high and low verbal ability group tended to disappear at the fourth grade level. In addition, there was strong support for finding consistently better performance with increased age-grade level, irrespective of social class, culture, or verbal ability.

The middle childhood years witness important changes as the child begins to interact with adults and peers in a wider world. During these years he becomes more responsible and independent, and he develops the

---

[3] Barbel Inhelder and Jean Piaget, *The Growth of Logical Thinking from Childhood to Adolescence,* trans. by A. Parsons and S. Milgram (New York: Basic Books, 1959), p. 29.

[4] J. D. H. Haney, "A Comparison of Socioeconomic Status, Verbal Ability, Grade Level, and Sex in the Performance of Piagetian-Type Tasks," ERIC (1971), ED 056 360.

skills and understandings that will enable him, through reading, cognitive development, and problem solving, to deal with concepts and phenomena for beyond the space and time of his immediate world.

Moral Development

An important goal of socialization in childhood is the development of moral character. For the child the developmental task is one of *learning to make ethical judgments and to apply ethical principles in determining right and wrong.* Morality has generally been defined as conscience, as a set of rules of social action internalized by the individual. Moral development is the increase in the internalization of these cultural rules. Ethical behavior, however, depends upon more than a knowledge of right and wrong; it also involves making moral judgments. We shall examine each of these dimensions of ethical behavior.

Some view moral character as "good habits" produced by training, example, and reward and punishment. These habits become internalized in one's forming his conscience. A more prevalent view, however, is that moral character is based on ego abilities of judgment, foresight, and reason. Both of these views relate to the question "At what age is ethical behavior formed?" Kohlberg,[5] from his review of the literature, concluded that moral character is not a product of development, since the evidence shows that resistance to cheating and stealing does not increase significantly or regularly with age from nursery school to high school. Hartshorne and May[6] found that the most influential factors determining resistance to the temptation to cheat are situational factors rather than a fixed individual moral trait of honesty. Thus, children are more likely to cheat in less risky situations than in more risky situations. These findings seem to undermine the view of moral character as a general set of "good habits" and cast doubt on the idea that moral character is formed gradually as part of the developmental process.

While moral behavior does not lend itself to an age-developmental analysis, acquiring *moral judgment* does seem to follow basic stages of development. Piaget[7] early theorized that children's growth in moral judgment corresponds to stages in their intellectual development. He states that intellectual growth and experiences of role taking in the peer group naturally transform perceptions of rules from external authoritarian com-

---

[5] Lawrence Kohlberg, "Development of Moral Character and Moral Ideology," in Martin L. Hoffman and Lois W. Hoffman, eds., *Review of Child Development Research* (New York: Russell Sage Foundation, 1964), pp. 383–431.

[6] Hugh Hartshorne and Mark A. May, *Studies in the Nature of Character:* Vol. 1, *Studies in Deceit;* Vol. 2, *Studies in Self-Control;* Vol. 3, *Studies in the Organization of Character* (New York: Macmillan Co., 1928–1930). See also Chapter 6, p. 159.

[7] Jean Piaget, *The Moral Judgment of the Child* (New York: Harcourt Brace Jovanovich, 1932).

mands to internal principles. Piaget points out that the morality of the preschool child is based upon an unquestioning respect for adult authority. The four-year-old reasons that taking someone else's toy is always wrong, regardless of the circumstances. The 10-year-old child, however, judges an act as bad in terms of the intent to do harm. Thus, the older child believes that if Gary accidentally runs into Philip, Gary should not be punished. The older child is more likely than the younger child to consider the diversity of views of right and wrong and to judge behavior by putting himself in the place of the person who has committed the misdeed.

A knowledge of these stages in children's moral development can assist the teacher in interpreting the child's responses in ethical situations. Instead of chastising a child for being bad or dishonest, the teacher can accept moral behavior that is appropriate to the child's stage of development. In addition, through individual counseling and class discussion the teacher can facilitate children's development of a more autonomous moral character in which internalized normal and logical principles of justice determine the individual's behavior in ethical situations.

Late Childhood

Late childhood, as it is to be described here, encompasses the period of development of boys (age nine to 11) and girls (age nine and 10) in the upper elementary years of grades four, five, and six. It is a period of slow, steady growth in height and weight; but there is a sharp decrease in rate of growth during the last few months of late childhood, just prior to the onset of the pubescent growth spurt. Wide differences in physical maturity are noticeable among children at this level. Some children in fourth, fifth, and sixth grades appear small and underdeveloped, while many of their classmates—tall, large, and well developed—are in the preadolescent and early adolescent stages of maturity. A few girls begin menstruating at nine and 10 years of age.

Late childhood may offer parents and teachers a breather from the stresses and problems of earlier periods of development. The youngster in late childhood is more responsible and dependable. He has developed a great many skills, he is more amenable to reason and logic, he is developing a strongly internalized sense of right and wrong, and he reveals a tremendous interest in and curiosity about the physical and social world in which he lives.

During late childhood, the peer group becomes increasingly important in the lives of children, but the interests and activities of boys and girls diverge more and more, as each sex group disdains the other and keeps pretty much to itself. Late childhood is a period of comparative calm in which children in general adjust smoothly to the problems that confront them.

There is some evidence that children in late childhood today are in many ways quite different from children at this age a decade ago. Today's children have grown up in a culture that is more open and have been more exposed to a broad range of stimuli, including sex and violence, which earlier were more often concealed from children. The schools, the mass media, the teenage world, and commerical interests all exert tremendous pressures toward precocity in encouraging children's emulation of teenage grooming, behavior, styles, and music preferences. Parents, too, often take the lead in promoting mixed parties and social activities normally associated with adolescent groups. Another characteristic of today's children in late childhood, especially those in middle class suburban settings, is the degree to which the child's life is organized around music lessons, dancing lessons, the Little League, and visits to the orthodontist. When one adds to this schedule homework and time each day for watching TV, it seems that the carefree childhood of building forts in the woods, collecting rocks, bicycling, playing, and talking with friends, going to summer camp, reading lots of books on all sorts of subjects, has all but disappeared. It seems that nowadays youngsters have too little time and too little fun just being children!

Before we discuss the changes and developmental tasks of late childhood, it may be useful to observe how two children, Cheryl and Stan, are responding to the demands and changes of this period.

Cheryl is nine years, nine months of age and is in the fourth grade of a third and fourth grade combination class. She has an older brother, Tim, who is 11, and two sisters, Nancy and Paula, who are five and three, respectively. Her father was killed the year before in an automobile accident.

October 6.   *For "Show and Tell" this morning Cheryl told about a teenager who goes to the same church as she does. Cheryl said the girl was simply "charming." "Yesterday at church she looked beautiful. She had on a navy blue chemise dress with huge white buttons for trimming. She had on a little blue hat, some blue pumps, and even blue hose. She has a real small waistline." Cheryl also stated that she didn't know this girl, "although she has noticed me, as she smiles at me." Cheryl hopes to make her acquaintance so she'll get some ideas on how to dress when she gets a little older.*

October 27.   *Cheryl was radiant as she rushed into the room this morning. Her eyes were simply dancing as she walked to her desk to put her library book away. She exclaimed, "Do you see anything different about me this morning?" I instantly knew that I'd better look Cheryl over fairly well before I answered. I had no need to worry, as Cheryl was bubbling with enthusiasm. She exclaimed, "Oh, Mrs. M., see my new tights! They're robin's egg blue. I simply am crazy about them." Cheryl opened the door and ran outside to show her new tights to all her friends.*

November 14.   When Miss B. brought her fifth grade class to visit our room, one boy wondered why we all had new chairs. Cheryl immediately spoke up and said, "We are the most privileged, so we get new seats." The boy gave Cheryl a sneering look, and Cheryl answered with a cool stare.

February 27.   Story written for language.

The Measure of Greatness

I think that a person rich or poor could be called great. A person does not have to be smart to be great. I think Abraham Lincoln was great even though he was poor and didn't have any schooling. And also there was George Washington who was rich and had schooling.

The greatest living person I know is my mother. The reason I think she is nice is because she is never cross or mean.

Cheryl Howe

March 31.   As I was writing some fourth grade assignments on the board Cheryl came up and said, "Oh, Mrs. M., I forgot to tell you. During Easter vacation I got a phone call. Guess who it was from?"

I hesitated a few seconds and asked, "Was it a boy or a girl?"

Cheryl: "A boy, and I really wasn't too thrilled. But I guess it's OK."

Teacher: "I give up. You'll have to just tell me."

Cheryl: "Well, it was Gary Grimes. He called one evening and told me he was moving. He will be going to a new school and won't see me anymore. He said that he liked me very much and he thought I liked him."

Cheryl went on to explain that she was so embarrassed but that she was courteous and kind to Gary.

Stan is 10 years, nine months of age and in the fifth grade. He laughs vigorously when something funny happens in the classroom and is always alert to do any favor I might ask of him. Although not a skilled leader in sports, he seems to show much enthusiasm and eagerness in participating in all games.

October 14.   While playing kickball today during the recreation period, Stan and Russ were continually getting together and trying to wrestle until the captain of the team said, "What's the matter with you two? You are not keeping your positions."

Stan remarked, "I just guess we aren't too interested today and we'd rather wrestle." Several other boys yelled at them and said, "Come on, Stan and Russ, we need your help." Both boys got to their positions and followed the game a little more closely.

November 17.   *In a conference with Stan's mother this after-noon, I learned that astronomy seems to be his greatest interest. When on a trip to New York with the family, they had taken him to the observatory, which he thoroughly enjoyed. Several times his father has taken him and his older brother to the Naval Observatory in Washington.*

November 24.   *Stan was sitting by my desk. Carl asked if he might buy a small picture of one of the girls. (She had returned her pictures without purchasing any.) Stan remarked, "Mrs. T., it's really fun sitting by your desk seeing how goofy some of these guys are. Imagine wanting to buy a girl's picture! I think too much of my money to spend it on a girl's picture. Carl must be in love." Carl looked at Stan with a delighted look on his face and remarked, "Sure, Stan, I want to buy Bee's picture. So what?" Stan shook his head and remarked again, "Buying a girl's picture!" I smiled at his remark and said, "Stan, maybe you'll think enough of a girl to buy her picture." Stan replied, "No, not me. That money smells too good."*

December 21.   *Stan came up to me and said he had hurt his hand and wrist yesterday. I asked how he hurt himself. He said, "You see, one of my friends and I were playing, and I guess he wanted to see who could be the best in boxing, and this is what I got, a bad hand. I don't think either of us was the winner. He went home with a hurt shoulder, and I got a sprained thumb, so that's why I'm gloomy. But one thing, I did come to school today and he didn't, so maybe he couldn't take it as well as I could. The other boy is Frank, in the sixth grade, a year older than I am, but I think I am a little taller and heavier than he is. I'll find out about him tonight when I get home. I'm glad I could come to school."*

March 23.   *Today we had a spelling contest. Before beginning, several asked Stan not to spell his words so loudly. He followed this suggestion. He and another boy tied as the best spellers. Stan's face was joyful. He wasn't boastful, but one could tell that he was pleased when several boys and girls said, "Stan, you are really a good speller." "Thank you" was his only reply.*

April 3.   *Stan seems to be noticing Bee a great deal today. She is one of the most popular girls in the room. He looked over at her and smiled several times. When he passed her desk, he'd pause to say something. While playing circle soccer, each time he'd kick the ball in Bee's direction. This seemed to please her, for I noticed she smiled each time the ball was kicked to her. When the group was ready to leave at 3 o'clock, I said, "Stan, I think something has happened to you."*

He said, "I'm curious. Can I stay in to find out?" Before I had time to answer, Stan returned to his seat and waited to talk with me. He asked what I had noticed.

I said, "I believe there is a girl in here you are showing a little attention to." With a pleased look he replied, "You mean Bee?"

I said, "Yes, Stan."

"You know, Mrs T., she is really pretty, a good sport, and good in schoolwork, and I do like her, but I'm not so sure she likes me."

I said, "I am pleased you see these good qualities. Bee is a fine girl."

May 3.   *Stan's mother came to bring Stan his baseball mitt, which he had forgotten. I spoke to his mother and she said, "Mrs. T., Stan was so enthusiastic about his new mitt, and now he doesn't want to play with the boys at noontime."*

I said, "Stan, what is the trouble? You showed me your mitt and were so happy about it."

He said, "Mrs. T., the boys just don't want me to play because I can't always hit the ball."

I said, "Stan, maybe the boys feel you need more practice. Why not practice with some of the boys after school and at noon until you become more skillful?"

He said, "Mother, don't leave my mitt. I'm not going to play." The mother insisted, but knowing the boys on the team, I could see Stan's point of view and I felt if I could talk with some of the boys they could help Stan. Stan said he didn't want me to do that. They'd think he was a sissy if I arranged to have him play. I asked Al if he'd help him with the skill in batting.

Al said, "I like Stan and even though he isn't such a great player, I think he should be on the team. He can do some things better than some of the others." Al urged Stan to play the next day. Stan had his mitt and brought it with him to the diamond. Later I noticed that Stan is on the team and seems to be very happy.

Physical Development

Late childhood is the period in which *physical prowess* and *athletic skills,* especially for boys, are more important than at any other time. Failure to learn the skills which enable one to participate adequately in the games and activities of the peer group is a grave handicap to being accepted by the group. The importance of being able to play well enough to make the team was keenly felt by Stan in the anecdote cited above. Stan recognized that he could not play ball as well as some of the boys; and, after some initial hesitation, he worked hard to improve himself in hitting and fielding.

The rapid *development of fine muscle control* during this period is revealed in improved athletic skills, skills in playing a musical instrument and use of tools, and in more legible handwriting and quality of artwork.

Arts and crafts hold considerable interest for children in late childhood. Boys may spend a morning or an afternoon working on a model airplane or car or building things with simple tools. Girls sew and weave, and both sexes reveal interests and skills in leather work, plastics, ceramics, and other art media.

The growth of body organs during late childhood has an important influence on behavior and development. Lungs and the digestive and circulatory systems are still growing. Since the heart lags behind the growth and development of other organs, overstimulation and excessive fatigue should be avoided. The eyes are much better developed and are able to accommodate to close work with less strain.[8]

For boys, this is a period of rough-and-tumble play. It is a time when boys test themselves against other boys by wrestling and occasional fights. Stan and his friend Russ started wrestling during kickball; later he spoke to the teacher of his injured hand, which came from his trying to outbox another boy. In late childhood, girls become physically less active. Cheryl played jump rope with the girls, but already in fourth grade she was more frequently a spectator than a participant in active games with boys.

Social Development

The peer group, which emerges in the latter part of the primary years, has by late childhood become an important social force in the lives of most of these children. *Being accepted by one's peers* and *playing roles in the peer group* are among the important developmental tasks which confront the child at this stage of his development. We noted earlier the important relationships between physical skills, physical maturity, and peer acceptance. Cultural differences, however, appear to exert limited influence on peer status during late childhood. If a child's behavior is acceptable to his peers, differences in socioeconomic background, race, and religion influence peer acceptance relatively little unless pressures are exerted on children by their parents.

As noted earlier, the beginnings of a strong conformity can be observed in late childhood. The peer group exerts an increasing influence on the dress, activities, and values of its members. Few children wish to risk rejection because of failure to conform. The peer group at this stage is made up of smaller clubs and cliques. Often these small groups form spontaneously and are informal and continuously changing. Frequently, clubs and cliques strive to maintain their identity and structure through use of secret language, secret rules, and secret passwords.

The most striking characteristic of most peer groups in late childhood is that there are really two peer groups, formed by the cleavage be-

[8] Gladys G. Jenkins, Helen Schacter, and William W. Bauer, *These Are Your Children*, 3rd ed. (Glenview, Ill.: Scott, Foresman and Co., 1966), pp. 130–219.

tween the sexes. In maintaining their preference for rough-and-tumble play, boys disdain weakness and feminine activities as "soft" and "sissyish." Girls perceive boys this age as rough, uncouth, ill-mannered, and not quite civilized. Girls and boys in late childhood do work and play together under the leadership of an adult, but in free play situations each child tends to participate in the activities of his own sex. At various times each sex group may respond to the other sex group by ignoring the other group, by criticism, and at times by antagonism and hostility. Stan left little doubt about his feelings toward girls: "Imagine wanting to buy a girl's picture! I think too much of my money to spend it on a girl's picture." The mutual disdain which Cheryl and a boy in another class felt for each other is reflected in his sneering look and her cool stare.

The boy's life in late childhood tends to be bound up in the life and activities of his gang. Many gangs center their attention on athletics and sports, some concentrate on maintaining their position and territory vis-à-vis neighboring gangs, while others seem to "have little organized purpose other than to serve as hideouts from adults where fellows may . . . exchange yarns of escapades and plan ever more daring, more dangerous activities."[9] It is from the gang that members gain further information about sex. Often it is communicated through ribald stories accompanied by raucous laughter. Though the stories, antics, practical joking, roughhousing, and secret communications seem silly and pointless to many adults, they are the means through which children in late childhood measure themselves against their peers in the group.

Clubs and formation of cliques are also focal points of girls' social interaction in late childhood. It has been suggested that girls are more concerned with form and verbal imagery than are boys at this age and that their clubs exist more for the practice they provide girls in exercising their verbal powers through the forms required by club life than for the sociability it affords. There is some indication, too, that girls' clubs tend to be more exclusive, more autocratic, and more tightly knit than do boys' gangs.[10]

Whereas boys gain prestige at this stage through athletic prowess, girls gain status in the group by their manner of dressing and grooming. They are much more conscious of their appearance than are boys. This strong interest in clothes was revealed in the excerpts from the case of Cheryl. By her detailed descriptions of the teenager she had seen in church, Cheryl revealed her strong admiration of this girl. Cheryl bubbled with enthusiasm in showing the teacher her robin's egg blue tights; and, in talking to a girl friend about her mother's new sweater that she tried on, she sighed, "It looked real dreamy on me."

In spite of the strong influence of the peer group in the lives of children in late childhood, the affection, confidence, and support of adults are

---

[9] Howard A. Lane and Mary Beauchamp, *Understanding Human Development* (Englewood Cliffs, N. J.: Prentice-Hall, 1959), p. 277.

[10] Lane and Beauchamp, pp. 281–282.

still very important. Thus, for these children, *relating to adults*—gaining their friendship, confidence, and approval—is an important continuing developmental task. The need for peer group belongingness and, at the same time, for the affection and approval of adults may be a source of conflict for the child if the differing expectations of each cannot be compromised or reconciled. Standards of the peer group come increasingly to prevail over those advocated by adults. At the same time, the efforts of adults to dominate, to manipulate, or to overprotect individuals or the group are deeply resented.

Because of the group's increased sensitivity to and fear of adult domination or manipulation, the parent or teacher who wishes to assist a child in gaining peer acceptance needs to exercise unusual tact. Stan was particularly sensitive to the unwanted interference by his mother in bringing his mitt to school and of his teacher's offer to ask the other boys to help him. Stan's ready smile, his willingness to help, and his frequent reporting to the teacher on peer activities and out-of-school experiences revealed a strong liking for his teacher. It was natural for Cheryl to identify strongly with her teacher, since she shared with her teacher her hopes and aspirations. It is also revealed in her statement "Mrs. M., I think you're a real common person. You usually wear such plain, attractive clothes." The teacher replied, "Thank you, Cheryl. That's the nicest compliment I've received in a long time."

Personal and Intellectual Development

Children register considerable progress during the years of late childhood in their development as persons. They are becoming more skilled in handling their emotions, in relating to others, and in coping with frustration. To the extent that children succeed in mastering developmental tasks of learning physical and game skills and gaining peer group acceptance, they grow in self-confidence. Stan revealed a new sense of self-esteem in his report of his boxing match with Frank.

Children at this stage are *learning more mature and more effective ways of adjusting to threat and frustration.* They can be more objective in seeing and accepting their own faults and shortcomings rather than projecting the blame onto others. Cheryl's progress in learning more appropriate adjustment patterns was shown in a variety of ways. In an anecdote presented in a previous chapter, Cheryl readily admitted her guilt in accusing Sue of cheating, and she apologized. She reported being courteous and kind to Gary, who unexpectedly telephoned and told Cheryl he liked her.

A child's growth in personal development at this stage is also shown in his *increased awareness of the opposite sex* and by his *increased acceptance of his own sex role.* We have noted the attachment for one's own sex and the antagonism directed toward the opposite sex, manifested during much of late childhood. This attachment to one's own sex extends over a longer period for boys than it does for girls.

In spite of their efforts to maintain their pose of disdain for the opposite sex, boys and girls are seldom able to mask their growing awareness of and interest in the opposite sex. The physical changes associated with approaching puberty make this growing awareness inevitable. In manifesting an awareness in the opposite sex at this stage, children are taking an important step toward *establishing heterosexual relationships,* an important developmental task faced in early adolescence. Cheryl reported that she wasn't too thrilled by Gary's saying that he liked her. Stan's sudden change in attitude toward girls is not untypical and is rather amusing. One can guess that some boys may be revealing their growing awareness in girls "safely" by teasing male peers who express this interest more overtly.

Boys and girls indicate an acceptance of their sex roles through characteristic behavior and modes of response that have already been described. Thus, boys show their masculinity by being tough and brave, playing hard and rough, and showing interest in sports. Girls express their femininity in their grooming, in their interest in clothes, and in their development of social and verbal skills.

Late childhood is a period of marked *development of intellectual skills* and interests. Most children at this stage have developed sufficient skill in reading to be able to use it to acquire a broad range of knowledge in many different fields. The average nine-year-old has a vocabulary of more than 10,000 words, which increases to nearly 14,000 words by age 11.[11] However, a range of difference of four or five years in reading ability can be expected in the same classroom and grade at this stage. A few 11-year-olds will be reading at adult levels.

Most children in late childhood are intensely curious about the physical and social world in which they live. They can distinguish between fantasy and reality, and they are oriented toward the world of reality. They exhibit a keen interest in science, in space travel, in other parts of the world, and in past events. This is a period when interest in collecting reaches a peak. A boy may collect rocks, stamps, or butterflies, while a girl may be adding to her collection of foreign dolls. Children's reading interests center in books about travel, science, nature, and biography.

Their wide interests and the broad scope of their reading enable children to make great strides in cognitive development. They are forming a great many concepts and are capable of abstract thought. Concepts such as gravity, space, power, and freedom are undergoing refinement of meaning. Stan's mother reported to the teacher Stan's strong interest in astronomy and his visits to observatories. Cheryl revealed in her language composition her understanding of the concept of "greatness."

The cognitive development of most children in late childhood (ages nine, 10, and 11) conforms to what Piaget has described as the latter phase of concrete operations. Children at this stage use logical operations in their solutions of problems rather than responding only on the basis of their

---

[11] Ruth Strang, *An Introduction to Child Study,* 4th ed. (New York: Macmillan Co., 1959), p. 455.

perceptions. The child's use of logical operations enables him to solve successfully conservation of number problems by age six or seven, conservation of area or mass problems by seven or eight, and conservation of volume problems (recognizing that equal volumes of water in different-sized or different-shaped containers are still equal) by age 11 or 12.

Other logical operations performed successfully by the 10- or 11-year-old include those which involve *seriation* (ability to arrange mentally elements according to increasing or decreasing size), *classification* (ordering objects according to a given criterion or concept), and *causality*. In the problem of propositional logic requiring the child to predict which objects will float and which will sink, the 10- or 11-year-old child strives to overcome the contradiction that certain large objects float while certain small ones sink. In striving for internal consistency, he may answer, "If the wood were the same size as the needle, it would be lighter."

Summary

Middle and late childhood are periods of development with their own important landmarks of growth. The years from age six to age 11 or 12 are known as the middle years, a period of tranquility marked by slow, steady growth. It is a period in which children reach out and extend their social development in forming friendships with peers and in joining together to form a peer society. Since nearly all children during these years are in school, this period is aptly called the school years—a time when great leaps in intellectual development occur. Because of the relative quiescence of genital development during most of middle and late childhood, these years are also referred to as the latency period.

Age six, the beginning of middle childhood, is a time when the child moves from his family into the larger world of the school and community. Some of the key developmental tasks of most American children at this stage are the following:

1.   *Gaining increased skill in using and controlling large muscles.*

2.   *Learning skills required in organized games and sports.*

3.   *Gaining increased control over fine muscles.*

4.   *Learning to relate to adults outside the family.*

5.   *Achieving some degree of independence of family.*

6.   *Gaining acceptance, roles, and prestige as a member of the peer group.*

7.   *Further learning of and adherence to the expectations of the culture.*

8.   *Developing a conscience.*

9. *Accepting one's sex role.*

10. *Learning appropriate symbol systems and developing conceptual abilities.*

11. *Developing physical and social concepts which relate to an ever changing world.*

Late childhood is the period of slow, steady growth experienced by children in the upper elementary grades prior to the onset of the pubescent growth spurt. The following developmental tasks engage the energies of most American children during the period of late childhood:

1. *Development of physical prowess and athletic skills (especially for boys).*

2. *Increased development of fine muscle control.*

3. *Gaining acceptance and playing roles in the peer group.*

4. *Developing and maintaining friendly relationships with adults.*

5. *Developing effective ways of adjusting to threat and frustration.*

6. *Increasing one's awareness of the opposite sex.*

7. *Further acceptance and learning of one's sex role.*

8. *Further development of intellectual skills.*

9. *Growth in cognitive development and use of abstractions.*

Study Questions

1. Mrs. Akin is very ambitious for her six-year-old daughter, Marjorie. Marjorie is small and shy, has a short attention span, and appears to be less developed than many others in her class. Miss Hoyt, Marjorie's first grade teacher, is providing Marjorie and other less mature children in her class with additional readiness experiences while the more mature children are beginning to read from books. Mrs. Akin is quite upset when she learns that Marjorie is not reading from books, as is the daughter of her next-door neighbor. If you were Miss Hoyt, how would you respond to Mrs. Akin?

2. Frank, who is in the fifth grade and has an IQ of 115, appears to be turned off by the academic aspects of school. He is absent a great deal and seldom completes written assignments. He is very much interested in cars, reads all the books he can get on the subject, and helps out at his father's service station after school. Frank is the star pitcher on his Little League team and is popular with the other chil-

dren. What developmental tasks is Frank working on as reflected in the above description? What can be done to make school a more meaningful part of Frank's life?

3. To what extent are the learning objectives and activities of a specific grade level or subject with which you are acquainted consonant with the developmental tasks that students at that maturity level are working on? Do school experiences provide opportunities to children for working on their developmental tasks, or are school experiences largely irrelevant to the developmental tasks of children? Discuss.

4. Children today are learning complex concepts and skills at an earlier age than did children of preceding decades. Cite examples to illustrate the changes in timing of onset of certain developmental tasks. What are some new tasks expected of children growing up today?

Suggested Readings

Lee, Harper. *To Kill a Mockingbird.* New York: J. B. Lippincott, 1960. Pulitzer Prize novel which portrays the childhood of a captivating young girl, Scout, and her experiences growing up in a small southern town a generation ago. Vividly portrayed are the human emotions and relationships within a warm, loving family and those of fear and hostility aroused in the community by an unfortunate racial incident. A rich, delightful picture of children and childhood.

Jenkins, Gladys G., Helen Schacter, and William W. Bauer. *These Are Your Children.* Third Edition. Glenview, Ill.: Scott, Foresman and Co., 1966. A generalized description of the physical, social, and mental development of children for each age from age five through middle and late childhood. Later chapters deal with the mature child, the preadolescent, and parent-child relationships.

Redl, Fritz. *When We Deal with Children.* New York: Collier Macmillan, 1966. An eminent child psychologist shares with the reader much of his knowledge of and experience in working with children. Various approaches to psychotherapy with children are discussed, and special attention is given to the problems of disturbed and delinquent children.

Stone, L. Joseph, and Joseph Church. *Childhood and Adolescence: A Psychology of the Growing Person.* Third Edition. New York: Random House, 1973. A comprehensive discussion of physical, social, and intellectual development from birth through adolescence. Included is a consideration of the child's capacities, needs, passions, and concerns and of the environmental conditions that help to shape his individuality.

Films

The Child Experts, 16 mm, sound, black and white, 40 min. New York 10011: Time-Life Films, 43 W. 16th St. This study, made in Britain, maintains that the way a child is brought up depends on the social class of his parents.

Class begins to affect a child when he is only six months old. At the age of five, more than half of a child's mental development is complete—before he even starts school. At age five a middle class child is substantially ahead of the working class child, and there is little evidence that the school redresses the imbalance.

"Dick"—A Fifth Grader, 16 mm, sound, black and white, 21 min. Bloomington: Audiovisual Center, Indiana University. Presents a candid view of a fifth grade pupil in a number of school situations. Dick is followed through a school day. Significant interludes are shown from each of his activities.

Home and Away, Children Growing Up Series, No. 5, 16 mm, sound, color, 26 min. New York 10011: Time-Life Films, 43 W. 16th St. At the age of five, a child usually has his first major confrontation with the outside world when he enters school. It is a giant leap for most children. And for some, adapting to a new environment and forming wider relationships with teachers and friends can be a disturbing experience. This film shows how these children can be helped to make an adjustment. It also looks at others who take this crucial experience in stride.

If These Were Your Children, Part 1. 16 mm, sound, black and white, 28 min. San Francisco 94120: Metropolitan Life Insurance Co. Discusses the basic principles of good mental health, explaining how to recognize early signs of emotional difficulties and how to find ways of meeting emotional needs of children. Depicts the activities and behavior of some second grade children.

Adolescence

If youth be a defect, it is one we outgrow only too soon.

James Russell Lowell

Adolescence is a period of biosocial transition between childhood and adulthood. The adolescent, far more variable than the infant in his growth and behavior, is at an in-between stage of development—at one instant displaying the behavior and feelings of a child and at other times acting quite grown up. So prone are we to dichotomize people as adults or children that we are perplexed about how to respond to persons who are in between and something of both.

Adolescence appears to generate mixed feelings and reactions in adults and in adolescents themselves. Understanding parents and teachers have come to accept elongated, rapidly maturing bodies, awkwardness, self-consciousness, rebelliousness, idealism, and wide swings in mood and activity as normal characteristics of adolescence. Early adolescence is a period when young people, because of rapid growth and maturing, are at times less attractive and less skillful than they were as children or will be as adults, and they have little experience and few resources for coping with new problems associated with these changes. For many adults and youth, adolescence is something to be endured. Something of the ambivalence of adults in their attitudes toward adolescence is revealed in this statement by Stone and Church[1]:

> [*Adolescence*] *is a phase that no one looks forward to, that adolescents themselves deny, and that only a few fading athletes and aging women look back on with regret and then usually with the reservation that it is their adolescent bodies they want, leaving their adult mentalities as they are.*

[1] L. Joseph Stone and Joseph Church, *Childhood and Adolescence: A Psychology of the Growing Person* (New York: Random House, 1957), p. 268.

Although the awkwardness and anxieties of early adolescence are frequently accompanied by a pervasive feeling of being out of step, the beauty, strength, and vitality of late adolescence and early adulthood are emulated by persons of all ages. Styles, TV commercials, pop music, help-wanted ads, and the mass media all seem to suggest that to be over 35 is one step from oblivion. The efforts of some adults' striving for eternal youth are reflected in the pathetic spectacle of the aging matron prancing around in miniskirt and boots and the graying middle-aged hippie sporting flowing hair, beard, and bell bottoms. Thus, there is a kind of dichotomy in attitudes toward adolescence. Early adolescence is accompanied by an anxious and uncomfortable feeling of being out of step, while late adolescence and early adulthood are focal points for adulation and envy of older adults as well as early adolescents. Most late adolescents, in turn, want to be accepted as full-fledged adults.

Puberty versus Adolescence

Before we discuss further the changes that occur during adolescence, it is necessary to distinguish in our terminology between the physical and sexual maturation of boys and girls (puberty) and certain behavioral characteristics of this maturity level (adolescence), characteristics that appear to be as much influenced by culture as by the physical changes of puberty. In speaking of the physical maturation of boys and girls, we will use the terms *prepuberty* (or *pubescence*), *puberty*, and *postpuberty*.

Pubescence is a period of about two years prior to puberty. During pubescence, physiological development occurs and reproductive organs mature. The onset of pubescence is marked by a spurt in physical growth, followed by changes in body proportion, the appearance of secondary sex characteristics, and the maturation of primary sex organs.

Puberty has been defined as the point of development at which biological changes reach a climax and sexual maturity is evidenced.[2] Puberty occurs in the girl with menarche, her first menstruation, and has been preceded by various body changes, including enlarging breasts, widening hips, and the appearance of pubic and underarm hair. Boys experience no such definite or dramatic sign as menstruation to mark their puberty. Puberty in boys is revealed by a variety of body changes, including growth of long bones of arms and legs, appearance of pubic and underarm hair, and hair on the upper lip and chin. At puberty, boys begin to experience nocturnal emissions. These are irregular, spontaneous expulsions of seminal fluid during sleep. Probably the most valid evidence of sexual maturity in boys is the presence from time to time of live spermatozoa in the urine.

Although puberty marks the beginning of sexual functioning, several more years of growth and development are required before the female

[2] Stone and Church, p. 269.

menstrual cycle becomes stabilized and the male becomes capable of ejaculating sperm in sufficient quantity to assure procreation. The age at which reproductive maturity occurs varies considerably and appears to be related to socioeconomic as well as geographical differences. Greulich[3] reports that reproductive maturity is earlier among those of higher socioeconomic status, those residing in temperate climates, and those favored by good nutrition. It appears later in those having inadequate diets, those with severe illnesses, and those who reside in tropical climates. Many primitive cultures take official note of the individual's sexual maturity in ceremonial observances called *puberty rites.*

Postpuberty is the name given to the several years following puberty. This period witnesses a progressive decrease in the velocity of growth toward adult body size, proportion, form, and capacities. This is the period during which the menstrual cycle becomes more regular and during which both boys and girls fill out and develop adult-like contours and physiques.

Adolescence is the period of development extending from the beginning of pubescence to the point at which the individual assumes the roles and responsibilities of adulthood. Culturally, adolescence is the period of transition between the dependency of childhood and the relative autonomy of adulthood. Psychologically, it is a period of adjustment to physical and social changes that distinguish child behavior from adult behavior. Chronologically, adolescence consists of the time span from approximately (depending on the individual and the culture) 12 or 13 until the late teens or early twenties.

Adolescence as a period of development appears to be a relatively recent phenomenon peculiar to Western civilization. In other societies such a period simply does not exist, and at puberty the individual passes directly from childhood to adulthood without going through any transitional stages. There may be initiation rites of some sort, but once these have been successfully passed, the individual is accorded full adult status. This absence of a sharp break between childhood and adolescence existed in the United States during the period when it was largely an agrarian, frontier society. With the enactment of compulsory school laws, however, the requirement of going to school often postponed the entry of the young person into an adult role. As a result, the term *adolescence* came to describe a period when the individual is, in many respects, ready for but not permitted to accede to adult roles and status.[4]

The term *adolescence* is probably most imprecise when it is used to refer to stereotyped behavior characteristics of some individuals at this age. The Franks[5] point out that rebelliousness, moodiness, irritability, crying spells, or outbursts of anger may occur before puberty in some children

---

[3] W. W. Greulich, "Physical Changes in Adolescence," in Nelson B. Henry, ed. *Forty-Third Yearbook: Part 1, Adolescence,* National Society for the Study of Education (Chicago: University of Chicago Press, 1944), p. 29.

[4] Nancy C. Ralston and G. P. Thomas, "America's Artificial Adolescents," *Adolescence,* 6 (Spring 1972), 137–142.

[5] Mary Frank and Lawrence K. Frank, *Your Adolescent at Home and in School* (New York: Viking Press, 1956), p. 36.

and may not appear at all in other children. A number of different explanations have been offered to explain the behavior changes which occur during the five- to eight-year period separating childhood and adulthood. We shall examine some of these explanations in the discussion of theories of adolescence which follows.

Theories of Adolescence

The marked interest in adolescent behavior and development manifested during this century has stimulated the development of numerous theories of adolescence.[6] Hall,[7] one of the earliest investigators of and writers on the psychology of adolescence, described adolescence as a time of inner turmoil, a period of storm and stress. He perceived the emotional life of the adolescent as oscillating between contradictory tendencies of energy, excitation, laughter, and euphoria and indifference, lethargy, gloom, and melancholy. This emotional turmoil was believed to result from the physiological upheaval associated with puberty. Studies by anthropologists, however, reveal that in other cultures adolescence is not always a period of turmoil. Mead[8] found that in Samoa adolescence represents no period of crisis or stress but is an orderly development of a set of slowly maturing interests and activities. Little support was found, too, for Hall's law of recapitulation, which postulates that the individual relives the development of the human race from early animal-like primitiveness to more civilized ways of life.

The relationships in pubescence between physiological changes and behavioral changes are recognized in Sigmund Freud's theory of psychosexual development, described in earlier chapters. Pubescent development during the genital period is marked by an awakening sexuality and increases in nervous excitement, anxiety, and personality disturbances. These disturbances and anxieties arise from the continuing struggle during pubescence between the biological-instinctual id forces and the socially responsive superego. Anna Freud[9] identifies two principal defense mechanisms which are typically used during pubescence to reduce anxiety: (1) *asceticism*, a self-discipline and withdrawal reflecting a distrust of all instinctual wishes, and (2) increased *intellectualization*, a repressing of libidinal thoughts through engagement in intellectual interests.

---

[6] Only a few representative theories are considered here. For a more comprehensive treatment of the topic, see Rolf E. Muuss, *Theories of Adolescence* (New York: Random House, 1962).

[7] G. Stanley Hall, *Adolescence*, Vols. 1 and 2 (New York: Appleton-Century-Crofts, 1916).

[8] Margaret Mead, *Coming of Age in Samoa* (New York: William Morrow, 1939), p. 157.

[9] Anna Freud, *The Ego and the Mechanism of Defence*, trans. by C. Barnes (New York: International University Press, 1948).

Erikson,[10] in his eight stages of man (presented in Chapter 8), posits the establishment of ego identity during pubescence. He suggests that the rapid body growth, genital maturity, and sexual awareness of pubescence foment a psychological revolution within the adolescent, threatening his body image and ego identity. The adolescent then must reestablish his ego identity, in the light of earlier experiences, and accept his body changes and libidinal feelings as a part of himself. In order to establish ego identity, the individual must integrate his vocational ambitions and aspirations and the qualities acquired through earlier identifications in imitation of parents, falling in love, and admiration of heroes.

Our observations of children and youth strongly suggest that the early and late periods of the five- to eight-year span between childhood and adulthood are rather distinct and qualitatively quite different from one another. In the following sections, we shall highlight some of these differences and at the same time note common trends in preadolescence, early adolescence, and late adolescence.

Preadolescence

Preadolescence, as the term implies, is a period in the developmental span between childhood and adolescence. In our use of the term, *preadolescence* is a period of one to two years encompassing the latter part of late childhood and the early part of early adolescence. Preadolescence has also been identified as the period when the childhood personality is broken up so that it can be modified into the personality of the adult.[11] It is a period of hyperactivity, rebelliousness, moodiness, and irritability. These behaviors, representing temporary developmental discordance and maladjustment, are the young person's responses as he copes with the disorganization of his childhood personality. His disturbing behavior is particularly trying and baffling to adults who live or work with him. Redl expresses this well when he refers to preadolescence as "the phase when the nicest children begin to behave in a most awful way."[12]

Preadolescence, overlapping as it does both late childhood and early adolescence, contains some of the characteristics of each. One of the most striking characteristics of preadolescents is their restlessness and hyperactivity. They appear to be continually in motion—tapping pencils, manipulating any one of the many objects they carry in their pockets, playing with their hair. Preadolescence is the period when the boy and girl, as they begin

---

[10] Erik Erikson, *Childhood and Society* (New York: W. W. Norton & Co., 1950), pp. 227–229.

[11] Fritz Redl, "Preadolescents—What Makes Them Tick?" *Child Study*, 21 (1944), 58–59.

[12] Redl, pp. 58–59.

to mature physically, gain the first glimpses of the man or woman each will become. Both sexes are becoming aware of the grown-up body and the desirability of grown-up attractiveness.

Before proceeding further with a discussion of the characteristics and developmental tasks of preadolescence, we shall present descriptions of two preadolescents found in excerpts from the case of Deke and the case of Babs:

Deke is a boy 12 years, five months of age who is in the sixth grade. The first day of school he remained rather close to a group of five or six other boys. This was evidenced by their motions of "Here, sit here" and "I saved this for you." In September, Deke was 63 inches tall and weighed 106 pounds.

October 29.   Today from 2:00 to 3:15 we had our Halloween party. The group played three team games. While refreshments were served by the students on the committee, Deke, Dan, Fred, Carl, and Earl pulled their chairs in together so that they were partially facing one another. They were giggling, talking, seeming to pay no attention to the others. Presently Deke got up and came to the table where the remaining refreshments were placed. He served himself to the balance of about four chocolate-covered peanut butter cookies. He passed them to the boys near him. They continued to giggle.

Later Earl said, "Do you know what we were laughing about at the party?" "No," I replied. "Well, Carl put some ice cream in his cider. Then we all did. We dipped our cookies in that. It was good!" he said.

November 3.   Deke is very good at soccer. He is after the ball, often getting a kick at it or stopping it. In punt ball, Deke usually gives it a good kick, getting it high in the air; but often it is caught on the fly. He catches the ball frequently. He is taller than any of the other boys but usually jumps up, getting both feet off the ground to catch the ball. He sort of cradles his arms to get it.

November 12.   During our short rest period in the classroom we were playing human tic-tac-toe. Alice was leader. After her turn was up, she chose Deke to take her place. The girls chose boys to take their places, and the boys in turn chose girls. Deke was leader in the last part of the game.

December 13.   Before 9 o'clock, Deke, with about eight boys standing around him, was showing a card trick. They walked closer to show it to me. During this time they were laughing and saying, "How did you do it?" Finally, he began to show another trick about finding it in another's hands. First he tried the left and then the right. Then he pretended to try the arms. The "trick" was finished when the hands were around the other person's neck. They all laughed. Fred said, "He showed that to us yesterday. John tried it on Cora. She got away and ran." They thought this was funny too, as they laughed again.

January 4.   As I walked by the table where Deke, Earl, Fred, Dan, Carl, and Ben were sitting with their heads close together, Ben said, "Mrs. G., we don't know whether to let John in with us or not." It was then that I realized that John was sitting at the end of the table. There are only six places to sit, but he pulled up a chair. I said, "Why, what do you mean?" "I'm with the six musketeers, and he makes seven," he explained. "He knows some big words and we know some little words. He might get something on us." All the while John was just sitting there, grinning. "Let me know what you decide," I said. "OK," he replied.

I have been under the impression that it was a question as to who was the sixth musketeer, Ben or John. Ben was doing the talking. Apparently, he feels himself pretty well in with the group. All this time Deke did not say a word.

January 8 (at the Teacher's Home).   I heard children's voices and pretty soon my doorbell rang. Deke, Helen, the girl who had invited him to the square dance, and Fay came in. They were all talking in happy voices about who was at the dance, who went with whom, and how much they ate (the last in some detail). Deke said Carl hadn't come because his mother was "kinda strict on him." Earl had come, but his mother came afterwards to take him home. Deke was to be taken home that night by Helen's father.

March 22.   For several weeks Deke has seemed far more restless. He is growing quite tall and is thin. I have often noticed him stretching his long legs out to rest on another desk or chair. He pushes his desk up and leans back with his hands clasped over his head.

He has found it hard to be still while making a small houseboat model, and he always seems to be talking. His interest in the hunters and trappers in our study of the West has been great. He found a picture of a trapper, and after planning individually with me, he enlarged the picture using the projector. While coloring with chalk and completing the picture, I noticed no need for "help" from his friends. He worked rapidly, using big swinging movements with his arms.

He has much to tell, not to me anymore, but to the boys in the room. Lately he pays more attention to Fred than to any of the others in the musketeer group. In fact, that little group is no longer so much in evidence. Several times recently they have divided up, usually three at one table with other boys and the other three at another table with still others. Over this period, the others sitting at the tables with the divided group have not been the same every day.

Babs is 10 years, four months old and is in the fifth grade. She is about the same size as the other girls in her class. Babs is in a hurry whenever she does anything. She is always running. Babs wears very attractive clothes. She wears most colors well, but her favorite dresses are pink with ruffles and lace. She said, "I love fancy clothes." She always looks neat and takes very good care of her clothes. She polishes her own shoes and puts her hair up in curlers. She has a shoulder bob.

October 27.   Babs and several girls pretend they have letters on the playground. They show these letters to certain boys and say, "I have a letter, but you can't see it." Then the boys chase them and try to get the letters. They seem to enjoy this because it goes on almost every recess. Babs told me, "I think the boys are so nosey. They always want to see what we write!"

November 10.   Some boys and girls were working on a Thanksgiving play. John said, "I will not have anything to do with the play if Babs is in it; she always wants to be boss, and I won't have an old girl bossing me around." This was said before the whole room, and all the boys agreed with John. The girls said they didn't want to be in it anyway. Babs said, "You will need us to play the Pilgrims' mothers and the girls." John also added, "We would rather wear dresses and be girls ourselves." To which Babs replied, "All right, have your old play, and don't call on me to help you when you get in a tight place." She made a face at him. John was director of the play and picked the characters. When he wanted a Pilgrim mother, he picked Babs and gave her the following reason: "I know you can get the costume and I know you can learn the part, but remember, you are not the boss this time."

December 7.   Today Babs was wearing a very pretty yellow wool skirt and white blouse. She looked very pretty, but I did not say anything about it. At recess she came to show me some dirt she had gotten on her skirt. I admired her outfit and said she looked very nice. She said, "Mother doesn't like me in skirts. She says they make me look too old."
I said, "I guess Mother wants to keep her baby."
She said, "She still calls me 'Baby,' but I think I'm too big for that now."

December 8.   Babs certainly has a way with the boys. She talks to them a lot and rolls her eyes and smiles when they seem willing to do anything she wants. I watched her this morning getting a boy to do her arithmetic. She told him how to do it, and he did all the work.

January 11.   Babs' sister came in to talk to me this morning. She told me Babs was talking in her sleep last night. They have separate rooms, but they are close. While she was talking Babs came in and heard her. Babs said, "She is just saying that to tease me. She is always teasing me about something. She talks in her sleep all the time about her boy friends." Babs' sister blushed and said, "She means she talks about her boy friends."

February 24.   Today on the playground, Jackson, a sixth grade boy, said to me, "Babs is always hitting me and pulling my sweater off." I sent for Babs and asked her about it. She started to cry and said, "He hit me first, and I am going to take care of myself." This is the first time I have seen Babs cry.

March 22.   Babs has been acting like a much older girl since she had her hair cut short. Some of the girls told me that Babs likes a boy in the seventh grade. He lives near her and takes her for rides on his bicycle in the evenings.
     Today she was with three sixth grade girls. They were walking past the high school looking up at the windows. Later in the day I heard Babs tell some girls that she has a boy friend in high school.

Physical Development

Preadolescence witnesses a brief slowing down of growth just prior to the onset of the rapid lengthening of arms and legs during pubescence. The physical and sexual maturing of many preadolescent girls is marked by developing breasts, widening hips, a more feminine figure, and the onset of menstruation. An important developmental task of the preadolescent, therefore, is *developing a readiness for and an acceptance of the body changes* that take place as one grows toward physical and sexual maturity. Evidence of these physical changes was revealed in the last entry in the case of Deke, in which the teacher describes him as growing quite tall and thin. The physical changes Babs is experiencing can be inferred from the several evidences of her strong interest in boys and in grooming.

The restlessness and hyperactivity of preadolescence alluded to earlier are also evident in the descriptions of Deke and Babs. Deke is active in sports and appears restless, while Babs has been described as in a hurry and always running. In spite of his restlessness, the preadolescent's endurance is usually not high, and he may often become overtired. Rather wide swings between hyperactivity and listlessness can be observed in some adolescents.

Emotional Development

A persistent developmental task of preadolescence is the *developing of appropriate ways of adjusting to new feelings evoked by changes in maturity and changes in one's perceptions of parents, peers, and self.* Boys and girls who have great affection for their parents will at this stage, nevertheless, often respond to their elders with irritation, distrust, and suspicion. They are easily offended and are quick to complain that adults do not understand them or treat them fairly. They are very sensitive, self-conscious, and easily hurt. At other times they appear to be unable to control their emotions and frequently lose themselves in anger, fear, or love. Many of the preadolescent's frustrations result from conflicts between parents and peers, or from an awareness of a lack of social skills or a failure to mature at the same rate as others. It will be recalled from Chapter 4 that the late-maturing boy often feels out of place with peers because of differences in his rate of maturing.

Conflict between the preadolescent and his parents often arises over his manner of dress, his friends, the ways he spends his time, the condition of his room, his general behavior, and his seeming lack of respect and consideration for others. His resistance to these demands and expectations is a first step toward *asserting his independence of adults*. Although he may act at times like a child, he resists efforts of adults to treat him as a child. However, even though he is restive under adult prodding and restrictions, the preadolescent is not ready for, nor does he really want, complete independence from his family.

In expressing her independence of adults, the preadolescent girl develops new feelings about herself and her relationships with members of her family. She may express her growing independence through criticisms of her mother's choice of clothes and personal grooming, the house decor, or her mother's overprotectiveness. In spite of this criticism, however, the daughter remains dependent upon her mother for evidences of acceptance and affection. The preadolescent girl is often ambivalent in her feelings toward younger siblings. At one moment she may express disdain for their immature behavior, while at the next moment she may be quite affectionate toward and protective of them.

The preadolescent boy's assertion of independence frequently brings him into conflict with his father. These conflicts arise when the son feels unable to meet his father's demands and expectations. If he feels inadequate and is anxious over whether he can meet his father's high standards, he may adjust by simply not trying. It is less damaging to his self-image to appear uncaring and lazy than to appear incompetent. The understanding father can help his son discover his individuality in the family by allowing him leeway in making decisions and by not criticizing his mistakes. The failure of the father to respect the boy's need for independent action causes many boys to struggle for a lifetime to demonstrate their worth to their fathers. The mother's love and admiration continue to be important to the preadolescent son. A boy must be able to feel that he will have his mother's love even if he is different from his father. His love for his parents and their love for him become part of his understanding of others and his whole attitude toward life.[13]

---

[13] Frank and Frank, pp. 55–58.

Every preadolescent faces the important developmental task of *forming and strengthening affectional relationships with adults within and outside the family*. The giggling, silly behavior of Deke and some of his friends is characteristic of the kind of preadolescent activity that many adults find annoying. Yet the many contacts which Deke and his friends initiated with the teacher indicate their desire and need for her friendship and affection. Similarly, Babs, on several occasions, related to the teacher and sought her support. Frequently, the preadolescent develops a strong identification with a young adult, who becomes the preadolescent's ideal. For the preadolescent girl, the ideal is a paragon of poise and femininity; for the boy, the ideal is a model of strength and masculine self-assurance.

Social Development

In preadolescence the importance of the peer clique or gang is even more evident than it was in late childhood. A continuing developmental task is that of *achieving acceptance and roles in a changing peer group*. Although the need for adult approval is still very important, the preadolescent frequently spends more time with his friends and is more responsive to their ideas and values than to those of parents and other adults.

We have noted, too, that at this stage there is an increased striving to conform to the peer group in matters of dress, language, behavior, and values. A further developmental task posed for the preadolescent is that of *accepting, learning, and adhering to the codes, standards, and values of the peer group*. An unspoken and unwritten code develops among members of the peer group and defines in peer terms what is good and bad, acceptable and not acceptable. In general, the peer code calls for supporting one's peers in conflicts with adults. It also requires that one maintain his independence from adults, and anything that smacks of being teacher's pet is beyond the pale. The pressure on the individual to adhere to the peer code is revealed in the boys' objections to Babs' being in the play because she seemed to want to boss others.

Frequently, the preadolescent must in some way reconcile the sharp differences between peer and adult codes and values. He wishes to be admired by his pals on a peer group basis; at the same time, he wishes that his parents would relax their demands so that somehow he can maintain the approval of both parents and peers. The wise adult avoids placing the preadolescent in situations that provoke a serious conflict between adult and peer standards.

The marked tendency in late childhood for boys and girls to prefer members of their own sex group and to show disdain for members of the opposite sex can also be observed in preadolescence. Boys see girls as weak and inferior, and frequently judge girls as OK only to the degree that they are like boys. Some girls may too readily accept the interpretation of boys and respond with a frantic imitation of boyish behavior in a negation of their feminine role. They dress like boys, play boys' games, and use tomboy language. For most girls, however, this period of identifying and competing with boys is brief. With the onset of pubescence, their behavior and interests are increasingly feminine.

The onset of preadolescence is also characterized by a masked but awakening interest in the opposite sex. This interest is manifested in the preadolescent's ambivalent attitudes toward the opposite sex. The preadolescent deals with this ambivalence by maintaining a strong identity with his own sex group while at the same time experimenting briefly with heterosexual relationships and activities. This phenomenon is clearly evident in the cases of Deke and Babs. Deke was most frequently observed in interaction with his close pals, the "six musketeers." We do see Deke and other boys, however, choosing girls in a game of human tic-tac-toe, showing girls card tricks, and accepting from girls invitations to square dances. Amusingly, in the anecdote of January 8 in their report to the teacher, Deke and his friends talked more about how much each person ate at the square dance than about any other aspect of the boy-girl event. The ambivalence of Babs toward her own sex group and toward boys is strikingly shown. Babs is frequently in conflict with some boys her age, but she seems to have a way with other boys in getting them to do things for her. The interest of the preadolescent girl in older boys is also evident in the case of Babs, who is reported to have boy friends two or three years older than herself.

Psychological Development

In preadolescence the brain and nervous system have nearly reached adult proportions, but preadolescent youngsters still lack the experiences that would enable them to solve adult problems and to respond in adult ways. Their interest in physical science remains strong, especially for boys, and they show an increasing interest in human relationships. A reexamination of values may begin about this time. Preadolescents reveal a strong valuing of justice and fair play, and they are likely to challenge adults or peers who violate these codes. Preadolescents are developing a stronger conscience, and with this they often experience intense feelings of guilt. Some may begin to question the religious teachings of church and home. They are likely also to be critical of people who do not live up to their ideals.

Blair and Burton[14] have identified three trends in the intellectual development of preadolescents: a strong focus on reality, the capability to use causal relationships effectively in thinking about physical, mechanical, and natural phenomena, and wide reading and rapid educational achievement. The preadolescent's interest in the larger world is manifested in increased awareness of world events, of social and economic problems, and of the advances of science and technology. Through reading and exposure to other

[14] Arthur W. Blair and William H. Burton, *Growth and Development of the Preadolescent* (New York: Appleton-Century-Crofts, 1951), pp. 148–177.

mass media, preadolescents learn about their world and explore specific intellectual interests. At this time they are capable of applying a scientific problem-solving approach to increasingly complex problems. As they pursue intellectual interests, manual and manipulatory skills, such as those required in conducting home experiments in chemistry and building models, are further developed and refined.

In these activities preadolescents are working on the continuing developmental task of *refining intellectual skills, understandings, attitudes, and interests appropriate to a phase of development marked by the beginnings of physical change and increased maturity.* Their interests are influenced by their rapidly changing bodies, their strong feelings and emotional reactions, and their awareness of the new roles and expectations they must fulfill as they progress toward adulthood.

Preadolescence is a relatively brief period of transition from childhood to adolescence. It is a time when boys and girls more and more are oriented to the people, events, and phenomena of the outside world. Parents and home are taken more or less for granted, and one's life and activities center in the peer group. It is a period of marked swings and fluctuations in activity, behavior, and emotions. Games and physical activities are important. It is a time of self-examination and self-assessment. Finally, it is a period marked by idealism, curiosity, a focus on reality, increased interest in causal relationships, and a real growth in intellectual powers.

Early Adolescence

The central theme in adolescence is the rediscovery of one's self. In the transition from the dependency of childhood to the independence of adulthood, the adolescent must adjust to an almost new body. The maturing body is the symbol of a new and changing self. The early adolescent must incorporate into his self-concept new feelings, a new body image, and new conceptions of his role and place in a changing world. The search for self is reflected in an intensified self-awareness, frequently manifested in increased self-consciousness.

Early adolescence, as we noted earlier, is marked by the rapid growth of the long bones, changes in body proportion, and evidences of sexual maturation associated with pubescence. Early adolescence extends from the beginning of the pubescent growth spurt until about a year after puberty, when the individual's new biological organization has become stabilized. For most individuals, early adolescence encompasses roughly the years of junior high school and possibly a year or two beyond. During this period greater stability in behavior, biological organization, and sexual functioning is being achieved. Many of the developmental tasks of preadolescence are encountered in a different form or at a higher level in early adolescence.

Early adolescence poses a dilemma of core values in which the young person is faced with having to integrate partially contradictory value themes of social *acceptance* and social *achievement*.[15] The early adolescent is strongly motivated toward achieving peer acceptance, at first among same-sex peers and later with those of the opposite sex. Yet this striving for peer acceptance may be inconsistent with equally strong drives for achievement. Some forms of achievement, such as earning high grades in school, may earn the early adolescent little popularity with peers. Peer group and dating activities beginning about age 13 in turn often take much time and attention away from studying. Thus, each early adolescent must seek in his own unique way to reconcile these equally attractive but often conflicting motives.

The great variation among early adolescents in growth, maturity, and behavior points to the uniqueness of each individual. Excerpts from the cases of Doris and Dennis reveal how two young people attempted to work through the developmental tasks and adjustments of early adolescence.

Doris is 14 years old and in the ninth grade. She is an adopted child of Spanish ancestry and an only child. Last year a recommendation was sent home that she follow the standard course of study. The next morning she came to me in tears. She said, "Daddy is angry about my low rating. He called me stupid and dumb. He said I must be playing around in school. Daddy always got good grades in school, and he expects me to do it too."

October 16.   *I have watched Doris several times after school as she was waiting for her bus. She stands around with a group of boys and girls. She does very little talking but laughs a great deal and rolls her eyes. She handles her hair a great deal, lifting it from her shoulders.*

October 21.   *Today, in a conference, Doris's father said, "Jim, her boy friend, came by a week ago Saturday afternoon. She had just washed her hair and had put it up in curlers. She asked her mother to tell him she wasn't at home. She didn't want him to see her that way. Her mother finally agreed and lied for her. The boy went on to another girl's house. This girl told him Doris was home. He saw her at church on Sunday and asked why she had her mother lie for her. Doris told him that she didn't want him to see her in curlers. He said, 'Don't ever lie again. I came to see you, not your hair.'"*

October 22.   *Doris doesn't talk much in the group. She rolls her big brown eyes, arches her brows, and flashes her teeth, which are large, white, and square. Once she said to me, "My teeth are too big." Earlier this morning I saw her wearing her glasses. I asked her*

[15] Chad Gordon, "Social Characteristics of Adolescence," *Daedalus*, Vol. 100, No. 4 (Fall 1971), 931–960.

about them, and she said, "I never wear them in the halls, but I always wear them in class."

October 31.   *This afternoon before the Halloween dance Doris went to the mirror in the home arts room and arranged her hair. Then she repaired her lipstick. Her bangs were curled but still reached to her eyebrows. She stood for a moment, rolling her eyes, lifted her shoulders, and continued to primp before the mirror.*

She changed to a red skirt for the dance. She had red flowers in her hair. One of the teachers said to me during the dance, "Did you see Doris? She looks more like a gypsy than anything else."

Doris was popular during the dance. She didn't miss one, and she danced better than the average child. Jim was her partner very often.

November 18.   *In a conference with Doris, I told her that her father was very interested in her grades and how she was getting along. "He seems to think a great deal of you," I said.*

"Yes, I guess he does," she replied, "but I wish he would let me go."

"Go where?" I asked.

"Oh, I don't know, just be free or something," she said. "Some of the girls in our neighborhood want to get an apartment and go on our own."

I said, "That will take money."

"We are going to get jobs when we are older and try it. I told Mama what we were planning to do. She said we couldn't do it, but when I insisted that we were, she said that she and Daddy would sell the house and buy a trailer and tour the country. They would be free too." She raised her shoulders, put her head on one side, and laughed. "We would all have fun, and maybe I would wish I were with them. I like to go places, but I don't want to do it with my parents."

January 26.   *This afternoon during our conference she talked mostly without prompting. She laughed now and then, rolled her eyes, tilted her head from side to side, and lifted her shoulders. She has a new bronze rinse on her hair. I noticed how very neat and clean she was. Her yellow blouse was trimmed with lace and was very becoming. Her fingernails were well manicured and tinted with pink polish. I noticed her hands are very beautiful. I asked her how much she weighed.*

"Just exactly a hundred pounds," she said, "and I'm just five feet tall."

February 6.   *Doris was elected by her homeroom to be candidate for Queen of the Sweetheart Dance, to be held on February 13. I passed her in the hall and stopped to congratulate her. Her face was all smiles. She thanked me as she lifted her hair from her shoulders, spreading it out carefully. She moved on, swinging her skirts.*

February 13.   For the dance today Doris was dressed in a red and white dress. Her hair hung loosely on her shoulders, and she had flowers in her hair. When the winners were announced, Doris was not among them. I saw her a few minutes after the coronation. She was dancing with a very popular boy. She and her partner later joined in the grand march. They walked along hand in hand grinning at each other. She danced every dance, and several times I saw her laughing up at her partner.

April 8.   In a conference today Doris said, "My problem is to find the right boy. I don't have a boy friend now. There are three boys in this school who want to go with me, but I don't want any of them. Those boys who want to go with me I don't want, those I want I can't get. There are three high school boys I like, one in particular, but none of them will look at me. I'll have a problem when it comes to finding a husband. I'll have to find one who is a member of the church. Mama wouldn't mind too much if he weren't a member, but it would break Daddy's heart if I married somebody outside the church."

I asked, "What about your Navy career?"

She answered, "I still have that in mind, but only if I don't find someone to marry when I finish high school. I really want to get married because I want to have a baby. I love babies. I want to have a lot of kids. I wish I had a brother or a sister. I sure envy the girls who have brothers especially."

Dennis, who was introduced in Chapter 7, is 14 years old and is in the ninth grade. He is 6 feet, 1 inch tall, weighs 169 pounds, and has wavy brown hair and blue eyes. The following is the first paragraph of his "autobiography."

On September the 8th, 19—, a future Vice President was born. He weighed eight pounds and eight ounces, and he wasn't wearing a thing. The reason he wasn't born a future President is that his parents had moved out of their log cabin three months before he was born. In short I was born. At least that's what the birth certificate says.

The following are excerpts from Dennis's case record.

September 11.   After giving Dennis his test paper at the end of English period, I added, "Please stay a minute after class." After the other students had gone, I turned around to Dennis and said, "Dennis, you did a nice job of bull slinging on your test paper yester-

day, and I'd like for you to cease trying to make a monkey out of me. Is that clear?"

Dennis laughed and said, "Now don't get mad, Miss Neal. Miss R. and I can't get along at all, and I'd hate to have two against me."

"All right, Dennis," I remarked, "but let's leave our humor for picnics and such."

He asked, "Is that all?" and I nodded in reply. He crushed the test paper in his hands and left the room.

October 3.   As we left school this afternoon I followed some children down the flight of steps from the second to the first floor. Dennis happened to be right in front of me, and he had gotten a lock of Laura's hair and was apparently pulling at it. At that moment, Laura whirled around and shouted, "Dennis, I don't believe you have a lick of sense. I've a good mind to slap your face." Laura was talking by the time she turned around. However, when she saw me she said, "I'm sorry I yelled, Miss Neal, but Dennis never shows any manners."

Before I could say a word, Dennis shrugged his shoulders and said, as if in disgust, "These women!" He took two large steps and was out of the building.

Laura added, "Don't you think he's rude?"

I said, "I don't think he meant any harm."

Laura replied, "Well, he sure is silly."

October 20.   This morning just as I arrived at school I met Dennis. I immediately thought of the Halloween Carnival. I spoke: "Hi, Dennis. Did you see about any prizes for my Bingo stand?"

Dennis at first clapped his hand over his mouth. Then he said, "Gosh! Miss Neal, I forgot, but don't worry. I'll get you some."

I came on into the building with two of my teaching companions, Miss R. and Miss T. When we were out of hearing distance for Dennis, Miss R. stated, "I wonder if you had better rely on Dennis. I'd be afraid to."

November 12.   As classes were dismissed today I heard Miss R. say, "Dennis, if you don't keep your hat off your head until you leave the building, I don't know what I'm going to do." Dennis was wearing a long billed straw cap. He lifted the hat about 12 inches from the top of his head and just held it suspended there. I decided to watch, and he kept the cap in this position until he left the building. Then he just dropped it on his head again. It landed sort of drooped over one eye. Joan and Bertha were watching too, and they laughed.

December 11.   The class had asked me to chaperone their party planned for Saturday night. Today plans were submitted and seemed rather complete except for the Recreation Committee, which had no report. I asked, "Who's chairman of the Recreation Commit-

tee?" Dennis raised his hand. I said, "I'll have to see the type of rec-
reation you've planned before I'll OK chaperoning the party."

Dennis said with a giggle, "Oh, we'll play 'Post Office' and 'Spin
the Lid.' "

"No, you won't under my supervision," I remarked.

Dennis continued, "Well, I guess we'll have to move the party
to my house."

"Well, if that's your choice for recreation, I imagine you'll have
to," I added.

Doris said, "Miss Neal, we'll just dance if you'll come." I asked
if that was agreeable to the rest of the class. It was, so I consented to
chaperone.

Physical Development

Earlier in this chapter we noted that the pubescent growth spurt,
which begins to taper off after puberty, leaves one nearly an adult in physique and appearance. Sex organs mature, and the secondary sex characteristics of deepening voice, shoulder development of boys, development of
breasts and hips of girls, and adult distribution of body hair are clearly evident. The startling physical changes which take place over a summer have a
profound effect on the young person himself. In his gawky appearance, his
awkwardness, and his sexual maturity, he becomes acutely aware of his
changing body. An unavoidable and insistent developmental task faced by
every early adolescent is *his acceptance and adjustment to his changing,*
maturing body. Contours of the body and face become mature. The face
becomes more tapered and elongated. Muscles of boys become firm and
hard, and, as sexual maturity is attained, growth of the bones is completed.
Toward the end of early adolescence, girls (at about 14) and boys (around
15) look more like adults than like children.[16]

One will recall that early adolescents are extremely sensitive about
their appearance. They tend to evaluate themselves physically against a
Hollywood ideal, and it is no wonder that most find themselves lacking and
reveal great concern about their physical characteristics. They worry about
their stature and size, their muscular strength (boys), their shapeliness
(girls), their facial features, their complexions. It will be recalled, too, that
early-maturing boys achieve a marked advantage over late-maturing boys in
sports competition, social relationships, and personal adjustment.

An aspect of accepting and adjusting to a changing body is that of
accepting one's sexual maturing and one's sexuality as a male or female. In
early adolescence, the distinctions between male and female are sharply

---

[16] Edward C. Britton and J. Merritt Winans, *Growing from Infancy to Adulthood*
(New York: Appleton-Century-Crofts, 1958), p. 70.

drawn. It is at this time that one not only accepts maleness or femaleness but also begins to value it. The adolescent boy learns to express his masculinity, and the adolescent girl learns to express her femininity, in ways that are appropriate to the situation. Lack of accurate information about sex may make it more difficult to accept one's sexuality. Because of this lack of information, many adolescent boys and girls become anxious, overcurious, and misinformed about sex. Feelings related to sex become more serious and intense because nothing in the adolescent's experience prepares him for dealing with and accepting his own sexuality. Frequently, parents themselves are embarrassed to discuss the problem.

We need to remember that sex has a different meaning at each stage of development and that the meaning may be quite different for different persons at the same stage of development. While sexual drives are awakened at puberty, there are vast individual and cultural variations in the way these drives influence the early adolescent's behavior. Some early adolescent boys continue to feel uncomfortable with girls. Many of both sexes manifest their interest in the opposite sex by talking, joking, teasing, flirting, and dancing with them. The percentage of early adolescents who engage in sexual intercourse is probably quite small, but among those who do, there will be a few girls in some communities who become pregnant before the age of 15.

What appears to be common to all early adolescents, however, is an intensified emotionality which may or may not be experienced as sexual. This emotionality is experienced as part of self rather than as being merely a response to events in the objective world.[17] The adolescent's total personality, his past feelings about his body, his capacities and abilities, and his feelings of self-worth strongly influence his feelings and attitudes toward sex and his approach to the opposite sex.[18] Attitudes that sex is dirty, women are untouchable, and men cannot be trusted not only handicap the young person's heterosexual adjustment but may also make more difficult his later marital adjustment.

Acceptance of one's sexuality is also important in one's *acceptance and learning of his sex role*, which was discussed in Chapter 6. Many of the developmental tasks discussed in this section are reflected in the early adolescent's interest in and concern over grooming. This was particularly evident in the case of Doris. She was frequently observed primping, lifting her hair from her shoulders, and swinging her skirts as she walked down the hall. It is reflected, too, in the anecdote of October 21, where it was reported that Doris and her mother lied so that her boy friend would not see her with her hair done up in curlers. It seems, further, that Doris has learned that rolling her eyes and arching her brows are feminine ways of responding in the company of boys.

---

[17] Lawrence Kohlberg and Carol Gilligan, "The Adolescent as a Philosopher: The Discovery of Self in the Postconvention World," *Daedalus*, Vol. 100, No. 4 (Fall 1971), 1,051–1,086.

[18] Frank and Frank, pp. 108–112.

Social and Emotional Development

Being accepted and playing roles as a member of the peer group is a continuing developmental task, and at no stage of development is this task more important than in early adolescence. At this stage, boys and girls will slavishly conform to group codes and standards for no other reason than that "everyone is doing it."

We have noted that most early adolescents are strongly attached to their own sex group. Some 12-year-old boys will look disdainfully at a female classmate and say, "Ugh, she's only a girl. What can you expect?" This deprecatory comment, however, may be an effort to mask their liking for this particular girl. Friendship choices at this stage are based more frequently than heretofore on similarity of physical maturity, abilities, interests, and socioeconomic status. Boys appear to have a wide circle of casual friends, whereas girls are more likely to have a small circle of intimate friends. Girls, throughout their teen years, maintain closer ties with girl friends than with boy friends.[19] For the early adolescent boy, skill in sports earns acceptance and prestige in the peer group, whereas for girls, nice clothes, grooming, and good looks bring peer acceptance and prestige. Social poise and skills in dancing, conversation, dating, and organizing social activities and clubs are also important assets for achieving peer status in early adolescence.

By age 14, most boys shift toward a positive but masked interest in the opposite sex. This interest is likely to be manifested in boys' watching girls and then rejoining their male clique to talk about girls. As young people learn appropriate ways of responding to peers, they are working on the crucial task of *establishing heterosexual relationships*. Early adolescents vary a great deal in the timing of this task and in the ways they work on it. Girls, as compared with boys of the same age, are more advanced in seeking the attention of the opposite sex and taking the initiative in dancing and at parties. A number of boys and the more immature girls tend to hold back in their relationships with the opposite sex. But, by age 14, more than half of both the boys and the girls are dating.[20]

The cultural patterns of the home and community may make it difficult for the young person to form satisfying heterosexual relationships. Ambitious parents may push early adolescents into heterosexual activities before they are ready. The need to conform and to be popular may force some young people to act in ways that are incompatible with their temperaments and interests. Finally, the confusion among both adults and adolescents with regard to feelings and attitudes about sex can impede natural, healthy heterosexual development.[21]

[19] Britton and Winans, pp. 74–75.

[20] Britton and Winans, pp. 76–77.

[21] Howard A. Lane and Mary Beauchamp, *Understanding Human Development* (Englewood Cliffs, N. J.: Prentice-Hall, 1959), pp. 320–322.

We note that Doris is very much aware of boys and is fairly well advanced in heterosexual development. Her heterosexual interests are revealed in her primping, rolling her eyes, swinging her skirts, talking about boy friends, attending school dances, and expressing interest in getting married. Dennis is preoccupied with working on heterosexual development, but because of adjustment problems and failure to live up to peer standards, Dennis appears to be making only limited progress in heterosexual development.

Another developmental task of primary importance in early adolescence is *achieving some measure of emancipation from parents and teachers.* The ease or difficulty the adolescent experiences with this task will depend largely upon his parents' attitudes and expectations. It is common for parents with the best of intentions to expect and require absolute obedience from their children beginning in early childhood. Even when the parent-child relationship is benevolent and loving, the child may seldom be permitted to decide things for himself.

Frequently, the efforts of the adolescent to assert his independence will be reflected in negative and unconventional behavior. The adolescent is likely to rebel against cleaning up his room, to be rude and disrespectful, to appear in sloppy or outrageous dress, to flaunt his parents' wishes concerning his friends, and to give forth with emotional outbursts when met with parental refusal or disapproval. In addition, he may become critical of his parents—their dress, their attitudes, the car they drive, and the appearance of the home. Girls especially want their home to be attractive to friends. Often, they are critical about the house and its furnishings, and they seem to want perfection.[22] All these behaviors, which are frequently so disturbing to adults, are symptoms of the adolescent's striving for independence.

The adolescent's negative behavior and rejection of adults appear in part to be a response to the disorganization that follows the breakdown of the childhood personality (as suggested by Redl[23]) and the need to challenge parental authority "as the price of his own individual maturation and acceptance by his own age group."[24] Frank reminds parents that their adolescent offspring really do not want complete freedom. Rather, they wish to be released from parental control and conformity so that they can comply with the often more exacting requirements of their own age and sex group.[25] Moreover, there is evidence that adolescents really depend upon parents and teachers to set rules and expectations for their conduct, and even though teenagers may protest, they would feel let down by adults if the latter did not establish some limits.

The early adolescent's striving for independence is vividly portrayed

---

[22] Britton and Winans, p. 78.

[23] Redl, pp. 58–59.

[24] Lawrence K. Frank, "The Adolescent and the Family," in Nelson B. Henry, ed., *Forty-Third Yearbook: Part 1, Adolescence,* National Society for the Study of Education (Chicago: University of Chicago Press, 1944), p. 247.

[25] Frank, pp. 240–254.

in the cases of Doris and Dennis. Doris speaks to the counselor about her conflict with her father and his distrust of her, her desires to be free and to join with other girls in leaving home and living in an apartment, and her desire to get married. We know little of Dennis's relations with his family; but Dennis is working hard on achieving independence of his teachers, as shown in his baiting of teachers, his wearing his hat in school, and his testing the limits of teachers' patience for tolerating his unconventional behavior.

Cognitive Development

Early adolescence is a period of important gains in cognitive development. In Piaget's theory of intellectual development, 11 to 15 years of age marks the *period of formal operations*, in which the early adolescent develops the ability to solve a broad range of problems through the use of logical operations. Formal thought and concrete thought both employ logical operations, but concrete thought is limited to tangible problems whose solutions depend heavily on the use of perceptual data. Formal operations, on the other hand, are required in solving complex verbal problems, hypothetical problems, and problems involving future time orientation. The period of formal operations is marked by an increase in the individual's ability to organize data, reason scientifically, and generate hypotheses.

The shift from concrete to formal operational thought is illustrated in the following problem, used by Peel[26] in a study of cognitive development during late childhood and early adolescence.

> *Only brave pilots are allowed to fly over high mountains. A fighter pilot flying over the Alps collided with an aerial cable-way and cut a main cable, causing some cars to fall to the glacier below. Several people were killed. Why did this happen?*

The answer of the child using concrete operations is a simplistic explanation based upon his perceptions. He responds: "I think that the pilot was not very good at flying. He would have been better off if he had kept on fighting." The response of the early adolescent using formal operational thought, on the other hand, reveals greater skill in use of hypotheses and a more sophisticated understanding of causality. He states: "He was either not informed of the mountain railway on his route or he was flying too low. Also, his flying compass may have been affected by something before or after takeoff, thus setting him offcourse and causing a collision with the cable."

[26] E. A. Peel, *The Psychological Basis of Education*, 2nd ed. (Edinburgh and London: Oliver and Boyd, 1967).

In the problem of propositional logic requiring one to predict which objects will sink and which will float, the child at 11 or 12 begins to group and systematize his classifications so that he can consider all possible combinations in each case. In the latter part of the stage of concrete operations, he has made significant progress toward internal consistency in searching for a single explanation, but the discovery of the law or principle (explanation) must await the stage of formal operational thought. In the problem of the floating bodies and specific gravity, the key to the principle is relating the weight of the object being considered to the weight of an equal volume of water, a relationship the young person has had no opportunity to observe in the testing situation. At the beginning of the stage of formal operations, the child recognizes that the kind of material (wood, steel, aluminum, stone) and the surface properties or dimensions (thin and flat or long and narrow) influence whether or not a given object will float, but he has not discovered the law of specific gravity. By age 13 or 14, however, the young adolescent not only has discovered the law but can state it and describe a procedure for verifying it. This is revealed in the statement of one subject: "I take a wooden cube and a plastic cube that I fill with water. I weigh them, and the difference can be seen on a scale according to whether an object is heavier or lighter than water."[27]

We note, then, that the early adolescent can deal with multiple attributes simultaneously and is not limited to a one-at-a-time analysis. This ability enables him to think about events as arrangements of multiple dimensions. He comes to understand and to accept the fact that what has happened may depend upon an event that is not immediately observable. His father's anger, for example, may be provoked by any number of reasons. It may be the result of yesterday's poor report card rather than anything the son has done today.

Kagan[28] points out that the adolescent can accept a relativistic view, so that he is not troubled by the fact that seeming discourtesy is a product of both the situation and the actor. The adolescent can excuse a hostile greeting from a friend, for example, if he believes the reason for the hostility is an event which occurred hours earlier in another context. The younger child, however, sees the hostile greeting as something that is connected with what the recipient of the greeting has done or with something in the immediate situation.

The cognitive development of the early adolescent is also reflected in the way he organizes, reconciles, and integrates his beliefs. The early adolescent tends to examine his beliefs in sets and to search for inconsistencies among them and between beliefs and related actions. This cognitive operation depends partly upon previously acquired abilities, since critical examination of the logic of a set of related beliefs requires a capacity to consider

---

[27] Barbel Inhelder and Jean Piaget, *The Growth of Logical Thinking from Childhood to Adolescence*, trans. by Anne Parsons and Stanley Hilgram (New York: Basic Books, 1958), p. 44.

[28] Jerome Kagan, "A Conception of Early Adolescence," *Daedalus*, Vol. 100, No. 4 (Fall 1971), 997–1,012.

multiple issues simultaneously. Thus, the 14-year-old may ponder the inconsistencies among the following propositions:

1. *Sexual activity—self-administerd or heterosexually experienced —is bad.*

2. *Sexuality provides pleasure.*

3. *If sex is pleasant, it should not be bad.*

Increased masturbation at puberty forces the child to deal with the fact that he is violating a strong prohibition. However, since the strong sensory pleasure cannot be denied, the violation must in some manner be rationalized. The most likely rationalization is that the first proposition is not tenable. Similarly, the young person is likely to question many other standards, and he begins to examine all prohibitions with the same skepticism.[29]

Self-Development

Perhaps the most pressing developmental task facing the adolescent is that of *searching for and achieving a sense of self-identity*. It will be recalled that the integration of self in the form of ego identity in adolescence is the fifth stage of Erikson's eight stages of man.[30] Mention has been made also of the breaking up of the childhood personality evident in preadolescence[31] and of the maturing body as a symbol of new feelings and attitudes toward self, toward others, and toward life.[32]

The adolescent's search for a sense of self-identity is revealed in a variety of ways. Becoming independent of parents and teachers and gaining acceptance of peers are important steps in achieving a sense of personal identity. Possessing the ability to cope effectively with one's environment also contributes to a sense of identity. One's choice of and preparation for a vocation is a particularly crucial step in achieving this task. Whether the boy chooses a career in business, government, or the military service, and whether the girl chooses marriage or a career, will profoundly influence the sense of self-identity of each. Although the quest for self-identity is a significant developmental task of adolescence and early childhood, the elaboration,

[29] Kagan, pp. 997–1,012.

[30] Erikson, pp. 227–229.

[31] Redl, pp. 58–59.

[32] Herbert R. Stolz and Lois M. Stolz, "Adolescent Problems Related to Somatic Variations," in Nelson B. Henry, ed., *Forty-Third Yearbook: Part 1, Adolescence*, National Society for the Study of Education (Chicago: University of Chicago Press, 1944), pp. 80–99.

reaffirmation, or modification of one's self-identity remains an uncompleted task which the individual works on throughout adult life.

There is ample evidence that both Doris and Dennis are working on the task of achieving self-identity. Doris wants very much to see herself as worthy of her father's trust and as feminine, well groomed, and attractive to boys. Her search for self-identity is also reflected in her talk about leaving home, joining the Navy, and getting married. Dennis's search for self-identity appears to be complicated by adjustment problems that bring him into conflict with teachers and peers.

Adolescents are faced with *developing adjustment patterns which are appropriate to their increased maturity.* The complexities and difficulties involved in working on and achieving the developmental tasks of early adolescence make severe demands upon the adolescent's emotional resources. Thus, we can suppose that Dennis's roles of teacher baiter and peer group tease are patterns of adjustment to unspecified problems in interpersonal relationships. Whether Dennis continues to play these roles will depend upon the opportunities he has and the satisfactions he gains in playing socially more appropriate roles. Schoeppe, Haggard, and Havighurst[33] conclude from a study of 16-year-old boys and girls that if the adolescent is to accomplish successfully the developmental tasks required in his society, it is imperative that he master his impulsivity and accept himself, so that he can mobilize his energy to deal effectively with the social and cultural forces which impinge upon him.

Late Adolescence

The boy or girl entering late adolescence has many more of the characteristics of adulthood than of childhood. This stage encompasses roughly the ages of 15 to 18 (the senior high school years). Designating these ages as late adolescence is, however, arbitrary; differences in timing and rates of physical maturing produce considerable overlap in arbitrarily set ages for early adolescence, late adolescence, and early adulthood. Some at age 16 who are married or are employed full time are obviously in the role of a young adult, whereas other, equally mature 16-year-olds who face many years of additional schooling may find themselves in the more dependent role of the late adolescent until they are well into their twenties. We shall discuss early adulthood (college and/or early years on the job) in the first part of the next chapter.

Young people in late adolescence represent a broad range of interests, life goals, activities, and achievements. Individual differences in capacities, abilities, and talents have been magnified or blunted by more than 15

---

[33] Aileen Schoeppe, Ernest A. Haggard, and Robert J. Havighurst, "Some Factors Affecting 16-Year-Olds' Success in Five Developmental Tasks," *Journal of Abnormal and Social Psychology,* 48 (January 1953), 42–52.

years of environmental differences in family relationships, socioeconomic status, ethnic background, culture, community, and opportunities for higher education. Late adolescents, who a few years before (in elementary school and junior high school) seemed almost indistinguishable from one another, now differ greatly with respect to present role, situation, and the immediate future. While the lives of most 15- to 18-year-olds revolve around high school, home, peers, and community, many also have part-time jobs and/or are actively involved in volunteer work and community activities. Many look forward at the conclusion of high school to full-time employment, military service, marriage, homemaking, and parenthood—activities which those who have dropped out of school are already engaged in. Still others face several years of additional schooling and, for many, continued dependence upon their parents for financial support.

Many of the developmental tasks of late adolescence–early adulthood will be familiar to the reader, since they have been encountered earlier in this chapter. In the context of approaching adulthood, however, each developmental task of late adolescence is a very different learning from its antecedent. In heterosexual development, for example, learning what one does on a date is a world apart from building a relationship of mutual understanding, trust, love, and respect in courtship.

Again, for a clearer understanding of this last developmental stage, we will now present brief excerpts from case records of a boy and a girl in late adolescence–early adulthood.

> *Phil Watson is 17 years old and a junior in high school. Last spring he was elected president of this year's junior class. He is six feet tall and weighs 150 pounds. He has been active in extracurricular activities, but his main interest has been the debate team.*

> September 18.   *The assignment was to write a paragraph about a picture I passed around the class. The picture was an optical illusion which showed a woman sitting at a dressing table before a mirror. From one view she was a beautiful lady; from the other she was a hideous death's-head. This is Phil's paragraph:*

> *Life is the essence of beauty. Beauty to most means only all; and yet I ask is beauty anything?*
> *I know not for what purpose a person should live if they're not beautiful. For to most beauty is all. To please all is to be happy, is it not? So I have been told. Yet, I ask again, is beauty anything? Why should you try if you are lost and ugly? You cannot win. For to most beauty is all. Still I ask is beauty anything?*
> *Ugly one, try not to change thy face. I am dead and God is ugly like us. I know not for what purpose a person should live if he is not beautiful.*

> October 20.   *This afternoon Mrs. Thompson, the guidance counselor, indicated that Phil had been in the guidance office to get*

information about colleges, their costs, and opportunities for scholarship help. He said, "No one in my family has ever attended college, but I would like to." He will need some type of scholarship aid, as his family has very modest means and can give him very little help. He has indicated an interest in being a teacher, but except for English many of his grades have been poor, especially in math and science.

He would like to go away to school but is afraid his limited finances will not permit it. Phil indicated that he earns 25 dollars a month with his paper route, but from his earnings he has to buy his own clothes and pay his school expenses.

November 10.   In the period between classes, I noticed Phil walking with his girl friend, Sue Bently, to her next class. She never took her eyes off him as he chatted and smiled at her. He was the last one to enter the classroom just as the bell rang.

Today I played a record of a reading of Walt Whitman's "Song of Myself." After the record I asked, "What connections did Whitman draw between the grass and death?" Phil raised his hand and I called on him.

"He called it the hair of graves at first. Later it is compared to a white-haired old lady, an old man's beard y'know. It is always the hair of the grave. It, well—it's just another part of life."

"Why did he make these comparisons?" I asked.

Phil continued, "It seems like he was looking for a chance to give a new view of death. He was glorifying it. Obviously, he means that death is a lot luckier than people think—that's what the last line says."

Later in the discussion I asked, "What about the image of grass growing from the roof of a dead person's mouth—that's pretty stark, isn't it?" Phil's hand shot up, and I nodded.

"Yeah, but like in 'Thanatopsis' where he goes into decomposition—that's not romantic. It seems even more realistic than this. After all, he was trying to be scientific. And he just flat says that death is nothing"—pause and then with greater emphasis—"but mingling of the elements." He continued, "In that poem ya gotta take the essential part—without the two ends he tacked on—they're no good!" Phil and I laughed, but most of the class appeared to have lost the train of thought, as they looked blank and didn't respond.

February 23.   Today I accompanied the debate teams, affirmative and negative, to the State Debate Tournament. Both of our teams were eliminated in the fourth round, but Phil came through with the highest rating in the discussion to win $10.00 in cash and a gold pin.

Out of approximately 500 speech contestants, Phil was also elected president of the State High School Speech Association for the coming year. His acceptance speech was actually a piece of art in my viewpoint. Students from many of the large high schools congratulated him, and he shook hands with many, many students in the meeting. Throughout this period, Phil maintained his poise and wore a smile.

One of the members of my group said, "Oh! Miss Foster, aren't you proud of Phil? He's just the smartest and most handsome boy in the entire group."

I nodded and smiled my approval.

March 13.   We received word today that Phil's father was taken to the hospital today with a serious heart condition. This afternoon I talked to Phil after school and tried to comfort him. He said, "I don't know whether I can stay in school or not. If Dad is in the hospital for very long, I'll have to quit and get a job to support my mother and brother and sister."

"I believe there are a lot of people who would be willing to help," I countered.

"It looks like this is the end of my hopes to go to college," he said sadly.

"Anybody who has a strong enough desire to get a college education will get there eventually," I reassured him. "I'm sure you will find a way, and we'll help you all we can."

"Thanks for everything," he said as he left to meet his girl friend, Sue. Later I spoke to Mrs. Thompson, and she suggested that she was sure Phil could finish high school by participating in the work-study program.

"Phil wants to be a teacher," I said. "I hope he can be helped to reach his goal, for he is the kind of person we need in teaching." She heartily agreed as we said goodbye.

A few brief excerpts from the case of Susan were presented in Chapter 7. She is a high school senior, is 17 years, nine months of age, and her most recent total IQ on the California Test of Mental Maturity was 104.

October 8.   In a conference after class Susan said she disagreed with a statement I had made in class, that college was not only for vocational training but was also fine for women who had marriage and a family as their only goal in life, if they had college-level ability. Suzy told me that she could see no value in college for herself because she would be married in three or four years. She added that most of her boy friends have been college students and that now she is going with a boy who's attending State University. We talked for some time on how she might find more in common with her husband and tastes more consistent with his if she were to go to college. In response, she said that she had artistic and cultural tastes already.

I realized more and more that I was in effect persuading her to go to college, so I tried to draw the subject to a conclusion. Finally, she said, "You know, my parents want me to go to college, but I still don't see that it will help me. I will work for a few years, then get married."

November 4.   *Susan is neither attractive nor homely. She dresses in style and with obvious care. She gives me a pleasant, neat impression. She wears dark horn-rimmed glasses almost all the time, an average amount of makeup, and has a very ready smile. Her teeth are even and seem well cared for. She is five feet, four inches tall and weighs 130.*

For two years, Suzy has had a part-time job as credit interviewer for the Blakely Department Store. She works three evenings a week, taking credit applications and opening accounts for people. She tells me that she enjoys her work very much, mostly because she likes the contact with different types of people. A good part of her job consists of typing forms from information gathered in asking questions of the applicant.

November 24.   *Just as she was leaving today, Suzy came over to me and said, "Look what the turkey brought me." She held her left hand out and on the third finger was the Bancroft school ring, the private military school Jack had attended.*

I said, "It looks like Jack is back." She went on to say that after she had come home from a walk on Thursday her mother said, "Someone's in the living room to see you." She dramatically described her surprise at seeing Jack there. Then she explained that her mother is afraid she will lose the ring because it is too big for her finger. "Jack is going to get a solid gold band to make it smaller."

I said, "That might make it more permanent."

Suzy smiled and said, "I hope so," and was gone out the door.

January 6.   *In the course of conversation today, I mentioned that her mother seems to like Jack. She said that both her parents like him very much, but they don't want her to marry until he gets out of the Navy (two and a half years). I asked her how she felt about that, and she said they both wanted to marry sooner but that they hadn't set any date yet, as things were too indefinite with Jack. She added that when they did set a date she thought her parents would agree. I said, "Suppose they don't."*

"I'm sure they will," she said, "but if they don't, I guess we'll just go ahead."

February 11.   *Suzy told me today that Jack sent her a telegram saying he had been selected for Naval ROTC. I congratulated her and remarked how wonderful it would be to have a college education and be paid for it. There were several other students in the office at the time, and I felt she was enjoying impressing them, especially when she said, "I told his mother that I'm going to be an ad-*

miral's wife." Then she said she thought there was a requirement that NROTC men could not be married. I gave her a copy of the NROTC handbook so she could look up the requirement. She was still smiling when she read it and said, "Oh, my goodness, four years. He can get married when he graduates." She kept smiling and said, "Well—." She then put the book down and left the office.

Physical Development

During the late adolescent period the individual attains his adult height. It is during this period that boys finally catch up to girls in physical maturity. The late adolescent has come to some kind of terms with the realities of his body type and appearance, and he is likely to have incorporated these realities of his self-image. This is reflected in the findings of a study by Clifford,[34] who investigated the extent to which 340 males and females aged 11 to 19 expressed satisfaction or dissatisfaction with their bodies and self-images. Both sexes expressed the same degree of relative dissatisfaction with aspects of their bodies associated with growth—height, weight, chest, waist, and hips—the last four of which may suggest concerns over weight gains that reflect in part the advantages of an affluent society. There is some evidence from this study that height, weight, and physique are common concerns of nearly all adolescents, no matter where they are in the growth process. The finding that females, regardless of age, express greater dissatisfaction with themselves and their bodies than do males may be due to heightened self-awareness and emphasis by women on clothing, personal adornment, standards of beauty, and feminine appearance.

Physical size, strength, skill, and daring are desired qualities of manliness. The period of late adolescence is a time when individuals are at their peak of physical efficiency and coordination. Recognition, adulation, and honor tend to be reserved to the few well-developed, well-coordinated boys who participate in varsity athletics.

Every boy needs to see himself as physically adequate. A few boys, as in the case of Shorty Doyle in Chapter 4, attempt to compensate for their felt physical inadequacy by exaggerated attempts at getting attention, boastfulness, and bravado. As young people seek a measure of self-identity in their choice of a vocation, the *development of physical skills required for success in one's chosen vocation* tends to overshadow athletic skills.

Learning vocational skills depends as much upon one's possessing the requisite emotional and intellectual qualities as it does upon physical development and coordination. The late adolescent tends to spend more and more time learning skills in activities closely related to his educational and vocational interests. In short, possessing the necessary physical qualifica-

---

[34] Edward Clifford, "Body Satisfaction in Adolescence," *Perceptual and Motor Skills*, 33 (August 1971), 119–125.

tions will be an important consideration in one's choice of a vocation. Medical students who lack finger dexterity are likely to choose a specialty other than surgery.

As we have noted throughout this chapter, girls assess their physical characteristics and appearance in relation to their contribution in making them attractive to boys. Susan is concerned about her figure, hair, and grooming. She is described as neat, well dressed, and very feminine in her appearance. Her typing skill will enable her to hold a job until she marries, but it is probably secondary to the qualities of feminine appearance and figure described above. Phil is tall and rather good looking. Since most of his energies are devoted to intellectual interests and leadership in extracurricular activities, physical skills appear to be relatively unimportant to him.

Social Development

The peer group, often labeled "the crowd," continues to be important to the late adolescent. At this age some are becoming independent of the group, but for many, peers remain an important influence in their lives. One picture of peer influence in late adolescence is suggested by Coleman's findings cited in an earlier chapter. It may be recalled that in order to get into the top crowd, a girl needed to have a nice personality, good looks, and nice clothes, but she also had to have a good reputation. For boys, athletic ability and having a car were important for being accepted into the top status group. Academic success was not valued by either sex group. The leading crowds of boys wanted to be remembered as star athletes; they were far less interested than were the rest of the student body in being recognized as brilliant students. Similarly, leading crowds of girls were oriented away from thinking of themselves as a brilliant student and toward the image of an activities leader or the most popular girl in the school.[35]

For some late adolescents, peer relationships are strongly related to the use of drugs. For some, drug use is the result of peer relationships, while, for others, the person's decision to use drugs leads him to choose friends who also use drugs. Robinson,[36] in a study of two groups of late adolescent girls attending urban and suburban high schools, found that the marijuana smokers were girls who moved into peer group relationships to find satisfactions lacking in relationships with family and to find security as they coped with their identity crises. The values of the peer group of marijuana users were demonstrated in their struggles against authority, repudiation of "Establishment" values, and use of marijuana.

The thoughts, efforts, and concerns of the boy and girl in late adolescence center mainly on making themselves acceptable to the opposite sex.

[35] James S. Coleman, *The Adolescent Society* (New York: Free Press, 1963), p. 142.

[36] Lisa Robinson, "Marijuana Use in High School Girls: A Psychosocial Case Study" (unpublished doctor's dissertation, University of Maryland, 1970).

The developmental task each is working on is that of *acquiring the skills, attitudes, and understanding which enable one to develop and to grow in a close personal affectional relationship with an esteemed person of the opposite sex.* This is, of course, a continuation of the task of heterosexual development which began in preadolescence. In early adolescence, heterosexual relationships began with nondating mixed parties and pairing off, followed by various trials and periods of "going steady" with one or more partners. For some late adolescents, heterosexual development culminates in *choosing a life mate,* followed by courtship and marriage. For other late adolescents who face additional years in school, the further development of heterosexuality centers in maintaining a close, affectional, sometimes intense, often intimate relationship with one person or a succession of persons of the opposite sex.

Although many teenage boys do not think much about girls during the first two years of high school, they are very conscious of them and reveal their anxieties over what to do and say in heterosexual encounters. In the latter part of high school, their curiosity about girls enables boys to overcome their anxiety regarding girls. One study[37] concluded that the typical middle class late adolescent boy does not experiment much with sexuality. He is likely to engage in kissing, necking, and petting, but he is not likely to get too involved with a girl at this stage, since sexual closeness is rather frightening. It is much safer just to daydream about girls. In this study of middle class youth, it was estimated that not more than 10 percent had had sexual intercourse by the end of high school. Late adolescent girls are generally more advanced and sophisticated in their heterosexual development, but they also reveal great variation in the frequency and intensity of their relationships with boys.

In Coleman's study, a girl's reputation was crucial to her acceptance by both sexes. This posed a dilemma for some girls, since the approaches they used in becoming successful with boys could endanger their good reputations. Middle class adolescent boys in this study tended to choose active rather than passive girls. Passive girls were those who were seen as conforming to parental expectations and school assignments and as getting high grades. Middle class boys, in expressing their liberation from parental control, tended to seek partners in liberation, not girls responding to the controls of childhood. Coleman points out that traditionally in adolescence, and still more so among working class boys, the relevant dichotomy is the *good* girl, one whom the boy respects and admires, versus the *bad* girl, one the boy exploits and has fun with. Among modern middle class adolescents, however, this dichotomy is replaced by the *active* girl versus the *passive* girl —the first to respect and have fun with, the second to ignore.[38]

Success in dating is related to many other developmental tasks. Foremost among these is one's acceptance and learning of his sex role. Being

[37] Daniel Offer, "Sexual Behavior of a Group of Normal Adolescents," *Medical Aspects of Human Sexuality,* 5 (September 1971), 40–49.

[38] Coleman, p. 172.

mature, responsible, considerate, and able to relate to others is also important. For girls, good looks, grooming, and nice clothes are important assets that increase their attractiveness to boys. Girls, in turn, expect their beaus to be strong, poised, and self-assured. As the boy grows up, he must ascertain what girls expect of him. He is expected to take the lead, but he must learn the proper balance between leading and being overassertive.

The involvement of the late adolescent in heterosexual relationships which culminate in finding a life mate is clearly shown in the case of Susan. Early in the record, Susan is dating several boys. She wants to get married and seems to feel that going to college will not necessarily further that goal in her case. By Thanksgiving, Susan has a strong involvement with Jack, an involvement she hopes and expects will lead to marriage. Phil and Sue Bently have a strong interest in each other, but for Phil marriage appears to be some years away. His strong desire to attend college and the crisis of his father's illness are far more pressing at the moment. Most late adolescents have numerous experiences of falling in and out of love. Sometimes these experiences are painful, but they also can be helpful and developmental in giving the young person perspective in his choosing a life mate.

Another developmental task in late adolescence, a task encountered earlier, is that of *achieving independence of parents and family*. We noted that in early adolescence the task of gaining emancipation from parents centered in conflicts involving home duties, clothes, and choice of friends. In late adolescence independence of family is manifested in a variety of ways. Often it is facilitated by the adolescent's having a part-time job, choosing his friends, buying his own clothes, being able to come and go as he pleases, and perhaps having his own car. For a few adolescents, assertion of independence of adults is expressed in rebelliousness and defiance through the use of drugs. In one survey,[39] 33 percent of the respondents indicated that youth who turn to drugs are expressing rebellion in challenging the law, defying parents and other authorities, and retaliating against prim and prudish regulations.

However, even though the late adolescent achieves independence from his family, his parents are still important to him. Coleman found that the high school adolescents' allegiance in the 10 Midwest high schools he studied was shared about equally between parents and peers. When adolescent boys and girls were asked whose disapproval of joining a school club would be hardest to take, 54 percent said parents, 43 percent said friends, and 3 percent said teachers. Thus, adolescents "look forward to their peers and backward to their parents."[40] Where the adolescent and his parents have maintained rapport and mutual respect, the parents' influence tends to remain strong.

The gaining of some measure of financial independence appears to be an important aspect of the task of achieving independence in late adoles-

---

[39] Elizabeth Herzog, C. E. Sudia, and J. Harwood, "Drug Use among the Young," *Children*, 17 (November–December 1970), 207–212.

[40] Coleman, p. 5.

cence. By age 16 or 18, most young people have the capabilities for holding down a full-time or part-time job. Young people who look forward to several years of additional education beyond high school may have fewer opportunities for gaining economic independence from their parents. Most college students, however, earn some portion of their personal and college expenses. Those late adolescents who suffer the greatest frustration from failure to achieve a measure of economic independence are probably members of minority groups and those in disadvantaged areas who are unable to gain employment and have neither the interest, nor the qualifications, nor the financial support for further schooling. It is no wonder that these young people feel bitter at being discarded by society before they have even gotten a start in adult life.

The achieving of independence from parents and families manifests itself in a variety of ways, each of which may be a source of conflict. Besides earning enough money for clothes and personal expenses, there is the selection of clothes, the issue of frequency of going out and the hour of return, the use of the family car, the choice of staying in school or going to work, driving and owning a car, taking a full-time job, living away from home, getting married, joining the armed forces, and voting.

It is important to note that along with the young person's desire for independence goes his desire for developing and maintaining good relationships. As the stresses of growing up diminish, the late adolescent–early adult and his parents may interact with and enjoy each other on more egalitarian terms.

Susan expressed her growing independence in many ways. Case record excerpts report her decision not to go to college, her working part time as a typist in the Blakely Department Store, and her intention of getting married whether her parents approve or not. Her good relationship with her parents is revealed in her statement that she was sure her parents would approve of her getting married when the time came. The record of Phil states that he earns 25 dollars a month from his paper route, from which he buys his own clothes and pays his school expenses. Not reported were his trips taken with another boy the previous summer to New York, Boston, and Atlantic City. It is certain, too, that the increased responsibility he must assume in helping to support his mother and family will give him an increased feeling of being mature and playing an adult role.

Psychological and Personal Development

Although mental development continues throughout late adolescence and beyond, the young person during this period reaches a peak in his capacity to learn. Certainly one of the most important developmental tasks in the individual's life is his *choosing, preparing for, and entering a life vocation.* Late adolescents reveal greater stability and are more realistic in their choice of a vocation.

Considerable shifting in occupational choices occurs during late adolescence and even in the twenties, after one has finished school and gone to work. Of pressing concern to late adolescents is their appraisal of their own abilities in relation to job interests and opportunities. Young people keep asking themselves: "I wonder if I'm good enough for this?" "Will I gain satisfaction in this work and can I continue to grow?" Many youth who go on to college do not have a firm vocational choice, as evidenced by the finding of some universities that prior to graduation more than half of the students change their choice of major field and a sizable number change to a different college.

To assist students in making realistic vocational choices, guidance and personnel services in schools and colleges make available to students test results, occupational information, and counseling which provide them with a sounder basis for choosing a vocation. Without adequate occupational information and a realistic assessment of interests and abilities, choices tend to be based less on objective knowledge of self and more on the aspirations of parents or the prestige that society attaches to certain vocations.

Vocational choices of girls usually create fewer anxieties. Although many girls look forward to marriage, the immediate focus of most is upon qualifying for employment in their young adult years prior to and perhaps extending into the early years of marriage. This was the situation that Susan faced as she considered her employer's offer of a full-time job while she waited for Jack to finish his Navy enlistment or complete Naval ROTC. Phil Watson hoped to become a teacher, and he was faced with finding the ways and the means of completing his education while at the same time fulfilling his responsibilities to his family.

Another developmental task which faces most late adolescents is that of *crystallizing a system of values and developing a philosophy of life*. It is natural for youth on the threshold of adult life to feel apprehensive and uncertain as to what is right and what they want their lives to stand for. As they take on the roles and responsibilities of adult life, they face choices and decisions for which there is no sure guide. They long ago were made aware of the fallibility of adults and of the discrepancies between people's verbally expressed beliefs and values and what they do or fail to do in their daily lives.

In late adolescence, a youth searches for and incorporates into his self-image those beliefs, convictions, values, and aspirations which will direct his future activities and give whatever meaning and purpose his life will have. Late adolescence marks a shift, for instance, in the young person's development of political thought and consciousness. By age 15 or 16, the adolescent is capable of abstract thinking. He is no longer as authoritarian in his views of the political system, and he has the capacity for acquiring an ideology—a set of beliefs and values concerning man and society. There is some evidence, too, that the contemporay late adolescent is less idealistic and more antiutopian than were his older brothers and sisters when they were that age. This anti-idealistic attitude may reflect a striving toward realism; the responses of contemporary American youth reveal their concern with taking political action to facilitate harmony between factions within a community, with reducing differences in status among members of a community, and with finding a balance between the rights of the individual and the rights of the group.[41]

Late adolescence is a period when the influence of the church and its teachings diminish for many youth. The late adolescent–young adult looks to fresh sources for answers to age-old questions of what kind of universe this is and where he stands in it. We can expect him to become disillusioned, perhaps bitter, about the injustices and lack of love which appear to be so prevalent in the world about him. Most young people, however, come to see in clearer perspective the good as well as the bad and to reaffirm most of the values and beliefs taught by their homes, churches, schools, and communities. In the case excerpts, Susan valued and trusted her own feelings about college, getting a job, and marriage. Phil, through the encouragement of his teacher, sought to clarify his values and beliefs about the nature of life and the universe through a study of literature.

This and the two preceding chapters have presented the principal characteristics and developmental tasks from birth to physiological maturity. The reader should again be cautioned, however, that no attempt has been made to arrive at an all-inclusive list of developmental tasks. Different cultures and different levels of society set different demands and expectations for children and youth, and these demands and expectancies are constantly changing. A knowledge of developmental tasks provides us with a framework for interpreting the information we have about an individual, but permits only a general assessment of development. The framework of developmental tasks is not a prescription, for each individual works on each common task in his own time and in his own unique way. Although developmental tasks will continue to be used as an integrating concept in describing adulthood in the next chapter, it may be useful to pause here and examine the application of this concept to facilitating classroom learning.

Developmental Tasks and Education

Developmental tasks are the milestones on the journey of development and becoming. In achieving these tasks, one moves toward increased independence, self-realization, and self-enhancement. The developmental-task concept, as we have noted, is an integrating concept which the educator can use in assessing an individual student's development. The individual's self-concept, how he sees and feels about himself and about his world, can also be used as an integrating concept in seeking an understanding of development.

---

[41] Joseph Adelson, "The Political Imagination of the Young Adolescent," *Daedalus*, Vol. 100, No. 4 (Fall 1971), 1,013–1,050.

Developmental tasks are common learnings which face individuals growing up in a specific society or subculture. The mastery of these tasks is made possible by the individual's achieving the maturation which a specific task requires for its successful completion. The culture in essence says: "This learning (such as walking, reading, gaining acceptance of peers) is an important step in your own development. Learning the task is related to your being approved by society, your personal happiness, and your success with later developmental tasks." Self-processes play an important role, for unless the learning of the task is related to an individual's motives, goals, and values, he is unlikely to work on the task or to master it.

Since the culture has an important stake in youth's learning the developmental tasks appropriate to their maturity level, one may ask how the school and its curricula assist students in their learning of developmental tasks. Obviously, there is no simple answer to this question. The curricula of most schools place considerably more emphasis upon students' increasing their knowledge and skills in academic areas than upon acquiring broad general learnings that are related to their growing up.

Most schools do a fairly effective job of helping children to learn to read, to develop concepts related to the physical and social world, and to gain coordination of large and fine muscles. Most schools, however, appear to do little in helping children and youth to accept and to learn their sex roles, win acceptance in the peer group, develop heterosexual relationships, accept a changing body, gain independence, or achieve a sense of self-identity. Because of the limited opportunities for working on developmental tasks through classroom learning experiences, many adolescents can be observed exploiting the three-to-five minute break between periods, the lunch period, and the period after school in working on peer acceptance, heterosexual relationships, and the clarification of their sex roles.

Some would argue that the school provides students with opportunities to work on their developmental tasks in the broad range of clubs and extracurricular activities that the school offers. This may be in part true, but the experiences offered are seldom systematic, nor does the whole student body participate in them. Schools where nonintellectual activities overshadow the academic program may reflect the efforts of students to master important developmental tasks outside an academic program that may not be sufficiently responsive to the developmental tasks and the school program can be interrelated.

First of all, teachers can develop increased sensitivity to and understanding of the sequence of changes and learnings which occur at successive stages of development. Education must be seen as facilitating each student's development and learning rather than only imparting skills and knowledge. Each student brings a unique developmental history and readiness to the common tasks of growing up, and each encounters some problems of adjustment which will influence his ability to master these tasks. A central theme of this book is that guidance of any individual child requires knowledge of the unique and specific features of his life history and of his immediate milieu, as well as recognition of the principles of development, including his developmental tasks. This has been illustrated in the several case illustrations appearing in this and the preceding chapter, as well as in other parts of the book.

Second, in implementing the preceding principle, teachers can incorporate into school experiences many opportunities which permit and encourage students to work on their developmental tasks. The following are suggestions:

1.   *Provide frequent opportunities for students to form into groups of their own choosing for committees, projects, and panel discussions (peer group acceptance). Form groups which include both boys and girls (heterosexual development).*

2.   *Plan for student-led discussions of current events, mathematics needed in daily life, analysis of literary works and figures, and so on. Encourage all students to express their viewpoints and feelings (achieving independence).*

3.   *Plan and present a high school career conference (planning and preparing for a vocation).*

4.   *Encourage understanding of self and others through autobiographies, themes, written reactions to readings, field trips, and discussion of events of national and international significance. Explore with students the feelings, attitudes, and motives of literary or historical figures, or those which relate to a school problem or situation (achieving self-identity).*

5.   *Assist students, through appropriate questions, comments, and discussions of their statements, to achieve clarification of personal values and beliefs. Analyze the philosophies and value commitments of historical and literary figures, writers, and artists, and the commitments of one's own culture in contrast to those of other cultures (achieving self-identity, clarifying one's values).*

Third, teachers can become sensitive to the dangers of overloading children with demands irrelevant to the developmental tasks at hand. They can also avoid making too rigid the cultural expectations for accomplishing each task. There has been considerable question regarding the value of homework. Many students underachieve or drop out of school because school assignments often appear irrelevant to their needs.

Finally, educators can interpret what they know about the student's developmental needs and progress to parents, other teachers, youth leaders, physicians, and others who are in a position to help the student. It is clear that if the optimum development, learning, and mental health of the individual student is to be realized, all persons and agencies who play prominent roles in his life must be in communication with one another and work cooperatively in the best interest of the student.

Summary

Adolescence is a period of biosocial transition between childhood and adulthood which has been of special interest to parents, educators, psychologists, and the culture at large. Adolescence is a period of feeling out of place and out of step, but in its later phases it is a period which many children and adults seek to emulate.

Many theories have been developed to explain the variable behavior and conflicting tendencies which characterize adolescence in our culture. G. Stanley Hall described adolescence as a time of inner turmoil, a period of storm and stress. Freud viewed the developmental process of adolescence as a dynamic struggle between the biological-instinctual id forces and the socially responsive superego. In Erikson's formulation, a major task in adolescence is one's reestablishment of his ego identity in accepting as part of himself his body changes and libidinal feelings.

Important distinctions have been made between the terms *puberty* and *adolescence*. Puberty is the point of development at which biological changes reach a climax and sexual maturity is achieved. Adolescence is the period of development and change extending from the beginning of pubescence to the point at which the individual assumes the roles and responsibilities of adulthood.

Preadolescence is a period of one to two years encompassing the latter part of late childhood and the early part of early adolescence, a period in which the young person's behavior reflects the temporary developmental discordance and adjustment to the disorganization of his childhood personality. Developmental tasks identified in preadolescence include the following:

1. *Developing a readiness for and an acceptance of body changes which mark one's growth toward physical and sexual maturity.*

2. *Developing appropriate patterns for adjusting to new feelings about one's changing body, maturation, parents, peers, and self.*

3. *Asserting one's independence of adults.*

4. *Forming and strengthening affectional relationships with adults within and outside the family.*

5. *Achieving acceptance and roles in a changing peer group.*

6. *Accepting, learning, and adhering to peer group codes, standards, and values.*

7.   *Developing intellectual skills and concepts appropriate to a period of physical change and increasing maturity.*

The central theme in adolescence is the rediscovery of one's self. The early adolescent must incorporate into his self-concept new feelings, a new body image, and new concepts of his roles and place in a changing world. The developmental tasks which early adolescents work on include:

1.   *Accepting and adjusting to a changing, maturing body.*

2.   *Accepting one's sexual maturing and one's sexuality as a male or female.*

3.   *Accepting and learning one's sex role.*

4.   *Being accepted and playing roles as a member of the peer group.*

5.   *Reestablishing heterosexual relationships.*

6.   *Achieving some measure of emancipation from parents and teachers.*

7.   *Searching for and achieving a sense of self-identity.*

8.   *Developing adjustment patterns appropriate to one's increased maturity.*

Young people in late adolescence represent a broad range of interests, goals, activities, and achievements. Although many of the developmental tasks of this period are similar to those of an earlier period, they often involve very different learnings from their earlier antecedents. These developmental tasks include:

1.   *Developing physical skills, knowledge, and competencies required for success in one's chosen vocation.*

2.   *Acquiring skills, attitudes, and understandings which enable one to develop and to grow in a close personal affectional relationship with an esteemed person of the opposite sex.*

3.   *Choosing a life mate.*

4.   *Achieving independence of parents and family.*

5.   *Choosing, preparing for, and entering a life vocation.*

6.   *Crystallizing a system of values and developing a philosophy of life.*

Achievement of developmental tasks appropriate to one's level of maturity is a strong expectation of one's culture as well as evidence of the individual's developing and becoming. The school, as an agency of the culture, has an important stake in assisting students to master their developmental tasks. Teachers, in their selection of process and content of learning experiences, are able to help students achieve their developmental tasks.

Study Questions

1. As you look back on your own adolescence, what were the most important events or experiences which were evidence of your achieving independence from adults? How were the behaviors you learned in achieving independence different from those of some of your friends or classmates who were members of a different subculture from yours?

2. In one large public university 60 percent of the undergraduate student body sometime during their four years changed their major field, and 40 percent transferred to a different college on campus. What developmental tasks appear to be associated with these decisions to change major or change colleges?

3. Henry Baldwin, age 17, is a well-developed, mature looking young man. He is outwardly friendly to all, but appears to have no interest in heterosexual relationships. Should Henry be guided toward taking some first steps in working on this developmental task, or should one wait for Henry to indicate a readiness for working on the task?

4. Chapters 3–9 have portrayed human development and learning as being influenced and shaped by a series of interrelated dynamic processes. Chapters 11 and 12, in contrast, have employed the developmental task concept to present a normative picture of what boys and girls generally are like during each period of childhood and adolescence. Disregarding differences in amount of material presented, list the advantages and disadvantages of each approach to studying human development and learning.

Suggested Readings

Coleman, James S. *The Adolescent Society.* New York: Free Press, 1961. A study of adolescent social climates and the relation of these to the behavior, learning, and values of adolescents in 10 midwestern high schools. Chapters 8, 9, and 10 are particularly informative in showing the psychological and scholastic effects of the social system on the way adolescents feel about themselves and in indicating the sources of adolescent value systems.

Conger, John Janeway. *Adolescence and Youth: Psychological Development in a Changing World.* New York: Harper & Row, 1973. Describes youth in a rapidly changing, complex society. The book seeks to show how the adolescent's development—psychological, social, cognitive, and physical— is influenced by changes in such institutions as the family, schools, and the world of work as well as by the divisions and conflicts taking place in society generally. Successive chapters are devoted to such basic principles of development as maturation, learning, cognition, motivation, identification, identity formation, and psychological defense mechanisms as these relate to adolescence. Findings from empirical research are cited to support and clarify the principles of development that are discussed.

Douvan, Elizabeth, and Joseph Adelson. *The Adolescent Experience.* New York: John Wiley, 1966. Reports the findings of two national interview studies involving 3,000 adolescents between the ages of 14 and 16. The authors conclude that the American teenager is less rebellious and disturbed than some would have us believe. Sex differences in adolescent development appear to be far more critical than has been heretofore realized.

Friedenberg, Edgar Z. *Coming of Age in America.* New York: Random House, 1965. A study of adolescence in the American secondary school. Examines the conflicts of choices that confront students between their personal commitments, values, and ambitions on the one hand and the values and interests of the group or institution on the other. Proposes new, more flexible, humane ways of facilitating the development and learning of youth.

Grinder, Robert E. *Adolescence.* New York: John Wiley, 1973. Provides a comprehensive view of development during the second decade of life. Emphasizes what it means to be an adolescent in today's world. Describes adolescence in terms of the familiar topics of physical development, adjustment, cognitive development, peers and youth culture, heterosexual relations, identification and identity formation, and career planning. Throughout, special attention is given to the interrelationships among the crucial factors in adolescent development.

Kagan, Jerome, and Robert Coles, eds. *Twelve to Sixteen: Early Adolescence.* New York: W. W. Norton & Co., 1971. Points out that less is known about early adolescence than other periods of development and makes a plea for more systematic study of early adolescence. The book consists of informative, well-documented papers on growth, social characteristics, cognitive and personality development, peers, family, and school as they shape the lives of early adolescents.

McCandless, Boyd R. *Adolescents: Behavior and Development.* Hinsdale, Ill.: Dryden Press, 1970. Focuses upon specific biological, personal, and social changes that shape adolescent behavior and development. The conceptual framework used is one which blends together concepts of drive theory, psychology of change, and self-concept.

Rogers, Dorothy, ed. *Issues in Adolescent Psychology.* New York: Appleton-Century-Crofts, 1969. A book of readings which presents a variety of points of view on a broad range of adolescent issues. Theories of adolescence, motivation, alienated youth, social-sex role, conflict between generations, youth as political activists, and youth in other cultures are some of the topics treated.

Salinger, J. D. *Catcher in the Rye.* Boston: Little, Brown and Co., 1953. Describes the weekend experiences of Holden Caulfield, beginning with his dismissal from Pency Prep for academic failure and ending with his reaching home in New York City. The raw feelings of this disturbed late adolescent are vividly described as he searches for meaning, understanding, and acceptance in relationships with both friends and strangers.

Films

"Alice"—A High School Junior, 16 mm, sound, black and white, 22 min. Bloomington: Audiovisual Center, Indiana University. Presents a candid view of an
eleventh grade pupil in a number of school situations. Alice is followed
throughout a school day from the time she arrives until the last class for
that day is over. Significant interludes are shown from each of her activities.

I Just Don't Dig Him, 16 mm, sound, black and white, 11 min. New York 10003:
New York University Film Library, 26 Washington Place. Dramatizes the
problem of communication between father and son caused by the stereotyped attitudes each has toward the other. When 14-year-old-Ken comes
home very late one night, he and his worried father have an argument.
The event on the following day subtly suggests how father and son can
learn to accept each other more realistically as individuals with strengths
and weaknesses.

No Reason to Stay, 16 mm, sound, black and white, 29 min. Berkeley 94720: Extension Media Center, University of California. Christopher Wood rebels
against the dull rounds of drill, memorization, and routine—the lack of
anything meaningful in his education. Here is the sort of rebelliousness
felt and expressed by many students today toward uninteresting, sterile
classes. The parents fail to understand, and so do the teachers. Presents
a deliberately biased view of one dropout and what he dropped out of.

Nobody Waved Goodby, 16 mm, sound, black and white, 80 min. New York:
Brandon Films, 221 W. 57th St. A study of delinquency in the affluent
society as observed in a study of a young boy who rejects the middle
class conventions and goals of his parents to strike out for himself. Shows
his gradual deterioration, his conflicts at home and at school, and the
ultimate rejection of his girl friend when he drives off in a stolen car.

Adulthood

14

Grow old along with me
The best is yet to be
The last of life, for which the first was made.

Robert Browning

Adulthood is a status and a level of development toward which the individual has been striving since the beginning of his life. Adult status confers upon the person a degree of independence he has not known before, together with its attendant rights, privileges, and responsibilities. Becoming an adult is important, therefore, because it marks the individual's entry into full-status membership in society. Table 14–1 lists the stages of the life cycle in contemporary, urban, middle class America, including the stages of childhood and adolescence, already discussed, and the stages of adulthood, described in this chapter. The table also presents the approximate ages, most significant others, and the major dilemma of value themes for each stage of development.

The designation of the period from age 18 to death as the adult years is admittedly arbitrary; some aspects of adulthood are achieved before age 18 and others are achieved afterward. One evidence of adulthood, for example, is the capacity for procreation, a capacity most persons acquire during the late adolescent years. Driving an automobile requires a level of skill, maturity, and responsibility that is generally associated with adult status, yet most young people in the United States are granted this privilege at age 16 if they pass a driving test. Fighting and dying for one's country as a member of the Armed Forces is a commitment worthy of adult status which some young people undertake as early as age 17. In the context of law, adult status implies a presumed level of maturity and responsibility that is reflected in procedures and penalties applied to adult criminal offenders which are different from those applied in the case of juvenile offenders. Legally, one attains his majority at age 21, but like the voting age (lowered in national elections to age 18), the age at which one legally is an adult is being lowered in many states.

While the terms *adulthood* and *maturity* are frequently used interchangeably, they have somewhat different meanings. *Adulthood* designates

Table 14–1.   Stages in the Life Cycle in Contemporary, Urban, Middle Class America

Life Cycle Stage	Approximate Ages	Most Significant Others	Major Dilemma of Value Themes, Erikson's Eight Stages of Man*
1. Infancy	Birth–2½ years	Mother, father	Trust versus mistrust
2. Early childhood	2½–6 years	Mother, father, siblings, playmates	Autonomy versus shame, doubt
3. Middle childhood	6–9 years	Parents, teacher, same-sex peers	Initiative versus guilt
4. Late childhood	9–12 years	Parents, same-sex peers, teacher	Industry versus inferiority
5. Early adolescence	12–15 years	Parents, same-sex peers, opposite-sex peers, teachers	Identity versus role diffusion
6. Late adolescence	15–18 years	Same-sex peers, opposite-sex peers, parents, teachers	↓
7. Early adulthood	18–30 years	Loved one, husband or wife, children, employer, friends	Intimacy versus isolation
8. Middle adulthood	30–45 years	Wife or husband, children, superiors, colleagues, friends, parents	Generativity versus stagnation
9. Maturity	45 years to retirement	Wife or husband, children, colleagues, friends	↓
10. Old age	Retirement to death	Remaining family, long-term friends, neighbors	Ego integrity versus disgust, despair

*Erik Erikson, *Childhood and Society* (New York: W. W. Norton & Co., 1950), pp. 219–234. These terms are explained on p. 241 and in the following pages of this chapter.

a status and a level of development. The term *maturity,* on the other hand, connotes in some contexts a point in the span of development and in other contexts a progression, quality, and direction of development. Physical maturity is a point in development defined in terms of skeletal age (assessed by X rays of hand and wrist) and in terms of indexes of sexual maturation. No such well-defined points have been identified for the other dimensions of development—social, emotional, and intellectual. Although we can evaluate other people's behavior against behavioral norms for social, emotional, and intellectual development at specific ages or stages of growth, these norms do not have widespread acceptance. Moreover, who among us can say that he has reached a point in social, emotional, or intellectual development beyond which no further growth is possible? As long as we live, further growth in each of these aspects of development is possible. Growth and development in these areas—as, indeed, in life itself—are open-ended. Although we are using the term *maturity* (for lack of a better term) to designate a later stage of adulthood, *maturity* is most meaningful when it is used to signify the progress, quality, and direction of one's social, emotional, and intellectual development in relation to behaviorally defined norms for each kind of development. Viewed in this way, some children and adolescents may be more mature in one or more of these aspects of development than some adults.

Probably the most significant aspect of adulthood for the individual is his feeling and perceiving himself to be an adult. To incorporate this percept into his self-image, one must be treated as an adult. Any person, regardless of his age, is unlikely to see himself as an adult or to act like one if parents or an extended period of schooling keep him dependent. Most young people view adulthood as where the action is—as providing opportunities for increased growth and self-enhancement through one's chosen vocation, marriage, family, and other mature affectional ties, and through shared efforts with others as full participants in trying to make society work. Initial progress toward these goals takes place during early adulthood, the period of development we shall examine next.

Early Adulthood

For many persons, the direction their lives will take is established in early adulthood, the period of 18 to 30 years of age. It is a time when young people strive to gain and maintain their foothold on lower rungs of the ladder that they will climb in their progress toward lifetime goals. Young adults are individualistic, egocentric, and often rather lonely. They are individualistic in their choices of vocations, schools they attend, life styles they emulate, and ways they go about achieving their goals. Their egocentrism is reflected in their tendency to be introspective and in their anxiety over whether they will "make it"—however this may be defined—on the job, as a man or woman, husband or wife, parent, and neighbor. Young adults are lonely because for most it is the first time they are really on their own. Taking a job or going to college often takes the young adult away from primary ties of family and peers which have provided much-needed support in his growing up.

Early adulthood is unique as a stage of development because it marks a transition from an age-graded to a social-status-graded society.[1]

[1] Robert J. Havighurst, *Developmental Tasks and Education*, 3rd ed. (New York: David McKay Co., 1972), p. 84.

As one progresses through childhood and adolescence, he gains new privileges and assumes new responsibilities at successive maturity levels primarily because he is thought to be old enough for these things. The early adolescent girl, for example, is permitted to visit a friend in the evening or to stay up later to watch TV, privileges which are denied the fifth grade sibling in late childhood. The older .child, in turn, is made responsible for the care and safety of the baby brother or for preparing dinner during the parents' absence, responsibilities which are not expected of the younger child. People are grouped and responded to in the adult society, however, not so much in terms of any age-grade status but more in terms of their skill, strength, knowledge, education, and family connections. Achieving life goals is not nearly so much a matter of attaining them by waiting until one grows up as it is of planning and carrying out strategies that will overcome obstacles in attaining them. Much of the young adult's time and efforts are devoted to devising and carrying out strategies for developing a satisfactory living arrangement, completing his education, getting established in a vocation, discovering and adopting a life style, and choosing a mate.

An indication of the ways two young adults worked toward achieving the developmental tasks of early adulthood is revealed in the following excerpts from the cases of Karen Brownell and Ron Thomas.

Karen Brownell grew up in a medium-sized college town in the Midwest. Her father, a professor of economics in the local college, and her mother, an artist whose paintings were frequently exhibited, had instilled in Karen and her two younger brothers the values of honesty, hard work, fair play, equality, kindness, humility, and a liberal point of view on political issues. During high school Karen made high grades and was active in a number of school activities, including being a member of the debate team and writing for the school paper.

Karen was indistinguishable from the other freshman girls entering a state university in a neighboring state. She continued to pursue her interest in journalism and debate and through these contacts met several of the leaders of protest groups which were active on that campus during these years. Karen found herself drawn into these activist groups and attended more and more of their meetings. She saw many of their aims of stopping the war, nondiscrimination in housing, and equal opportunity for women as clearly consistent with the core values she had acquired from her family. She participated in a number of protest demonstrations on campus as well as in the protest marches for peace held in Washington, D. C., in 1970 and 1971. Karen's parents were concerned over the depth of her involvement in political activity, but they said little. At various times they seemed proud that Karen was working directly on problems and issues which they strongly though covertly supported.

Karen's interpersonal relationships and life style changed markedly during her four years at the university. After living during her freshman year in a university dormitory, she moved at the beginning of her sophomore year into an apartment wth two other girls. She dated several boys during the first two years, but in her junior year she began to develop a strong attachment to Kevin, who was also active in protests and the peace movement. Although she had some reservations at first, she finally moved into Kevin's apartment and lived with him for most of her last two undergraduate years.

So involved had Karen become in political activities that she had not given much thought to what she would do after graduating. Marriage didn't seem very likely just yet. She and Kevin got along well together, but he still had three years of law school ahead of him; besides, she was not really sure he was the one. Although her parents were liberal, she wasn't sure how they would take Kevin's vehemently expressed radical ideas, to say nothing of his full beard and shoulder-length hair. With a degree in English literature, Karen vaguely thought of going on to graduate school, but she was a bit tired of school.

After a summer at home following graduation, Karen set out with only 200 dollars for Boston because, as she expressed it, "That's where the action is!" She found a group living arrangement with seven other young men and women in a large rented house in Cambridge. It was difficult to get a job, but she did manage to support herself the first year by working in a succession of low-paying clerical jobs in banks and insurance companies. That first year in Boston, Karen attended many meetings of the New Left and participated in a number of their protest marches. She believed as fervently as ever in the movement's goals, but somehow it seemed different from the movement she remembered on campus in the Midwest. These leaders in Boston seemed so young, hot headed, impractical, and radical. During her second year in Boston, she joined a publishing firm as a trainee in the editorial department. The work was interesting, and she was challenged by the opportunities for advancement there. Soon after that she began dating Jim, who worked in the same office. As Karen reflected on the past few years, she felt that she had changed a lot; but as she moved back toward more stable living patterns reminiscent of the home she left six years ago, she wondered at times how much she really had changed.

Ron Thomas grew up in a medium-sized city in the South. His father, an electrician, provided a modest but adequate home and standard of living for the family of five. The family were staunch Baptists and attended services regularly on Sunday and during the week. Ron's major interest in high school was sports, and during his senior year he gained considerable fame in that part of the state as a linebacker on the local football team.

During his senior year in high school, Ron was undecided

about what he wanted to do after graduation. He finally decided to accept a football scholarship at the state university 50 miles away. That fall he found it increasingly difficult to keep up with his studies, especially with football taking so much of his time. Ron barely scraped through academically during his freshman year, but significant changes were occurring in his attitudes and beliefs. Having seen blacks in a subservient status at home, Ron had come to college with stereotyped attitudes toward blacks as being lazy and inferior. At State, however, Ron became close friends with two blacks on the football team. He soon realized that many statements about blacks made by his parents and respected citizens of his home town simply were not true. When he went home, Ron often argued with family and friends. Afterward he felt very uncomfortable and sensed that he was growing apart from the people he had always known and respected.

A major crisis occurred in Ron's life during the first semester of his sophomore year. Early in the season it became evident that he and the football coach were not getting along. As a result, he found himself on the bench while other, less able teammates were playing during most of the game. He was failing in three subjects, and to top it off, Wanda, his steady since early in his freshman year, broke off and started going with someone else. Ron was so depressed that he dropped out of school at midsemester even though this meant he was sure to be drafted and sent to Vietnam.

Fresh out of basic training, Ron was convinced of the rightness of America's being in Vietnam to help the South Vietnamese defend themselves against the Communists. After being there for several months and seeing what the war was doing to the country and its people, however, Ron became more and more convinced that America's participation in the war was wrong and futile. On March 18 Ron's patrol was ambushed by the Viet Cong, and Ron was severely wounded. He guessed that he might not have made it if a black medic had not crawled out and pulled him back to safety.

After his discharge Ron returned to his home town and finally landed a job at the local paper mill. Six months later he married Sharon, whom he had remembered as a freckle-faced junior in high school but who since had grown into a beautiful young woman. During the first year of marriage, they both worked, furnished a nice apartment, bought a car, and were very happy together.

During their second year of marriage, life did not go quite as smoothly. Sharon became pregnant and gave up her job, which meant that their standard of living had to be drastically reduced. Ron took a second job, but even then it was difficult to make ends meet. Ron's relationship with Sharon during this period had its ups and downs. Sharon's interest in sex cooled during her pregnancy, and after their son, Robbie, was born, Ron felt neglected because Sharon spent so much time with the baby. Sharon expected Ron to give her more help around the house and in caring for Robbie even though

Ron came home from his two jobs exhausted. Sharon also wanted Ron to take her places so she could get out of the house, but he preferred to spend an evening with the boys playing poker.

On top of his domestic problems, Ron found himself increasingly estranged from the dominant values of his parents and the community. He was appalled at the verbal abuse of welfare recipients—most of whom were black—and of black children when they entered previously all-white schools as the result of court-ordered desegregation. Ron became disillusioned with the church because it seemed unable or unwilling to take effective action, and he stopped going to church. Because of his dependence upon work to support his family, Ron felt trapped into staying in that community. Fortunately, however, a few months later, an army buddy wrote to Ron inviting him to join him in his sporting goods business. Ron accepted the offer with alacrity, packed up, and set out with Sharon and Robbie to begin a new life in Atlanta.

Achieving Personal Autonomy

Achieving a measure of personal autonomy is a lifelong developmental task, but it has special significance for those in late adolescence and early adulthood. Only by expressing his autonomy in mature and responsible ways can one be convinced that he is indeed an adult. Frequently, the young adult expresses his autonomy by moving out of his parents' house and establishing, often with others, a home of his own. Sometimes this split is precipitated by parent–young adult conflict, but the conflict may only be a reflection of the young adult's strong need to be on his own. Many, like Karen and Ron, achieve this level of autonomy when they go away to college. Each sought to remain physically independent of his family after years at the university or in the army. Karen set out for Boston soon after graduation, while Ron married and established his own home soon after his discharge. The degree of success of the young adult in achieving this kind of autonomy depends upon his financial status and job opportunities, for living apart from parents obviously costs money. For this reason, a high unemployment rate among young adults is a double blow. Being denied a job not only undermines one's self-esteem but also threatens one's sense of autonomy.

The difficulty of achieving autonomy as an adult is only slightly different for the young person who faces many years of higher education before he is qualified to start his chosen career. The academic demands made on many of these young adults prevent them from assuming the normal adult responsibilities of marriage, starting a family, and gainful employment—even though they are physically and psychologically ready to assume these duties. Young people attempt to solve these problems in a variety of ways. In some cases the student marries in spite of his lack of economic independence, and his wife works to finance his education. If this support is not sufficient or if children enter the picture, the student may work also, often full time, in addition to pursuing his studies. As a last resort the couple may be subsidized by parents—a solution which compromises young adults' sense of independence. Single students often face the same kinds of problems, and their solutions are similar.[2]

Sexual Relationships

In early adulthood a major dilemma in value themes is, according to Erikson, intimacy versus isolation. The growing amount of literature on human sexual behavior and sexual response[3] points to the high level of sex drive experienced by members of both sexes during early adulthood. Upon leaving his parents, the young adult often experiences a sense of isolation and insecurity which is only partially assuaged in relationships with members of his own sex. The need to work on the task of relating to the opposite sex, first encountered in early adolescence, becomes much more intense in early adulthood. This need for heterosexuality is manifested in a desire for greater intimacy with a member of the opposite sex, an intimacy which may or may not involve sexual relationships. This desire for intimacy and for avoiding isolation poses for the young adult the developmental task of *developing appropriate ways of satisfying one's sex drives.*

Differences in strength of sex drives, in cultural backgrounds and mores, and in personal values and adjustment patterns make the achievement of this task a different experience for every young adult. Many will seek satisfactory outlets for their sex drives through working on the related developmental task of selecting a mate in the activities of courtship. This is the culturally approved way—and for most persons the most satisfying way—of satisfying sex drives. For other young adults, however, early marriage may be neither desirable nor feasible because of the lack of a job or because of commitment by the man and/or woman to further education. Thus, for many young adults, finding satisfactory outlets for sex drives and choosing a life mate may be quite distinct and appear at different times during early adulthood.

Older adults feel certain that there has been a marked change in sexual attitudes and practices over the last generation. The widespread use of the pill and other contraceptive devices, the liberalization of laws governing abortion, and the increased services of family-planning clinics to both married and unmarried women lend credence to the impression of greater

[2] Nancy C. Ralston and G. P. Thomas, "America's Artificial Adolescents," *Adolescence,* 6 (Spring 1972), 137–142.

[3] See Alfred C. Kinsey, Wardell B. Pomeroy, and Clyde R. Martin, *Sexual Behavior in the Human Male* (Philadelphia: W. B. Saunders, 1948); William H. Masters and Virginia E. Johnson, *Human Sexual Response* (Boston: Little, Brown and Co., 1966); and David Reuben, *Everything You Always Wanted to Know about Sex but Were Afraid to Ask* (New York: David McKay Co., 1969).

freedom and permissiveness in sexual practices. Yet some maintain that the available evidence suggests that there has been no significant change in the *frequency* of premarital petting and coitus since the 1920s. Kinsey, for example, has pointed out that "there has been little recognition that premarital petting and coital patterns established then [1920s] are still with us."[4] It appears, then, that the parents and even some of the grandparents of today were the youth who introduced the new patterns of sexual behavior about 50 years ago.[5] Reports of swinging and wife swapping among some middle-aged adults seem to add support to the view that extramarital sex may have been almost as prevalent at other times and in other generations as it is now.

There seems to be little question, however, that young people today are more frank in discussing sex and less inclined to pass judgment on the sexual behavior of others. The marked shift in the attitudes of contemporary young adults compared to those held by earlier generations centers in a disavowal that premarital sex is shameful or that it harms the prospect of happiness in marriage. This shift in attitudes is also reflected in a change in premarital sexual behavior among young adults. Earlier studies showed that the nonvirgin bride usually had sexual relations with only one man before marriage, the man she subsequently married. More recent studies, however, show increasing rates of sexual intercourse among young women without regard to expectations of marriage. A survey of female students at an urban university in 1968 revealed that, of those who had premarital coitus, only 19 percent had first experienced it while they were engaged to be married. Fully three-fourths had first experienced sexual intercourse in a dating relationship—not necessarily even a "going steady" dating relationship. Not only did many of these woman feel no necessity to have a commitment to marriage, but they also felt no remorse. This finding may indeed reflect the first significant change in premarital sexual behavior since the 1920s.[6]

Further evidence of this shift in attitudes toward premarital sex is contained in the results of a Gallup poll conducted on 55 campuses in the spring of 1970. This poll showed that three-fourths of the students questioned said that virginity is not an important consideration in choosing the person they would marry. An equal proportion of men and women responding to the question felt this way. It appears, too, that virginity becomes less and less valued at successive levels of higher education—68 percent of the freshman, 80 percent of the seniors, and 83 percent of the graduate students did not value virginity in a prospective mate. A generation gap is indicated in the results of a Gallup poll taken the preceding year which showed that 68 percent of the adults questioned said that premarital sex is wrong.

---

[4] Alfred C. Kinsey et al., *Sexual Behavior in the Human Female* (Philadelphia: W. B. Saunders, 1953), p. 300.

[5] Robert R. Bell, "Parent-Child Conflict in Sexual Values," *Journal of Social Issues*, 22 (April 1966), 35.

[6] Robert R. Bell and J. B. Chaskes, "Premarital Sexual Experience among Coeds: 1958 and 1968," *Journal of Marriage and Family*, 32 (February 1970), 84.

Although the figures in the 1970 survey apply only to college students, we have little reason to expect any marked differences in sexual attitudes and sexual behavior between college youth and the total population of young adults. Some differences have been noted, however, in the way various social groups deal with this task of satisfying one's sexual drives. Middle class boys are more likely to practice masturbation, while lower class youth show a preference for heterosexual intercourse. Our case record excerpts suggest that Karen's developing a stable affectional tie with a boy friend that included sexual relationships appears to be typical of the attitudes and behavior of college youth described above. From the excerpts we have no way of knowing the extent of Ron's premarital sexual experience, but it is evident that his primary mode of satisfying sexual drives was in a marriage relationship.

It is probably naive for older adults to expect any reversion among the young to an earlier era favoring chastity and Puritan morals. Rather, it appears that openness and permissiveness in sexual expression are likely to increase at all levels of society. This is not to say, however, that we should abandon rules and safeguards. Above all, *one should be responsible in his sexual behavior, as in other areas of adult life.* This suggests that sex is probably most meaningful and satisfying when one has reached a stable degree of emotional and social maturity. Impulsive sex generated in a moment of unthinking passion is often followed by feelings of disgust and disappointment. Dissatisfaction with early sex experiences is probably much more the result of the immaturities and hangups of one or both participants than of faulty technique. So much has been promised in the popular literature regarding each partner's right to experience a particular kind of orgasm and to gain sexual fulfillment that many persons are bound to experience disappointment—not realizing that a sexual relationship grows as the human relationship with that person grows. Because meaningful sexual expression requires an openness and an intimate fusion between two persons, most of us do not want to be that intimate with just anybody. Thus, without invoking any traditional moralities, one can find good psychological reasons for waiting until he has achieved responsible adulthood—whether married or unmarried—before he seeks sexual fulfillment.[7]

Forming Affectional Ties in Early Adulthood

For most adults the satisfaction of sexual drives is best achieved in marriage. Early adulthood is the period when most persons marry (the first time, at least), and so, much time, energy, emotion, and resources are spent in *finding and courting a marriage partner.* Some young adults who do not marry form nonsexual affectional ties with friends of the same and

---

[7] Joseph Stone and Joseph Church, *Childhood and Adolescence: A Psychology of the Growing Person,* 2nd ed. (New York: Random House, 1968), pp. 484–491.

opposite sex. In addition, they may have affectional ties with the families of married brothers and sisters. As noted earlier, changing life styles result in the forming of an often temporary, sometimes stable relationship by a young adult male and female outside of marriage. In view of the high incidence of divorce in contemporary America, the emotional security and satisfaction experienced by an unwed couple may be greater than that found in some marriages. The key to happiness and satisfaction lies in the maturity and commitment of the partners rather than to whether or not the relationship is formalized. Most young people, however, conform to cultural expectations by formalizing their commitment in marriage vows, thereby establishing a relationship through which they can grow and build a life together.

To make marriage work, one must work at the task of *learning to live with one's spouse and becoming a satisfying husband or wife.* The closeness of marriage provides the real test of one's maturity as an adult. In successful marriages the love, stability, sacrifice, and commitment of each partner are more than adequate for overcoming the stresses which most marriages encounter. Marriage at its best provides a unique opportunity for the personal growth of each of the partners. The recent growth in movements seeking equal rights for women suggests that attitudes and practices which stereotype and restrict the roles women play in the home and in society may thwart the personal growth of the wife. Similarly, the stereotyping of men's roles may also limit development. A task of marriage is *providing opportunities for both husband and wife to assume roles that promote the satisfaction and growth of each other.*

A major goal of most marriages is procreation. Many couples seek fulfillment in their marriage through *becoming parents and raising children.* Raising a child well demands great sacrifices on the part of both mother and father, but these sacrifices may, in turn, enhance the personal growth of both parents. At the beginning of Chapter 11, it was noted that, with the recent decline in the birth rate and the trend toward stabilization in population growth, the direction in the future is toward smaller families. The decline in the birth rate has been so sharp that we are already approaching a "zero population" growth rate, which was not expected to be reached for some decades. For some young adults, procreation and child rearing seems to be temporarily out of style;[8] for others, having and rearing children is no longer mandatory. Continued decline in the birth rate would have profound effects on the people and way of life of future generations which at present can only be imagined. If, however, population growth stabilizes—that is, does not suffer a net loss—the resources and research findings which a growing technological society makes available can enhance the personal fulfillment of children and adults alike.

Although the young person may confirm his adulthood and his sense of autonomy by leaving his parents' home, he still needs his parents. Conflicts between young adults and their parents may temporarily strain family

---

[8] See "Childlessness," *New York Times Magazine,* December 24, 1972.

ties, but the young adult often is lonely, and he becomes discouraged as he encounters setbacks in seeking to establish himself in the adult world. He needs a home base to which he can return periodically for reassurance and support. Parents who, despite conflict between the generations, maintain communication with their young adult sons and daughters provide continuing affectional ties that are important to the security and well-being of both parents and their adult offspring.

The Generation Gap

Frequently, however, changing mores and different values produce ongoing conflict between the late adolescent–young adult and his parents—a phenomenon often referred to as a *generation gap*. Disagreements between parents and their offspring center in sexual behavior, the use of drugs, and the validity of traditional life styles, goals, and social and political institutions.

We have noted that today's youth are more tolerant of premarital sex than their parents are. Parents who are strongly committed to monogamy often are deeply disturbed to learn that many youth engage in coital relations with a succession of partners for whom they have no deep or lasting feeling. Since parents and their grown children seldom discuss sex openly, the parent likely does not ask questions and does not want to know about his child's sexual experiences; yet he remains apprehensive about the welfare of his son or daughter.

The drug culture is a phenomenon that is largely unknown to the vast majority of older adults. Accounts of persons getting hooked on drugs, of crimes committed to support a habit, and of lethal overdoses all cause older adults to fear the worst. There is disagreement between the generations over the legalization of marijuana, since no study has yet reported the long-term effects of using the drug. Neither is the parent mollified by being told that only a small fraction of marijuana users go on to hard drugs, since "the one who does and gets hooked could be my son or daughter."

What is probably most disturbing to many parents of young adults, however, is the seeming rejection by some youth of cultural and personal values which undergird everything the parents believe in. Parents disdain the counterculture, the hippies, and the revolutionaries, who appear to reject contemporary culture and its institutions of work, family, law, and government. While radicals of other times have frequently questioned the social forms of authority, competitive achievement, and the nuclear family, seldom have revolutionaries, as in contemporary society, attacked the realities of work, making a living, child rearing, and the organized social order. Equally disturbing to some parents are the statements of a few radicals which seem to question the supreme reality of adulthood—being a parent and raising children. In talking of revolution, extremists among the radical youth do not dwell on adult society being evil and resistant to rational change; they contend that there is no real social order worth saving at all.[9]

While few doubt the existence of a generation gap between parents and youth, the gap itself may be somewhat exaggerated. In one survey[10] 57 percent of the youth responding stated that they got along fine with their parents and enjoyed their company. Seventy-five percent believed that their parents lived up to their own ideals, and an equal proportion of the youth were in general agreement with their parents' ideals. Although a growing minority of youth have been alienated from a society that they view as unjust, violent, hypocritical, impersonal, and immoral, the average young person shares many of the traditional values of his parents: competition, excellence, respect for property, hard work, and success.

Values and Adjustment

The young adult, through his broadening experience, has had an opportunity to test and to refine some of the values which were crystallized in late adolescence. As a result of this process of value refinement and change, contemporary youth appear to have a greater concern than did their parents at the same age, or do now, with such issues as social class discrimination and racial prejudice. Contemporary youth are far more willing than their parents to support school integration and to have blacks or members of other minority groups as neighbors. This attitude of tolerance is reflected in their willingness to let others "do their own thing." Especially evident is the high value they place on open, honest, and meaningful relationships with others.

Most young adults are interested in job success as conventionally defined, but they seem less concerned with achieving status and recognition by society than they are in performing work that is meaningful, enjoyable, and significant. Today's youth are more skeptical of the lessons to be learned from the past and are inclined to view the future as either unpredictable or full of options that need not be explored yet. As members of the "new generation," they look to the present in searching for the meaning of uncertainty and irrationality. The overarching value espoused by contemporary youth, irrespective of social status and culture, is that of the friendship and love which should permeate all human relationships.[11]

One way that adults may gain a better understanding of contemporary youth is through analyzing the shift in the values of youth during

---

[9] Lawrence Kohlberg and Carol Gilligan, "The Adolescent as a Philosopher: The Discovery of Self in a Postconvention World," *Daedalus*, Vol. 100, No. 4 (Fall 1971), 1,051–1,086.

[10] John J. Conger, "A World They Never Knew: The Family and Social Change," *Daedalus*, Vol. 100, No. 4 (Fall 1971), 1,105–1,138.

[11] Conger, pp. 1,105–1,138.

the past few generations. Getzels[12] has studied the shift from "traditional values" (which guided American youth prior to 1940) through the "transitional values" of the late 1940s and early 1950s to the "emergent values" of the middle and late 1960s. The dominant values in each group are presented in Table 14–2.

Table 14–2.   Transformation of National Secular Values

Traditional Values (Classical American Image)	Transitional Values (Late Forties–Middle Fifties)	Emergent Values (Middle-Late Sixties)
Work-success ethic	Sociability	Social responsibility
Future-time orientation	Present-time orientation	Relevance
Independence	Conformity	Authenticity
Puritan morality	Moral relativism	Moral commitment

Source: J. W. Getzels, "On the Transformation of Values: A Decade after Port Huron," *School Review*, 80 (August 1972), 505–519. Reproduced by permission of The University of Chicago Press.

Getzels found that the shift from the transitional ethic of *sociability* to the emergent ethic of *social responsibility* is reflected in the responses of a majority of forward-thinking college youth who indicated that high in their personal values were "bringing about needed change in society" and "providing greater opportunity for black people." The change from the transitional *future-time orientation* to the emergent ethic of *relevance* is revealed in answers to the question "What would have a very great influence on your career?" Instead of responding "money," an overwhelming majority answered: "Opportunity to make a meaningful contribution." The shift from *conformity* as a value to *authenticity* as a value is reflected in such statements as "We want a society that tolerates candor and spontaneity" and "We want to retain control over our own lives." Finally, the shift from *moral relativism* as a value to *moral commitment* as a value is reflected in statements by youth such as "Civil disobedience is justified if it is non-violent and protesters are willing to accept the penalties." Getzels indicates that while the direction of value change is toward emergent values, we are still in a stage of transition, with some holding to traditional values, others following transitional values, and still others espousing emergent values.

The considerable attention given to campus protests and riots in recent years has led to an increased interest in understanding the motiva-

[12] Jacob W. Getzels, "On the Transformation of Values: A Decade after Port Huron," *School Review*, 80 (August 1972), 505–519.

tions and values of campus rebels. Although radical youth may unite in common cause in protesting against American foreign policy, racial injustice, or university restrictions, the motives and the types of youth participating in protests are often quite diverse. Keniston[13] identifies and describes two types of youthful dissenters: the culturally alienated and the student activist.

The growing alienation of man from man and of man from the universe has afflicted not only a considerable number of our youth but persons of all ages and other cultures as well. This alienation is reflected in the discontinuities of psychological development, in the tenuous relationship between man and society, in our concern over national purposes, and in the breakdown of established values. Alienated youth in America tend to reject their culture and to seek a new society. Their alienation takes the form of a rebellion without cause, a rejection without program, and a disavowal of what is without a vision of what should be. Keniston points out that the alienated youth, in contrast to the student activist, is more likely to be disturbed psychologically and far too pessimistic and too much opposed to the system to demonstrate his disapproval in any organized way. Thus, his demonstrations of dissent are more personal and manifested in nonconformity of behavior, ideology, and dress and in efforts to intensify his own subjective experiences through drugs. While both the alienated and the activist come from similar middle class backgrounds, the activist more frequently accepts the basic political and social values of his parents; the alienated rejects his parents' values.

In contrast to the alienated, the activist expresses a basic belief in American ideals and a belief in the desirability of political and social ideals. He believes in America, but he wishes to correct the injustices in American life so as to improve society. Activists are more responsive to the denial of civil rights on and off campus, particularly when political pressures seem to be responsible for unjust policies. Activists push for student power and student participation in decisions affecting campus life, such as removal of a ban on controversial speakers' being invited to campus, censorship of student publications, and limitations on off-campus political activity. Activists are not really rebelling against explicit parental values but are seeking to live out their parents' values in practice. Many youthful civil rights demonstrators, for example, indicate their willingness to risk jail or injury in standing up for values and beliefs which their parents did not have the courage or the opportunity to practice or to fight for. Consequently, parents frequently give their activist children support and may be secretly proud of efforts to implement ideals which the parents support by words but not by actions.

[13] Kenneth Keniston, "The Sources of Student Dissent," *Journal of Social Issues*, 23 (1967), 108–137. See also Kenneth Keniston, *The Uncommitted* (New York: Harcourt Brace Jovanovich, 1965); and Kenneth Keniston, *Young Radicals: Notes on Committed Youth* (New York: Harcourt Brace Jovanovich, 1968).

Drug Use

Studies of college-age youth reveal that types and frequency of drug use are associated with specific patterns of values and adjustment.[14] The public's impression of very high rates of drug use among college youth is due in part to the high visibility of colleges where drug use is most prevalent. There are, however, wide differences in drug use by students in different types of institutions and in different parts of the country.[15] The relationship between "intellectual climate" and drug use is very close. The highest rates of drug use are found at small, progressive, liberal arts colleges with a nonvocational orientation; high student intellectual caliber as measured by College Boards; close student-faculty relationships; and great value placed on the academic independence, intellectual interests, and personal freedom of students. Schools that are low in drug use by students are state teachers colleges, junior colleges, community colleges, the smaller religious and denominational colleges, and most Catholic colleges and universities. Within a large university, rates of drug use among students vary within the different colleges: Arts and sciences, the graduate school, and the schools of drama, music, art, and architecture have the highest rates; the schools of business administration, engineering, agriculture, and education have the lowest rates.

Keniston[16] classifies college-age drug users into two categories: heads and seekers. These classifications correspond very closely in many respects to the alienated and activist students described above. *Heads* are a relatively small but highly visible group of students who use drugs often and regularly, frequently experimenting with a variety of different drugs. But even among the heads, drug use does not invariably constitute the deeply psychopathological and self-destructive phenomenon that it is often believed to be. Many heads show little or no ill effects from their frequent use of drugs. A number of students who use marijuana routinely, for example, do not experience the "bad trips" or loss of motivation sometimes thought to accompany even casual drug experimentation. A smaller group of heads suffer serious ill effects from even a single experience with hallucinogens. Students with preexisting pathology are most vulnerable. These are students who seem to experiment with drugs under conditions that even experienced drug users consider adverse—intense depression, personal isolation, and unpleasant surroundings. More important than the highly dramatic but usually reversible drug psychosis is the danger of lapsing into a relatively enduring personal disorganization that is manifested in a virtually total and appar-

---

[14] See Chapters 4 and 9 for discussions of the effects of drugs on the body, personality, and adjustment.

[15] J. V. Toohey, "An Analysis of Drug Use Behavior at Five Universities," *Journal of School Health*, 41 (November 1971), 464–468.

[16] Kenneth Keniston, "Heads and Seekers: Drugs on Campus, Countercultures, and American Society," *The American Scholar*, 38 (Winter 1968–1969), 97–112.

ently destructive immersion in a drug-using hippie culture. Some persons may remain in a hippie subculture indefinitely, while others return to the world of action and commitment after spending a limited time in a drug-using culture. Unlike most seekers, heads are alienated from American society, and they often feel separated from self and others as well.

Seekers use drugs only occasionally as part of a more general pattern of experimentation and search for relevance both within and outside the college experience. They seek through the use of drugs some way of intensifying experience, expanding awareness, breaking out of deadness and flatness, or overcoming depression. Marijuana and the more powerful hallucinogens seem to be used by students who are seeking increased intensity, heightened sensations and perceptiveness, and perhaps increased understanding. The last is of prime importance to seekers, since they are more inclined to blame themselves than others for the inadequacies of their lives, and they frequently seek through self-analysis to change their personalities. Seekers are intellectual, usually better-than-average students, and often uncertain of their future career plans. They are likely to be critical of American society but not alienated from it. Drug use by college students in America may reflect their frustration at finding no appropriate ways of using their intelligence and idealism to reform our society.

Becoming Established in a Vocation

One of the most important developmental tasks encountered by young adults is *preparing for and becoming established in a vocation*. Holding a job is vital if one is to acquire the financial resources needed to feel and to act independently as an adult. Moreover, one's choice of a vocation defines an important aspect of one's self-concept and contributes to his sense of self-identity.

Occupational choice is first expressed in childhood and seems to progress through three phases: fantasy choice, tentative choice, and realistic choice. Most adolescents are in the phase of tentative choice, which for many may carry over into early adulthood. The young adult's increasing ability to estimate the reality of his interests, aptitudes, and values through widening experience in school and work enables him to move toward a realistic choice of occupation.[17] However, changing technology and the changing economy cause some jobs to be in short supply and others to become obsolete, thereby further complicating the career plans of young people.

Girls' fantasy choices of actress, model, or airline stewardess expressed in early adolescence may be psychological strategies for dealing with unconscious desires for marriage which will not be realized until some

[17] Eli Ginzberg et al., *Occupational Choice* (New York: Columbia University Press, 1951).

years later. Observations of girls in later high school years reveal a pattern of sharply declining career interest on the part of many girls. This decline of career interest as marriage interest rises is obscured by the scholastic success of girls.[18] Toward the end of high school, boys are becoming involved in the necessity of making a career decision, while girls are increasingly drawn toward marriage. Girls express a variety of marriage-career and goal patterns: marriage after high school; a job and then marriage; college or post–high school education followed by brief work experience, then marriage; college and marriage at the same time; marriage and a career at the same time until the arrival of children; and occasionally a career without marriage or with marriage occurring sometime later.

The tentativeness of the career choices of many young adults is reflected in their frequent change of jobs and change of vocation during the early years of their work careers. Even college youth are not immune from this trend, for a large proportion of college youth change academic majors, and a fair proportion change colleges or programs one or more times during their undergraduate years. Excerpts from the cases of Karen and Ron reveal for both some experimentation and shift of career choice during their early work experience.

Middle Adulthood

The middle adult years, encompassing the period between ages 30 and 45, is a time when one's intellectual and productive capacities are at a peak. The payoff for the long years of struggle and sacrifice in bearing children and becoming established in a career is at last realized during the middle adult years. Erikson identifies the major psychological task of middle age as that of *generativity*, that of passing on a fair world to the next generation. This is accomplished within the family by helping children develop their full potential and in the larger society through assuming greater civic and social responsibility.

It is during the middle adult years that one's children grow to adulthood. Earlier chapters emphasized the critical influence which parents exert on children's emotional security, socialization, and personality development beginning with their children's infancy and early childhood. The middle adult years provide parents with an opportunity to build on this base as their children grow into late childhood, adolescence, and early adulthood. At the same time, it is a critical period in one's career development. The achievement of or the likelihood of achieving a position of status, prestige, power, or influence in one's company, organization, or profession is realized by most persons during their middle adult years. If one is going

---

[18] Esther Matthews, "Career Development of Girls," *Vocational Guidance Quarterly*, 2 (1963), 273–277.

to achieve his career goals, these years offer the best opportunities for achieving them or at least progressing within striking distance.

We can gain some understanding of the middle adult years through these excerpts from the case of Frank and Edith Sargent:

> *Frank, age 40, is a college graduate and middle-level executive with Westinghouse, and Edith, his wife, age 38, is a full-time home-maker and mother of their three children: Philip, 15, Mary, 12, and Ted, eight. The family moved frequently during the early years of marriage as Frank was given promotions and assignments in different parts of the company organization in different cities. He has been in his present assignment three years and expects to remain in this area indefinitely. The family lives in a spacious, comfortable, 50,000 dollar ranch-style house in suburban Los Angeles.*
>
> *The Sargents have been a closely knit family. When the children were small, Frank was so engrossed in his work that he was unable to spend much time with his family. He has been promoted frequently and has provided his family with a comfortable living in a nice neighborhood with swimming pool, two cars, music lessons, bicycles, trampoline, sports equipment, and expensive vacations. Philip, the older son, seems to show the effects of infrequent contacts with his father during the period when Frank was preoccupied with his job. Philip does well in school but has avoided sports and active play with the other boys, retreating instead into a world of books. He is painfully shy around girls. Mary is active and outgoing like her mother. She is very popular with peers and has become a skilled pianist. She has also won several medals in local swimming meets. Frank is trying to spend more time with the family and is presently helping to coach Ted's Little League baseball team.*
>
> *Edith has been preoccupied with the home and raising her children. The Sargents have friends in for dinner frequently, and there is a continuous round of chauffeuring the children to their various activities. Edith is fairly well satisfied with her marriage, but there does seem to be something missing. Frank is not as attentive as he once was, and the children are not as dependent upon her as they were when they were smaller. Edith is becoming increasingly dissatisfied with her role as a housewife. She is already thinking of completing her college education, which was interrupted by marriage, and of qualifying for full-time employment as either a teacher or a social worker.*

Helping Children Grow to Adulthood

Since most middle-aged adults are members of families with teenage children, it may be useful to examine the tasks of husband, wife, and children as these members of the family grow in relation to one another. A major task of parents in middle adulthood is *nurturing and rearing their children to become responsible, well-adjusted adults.* The early years of middle adulthood are a time when children look to the same-sex parent as a model for the development of sex role. A child who has accepted and learned a well-defined sex role and is secure in his parents' love has a strong advantage in gaining the acceptance of his peers—an important developmental task of middle and late childhood. Frank's helping coach Ted's Little League team has had a favorable effect on Ted's development, but Philip's lack of identification with peers reflects the lack of an early close father-son relationship. Mary's development appears to have been favorably influenced by the continuous close relationship with her mother.

The middle-aged adult task of nurturing and rearing offspring changes in character as children become teenagers. Since achieving independence of adults is a major developmental task of adolescence, this is a time of potential conflict for parents and teenagers. Adolescents need to achieve independence of adults as they seek to win the acceptance of peers. If the adolescent spends a great deal of time in activities with friends whom parents do not know or approve of, considerable tension may develop between the parents and the teenager. If the parents are uninformed about the teenager's whereabouts, they may fear the worst—that their son or daughter may be mixed up with bad companions in drinking, drugs, sex, or crime. Parents need to demonstrate their trust in the teenager, and the teenager should recognize their genuine concern over his welfare. Open communication between parents and their adolescent children is essential if conflicts are to be resolved. Teenagers need and want their parents, but they also want to be free to grow in their own way. If communication breaks down and adolescents become estranged from parents, there is a greater likelihood that the adolescent may drop out of school, run away from home, become unduly dependent upon peers, turn to drugs, or "cop out." Although Philip Sargent does not manifest any such behavior, his poor relationships with peers and his tendency to withdraw into himself are potential sources of concern.

The Changing Role of Wife and Mother

Many wives and mothers experience some degree of restlessness and dissatisfaction with their homemaking role as they reach their late thirties and early forties. Women during this period continue to have an intense desire to be useful and needed. As the last child enters school and her husband's career direction becomes established, she may have time on her hands because the family makes fewer demands on her. For some women, this change in role may precipitate an identity crisis in which the wife questions her own role and significance in the larger society. This search for meaning and significance in their lives has sparked a drive in some women to improve their opportunities for personal development through vigorous support of women's rights legislation and practices.

Women in middle adulthood may adapt to this change in role through enrolling in school or college, entering part- or full-time employment, increasing their participation in civic affairs, or resuming earlier hobbies and interests. The active, intelligent, middle-adult woman with a highly developed sense of values and rich life experience has a much better idea than a younger woman of where she would like to go in the world of work. She is also likely to have a greater commitment to her job because her marriage-family goals have been largely accomplished. The degree to which middle-aged women have adapted to this role change is reflected in statistics which show that 51 percent of the women aged 30 to 54 in the United States are employed in the work force, many having acquired the job after rearing a family.[19] Our case record excerpts on the Sargents show that Edith is seriously considering the alternatives for new roles which have been brought on by a further need for self-identity and the diminishing dependence of her family on her.

Achieving Satisfaction in One's Vocation

As noted earlier, the middle adult years of 30 to 45 are the most favorable period for *achieving satisfaction in one's vocation*. It is a time when intellectual and physical power and experience combine to create the capacities for optimum development and performance of work skills. During this period most men attain the highest status of their careers. Frank Sargent's position with his company and his salary status are evidence of his having achieved a measure of success in his vocation. Some wives who enter employment during this period quickly achieve the highest job status they are likely to attain, while others with specialized skills and training may continue to advance to positions of greater status and responsibility.

Assuming Social and Civic Responsibility

The middle-aged adult achieves the psychosocial task of generating and passing on a decent, fair world to the next generation not only through the nurturance of his children but also by trying to improve society through *assuming civic and social responsibility*. A family's development and well-being are influenced by the quality and resources of the community's political life. Hence, parents—especially those in middle class suburban areas—become active in PTAs, church groups, service clubs, school, library, or hospital boards, Scouts, Little League, youth clubs, civic associations, political parties, or nonpartisan political action groups. Participation in and support of civic groups vary widely among middle-aged

[19] *1970 Census of Population: Detailed Characteristics, United States Summary* (Washington, D. C.: U. S. Government Printing Office, 1973), Table 219.

adults and vary with the individual at different times in his adult life. Job demands and striving for vocational success explain in part the limited participation in community affairs by some middle-aged adults. Some corporations, however, encourage active community involvement of their executives and workers as an important part of the employee's job. Some middle-aged women seem to make a career of participating and assuming roles of leadership in a variety of community activities. Edith Sargent was quite active in the PTA and in church work, while Frank became involved in coaching Ted's Little League baseball team.

Maturity

Some writers prefer to include the years from age 45 to retirement as part of the middle adult years, but we prefer to call the latter half of the productive adult years the age of maturity. In using the term *maturity*, we do not mean to suggest that the adult has reached any highest point of development. As noted earlier, we prefer to think of maturity as open-ended —a process of continuous developing and becoming. The term as used here, however, refers to a level of development in which some decrease in physical strength, dexterity, speed, and vigor can be noted, but in which the keenness of intellectual powers and the wisdom of experience remain undiminished.

For many, the mature years are the prime of life. Mature adults usually are at the peak of their productive capacities. Their slightly lower physical vigor is more than compensated for by manual and intellectual skills which have been sharpened by more than 20 years of adult living. They are at a peak of their earning power, reflected in the comfortable home and the material advantages of good food, expensive clothes, car, vacations, and good educations for their children which a good income can provide. This is a period, too, when their service and skills are recognized by election to the school board, city council, or church vestry. It is a time when their opinions are listened to by other adults, and their social status is established. In short, it is a time when they come to a realization that they have "made it"—or that they have achieved about as much as they are going to achieve in the way of worldly success or acclaim.

The age of maturity has its other side, however. Children are entering their last years of high school, military service, or college. While the parents are freed from the close supervision and care required when children were younger, the satisfactions of parenthood experienced when children were younger are often followed by perplexity over how to cope with the "now generation," with its alternative hair and dress styles, innovative life styles, new morality, and profound irreverence for established ways.

The mature years can be distinguished from the preceding, middle adult years by the significant physical changes that occur during the former period. The aging of body tissues which has been going on since early life is reflected in the slowing down of the body. The diminishing physical strength and neuromuscular skills have already been noted. A significant change in women is menopause, which occurs over a period of several years, usually between the ages of 45 and 55. The cessation of ovarian activity is accompanied by changes in the endocrine system. Physical symptoms of menopause include hot and cold flashes, dizziness, sweating, insomnia, and excitability. Other symptoms of aging are the growth of stiff hair in the nose, ears, and eyebrows of men, growth of hair on the upper lip of women, drying and wrinkling of the skin, accumulation of fat at the waist and hips ("middle age spread"), and decrease in the elasticity of the lens of the eye, making the task of focusing on objects at varying distances more difficult. The mature years are also a period of increased incidence of disability or death from heart attacks, hypertension, and cancer.

A description of the life and developmental tasks of the mature adult years follows in these excerpts from the case of Bart and Helen Richards.

When the family counselor first talked with Bart and Helen, they had come for help in understanding their adolescent and young adult children. Bart is a self-made man and at age 52 is the owner of a successful construction business. Since their marriage, Helen has been a full-time housewife. Their three children are Keith, 25, now somewhere in Europe, Kathie, 22, a college senior, and Fred, 18, a high school senior.

In the initial interview the parents poured out their anguish over their older son, Keith. Bart had always had difficulty in relating to Keith because of Keith's appearing rather feminine in his behavior and attitudes. Bart tried to interest him in sports, but Keith's interest revolved around music and philosophy. Keith became quite skilled on the guitar, and in high school he was the leader of a rock band. Bart and Helen were eager for their children to have a college education, an opportunity they had missed.

Their conflict with Keith began in high school and centered in his staying out until all hours playing with his band or sitting in cabarets listening to rock groups. Bart and Helen continued to feud with Keith over his shoulder-length hair, the hairy male animals he ran with, and his wrecking the family car. Periodically during the last year of high school, Keith moved out of the house and stayed with a friend. Various efforts were made to patch up their differences, with Keith coming home for a while but with further conflict always following. The parents were especially concerned that Keith ignored girls, preferring to spend his time with a small group of male friends. Keith dropped out of college during his sophomore year, and he and his friends went to New York to work and live. The psychiatrist to whom the parents sent Keith before he dropped out of college diagnosed Keith as an active homosexual. Keith, however, refused to begin psychiatric treatment. The family has had little contact with Keith for the past four years. Nine months ago Keith went to Europe, and recently his sister, Kathie, received from him a card sent from Istanbul.

The interview revealed that a similar pattern of conflict has continued in the relationship between the parents and Kathie. Bart and Helen have attempted to avoid the mistakes they made with Keith by being less strict with Kathie, but this approach seems to have encouraged Kathie to test the limits even further. Kathie is a classic example of the alienated young adult. She is critical of her parents and blames society's mess on the older generation. She has done well in school but appears to have no career plans except to be a professional revolutionary. Now in her last year of college, Kathie is living in a commune with five other young adults.

The parents' relationship with Fred, now in high school, seems tranquil at present. Bart and Helen express hope that the counselor can help them to avoid in their relationship with Fred the mistakes they made with their older children. As the counselor talked with Helen alone, he learned that Helen's problems are aggravated by an endocrine imbalance and symptoms associated with menopause. Medication seems to offer only limited relief. Helen is also worried about Bart. He has attempted to adjust to his anguish over what has happened to the older children by spending more and more time away from home on his business. Helen feels neglected, and she wonders whether Bart is having an affair with the attractive secretary he recently hired. It gradually came out that their sex life has become increasingly unsatisfactory because of her husband's growing impotence. She hoped that with the children on their own, she and Bart might regain the happy relationship of the early years of their marriage, but he just seems to bury himself deeper in his work. Helen believes that she should have taken a job or become much more involved in community organizations and service. Now it seems too late to change. The future seems to have little to offer, and Helen is depressed.

Changing Relationships

Maturity is a period when parents watch their children grow into adulthood, leave home, and take their places as full-fledged members of society. The parental role of direct responsibility for nurturing and caring for children and guiding their development has come to an end. The developmental task of the mature adult in relation to his child is one of *building a new relationship with the grown child that acknowledges and respects each's independence, uniqueness, and maturity.* The young adult's taking his place in the world is a fulfillment of one of the parents' most cherished goals. It's fulfillment is manifested in the parents' pride at the son's or daughter's wedding, the birth of a grandchild, and the son or daughter's educational, vocational, and creative attainments. The lack of a parent-child relationship which respects each's independence, uniqueness, and maturity leads to bitterness and a feeling by the parent that he has failed in one of life's most important tasks. Such was the experience of Bart and Helen in their relationships with Keith and Kathie.

The mature years frequently are a time when a change in the husband-wife relationship occurs. Maturity is a period in which *each partner learns to relate to the other as a person*. With the years of child bearing and child rearing coming to an end, husband and wife have an opportunity to draw closer and to renew their relationship. The husband needs the encouragement and appreciation he received from his wife early in their marriage, for he may be facing the disappointment that he will never achieve some of his cherished aspirations. The husband, in turn, should understand the void his wife feels as she must find interests to replace the children who have left and must cope with the problems associated with menopause. Unfortunately, some couples reach maturity and find that they have little relationship left to preserve or renew. Sometimes the husband has devoted so much time to his work that he is virtually a stranger to his family. An occasional husband drifts into an affair with a younger woman in an effort to demonstrate to himself that he is still very much a man and is by no means over the hill. With some couples, the conflicts which were muted while the children were growing up break forth with new intensity. As a result, marriages of 25 or 30 years end in divorce. The case record excerpts of the Richards reveal the need of Bart and Helen to rebuild their relationship. They had grown apart, and Helen imagined that Bart was having an affair.

The mature adult is likely to face the task of *assisting and providing for aging parents*. Parents who are in early years of retirement often are able to remain independent in their own home, but as the infirmities of age take their toll, the mature adult is often called upon to provide financial help or physical care for an aging parent. Although there may be real advantages for a couple with children to have their grandparents living with them, it often happens that neither generation wants to live with the other. This may mean locating parents near a relative or a member of the immediate family who can assist the parents when needed.

Adjusting to Physical Change

An inescapable task of the mature adult years is that of *adjusting to declining energy and to physical changes that evidence the processes of aging*. It is a period of changes brought on by menopause, lessened ability of the eye to accommodate to objects at varying distances, lowered energy, and diminished sex drive. We commented on these physical changes earlier and noted that Helen's experiencing menopause and Bart's growing sexual impotence were important influences on their marital relationship and their relationships with their children.

Reflection and Personal Assessment

The mature years are a time when one *comes to terms with what he is in relation to his lifetime goals and aspirations.* In one's youth many of life's goals appear to be within reach, and achieving them seems to depend only upon a reasonable amount of intelligence, hard work, and good breaks. One of the realities facing the mature adult is that he has probably achieved just about as much as he is going to achieve in the way of worldly success— position, power, status, influence, and wealth. Maturity is a time when youthful dreams fade and one faces the reality that he will not become president of the company, be elected to political office, become independently wealthy, or achieve national recognition for his scholarly contributions. Bart Richards did feel that he was a success in his work, but success in business did not completely assuage his bitterness over his estrangement from Keith and Kathie.

Old Age

As more and more of our population live longer and the number of aged people increases, the greater is our need for understanding this later period of human development. At present about 20 million Americans are senior citizens, and their proportion of the total population is increasing steadily. A man who retires from his job at age 65 can expect to live another 14 years, a woman of the same age can expect to live another 18 years.

The retirement years are not a period of inactivity but a time when familiar vocational activities are replaced by new experiences and new pursuits. Learning continues to play a vital role in the retiree's adjustment to new experiences and a changed status, just as it did in the preceding periods of life. The retiree finds that learning new behavior patterns is frequently required for adjusting to decreased income, moving to a smaller house, making new friends, acquiring new skills and hobbies, and adjusting to a crippling illness, an accident, or the death of a spouse.

Erikson[20] has suggested that the value theme in old age is the achievement of *ego integrity,* that is, an acceptance of oneself and a willingness to defend the dignity of his own life style against all physical and economic threats. Failure to achieve ego integrity leads to a feeling of despair, the feeling that life is too short for an attempt to start another life and try out alternative roads to integrity.

Some of the different ways retirees seek to achieve ego integrity are

---

[20] Erik Erikson, *Childhood and Society* (New York: W. W. Norton & Co., 1950), pp. 219–234.

revealed in these excerpts from the cases of Howard and Frances Parker and Ed Hamilton:

For some years prior to his retiring from teaching, Howard Parker and his wife, Frances, had spent their vacations buying and refinishing antique furniture. With his background as a history teacher, Howard quickly became engrossed in learning as much as he could about the origin, history, and authenticity of the pieces he acquired. Soon the Parkers turned a part of their home into an antique furniture shop. Retirement freed them to devote more time to their passion for antiquing. Howard seems to get particular pleasure from finding pieces to fit exactly the character and decor of the customer's home. When the information is available, he includes with each piece he sells a typed statement of its history.

Howard and Frances make sure that their antique business does not interfere with other things they find pleasurable. They do not hesitate to close their shop and take off for a week to visit their children and grandchildren. Their interest in travel gives them further opportunity to look for and bring back valuable antiques. Service in their local church has always meant much to them, and they have found that visiting shut-ins is a particularly satisfying experience. The more leisurely life style also enables them to entertain frequently their close, long-time friends.

The Parkers' active involvement in the social life and activities of the church brings them into contact with persons of all ages. Their work on interdenominational committees enables them to know persons from other parts of the community. Being accepted by persons of all ages and backgrounds and being able to work and help others gives Howard and Frances special pleasure.

While the Parkers feel that they can continue their life style indefinitely, they realize that any situation can change suddenly. They foresee the day when they will have to give up their antique shop. At that time they expect they may find it more difficult to make ends meet on just their pension and Social Security, especially in times of steep inflation. They wonder, too, what the survivor will do when one of them dies. Tentatively, when their present living arrangement becomes too much to cope with, the Parkers plan to sell their house and enter a nearby retirement home.

Ed Hamilton was particularly bitter when the company for which he had worked for 27 years forced him into retirement at age 58. The past 10 years of retirement have been filled with much unhappiness for Ed. His whole life had been wrapped up in the company. At retirement he was suddenly cut off from life-long associates. An unsatisfactory marriage ended in divorce 15 years ago. He enjoys visits with his two grown children, but he realizes that they have their own lives to live.

Shortly after retirement Ed moved to Florida, but he soon returned to the more familiar surroundings of his home town. In the years since, Ed has become increasingly lonely. Many of his friends have moved away, and others have died. A heart condition that the doctor has recently diagnosed gives Ed particular concern. He wonders who will take care of him if he becomes incapacitated. With advancing age, few friends, and possible physical disability, Ed Hamilton is becoming increasingly bitter over his lot and over life in general.

Changing Roles and Status

The initial and often the most difficult task of the retirement years is *adjusting to giving up significant roles one has had over a long and active life.* One day the individual is president of Emerson Manufacturing Company, teacher of senior English at Washington High School, or welder at station 37 on the Lordstown assembly line, and the next day he is something else—a retiree. The nature of the work one has been doing is often an important determinant of his attitude toward and adjustment to retirement. It appears that retirement is more readily accepted by those in high prestige and low prestige positions than in middle class positions. Individuals in high prestige occupations, such as medicine, law, teaching, and the ministry, tend to be satisfied in retirement if they felt successful and satisfied with their work and if they have some chance to continue their former work activities. Retirees from low prestige positions also adjust readily to retirement because they had little personal involvement in their jobs. Among middle class workers, however, those who liked their work and miss it have less of a chance to recapture in retirement those features that they liked. In general, persons retired from high prestige positions find retirement better than they expected, while semiskilled workers often do not find it as attractive as they thought they would.[21] Howard Parker made a smooth transition into retirement because he developed further a hobby and an avocation started during preretirement years. Ed Hamilton's adjustment to retirement was poor in part because he had it forced on him and he was unprepared for it.

Successful adjustment in retirement depends in large measure on *developing satisfying leisure time activities.* Case studies of successful and unsuccessful retirement indicate that it is not the activities themselves

---

[21] Kurt W. Back, "The Ambiguity of Retirement," in Ewald W. Busse and Eric Pfeiffer, eds., *Behavior and Adaptation in Late Life* (Boston: Little, Brown and Co., 1969), pp. 93–114.

but the meaning that the individual gives to the activities which determines his adjustment.[22] Puttering around with toys may be the last resort of a desperate, bored man, but it may also be a satisfying activity for a man who likes to work with his hands and whose life style has consisted in general of devotion to others, especially if the toys are for his grandchildren.[23] It seems clear that life cannot become suddenly meaningful in retirement if it was not meaningful before. Many of the morale problems attributed to retirement may in reality be a function of the total life style of the person. This was evident in the contrasting case histories of Howard Parker and Ed Hamilton.

Changes in Life Styles

Sooner or later all retirees face the task of *adjusting to decreasing physical strength and health.* Almost every cell and cellular system in the human body ages. The aging person is most vulnerable to disease and organic breakdown in the cardiovascular system, the kidneys, and the joints. Heart disease often comes on slowly and makes an invalid out of a person before it kills him. Hence, a large proportion of older people must adjust to the invalidism of heart disease, while another considerable group must adjust to invalidism or reduced activity caused by arthritis or other disabilities. The special problem in the elderly is that a given illness is usually superimposed on an assortment of preexisting chronic illnesses and on organ systems which have lost their wide margin of reserve capacity. Because of the delicately balanced physiological mechanism of the elderly, even a minor illness can have major consequences.

One of the first realities encountered in retirement is the *need to adjust to a reduced income.* Although the number of persons covered by private pension plans has increased markedly in recent years, restrictions limiting those who qualify for pensions mean that large numbers of retirees must live on very low incomes. Maintaining an adequate standard of living on a fixed income is particularly difficult in a period of high inflation and continuously rising prices. It is estimated that in the United States 30 to 40 percent of the aged live in poverty.[24] Some retirees must return to work, often in low paying jobs, in order to make ends meet. In spite of periodic increases in Social Security benefits, the loss of dignity and the insecurity

---

[22] M. E. Linder, "Preparation for the Leisure of Later Maturity," and G. H. Saule, "Free Time—Man's New Resource," in W. Donahue, D. H. Coons, and H. K. Maurice, eds., *Free Time: Challenge to Later Maturity* (Ann Arbor: University of Michigan Press, 1958).

[23] Charlotte Buhler, "Meaningful Living in the Mature Years," in R. W. Kleemeier, ed., *Aging and Leisure* (New York: Oxford University Press, 1961).

[24] Juanita M. Kreps, "Economics of Retirement," in Busse and Pfeiffer, eds., *Behavior and Adaptation in Late Life*, p. 72.

many of our elderly are subjected to constitute a remediable human tragedy.

Inadequate income, failing health, and/or loss of spouse frequently confront the aged with *having to establish satisfactory living arrangements*. The majority of elderly men and women live in families, maintaining their own household with a spouse or living with a relative in either their own home or the relative's home. With advancing age and widowhood, the proportion of old people living alone or living in the homes of relatives increases markedly. Because of the higher incidence of widowhood among older women, more than twice as many older women live alone than do older men. Only a small proportion (about 5 percent) of the aged population live in institutions.[25] Many retirees who can afford it move to homes in retirement communities in the milder climates of Florida, Arizona, and California. Others prefer to remain in their home communities because of limited income or because of their deep roots in the community. As physical strength wanes, old people must relinquish some of their independence. Increasingly, the reasonably healthy aged turn to the congregate living arrangements of retirement hotels, while the aged who require specialized or continuous care live in nursing homes and hospitals.

Intellectual and Sexual Capacities and Interests

A further developmental task of old age is *adjusting to changing intellectual and sexual capacities and interests*. Studies of intellectual and cognitive changes associated with aging reveal no decline in intellectual functioning from age 62 to 72 and only a modest decline from age 74 to 86.[26] The ability of older people to manipulate words is maintained with advancing age, but their ability to manipulate symbols on the basis of coordinated perceptual motor skills decreases somewhat with age. In general, older persons with average IQs do better at more slowly paced (or self-paced) tasks than in more rapidly paced learning situations. Older persons engage in less risk-taking behavior, as indicated in their tendency to withhold answers, especially on timed tests. The elderly, too, often are apprehensive in testing situations because of their lack of recent experience with tests and because of fear that they may be losing their intellectual ability.[27]

The limited information available on the sexual behavior of the elderly reveals that (1) sexual interest and coital activity are by no means rare in persons over age 60 and (2) patterns of sexual interest and coital activity

[25] Ethel Shenas, "Living Arrangements and Housing of Old People," in Busse and Pfeiffer, eds., *Behavior and Adaptation in Late Life*, pp. 129–149.

[26] Carl Eisdorfer and F. Wilkie, "Longitudinal Changes with Advancing Age," paper presented at the annual convention of the American Psychological Association, San Francisco, September 1968.

[27] Carl Eisdorfer, "Intellectual and Cognitive Changes in the Aged," in Busse and Pfeiffer, eds., *Behavior and Adaptation in Late Life*, pp. 237–250.

differ substantially for men and women of the same age. One longitudinal study[28] showed that about 80 percent of a group of healthy, active men aged 60 or older reported continuing sexual interest, and 70 percent of the men in this group were still sexually active. Ten years later about the same proportion of the men were still interested in sex, but only 25 percent of the men reported that they were still sexually active. Among the group of healthy, active women, about one third reported continuing sexual interest at age 60, and the proportion did not change significantly over the next 10 years. Only about 20 percent of these women at age 60 reported that they were having sexual intercourse regularly, and again, this proportion did not decline over the next 10 years. The median of cessation of intercourse occurred nearly a decade earlier in women than in men (ages 60 and 68, respectively), but according to both men and women respondents, it was the man who was responsible for the cessation of sexual activity.

Facing Death

Finally, a developmental task that intrudes increasingly into the consciousness of the older person is *accepting and coming to terms with the reality of his own approaching death.* One event which brings the knowledge of this reality closer is the death of one's spouse. Often this calls for a major change in the life style of the survivor. It may mean that the survivor will have to move into the home of one of his children or another relative, move to a retirement home, or try to live alone. Older people try to adjust to the reality of their own eventual demise in a variety of ways. Some try to exclude it from consciousness by thinking, "Inevitable, except for me," or "Not for a long time yet." A second method is to withdraw from others so as to protect oneself from the painful loss through death of significant others. A third pattern involves attempts at mastery or resolution. Such persons may become vigorously active in hobbies, travel, or civic enterprises or become absorbed in creative activity, thereby keeping death at arm's length, often physically as well as psychologically. Still another mechanism is the life review, in which the individual recalls some of the major events and relationships in his past life. Recalling one's significant contributions may help some people to accept approaching death, but for others it may lead to depression in a realization that they have missed the boat and that it is now too late to repair previous mistakes.[29] With death, the cycle of life is now complete.

[28] Eric Pfeiffer, "Sexual Behavior in Old Age," in Busse and Pfeiffer, eds., *Behavior and Adaptation in Late Life,* pp. 151–162.

[29] Frances C. Jeffers and Adriaan Verwoerdt, "How the Old Face Death," in Busse and Pfeiffer, eds., *Behavior and Adaptation in Late Life,* pp. 163–181.

Summary

Adulthood is the status and level of development toward which the individual has been striving since the beginning of life. The term *adulthood* designates a status and level of development, while the term *maturity* connotes in some contexts a point in the span of development and in other contexts a progression, quality, and direction of development. Probably the most significant aspect of adulthood for the individual is feeling and perceiving himself to be an adult. Adulthood can be roughly divided into four stages: (1) early adulthood (ages 18–30), (2) middle adulthood (ages 30–45), (3) maturity (age 45 to retirement), and (4) old age (retirement to death).

Early adulthood is unique as a stage of development because it marks a transition from an age-graded to a social-status-graded society. Most persons in early adulthood are confronted with the following developmental tasks:

1.   *Achieving a measure of personal autonomy.*

2.   *Developing appropriate ways of satisfying one's sex drives.*

3.   *Developing an affectional relationship with a marriage partner and/or close friends.*

4.   *For couples, becoming parents and raising children.*

5.   *Learning to relate to parents and other older adults in ways that minimize the "generation gap."*

6.   *Testing and refining a set of values.*

7.   *Learning appropriate ways for coping with anxiety and alienation.*

8.   *Preparing for and becoming established in a vocation.*

The middle adult years, from age 30 to 45, are a time when one's intellectual and productive capacities are at a peak. A major psychological task of middle age is that of passing on a fair world to the next generation. The principal developmental tasks of this period are:

1.   *Nurturing and rearing children to become responsible, well-adjusted adults.*

2.   *Developing new interests and skills to replace family-centered ones that are no longer needed.*

3.   *Achieving satisfaction in one's vocation.*

4.   *Assuming social and civil responsibility.*

The mature years, beginning at age 45 and extending to retirement, are a period of development in which some decrease in physical strength, dexterity, speed, and vigor can be noted, but the keenness of intellectual powers and wisdom remain undiminished. Maturity is the prime of life for many people; this is a time when productive capacities are still at their peak. The important developmental tasks of maturity are:

1.   *Building a new relationship with grown children that acknowledges and respects each's independence, uniqueness, and maturity.*

2.   *Learning to relate to one's spouse as a person.*

3.   *Assisting and providing for aging parents.*

4.   *Adjusting to declining energy and physical changes that evidence the processes of aging.*

5.   *Coming to terms with what one is in relation to lifetime goals and aspirations.*

Old age is not a period of inactivity but a time when familiar vocational activities are replaced by new experiences and new pursuits. The value theme in old age is the achievement of *ego integrity,* an acceptance of oneself and a willingness to defend the dignity of one's own life style against physical and economic threats. The developmental tasks of old age include:

1.   *Adjusting to giving up significant roles one has had over a long and active life.*

2.   *Developing satisfying leisure time activities.*

3.   *Adjusting to decreasing physical strength and health.*

4.   *Adjusting to a reduced income.*

5.   *Establishing satisfactory living arrangements.*

6.   *Adjusting to changing intellectual and sexual capacities and interests.*

7.   *Accepting and coming to terms with the reality of one's own approaching death.*

Study Questions

1. As you reflect upon your own experiences in early adulthood, which developmental tasks have been easiest to achieve and which have proved most difficult? What resources and people have been the most helpful in assisting you to cope with the problems of early adulthood?

2. Which values expressed by young adults are most likely to be incorporated into the larger American culture? Which values are likely to prove most transient?

3. How different do you think the rearing and socialization of children born to today's young adults are likely to be from their own rearing and socialization a generation ago? Discuss.

4. What draws some alienated young adults back into established society while others of their contemporaries remain permanently outside the mainstream of society?

5. What kinds of forums or institutions might be developed which would enhance open communication between adults of all ages? What kinds of help might people at each level of adulthood render to persons at other levels of adulthood?

Suggested Readings

Busse, Ewald W., and Eric Pfeiffer, eds. *Behavior and Adaptation in Late Life.* Boston: Little, Brown and Co., 1969. A book of readings which report research findings of studies on aging carried out by the Duke University Center for the Study of Aging and Human Development. Authoritative findings presented on the medical, social, and psychological factors associated with aging.

Goodman, Paul. *Growing Up Absurd.* New York: Random House, 1960. Interprets the feelings and disaffection of the beatnik generation of the late 1950s. The book is highly critical of the American culture and its treatment of youth.

Keniston, Kenneth. *Young Radicals: Notes on Committed Youth.* New York: Harcourt Brace Jovanovich, 1968. A study of the young adult activists who participated in a summer program in 1967 which sought to organize new groups to oppose the war in Southeast Asia. Analyzes the backgrounds, motives, goals, work, and crises of a highly committed group of radical young Americans.

Peterson, James A. *Married Love in the Middle Years.* New York: Association Press, 1968. Describes the crises of middle age and some of the ways these crises can be resolved. The middle age crises arise because past devotion and communication are inadequate for meeting the new problems of this period. Suggests that if the fears and needs of husband and wife can be openly shared, solutions to problems can be worked out.

Sherif, Muzafer, and Carolyn W. Sherif, eds. *Problems of Youth: Transition to Adulthood in a Changing World.* Chicago: Aldine Publishing Co., 1965. A book of readings which discuss youth and the families, subcultures, age mate groups, and adolescent values and attitudes of youth in different cultures and subcultures. Delineates the problems that youth face in achieving adulthood in a world fraught with tremendous problems of rapid social change.

Simon, Anne W. *The New Years.* New York: Alfred A. Knopf, 1968. Describes a new kind of middle age never known by any previous society which is the result of radical change in most aspects of life marked by vastly expanded scientific knowledge, increased productivity, improvement in health, and extended life expectancy. Suggests that maturity will be a time of life to grow up for, to be enjoyed, and to be used for greater fulfillment.

Films

A Nice Kid Like You, 16 mm, sound, black and white, 38 min. Berkeley 94720: Extension Media Center, University of California. In small groups and individual interviews, college students discuss various topics—drugs, sex, parents, and failures of modern America. They express their opinions forthrightly.

Marriage under Stress, 16 mm, sound, black and white, 40 min. New York 10011: Time-Life Films, 43 W. 16th St. Points out that often the first real stress of marriage comes with the arrival of children. Some couples who can cope with economic uncertainty, emotional insecurity, and sexual incompatibility may not be prepared to rear children. The film shows that marrying again does not always eliminate problems and that the aftermath of bitterness may make the children into a common battleground between divorced and remarried parents.

The Critical Decades, 16 mm, sound, black and white, 30 min. Washington, D. C. 20409: U. S. National Audiovisual Center, National Archives and Records Service. A small-town physician compares some of his active elderly patients with three middle-aged patients in order to emphasize the importance of planning and sensible living for maintaining good health in middle and later life.

The Key Maker, 16 mm, sound, color, 20 min. Los Angeles: Department of Cinema, University of Southern California. A study of an elderly retired locksmith who is not willing to give up vitality in living, as his neighboring contemporaries have done.

Part Four

**Learning and the
Educative Process**

The Nature and Theories of Learning

Learning is but an adjunct to ourself,
And where we are our learning likewise is.

William Shakespeare

Learning is a universal, lifelong activity in which individuals modify their behavior in coping with and adapting to their environment. Learning occurs in a wide variety of situations and at all levels of animal life—from the conditioned reflexes of lower animals to the complex cognitive processes of man.

Early evidence of learning among low forms of life was reported by Day and Bentley,[1] who found that paramecia can, after repeated trials, reduce the time required for them to turn around in a capillary tube. More recently, studies have revealed that the planarium, a simple flatworm, through a series of stimuli involving light coupled with electric shock, can be conditioned to flex its body in response to the light stimulus alone.[2] However, though lower forms of life do learn, their learning is slow, limited, and not very important to their existence. Protozoa, for example, are practically mature at birth; instinctive responses which begin functioning at birth provide them with most of the behaviors they will ever use.[3]

Man, on the other hand, the highest form of animal life, is also the most helpless at birth, has the longest period of infancy, and has the greatest capacity for profiting from experience. Learned responses constitute the overwhelming proportion of his behavioral repertoire. The change in proportions between innate and learned components of behavior at various points on the ascending scale of animal life is shown in Figure 15.1.

---

[1] L. M. Day and M. Bentley, "A Note on Learning in Paramecium," *Journal of Animal Behavior,* 1 (1911), 167.

[2] R. Thompson and J. V. McConnell, "Classical Conditioning in the Planarium, Dugesia dorotcephala," *Journal of Comparative and Physiological Psychology,* 48 (1955), 65–68.

[3] James M. Sawrey and Charles W. Telford, *Educational Psychology,* 2nd ed. (Boston: Allyn & Bacon, 1964), pp. 93–94.

Figure 15–1.   The Relationship of Components of Behavior to Level of Animal Life

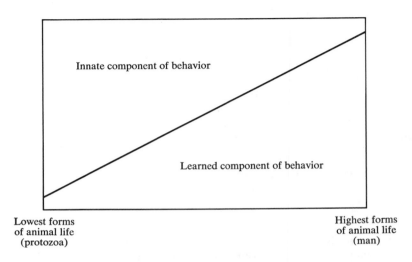

Source: James M. Sawrey and Charles W. Telford, *Educational Psychology*, 2nd ed. (Boston: Allyn & Bacon, 1964), p. 94. Reproduced by permission.

Learning as Process and Product

The term *learning* refers to both a process and a product. Some of the processes involved in the transactions that take place between the organism and its environment are the familiar ones of sensing, perceiving, feeling, symbolizing, remembering, abstracting, thinking, and behaving. Each of these is anything but simple.

There is evidence, for example, that biochemical changes within the body may influence behavior. When planaria that have been conditioned to respond to light are cut in half, both of the regenerated organisms that are then formed—one from the head segment and one from the tail segment—also respond to light. According to one hypothesis, the memory retention of the planarium is related to the presence of some biochemical substance in the body of the worm. Other investigations appear to substantiate this hypothesis. When conditioned planaria are cut up and fed to unconditioned planaria, the cannibalistic worms learn much faster than those on a less educated diet. Investigators have hypothesized that RNA (ribonucleic acid, a protein-like substance found in all cells which transmits from the nucleus to the cytoplasm coded genetic information obtained from the DNA, desoxyribonucleic acid, molecule) might be the substance responsible for memory retention in the planarium. When the bottom half of the planarium is treated with a substance that destroys RNA, this half becomes a worm with no learning and hence no memory at all.[4] In other experiments, rats trained to walk a tightwire were found to have more RNA in their brain cells than did untrained rats. In another study, untrained rats injected with RNA taken from the brains of trained rats manifested a significant tendency (as compared to controls) to perform the same learned response as did the trained rats, that is, to approach the food cup when the click, unaccompanied by food, was presented.[5] It is clear that processes of learning involve not only psychological and behavioral components but physiological, biochemical factors as well.

Most of us, however, are more accustomed to thinking of learning as an outcome or product than as a process. Our references to and many of our conceptions of learning are frequently limited to those changes that are acquired in school or other formal teaching-learning situations. Intuitively, however, we know that learning also has occurred when a baby is able to grasp a ball, to walk, or to talk; when a teenager acquires a taste for pizza or learns to ride a motorcycle; and when a young mother learns to distinguish between the different kinds of cries her infant emits. We often overlook these and similar kinds of learning because they are not usually associated with a school setting.

Also included in a broad concept of learning are the formation, modification, and breaking of habits; the acquiring of interests, attitudes, and values; the development of tastes and preferences; and the formation of biases and prejudices. Learning is involved in the synthesis and application of knowledge in reasoning, thinking, theory building, and problem solving, and in our deepest feelings and emotions, our self-concepts, and, indeed, our total personalities. (Further discussion and elaboration of the various kinds and outcomes of learning will be found in Chapters 17 and 18.)

Definition of Learning

The term *learning* does not lend itself to any simple or universally accepted definition, but a common and somewhat useful definition, frequently cited by psychologists and educators, is that *learning is a modification of behavior as a result of experience or training.*

Some of the advantages and disadvantages of this definition are immediately apparent. By limiting the types of changes under consideration to those resulting from experience or training, the definition excludes

---

[4] J. V. McConnell, A. L. Jacobson, and D. P. Kimble, "The Effects of Regeneration upon Retention of a Conditioned Response in a Planarium," *Journal of Comparative and Physiological Psychology*, 52 (1959), 1–5.

[5] Frank R. Babish et al., "Transfer of a Response to Naive Rats by Injection of Ribonucleic Acid Extracted from Trained Rats," *Science*, 149 (August 6, 1965), 656–657.

behavioral changes due to innate response tendencies, maturation, or temporary states such as fatigue or the use of drugs. The definition also excludes changes that are not manifested in modifications of behavior. All of us, for example, can recall an experience or an idea that has changed the way we feel or think, but in a way that has not affected our overt behavior. The importance of recognizing the existence of both overt and covert behavioral changes is emphasized by Hilgard,[6] who distinguishes between *learning* (covert) and *performance* (overt). He points out that learning can only be inferred from performance.

Since both overt and covert changes constitute learning, some theorists prefer to define learning in terms of "modification in the learner" instead of "modification in behavior." Others limit their definition of learning to the relatively permanent changes associated with training or experience, while still others feel there is no good reason to limit a definition of learning to permanent changes.

Clearly, there are many kinds, expressions, and levels of learning. In substance, however, there is little conflict over the definition of learning between rival theories and points of view. The differences of opinion that do exist have actually arisen from differences in interpretations of the findings of particular experiments.

Nature of the Learning Process

Three sets of variables must be considered in any study of the learning process: (1) the *stimulus* or situation, which consists of one or more sensations in the body or environmental changes; (2) the *organism*—that is, the internal processes that intervene between stimulus and response; and (3) the *response*—the overt and covert activities that modify the initial stimulus (eating candy reduces hunger). The relationships among these variables are shown in Figure 15–2, which depicts the structure of the learning process.

This paradigm of the learning process is similar to the model of the human behavior cycle described in Chapter 8. The impetus for learning, as in the activation of the human behavior cycle, is a stimulus. Instead of thinking of a single stimulus, however, we should probably think of a set of stimuli (sensations of touch, sight, hearing, taste, smell, and kinesthesia) impinging on the receptor organs at any given moment. A set of stimuli conveys information. If an organism is to change in ways that characterize learning, it must receive some kind of message, or input. Without some kind of patterned stimulation, the individual has difficulty maintaining his psychological organization.

---

[6] Ernest R. Hilgard and Gordon H. Bower, *Theories of Learning*, 3rd ed. (New York: Appleton-Century-Crofts, 1966), p. 5.

Figure 15-2. The Structure of Learning Activity

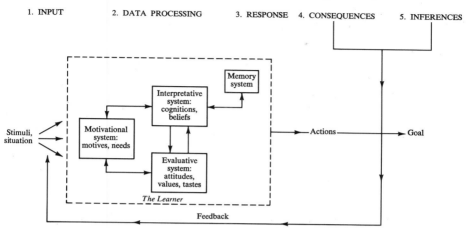

Source: Frederick J. McDonald, *Educational Psychology*, 2nd ed. (Belmont, Calif.: Wadsworth Publishing Co., 1965), p. 77.

The variables referred to by the term *organism* include all processes and events that occur inside the organism between the onset of the sensation and the emitting of a response. These processes and events are referred to as *intervening variables* in some theories and *mediating variables* in other theories. As shown in Figure 15–2, the variables labeled "organism" include a motivational system (which arouses and directs the individual's energies toward specific goals); a perceptual-interpretative system (which differentiates, integrates, and ascribes meaning to sensory stimulation); a memory system (consisting of acquired concepts, knowledge, and skills); and an evaluative system (attitudes, values, and tastes). These variables are psychological, are not open to direct observation and study, and, therefore, must be inferred from the organism's behavior.

Response is a general term used to refer to whatever the organism does or does not do after the stimulus and organism steps in the S-O-R sequence of activities. Often, we think of response as some observable behavior. We look for some movement or action of the body or its parts—perhaps a verbal response, a nod of the head, a frown or smile, or even a flick of an eyelash. Teachers become alert to actions or words that confirm a student's grasp of the concept of gravity, his mastery of a rule of grammar, or his ability to apply a historical principle to a current political problem. Even when he is making no observable response, however, a learner is probably learning something. A student who registers no movement, comment, or change of expression to the statement "Trade barriers restrict free trade and economic growth" may store the principle in his memory, may try to think of examples of the principle or relate it to other economic concepts, or may view the principle as further evidence that economics is dull. To determine whether any learning has occurred, the teacher must await some future situation in which some statement or application of this principle is relevant. It is possible, of course, that the learner was attending to other internal or external stimuli, so that no stimuli symbolizing trade barriers, free trade, and economic growth were received, no relevant response occurred, and, presumably, the desired learning did not take place.

The nature of the response is far more complex than this brief description suggests. The reponse consists of much more than a movement or an oral or written statement. It includes activities at various levels—brain, nervous system, muscles, glands, and other internal organs. As we well know, the many activities that comprise a response are different for every learner.

Figure 15–2 shows that "response" is not the end of the learning process. The consequences of the response and the inferences to be drawn from these consequences provide continuous feedback in the form of new stimuli, or input. On previous occasions, for example, the hungry child has gone to the kitchen counter where he has found the cookie jar and gotten a cookie. The nth time he is hungry (stimulus), he goes to the counter (response) but does not find the cookie jar or get a cookie. The consequences of this response produce *feedback*, which provides new stimulus input. The consequences of successive unsuccessful responses in looking for the cookie jar and the successful response of finding the cookie jar in the cupboard all produce feedback and new stimulus input.

Each learning theory varies in the relative importance it assigns to stimulus-organism-response (S-O-R) variables in the learning process. Stimulus-response theories quite naturally emphasize the observable variables S and R, while cognitive field theories give primary emphasis to the structuring of the cognitive field and to goal setting, which occur within O (organism). As we analyze learning in relation to any learning theory, we shall need to focus on the individual variables in the learning process and to analyze the influence of each on other variables and on the total sequence of events.

Theories of Learning

There is a real need for every educator to develop a personal theory of learning. The first step in the development of an adequate, consistent personal learning theory is gaining a basic knowledge and understanding of the major learning theories found in the literature of psychology. An educator may embrace an existing theory in its totality. More frequently, however, he will probably select from various theories those principles, laws, or postulates that correlate most directly and consistently with his own findings, predilections, biases, and speculations. These become organized and synthesized into a personal theory of learning which evolves, changes, and becomes further refined as the educator continues to study and to analyze the processes through which people learn.

Two Views of Learning

Scientific learning theories and systems of psychology developed in America after 1900 can be roughly classified under two broad headings: stimulus-response (also called "association") theories and cognitive field theories. These two types of learning theory differ first of all in their philosophical premises and in their conceptions of the nature of man. In general, S-R theorists hold that the learner is essentially passive, that his behavior is controlled by internal and external forces. Cognitive field theorists, on the other hand, believe that the learner's own purposes, motives, perceptions, and cognitions influence and are influenced by inter-actions with the psychological environment.

Stimulus-response theories have often been described as molecular, reductionist, and mechanistic because they study small, irreducible ele-ments of learning and use many of the same terms and experimental procedures emphasized in the natural sciences. S-R theories focus on be-havior, emphasizing *conditioning;* that is, they seek to discover and to refine the principles or laws whereby a *stimulus* or *situation* in an external or internal environment becomes associated with some aspect of behavior called *response.*

Cognitive field theories are frequently described as molar and relativistic. They contend that any idea or object derives its qualities from and has meaning only in relation to other components of the total situa-tion. Reality for the cognitive field theorists is the meanings which the individual acquires as he interacts with his environment.

S-R theorists and cognitive field theorists both use the methods of scientific inquiry in their study of learning. They differ, however, in the assumptions they make and the ends they seek. The cognitive field theorist relies largely on inferences drawn from data on the learner's perceptions, insights, and cognitions; the S-R theorist usually restricts his investigations to those events that can be directly observed and measured. Some learning theories seem to be better adapted for explaining certain types of learning, while other learning theories appear to be better suited for explaining other types of learning. We shall examine next this relationship between types and theories of learning.

A Taxonomy of Types and Theories of Learning

The history of psychology is studded with conflicts between rival learning theories, but it is increasingly evident that, despite optimistic claims, no one learning theory can at present provide adequate explanations for all of the many types of learning. Some theories have been more successful in explaining psychomotor skills and the learning of attitudes; other theories offer better explanations of cognitive and problem-solving learning. As a result, a number of learning theorists recently have tried to produce a taxonomy of types of learning.

One such taxonomy of types of learning has been developed by Gagné.[7] From observations of everyday occurrences, Gagné has identified eight types of learning, each of which requires a different set of conditions. The conditions of learning are the events that must take place if a particular learning is to occur. The conditions of learning include events within the learner (such as drive level, previous learning, and satisfaction) and events in the learning situation (such as the task itself). Knowledge of these conditions enables the teacher to provide appropriate guidance in promoting learning activities. The eight types of learning identified by Gagné appear in a hierarchy of levels of complexity:

Type 1: Signal learning. *The individual learns to make a general, diffuse response to a signal. This is the classical conditioned response of Pavlov [and the behaviorism of Watson].*

Type 2: Stimulus-response learning. *The learner acquires a precise response to a discriminated stimulus. What is learned is a connection (Thorndike) or a discriminated operant (Skinner), sometimes called an instrumental response (Kimble).*

Type 3: Chaining. *What is acquired is a chain of two or more stimulus-response connections. The conditions for such learning have been described by [Guthrie,] Skinner and others.*

Type 4: Verbal association. *Verbal association is the learning of chains that are verbal. Basically, the conditions resemble those for other (motor) chains. However, the presence of language in the human being makes this a special type because internal links may be selected from the individual's previously learned repertoire of language.*

Type 5: Multiple discrimination. *The individual learns to make* n *different identifying responses to* n *different stimuli, which may resemble each other in physical appearance to a greater or lesser degree. Although the learning of each stimulus-response connection is a simple type-2 occurrence, the connections tend to interfere with each other's retention.*

[7] Robert M. Gagné, *The Conditions of Learning*, 2nd ed. (New York: Holt, Rinehart and Winston, 1970).

Type 6: Concept learning. *The learner acquires a capability of making a common response to a class of stimuli that may differ from each other widely in physical appearance. He is able to make a response that identifies an entire class of objects or events (Kendler).*

Type 7: Principle learning. *In simplest terms a principle is a chain of two or more concepts. It functions to control behavior in the manner suggested by a verbalized rule of the form "If A, then B," where A and B are concepts. However, it must be carefully distinguished from the mere verbal sequence "If A, then B," which, of course, may be learned as type 4.*

Type 8: Problem solving. *Problem solving is a kind of learning that requires the internal events usually called thinking. Two or more previously acquired principles are somehow combined to produce a new capability that can be shown to depend on a "higher-order" principle.*[8]

This taxonomy is one way of classifying different kinds of learning and of relating each to the learning theory or theories best suited for explaining it. Gagné suggests that principles and generalizations emerging from learning theory may prove useful only as they are related to the kinds of capability being learned. Other writings by Gagné analyze the individual skills and understandings required at each level or step in a specific learning. He relates each of these skills and understandings to one or more of the eight types of learning summarized above. Through an analysis of this kind, what is known about the types or conditions of learning can be used to facilitate specific learning performances.

Stimulus-Response Learning

Stimulus-response theory emphasizes conditioning. *Conditioning* is a type of learning which occurs when one or more stimuli (S) are connected or strengthened through association with one or more responses (R). Conditioning usually involves the repeated association of a particular stimulus and a particular response, such as in the forming of habits. Learning acquired through conditioning is of two types: classical conditioning and operant conditioning.

---

[8] From Chapter 2 of *The Conditions of Learning* by Robert M. Gagné. Copyright © 1970 by Holt, Rinehart and Winston, Inc. Reprinted by permission of Holt, Rinehart and Winston, Inc. Bracketed material inserted by this writer.

Classical Conditioning

Classical conditioning describes a process whereby a given response is elicited by specific stimuli. The essential feature of this kind of learning is that a stimulus occurs in the presence of a response that it does not ordinarily elicit and, through becoming linked with the response, acquires the property of eliciting that response. For example, when a buzzer (neutral stimulus) in successive pairings with a puff of air (unconditioned stimulus) elicits a blink of the eye (reflex response), learning by conditioning has occurred when the buzzer alone evokes the eye blink. Virtually any neutral stimulus (a color, a bell, even an odor), through successive pairings with the puff of air, can become a conditioned stimulus. The one-time neutral stimulus (now the *conditioned stimulus*), having heretofore served as a signal for the puff of air, is now capable of eliciting the eye blink even when the puff of air is eliminated. The law of conditioning thus states that when a neutral stimulus is paired with an unconditioned stimulus (UCS) over several trials, a conditioned stimulus (CS) results, which has by itself the ability to evoke the conditioned response (CR). Classical conditioning is an example of Gagné's type 1, signal learning, and applies only to involuntary behavior; that is, to reflexes and responses controlled by the autonomic nervous system. The term given to classical conditioning by B. F. Skinner is *respondent behavior*, since the eye blink is a response to a stimulus (buzzer) which elicits it.

The elements of classical conditioning described above were first identified by Ivan Pavlov (1849–1936),[9] a Russian physiologist whose work profoundly influenced the development of learning theory in the United States. While studying certain digestive reflexes of dogs, Pavlov noted that these laboratory animals would salivate at the mere sight of food. In one of Pavlov's often cited experiments, a hungry dog was fastened comfortably, but securely, to a laboratory table in a stimulus-free room and fed powdered meat. Shortly before the meat was given, a bell was rung. The dog's reaction to the food—the extent of his salivation—was measured at each feeding. At first, the dog salivated only upon presentation of the food. After about 30 trials, however, the dog salivated just as much at the sound of the bell. After 30 trials, then, conditioning had occurred, since the ringing of the bell alone was sufficient to elicit salivation (see Figure 15–3). If food was not presented after the ringing of the bell, the conditioned response (salivation) gradually decreased and finally ceased. This process is known as *extinction*.

In other experiments, Pavlov discovered a principle of *stimulus generalization*. He found that stimuli similar to but not identical with the conditioned stimulus will also evoke the conditioned response. Thus, the

---

[9] See Ivan P. Pavlov, *Conditioned Reflexes*, trans. by G. V. Anrep (London: Oxford University Press, 1927).

Figure 15–3. Relationships between stimuli and responses before and after simple conditioning. Dotted line represents potential connection; solid line represents functional connection.

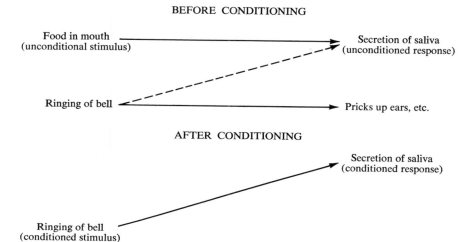

BEFORE CONDITIONING

Food in mouth
(unconditional stimulus)   Secretion of saliva
                                            (unconditioned response)

Ringing of bell   Pricks up ears, etc.

AFTER CONDITIONING

                                            Secretion of saliva
                                            (conditioned response)

Ringing of bell
(conditioned stimulus)

Source: James M. Sawrey and Charles W. Telford, *Educational Psychology*, 2nd ed. (Boston: Allyn & Bacon, 1964), p. 99. Reproduced by permission.

sounding of a tone which is slightly higher or lower in pitch than the original tone has the property of eliciting the same conditioned response. The less similar the new stimulus to the original one, however, the weaker the conditioned response. Pavlov found that *stimulus discrimination* is achieved when the animal salivates (conditioned response) to a tone of 440 vibrations per minute, but does not salivate to tones of 420 or 460 vibrations per minute. He also demonstrated that *higher order conditioning* occurs when the conditioned response (salivation) is evoked after repeated pairings of a second neutral stimulus (electric shock becoming the new conditioned stimulus) and the first neutral stimulus (the bell becoming the new unconditioned stimulus).

When Pavlov's work was introduced into the United States, it found ready acceptance in a school of psychology known as behaviorism, whose basic ideas were first expounded by John B. Watson (1878–1958).[10] *Behaviorism*, an environmentalist psychology, sought completely objective explanations of behavior, avoiding any consideration of consciousness or other mental factors. Watson extended Pavlov's classical conditioning model, developed from animal experiments, to studies of human behavior,

[10] John B. Watson, *Psychology from the Standpoint of a Behaviorist* (Philadelphia: J. B. Lippincott Co., 1919).

and expanded the reflex arc concept to include responses that are non-reflective and complex.

Watson believed that if the proper stimuli were presented, specific responses could be elicited in an individual from early infancy; thus, the individual could be molded into any type of person desired. Using the classical conditioning model in one of his most famous experiments, Watson[11] conditioned Albert, an 11-month-old boy, to fear a white rat toward which he had previously responded in a positive, friendly manner. One day, as the boy reached out to touch the rat, Watson produced a loud noise by striking an iron bar behind Albert's head just as he touched the rat. Albert jumped and fell forward, burying his face in the mattress. With successive repetitions of this procedure, various other fear responses were evoked in Albert. Presentation of a rabbit and a sealskin coat also evoked fear and withdrawal behavior in Albert, a phenomenon referred to above as stimulus generalization. Watson suggested by this experiment that fear is a conditioned (learned) reaction. In a later replication of this experiment. M. C. Jones[12] demonstrated that by showing a rabbit to the child at a distance, then moving the rabbit closer on successive days and omitting the loud noise, fear as a conditioned response can be unlearned (extinguished).

Applications of Classical Conditioning

The results of experiments in conditioning reflexes (such as salivation or eye blink) appear to have only limited application outside the laboratory. Classical conditioning as it relates to our learning fears, anxieties, and phobias, however, is a much more common and pervasive type of human learning than most persons realize. A child who is bitten or frightened by a ferocious dog can be conditioned to fear all dogs, even small, friendly, tail-wagging puppies. An adult responds with aversion to a particular seafood or vegetable because of its association with a particular traumatic experience. These fears or aversions can be extinguished by detaching the fear-evoking stimulus (dog, food, or other object) from the experiencing of fear elicited by the pain of being bitten, indigestion, or discomfort.

Lazarus[13] relates how he extinguished a 10-year-old-boy's fear of cars. Two years earlier the boy had been in a car accident. Lazarus began by playing with toy cars himself, time and time again acting out versions of accidents between the toy cars while the boy watched from a distance. As

[11] John B. Watson and R. Rayner, "Conditioned Emotional Reactions," *Journal of Experimental Psychology*, 3 (1920), 1–14.

[12] Mary Cover Jones, "A Laboratory Study of Fear: The Case of Peter," *Pedagogical Seminary and Journal of Genetic Psychology*, 31 (1924), 308–315.

[13] A. A. Lazarus, "The Elimination of Children's Phobias by Deconditioning," in H. J. Eysenck, ed., *Behavior Therapy and Neurosis* (London: Pergamon, 1960), pp. 114–122.

the child moved successively closer to the cars, Lazarus popped a piece of chocolate into the boy's mouth. After each "accident" with the toy cars, if the boy evidenced no fear, he was given a chocolate. During subsequent days and weeks, Lazarus and the boy played "accident" games with the toy cars and spent long hours discussing the accident in which the boy was involved. One day Lazarus discovered that he was out of chocolates and suggested to the boy that they both go in his car to get some. The boy's response in accompanying him without hesitation and his pleasure expressed during the extensive drive around town indicated that the boy's fear of cars had been extinguished.

Some fears involving a particular classroom learning activity may, through reinforcement, become generalized and transferred to an infinite number of stimuli or events. If Ted, for example, is sharply criticized for his poor reading, he becomes conditioned to dislike and to avoid reading. He feigns illness and sometimes actually becomes ill when faced with a reading assignment. These responses are reinforced as the result of disapprobation of poor reading shown by parents, teachers, and peers. Over a period of years, Ted's initial conditioned response of anxiety about reading may become generalized to an avoidance and dislike of other school subjects, his teacher, all teachers, all women who look or act like his teacher, this school, this school system, all schools and school systems, education in general, and life in general. This would be an example of the higher order conditioning of signal learning (type 1).

Other stimuli (words, smiles, colors, objects) can serve as conditioned stimuli in eliciting pleasant feelings and responses via classical conditioning. Candlelight and soft music during dinner evoke a pleasurable response. Similarly, light, colors, pictures, displays, and arrangement of furniture can serve as signals for the pleasant feelings that are associated with a favorable climate for learning. Other stimuli, such as the teacher's smile, enthusiasm, acceptance, and encouragement of pupils, can become generalized and evoke pleasant feelings and positive responses in students. While most learning is probably more than simple conditioning or association, it is nevertheless likely that these processes play some part in almost every learning experience.

Operant Conditioning

A second and much more important class of behaviors that can be conditioned are those which are not elicited by any known stimuli but are simply *emitted* by the organism. Most behavior such as walking, talking, eating, working, and playing is of this sort. These behaviors fit Gagné's type 2 (stimulus-response), type 3 (chaining), and type 4 (verbal association) learning. Sometimes behavior that is emitted is referred to as instrumental behavior, but more frequently it is known as *operant behavior*, the term given it by B. F. Skinner. Whereas respondent behavior (such as the eye blink in classical conditioning) is a response to stimuli (buzzer and puff of air), operant behavior operates in the environment. The pigeon moves about the cage and the small child moves about the room. Through a sequence of movements the pigeon pecks a disk and receives food, and through a different sequence of movements the child finds a cookie in the cupboard. Behavior (such as pecking the disk or going to the cupboard) which is followed by the presentation of food is said to be reinforced. *Reinforcement* is simply any event or stimulus which increases the probability of a response's recurring. Thus, food is the reinforcement, and the behavior of pecking the disk or going to the cupboard is called an operant. The law of operant conditioning states that "if the occurrence of an operant is followed by the presentation of a reinforcing stimulus, the strength of the operant is increased."[14]

Reinforcers can be either positive or negative. *Positive reinforcers* are usually rewards; *negative reinforcers* are aversive stimuli such as shock, pain, or discomfort, stimuli the individual commonly seeks to avoid. Whereas reinforcement results from the *occurrence* of a positive reinforcer, it also results from the *termination* of a negative reinforcer. For example, one may acquire an operant of going to a particular berry patch for delicious strawberries, a positive reinforcer. Over a period of time his body chemistry changes, and he becomes allergic to strawberries. Now the pain and discomfort of eating strawberries make strawberries a negative reinforcer. If the pain and discomfort of eating strawberries is terminated by taking a prescription drug, the removal of the negative reinforcer (pain, discomfort) strengthens the original operant of going to the berry patch and eating strawberries. Thus, a response can be reinforced either by presenting a positive reinforcer or by removing a negative reinforcer.

Negative reinforcement seems to be related to punishment, but the exact relationship is not obvious. Reinforcement results from the removal of a negative reinforcer, whereas punishment involves the presentation of a negative reinforcer. The punishment of scolding a student for inattention in school is likely to be followed by the student's holding negative feelings about the teacher, the source of the punishment. The attending behavior of the student is temporarily increased, but it is directed toward the teacher rather than toward the lesson or learning activity. When the punishment is removed, the emotional effects soon wear off and the inattention again recurs, often more pronounced than before the punishment. Used as a negative reinforcer, the elimination of scolding permits the attending behavior of other students to continue, since they are not distracted by the teacher's scolding a fellow student.

An important characteristic of reinforcers, both positive and negative, is that they can be conditioned. If a stimulus is paired with a positive reinforcer, the stimulus tends to acquire the capacity to reinforce behavior. Such a stimulus is called a *secondary reinforcer*. A young child who acquires operants of walking, talking, and using the toilet is likely to be re-

---

[14] B. F. Skinner, *The Behavior of Organisms* (New York: Appleton-Century-Crofts, 1938), p. 21.

inforced not only by food (primary reinforcement), but also by praise, a smile, and a hug (secondary reinforcements) as well. Fear can also be a secondary reinforcer, as when it is paired with the discomfort an adolescent experiences when he is punished by being ridiculed before peers, being given poor grades, or having privileges withheld. Fear serves to reinforce avoidance of critical adults or situations where he feels vulnerable or inadequate. Grades, honors, words, gestures, and money are other familiar examples of secondary reinforcers. The importance of secondary reinforcers in human learning becomes evident when we realize that most people acquire social behaviors and academic skills in response to something other than the physiological (primary) drives of hunger and thirst. As we noted in previous chapters, a teacher or parent is well advised to identify the specific stimuli (such as praise, recognition, or appropriate model) which are reinforcing for a particular student and to use these reinforcers in facilitating the operant learning of that individual.

Skinner and his followers have found that the number of responses the learner emits per unit of time varies according to the *schedule of reinforcement* employed. The reinforcement of operants can be either continuous or intermittent. *Continuous reinforcement* is the reinforcing of every response; *intermittent reinforcement* is the reinforcing of part of the responses. Intermittent reinforcements can be delivered according to a *ratio* (one reinforcement per number of emitted responses) or according to a time *interval* (one reinforcement per unit of time). Ratio and interval schedules of reinforcement can be either fixed or variable. Thus, the experimenter can employ a fixed ratio, a variable ratio, a fixed interval, a variable interval, or a mixed schedule of reinforcement.

Studies of various schedules of reinforcement reveal that each schedule has its own characteristic response curve. The major finding emerging from these studies is that organisms will emit more responses per reinforcement under any kind of intermittent reinforcement than under continuous reinforcement. If reinforcement is finally terminated altogether, resistance to extinction is also greater after intermittent reinforcement than after continuous reinforcement. Thus, a student can be expected to complete more problems per unit of time in his seat work assignment if he receives occasional praise after completing several problems than if he is praised or rewarded for every problem completed. Reinforcing every correct response, however, is more effective for progressing through a programed learning sequence or learning a complex skill (such as driving a car) through shaping the learner's behavior, a topic we shall consider next.

A technique which Skinner used to train animals to perform complex acts that are outside their normal range of behavior is called *shaping*. Behavior is shaped through a series of approximations, each made possible by reinforcing certain responses and not others. Thus, behavior is gradually brought closer and closer to the desired pattern.

The technique of shaping behavior has been used extensively in human learning. Children's responses are shaped by socialization processes toward desired social behaviors; the responses of retardates and the emotionally disturbed can be shaped in the learning of simple skills; and the classroom teacher shapes students' behaviors toward goals in reciting, preparing a report, learning shorthand, and observing proper deportment. Each of these behaviors is an example of Gagné's type 3 (chaining) and type 4 (verbal association) learning. Since many of these activities require the learner to make responses to different but similar stimuli, type 5, multiple discrimination learning, may also be involved.

Another procedure that has frequently been used to influence the behavior of others is differential reinforcement. *Differential reinforcement* is reinforcing certain behaviors in the subject's response repertoire and not other's. The story is frequently told of the psychology class which, after being introduced to the principles of operant conditioning, proceeded to apply the principles in bringing under their control the behavior of the psychology professor. It seems that this professor lectured most of the period from the front left side of the lecture hall, which made it difficult for students on the far right to hear him. Only occasionally did the professor move to the right side of the room to write something on the board. In an effort to modify the professor's behavior of remaining on the left side of the room, students responded with smiles and nods as the professor moved toward the right side of the room. Pretty soon most of his lecturing was being done on the right side of the room. So elated were the students by their success in using differential reinforcement that they reinforced the professor by smiles and nods when he lectured pacing back and forth in front of the class. When informed some time later of what had occurred, the professor could only shake his head in disbelief, saying, "And I thought that the class's responsiveness was because I was in such good form on those occasions!"

Differential reinforcement has been used in inducing subjects to use a preponderance of plural nouns or expressions of opinion simply by the experimenter's reinforcing these responses by saying "Um hm" whenever the subjects emitted plural nouns or opinions.[15] Differential reinforcement can also be a directing influence on the client's behavior in the nondirective, or client-centered, therapy of Carl Rogers. In client-centered therapy the therapist seeks to develop an accepting, empathic relationship with the client that is "facilitative of personal growth and integration." Rogers contends that the verbal responses of the client who is making progress in therapy are moving him toward healthier adjustment because of the general therapeutic climate, not because of the therapist's differential positive reinforcement of "positive" or "healthy" verbal responses by the client. To test this contention, Truax[16] analyzed client statements and Rogers' responses form recordings of Rogers' therapy sessions with a long-term client. Truax found that for five of nine categories of client statements, Rogers

[15] Joel Greenspoon, "The Reinforcing Effect of Two Spoken Sounds on the Frequency of Two Responses," *American Journal of Psychology*, 68 (1955), 409–416; William S. Verplanck, "The Control of the Content of Conversation: Reinforcement of Statements of Opinion," *Journal of Abnormal and Social Psychology*, 51 (1955), 668–676.

[16] Charles B. Truax, "Reinforcement and Nonreinforcement in Rogerian Psychotherapy," *Journal of Abnormal and Social Psychology*, 71 (1966), 1–9.

did respond differently, providing positive reinforcement in the form of understanding, warmth, and affirmation for "healthy" statements and neglecting to respond in this way if client statements were not "healthy." In the category of clarity-ambiguity, for example, Rogers offered positive reinforcement for statements which reflected clarity but withheld reinforcement for ambiguous statements. As the result of Rogers' providing warmth, understanding, and affirmation to some statements but not to others, the former statements were found to increase in frequency while the latter did not. Regardless of Rogers' stated intent, it appears that he differentially reinforced the client's responses when they were consistent with Rogers' notion of "healthy." One can predict, then, that as therapy continues, the client's verbal behavior will begin to generalize to situations outside the therapy session. The client becomes more optimistic, relaxed, and clearer than before. Friends and acquaintances see this change and respond to it favorably, thus reinforcing his new personality. Soon it can be maintained by persons other than the therapist, and therapy can be terminated.

With this brief presentation of the principles of operant conditioning in mind, we shall consider next its various applications in human learning.

Applications of Operant Conditioning

Operant conditioning has been applied to a wide range of behavior and learning problems involving both animals and humans in a variety of contexts. One familiar application is programed learning, which was introduced by Skinner and others in the 1950s. Skinner noted that the inefficiency of some teaching procedures can be overcome by presenting a series of stimuli to which the child is to respond, by reinforcing the child's correct response immediately instead of after a lapse of time, and by step-by-step reinforcement of a series of progressive approximations toward the final desired behavior.

Programed learning. Skinner's system of operant reinforcement has been applied in the selection and programing of material for use with teaching machines or programed texts. Effective learning through the use of programed learning media requires that the student take the initiative in composing his response, rather than selecting his response from among a set of alternatives. In programed learning, again following Skinner's suggestion, the student passes through a carefully designed sequence of small, easy steps toward the desired behavior.

The student using Skinner's machines or programed texts is presented with a graduated series of questions, each of which calls for an answer that has been presented in or suggested by the previous material. Each question is in the form of an incomplete statement, and the student responds by writing a word or phrase which completes the statement. He then moves a device that exposes the correct answer; compares it with his response; and then, if his answer is correct, moves a lever which brings up the next question. Correct answers thus are reinforced by the exposed printed answer. Programed instruction is also presented in the form of a scrambled textbook. Figure 15–4 presents items from a page of a book programed for self-instruction in English grammar.

In programed instruction, the choice and the sequential ordering of information and questions are of primary importance. If materials to be learned are properly prepared and presented in sequential order, Skinner finds that they are highly effective. Skinner summarizes the advantages of this type of instruction:

1.   *Learning is more effective when it involves the active participation of the learner. Since the student is continually reading and answering questions, he is always busy with learning activities. He does not sit passively listening to a lecture or watching a demonstration but must make an overt response in answering each question that is posed.*

2.   *The learning of concepts and principles is facilitated when they are presented in small sequential steps, beginning with the simple and leading to more complex concepts and principles. The student is less likely to get "lost" because wherever he is in the program he has been able to answer every question up to that point. The teaching machine operates like a good tutor in making sure that a particular point is understood before the student moves on. Lectures and textbooks, on the other hand, often proceed without ascertaining whether the student understands and thus may leave him behind.*

3.   *Learning is facilitated when the learner is permitted to proceed as slowly or quickly as he is able and as he wishes with no pressure being exerted to complete a question or section within a specified period of time. Thus, the student does not have to cope with concepts until he is ready for them. Programed learning is self-paced, with the only requirement being a correct response before the learner is permitted to proceed with new material.*

4.   *Like a skillful tutor, the machine helps the student come up with the correct answer. The student is helped by the orderly construction of the program and in part by the hints and suggestions which may be derived from the verbal material.*

5.   *Finally, the machine provides reinforcement for every correct response. This immediate feedback enables the student to learn more efficiently with minimum loss of time and effort; it contributes, too, toward maintaining his interest in learning.*[17]

[17] B. F. Skinner, "Teaching Machines," *Science*, 128 (October 24, 1958), 969–977. Reprinted by permission.

Figure 15–4. A page from a programed learning textbook. The student is instructed to cover up the answers with a leatherette strip which serves as a guide. After answering the question, he moves the guide down so that it reveals the correct answer.

-1333-

Only an_____can modify a verb.	adverb
Many adverbs end in_____.	ly
When they modify the verb, these adverbs usually tell us something about the _____ of the verb.	action
Adverbs ending in____seldom modify linking verbs.	ly
Do they often modify verbs of action?	yes

-1334-

Some of the following sentences contain linking verbs. The others contain verbs of action.

The linking verbs are followed by adjectives which modify the_____ of the sentence.	subject
The verbs of action are followed by adverbs ending in _ly_ which modify the_____.	verb

In each sentence select the correct form of the adjective or adverb:

A rose smells - sweet/sweetly.	sweet
This food tastes - bad/badly.	bad
The professor speaks - rapid/rapidly.	rapidly
You sing - good/well.	well
He felt - quick/quickly/ - for the door knob.	quickly
He polished - vigorous/vigorously.	vigorously
The play ended - happy/happily.	happily
The snake struck - vicious/viciously	viciously

Source: M. W. Sullivan, *Programmed English* (New York: Macmillan Co., 1963). Reprinted by permission.

Advocates of programed instruction point out that neither teaching machines nor programed texts are intended to replace the teacher. Rather, these media serve to supplement the teacher's activities and to free him to help slower students and those with individual problems. Skinner's method of having all students go through the same sequence of items, or frames, is called *linear programing*. A contrasting type of program, called a *branching program*, provides several different sequences of items. This type of program seeks to make greater provision for individual differences, since the particular route a learner follows is determined by his response at some preceding "choice point."

Programed learning media appear to be most useful in the learning and recognition of verbal definitions and concepts, and most programed learning materials contain many such items. Thus, Gagné's type 4 (verbal association) learning appears to be most characteristic of programed learning material. Less frequently, the learner may be asked to identify a concept (type 6—concept learning), to apply a rule (type 7—principle learning), or to utilize two or more previously learned principles in solving a problem (type 8—problem solving).

As with so many problems and issues in education, the answers to the question of whether programed learning is superior to traditional patterns of instruction are equivocal, since the findings of different studies are inconsistent. Some studies show that programed instruction may produce greater initial gains in achievement, but that often these gains are not maintained. The chief complaint of good students is that programed material quickly becomes boring; the individual must follow a prescribed series of steps and has little or no opportunity to relate, to evaluate, to reflect, or to make an intuitive leap that may short-cut the step-by-step sequence. Advocates of programed instruction contend, however, that improved programs can eliminate many of these disadvantages and deficiencies.

Extinguishing undesirable behavior.   There are numerous examples of antisocial or undesirable behaviors in children as well as adults which parents, teachers, therapists, counselors, physicians—indeed, all of us— would like to see changed in people with whom we work and live. The procedures which have been developed in applying operant conditioning principles to change human behavior are called *behavior modification* or *behavioral therapy*. An important tool for modifying undesirable behavior is extinction. It will be recalled that this consists of withdrawing the reward or reinforcement which seems to be associated with the undesirable behavior.

A common type of misbehavior observed in many classrooms is that of the child who frequently disrupts the class by a tantrum—crying, kicking, and screaming. Invariably, the teacher takes some action, whether it is trying to calm the child, scolding him, or removing him from the classroom, while the other children watch and comment. A favorite hypothesis for explaining the misbehavior is that it is caused by someone's teasing him or his being frustrated by the assignment. Characteristically, neither a comforting, permissive response nor a punitive response from the teacher diminishes the incidence of the misbehavior.

One teacher who had such a student in class felt that the attention this boy was getting from classmates and teacher might be reinforcing the tantrum behavior. The next time the tantrum occurred outside the classroom, she had the boy brought kicking and screaming into the classroom and placed in his seat. The teacher closed the door and waited. She told him that when he finished crying, they could start working. The boy cried for seven or eight minutes and then said he was ready to work. The teacher went to his desk to help him with his English assignment, and the boy was very cooperative for the rest of the class period. After several weeks of extinction, the tantrums disappeared completely.[18] This case indicates that the teacher's comforting or punishing a child's misbehavior may not be a deterrent but may instead reinforce the undesirable behavior. Once the undesirable behavior is extinguished, the teacher or parent can give the child attention and recognition as a *contingency reinforcement* for desirable behavior.

In the following case record excerpt, a kindergarten teacher describes how, with the help of Mrs. M., a fellow teacher, contingency reinforcement was used to modify the tantrum behavior of five-year-old Teddy.

The plan was as follows: If the teacher noticed Teddy sitting in his chair, he would be reinforced on an intermittent schedule. Unacceptable behavior was to be ignored. Mrs. M. began by drawing a picture on the blackboard of a happy-faced boy sitting in a chair. Teddy was brought to the blackboard and was asked if he liked chewing gum. He nodded. Then Mrs. M. told Teddy that if he sat in his chair long enough he could have his gum. She set up a contract agreement. Every time she came into the room and found Teddy sitting in his chair, she would draw a happy face under the picture of the boy at the blackboard. If Teddy could get 10 happy faces by the end of the day, he could have the stick of chewing gum.

At that point she told Teddy to go to his seat so that she could give him his first happy face. He darted for his chair, and Mrs. M. drew the happy face. Then she went to his chair and congratulated him. She smiled, reminded Teddy that she would be back soon, and left the room. She returned within a few minutes, and Teddy was still in his chair. The elapsed time between Mrs. M.'s visits to the classroom grew longer, but by the end of the day Teddy had received 10 happy faces and was rewarded with a stick of chewing gum.

The next day the classroom teacher took over the task of providing the reinforcement. If the teacher was too busy to notice, Teddy reminded her that he had been sitting in his chair for a time. During the following days the periods between reinforcements were lengthened so that by the end of two weeks Teddy waited three days before

[18] E. H. Zimmerman and J. Zimmerman, "The Alteration of Behavior in the Classroom," *Journal of the Experimental Analysis of Behavior,* 5 (1962), 59–60.

receiving his gum reward. After the sitting behavior was well estab-
lished, the teacher began shaping Teddy's behavior by having him
sitting plus interacting (working, helping, talking, playing) with an-
other classmate before he could receive the happy face on the board.
During this period of using contingency reinforcement, the teacher
noted that Teddy's tantrums and disruptive behavior had markedly
decreased.

Undesirable behaviors can also be extinguished by *withdrawal of con-*
tingency reinforcements. Wetzel[19] describes the use of this technique in
modifying the chronic stealing of Mike, an eight-year-old boy in a training
home for disturbed children. A periodic frisking of Mike and his locker revealed numerous articles taken not only from other children within the
institution but also from the psychologist, social workers, janitors, and
other staff members. When confronted with the evidence, Mike would deny
guilt or place the blame on others and then would accuse others of not
trusting him. The staff noted that Maria, the Mexican cook for the pupils
and staff, had developed a fondness for Mike, who was himself of Mexican
extraction. She spent a great deal of time talking to him, and Mike seemed
to enjoy her company immensely. Maria's interaction with Mike was highly
reinforcing to him. A plan for extinguishing Mike's stealing was developed
whereby if Mike was observed to steal even one article, no matter how insignificant, Maria came to Mike and said, "Mike, it has been reported to me
that you were stealing. Because of your stealing, I cannot spend any more
time with you today." Then she would walk away and say nothing further.
During the next several weeks there were occasional slips in Mike's behavior. In time, however, the stealing was apparently eliminated; several
months went by during which no stolen item was found in Mike's possession. A short time after announcing to the staff that he was not going to
steal anymore, Mike bought with money he had earned items which he gave
to other children, claiming that he was paying them back for things he had
taken.

Withdrawal of contingent reinforcement has also been used to
eliminate cigarette smoking.[20] Twenty-five persons in a college community
who smoked more than a pack of cigarettes a day indicated a desire to stop
smoking by paying a deposit of 50 dollars each and agreeing to the following contract:

1.   The participant pledged that he would not smoke or otherwise
     use tobacco in any form for a period of 15 weeks.

---

[19] Ralph J. Wetzel, "The Use of Behavioral Techniques in a Case of Compulsive
Stealing," *Journal of Consulting Psychology*, 30 (1966), 367–374.

[20] Thomas J. Tighe and R. Elliott, "Breaking the Cigarette Habit: Effects of a
Technique Involving Threatened Loss of Money," paper presented at the American Psychological Association convention, Washington, D. C., 1967.

2. *If the participant refrained from using tobacco for two days, 10 dollars of his money would be returned. If he abstained for two weeks from the beginning date, he would receive an additional 10 dollars; if he abstained for 11 weeks, he would receive 15 dollars; and if he finished the full 15 weeks without smoking, he would receive the remaining 15 dollars of his deposit.*

3. *If the participant smoked or otherwise used tobacco at any time during the 15-week period, he would report the fact and forfeit all the money that had not been returned to him. The money that he forfeited was to be equally divided among the participants who succeeded in abstaining from smoking for the entire 15-week period.*

4. *The participant agreed to read an article on the physical effects of smoking. This particular article pointed out in great and gory detail some of the more harmful effects attributed to cigarette smoking.*

5. *The individual agreed to have his name published in the notices section of the campus newspaper indicating that he was a participant in a program in which he agreed not to smoke for 15 weeks or forfeit money if he did.*

The results of this procedure were striking. Twenty-one of the 25 participants went for the entire 15 weeks without smoking and received all their money back. A follow-up 17 months later revealed that 46 percent of those who participated in the study were still not smoking.

Helping exceptional children.   The use of principles of operant conditioning has proved especially effective in treating the behavior and learning problems of various types of exceptional children. As one example, contingency reinforcement has been used in the treatment of children with cerebral palsy in helping them to improve their classroom behavior[21] and their motor skills.[22] Since cerebral palsy involves impaired neurological functioning due to aberrant structure, growth, or development of the central nervous system, the development of motor skills is a matter of great concern in the habilitation of the cerebral palsied. In shaping behavior of the cerebral palsied child for teaching him motor skills, it is necessary to reduce each skill to its component parts and arrange the components in rank order from easiest to most difficult. The physical therapist begins training with that component which the child can perform easily. As the

[21] Martin C. Stone, "Behavior Shaping in a Classroom with Cerebral Palsy," *Exceptional Children*, 38 (May 1970), 674–677.

[22] Mary L. Kolderie, "Behavior Modification in the Treatment of Children with Cerebral Palsy," *Physical Therapy*, 51 (1971), 1,083–1,091.

child's performance improves, other components are required before a re-inforcer is given, until, finally, he can perform the entire motor skill. One 10-year-old girl with athetoid cerebral palsy (characterized by involuntary and uncontrollable motion) was just beginning to learn to crawl and could walk only with much assistance. The program began with development of skills in rolling over and sitting up, then progressed to balancing and crawling on hands and knees, and finally to standing and walking.

Reinforcement contingencies have been found equally effective in increasing the attention that children with learning disabilities give to learning tasks. In one study[23] children aged 10 to 13 with learning disabilities were awarded free time activities and privileges for completing weekly assignments in academic subjects during a baseline period. Grades of A, B, C, and "incomplete" were also given. During the experimental period, the procedures of the baseline period were continued, but, in addition, each child was paid a dime, a nickel, or a penny for each A, B, or C grade earned, respectively. A marked increase in attending to reading and arithmetic occurred in the pay period compared with the baseline period (68 to 86 percent). At the end of the school year, all 10 students were working one to four levels above their starting levels in all academic areas, and six of the 10 returned to regular classrooms one grade higher and were promoted again at the end of the year. This study indicates that a reinforcement system with grades as tokens and allowance money as backup reinforcers can increase the levels of academic behavior of highly distractable and disruptive children beyond those reinforcers that are generally available in schools.

Increasing academic performance.   One of the most striking successes in the use of reinforcement procedures for improving reading performance is described by Staats and Butterfield[24] in their treatment of a 14-year-old nonreading disadvantaged juvenile delinquent. Juan was the fifth child in a Mexican-American family of 11 children. The parents' techniques for controlling their children's behavior consisted of physical and verbal abuse. Juan had a long history of antisocial behavior, having been referred to the juvenile authorities nine times for such things as running away, burglary, incorrigibility, and truancy. His verbal and performance IQs on the Wechsler Bellevue Form I were 77 and 106, respectively, for a full scale IQ of 90. His reading level was second grade. Juan's tutor viewed reading as a series of responses which could be conditioned if appropriate reinforcements were used. The reading material consisted of specially prepared stories from the Science Research Associates (SRA) reading kit materials. A list was made of each different word that appeared in the stories. The words, each printed on a separate card, were to act as discriminative stimuli for

---

[23] Cedric Benson et al., "Behavior Modification of Children with Learning Disabilities Using Grades as Tokens and Allowances as Backup Reinforcers," *Exceptional Children*, 38 (Summer 1968), 745–751.

[24] Arthur W. Staats and William H. Butterfield, "Treatment of Nonreading in a Culturally Deprived Juvenile Delinquent: An Application of Reinforcement Principles," *Child Development*, 36 (December 1965), 925–941.

Juan's responses of pronouncing these words. The procedure for each story in the series commenced with the tutor presenting individually on cards the new words introduced in that story. Juan was asked to pronounce each word. A correct response to a word stimulus was reinforced with a middle value token. When Juan gave an incorrect response or no response, the tutor gave the correct response. Juan repeated the word while looking at the stimulus word.

After completing the vocabulary materials, each paragraph of the story was individually presented to Juan in the order each appeared in the story. Juan was asked to read orally each word in the paragraph and was given a high value token for each paragraph read. Next, he was asked to read the story and to answer the questions listed after the story. Reinforcement was given on a variable interval schedule for attentive behavior during silent reading and for each correct answer to the questions. Of the 761 new words presented during the vocabulary training, Juan recognized 585 of them during the oral reading phase. When tested 10 to 15 days later, Juan read correctly 430 of the 761 new words. During four and a half months of training, which involved 40 hours of reading training and the emission of an estimated 64,307 single-word reading responses, Juan earned tokens worth $20.31 and advanced from the 2.0 to the 4.3 grade level on the California Reading Test. Thus, he progressed more in those four and one-half months in reading than he had in the preceding eight and one-half years in school.

Other studies have investigated the differential effects of various reinforcements in promoting the school learning of different groups of students. Pikulski[25] compared the achievements of lower and middle class kindergarten children when various types of reinforcers were used in a word recognition task. The first reinforcer was the knowledge that one had gotten the word correct, the second or "social" reinforcer was the praise of the teacher and a smile, and the third or "material" reinforcer was candy. Pikulski found that middle class children and lower class girls responded best to social reinforcement, while lower class boys responded equally well to all three. In a replication[26] of this study with 60 lower class first graders, Pikulski changed the schedule of reinforcement. Instead of rewarding every correct word, the child was rewarded after a series of 20 words was learned successfully. The three reinforcers were the same. Pikulski found that girls responded best to social reinforcers, next best to the material reinforcers, and least well to feedback reinforcers. The boys, however, did qually well with social and material reinforcers, both yielding better results than knowledge of results alone. In another study[27] 30 black elementary school children in an urban ghetto whose reading performances were massively

[25] John J. Pikulski, "Effects of Reinforcement on Word Recognition," *The Reading Teacher*, 23 (March 1970), 516–522.

[26] John J. Pikulski, "Candy, Word Recognition, and the Disadvantaged," *The Reading Teacher*, 25 (December 1971), 243–246.

[27] Carl A. Clark and Herbert J. Walberg, "The Influence of Massive Rewards on Reading Achievement in Potential Urban Dropouts," *American Educational Research Journal*, 5 (1968), 305–310.

rewarded by teacher praise (tallied by each child) scored significantly higher on the SRA Reading Test than did the control groups, who received moderate amounts of teacher praise. These findings suggest that, especially for girls, social reinforcers are as effective as material reinforcers in promoting the language development of disadvantaged children.

Use of token economies.   Extending the use of contingency reinforcement to groups of subjects in an institution or a classroom requires the development of a systematic procedure for identifying and reinforcing the desired behaviors that appear in a group situation. In implementing such a procedure, it usually is necessary to establish a medium of exchange, so that an accounting can be made of reinforcements earned by individuals in the groups. Since the medium of exchange usually involves some kind of token, the general name given to a system that employs tokens as contingent reinforcers is *token economy*.[28] The token may be a piece of cardboard or paper, a poker chip, or a bottle cap. The recipient collects them and later uses them like money to purchase candy, comic books, or some privilege or amenity. Tokens are also a training device to help teachers, therapists, and hospital attendants learn to observe behaviors, to respond contingently, and to arrange the environment so as to maximize the possibility of the student's or patient's receiving rewarding stimuli. The use of tokens serves to reduce the logistics and record keeping involved in dispencing reinforcements in a group situation where several individuals may be earning reinforcements simultaneously.

An alternative to using a token economy in a school classroom is that of providing reinforcement outside the classroom. McIntire, Davis, and Pumroy[29] describe a study in which all the students in one fifth grade and one sixth grade classroom were differentially reinforced in accordance with the scores each earned on spelling and math assignments. Students who scored 90 percent or better *or* increased their score by 10 percentage points from the last session were reinforced by being allowed to engage in any activity in a special projects room: baking and cooking, making ceramic ashtrays, or working with teaching machines. Children whose score was within 10 points of their previous score were permitted to work with ceramics or teaching machines; those children whose score went down more than 10 points from the last session were permitted to work only with teaching machines.

The experimental period was divided into three phases. During phase 1 both the arithmetic and the spelling papers counted in both classrooms

[28] See Teodoro Ayllon and Nathan H. Azrin, *The Token Economy* (New York: Appleton-Century-Crofts, 1968); Garth J. Blackham and Adolph Silberman, *Modification of Child Behavior* (Belmont, Calif.: Wadsworth Publishing Co., 1971); Albert Bandura, *Principles of Behavior Modification* (New York: Holt, Rinehart and Winston, 1969); Leonard Krasner and Leonard P. Ullman, *Case Studies in Behavior Modification* (New York: Holt, Rinehart and Winston, 1965).

[29] Roger McIntire, Gayle Davis, and Donald Pumroy, "Improved Performance by Reinforcement," paper presented at the annual convention of the American Psychological Association, Miami Beach, Florida, 1970.

in calculating students' scores for the project room. At the beginning of phase 2, the fifth grade was told that spelling papers would no longer count in calculating scores, while the sixth grade was told that math papers would no longer count. At the beginning of phase 3, the fifth grade was told that math papers would not count but that spelling papers would. Contingencies for the sixth grade were also reversed; they were told that spelling papers no longer counted but that math papers did. This condition continued until the end of the experiment.

The results of this study indicate that for the fifth grade the shift in the contingencies of reinforcement during phases 2 and 3 produced significant expected changes in spelling and reading scores. For the sixth grade the shift in contingencies was ineffective for spelling scores but effective for math scores, although not nearly as striking as for the fifth grade. These findings demonstrate that written assignments, including tests and homework, can be brought under operant control. They further demonstrate the efficacy of delaying reinforcement for performance of classroom skills until another time and place.

The uses of operant conditioning: A further look.　　　The evidence pointing to the effectiveness of operant conditioning in changing human behavior is impressive. A closer examination of the evidence, however, indicates that the use of reinforcement contingencies is probably most successful in changing behavior in situations where the performance criterion is quite specific and in situations where the need for and reliance on external guidance and control in modifying behavior is very great. These characteristics seem to be most evident in special-education or institutional settings where the goal is the elimination of undesirable behavior (through extinction or contingency withdrawal) in emotionally disturbed and mentally retarded subjects. The success of the behavior modification seems to hinge on identifying and using with a given subject appropriate and adequate reinforcers. Frequent mention is made in the literature, for example, of the need for backup reinforcers (food or other material rewards, for example) to back up praise or knowledge of success.

Two key questions that are raised in assessing the long-term effects of operant conditioning are "How permanent are the behavior changes that have been brought about by reinforcement contingencies?" and "Will the desired behavior be extinguished if the material reinforcements are withdrawn or if the subject leaves the setting where the conditioning occured?" The answers to these questions seem to depend again upon the adequacy of the reinforcers available to the subject after the training experience. If social approval or knowledge-of-results stimuli prove adequate as reinforcers after training has been completed, the behavior change is likely to continue. If they do not prove adequate or if the reinforcers used during training are discontinued, the behavior will be extinguished and the effects of the training largely nullified.

Many would not go as far as Skinner in saying that operant conditioning and behavioral engineering have the primary roles in shaping human behavior. Some persons learn much more quickly and effectively in an environment where they are free to inquire and to discover ideas, principles, and solutions to problems by themselves in an environment rich in resources. Cognitive field theories, which we shall consider next, appear to be more facilitative of this type of learning.

Cognitive Field Theories of Learning

Cognitive field theories of learning, with their emphasis upon perception, cognition, goals, personal meaning, and the immediate situation, contrast sharply with stimulus-response theories—particularly with respect to motivation. S-R theorists believe that the learner is motivated primarily by organic drives and by successful (rewarded or otherwise reinforced) learning experiences. Cognitive field psychologists, in contrast, believe that the individual is motivated primarily by his need to grasp the *holistic meaning* of perceived phenomena.

Gestalt Theory

Gestalt psychology began with psychological studies of visual perception. In 1912, Max Wertheimer demonstrated that two fine parallel lines that are close together will be seen as one and that two optical stimuli perceived by the human eye in quick succession convey the illusion of movement. This illusion of motion has been called the *phi phenomenon*, and it is exemplified in the series of individual pictures seen in rapid succession in the modern motion picture. Such experiments in perception became the basis for a radically different view of learning that became known as Gestalt psychology.

Gestalt psychology is based on the premise that there is an essential unity in nature and that each phenomenon of nature is a whole, not merely the sum of its parts. Initially, a perceiver responds to a stimulus pattern as a whole; he perceives a total configuration, or *Gestalt*. After this response to the whole, the perceiver differentiates the whole into separate components. That part of the perceptual image which the perceiver differentiates most sharply and focuses his attention upon is called the *figure*. The less differentiated portions of the image serve as background and are called *ground*. *Figure* and *ground*, therefore, refer to the relationships between more differentiated and less differentiated portions of a perceptual image.

The concepts of Gestalt, figure, and ground are illustrated in Figure 15–5. Some will see the top figure as a comb for holding a woman's hair in place. Others will see it as a traffic officer with a white glove raised in front of his face. Some may see the bottom figure as a black Maltese cross; others, as a white propeller. When one is focusing on one of these images, the other is in the "ground"—and vice versa. Being attentive to anything means perceiving it in its "figural" form rather than as "ground."

Figure 15–5.   Conventional "Reversible" Figures

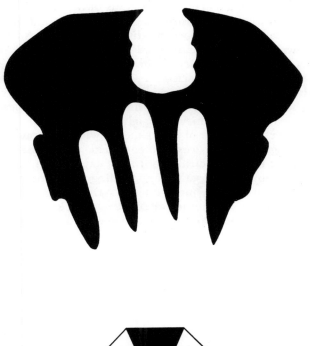

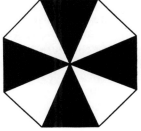

Source: George W. Hartmann, "The Field Theory of Learning and Its Educational Consequences," in Nelson B. Henry, ed., *The Psychology of Learning*, Part 1, Forty-First Yearbook of the National Society for the Study of Education (Chicago: University of Chicago Press, 1942), p. 176. Reproduced by permission.

Fundamental to a cognitive field theory of learning is the proposition that the individual confers form, configuration, and meaning on what he perceives. A basic law of Gestalt psychology is the law of *Pragnanz*, which states that a person will impose order on a disorganized perceptual field in a predictable way, a way that produces "good" Gestalts—images that are simple and symmetrical.

Motivational dynamics in Gestalt learning are inferred in the law of *closure*, which states that an individual will seek to complete an open or incomplete figure or design. Thus, he will "see" a 330-degree arc as a circle and a silhouette as a person even when details of face and body are missing. Achieving completeness, or closure, is satisfying, whereas lack of completion is accompanied by tension and dissatisfaction. Closure represents a goal or end toward which the individual is striving as he seeks to perceive unity, completeness, and stability in the objects and events he encounters.

Another concept emphasized in Gestalt psychology is insight—the "sudden flash" that occurs when an individual successfully grasps the key to a problem which previously baffled him. Evidence that learning occurs only when the learner has achieved insight into the problem was obtained initially by Kohler in a series of experiments with chimpanzees.[30] In these experiments, hungry chimpanzees in a cage had to devise a way to reach a banana placed just beyond their reach. In one experiment, the chimps could solve the problem by using a stick or standing on a box. In other experiments, the solution was made more difficult—the chimpanzee was required to place one box on top of another or to fit two sticks together in order to reach the banana. In reporting these experiments, Kohler emphasized that the solution always seemed to come to the chimpanzee abruptly, as a flash of insight that occurred when relations were perceived in the entire perceptual field. These successful responses, occurring as flashes of insight, tended to be permanent and to carry over to later experiences.

Gestalt theory appears to be most relevant in explaining the cognitive types of learning in Gagné's taxonomy. Recognizing a type of aircraft by its silhouette or grasping the key to a puzzle requires that one distinguish between many different stimuli resembling one another in physical appearance—an example of type 5 (multiple discrimination) learning. Acquiring the key to a problem usually involves the learning of a new concept (type 6, concept learning), as, for instance, the chimps learned to "lengthen their arms" in order to obtain food. The solution to most problems involves the development and application of principles exemplified by type 7 (principle) and type 8 (problem-solving) learning.

Lewin's Topological Psychology

While the early Gestaltists focused upon the structure and properties of perceptual configurations and on learning by insight, Kurt Lewin (1890–1947)[31] gave his attention to the individual's subjective structuring of his field and to the psychological variables which influence this structuring. Thus, Lewin's field theory comes close to merging learning theory (how

---

[30] Wolfgang Kohler, *The Mentality of Apes*, trans. by Ella Winter (New York: Harcourt Brace Jovanovich, 1927).

[31] See Kurt Lewin, *Principles of Topological Psychology* (New York: McGraw-Hill Book Co., 1935).

learning takes place) and personality theory (why the individual behaves as he does).

A basic construct of Lewin's theory is that of life space (Lewin's name for cognitive field), the individual's world of reality. *Life space* can be defined as the totality of facts and events which determines one's behavior at any given time. Conceptually and graphically, one's life space is represented as a two-dimensional area containing the person himself, the goals he is striving to achieve, the "negative" goals he is striving to avoid, the forces which push him toward or away from goals, and the paths he can take to achieve his goals. Lewin used the term *topology* (a nonmetrical geometry of spaces which includes such concepts as "inside," "outside," and "boundary") to describe his psychology because he believed that the person-environment relationship could best be presented as topological space.

Life space, a person's psychological space, may or may not include elements of his physical or geographical environment. A person, for example, may be unaware of slow-growing cancer in his body. The cancer is physically present but is not represented in his life space. On the other hand, a person may believe he has cancer though all tests for cancer are negative. In this case, cancer is physically absent but is very much present in the person's life space. His perception of his having cancer will influence his behavior; he may give up his job, go from clinic to clinic for diagnosis and treatment, or bemoan his fate. Thus, a fundamental principle of Lewin's theory is that behavior at the time it occurs is determined by the person's life space. This principle and the main constructs of Lewin's system are illustrated in Figure 15–6, a topological representation of Peter in a classroom situation in which he is required to read.

In Figure 15–6, Peter (P) must improve his reading $(-Rdg)$ in order to pass to the next grade $(+G)$. A is the point at which movement can be initiated. The symbols prefixed $_fA+$ represent forces acting at point A to

Figure 15–6.   Topological Representation of the Life Space of Boy P Whose Goal of Passing to the Next Grade Requires That He Improve in His Reading

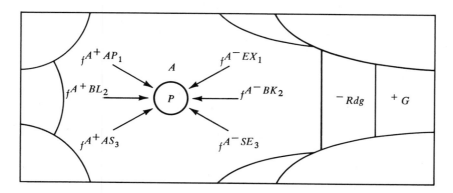

push Peter toward the goal, while symbols prefixed $_fA-$ represent negative forces acting at point A to push him away from the goal. Positive forces (on the left) include $+AP_1$, love and approval of parents, which Peter can maintain by success in school; $+BL_2$, belonging in the peer group, which he can maintain if he is promoted with his class; and $+AS_3$, the aspiration to be admitted to a good technical school to pursue his long-time goal of studying electronics. Negative forces (on the right) include $-EX_1$, past experiences in reading, in which Peter has done poorly; $-BK_2$, the uninteresting stories and books he is required to read; and $-SE_3$, the low self-esteem he feels with respect to reading and to academic situations in general. Peter's locomotion, or movements, in relation to reading and passing to the next grade will depend upon the resolution of the vectors of forces, represented by arrows.

It appears that Peter's responses in this situation will depend largely on perceptual and cognitive types of learning. In making some progress in his reading, he has learned that the same printed word symbol often has different meanings (Gagné's type 5—multiple discrimination—learning). He responds to clearly formed concepts of "reading," "promotion," "teacher," "parents," "approval," "education," and "electronics" (type 6, concept learning). Finally, the movements Peter makes in dealing with the issue of improving his reading are likely to involve type 3, type 7, and type 8 (chaining, principle, and problem-solving) learning.

Lewin's theory provided the impetus for important breakthroughs in behavioral science research. The influence of his ideas on the development of phenomenological self theory and on investigations of social-emotional climate, group behavior, and learning have been substantial. Discussions of these influences appear elsewhere in this book.

Bruner and Cognitive Learning

Much of the impetus for continuing the ideas and work of Gestalt psychologists and of Lewin is to be found in the areas of perceptual psychology and cognitive learning. Jerome Bruner's contributions in both of these areas have important implications for classroom learning. Like the field theorists who regard learning as a restructuring of thought patterns, Bruner stresses the importance of structure in promoting cognitive learning. Much of school learning, especially the academic subjects such as English, mathematics, science, social studies, and foreign languages, is cognitive in nature; that is, these subjects require the student to learn facts, concepts, and principles and to utilize them in thinking and problem-solving activities. As the student progresses through school, the language skills of speaking, reading, and writing are important tools for increasing cognitive learning. Bruner believes that the key to understanding a field of knowledge lies in the student's *grasping the underlying principles that give meaning and structure to that subject*. He cites four advantages of focusing upon structure in studying a subject:

1. *Understanding the fundamentals makes a subject more comprehensible.*

2. *Structuring information facilitates retention. Unless details are organized into a pattern, they are rapidly forgotten.*

3. *Understanding fundamental principles and ideas facilitates their transfer to new situations.*

4. *Structuring information enables one to narrow the gap between elementary and advanced knowledge.*[32]

Bruner also contends that the learner is more likely to acquire a better understanding of facts, concepts, and principles if he has discovered them for himself than if he has read about them or has had the material explained to him. In *discovery learning* the key concepts and principles of what is to be learned are not given but must be independently discovered by the learner, and then he must rearrange this information and integrate it into his cognitive structure (fund of knowledge) in relation to its personal meaning for him.

The efficacy of independent discovery methods in promoting school learning has been hotly debated by psychologists and educators. Bruner[33] suggests four advantages of learning by discovery:

1. *Discovery learning increases the learner's ability to learn related material.*

2. *It fosters an interest in the activity itself rather than in rewards which follow from the activity.*

3. *It develops one's ability to approach problems in a way more likely to lead to a solution.*

4. *It aids memory in making material that is learned easier to retrieve or to reconstruct.*

It may be recalled that a study by Kersh[34] cited in Chapter 3 appears to support the claim that discovery learning promotes intrinsic motives when the learner pursues his interest in a topic for its own sake rather than for a grade. The findings of other studies, including a later study by Kersh,[35] on the other claims for discovery learning are equivocal.

[32] Jerome S. Bruner, *The Process of Education* (Cambridge, Mass.: Harvard University Press, 1960), pp. 23–26.

[33] Jerome S. Bruner, "The Act of Discovery," *Harvard Educational Review*, 31 (1961), 21–32.

[34] See pp. 76–77.

[35] Bert Y. Kersh, "The Motivating Effect on Learning by Directed Discovery," *Journal of Educational Psychology*, 53 (1962), 65–71.

Both Skinner and D. P. Ausubel have offered criticisms of discovery learning. Skinner[36] focuses on the practical problems which the teacher faces in using discovery methods. Should the teacher pretend that he himself does not know? Or, for the purpose of encouraging joint ventures in discovery, is the teacher to teach only those things he himself has not yet learned? If the teacher is to be responsive to the learning needs of all the students in the class, how are a few good students to be prevented from making all the discoveries? Ausubel[37] suggests that the real job of schools is to develop more efficient and appropriate ways of selecting, organizing, and presenting significant knowledge to students so that they can retain it meaningfully. We shall examine next Ausubel's ideas on how this knowledge can be acquired.

Ausubel and Meaningful Verbal Learning

While Bruner favors discovery learning for increasing cognitive development, Ausubel[38] believes that cognitive development is more likely to be achieved through *reception learning*, that is, through the learner's internalizing information which has been selected, organized, and presented by lectures, textbooks, or programed instruction. Both Bruner and Ausubel, however, are in fairly close agreement in their emphasis upon organizing and structuring the verbal material to be learned and upon structuring the cognitive processes of the learner. As noted earlier, Bruner believes that the learning of any discipline (such as English or biology) is facilitated if the learner is able to grasp the underlying principles that give meaning and structure to that subject. Ausubel contends that it is the way in which information is organized in the learner's cognitive structure that determines how well new material is learned and retained. The individual's cognitive structure is simply the organization, stability, and clarity of his knowledge at a given time.

Ausubel's cognitive theory seeks to explain how the individual learns and retains meaningful but unfamiliar concepts. An object or an idea has meaning, according to Ausubel, when it elicits a mental image that is equivalent to the object. Similarly, a concept acquires increased meaning (through familiarity) after it has been retained in the mind. Thus, for an external stimulus or concept to have meaning, there must be some mental image within the learner to which it can be related. One's cognitive structure consists of the totality of these more or less stable concepts, which are organized in a hierarchy with the most general, inclusive, abstract concepts

---

[36] B. F. Skinner, *The Technology of Teaching* (New York: Appleton-Century-Crofts, 1968), pp. 110–111.

[37] David P. Ausubel, "Learning by Discovery: Rationale and Mystique," *Bulletin of the National Association for Secondary School Principals*, 45 (December 1961), 18–58.

[38] David P. Ausubel, *The Psychology of Meaningful Verbal Learning* (New York: Grune and Stratton, 1963).

at the apex of the hierarchy and the most specific, highly differentiated concepts at the base of the hierarchy. Ausubel contends that in teaching specific meaningful but unfamiliar verbal material, one should relate it to a more general, inclusive concept in the learner's cognitive structure hierarchy. Thus, before one can understand the process of glycolysis or other biochemical changes in digestion and circulation, he must first have acquired more general, inclusive concepts such as "metabolism."

This process of organizing specific concepts under more general, inclusive, higher order concepts is called *subsumption*. To subsume is to incorporate meaningful material into one's existing cognitive structure. When one subsumes, he learns. The meaningfulness of what is learned depends upon the appropriateness and adequacy of the subsumers. A subsumer is appropriate in the degree to which the material being learned can be subsumed under it. If the material is totally unfamiliar, the learner lacks a subsumer under which it can be placed. *Glycolysis* would be a meaningless term if one lacked the more inclusive concept "metabolism" or some other appropriate subsumer. Thus, if the students do not already possess appropriate subsumers (which Ausubel also calls "advance organizers"), Ausubel recommends that these be presented to them before they are introduced to new, more specific or more specialized concepts.

Applications of Cognitive Field Theories

Since cognitive field theories relate more directly to the verbal and cognitive content of school learning, they offer a number of applications to learning in the classroom. From the preceding discussion we can expect the application of cognitive field theories to center on figure-ground and whole-part relationships, differentiations of perceptual field and life space, discovery learning, and the structuring of content and the learner's cognitions. Because of the central role of the learner's goals, purposes, and cognitions in cognitive field learning, it is evident, too, that the teacher's knowledge of his students is much more crucial in promoting cognitive learning than it is in the case of stimulus-response learning.

Whole-part and insight learning. Figure-ground relationships and principles of perception derived from Gestalt psychology point to a fundamental truth about many kinds of psychomotor and cognitive learning: In these areas learning is facilitated by moving from the whole task to part to restructured whole. Thus, if one applies the whole-part-whole principle to learning a piano piece or memorizing a poem, he would play or read through the whole piece or poem and note its broad outline or tempo and rhythm and its general structure. Next, parts of the whole would be identified for analysis and practice. The final step would be to integrate the individual parts into a restructured whole rendition of the piano piece or recitation of the poem. Similar steps would be followed in perfecting one's golf swing, tennis serve, or swimming stroke.

Learning by insight appears to have important applications to classroom learning. After showing children how to find the area of a rectangle by dividing the rectangle into small squares, Wertheimer asked the children to find the area of a parallelogram.[39] One child, seeing that the projecting ends of the parallelogram made the problem more difficult, asked for scissors, cut off one end, and fitted it against the other end, thus making the parallelogram into a rectangle. Another child achieved the same result by bending the parallelogram into a ring, so that the two ends fit together, and then cutting the ring vertically to make a rectangle. Each child's insight into the correct relationship between two geometric figures enabled him to achieve a solution through a restructuring of the problem. Each child changed the parallelogram into a better Gestalt.

Insight learning can be observed in a broad range of problem-solving tasks encountered in school, such as unraveling the plot or analyzing the motives of characters in a novel, play, or short story, solving problems in math or physics, and identifying cells under a microscope. Insight learning plays an increasingly important role in students' attainment of higher level cognitive learning objectives, such as analysis, synthesis, and evaluation. Learning by insight is more efficient than rote or trial and error learning because it allows for more rapid learning and greater retention and is more readily transferred to new situations.

Discovery learning.   Bruner[40] describes an application of discovery learning in social studies as follows:

> *One experiment which I can report provides encouragement. It was devised and carried out by the research group with which I am associated at Harvard in collaboration with teachers in the fifth grade of a good public school. It is on the unpromising topic of the geography of the North Central States and is currently in progress so that I cannot give all of the results. We hit upon the happy idea of presenting this chunk of geography not as a set of knowns, but as a set of unknowns. One class was presented blank maps, containing only tracings of the rivers and lakes of the area as well as the natural resources. They were asked as a first exercise to indicate where the principal cities, . . . railroads, and . . . main highways would be located. Books and maps were not permitted and "looking up the facts" was cast in a sinful light. Upon completing this exercise, a class discussion was begun in which the children attempted to justify why the major city would be here, a large city there, a railroad on this line, etc.*
>
> *The discussion was a hot one. After an hour and much plead-*

---

[39] Max Wertheimer, *Productive Thinking* (New York: Harper & Row, 1945), p. 48.

[40] Jerome S. Bruner, "Learning and Thinking," *Harvard Educational Review*, 29 (1959), 184–192. Reprinted by permission.

Figure 15–7.   A Partial List in Hierarchical Form of the Most General and Inclusive Concepts (Advance Organizers) in Biology

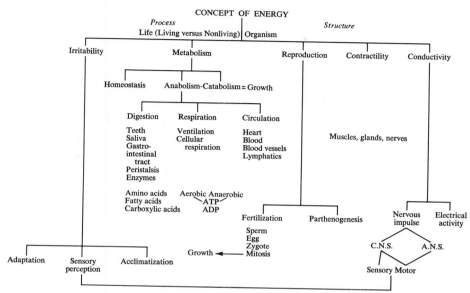

ing, permission was given to consult the rolled up wall map. I will never forget one young student, as he pointed his finger at the foot of Lake Michigan, shouting, "Yipee, Chicago is at the end of the point-ing-down lake." And another replying, "Well, OK: but Chicago's no good for the rivers and it should be here where there is a big city [St. Louis]." These children were thinking, and learning was an instru-ment for checking and improving the process. To at least a half dozen children in the class it is not a matter of indifference that no big city is to be found at the junction of Lake Huron, Lake Michigan, and Lake Ontario. They were slightly shaken up transportation theorists when the facts were in.

The children in another class, taught conventionally, got their facts all right, sitting down, benchbound. And that was that. . . . One group learned geography as a set of rational acts of induction—that cities spring up where there is water, where there are natural re-sources, where there are things to be processed and shipped. The other group learned passively that there were arbitrary cities at arbi-trary places by arbitrary bodies of water and arbitrary sources of supply. One learned geography as a form of activity. The other stored some names and positions as a passive form of registration.

Cognitive structure and verbal learning.   As described in an earlier sec-tion, Ausubel contends that an individual's existing cognitive structure—the organization, stability, and clarity of his knowledge at a given time—is the principal factor influencing his learning and retention of new material. Ausubel hypothesizes that a student will have difficulty learning unfamiliar concepts if he has not acquired the more general, inclusive, and overarching concepts under which the unfamiliar concepts can be grouped and related. Figure 15–7 presents in hierarchical form a partial list of the most general and inclusive concepts in biology which a student should have before he is introduced to more specific concepts and content. For example, it is important for the student to know and understand the general concepts of energy, life processes, reproduction, fertilization, differentiation, growth, and enzyme before he is introduced to the more specific concepts of gene, chromosome, DNA, mitosis, meiosis, and centriole. If the student does not already possess the more general, inclusive concepts (which Ausubel calls "advance organizers"), Ausubel recommends that he be given them before he is introduced to new, more specific or more specialized concepts.

Summary

Learning is a universal, lifelong process in which individuals modify their behavior in coping with and adapting to their environment. Capacity for learning and the importance of learning in the life of the species increase with the greater complexity of organization of higher animals. For man, the highest form of animal life, learned responses constitute the overwhelming majority of his behavioral repertoire.

Learning is both a process and a product. Learning has been defined as a modification of behavior as the result of experience or training. A useful distinction can be drawn between the term *performance*, what the learner does, and the term *learning*, which must always be inferred from performance.

A general model of learning useful in any study of the learning process consists of three sets of variables: *stimulus* or *situation* variables; *organism* variables, internal processes or events which intervene between stimulus and response; and *response* variables, overt and covert activities which relate to conditions of stimulation. Each learning theory tends to emphasize and to elaborate on certain interrelationships within the situation-organism-response model in preference to other interrelationships within the model.

Scientific learning theories and systems of psychology can be roughly classified under two broad headings: *stimulus-response theories* and *cognitive field theories*. In general, S-R theorists hold that the learner is essentially passive, that his behavior is controlled by internal and external forces. Cognitive field theorists, on the other hand, believe that the learner's own purposes, motives, perceptions, and cognitions influence and are influenced by interactions with the psychological environment.

A growing recognition by psychologists that there are several different types of learning, each of which appears to fit one kind of learning theory more readily than others, has resulted in several attempts to produce a taxonomy of learning types. One such taxonomy, developed by Robert M. Gagné, identifies and describes eight types of learning, each of which requires a different set of conditions. Types 1 (signal), 2 (stimulus-response), 3 (chaining), and 4 (verbal association) exemplify stimulus-response association learning; types 5 (multiple discrimination), 6 (concept), 7 (principle), and 8 (problem solving) are explained more readily by cognitive field theories of learning.

Stimulus-response learning emphasizes *conditioning,* a type of learning which occurs when one or more stimuli (S) are connected or strengthened through association with one or more responses (R). Learning acquired through conditioning is of two types: classical conditioning and operant conditioning.

In *classical conditioning* a stimulus occurs in the presence of a response that it does not ordinarily elicit and, through becoming linked to the response, acquires the property of eliciting that response. Classical conditioning relates to the conditioning of reflexes, such as the salivation in dogs studied by Pavlov, as well as responses controlled by the autonomic nervous system, such as feelings and emotions. The applications of classical conditioning center in the extinction of fears and phobias through the elimination of the unconditioned stimulus. Some fears involving antipathy toward a particular classroom activity such as reading may through *reinforcement* become generalized and transfered to a large number of stimuli and events.

A second class of behaviors that can be conditioned are those which are not elicited by any known stimuli but are simply emitted by the organism. Emitted behavior is sometimes called instrumental behavior, but more frequently it is known as operant behavior because it is behavior that operates in the environment. In *operant conditioning,* reinforcement is presented after the emitting of an operant (response), and this increases the probability of the response's recurring. Both positive and negative reinforcers serve to condition operants. Secondary reinforcers (such as praise or money), because they are much more numerous and adaptable than primary reinforcers (food), are especially important in facilitating human learning. In general, operants conditioned by intermittent reinforcement are more resistant to extinction than are those conditioned by continuous reinforcement. Through shaping, reinforcing behavior through a series of approximations, both animals and humans can be conditioned to perform complex acts that are not in their immediate response repertoire.

Operant conditioning has been applied to a broad range of behavior and learning problems involving both animals and humans in a variety of contexts. A direct application of operant conditioning to education is the development of programed instructional materials. Undesirable behavior can be extinguished by techniques of operant conditioning called *behavior modification* or *behavioral therapy.* Reinforcement procedures have also been used to improve the academic performance of individuals and groups of students. The use of reinforcement contingencies seems to be most effective in changing behavior where the performance criterion is quite specific and where the need for and reliance on external guidance and control for modifying behavior is very great.

Cognitive field theories of learning, with their emphasis on perception, cognition, goals, and personal meaning, offer a view of learning which contrasts sharply with that of the stimulus-response theorists. A fundamental proposition of cognitive field theory is that the individual confers form, configuration, and meaning on what he perceives. Learning, according to Gestalt theory, requires the learner to achieve insight into the solution of the problem. Insight, achieved when the individual successfully grasps the key to a previously baffling problem, may occur quite suddenly.

Kurt Lewin expanded cognitive field theory by drawing into it the psychological variables which influence the structuring of one's cognitive field. A key construct in Lewin's theory is the individual's *life space*, the totality of facts and events which determines the individual's behavior at any given time.

Jerome Bruner describes how cognitive learning can be increased through helping the student grasp the underlying principles which give meaning and structure to the subject being studied. He also contends that the learner will acquire a better understanding of facts, concepts, and principles if he discovers them for himself than if he reads about them or has them explained to him. B. F. Skinner and D. P. Ausubel offer criticisms of *discovery learning*, citing in its stead the advantages of *reception learning*. Ausubel describes how unfamiliar meaningful verbal material can be learned more easily and better if it is organized under more general, inclusive, higher order concepts, which he calls "subsumers" or "advance organizers".

Cognitive field theories offer many applications for classroom learning. Psychomotor and cognitive learning is facilitated by focusing on the whole task, analyzing the parts, and finally restructuring the whole. Insight learning plays an increasingly important role in the study of most school subjects and in higher cognitive processes. Discovery learning enables students to learn concepts inductively instead of receiving information in predigested form. Verbal learning, as Ausubel suggests, is more likely to be learned and retained if the learner acquires and uses general and inclusive concepts under which he can organize and relate new verbal material.

Study Questions

1. Describe two or three examples of the best teaching you have ever observed. Identify the common elements in each. What theories of learning were being employed?

2. Nick Rogers, a seven-year-old in the second grade, shows a strong dislike for reading. He stays away from the reading circle, avoids all books, even picture books, and feigns a headache when it is time for his group to read. Mrs. Nichols, his teacher this year, learned from his mother that Nick was late in starting to read last year. Last year's teacher sometimes became impatient with Nick when he was

unable to recognize a word that he had just read a moment before. His father became concerned about his slow progress in reading and ordered that Nick read for him every night. If you were Mrs. Nichols, how would you work with Nick to bring about a change in his attitude and his feelings about reading? What principles of learning would you seek to apply?

3. Elsie Kramer has a special education class of retarded learners aged nine to 12. Ted and Phil, two of the larger boys, make it difficult for the other children to do their work because of their loud talking and walking around the room. Elsie has scolded them and tried a variety of punishments, but their disturbing behavior seems to persist. If you were Elsie, what strategy would you use to change Ted's and Phil's behavior?

4. Forrest Lee, a high school junior, does well on tests in science, history, and English which ask for a recall of facts that were presented in class or in the text, but he does poorly on essay tests which ask him to contrast the style of two writers or to discuss the interrelationships between the Industrial Revolution and colonialism in Europe during the eighteenth century. What strategy would you devise for helping Forrest to improve his performance on essay-type discussion questions?

Suggested Readings

Bigge, Morris L. *Learning Theories for Teachers.* Second Edition. New York: Harper & Row, 1972. Presents in Socratic form a comprehensive review of current psychological learning theories. Contrasts stimulus-response and cognitive field theories in general and analyzes the contributions of each to learning and teaching.

Bruner, Jerome S. *The Process of Education.* Cambridge, Mass.: Harvard University Press, 1960. Report of the Woods Hole conference of scientists, scholars, and educators who met in 1959 to discuss how education in science might be improved in primary and secondary schools. The report suggests that the key to improving school learning lies in structuring the content of material to be taught, improving readiness for learning, encouraging intuitive methods of thinking, and stimulating in students an interest in learning for its own sake.

Bugelski, B. R. *The Psychology of Learning Applied to Teaching.* Second Edition. Indianapolis: Bobbs-Merrill Co., 1971. Examines the major stimulus-response learning theories and points out succinctly the applications of each for classroom learning. The latter half of the book focuses upon recurring issues in learning: attention, reinforcement, forgetting, extinction, transfer, and understanding, as well as the development of some of the newer technological and instructional media.

Gagné, Robert M. *The Conditions of Learning.* Second Edition. New York: Holt, Rinehart and Winston, 1970. Describes eight types of learning, from simple signal stimulus-response learning to complex problem solving. The eight varieties of learning are fundamental in the development of hierarchical learning sets. These sets identify the goals and sequential learning steps required for learning a skill or concept.

Hilgard, Ernest R., ed. *Theories of Learning and Instruction.* Part 1, Sixty-Third Yearbook of the National Society for the Study of Education. Chicago: University of Chicago Press, 1964. Reviews the contributions and implications of historical stimulus-response and cognitive field theories to education. Considers the role of motivation, readiness, creative thinking, programmed instruction, and other issues in learning and instruction.

Skinner, B. F. *The Technology of Teaching.* New York: Appleton-Century-Crofts, 1968. Eleven essays which describe the role and applications of operant learning principles in facilitating human learning. Describes the use of teaching machines in classroom learning, why teachers fail, and the conditions which enhance and limit school learning.

Films

Focus on Behavior: Learning about Learning, 16 mm, sound, black and white, 30 min. Bloomington: Audiovisual Center, Indiana University. Describes the approaches used by Skinner, Harlow, Spence, and the Kendlers in developing new theoretical concepts about man's ability to learn.

Learning through Inquiry, 16 mm, sound, color, 22 min. Melbourne, Fla. 32901: Institute for Development of Educational Activities, P.O. Box 446. Explains the way in which the excitement of inquiry can be employed to facilitate a youngster's learning. Emphasizes learning by all students through direct observation and involvement of factual and human phenomena. Assists teachers in increasing their knowledge of techniques of inquiry.

Teaching Machines and Programmed Learning, 16 mm, sound, black and white, 28 min. Bloomington: Audiovisual Center, Indiana University. Presents B. F. Skinner, A. A. Lumsdaine, and Robert Glaser as each discusses teaching machines and programed learning. Skinner identifies the main features and rationale behind the use of teaching machines. Lumsdaine discusses various types of machines and current trends in programed material. Glaser describes the impact of programed learning upon the whole educational system.

Readiness for Learning

16

Feed the growing human being, feed him with the sort of experience for which from year to year he shows a natural craving.

William James

Few educators doubt the importance of readiness in human development and learning. There is ample evidence from research and from everyday experience that pupils learn more quickly, efficiently, and effectively when they are ready for a learning experience.

Too often, however, teachers think of readiness as something that occurs prior to the learning activity itself. They assume that if a student is placed in a class or is registered for a course, he is able and ready to learn the concepts and skills he will encounter. Further, they assume that if a student has an average or higher than average IQ, he can learn. These assumptions are questionable. We know from our study of human development and learning that individuals differ in every aspect of their development—including their "readiness." Therefore, some students will require help from the teacher to develop readiness for the learning tasks which the school is expected to teach.

What is readiness? The term in general connotes the presence within the learner of requisite conditions for his effective learning. Attempts to develop more detailed definitions of the term have generated considerable confusion and controversy. Some people hold that readiness is solely an inner dynamic, a product of maturation; to these people, readiness is almost synonymous with maturation. Others believe that readiness is also influenced by environmental, experiential, and psychological variables. A related disagreement has arisen over whether the learner is always in a natural state of readiness or whether readiness is something that must be nourished and developed. Bruner appears to feel that children are always ready to learn; in a frequently quoted statement, he says that "any subject can be taught effectively in some intellectually honest form to any child at any stage of development."[1] However, the view that readiness is a quality that requires development appears to enjoy wider acceptance.

---

[1] Jerome S. Bruner, *The Process of Education* (Cambridge, Mass.: Harvard University Press, 1960), p. 33.

For our purposes, we will define a learner's readiness in any situation as *the sum of his characteristics which make his behavior amenable to change.* One's readiness for learning depends on the interplay of dynamic processes described in Chapters 3 through 9: one's physical maturity and development; his experiences with adults and peers and his culture in general; and his needs, goals, learned ideas, skills, emotions, and adjustive patterns.

The student's state of readiness, then, is not the same from day to day but changes with increased maturation and added learning and experience. A student's readiness for some activities and skills may decrease, while his readiness for others may increase. For example, the child's readiness for boy-girl relationships is probably greater at ages six and 14 than at age 10. On the other hand, his readiness for baseball is probably greater at age 10 than at either six or 14.

Principles of Readiness

Cronbach[2] cites four principles that influence the development of readiness. First, *all aspects of development interact.* We might add that all aspects of development are also interrelated. We noted in Chapter 4, for example, that Betty Burroughs' early physical maturation contributed to her view of herself as out of place in the ninth grade, but gave her a readiness for interacting and learning with older adolescents. In Chapter 8, the case of Becky showed that an inadequate self-concept can influence intellectual development and achievement. Chapters 11 through 14 emphasized the serial appearance and interrelatedness of developmental tasks. Similarly, the development of affectional relationships in early life prepares the individual for satisfying peer relationships at a later age.

Second, *physiological maturing prepares one to profit from experience.* The need to have the physical maturation requisite for a specific learning is self-evident. An individual's readiness, however, is a result of both physical change and learning. One does not automatically begin to walk or read as soon as he is physically mature enough. Many trials, successes, and failures must occur before these activities are mastered.

Third, *experiences have a cumulative effect.* Successes or failures at earlier stages of development usually have a direct influence on related aspects of later development. A child's success in sports, his fascination with history, or his curiosity about stars and planets in elementary school provides him with a predisposition toward and a readiness for experiences and satisfactions in sports or in the study of history or astronomy in high school or college. Conversely, failure or lack of satisfaction in certain activi-

[2] Lee J. Cronbach, *Educational Psychology,* 2nd ed. (New York: Harcourt Brace Jovanovich, 1962), p. 89.

ties lessens one's readiness for those activities and leads him to avoid them on subsequent occasions.

Finally, *basic readiness for a particular activity is established during certain formative periods of life.* This principle suggests that there is an optimum time for initiating most learning tasks, a "teachable moment."[3] The formative period for the establishment of readiness for a physical skill, for instance, is age one to four; the formative period for the development of attitudes about one's intellectual ability is the first year or two of school, when success, failure, or conflict influences reactions to all subsequent schooling.[4]

Dimensions of Readiness

Maturation

Initially, the term *maturation* was used by geneticists and embryologists to designate the period of development in which an immature germ cell is converted into a mature one. This significant change, called meiosis, produces a reduction of chromosomes, so that a mature ovum or sperm has only half as many chromosomes as immature germ cells and other body cells. This quite specific definition has given way to more generalized and sometimes ambiguous and confusing usage by behavioral scientists. As a result, the term is now applied indiscriminately to different kinds of maturity—physical, sexual, skeletal, social, emotional, and mental. Furthermore, some of these types of maturation are difficult to assess. For instance, although physical maturation can be measured fairly reliably (by level of bone ossification in comparison to norms, chronological age at menarche, or the appearance and measurement of secondary sex characteristics), there is far less agreement about *social* or *emotional maturity.* At best, these terms refer to a score or percentile derived from a test of undetermined validity; more often, they reflect subjective assessments of some individuals by other individuals.

The terms *maturity* and *maturation* also imply the attainment of some end point or final goal, which is accompanied by the cessation of processes of growth and development. This notion too is somewhat misleading; for, as we have tried to show, the human being is an open, dynamic energy system which moves toward optimum development, a development that is limited only by the individual's capacities, his opportunities, and his level of organization (physiological and psychological). Maturation, therefore, is an open-ended process, and *maturity* is a relative rather than an absolute term.

---

[3] Robert J. Havighurst, *Human Development and Education* (New York: David McKay Co., 1953), p. 5.

[4] Cronbach, p. 90.

Maturation is not always clearly distinguishable from learning. *Maturation*, in the strict meaning of the term, refers to that process whereby behavior is modified as a result of the growth and development of physical structure. Learning, on the other hand, is the process by which behavior is originated or changed through practice or training. However, maturation and learning are interrelated processes; if an individual is not yet mature enough to learn a particular skill, practice and training alone will not enable him to learn it.

The negligible effect of practice in the absence of requisite maturation was demonstrated in a study by Gesell and Thompson,[5] who studied learning and maturation in two young girls, identical twins, labeled T and C. At the beginning of the study, the twins, at age 46 weeks, were essentially equal in all fields of behavior, including locomotion. Both were able to pull themselves to a standing position, to creep with equal facility, and to walk when held by two hands, and both were on the threshold of walking alone. Beginning at 46 weeks, twin T was given 10 minutes of stimulation and guidance every morning in stair climbing, creeping, pulling herself to a standing position, walking while holding on to a crib, and walking while holding on to the experimenter's hand. After the first three days of this training, the experimenter enticed T to climb as many steps as possible. Twin C was given no specific training until she was 53 weeks old.

At 52 weeks of age (after T had had six weeks of training), the twins were equal in creeping ability and expressed an equal eagerness to stand. T, however, was slightly better than C in standing alone momentarily and in lowering her body. At this time, C made an initial attempt to climb the stairs, while T could already climb them (in 26 seconds). The following week (when the twins were 53 weeks of age) twin C, although untrained, climbed the entire staircase, unassisted, in 45 seconds; the next day she did it in 40 seconds. Twin T had meanwhile reduced her time to 17 seconds.

Comparisons in the performances of the twins after T had had six weeks of training (at age 52 weeks) and C had had two weeks of training (at age 55 weeks) revealed that both climbed in a similar manner but that C climbed more rapidly. C also walked better than T when supported by one hand. Although T's training began seven weeks earlier and lasted three times as long (six weeks as opposed to two weeks), three weeks of added age nevertheless enabled C to surpass T in performance. Gesell and Thompson concluded that the maturity advantage of three weeks of age must have accounted for this superiority of C's performance.

The findings of this and other co-twin control studies suggest that maturation is a function of the passage of time and that practice given too early is likely to be ineffectual and in some cases detrimental. Although such indications of the importance of maturation in motor learning may not necessarily apply to cognitive learning, the idea of postponing practice until

[5] Arnold Gesell and Helen Thompson, "Learning and Maturation in Identical Infant Twins: An Experimental Analysis by the Method of Co-twin Control," in R. G. Barker, J. S. Kounin, and H. F. Wright, eds., *Child Behavior and Development* (New York: McGraw-Hill Book Co., 1943), pp. 209–227.

the child has attained the requisite level of maturity has nevertheless become a well accepted educational procedure.

A positive relationship between maturation and learning is also found among school children, as reported in the studies by Zeller and Simon cited in Chapter 4.[6] Zeller found that the young child with a less mature body figure formed by adipose tissue rather than muscles and joints was much less likely to be successful in school than a child with a more linear body outline in which muscles and arms and joints were clearly visible. Similarly, Simon found that first grade children who were less physically mature (as measured by indexes of head, waist, and leg circumference) were more likely to experience failure that children who were more physically mature.

Intelligence

Intelligence is another important aspect of readiness. Students assigned to a particular class are supposed to have sufficient intellectual aptitude to profit from that class. But how does a teacher know that all his students do have sufficient intellectual aptitude? To solve this dilemma, psychologists have tried to develop intelligence tests which discriminate between students who are most likely and students who are least likely to profit academically from school instruction. A pioneer in the development of such tests was Alfred Binet. In the early 1900s, Binet and his co-worker, Théodore Simon, developed a scale designed to measure complex functions of behavior, while avoiding measures of sensation and simple motor responses. In 1908, the Binet-Simon scale was brought to the United States and translated into English. Here it was modified, and from those modifications emerged the well-known Revised Stanford-Binet Scale. This is an individual test consisting of a series of tasks for each year from ages two to 14, followed by tasks for the levels of average and superior adult. Included in the scale are tasks which ask the testee to identify objects, to repeat digits from memory, to give the meaning of words, to identify verbal and pictorial absurdities, and to define abstract words. In early editions of the Revised Stanford-Binet Scale, the testee was given a score of so many months for each correct task completed at each year level. When added together, these scores yielded a *mental age* (MA), which corresponded to the performance of an average individual of that chronological age (CA). An individual's mental development (his intelligence quotient, or IQ) was determined by the following formula:

$$IQ = \frac{MA}{CA} \times 100.$$

That is, the individual's mental age is divided by his chronological age, and the result is multiplied by 100. More recently the IQ has been reported as

[6] See pp. 110–111.

the deviation IQ. The *deviation IQ* represents the extent to which an individual's score "deviates" from the mean of the standardization group which was tested in developing norms for the test. Although it is not based upon mental age, numerically the deviation IQ resembles the IQ score based on mental age. We need to remember that the IQ is never an absolute measure of intellectual aptitude but an indication of the rate at which the individual is achieving his intelligence. Thus, a five-year-old child with a mental age of eight would have an IQ of 160, whereas a 12-year-old child with the same mental age would have an IQ of 67.

Another individually administered intelligence test in common use is the Wechsler Intelligence Scale for Children (WISC), a series of performance (nonverbal) and verbal tests used throughout the age range. An individual's performance on the test yields a raw score which can be translated into an IQ score derived from the formula given above.

Individual tests, such as the Stanford-Binet and the Wechsler, permit the testing of only one individual by one examiner at a time. The individual test is frequently administered for the purpose of obtaining an accurate estimate of the intellectual aptitude of a student who has been referred by a teacher or school to psychological services for diagnosis of a learning or behavior problem. When properly administered, such a test yields a more valid measure of the rate of growth in intellectual aptitude than does a group test.

Group tests of intelligence were developed during World War I, when large numbers of recruits had to be classified and screened for various military jobs and assignments. The Army Alpha and Army Beta (nonlanguage) tests proved to be very successful for assessing the mental aptitudes of military personnel.

The period between the two world wars witnessed a tremendous growth in the development and use of standardized tests of all kinds. These tests yielded quantitative scores which were subjected to a variety of statistical treatments. The tremendous interest in education measurement gave rise in the 1920s and 1930s to what has been referred to as "the scientific movement in education." Numerous group intelligence, achievement, and other types of standardized tests were developed for use in elementary schools, high schools, and colleges. Some of these intelligence tests yield scores which are readily transformed into IQ scores; but a more common practice, especially in testing older students, has been to translate the raw test score into a percentile score. A person's percentile score indicates what percentage of the comparison group (such as eighth graders or college freshmen) received a lower score than he did. A comparison between IQ and percentile scores is shown in Table 16–1.

The reader may have noted that we have been discussing intelligence and intelligence testing for some pages without having defined the term *intelligence*. There have been many definitions of intelligence, but probably all are for one reason or another incomplete. In general, the term refers to one's capacities or abilities for learning. In discussing intelligence, Binet and Simon wrote, "To judge well, to comprehend well, to reason well, these

Table 16–1. A Guide for Interpreting IQ

IQ	Percentile Score	Prognosis or Interpretation
140	99	
130	96	
120	87	Likely to succeed in college
110	69	Level of median college entrant
100	50	Average of unselected population
90	23	Unlikely to complete traditional high school program
80	8	
70	3	

Source: Lee J. Cronbach, *Educational Psychology*, 2nd ed. (New York: Harcourt Brace Jovanovich, 1962), p. 192. Reproduced by permission.

are the essential activities of intelligence."[7] For Wechsler, who developed probably the most widely used individual intelligence scales for children and adults, "intelligence, operationally defined, is the aggregate or global capacity to act purposefully, to think rationally, and to deal effectively with the environment."[8]

Wechsler's definition identifies in very general terms the qualities of behavior which many would classify as "intelligent," but as a definition it falls short in at least two respects. First, its emphasis upon rational thinking seems to deny intelligence to animals below the level of primates, whereas, as Munn suggests, there appears to be "a more or less gradual transition from relatively simple sensorimotor learning of lower animals to higher types of symbolic processes exhibited by primates."[9] That is, intelligence is not an all-or-none affair; degrees of intelligence can be observed at all levels of animal life.

Second, studies of the structure of the intellect and of creativity (which will be discussed later) strongly suggest that there exist intellectual abilities and qualities which our present intelligence tests do not measure.[10] Consequently, in recent years psychologists have tended to avoid defining intelligence. Instead, they speak of intelligence as "that which the intelligence tests measure." While such a description may be realistic and practi-

---

[7] Alfred Binet and Théodore Simon, *The Development of Intelligence in Children*, trans. by Elizabeth S. Kite (Baltimore: Williams and Wilkins, 1916), p. 42.

[8] David Wechsler, *The Measurement and Appraisal of Adult Intelligence*, 4th ed. (Baltimore: Williams and Wilkins, 1958), p. 7.

[9] Norman L. Munn, *The Evolution and Growth of Human Behavior* (Boston: Houghton Mifflin Co., 1965), p. 409.

[10] J. P. Guilford, "Three Faces of Intellect," *The American Psychologist*, 14 (August 1959), 469–479.

cal, it, too, restricts the concept of intelligence to human beings, besides being vague.

The notion of fixed intelligence.   The view that one's IQ remains relatively constant throughout life permeated much of psychological and educational thinking during the first half of the twentieth century. Hunt[11] points out that this view was based on (1) the belief in fixed intelligence—that is, the belief that intelligence is an innate dimension of personal capacity which increases at a fixed rate to a predetermined level; and (2) the belief in predetermined development—that is, the belief that behavioral organizations unfold more or less automatically as a function of physical growth and development.

The belief in fixed intelligence was initially based upon the finding that IQ scores are relatively stable after age six or seven. The average difference between individual scores on a test at that age and scores on a test 15 months later is only 5 IQ points, although in a few cases the differences may be up to 25 or 30 points. Longitudinal studies carried out in Berkeley, California, by Honzik et al.[12] and Bayley[13] show that correlations between the IQ scores of the same individuals in early adulthood are about .9; however, when adult IQ scores are compared with the IQ scores of these same individuals at age seven, the correlation drops to .7. The near zero correlation between adult IQ scores compared with IQ scores on tests administered to the same individuals in infancy suggests that the tests may be measuring different aspects of intelligence (infancy scales include more nonverbal factors), or it may reflect the development in the individual of new intellectual structures at successive maturity levels. In addition, the early belief in the hereditary determination of intelligence scores seemed to be supported by the comparison of correlations between intelligence test scores of persons with different degrees of genetic relationship, ranging from .85 for identical twins to .50 for siblings and for parents and their children to zero for unrelated children.

The belief in fixed intelligence came under strong attack in the *nature versus nurture* controversy of the 1930s. There ensued spirited debate and feverish investigations by both those who contended that intelligence is inherited and fixed (nature) and those who believed that intelligence can be changed if a child is placed in a favorable and stimulating environment (nurture). An important line of research aimed at resolving this issue centered in studies that investigated IQ changes in identical twins who had been separated and reared apart. An early study by Newman, Freeman, and

---

[11] J. McV. Hunt, *Intelligence and Experience* (New York: Ronald Press, 1961).

[12] Marjorie P. Honzik, Jean W. Macfarlane, and L. Allen, "The Stability of Mental Test Performance between Two and 18 Years," *Journal of Experimental Education*, 16 (1948), 309–324.

[13] Nancy Bayley, "Consistency and Variability in Growth from Birth to 18 Years," *Journal of Genetic Psychology*, 75 (1949), 165–196.

Holzinger[14] found that the average IQ difference for 19 pairs of twins who were reared apart was 8.2 IQ points. This finding offers scant support for the view that the environment is a major determiner of IQ, since the average change in IQ over successive testings for the total population is 5 points. A more recent report[15] tends to confirm the finding of negligible effects of the environment in influencing the IQ scores of identical twins reared in separate homes. In this study 122 pairs of twins—all Caucasians living in England, Denmark, and the United States—had been separated by the age of six months. These 122 pairs of twins had a range in IQ from 63 to 132 and a mean IQ of 97. The IQs of one member of these identical twins correlated .85 with the IQs of a twin sibling reared in another home. This correlation is higher than would be expected of ordinary siblings or even fraternal twins growing up together with their own families. The relationship between the foster home environments of each pair of twins (as measured by the occupational level of the breadwinner) yielded a zero correlation. Thus, studies of identical twins reared apart strongly suggest that their similar IQ scores are most likely the result of shared inheritance, with environmental influence playing an indeterminant role.

Somewhat more support for the view that environment exerts a significant influence on IQ is revealed in a study by Skodak and Skeels,[16] which found that the IQs of children in foster homes were 20 points higher than the IQs of their natural mothers. The relationship between the fathers' and the children's IQs could not be determined. The unexpected boost in IQ of these children was presumably due to the better social environment provided by the foster families.

The long-term effects of better environments on the intellectual and personal development of a different group of adopted children are documented in a follow-up study by Skeels[17] 21 years after the initial study. In the original study, the 13 children in the experimental group, all mentally retarded at the beginning of the study, experienced the effects of early intervention which consisted of a shift to a different institutional environment that provided an increase in the amount of developmental stimulation and intensity of relationships between the children and mother surrogates. After a variable period in this new institutional environment, 11 of the 13 children were placed in adoptive homes. Over a period of two years, the children in the experimental group showed a marked increase in mental growth, making an average gain of 28.5 IQ points, while the control group showed an

[14] H. H. Newman, F. N. Freeman, and K. J. Holzinger, *Twins: A Study of Heredity and Environment* (Chicago: University of Chicago Press, 1937).

[15] A. R. Jensen, cited in Richard Herrnstein, "I.Q.," *The Atlantic Monthly,* 228 (September 1971), 44–64.

[16] Marie Skodak and Harold M. Skeels, "A Final Follow-Up Study of 100 Adopted Children," *Journal of Genetic Psychology,* 75 (1945), 85–125.

[17] Harold M. Skeels, "Adult Status of Children with Contrasting Early Life Experiences," *Monographs of the Society for Research in Child Development,* Vol. 31, No. 3, Serial No. 105 (1966).

average loss of 26.2 IQ points. Skeels's follow-up study 21 years later revealed that the two groups maintained their divergent patterns of development into adulthood. All 13 children in the experimental group were self-supporting, largely in professional or business occupations, or married and functioning as housewives. The members of the control group, in contrast, were employed in larger proportion in menial occupations. In educational level, the median for the experimental group was completion of the twelfth grade, while the median for the control group was completion of less than the third grade. The IQs of the 28 offspring of the experimental group ranged from 86 to 125, with no indication of mental retardation or demonstrable abnormality.

The substantial correlation between cultural groups and IQ provides further evidence of the presumed influence of environment on intellectual development. Occupational level is one indicator of social class status. The relationship between social class and IQ is suggested by a study which reports the range of and median scores on the Army General Classification Test received by several thousand army air force enlisted men during World War II by civilian occupation. The relative standing of representative occupational groups is shown in Figure 16–1. Note the range of scores for each occupation and the amount of overlap between occupations. Although relationships of this kind enable us to predict whether a person is likely to succeed in a given occupation, we cannot assume that the brighter persons within the occupation are the more successful ones. Success in any occupation depends upon a variety of factors, only one of which may be intellectual ability.

While the foregoing data seem to indicate that the quality of the environment determines the *level of intellectual functioning* a person may achieve, most researchers have concluded that the *potential for intellectual development* is largely determined by heredity.[18] It has been estimated that IQ differences among U. S. and northern European white populations arise far more from genetic differences than from present environmental differences. It has been known for many years that white lower class and black groups have lower IQs, on the average, than white middle class groups. Most behavioral scientists[19] were content to explain these group differences in IQ as due to environmental differences between the groups in standards of living and in educational and job opportunities.

Intelligence and race.   The calm engendered by this widely held belief was suddenly shattered in 1969 by the publication of a long, scholarly article by Arthur Jensen[20] in the *Harvard Educational Review* which posed the

[18] For a review of studies, see L. Erlenmeyer-Kinling and I. F. Jarvik, *Science*, 142 (1963), 1,477.

[19] For a review of studies of the relationship between intelligence and race, see Thomas Pettigrew, *A Profile of the Negro American* (Princeton, N. J.: D. Van Nostrand Co., 1964), pp. 100–135.

[20] Arthur R. Jensen, "How Much Can We Boost IQ and Scholastic Achievement?" *Harvard Educational Review*, 39 (Winter 1969), 1–117.

Figure 16–1. Army General Classification Test score in relation to civilian occupation. Vertical lines indicate median scores.

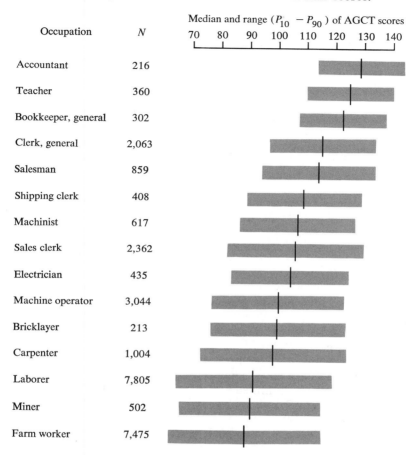

Source: A. Anastasi, *Differential Psychology*, 3rd ed. (New York: Macmillan Co., 1958), p. 516. Based on data from N. Stewart, "AGCT Scores of Army Personnel Grouped by Occupation," *Occupations*, 26 (1947), 5–41. Reprinted with permission of American Personnel and Guidance Association.

question "If individual differences in IQ within the white population as a whole can be attributed largely to heredity, is it not plausible that the average differences in IQ between social class groups and racial groups also reflect genetic differences?" Jensen raised this question as a way of suggesting one possible explanation for the disappointing results obtained by intervention and compensatory programs which had sought to reduce the experiential and language handicaps of disadvantaged black and white children. Many of the initial gains in IQ and language skills of Head Start children seemed to have disappeared when these children were tested in follow-up studies a year or two later. In view of the massive commitment of resources to improving the academic potential of disadvantaged students, Jensen contended that the discrepancy between their average and their expected performance cannot be completely or directly attributed to discrimination and inequalities of education. In the article he suggested that it is not unreasonable, in view of the fact that intelligence variation has a large genetic component, to hypothesize that genetic factors may play a part in accounting for IQ differences among groups.

The main thrust of Jensen's article is his contention that individuals with low IQs typically differ genetically from those with high IQs. He reiterates the well-established fact that the IQ test scores of blacks, on the average, are about 15 points below the average for whites. Similar discrepancies between blacks and whites are found in school achievement for grades one through 12. He cites one study which found that there was a much higher incidence of IQs below 75 among blacks than among whites at every socioeconomic level. In the two highest of these levels, the incidence among blacks was more than 13 times as high as for whites. Jensen believes that this finding supports his contention that there is a strong genetic component in intelligence; if environment is mainly responsible for IQ differences, one would expect to find a lesser white-black discrepancy at the upper socioeconomic levels. Finally, to buttress his argument, Jensen cites the Coleman report,[21] which found that in almost every way the environmental rating of American Indians is as far below the average for blacks as the latter is below that of whites. Yet, in tests of both ability and achievement, Indians average six to eight points above blacks.

Based on data from whites, Jensen estimates that the *heritability*—the proportion of the variation of a trait that is due to genetic factors—of IQ is about .80, or 80 percent. This estimate is very close to that made more than 35 years ago by Shuttleworth,[22] who estimated that the variation in tested IQ among schoolchildren is accounted for 75 percent by heredity, 21 percent by environment, and 4 percent by accidental factors. While most experts are in general agreement with this estimate of heritability of IQ for whites, no comparable estimate can be made for blacks because we do not know the heritability of IQ among blacks.

Jensen's hypothesis that the lower average intelligence and achievement of blacks is strongly influenced by genetic as well as environmental factors has generated heated debate. To propose genetically based racial and social class differences in IQ is anathema to most social scientists; they fear that the statements and misstatements emanating from a discussion of this issue may increase racial and ethnic prejudice and may further exacerbate hostile black-white feelings and relationships. Since the issue has been

[21] James S. Coleman et al., *Equality of Educational Opportunity* (Washington, D. C.: U. S. Department of Health, Education, and Welfare, 1966).

[22] Frank K. Shuttleworth, "The Nature versus Nurture Problem: II. The Contributions of Nature and Nurture to Individual Differences in Intelligence," *Journal of Educational Psychology*, 26 (1935), 655–681.

raised and projected into the public context of social and educational policies, a hard scientific look must be taken at what is known and what inferences can be drawn from that knowledge.

A main criticism of Jensen's hypothesis is that a statement concerning the genetic IQ differences between races is unwarranted at present. We
lack the information, conceptualization, and tools required for making a
definitive test of Jensen's hypothesis. Some have suggested, for example,
that one simply cannot make a hypothesis about genetic IQ differences between blacks and whites based upon an estimate of heritability of IQ for
whites only. Even if heritabilities of IQ are extremely high in all races, this
is no justification for equating within-group heritabilities (between parent
and offspring) and between-group heritabilities (between racial, ethnic, or
social class groups). Moreover, it is not known whether different racial
groups are equivalent in characteristics like IQ, and the differences in environments within and between races may have as yet unquantified effects.[23]

Other critics[24] suggest that at present a direct assault on the nature-
nurture problem of race differences in IQ is vulnerable to many criticisms.
Direct comparisons of estimated within-group heritabilities and the calculation of between-group heritabilities require assumptions that few investigators are likely to make. Many question, for example, whether all environmental differences are quantifiable, whether differences in environment
between blacks and whites can be assumed to affect IQ in the same way in
the two groups, or whether differences in environment between groups can
be statistically controlled. Scarr-Salapatek[25] suggests that indirect approaches to studying the problem may be more profitable. One could test,
for example, whether, if the population mean for blacks is 15 IQ points
lower than that for whites, the offspring of high-IQ black parents show
greater regression (toward a lower population mean) than the offspring of
whites with equally high IQs. Studies based on correlations between degree
of white admixture within the black group would avoid many of the pitfalls
of between-group comparisons.

Finally, how important is IQ anyway, whatever the degree of its
heritability? Jencks[26] points out that while intelligence scores are highly
correlated with school success as measured by achievement test scores and
school marks, men's IQs account for only 20 percent of the variance in
occupational status and 10 percent of the variance in incomes. Scarr-
Salapatek,[27] however, contends that heritability estimates may be useful in
predicting the results that can be expected from various types of interven-

[23] Sandra Scarr-Salapatek, "Unknowns in the IQ Equation," *Science*, 174 (December 17, 1971), 1,223–1,228.

[24] Walter F. Bodmer and Luigi L. Cavalli-Sforza, "Intelligence and Race," *Scientific American*, 223 (October 1970), 19–29.

[25] Scarr-Salapatek, pp. 1,223–1,228.

[26] Christopher Jencks, "What Color Is IQ? Intelligence and Race," *The New
Republic* (September 13, 1969).

[27] Scarr-Salapatek, pp. 1,223–1,228.

tion programs. If, for example, IQ tests which predict well achievement in the larger society show low heritabilities in the population, then simply providing better environments can be expected to improve average performance in that population. If, however, heritability of IQ is high and the environments sampled are largely favorable, then novel environmental programs are probably required to raise IQs and eugenic programs can be encouraged. Although at present we lack definitive information on the heritability of IQ, there is evidence that early intervention programs may be succeeding in raising IQs of some disadvantaged children. In one study described by Heber[28] ghetto children whose mothers' IQs were less than 70 were enrolled in an intervention program shortly after birth. Intensive tutoring of these children for several hours a day over a four-year period has produced an extremely large IQ difference between the experimental group (mean IQ 127) and a control group (mean IQ 90). If the tutored children maintain these gains in environments that are radically different from homes with retarded mothers, we will have some idea of what an optimum learning environment can accomplish in raising low IQs.

"Intelligence" and intelligence test scores.   It is important to distinguish between realized or effective intelligence (the intelligence that IQ tests in some degree measure) and the theoretical construct of native intelligence, for which we have no measure. An analogy has often been drawn between those two kinds of intelligence and one's inherited capacity for tallness *versus* his achieved height. Heredity not only sets the limits within which the individual may develop his physical attributes, but also determines the limits of his capacity for intellectual functioning. Realized intelligence is a measure of the extent to which one's inherited capacity for intellectual functioning has been achieved.

Our review of some of the issues and problems related to intelligence leads to the conclusion that educators need a balanced view when interpreting and using intelligence-test scores; either to ignore or to overrely on them is unwarranted. While intelligence is usually thought of in quantitative terms, we need to remember that it is not a substance or an entity within the organism. Rather, it is a *quality* of behavior and should always be interpreted as a descriptive term characterizing an action or an actor. Furthermore, any intelligence- or aptitude-test score is only an *estimate* of an individual's realized intelligence. Since an intelligence test samples performance on a limited number of intellectual abilities, any intelligence test score is subject to errors of sampling and measurement. Educators, therefore, should not rely on a single test score but should seek several independent measures of the student's intelligence. It is particularly unfortunate when parents or teachers view an IQ score as a fixed capacity rather than as an estimate of a student's rate of intellectual development. The story is told of a teacher who didn't try very hard with a boy whose IQ was

[28] R. Heber, *Rehabilitation of Families at Risk for Mental Retardation* (Madison: Regional Rehabilitation Center, University of Wisconsin, 1969).

87. She didn't feel guilty about her limited success in helping him to learn until she discovered that she had copied his locker number in the space intended for his IQ score. An IQ score is helpful in planning an educational program, but it should be used as only one of several estimates of a student's mental ability.

The preceding discussion suggests that the intellectual aptitudes of many children can be increased. There is a need to provide students with as stimulating and as enriched a learning environment as possible, for it is doubtful that the optimum intellectual abilities of our students are being realized in present educational programs. (This unrealized intellectual capacity appears to be most common among culturally disadvantaged children, a problem which will be considered in a later section of this chapter.) One should recall, too, that present intelligence tests, in sampling a child's verbal comprehension, word fluency, spatial relationships, and number and inductive abilities, measure only a few aspects of intellectual aptitude. Evidence of this is shown in the findings of Getzels and Jackson[29] in their study of a group of private school students whose average IQ was 132. They found that a number of children who scored in the top fifth in IQ did not score in the top fifth in creativity, while some in the top fifth in creativity were below the average IQ for that school.

Intellectual Development

Maturation level and intelligence test scores, by themselves, are no longer considered adequate indexes of readiness for learning. Previously cited studies which show that the IQs of many children can be increased by favorable home situations and enriched educational opportunities suggest that a child's *intellectual development*—his acquisition of modes and patterns of thinking in processing sensory data—may provide more useful clues to his readiness for learning than his IQ score. The concept of intellectual development focuses not only on the development and functioning of the somatic and cerebral structures involved in processing information, but also on the role of experience in the "development of those central organizations for the processing of information that are required to solve problems."[30]

A theory that conforms to this view of intelligence is Piaget's theory of intellectual development, which was described in detail in Chapters 11, 12, and 13. It will be recalled that Piaget identifies four stages of cognitive development which human beings pass through from birth to about 15 years of age. They are:

[29] Jacob W. Getzels and Philip W. Jackson, *Creativity and Intelligence* (New York: John Wiley, 1962).

[30] Hunt, p. 65.

1.   The period of sensorimotor intelligence (*birth–two years*). *The child does not yet "think" conceptually, but "cognitive" development can be observed.*

2.   The period of preoperational thought (*two–seven years*). *This period is characterized by the development of language and rapid conceptual development.*

3.   The period of concrete operations (*seven–11 years*). *During this period the child develops the ability to apply logical thought to* concrete *problems.*

4.   The period of formal operations (*11–15 years*). *During this period the child's cognitive structures reach their highest level of development, and the individual becomes able to apply logic to all classes of problems.*

Each stage of development carries with it possibilities for the acquisition of new abilities and new ways of processing information. Piaget hypothesizes that unless each of these abilities is used, it will not develop fully and will contribute little to the requirements of the next stage.

According to Piaget, cognitive structures called *schemata* are formed in the mind which enable the individual to adapt to and to organize his environment. Cognitive development occurs as schemata change, and this change may take place in two ways: (1) by *assimilation*, in which the person integrates new perceptual data into his existing schemata or cognitive structure; and (2) by *accommodation*, the process of forming new schemata or modifying old ones so as to integrate perceptual data that do not fit his existing schemata.

The teacher who has acquired a fundamental knowledge of Piaget's theory is in a position to provide readiness experiences for the child which will strengthen and extend the child's cognitive structures at his present period of development as well as stimulate the growth of structures appropriate to the next period of development. The early intervention programs for young infants provide readiness experiences preparing the child for the successive stages of sensorimotor development. Thus, the infant can be given many opportunities for varied sensory experiences by presenting him with a rattle, block, ball, teddy bear, or colorful plastic objects suspended from his crib which he may grasp, hit at, or put in his mouth. In addition, by being carried, pushed in a stroller, or walked from place to place, he can assimilate and accommodate sensory impressions of varied novel stimuli. These visual, auditory, tactual, and kinesthetic sensations become organized cognitively and expressed in *patterns of action*. As the child is talked to and played with and as he himself begins to use words to identify objects and to express himself, he is acquiring readiness for preoperational thought, a period in which conceptual development is enhanced through the child's increased use of vocabulary and language skills.

The curricula of a good nursery school, day care center, or intervention program such as Head Start provide numerous readiness experiences

that facilitate the development of preoperational thought. Listening to stories and records, looking at picture books, playing with blocks, trucks, and
dolls, and going on walks and trips all expose the child to a variety of stimuli which he assimilates or accommodates in forming concepts. The development of vocabulary and language skills provides the preschooler with
labels for an increasing number of objects and ideas which facilitate classifying in the forming of concepts. Having the child describe what he feels
when he puts his hand in a bag containing a variety of objects or encouraging him to move his body to music promotes conceptualization
through the use of other sensory modalities.

Piaget[31] describes how the child of six or seven manipulates objects
in his environment in developing the concepts of invariance and equivalence
of number, which ready him for later concrete thought. The child, for example, given eight red chips and eight blue chips, comes to realize through
arranging the chips in one-to-one correspondence that the two groups remain
equal in number regardless of the shape they take. At age seven, on the
average, the child can build a straight fence (of equal length sticks, each
stuck in modeling clay) consistently in any direction across a table, and
he will check the straightness of the fence by shutting one eye and sighting
along the row of sticks. In measuring the relative height of two towers of
blocks, the child will line up his shoulder with the top of his tower, mark
the spot opposite the base on his thigh with his hand, and walk over to the
model to see whether the heights of the two are the same. Arranging materials in ways that pose problems to the child provides readiness for the next
stages of cognitive development.

Similarly, Piaget-like tasks have been used to assess children's current level of cognitive development. Weisman and Safford[32] used six tasks
involving conservation of volume, one-to-one correspondence, cardinal number, reasoning, and left-right relationship to evaluate the level of cognitive
development of nine first grade children. The children's performance on
the tasks confirmed predictions that two of the children had good ability
but were not achieving, that one was neither verbal nor a high achiever,
and that others were either verbal nonachievers or nonverbal achievers.
These researchers concluded that Piaget-like tasks can be used as diagnostic
and instructional tools in assisting the teacher to gear instruction to the
readiness of individual pupils.

Experiential Readiness

As our discussion of intellectual development and readiness has indicated, a child's progress from the stage of concrete operations to the

---

[31] Jean Piaget, "How Children Form Mathematical Concepts," *Scientific American,* 189 (November 1953), 74–79.

[32] L. I. Weisman and P. L. Safford, "Piagetian Tasks as Classroom Evaluative
Tools," *Elementary School Journal,* 71 (March 1971), 329–338.

stage of formal operational thought depends upon his having the kinds of experiences which will enable him to develop appropriate thought structures. Experiential readiness has for many years been a major focus of teachers' efforts to help young children to acquire repertoires of experiences upon which academic skills and later learning can be built. If the kinds of experiences students have can increase their readiness for learning, then readiness is something that teachers and parents can do something about.

The crucial role of past experience in facilitating or limiting school learning is most clearly revealed in studies of the performance of children from culturally disadvantaged homes. It is in the area of language development, and especially in the abstract qualities of verbal functioning, that these children are likely to be most retarded. The impoverished home lacks the large variety of objects, utensils, toys, pictures, and so forth that serve as referents for language development in middle class homes.

Because he is not spoken to or read to very much by adults, and because his home enivironment is full of noise and distractions, the culturally disadvantaged child's auditory discrimination is often poor.[33] Auditory discrimination and general auditory responsiveness are presumably necessary for good verbal performance and reading ability.[34] The slum child is also inhibited in his development of concepts. His parents' everyday vocabulary is limited; stimulating conversation does not take place in the home; and there are few if any books, newspapers, or magazines in the home. As a result, the lower class child tends to respond mostly to the concrete, the tangible, and the immediate. Middle class children, on the other hand, are able to respond to abstract, categorical, and relational properties.[35] For example, if given a number of marbles, the lower class child will probably simply hold them in his hand and look at them, while the middle class child may count them and announce how many blue, red, and green ones there are. These cultural differences in the development of language and conceptual thinking become marked with increasing age.

One view of the parents' influence on the child's development of language and modes of thought has been expressed by Basil Bernstein.[36] Bernstein distinguishes between two types of families. One type stresses discipline and control; the other type stresses personal relationships. In the "discipline and control" families, a *restrictive* style of language—consisting of short, simple, and often unfinished sentences—predominates. This kind of language is easily understood but lacks the specificity and exactness needed for developing precise and well-differentiated concepts. In "personal

[33] David P. Ausubel, "The Effects of Cultural Deprivation on Learning Patterns," *Audiovisual Instruction*, 10 (January 1965), 10–12.

[34] Cynthia P. Deutsch, "Auditory Discrimination and Learning: Social Factors," *Merrill-Palmer Quarterly of Behavior and Development*, 10 (1964), 277–296.

[35] Ausubel, pp. 10–12.

[36] Basil Bernstein, "Social Class and Linguistic Development," in A. H. Halsey, Jean Floud, and C. Arnold Anderson, eds., *Education, Economy, and Society* (New York: Free Press, 1961).

relationship" families, an *elaborate* style of language prevails. In these families, communication is individualized and specific and provides for a wide range of linguistic and behavioral alternatives in interpersonal interaction.

Hess and Shipman[37] studied the effects of these contrasting family communication styles on children's perfomance in learning from their mothers a series of simple tasks, such as grouping toys by color or function and sorting blocks according to two characteristics. Their study investigated the relationships between the kind and quality of the mother-child interaction during the time her child worked on these cognitive tasks and the child's performance of the tasks. Mothers and children from four socioeconomic groups were studied: professionals, skilled workers, unskilled workers, and families on public assistance.

Bernstein's hypothesis about the relationship of family communication style and cognitive development appears to be substantiated by the findings of this study. Mothers of children who performed tasks correctly were more likely to give explicit information and instructions about the task and to offer support and help. In contrast, mothers of children who performed with less success tended to rely more on physical signs and nonverbal communication and were generally less explicit in their directions and expectations. In general, marked social class differences were found in the abilities of the children to learn from their mothers. Children from middle class homes ranked above children from lower socioeconomic levels in their performance of the tasks.

The culturally disadvantaged child's retardation in language and cognitive development tends to increase as he progresses through school. At the outset, in elementary school, he lacks readiness for learning because he has not made a complete transition from (in Piaget's terms) the concrete operational to the formal operational mode of thought. As a result, his progress in junior and senior high school subjects which require fluency in language and use of abstractions is limited.

Many programs attempting to overcome in part the experiential handicaps of culturally disadvantaged children and youth have been initiated or are being developed. Smith[38] suggests that slum children can be helped to experience their environment intellectually by being challenged to see, to distinguish, and to know about the objects in it. On a field trip, they should be encouraged to identify cities, buildings, animals, highways, rivers, and historical landmarks along the route.

Brunson[39] describes an approach used by high school social studies teachers to help culturally disadvantaged students to focus their attention on the main ideas of a presentation. Special tape-recorded lectures are produced, together with a guide sheet emphasizing the main ideas of the lec-

---

[37] Robert D. Hess and Virginia Shipman, "Early Blocks to Children's Learning," *Children,* 12 (September-October 1965), 189–194.

[38] Mildred B. Smith, "Reading for the Culturally Disadvantaged," *Educational Leadership,* 22 (March 1965), 398–403.

[39] F. Ward Brunson, "Creative Teaching of the Culturally Disadvantaged," *Audiovisual Instruction,* 10 (January 1965), 30–31.

ture. The guide sheet follows the sequence of the presentation, and the student fills in blanks as the presentation proceeds. Later, the guide sheet is discussed in class, and the student makes corrections where necessary.

Although such programs are unquestionably helpful, the effects of cultural differences in intellectual development are in part irreversible; a student with this type of background is often less able to profit from enriched and advanced levels of environmental stimulation. To facilitate the culturally disadvantaged child's transition to a more abstract level of cognitive functioning, Ausubel[40] suggests greater opportunities for the physical manipulation of objects, the use of abacuses, schematic models, and diagrams, and the use of illustrations and analogies drawn from everyday experience. In addition, programed instruction is a promising device—if each frame presents a complete rather than a fragmented concept.

Readiness and the Facilitation of Learning

What role does readiness play in the learning of school subjects? We shall next discuss readiness as it relates to reading, mathematics, and science.

Reading

Readiness for reading seems to be influenced by four factors: (1) intelligence, (2) physical factors, (3) experience and language development, and (4) personal and social development. The importance of intelligence in learning to read is indicated in the very high correlations (usually .90 or more) that are found between IQ scores (especially verbal IQ) and vocabulary and reading comprehension scores. Physical factors affecting reading ability include fatigue, illness, and physical disabilities, such as hearing loss, poor vision, or poor auditory or visual discrimination. The lack of unilateral dominance in children who are, for example, right-eyed and left-handed may influence readiness for reading, but the evidence is not clear.

The importance of experience and language development in learning to read was demonstrated in a study[41] which compared a conceptual language approach with a basal reader workbook approach for facilitating reading readiness in kindergarten children. Children who were encouraged to explore their interests and to conceptualize the ideas they gained from their exploration and experiences (conceptual language approach) scored

---

[40] Ausubel, pp. 10–12.

[41] C. M. O'Donnell and D. Raymond, "Developing Reading Readiness in Kindergarten," *Elementary English*, 49 (May 1972), 768–771.

significantly higher on reading tests at the end of the year than did the basal reader workbook group—even though the conceptual language approach involved no formal instruction in reading. The child's understanding of what he reads depends upon the knowledge he has acquired from his activities, his perceptions, his contacts with people and things, his emotional experiences, and his reactions to all of these. Experiential readiness for reading is measured by the extent to which the child can recall and represent in language the experiences he has had. The limitations on development and learning posed by immaturity in personal and social adjustment have been discussed at some length in previous chapters. A positive self-concept, for example, which includes the self-percept "I can read" is an important prerequisite for successful reading and language experiences.

Monroe and Rogers[42] suggest that a child's oral language skills can be evaluated by an analysis of the child's way of thinking—the quality of his ideas and the nature of his definitions of words—and the child's use of words—his ability to verbalize ideas and his command of sentence structure. Various scales have been developed for evaluating each of the child's oral language skills.

An issue which frequently arises in any discussion of readiness for reading is the desirability and efficacy of encouraging and helping children to learn to read prior to the first grade. Although most children do not achieve the requisite physical maturity until about six and a half years, some children show an interest in reading and do learn to read before they enter the first grade. In a group of 5,103 beginning first graders in California, Durkin[43] found 49 children from varied socioeconomic levels, with IQs ranging from 91 to 161, who read at grade levels from 1.5 to 4.6. In contrast to the findings of other studies, Durkin found that more than half of the early readers came from the blue collar class, while only 14 percent were from families of professional status. Family interviews revealed that these early readers had good memories and that they were persistent, curious, perfectionistic, and eager to keep up with older siblings. Even before they started kindergarten, in their drawing and scribbling they frequently drew letters copied from books or signs. The ability to make letters led to the question "How do you spell _____?" and ultimately to reading.

In a second study,[44] this time of 4,465 first graders enrolled in New York City public schools, Durkin identified 157 children as early readers. At the beginning of the first grade, the median reading level of these early readers was 2.0, and their median IQ on the Revised Stanford-Binet Scale was 133; their median gain in reading during the first grade was 1.4 years.

[42] Marion Monroe and Bernice Rogers, *Foundations for Reading* (Glenview, Ill.: Scott, Foresman and Co., 1964), pp. 24–48.

[43] Dolores Durkin, "Children Who Read before Grade One," *Reading Teacher*, 14 (January 1961), 163–166.

[44] Dolores Durkin, "Children Who Read before Grade One: A Second Study," *Elementary School Journal*, 44 (December 1963), 143–148.

A randomly selected group of 30 of these early readers were compared with a group of 30 matched first graders who could not read' when they entered first grade. Comparisons of the two groups revealed that early readers come from smaller families and walk and talk at earlier ages. They are more often content with quiet activities, such as drawing, coloring, and looking at books and pictures. They spend fewer hours watching TV but learn more from TV viewing than children who did not read at the beginning of first grade. The influence of parents of early readers appears to be important in encouraging these children to learn to read. When reading to their children, parents of early readers more often discuss pictures and point out particular words as they read, a procedure which is more likely to help a child learn to read.

Sutton,[45] in a study of the attitudes of kindergarten children who were given the opportunity to learn to read, found that about half of a group of 134 of these children voluntarily participated in the daily 10 to 15 minutes of reading instruction that was offered. Most of the children who participated looked upon reading as evidence of increased maturity and were highly motivated to learn to read. Results of a standardized reading test given in April revealed that 46 of these kindergarten children (more than one third) had achieved a reading level of at least the third month of the first grade. Their early success in reading increased their enthusiasm, so that by the following year most of them had become independent readers.

These studies suggest that where early reading occurs naturally, without pressure, it does not interfere with subsequent progress in reading at school and, indeed, may contribute to the child's development of a positive self-image and favorable attitudes toward learning.

Mathematics

With the advent of the "new math," the emphasis on readiness has shifted toward helping students discover the order and structure of mathematics. Less emphasis is placed upon processes and the acquisition of computational skill, and more emphasis is placed upon mathematics as a language or tool for expressing and dealing with ideas and concepts. Mathematical concepts once thought too difficult for young children to grasp are now introduced in the early grades, and these establish a readiness for mathematics experiences at higher grade levels.

Suppes[46] found that readiness among primary grade children for forming mathematical concepts is enhanced when the concepts are pre-

[45] Marjorie H. Sutton, "Attitudes of Young Children toward Reading," *Education*, 85 (December 1964), 238–241.

[46] Patrick Suppes, "The Formation of Mathematical Concepts in Primary Grade Children," in A. H. Passow and R. R. Leeper, eds., *Intellectual Development: Another Look* (Washington, D. C.: Association for Supervision and Curriculum Development, N.E.A., 1964), pp. 99–119.

sented precisely, with the help of consistent notation. Children early learn the notion of sets by manipulating concrete objects (such as beads, balls, pencils). They learn that numbers are properties of sets and that the operation of addition of numbers is simply a general way of combining families of sets of things without paying any particular attention to the things themselves. The leap in abstraction from groups of objects to numerals is accomplished, in set notation, in three steps. The first step is to portray the objects corresponding to a set (for example, five blocks) within a pair of brackets. The second step is to place the letter N in front of the bracket. This notation names a number and at the same time maintains the pictorial character of the set description. The final step is to introduce the Arabic numeral that corresponds to the set (in our example, 5). Introducing the student first to the easily comprehended operations on performed sets prepares him for the more difficult operations performed on numbers.

Other ways of increasing students' readiness for learning mathematical concepts and skills have also been suggested. One writer[47] suggests that students' readiness for ninth grade algebra will be enhanced if mathematics teachers in grades seven and eight emphasize "the factor point of view," "equation type of thinking," and "ordered pairs." Davis[48] ascertained the skills basic to success in algebra and then sought to teach these skills in the elementary grades, so that they would be learned well in advance by prospective algebra students. Brune[49] recommends the introduction of simple geometry in the lower grades, thereby enabling students to develop mathematical motivations that will be helpful in later studies.

Finally, readiness in mathematics as well as other subjects can be facilitated by the analysis of learning sets and hierarchies. It will be recalled (from Chapter 15) that Gagné[50] has developed a taxonomy of eight types of learning, increasing in complexity from signal learning (type 1) to problem-solving learning (type 8). Mastery of each lower or less complex type of learning confers upon the learner capabilities needed for achieving more complex learnings. For example, a student must have acquired concepts of time, velocity, and gravity before he can solve problems involving the speed of falling bodies. Thus, underlying every major educational objective is a hierarchy of subordinate capabilities that the learner must achieve before the final objective can be obtained. Such subordinate capabilities are called *learning sets*. The learning sets that must be mastered before a student is capable of "solving equations" are shown in Figure 16–2. Using the concept of learning sets, the teacher assists students to achieve readiness for particular learning by mapping the sequence of subordinate

[47] Francis J. Mueller, "Building Algebra Readiness in Grades Seven and Eight," *Arithmetic Teacher*, 6 (November 1959), 269–273.

[48] Robert B. Davis, "The 'Madison Project' of Syracuse University," *Mathematics Teacher*, 53 (November 1960), 571–575.

[49] Irvin H. Brune, "Geometry in the Grades," *Arithmetic Teacher*, 8 (May 1961), 210–219.

[50] Robert M. Gagné, *The Conditions of Learning*, 2nd ed. (New York: Holt, Rinehart and Winston, 1970).

Figure 16–2.   Proposed Hierarchy of Learning Sets in a Self-Instructional Program on Solving Equations

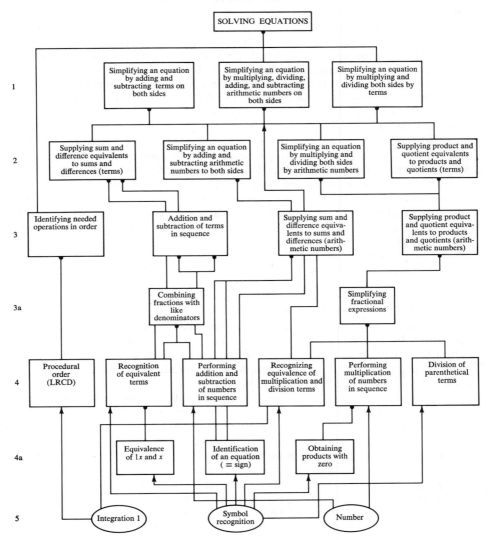

Source: Robert M. Gagné and Noel E. Paradise, "Abilities and Learning Sets in Knowledge Acquisition," *Psychological Monographs*, 75 (1961), 1–23. Copyright 1961 by the American Psychological Association, and reproduced by permission.

learning capabilities (such as those shown in Figure 16–2) prerequisite to attaining the desired educational goal, and organizing activities which provide students with opportunities for acquiring each of the subordinate capabilities or learning sets.

Gagné and Paradise[51] tested the validity of the hierarchy of learning sets for solving equations (Figure 16–2) in an experiment which sought to ascertain whether correlations of relevant abilities were higher than those of irrelevant abilities with measures of achievement in equation solving. After administering a learning program on equation solving to a group of 118 seventh graders in four different school classes, Gagné and Paradise found instances of positive transfer to each learning set from subordinate relevant learning sets throughout the hierarchy, with proportions ranging from .91 to 1.00. In addition, the rate of mastery of learning sets at progressively higher levels of the hierarchy was found to depend increasingly upon specific transfer from subordinate learning sets.

These and related studies suggest that a pupil is ready to learn the concepts and skills at a given level of difficulty if he has mastered the concepts and skills in the learning sets of the hierarchy below that level.

Science

Considerable study by educators and scientists during the past decade has been directed toward improving science curricula and the teaching of science in the elementary and secondary schools. While readiness for experiences in science is important at all levels, we shall consider here the problem of readiness as it is related to science education in the elementary schools.

Karplus,[52] a physicist, carried out a study of curriculum improvement in elementary science testing by teaching in first grade classrooms the methods and materials he had developed. For Karplus, the principal objective of the elementary school science program is the development of "scientific literacy," which provides the student with a conceptual structure and a means of communication which will enable him to interpret information obtained by others. Karplus deplores exclusive reliance on textbooks and other secondary sources and failure to use direct experiences to nourish pupils' development of scientific modes of thinking. Too often, he says, "the science course creates a second, separate, and relatively abstract structure that is not much used outside the school situation and which eventually atrophies or even results in resentment against science."[53]

[51] Robert M. Gagné and Noel E. Paradise, "Abilities and Learning Sets in Knowledge Acquisition," *Psychological Monographs*, 75 (1961), 1–23.

[52] Robert Karplus, "One Physicist Looks at Science Education," in A. H. Passow and R. R. Leeper, eds., *Intellectual Development: Another Look* (Washington, D. C.: Association for Supervision and Curriculum Development, N.E.A., 1964), pp. 78–98.

[53] Karplus, p. 82.

Karplus suggests that one of the first tasks of a science program is to reinforce a child's growing awareness of material objects and their properties. By utilizing children's everyday experiences, the elementary school teacher can assist students to understand such fundamental concepts as interaction, system, equilibrium, reversibility, and irreversibility. Common experiences such as scraping a knee, pulling or pushing a wagon, cutting paper, and sticking a stamp or label on paper are all examples of *interaction* (in which two or more objects affect or influence one another). When children are allowed to examine a display of many *systems* (including, perhaps, a pile of blocks, a burning candle, a spring, an ice cube in water, sugar crystals in water, and a stone in water), they may discover that some systems are in *equilibrium* (the pile of blocks, the spring, and the stone), while others are not in equilibrium (the burning candle and the sugar and the ice cube in water). Noting that undisturbed systems tend to come to equilibrium, the child is better able to cope with the concepts of *reversibility* and *irreversibility*. The teacher can then demonstrate these concepts by showing pupils a film composed of reversible and irreversible scenes and running it in both directions.

The kind of science program which Karplus has described, by introducing concepts that contribute to a scientific mode of thinking, builds a readiness for later science experiences.

Gagné[54] describes a similar approach used by the Commission on Science Education of the American Association for the Advancement of Science. The commission emphasizes the teaching of *processes* of science, in place of a science content approach, beginning in the elementary school. Exercises have been developed to increase children's understanding of such processes as observation, classification, communication, number relations, measurement, space relations, prediction, and inference. Children demonstrate these processes by performing various experiments and exercises. In one such experiment, fifth grade students formulate a method of measuring the energy of motion of a cylinder when it reaches the bottom of an inclined plane and pushes a block on the surface of a table. The children vary the slope of the plane and the initial position of the cylinder, and note the effects on the distance the block moves. In carrying out this experiment, children use the processes of observation, measurement, number relations, prediction, and inference in discovering a physical law: Work equals force times distance. Using this approach, pupils learn to carry out critical and disciplined thinking in connection with each of the processes of science.

[54] Robert M. Gagné, "Elementary Science: A New Scheme of Instruction," *Science*, 51 (January 1966), 49–53.

Summary

There is considerable evidence suggesting that pupils learn more quickly, efficiently, and effectively when they are ready for and can profit from a learning experience. Many misconceptions and conflicting views exist regarding the concept of readiness. A major disagreement is whether readiness is an inner dynamic present in the learner or whether it must be developed. By our definition, a learner's *readiness* in any situation is the sum total of all of his characteristics which make his behavior amenable to change.

Maturation, an important dimension of readiness, involves the changes in organic function and structure which precede and are prerequisite to learning. Misconceptions associated with the term *maturation* are reflected in its indiscriminate application to different kinds of maturity—physical, skeletal, social, mental, and emotional—and in the implication that there exists some end point of maturation at which the processes of growth and development cease. Studies of maturation and learning indicate in general that practice and training introduced prior to the time a child has gained the required physiological maturity tend to be ineffectual.

Intelligence is a second important dimension of readiness. The intelligence quotient, commonly called the IQ, is never an absolute measure of intellectual aptitude; it indicates only the rate at which the individual is achieving intelligence. Over the past half century the idea that intelligence is fixed—that is, the belief that it is an innate dimension of personal capacity which increases at a fixed rate to a predetermined level—has been enveloped in considerable controversy. A conclusion drawn from numerous studies of identical twins and studies of retarded children raised in favorable and less favorable home environments is that environment determines the level of intellectual functioning a person can achieve, but that the potential for intellectual development is largely determined by heredity. Recent discussion of this problem has centered in the question of whether differences in IQ between racial and social class groups are the result of genetic differences. Although there has been much, often heated debate on this issue, it appears that the information, conceptualization, and tools needed to make a definitive test of this hypothesis are presently not available.

According to Piaget's ontogenetic theory of intellectual development, readiness for learning depends upon the development of central processes that are reflected in patterns of action used by the child in processing and organizing information. During each of four stages of intellectual development, through a process which Piaget calls *assimilation*, the child uses in new situations information or responses from previous situations. The child varies his response to achieve an *accommodation* to the new situation, and, in this process, action patterns or schemata for conceptualizing and processing information are modified and new ones are formed.

The crucial role of past experience in providing a readiness for learning in school is most clearly revealed in studies of the performance of children from culturally disadvantaged homes. It is in the area of language development that these children are likely to be most retarded. The syntax and grammar learned out of school by the slum child limits his development of conceptual thinking. Many programs initiated in an effort to overcome the experiential handicaps of culturally disadvantaged children have had only limited success. The effects of cultural deprivation are in part irreversible.

The task of preparing students for experiences in reading, mathematics, and science has made readiness a problem of particular interest to educators. Studies seem to show that when early reading by young children occurs naturally and without pressure, it not only does not interfere with subsequent reading experiences in school, but it contributes to increased learning and self-development as well. Studies of children's readiness for experiences in mathematics suggest that a pupil is ready to learn the concepts or skills at a given level of difficulty or complexity if he has mastered the concepts and skills in the learning sets of the hierarchy below that level. The current emphasis in science education is upon introducing young children to concepts which contribute to a scientific mode of thinking and build a readiness for. later science experiences.

Study Questions

1.   Focus on the grade or subject you expect to teach. How will you go about ascertaining the states of readiness of your pupils for learning? What kinds of data will you need, and where will you obtain them?

2.   Do our schools, in their promotion and grouping policies, act on the belief that one's intelligence can be increased or on the belief that one's intelligence remains fixed?

3.   There has been a trend to introduce certain concepts, especially in mathematics and science, to students once thought too young to understand such concepts. How do you reconcile this with findings of studies of maturation and learning which indicate that practice and training are largely wasted if introduced prior to the time a child has gained the required physiological maturity?

4.   If genetic factors are later found to be the principal determinant of intelligence in all racial, ethnic, and social class groups, how would this finding influence your teaching your subject in a multiracial classroom?

5.   What factors discussed elsewhere in this book also have a bearing on the student's readiness for learning?

Suggested Readings

Environment, Heredity, and Intelligence. Cambridge, Mass.: Harvard Educational Review, 1969. Contains a reprint of Arthur Jensen's long, controversial article "How Much Can We Boost IQ and Scholastic Achievement?" in which he hypothesizes that social class and racial variations in intelligence cannot be accounted for solely by differences in environment, but are due in part to genetic differences. Included also are papers by critics of Jensen's thesis and Jensen's reply to his critics.

Hunt, J. McV. *Intelligence and Experience.* New York: Ronald Press, 1961. Examines the historical roots of the assumptions of fixed intelligence and predetermined development and documents the shift toward recognizing the crucial role of life experiences in the development of central processes of intelligence. Evidence of this shift from investigations of learning sets, programing of electronic computers, as well as Piaget's work investigating the development of intelligence and logical thinking in children is presented.

Ilg, Frances L., and Louise D. Ames. *School Readiness: Behavior Tests Used at the Gesell Institute.* New York: Harper & Row, 1964. Contains a test battery developed to assess readiness for school entrance. The rationale for the selection of particular tests, directions for administration and scoring, norms, and estimates of reliability are discussed.

Passow, A. Harry, and Robert R. Leeper, eds. *Intellectual Development: Another Look.* Washington, D. C.: Association for Supervision and Curriculum Development, N.E.A., 1964. Contains papers on intellectual development, cognitive processes, curiosity and exploration, inquiry training, and the development of concepts by primary grade children in the areas of mathematics and science. The paper by Almy presents a very clear description of Piaget's theory of intellectual development.

Tyler, Fred T. "Issues Related to Readiness to Learn," in Ernest R. Hilgard, ed., *Theories of Learning and Instruction.* Part 1. Sixty-Third Yearbook of the National Society for the Study of Education. Chicago: University of Chicago Press, 1964, pp. 210–239. Examines historical and theoretical issues relating to the concept of readiness. Considerable attention is given to the topic of maturation and some of the disagreements surrounding the use of this term. Presents a thorough analysis of the present status of the concept of readiness and its relationship to learning.

Films

Portrait of a Disadvantaged Child: Tommy Knight, 16 mm, sound, black and white, 16 min. Bloomington: Audiovisual Center, Indiana University. By following the events in a day of the life of a slum child, Tommy Knight, the viewer is introduced to the special problems, needs, and strengths of the inner city child and the factors hindering his ability to learn. Contrasted are the home life and parental attitudes of disadvantaged children, showing that some homes are supportive while others are neglectful.

The Outcomes of Learning: Cognitive

17

If all students are helped to the full utilization of their intellectual powers, we will have a better chance of surviving as a democracy in an age of enormous technological and social complexity.

Jerome S. Bruner

There are three major types of learning: *cognitive, psychomotor,* and *affective.* In this chapter we focus on cognitive learning and in the next on psychomotor and affective learning. Few if any behaviors, however, are purely cognitive, psychomotor, or affective, but one of these processes may predominate in a specific behavior pattern. Affective learning, in the form of likes and dislikes, tastes, and attitudes, accompanies all psychomotor and cognitive learning; psychomotor learning influences the development of cognitive structures; and perceptual and cognitive factors are involved in the learning of psychomotor skills.

Figure 17–1 portrays the hierarchies of learning outcomes, in which successively more complex behavioral patterns are formed from combinations of simpler behavior patterns. For example, while patterns of problem solving and creative thinking (column 3) presumably require factual information, concepts, and principles, they may also require verbal and graphic skills (psychomotor patterns) and be influenced by likes and dislikes (affective patterns). Similarly, the higher-level integrations listed in column 4 and the still higher levels of integration in column 5 are formed from unique combinations of simpler patterns of cognitive, psychomotor, and affective learning.

Also listed in Figure 17–1 are a number of learning outcomes which appear to be only marginally influenced by formal educational experiences: facial expressions, habitual postures and gestures, acquired likes and dislikes, personality, character, values, and locomotor and manipulatory skills. Formal school learning does not focus directly on some of these outcomes, but many of the patterns learned incidentally in and out of school may be more important than some of the patterns the school does emphasize.

Another classification of learning outcomes particularly relevant for

525

Figure 17–1.   A Classification of the Outcomes of Learning

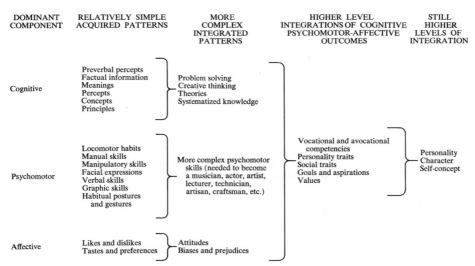

DOMINANT COMPONENT	RELATIVELY SIMPLE ACQUIRED PATTERNS	MORE COMPLEX INTEGRATED PATTERNS	HIGHER LEVEL INTEGRATIONS OF COGNITIVE PSYCHOMOTOR-AFFECTIVE OUTCOMES	STILL HIGHER LEVELS OF INTEGRATION
Cognitive	Preverbal percepts Factual information Meanings Percepts Concepts Principles	Problem solving Creative thinking Theories Systematized knowledge		
Psychomotor	Locomotor habits Manual skills Manipulatory skills Facial expressions Verbal skills Graphic skills Habitual postures and gestures	More complex psychomotor skills (needed to become a musician, actor, artist, lecturer, technician, artisan, craftsman, etc.)	Vocational and avocational competencies Personality traits Social traits Goals and aspirations Values	Personality Character Self-concept
Affective	Likes and dislikes Tastes and preferences	Attitudes Biases and prejudices		

Source: Modified from James M. Sawrey and Charles W. Telford, *Educational Psychology,* 2nd ed. (Boston: Allyn & Bacon, 1964), p. 95. Used by permission.

the school setting is a *taxonomy of educational objectives*[1] which has been developed for the cognitive and affective domains. The cognitive domain of the taxonomy consists of six broad areas of cognitive learning arranged in descending order of increasing complexity:

    1.   *Knowledge.*

    2.   *Comprehension.*

    3.   *Application.*

    4.   *Analysis.*

    5.   *Synthesis.*

    6.   *Evaluation.*

For each of these broad areas of cognitive learning, the taxonomy identifies specific learning outcomes in behavioral terms and suggests ways whereby each of these educational objectives can be evaluated. Listed under the broad area of "knowledge," for example, are the following specific learning outcomes:

[1] Benjamin S. Bloom, *Taxonomy of Educational Objectives, Handbook 1. Cognitive Domain* (New York: David McKay Co., 1956); David R. Krathwohl, Benjamin S. Bloom, and Bertram B. Masia, *Taxonomy of Educational Objectives, Handbook 2. Affective Domain* (New York: David McKay Co., 1964).

Knowledge of specifics.
 knowledge of terminology.
 knowledge of specific facts.

Knowledge of ways and means of dealing with specifics.
 knowledge of conventions.
 knowledge of trends and sequences.
 knowledge of classifications and categories.
 knowledge of criteria.
 knowledge of methodology.

Knowledge of the universals and abstractions in a field.
 knowledge of principles and generalizations.
 knowledge of theories and structures.

The taxonomy can assist the teacher in clarifying his educational objectives and modifying his teaching practices so that relevant, important outcomes of learning are identified and realized.

Cognitive Processes

In our description of intellectual development in the preceding chapter, the learner was viewed as an information processor, one who sorts and interpets sensory inputs in acquiring and organizing data. The processes through which one acquires, organizes, interrelates, and interprets the data of his experience are called *cognitive processes*. Cognitive processes include labeling, forming hypotheses, evaluating, and applying rules of transformation.[2]

The learner's initial cognitive task is to label the data acquired through sensory output. Piaget[3] and Bruner[4] have described how the very young child acquires labels through sensorimotor representations of external stimuli. When he learns to use spoken and written language, the child acquires symbolic labels. In accordance with these labels the child generates hypotheses. He then evaluates the meaning of the data suggested by the hypotheses he has made. Finally, he implements the hypothesis he has decided on, using an appropriate rule of transformation. The young child,

---

[2] Jerome Kagan, "A Developmental Approach to Conceptual Growth," in Herbert J. Klausmeier and Chester W. Harris, eds., *Analyses of Concept Learning* (New York: Academic Press, 1966), pp. 97–116.

[3] Jean Piaget, *The Psychology of Intelligence*, trans. by M. Piercy and D. E. Berlyne (London: Routledge & Kegan Paul, 1947).

[4] Jerome S. Bruner, "The Course of Cognitive Growth," *American Psychologist*, 19 (January 1964), 1–15.

for example, acquires a sensorimotor label (kinesthetic sensations, arm and leg movements) for having his snow suit put on. He hypothesizes that his mother is going to take him for a ride in the car. His positive evaluation of this anticipated experience is expressed in his smile. If his mother heads toward a neighbor's house, his initial hypothesis is replaced by a new one—that he is to be left with the neighbor while his mother goes shopping. His evaluative response to this new meaning is to start crying. The transformation rule which the child has learned and applied is "A change in clothing signals a change in activity."

Data acquired from experience, processed and transformed, become *cognitive outcomes* of increasing complexity—percepts, concepts, principles, hypotheses, theories. The developmental and hierarchical ordering of these cognitive outcomes is shown in Figure 17–2. Preverbal percepts are formed

Figure 17–2.   Developmental and Hierarchical Ordering of Cognitive Learning Outcomes

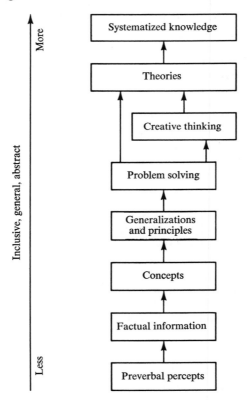

Source: Adapted from Herbert J. Klausmeier and William Goodwin, *Learning and Human Abilities*, 2nd ed. (New York: Harper & Row, 1966), p. 212. Used by permission.

as the infant gives labels to the sensorimotor data of his experience. The learning of language facilitates labeling and leads to an increase in factual information. Concepts are formed as objects or data are classified and grouped systematically. Generalizations and principles are formed by inter-relating two or more concepts. The application of two or more principles to produce a new capability is called problem solving. Problem solving in-volves forming and testing hypotheses and evaluating the results of tested hypotheses. Novel and original hypotheses and solutions to problems are evidence of creative (divergent) thinking. The products of either convergent thinking (common, conventional hypotheses and solutions) or divergent thinking become organized as theories—statements describing and ex-plaining the nature of various phenomena. Finally, the aggregate of what one knows and believes about various phenomena constitutes his body of systematized knowledge.

The arrangement in Figure 17–2 should not be interpreted as mean-ing that only successively higher outcomes are learned at successively higher maturational levels. For example, we acquire percepts and factual information throughout our lives. Also, as one moves up the hierarchy from preverbal percepts to systematized knowledge, the cognitive outcomes at successively higher levels are more inclusive, general, and abstract. It is well to remember, however, that in organizing knowledge systematically, one moves from the general to the specific as well as from the specific back to the general. We shall next discuss various aspects of cognitive learning: (1) concept formation, (2) generalizing, (3) problem solving, and (4) creativity.

Concept Formation

Before an individual can respond to the stimuli and events of his life, he must develop appropriate concepts. One is handicapped in solving problems in geometry, for instance, if he lacks the concepts of angle, point, or perpendicular; writing a story would be difficult without the concepts of sentence, plot, description, and characterization. Concepts influence all aspects of behavior. Moreover, the extension of knowledge depends upon the modification, refinement, or replacement of existing concepts. The de-velopment of space sciences, for example, had to await the refinement of old concepts and the development of new concepts relating to energy, mass, radiation, weightlessness, electronic computation, and data processing.

A major educational objective of the school, therefore, is to provide students with opportunities to develop and refine concepts needed to make adequate interpretations of and responses to life situations. A student, for example, will find that arithmetic concepts are inadequate for solving prob-lems of change in acceleration and deceleration of automobiles, airplanes, or rockets; for this, concepts of differential calculus are needed. The teacher, by assisting the student to clarify, broaden, and test his present concepts and to develop new ones, helps him to make better provisional responses in new situations. The most significant learning experiences are those that afford opportunities for the formation or refinement of concepts required for making wiser provisional responses in new situations. This application of learned concepts and skills to new situations is known as *transfer* and is of central importance in learning.

Concepts are formed when an individual perceives that two objects or qualities can be placed in the same class. Thus, a young child with two different teddy bears learns to put both of them into the same class, labeled "teddy bears." Later, he may put teddy bears into more inclusive classes, such as "stuffed animals" or "toys." The ability to categorize and classify allows the individual to cope with the otherwise overwhelming mass of detail registered by his senses.

A concept, then, is a classification of stimuli that have common characteristics. In forming a concept, a student must first *discriminate* between relevant and irrelevant features of the data. In forming a concept of "natural resources," for example, he must distinguish between the water resources of a given region and the dams and artificial lakes constructed to conserve water and to generate electricity. Second, the student must *generalize* by correctly identifying the several instances or exemplars that belong to the conceptual category. In generalizing, the student extends such a category as, for instance, "assets indigenous to a geographical region" to include minerals, soil, stones, plants, animals, and climatic conditions. In short, he must include all essential features and omit all nonessential features.

Concepts and Experience

The concepts that children acquire depend upon the kinds and qualities of experience they have had. Piaget's theory of intellectual development, presented in Chapters 11–13, emphasizes the role of experience in acquiring concepts. It will be recalled that Piaget's theory describes the growth in the child of cognitive structures (schemata) that are acquired through assimilation and accommodation as the child interacts with the environment. Concepts are formed as the child develops more complex and elaborate schemata at successive periods of development. Thus, during the sensorimotor period, the infant acquires the concept of object permanence when he searches with his eyes for a rattle that has disappeared from view. Recognizing himself in the mirror provides a rudimentary concept of self, while shaking a rattle and making a noise introduces him to the concept of causality.

Children acquire a great many concepts informally before they go to school. Development of vocabulary and language skills provides the child with labels that enable him to increase the number and complexity of concepts formed during the preoperational period of intellectual development. Most tests of reading readiness given in kindergarten and first grade measure the degree to which the child has grasped concepts such as "boy," "girl," "house," "tree," "largest," "smallest," "left," "right," "same," and "different." It will be recalled, however, that most preschool children have great difficulty in grasping the concept of invariance (or conservation); that is, that the amount, number, or volume of a substance remains the same regardless of change in shape or position. Thus, four- or five-year-olds will respond that there are more beads in an array of eight beads spaced far apart than there are in an array of eight beads spaced closer together. These responses of the young child remind us that during the preoperational period the child's thought processes are dominated by his perceptions.

The child who has progressed to what Piaget calls the concrete stage of intellectual development (approximately ages seven to 11) is able to form more complex concepts which involve more than a single dimension. It may be recalled that in order to identify correctly objects that float and objects that sink in water, the child, using concrete operations, must combine dimensions of size and weight in developing concepts of big-heavy, big-light, little-heavy, and little-light. During successive years in school, students acquire, both formally and informally, a great many concepts of increasing complexity and abstractness. The following excerpts from the cases of Tab and David reveal the understanding of the concept of gravity which these intellectually able boys in the first and fourth grades, respectively, had acquired.

> December 5.   *A story about Santa's reindeer being stolen by the Man in the Moon was told. When it came to the part where Santa flew out of his chair aboard the rocket ship as the ship was going into the stratosphere, Tab said, "I know why that happens. It's the same as why they can jump through the air many feet up there. It's the pull of gravity. He ought to have a safety belt." At the end of the story he said, "That isn't a true story, but it's a good one anyway."*

> December 14.   *In science class we were discussing gravity. Someone asked why an astronaut is weightless if gravity is always acting.*
>
> *"I can answer that, Mrs. D.," David said. "I read an article on that in one of my science magazines."*
>
> *"All right, David, suppose you explain it to the class," I said.*
>
> *David paused an instant as if trying to decide how to explain it in the simplest way. Then he said, "Well, you feel weight when something like the floor or ground resists the pull of gravity on you. When there is no resistance, as you fall, you are weightless. For instance, an astronaut becomes weightless when the rocket motors shut off because there is no force to resist the pull of gravity. He and the capsule are both weightless and falling freely together. He will remain weightless until some outside force acts on him."*
>
> *"Like what?" asked Roy.*
>
> *"Oh, like air resistance or rocket power," David replied.*

*This discussion, although fascinating to David, was completely
beyond the comprehension of the class, so I steered it into channels
which the group could understand.*

In the above anecdote David is shown employing the concepts of
gravity, force, and resistance in forming generalizations about gravity and
weightlessness. His skill in using hypotheses and his sophisticated understanding of causality are qualities of formal operational thought, which
Piaget suggests is usually not observed until the child is in early adolescence, between the ages of 11 and 15. In formal operational thought the
adolescent or adult needs a larger and more sophisticated array of verbal
and abstract concepts for solving complex problems. As adolescents become
involved in the complex problems of the physical and social world, they
have increasing need for such abstract concepts as justice, beauty, love,
society, and democracy.

The teacher, in helping students to crystallize, broaden, and refine
concepts, also aids them to recognize and to modify stereotypes. A *stereotype* can be defined as "a tendency to attribute generalized and simplified
characteristics to a group of people in the form of a verbal label."[5] Concepts
based on partial or distorted data relating to peoples, groups, movements,
or ideologies can be classed as stereotypes. Stereotypes, then, are the result
of inadequate conceptualizations. Not all Italians are artistic and impulsive,
nor are all Jews shrewd and mercenary, or all Americans industrious and
materialistic. Concepts which ascribe common behaviors or characteristics
to millions of individuals of a nationality or race are obviously inadequate,
distorted, and overgeneralized.

Schools have a responsibility to encourage students to avoid stereotypes by helping them to develop adequate, valid concepts of people, places,
and events. Teachers can help students to form more valid concepts by encouraging them (1) to examine their concepts, and, if necessary in the light
of additional information, to revise them; and (2) to form more careful and
accurate discriminations and generalizations from all the data available.
How this can be achieved is described in the next section.

Strategies for Developing Concepts

To learn how people form concepts, one must find out what influences a person to attend to some features of an object or event and to ignore others. A common strategy in the formation of concepts is the use of
examples and nonexamples. Learning concepts through the use of positive
examples is more effective, since the use of nonexamples, which forces the

---

[5] W. E. Vinacke, "Explorations in the Dynamic Processes of Sterotyping," *Journal
of Social Psychology*, 43 (1956), 105.

learner to memorize a multitude of things that a concept is not, is both difficult and inefficient.[6]

A more promising instructional strategy for facilitating concept attainment is reinforcement. Reinforcement is generally provided in the form of verbal feedback that informs the learner whether or not he has correctly identified the concept. Continuous (that is, 100 percent) reinforcement of both correct and incorrect responses seems to be more effective in teaching children concepts than intermittent reinforcement. Carpenter[7] found that children who were given feedback for every correct and incorrect response learned the concept in fewer trials and less time than did children in groups reinforced for only correct responses 100 percent, 50 percent, and 25 percent of the time. Immediate reinforcement, even if given on an intermittent schedule, seems to result in concepts' being learned more quickly than does delayed continuous reinforcement.[8] As in Skinner's description of shaping complex motor responses, the teacher may find that identifying and reinforcing intermediate steps in concept formation results in faster learning of a complex concept than does rewarding only the final performance.[9]

Has a person really learned a concept if he is unable to verbalize it? *The Taxonomy of Educational Objectives: Cognitive Domain*, cited earlier in the chapter, indicates that we can "know" something at several different levels. At an initial level of knowledge, we may be able to recognize, recall, or define the concept "catalyst." Increased knowledge or understanding of this concept may be indicated by our comprehending the concept well enough to cite examples or applying the concept in explaining certain chemical reactions. At still higher levels of cognition, we may demonstrate our understanding of this concept through analysis, synthesis, and evaluation in using the concept outside the field of chemistry to explain actions and reactions in social organizations, economics, group behavior, and cultural evolution.

Frequently learners are able to use or apply a concept but are unable to define it. Johnson and O'Reilly[10] studied the relationship between the classifying and defining processes in learning a concept. Three groups of 11- and 12-year-old children were given the task of learning the difference between two groups of birds. One group (pictorial) was asked to classify colored pictures of birds, while a second group (verbal) was asked to classify verbal descriptions. After performing the classification task, each child was asked to define the difference between the two groups of birds and to sort 10 cards containing pictures and verbal descriptions of the two kinds of

[6] Loy S. Braley, "Strategy Selections and Negative Instances in Concept Learning," *Journal of Educational Psychology*, 54 (June 1963), 154–159.

[7] Finley Carpenter, "Conceptualization as a Function of Differential Reinforcement," *Science Education*, 38 (1954), 284–294.

[8] G. Sax, "Concept Acquisition as a Function of Differing Schedules and Delays of Reinforcement," *Journal of Educational Psychology*, 51 (1960), 32–36.

[9] Carpenter, p. 293.

[10] Donald M. Johnson and Charlene A. O'Reilly, "Concept Attainment in Children: Classifying and Defining," *Journal of Educational Psychology*, 55 (April 1964), 71–74.

birds. The third group of children (pictorial-definition) received colored pictures to classify, but, after each five pictures, they were asked to define the difference between the two kinds of birds. They were given no evaluation of their answers. The verbal group learned the classification task most rapidly. Both the verbal and pictorial-definition groups were superior to the pictorial group in the accuracy of their definitions of the difference between the groups of birds. The most important finding, however, was that the pictorial-definition group gave almost twice as many definitions judged "good" as did the pictorial group. Thus, some learners do grasp a concept visually (in noting the difference in pictures of two groups of birds), but they may be unable to verbalize the concept in an acceptable definition. The findings show, however, that a small amount of practice in defining, even without knowledge of results (pictorial-definition group), markedly improves definitions of the concept.

Sensory modalities.   Learning concepts, as well as other types of learning, depends upon the adequacy and accuracy of sensory input—especially visual, auditory, tactual, and kinesthetic. These different kinds of input of stimuli are called *sensory modalities.* It appears that some people learn better through the use of one sensory mode than another. Preferred modes of sensory input in learning are often referred to as *learning modalities.* Thus, a city child's concept of "green plants" is likely to be limited to what he sees in a window box or in pictures or reads about (visual), or hears his teacher talk about (auditory). The rural child's concept of "green plants," however, is much more likely to include touching and smelling vegetables, flowers, and crops. Similarly, the young child learns a foreign language through hearing it spoken (auditory). An adolescent or an adult may learn the foreign language more readily through developing a sight vocabulary and through reading (visual). Modern methods of teaching foreign languages emphasize many sensory modalities: listening (auditory), speaking (auditory and kinesthetic—internal sensations of muscle movements), as well as reading (visual). Indeed, all three modalities may be used simultaneously, each reinforcing the others.

The integration of sensory modalities appears to be especially important in learning to read. Luria[11] suggests that the integration of sensory modalities can be facilitated when a weak sense modality is paired with a strong one. For example, if a child has poor visual perception, he will be helped with reading if he gets auditory feedback by hearing the words at the same time he sees them. Children with reading problems can often be helped by special training to strengthen specific modalities or aspects of visual perception.[12] Some children, for example, have difficulty in perceiving sequences of words and spatial relationships. Such children can be helped

[11] A. R. Luria, "The Problem of Cortical Defect and Recovery of Function," lecture to the Postgraduate Center for Psychotherapy, New York, March 1960.

[12] M. Frostig, "Visual Perception, Integrative Functions, and Academic Learning," *Journal of Learning Disabilities,* 5 (January 1972), 1–15.

by being given familiar objects such as beads, pegs, or drawn figures. When they can reproduce a pattern, putting beads or pegs of the correct shape and/or color in proper relationship to one another, they can use this skill to read short words by using color cues. As children copy with colored letters the sequences of the color pegs, they become aware that words are formed with sequences of letters, and thus they learn particular words.

Other children may have difficulties in form perception, in the perception of letters as well as words. A child who cannot perceive a letter as a whole can be helped to analyze and then synthesize the total Gestalt by dividing letters and numerals into parts, which can then be assembled and grouped. Perceptual skills can be further sharpened by helping the child to visualize letters or words. Visualization can be enhanced by writing or printing words in distinctive letters, so that they form vivid images which help to fix the words in the mind. Visualization is an important ability needed in all learning, including remembering facts, events, and relationships. Training in visualization can also be integrated with the teaching of arithmetic. Sticks of different colors and different lengths (called Cusienaire rods) can be used to represent numbers, thus helping the child to visualize the stair-step relationships of numbers.

Although the meaning of what we perceive is based upon sensations received from all our receptor organs, for some of us one sensory modality is dominant, while for others responding to the same stimuli, a different sensory modality is dominant. Difference in dominant modality is particularly well illustrated in the perception of the upright—perceiving our bodies or other objects as being in the vertical plane. Witkin[13] found that when subjects were placed in an adjustable chair that was tilted to some degree and were told to bring the chair to an upright position, some based their judgments of whether it was upright on the perceived "straightness" of objects around them, while others based their judgments on the "feelings" of their bodies in reaction to gravitational pull (kinesthetic) in relative independence of the visual field. Witkin found wide differences in response between persons who relied on body sensations (whom he labeled "field independent") to bring their chair upright and persons who had to be aligned with the tilted room (depended upon visual cues, and thus labeled "field dependent") before they could perceive themselves as upright.

Important sex differences emerged from these studies. Females as a group are more likely to be field dependent; males generally are more field independent. These differences in spatial orientation were also found to be correlated with learning and personality variables. Field-independent subjects excel field-dependent subjects in discovering simple figures hidden in the complex designs of the embedded figures test. The field-independent person was found to have a more definite sense of his role and status in the family. He usually functions with greater independence in a variety of situations, shows a greater desire and capacity for active striving in dealing with

[13] Herman A. Witkin et al., *Personality through Perception: An Experimental and Clinical Study* (New York: Harper & Row, 1954).

his environment, and has wide and better developed interests than the field-dependent person.

The specific implications of these studies may not be immediately evident, but they do emphasize the wide differences in sensory modalities and cognitive styles which students employ in their learning. A general implication of these studies is that teachers should respond to the varying sensory modalities and cognitive styles of students by organizing learning experiences which utilize a wide range of sensory input. As noted earlier, the teacher can, through the use of training materials, facilitate children's learning by strengthening those sensory modalities which are weak or less developed.

Conceptual Tempo

A person's cognitive development is shaped not only by the strategies he employs in forming concepts but also by tempo and motivational variables. Kagan,[14] in his studies of the cognitive styles of impulsive and reflective children, has found evidence which contradicts the common stereotypic belief that bright children think quickly in problem situations. The child who characteristically responds impulsively in trying to identify a concept or to solve a problem is likely to make more errors than the child who carefully considers the adequacy of several possible answers. To test this hypothesis, Kagan employed a Matching Familiar Figures test which asked children in grades one through three to match each of a group of familiar objects such as a tree or teddy bear (the standard) with one from an array of six strikingly similar images of the tree or teddy bear, only one of which was identical to the standard. As the child studied the array, the standard was available for comparison. The Haptic Visual Matching task was also used, in which the child first explores with his fingers a wooden form approximately three inches square hidden from view in a bag. After withdrawing his hand from the bag, he is asked to select from five visual stimuli the one he has explored with his fingers.

The results of both tests revealed that with increasing age children took a longer time and made fewer errors in selecting the correct response. At any age, however, children who responded quickly (impulsive) in performing these tasks made many more errors than did children who took longer (reflective). These findings suggest that the superior performance of the older child is due not to his having more mature cognitive structures, but to a slower, more thoughtful *conceptual tempo*, the disposition to reflect longer over the validity of his answer.

In another study Kagan[15] investigated the relationship between cog-

[14] Jerome Kagan, "Impulsive and Reflective Children: Significance of Conceptual Tempo," in John D. Krumboltz, ed., *Learning and the Educational Process* (Chicago: Rand McNally & Co., 1965), pp. 133–161.

[15] Jerome Kagan, "Reflection-Impulsivity and Reading Ability in Primary Children," *Child Development*, 36 (September 1965), 609–628.

nitive tempo (impulsive versus reflective) and word recognition among middle class first grade children. This study revealed that the longer a child delayed in selecting a figure which matched the standard in the Matching Familiar Figures test, the more accurate was his initial recognition of the word spoken by the examiner. The importance of delay was strikingly evident for low-verbal boys. Those low-verbal boys who delayed (were reflective) in responding were more accurate in recognizing letters than low-verbal boys who responded quickly (were impulsive). In a follow-up study a year later, those children, especially girls, who were of a reflective disposition made fewer errors in an oral reading task than did children who tended to be more impulsive in their cognitive responses.

These studies underscore the need for teachers to rid themselves of the stereotypic belief that the slow-responding student is less bright than the quick-responding student. Instead of categorizing a student as bright or dull, obedient or disobedient, timid or outgoing, teachers might better ascertain whether he is impulsive or reflective in his conceptual approach to problems. The child who tends to respond quickly and often incorrectly should be encouraged to take more time to study the alternatives carefully before answering. Finally, the teacher needs to consider his own tempo in the teaching-learning activity. Teachers with a rapid tempo may need to refrain from hurrying through presentations, reminding children that there is not much time left to complete the assignment, speaking fast, or offering a rapid flow of ideas. The teacher can encourage reflection by urging students to consider alternatives, to think about their answers, and to take time in responding.[16]

Development versus Learning in Concept Formation

Is the forming of concepts primarily the result of developmental processes and appropriate experiences, as Piaget suggests, or is it predominantly a function of learning? Gagné[17] poses this question and then hypothesizes that children in Piaget's experiments who are unable to conserve (to recognize the same volume of liquid in different-shaped containers) may fail in the task because they lack concrete knowledge of containers, volumes, areas, lengths, widths, heights, and liquids. Gagné believes, it may be recalled, that in order for a student to achieve a major educational objective (such as solving equations) he must first have acquired the subordinate capabilities that are needed to attain that objective. The subordinate capabilities are organized into what Gagné calls a hierarchy of learning sets or a cumulative learning sequence.

[16] Kagan, "Impulsive and Reflective Children," pp. 133–161.

[17] Robert M. Gagné, "Contributions of Learning to Human Development," *Psychological Review*, 75 (May 1968), 177–191.

Mouw and Hecht[18] sought to test Gagné's hypothesis that mental operations described by Piaget are more dependent upon learning than development. Mouw and Hecht trained third and fourth grade children so that they learned the concept of class inclusion; that is, of classifying various kinds of geometric figures (different kinds of triangles, rectangles, and so on) and pictures of different kinds of Ford and Chevrolet cars. They found that children who accomplished this task of putting objects into classes and subclasses also were successful in the transfer task of classifying maps of countries, states, and cities, and pictures of various foods. Furthermore, they found that fourth graders performed no better on the transfer task than did third graders. Since, according to Piaget's developmental theory, fourth graders would be expected to be superior to third graders, the results of this study seem to support Gagné's contention that acquiring a concept such as class inclusion might better be explained as the culmination of learning an organized system of concepts and principles than as the result of maturation.

We should bear in mind that most kinds of learning are influenced by both maturation and training or practice. Some, such as learning the concept of class inclusion described above, seem to be strongly influenced by prior learning, while other kinds which involve the acquisition of motor skills and patterns of logical thinking may be more dependent upon maturation. Teaching is probably most effective when children who are motivated and have the required maturational readiness are introduced to educational experiences which utilize their prior learning.

Generalizing

Generalizing is the act of deriving a general concept, principle, law, or theory from particular facts or observations. We noted that one forms a concept when he establishes a category with specified attributes; the concept becomes generalized as one finds and includes other examples in the category. The act of linking two or more concepts in meaningful combinations is a further example of generalizing. An interrelating of two or more concepts in the formula "If *A*, then *B*" results in the formation of a *principle*. Principles function to explain or to predict events and to control behavior. The use of concepts to form generalizations and principles and the use of these generalizations and principles to explain certain phenomena or events are illustrated in the following anecdotes from the case of David.

October 15.   *I had been reading supplementary material to the class on the Lewis and Clark Expedition. In his diary Lewis wrote, "I first tasted the water of the Great Columbia River." This*

[18] John T. Mouw and James T. Hecht, "Transfer of the 'Concept' of Class Inclusion," *Journal of Educational Psychology*, 64 (February 1973), 57–62.

entry was made soon after Lewis crossed the Continental Divide. The class did not understand what Lewis meant, since he was so far from the Columbia River at that time.

David raised his hand and said, "I can explain that. Lewis was drinking from the Lemki River which is one of the small tributaries of the Columbia River system. Its waters eventually flow into the Columbia."

I asked if everyone understood now what Lewis meant. Several hands went up. They did not understand what David meant by tributaries or river system.

"David, can you make your explanation clearer?" I asked.

He thought a minute and said, "Yes, m'am, I think I can." He walked to the board and said, "A river system looks something like the branches of a tree." He drew a picture of a tree. "Now here is the trunk, here are large branches, and from these grow small branches; from them grow tiny twigs, and from the twigs grow the leaves. In a river system the growth follows the opposite pattern. The leaves and tiny twigs represent very small streams and their sources which flow into larger streams or branches. These branches flow into larger streams and finally into the trunk or main river. The Lemki River begins just west of the Continental Divide and flows into the Salmon River. The Salmon flows into the Snake, which is a larger river. Then the Snake flows into the Columbia. So when Lewis drank from the Lemki River he was having his first drink from the Columbia."

After this explanation the class seemed to understand perfectly.

November 9.   In a unit of study on pioneer life, we read a story in which a little pioneer girl wanted to have her photograph made. She had to wait for a traveling photographer to come through.

I asked, "Why do you think she had to wait for a traveling photographer?"

Roy answered, "Because the pioneers were too poor to afford cameras."

Don offered, "There weren't many cameras in those days."

David had sat quietly listening to the discussion without contributing to it, but at this point he raised his eyebrows in his own personal mannerism and drawled, "Well, pioneers lived before the time of mass production. Those things were scarce and expensive. Because of this the ordinary family did not have them. Mass production is the reason we have cameras and many other luxuries today at prices people can afford."

In the October 15 entry, David used the concepts of Continental Divide, river tributaries, river system, tree, trunk, branches, and twig to develop generalizations explaining a statement in Lewis's diary. By analogy, David used a familiar generalization, "Leaves, twigs, branches, and trunk form a tree," to derive another generalization, "Mountain streams and the successively larger rivers formed by the flow of water are the tributaries of a river system." David also used the generalization "Water flows toward and collects in points of lowest elevation." The November 9 anecdote reveals that David used concepts of pioneer life, photography, traveling photographer, camera, money, income, scarce, expensive, products, and mass production to form two generalizations: "Mass production permits cameras and other products to be manufactured at prices people can afford" and "The advantages of mass production were not available to pioneer families."

Often, a statement of relationships between two or more concepts is made without sufficient evidence to support it as a generalization. Such statements, called *hypotheses*, are useful tools in scientific inquiry. Hypotheses that are supported by subsequent empirical tests become generalizations. The statement "There is a greater incidence of lung cancer and heart disease among persons who have been heavy smokers than among nonsmokers" is a generalization supported by evidence. The statement "Smoking causes lung cancer" remains a hypothesis suggested by the above generalization. Statements of the stable or invariable relationships between certain concepts in mathematics and physics are called *laws*. The following are examples of laws: "The angle of incidence equals the angle of reflection" and "The pressure of a gas is inversely proportional to its volume if its temperature remains constant."

Generalizations can be acquired in either of two ways: by *deduction* from laws, premises, or other generalizations; or by *induction*, in which specific instances are combined. Both processes are indispensable tools in reasoning and problem solving. Because of the characteristics of their data, some disciplines, such as philosophy and mathematics, usually employ deductive methods in solving problems and extending knowledge; other disciplines, such as the natural and social sciences, more often employ inductive methods. Deductive and inductive methods are most effectively used in tandem, with conclusions reached using one method being verified and checked by the other method. Few conclusions can be drawn regarding the superiority of either method. There is some evidence that children taught by deductive methods perform better if tested on the kinds of materials they had used in learning the generalizations. Children taught by the inductive method, however, realize greater transfer benefits—that is, they are better able to utilize the generalization in learning new material.

Thinking is another process or activity generally associated with cognitive functioning and development. Statements of educational objectives frequently include "the development of critical thinking." However, the term *thinking* has so many meanings (such as, "ponder," "reflect," "believe," "consider," "reason," "speculate," "deliberate") that it is not very useful as a description of cognitive processes unless it is clearly defined. For our purposes, we will define *thinking* as a generic term that refers to the mental activities of (1) organizing, manipulating, and interrelating facts and concepts, (2) forming and testing hypotheses, and (3) evaluating and interpreting evidence.

Many of our ideas about thinking as a process can be traced to the steps or phases of reflective thinking suggested by Dewey:[19]

1. *Suggestions of a possible solution.*

2. *Intellectualization of the difficulty or felt need.*

3. *Use of one hypothesis after another to initiate and to guide observation and the collection of data.*

4. *Mental elaboration of the idea or supposition.*

5. *Testing of hypotheses by overt or imaginative action.*

These steps, or variations of them, describe the scientific method of problem solving and were introduced in Chapter 2.

Taba[20] has analyzed strategies used by teachers in promoting thinking in elementary school children. The following strategies are intended to evoke children's thinking in classroom discussion.

1. Focusing *questions or remarks so as to establish both the content of the topic under consideration and the cognitive operations to be performed. Example: "What events and conditions favor the mobility of people in an underdeveloped country?"*

2. Extending *thought on the same level, which allows a sufficient amount of assimilation before thought is lifted to another level. This is essentially a strategy of inducing a number of students to respond to the same questions, rather than of pursuing a line of inquiry with the same student. Example: "What are some other reasons why people migrated westward?"*

3. Lifting *of the level of thought occurs when the teacher or child either gives or seeks information that shifts the thought to a higher level than a previously established one. Example: "What are some of the ways that the United States might be different today if it had been settled from west to east?"*

4. Controlling *thought, which occurs when the teacher does things for students that they should do for themselves. Example (a definition supplied by the teacher): "A homesteader is one who stakes out a land claim, erects buildings, and lives on the land."*

[19] John Dewey, *How We Think* (New York: D. C. Heath & Co., 1933).

[20] Hilda Taba, *Thinking in Elementary School Children*, Cooperative Research Project No. 1574 (Washington, D. C.: U. S. Office of Education, Department of Health, Education, and Welfare, 1964).

From her analyses of these teacher strategies, Taba concludes that transformations of concrete operations into formal ones begin in the second grade and increase slowly through the third and fourth grades; finally, in the fifth and sixth grades, formal thought represents approximately one sixth of all thought units offered. This suggests a somewhat earlier beginning of formal thought processes than has been postulated by Piaget. Taba views the development of thought as a continuous stream rather than as an accretion of specific skills. Taba concludes that the questions teachers ask are especially crucial in either limiting or enhancing the capacity of students to think.

More recently, Taba's strategies have been extended to include the following:

1. *Concept development.*

2. *Interpretation of data (arriving at generalizations).*

3. *Application of generalizations.*

4. *Interpretations of feelings, attitudes, and values.*

Trezise[21] describes how these strategies can be used in English classes, particularly in discussions of stories, novels, and poems which involve individual interpretations. First, the English teacher asks such questions as "What happened in the story you read?" in eliciting data from which concepts in the story can be identified and verbalized. The teacher then continues with a different type of question to elicit from students inferences about the way someone might have felt, such as "What do you think Macbeth felt when he entered Duncan's chamber?" The skilled teacher elicits as many inferences as possible about what the students think Macbeth might have felt and always asks why they think Macbeth would have felt that way. Next, the teacher leads students into a discussion that attempts to relate what they have been reading and discussing to their own lives. "Has anything like this happened to you? How did you feel?" Finally, the teacher asks the students to make an overall generalization on the basis of their discussion.

The teacher need not ask all these questions, as shown in the following anecdote, which reveals the strategies David's teacher used in encouraging thinking among her pupils.

October 26.   *We were discussing the Cuban blockade in class. The morning TV news had stated that the United States knew the positions of some 25 Russian ships. Roy asked, "How is that possible?" "By radar," David answered.*

---

[21] R. L. Trezise, "The Hilda Taba Teaching Strategies in English and Reading Classes," *English Journal*, 61 (April 1972), 577–580.

"I've seen radar screens on TV shows, but I don't understand how it works," remarked Roy.

David replied, "It's simple. Radio waves are sent out from a transmitter into space. When they strike an object they bounce back to their source, which has a receiver. We know the speed of radio waves, so the time they take to go and return gives us the distance to the object."

"But how do we know the objects they hit aren't our own ships at sea?" asked Roy.

"Because we know the location of our ships from their radio reports. There were none in the area where the Russian ships were," said David.

"Where were the radar stations that located the ships?" asked Carl.

"They were on our ships at sea. You see, radio waves can't follow the curvature of the earth, so ships at sea carry radar equipment and can locate objects if they are too far from our land-based radar stations," David explained.

Problem Solving

Problem solving is perhaps the most unique, complex, and significant of human abilities. Problem solving and creative behavior evidence a high level of cognitive development. The quality of problem-solving performance is dependent upon the availability of a broad range of concepts and generalizations and the development of thinking abilities. The full resources of one's development and learning are committed to solving the many kinds of problems he encounters in his daily life. The success one has in solving both mundane and challenging intellectual problems influences his concept of himself as a problem solver. A favorable image of self as problem solver is an impetus for continued problem-seeking, problem-solving behavior.

Problem-solving behavior occurs in response to a problem situation. One is confronted with a problem situation when he must choose and prepare for a vocation, when his income will not cover all his expenses, or when his car will not start. The student at school may be confronted during any one day with a wide variety of problems: proving a theorem in geometry, diagramming a sentence, identifying the elements in a chemical solution, finding ways of improving the student body's school spirit, or getting elected to class office. Scientists are confronted with problems of overpopulation, finding a cure for cancer, and reaching planets in outer space. Problem situations, then, are unique to the individual, may be general or specific, vary in complexity and importance, and may be of short or long duration.[22]

[22] See Frederick J. McDonald, *Educational Psychology*, 2nd ed. (Belmont, Calif.: Wadsworth Publishing Co., 1965), p. 254.

A distinction can be made between problems whose solutions are known to someone and problems whose solutions are unknown. Solving a puzzle or an equation is an example of the first type, while achieving a permanent peace is an example of the second. "A problem situation exists, then, when there is a goal to be attained, but the individual sees no well-defined, well-established means of attaining it; or when the goal is so vaguely defined or unclear to the person that he cannot determine what are relevant means for attaining it."[23]

We shall identify and discuss each step in problem solving in relation to a concrete problem. Ed Richardson, an eighth grader, inherited an old grandfather's clock from his grandmother. After repairing, oiling, and refurbishing it, he found that it continuously lost time. The first step in problem solving is a recognition of a felt need, which is manifested in a *goal to be achieved*—in this case, developing a more reliable clock. Since Ed was uncertain whether the difficulty was in the clock mechanism or with the pendulum, it was necessary for him to *analyze the situation.* Ed tested the gear mechanisms and other moving parts and found that all moved freely. It soon became clear, in the *redefinition of the problem*, that restoring the accuracy of the clock would involve correcting the speed of the pendulum.

Ed's preliminary analysis of the situation led to his *making several hypotheses* for increasing the velocity of the pendulum. He could (1) lighten the weight, (2) shorten the pendulum arm, (3) release the pendulum weight from a higher point on the arc, (4) increase the force used in starting the pendulum swinging, or (5) use some combination of these variables. By *testing each hypothesis* while holding each of the other variables constant, Ed found that only changing the length of the pendulum arm influenced its velocity. Weight, height of the drop, and force of the push in starting it were excluded as influences on the velocity of the pendulum. The *generalization* emerging from the solution to this problem is that shortening the arm of a pendulum increases the velocity of the pendulum, while lengthening the arm decreases its velocity.

Suchman[24] describes a procedure for helping elementary school children to improve their problem-solving performance through developing skills in inquiry. A sixth grade class observes a film clip of a man holding a long metal blade with a wooden handle. When the blade is held over a flame, it bends downward. After heating, the blade is plunged into a tank of water and it straightens out again. When the blade is turned over and heated again, the blade bends upward. The children are asked to find out why the events in the filmed episode occurred. To gather the information they need, they must ask questions. Restricting them to questions which can be answered "yes" or "no" requires the children to think through and to structure their own questions.

[23] McDonald, p. 253.

[24] J. Richard Suchman, *The Elementary School Training Program in Scientific Inquiry* (Urbana: University of Illinois Press, 1962).

Suchman found that children ask three types of questions about the filmed episode. Questions which seek information on temperature, pressure, shape of objects, or events in the episode are called *verification* questions (for example, "When heated, does the blade always bend in the same direction?"). In a second type of question, called *abstract-conceptual* questions, the child asks for a direct verification of his own hypothesis, thus avoiding having to gather data and make his own inferences (for example, "Does the bending of the blade have anything to do with the heat?"). A third type of question, called *concrete-inferential* questions, is much like an experiment in that the child manipulates a variable and then asks what the outcome of this manipulation would be (for example, "If we made the flame hotter, would the blade bend further?"). In this type of question, the child makes his own inference as to causality from the data he obtains. The object of inquiry training, according to Suchman, is to increase the amount of verification and experimentation undertaken by a child on his own, and to reduce the number of attempts he makes to pick the brains of the teacher with abstract-conceptual questions.

Suchman found that inquiry-trained groups asked significantly more verification questions than did control groups and significantly fewer abstract-conceptual questions. The two groups did not differ, however, in their use of experimentation; nor were there significant group differences on tests measuring knowledge of concepts. In spite of the negative nature of some of his results, Suchman concludes that inquiry training has a marked effect on the motivation, autonomy, and question-asking fluency of children: "They clearly enjoy having the freedom and power to gather their own data in their quest for assimilation."[25]

Numerous studies[26] suggest that young children are able to perform rather advanced problem-solving tasks, but that this ability tends to extinguish quickly, is subject to interference, and does not transfer to other tasks. These findings are seen by some as invalidating stimulus-response explanations of concept formation and supporting Piaget's theory that a child's performance of a given cognitive task must await his attainment of the requisite stage of intellectual development. Anderson,[27] however, hypothesizes that first grade children who are given suitable training will acquire a rather advanced problem-solving skill. Anderson formed 60 first graders in the highest third of the mental age distribution into two groups, a training group and a control group. Three times a week, members of the training group were given individual 20-minute training sessions in identifying a range of concepts (geometric figures, leaf facsimiles, cowboys with

[25] Suchman, p. 126.

[26] See, for example, David P. Ausubel and N. M. Schiff, "The Effect of Incidental and Experimentally Induced Experience in the Learning of Relevant and Irrelevant Causal Relationships by Children," *Journal of Genetic Psychology*, 84 (1954), 109–123; and Susan M. Ervin, "Training and a Logical Operation by Children," *Child Development* (September 1960), pp. 555–563.

[27] Richard C. Anderson, "Can First Graders Learn an Advanced Problem-Solving Skill?" *Journal of Educational Psychology*, 56 (December 1965), 283–294.

varying features, and a pegboard game). After the training, both groups were tested on problems that required them to identify concepts similar to those presented earlier only to the training group. Anderson found that children receiving training solved more problems involving retention with fewer unnecessary trials; they also solved more transfer problems and solved them more efficiently than did the control group. Anderson interprets these findings as supporting a stimulus-response theory of concept development.

Many of the issues and variables that relate to learning in general can also be observed in problem solving. The reader will recall that puzzle boxes and problem-solving tasks are used by both cognitive field theorists (who favor an insight explanation of learning) and stimulus-response theorists (who favor a trial-and-confirmation explanation of problem solving). It appears that many puzzle-like problems lend themselves to a sudden solution, with few trials required once key concepts or relationships are grasped. "With six matches of equal length, make four and only four equilateral triangles" is a problem whose solution is dependent upon insight. Other problems lend themselves more readily to a trial-and-confirmation strategy —"Given: Three jars holding three, five, and eight quarts, respectively. The first two are empty, and the third is filled with water. Divide the liquid into two equal parts using only the three jars."

Success and failure appear to have a marked influence on problem-solving behavior.[28] Students who consistently fail in solving problems spend more time working on problems, evidence greater tension, have a stronger desire to give up and substitute a different goal, and, while working on the problem, engage in more fantasy and use less realistic problem-solving behavior. Schroder and Hunt[29] found that students who withdraw from a problem-solving situation prior to achieving a solution set higher goals originally, use fewer alternative solutions in attempting to solve the problem, and perform less effectively after failure than do those who achieve solutions.

Set

An individual's problem-solving performance is greatly influenced by his predisposition to perceive, to approach, and to respond to a given problem situation in a certain way. This predisposition is what psychologists call *set*. For most of us, a two-dimensional set will prevent, initially, our grasping the solution to the problem of forming four equilateral triangles with six matches of equal length. The influence of set is most evident when

[28] See B. Lantz, "Some Dynamic Aspects of Success and Failure," *Psychological Monographs*, 271 (1945).

[29] H. M. Schroder and D. E. Hunt, "Failure Avoidance in Situational Interpretation and Problem Solving," *Psychological Monographs*, 342 (1957).

individuals taught to solve problems by one method persist in applying that method to problems even when it repeatedly fails to solve them. Thus, set promotes positive transfer to problems of the same class but produces negative transfer to problems of other classes. Negative transfer was demonstrated in a study by Birch and Rabinowitz[30] involving the problem of tying together two strings suspended from the ceiling and placed sufficiently far apart that they could not be held at the same time. The problem could have been solved by attaching a weight to one string, thus making it into a pendulum. Subjects had available to them an electrical switching relay they had used in a previous problem, but they were unable to see this object as a possible weight for making a pendulum.

The set a student has prior to his beginning a learning activity is shaped by many factors. The instructions a teacher gives a class for doing an assignment may significantly influence the learning of the class. The learning produced, for example, if the teacher instructs the class to note similarities and differences is likely to be different from that emerging if he tells students to read and memorize.[31] The socialization patterns a student has experienced may also influence set by encouraging either convergent thinking or novelty, originality, and divergent thinking. Some persons may be open, flexible, and creative in dealing with some types of problems, but fixed, unyielding, and conventional in dealing with other types. A successful businessman, for example, may exhibit great flexibility and creativity in producing or marketing new products, but may remain very rigid in his approach to certain social and political problems. Most persons do feel more comfortable using patterns that have proven successful in the past. By the very nature of the task, however, problem solving calls for new, fresh, and original approaches.

The evidence indicates that a learner's set can be a strong deterrent to his solving of problems that require new approaches; but the evidence also shows that the teacher can help to modify the learner's set. The inhibiting effects of set can be reduced if teachers introduce students to problems that require different and varied approaches. Greater emphasis also should be given to the methods and processes involved in solving a problem, and less stress should be given to problems that require only one correct answer.

Transfer and Problem Solving

An important concern of the teacher in facilitating learning should be to assure that concepts and skills that students learn in one situation will be applied—in adapted form if necessary—in other situations. Do stu-

---

[30] H. G. Birch and H. S. Rabinowitz, "The Negative Effect of Previous Experience in Productive Thinking," *Journal of Experimental Psychology*, 41 (1951), 121–125.

[31] See M. C. Wittrock, "Effects of Certain Sets upon Complex Learning Material," *Journal of Educational Psychology*, 54 (April 1963), 85–88.

dents who write, spell, and punctuate correctly on tests and exercises also spell and punctuate correctly in letters and themes? Do students who learn the Pythagorean theorem in geometry apply this theorem later in trigonometry? Evidences of *transfer* are often used as a measure of learning.

In no outcome of learning is transfer of greater importance than in problem solving. Solving a problem facing one at a particular moment may be of immediate practical value, but, since problem solving is a lifelong activity, the skills, methods, and insights gained in solving a particular problem have significance only as they can be transferred in the solving of other problems.

The advantages of knowing and applying generalizations in solving new but related problems were demonstrated in an early experiment by Judd.[32] Two groups of boys were given practice in throwing darts at a target submerged in a foot of water until both groups had developed approximately the same level of proficiency. At the beginning of the experiment, one group had been given an explanation of the principles involved in the refraction of light. Initially, this information appeared to have little influence on their performance in throwing darts. However, when the depth of the water was changed from 12 to four inches, the group which had been given the principle of refraction of light adjusted quickly to the new situation, while the group lacking the principle had difficulty adjusting.

Other studies show that transfer is increased when students derive principles for themselves. Haslerud and Meyers[33] gave a group of students two kinds of problems: (1) problems for which both the principles of solution and their application were explained and (2) problems for which no directions relevant to solutions were given. On a test measuring transfer, after a practice test, students' scores increased significantly on those problems which required them to derive the principle in order to solve the problem. Haslerud and Meyers suggest that a specific explanation blocks transfer because it prevents the student from anticipating new applications of the principles.

Transfer in problem solving is facilitated when the student understands the principles involved in the solution of the original problem. The teacher has an important role in this process. The teacher can assist students in applying problem-solving learning to other situations by showing that a principle of solution is relevant to other problems, by having students apply a principle to a wide variety of problems, by preparing students to recognize problems similar to those on which they have worked, and by helping students to become aware of and to anticipate the usefulness of previously learned principles in solving new problems.[34]

---

[32] Charles H. Judd, "The Relation of Special Training to Special Intelligence," *Educational Review*, 36 (1908), 28–42. For a similar study, see G. Hendrickson and W. H. Schroeder, "Transfer of Training and Learning to Hit a Submerged Target," *Journal of Educational Psychology*, 32 (1941), 205–213.

[33] George M. Haslerud and S. Meyers, "The Transfer Value of Given and Individually Derived Principles," *Journal of Educational Psychology*, 49 (1958), 293–298.

[34] McDonald, p. 282.

Creativity

There is no general agreement on what creativity is. Members of one symposium[35] variously defined creativity as life itself, as a way of life, as optimum growth in social interaction, and as a maximum of self-actualizing. McKinnon[36] has defined creativity as "a process extended in time and characterized by originality, adaptiveness, and realization." He elaborates:

> If a response is to lay claim to being a part of the creative process, it must to some extent be adaptive to, or of, reality. It must serve to solve a problem, fit a situation, or accomplish some recognizable goal. And, thirdly, true creativity involves a sustaining of original insight, an evaluation and elaboration of it, a developing of it to the full.[37]

Some writers have found it useful to distinguish between creative behavior and original behavior. Original behavior is that behavior "which occurs relatively infrequently, is uncommon under given conditions, and is relevant to those conditions."[38] Originality, thus defined, can be more easily translated into behavioral terms and studied in relation to problem solving. Creative behavior, on the other hand, is behavior that *results* in products or achievements judged to be creative by relevant judges.[39]

Creativity and Intelligence

Since the term *gifted* has often been used to describe both creative individuals and those of high intelligence, it is not surprising that highly creative and highly intelligent persons have been pictured as sharing many of the same qualities. Studies have shown rather consistently, however, that while creative persons are generally above average in intelligence, the qualities associated with the highly creative person and the highly intelligent person are sufficiently different as to make each type independent and dis-

---

[35] Harold H. Anderson, ed., *Creativity and Its Cultivation* (New York: Harper & Row, 1959).

[36] Donald W. McKinnon, "The Nature and Nurture of Creative Talent," *American Psychologist*, 16 (July 1962), 484–495.

[37] McKinnon, p. 485.

[38] I. Maltzman, "On the Training of Originality," *Psychological Review*, 67 (1960), 229.

[39] McDonald, p. 293.

tinctive. Taylor[40] points out that traditional intelligence tests cover only a very few of the dimensions of the mind and suggests that IQ may be only one of the several types of intellectual gifts.

Getzels and Jackson[41] identified a group of "high-creative" adolescents who scored at the eightieth percentile in tests of creativity but below it in IQ. A group of "high-IQ" students from the same population scored at the eightieth percentile or above in IQ but scored below it on tests of creativity. The mean IQ of the high-creative group was below the school mean and 23 points below the mean of the high-IQ group. McKinnon[42] found, in studies of creative mathematicians and architects, essentially a zero relationship between creativity and intelligence. He concluded that it is just not true that the more intelligent person is necessarily the more creative one.

Studies show that high-IQ students are generally preferred over average students by their teachers, while highly creative students tend to be less preferred. Nuss[43] found that creativity as measured by a creativity test is relatively independent of intelligence, but that creativity as measured by teachers' ratings is positively associated with intelligence. The same was true in the case of creativity and scholastic achievement. In the study by Getzels and Jackson cited above, a close relationship was found between the qualities high-IQ students value in themselves and the qualities they believe lead to success, suggesting that high-IQ students are highly success oriented. The very low relationship found between the qualities high-creative students value in themselves and those they believe lead to success suggests that high-creative students are not highly success oriented, at least not by conventional adult standards.

Encouraging Creativity

Carl Rogers has set forth a tentative theory of creativity relating to the nature of the creative act, the conditions under which it occurs, and the manner in which it can be fostered. Rogers defines the creative process as "the emergence in action of a novel relational product, growing out of the uniqueness of the individual on the one hand, and the materials, events, people, or circumstances of his life on the other."[44] The motivation for crea-

---

[40] Calvin W. Taylor, "A Tentative Description of the Creative Individual," in Walter B. Waetjen, ed., *Human Variability and Learning* (Washington, D. C.: Association for Supervision and Curriculum Development, N.E.A., 1961), pp. 62–79.

[41] Jacob W. Getzels and Philip W. Jackson, *Creativity and Intelligence* (New York: John Wiley, 1962), pp. 13–76.

[42] McKinnon, pp. 487–488.

[43] Eugene M. Nuss, "An Exploration of the Relationship between Creativity and Certain Personal-Social Variables" (unpublished doctor's dissertation, University of Maryland, 1961).

[44] Carl R. Rogers, "Toward a Theory of Creativity," in Anderson, p. 71.

tivity is the directional trend which is evident in all organic life: the urge to expand, extend, develop, and mature. Rogers postulates that persons who possess an openness to experience, an internal locus of evaluation, and an ability to toy with elements will, in a climate of psychological freedom, form a greater number of creative products.

Hamby[45] tested parts of Rogers' theory in an investigation of the relationship between teacher behavior and change in children's creative performance. She hypothesized that fourth grade children in art classes under a nondirective, nonevaluative teacher would show greater gains in creativity and self-concept than would fourth grade students in art classes under a directive, evaluative teacher. With nondirective, nonevaluative structuring, the teacher was endeavoring to establish a climate of psychological safety and freedom and to encourage openness to experience and self-evaluation.

Children in art classes under nondirective, nonevaluative structuring made significantly higher scores than did children under directive, evaluative structuring on only two of 21 subtests of the Verbal Battery, Minnesota Tests of Creative Thinking. At the end of an eight-week period, children in nondirective, nonevaluative art classes received significantly higher scores than children in directive, evaluative art classes on judges' evaluations of the creativity of their art products; at the end of 16 weeks, however, the scores of the two groups were not significantly different.

Torrance[46] conducted a study of another teaching method designed to stimulate the flow of creative ideas among children in grades three through six. Each child was encouraged to have an "idea trap"—a small note pad on which he was to record his ideas any time they came to him. The children were urged to write down their ideas for poems, stories, jokes, songs, inventions, and cartoons. Every Friday, each pupil was asked to select from his idea trap one idea for possible use in a weekly magazine, *Ideas of the Week*. At the beginning and end of the six-week study, each pupil wrote an imaginary story. The stories were scored using scales developed for evaluating creativity.

Torrance found that children in grades three to six can be stimulated to do a great deal of creative work. The third graders were highest in productivity and showed significant growth in creative writing as measured by pretraining and posttraining stories. The fourth and sixth graders also showed growth on two of the three measures of creativity. The fifth graders, however, showed regressive trends. There was evidence in this study that the children had learned to value more highly their own ideas—indeed, they objected rather violently to the small amount of editing that was done on their creative writing. Torrance presents the following principles to guide teachers in encouraging and rewarding children's creative thinking:

---

[45] Trudy M. Hamby, "An Investigation of the Relationship between Teacher Structuring and Change in Children's Creative Performance and Self-Ideal Self-Reports" (unpublished doctor's dissertation, University of Maryland, 1966).

[46] E. Paul Torrance, *Rewarding Creative Behavior* (Englewood Cliffs, N. J.: Prentice-Hall, 1965).

1.   *Be respectful of children's questions.*

2.   *Be respectful of imaginative and unusual ideas.*

3.   *Show pupils their ideas have value.*

4.   *Give opportunities for practice or experimentation without evaluation.*

5.   *Encourage and evaluate self-initiated learning.*

6.   *Evaluate in ways that foster the pupil's ability to see the causes and consequences of his behavior.*[47]

Structure of the Intellect

An overview of the aspects and dimensions of cognitive functioning that have been discussed in this chapter is provided by Guilford's investigations into human intelligence. His model of the structure of the intellect (see Figure 17–3) is organized in relation to three major aspects of cognitive functioning: *operations, products,* and *contents.* An *ability* is a combination of an operation, a content, and a product. In identifying five kinds of operations, four kinds of contents, and six kinds of products, Guilford hypothesizes that there are 120 possible abilities in the human cognitive domain. He describes each of the operations, contents, and products as follows:

OPERATIONS	*Major kinds of intellectual activities or processes; things that the organism does with the raw materials of information, information being defined as "that which the organism discriminates."*
Cognition	*Immediate discovery, awareness, rediscovery, or recognition of information in various forms; comprehension or understanding.*
Memory	*Retention of storage, with some degree of availability, of information in the same form it was committed to storage and in response to the same cues in connection with which it was learned.*
Divergent production	*Generation of information from given information, where emphasis is upon variety and quantity of out-*

[47] Torrance, pp. 314–319. See also G. A. Davis, "Teaching for Creativity: Some Guiding Lights," *Journal of Research and Development in Education,* 4 (Spring 1971), 29–34.

put from the same source. Likely to involve what has been called transfer. This operation is most clearly involved in aptitudes of creative potential.

Convergent
production

Generation of information from given information, where the emphasis is upon achieving unique or conventionally accepted best outcomes. It is likely the given (cue) information fully determines the response.

Evaluation

Reaching decisions or making judgments concerning criterion satisfaction (correctness, suitability, adequacy, desirability, etc.) of information.

CONTENTS

Broad classes or types of information discriminable by the organism.

Figural

Information in concrete form, as perceived or as recalled, possibly in the form of images. The term figural *minimally implies figure-ground perceptual organization. Visual spatial information is figural. Different sense modalities may be involved, e.g., visual kinesthetic.*

Symbolic

Information in the form of denotative signs, having no significance in and of themselves, such as letters, numbers, musical notations, codes, and words, when meanings and form are not considered.

Semantic

Information in the form of meanings to which words commonly become attached, hence most notable in verbal thinking and in verbal communication but not identical with words. Meaningful pictures also often convey semantic information.

Behavioral

Information, essentially nonverbal, involved in human interactions where the attitudes, needs, desires, moods, intentions, perceptions, thoughts, etc. of other people or ourselves are involved.

PRODUCTS

Forms that information takes in the organism's processing of it.

Units

Relatively segregated or circumscribed items of information having "thing" character. May be close to Gestalt psychology's "figure on a ground."

Classes

Conceptions underlying sets of items of information grouped by virtue of their common properties.

Relations	Connections between items of information based upon variables or points of contact that apply to them. Relational connections are more meaningful and definable than implications.
Systems	Organized or structured aggregates of items of information; complexes of interrelated or interacting parts.
Transformations	Changes of various kinds (redefinition, shifts, or modification) in existing information or in its function.
Implications	Extrapolations of information, in the form of expectancies, predictons, known or suspected antecedents, concomitants, or consequences. The connection between the given information and the extrapolated is more general and less definable than a relational connection.[48]

Teachers may find this model useful for identifying and defining specific learning outcomes. Learning the multiplication table, for example, would be representative of the memory-symbolic-classes cell, while ascertaining the geographical position of Chicago by interpreting a map would be representative of the convergent-semantic-relations cell. Thus far, Guilford has identified more than 80 of the possible 120 abilities of his model.[49]

Guilford's model, especially those elements of it relating to convergent and divergent thinking, has stimulated considerable interest and investigation. Each kind of thinking appears to be associated with a distinctive personality pattern. Getzels and Jackson,[50] for example, found that adolescents high in divergent thinking and highly creative in their nonverbal productions are more stimulus-free (in that they tend to structure a task in their own terms), more fanciful and humorous, and tend to express more aggression and violence. High-divergent, high-creative adolescents tend to produce new forms, to risk joining dissimilar articles, and to go off in new directions. High-IQ adolescents, on the other hand, tend to focus on the usual, the right answer or the socially acceptable answer, and to shy away from the risk and uncertainty of the unknown.

[48] J. P. Guilford and Ralph Hoepfner, *Structure-of-Intellect Factors and Their Tests, 1966,* reports from the Psychological Laboratory, University of Southern California, Los Angeles, California, Report No. 36, 1966, pp. 3–4. Used here by permission.

[49] J. P. Guilford, "Intelligence: 1965 Model," *American Psychologist,* 21 (January 1966), 20–26.

[50] Getzels and Jackson, pp. 50–52.

Figure 17–3.   Model of the Structure of the Intellect

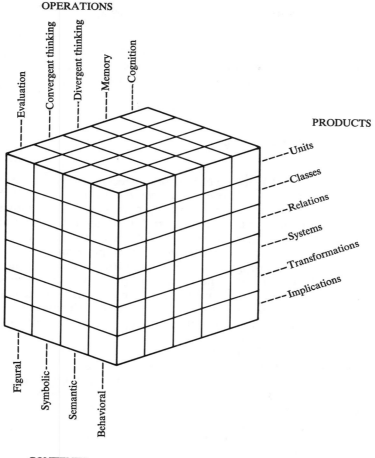

CONTENTS

Source: J. P. Guilford, "Three Faces of Intellect," *American Psychologist*, 14 (1959), 470. Reproduced by permission.

Gallagher,[51] using a system for classifying verbal statements developed from Guilford's model of the structure of the intellect, analyzed the productive thought processes displayed in the classroom by intellectually gifted adolescents and their teachers. Gallagher found that in nearly all

[51] James J. Gallagher, *Productive Thinking of Gifted Children*, Cooperative Research Project No. 965 (Washington, D.C.: U.S. Office of Education, Department of Health, Education, and Welfare, 1963).

class sessions, 50 percent or more of the questions teachers asked related to cognitive memory operations. The second most frequently used category was that of convergent thinking, with a much smaller proportion of questions calling for divergent thinking or evaluation. The patterns of thought expressed by students were closely related to the kinds of questions they were asked. The findings of this study underscore the crucial role played by the teacher as the initiator and determiner of the kinds of thought processes expressed by children in the classroom.

Summary

The outcomes of learning can be organized into three major types or categories: *cognitive, psychomotor,* and *affective.* Although a given behavior pattern may be predominantly cognitive, psychomotor, or affective, the three types of outcomes and processes are interrelated. Learning outcomes become organized into hierarchies, in which more complex behavior patterns and integrations are formed from simpler patterns.

The processes through which one acquires, organizes, interrelates, and interprets the data of his experience are called cognitive processes. The data acquired, processed, and transformed are cognitive outcomes of increasing complexity: preverbal percepts, factual information, concepts, generalizations and principles, problem solving, creative thinking, theories, and systematized knowledge.

A *concept* is a classification of stimuli that have common characteristics. In forming concepts, one must discriminate between relevant and irrelevant features of the data and generalize by correctly identifying the several instances or exemplars which belong to this category of concept. The concepts that children and youth acquire depend upon the kinds and qualities of experiences they have. The teacher's failure to utilize illustrations of concepts drawn from students' experiences often results in misunderstanding and incomplete learning. Schools also have a responsibility to encourage pupils to avoid stereotypes by helping them to develop adequate, valid concepts of people, places, and events.

Studies of strategies used in teaching concepts reveal that students given 100-percent, immediate reinforcement learn concepts more quickly than do students given partial or delayed reinforcement. Although learners may use or apply a concept without defining it, the ability to verbalize a concept can be increased by practice in defining it.

Learning concepts, as well as other types of learning, depends upon the adequacy and accuracy of sensory input—visual, auditory, tactual, and kinesthetic. Integration of these *sensory modalities* facilitates concept attainment and is especially important in learning to read. Differences in sensory modalities, as these influence perception and learning, are revealed in the differential responses of field-dependent (responding to visual cues) and field-independent (responding to body sensations) subjects in aligning themselves with the vertical.

Studies of *conceptual tempo* reveal that cognitive development is more likely to be enhanced if the child carefully considers the adequacy of several possible answers to a problem (reflective) instead of making a quick, ill-considered response (impulsive). The learning of some types of concepts seems to be strongly influenced by prior learning, while other kinds of learning, such as the acquisition of motor skills and patterns of logical thinking, seem to be more dependent upon maturation.

Generalizing is the act of deriving a general concept, principle, law, or theory from particular facts or observations. Generalizations can be acquired in either of two ways: by *deduction* from laws, premises, or other generalizations; or, by *induction*, in which specific instances are combined. In reasoning and problem solving, deductive and inductive methods are most effectively used in tandem, with conclusions reached using one method being verified and checked by the other method.

Problem solving—the most unique, complex, and significant of human abilities—is dependent upon the availability of a broad range of concepts and generalizations and the development of thinking abilities. The steps in problem solving include (1) identifying a goal to be achieved, (2) analyzing the situation, (3) redefining the problem, (4) making hypotheses, (5) testing each hypothesis, and (6) generalizing from the findings emerging from tests of hypotheses. The problem-solving abilities of elementary school children can be improved by improving their skills in inquiry. Through inquiry training, children are encouraged to undertake their own verification and experimentation instead of attempting to pick the brains of others in order to avoid gathering data and making independent inferences.

Problem-solving performance is greatly influenced by *set*, one's predisposition to perceive, to approach, and to respond to a given problem situation in a certain way. The learner's set is a strong deterrent to his solving of problems that require new approaches, but the limiting effects of set can be reduced if teachers give children practice with problems that require different and varied approaches. Studies show that *transfer* from one problem-solving situation to another is facilitated when the student understands the principles involved in the solution of the first problem.

Creativity often involves a high development of cognitive abilities. However, while creative persons are generally above average in intelligence, the qualities associated with highly intelligent persons and with highly creative persons are sufficiently different as to make each type independent and distinctive. The view that creativity is a quality that can, to some degree, be nurtured and developed in all students has prompted educators to develop programs which give greater emphasis and encouragement to creativity.

The major aspects and dimensions of cognitive functioning are represented in Guilford's model of the structure of the intellect. The various combinations of the components of the three major aspects of cognitive functioning—*operations, products,* and *contents*—indicate the abilities possible in the human cognitive domain.

Study Questions

1.   The terms *knowledge, comprehension,* and *understanding* are frequently used in describing cognitive processes and outcomes. What distinctions would you make between these terms?

2.   Identify one or more concepts you would expect your students to master. Describe the steps of the instructional strategies you would use in helping your students acquire these concepts. How would you provide in your selection of teaching strategies for individual differences among students?

3.   How might you identify the preferred sensory modalities of your students? What concepts in your subject field could you teach by utilizing the sense of touch and the sense of body awareness?

4.   What explanations can you offer about why our schools in the past have seemed to fail to give strong emphasis and encouragement to nurturing of creativity?

Suggested Readings

Almy, Millie. *Young Children's Thinking.* New York: Teachers College Press, Columbia University, 1966. Explores some of Piaget's theories about young children's thinking and considers the significance of these theories for early childhood education in the United States. Reports two studies of young American children which test Piaget's theories of the thought processes of young children involving conservation of number. Discusses implications for curriculum planning in early childhood and for further research on changes in thought processes in children from ages five to seven.

Bloom, Benjamin S., ed. *Taxonomy of Educational Objectives. Handbook I. Cognitive Domain.* New York: David McKay Co., 1956. Identifies major dimensions and types of cognitive learning: knowledge, comprehension, application, analysis, synthesis, and evaluation. Provides helpful hints on how each of the cognitive learning objectives in various subject fields can be stated and suggests appropriate ways for evaluating each.

Bruner, Jerome S., Rose R. Olver, and Patricia M. Greenfield. *Studies in Cognitive Growth.* New York: John Wiley, 1966. A theoretical assessment of the processes of cognitive development in children which focuses on how children come to develop different strategies of problem solving using a wide variety of experimental techniques. The book examines the growth of three systems for representing information—through action, through imagery, and through symbolization of language. The authors are as much concerned with the cultural patterning of cognition as with growth from a purely maturational point of view.

Getzels, Jacob W., and Philip W. Jackson. *Creativity and Intelligence*. New York: John Wiley, 1962. Reports research which shows that highly creative persons and highly intelligent persons differ significantly in personal values, imaginative productions, career goals, and family backgrounds. The implications of these findings for teaching and learning are discussed.

Inhelder, Barbel, and Jean Piaget. *The Growth of Logical Thinking from Childhood to Adolescence*. New York: Basic Books, 1958. Describes studies of the development of formal psychological structures which "mark the completion of the operational development of intelligence."

Films

My Name Is Children, 16 mm, sound, black and white, 60 min. Bloomington: Audiovisual Center, Indiana University. This film shows how one school is using an inquiry approach to motivate its students to learn. Children are seen working alone, in small groups, and in large groups. The teachers coordinate their plans and discuss individual student problems in daily meetings. The children are deeply involved in their learning of subjects from dinosaurs and democracy to bees and propaganda methods.

The Outcomes of Learning: Psychomotor and Affective

There's only one corner of the universe you can be sure of improving and that's your own self.

Aldous Huxley

Optimum self-development and psychological health depend upon the full development and integration of all of man's powers. This suggests that effective functioning as a person requires the harmonious blending of affective, cognitive, and psychomotor components of behavior. An individual's full development requires not only cognitive abilities, but also an adequate repertoire of psychomotor skills and affective responses.

Psychomotor Learning

The term *psychomotor* refers to a class of responses which involve the coordination of the body or any of its parts. Rather than viewing psychomotor behavior as a series of motor responses made to reach some goal, it may be more useful to view such behavior as *information-processing* activity guided by some general plan or program.[1] Thus, skilled psychomotor performance can be viewed as involving the coordination and sequencing of the biochemical and electrochemical activities of muscles, glands, and nerves in the translation, transmission, collation, storage, and in some cases the reduction and the generation of information. Central to all information processing is the general concept of *coding*—a system for representing information relating to neurophysiological processes, inputs to man's sensory channels, as well as his motor responses. This emphasis upon information processing and coding has resulted in a lessening of the sharp distinctions between verbal and motor learning, since the same

---

[1] P. M. Fitts, "Perceptual-Motor Skill Learning," in A. W. Melton, ed., *Categories of Human Learning* (New York: Academic Press, 1964), pp. 243–285.

processes seem to be involved in both types of learning. We shall begin our study of psychomotor learning by identifying and discussing the characteristics of psychomotor skill.

Characteristics of Psychomotor Skill

Accurate conception of the task.   The initial characteristic of an effective psychomotor performance is a clear conception of the goal to be achieved and of the general task and subtasks that must be executed in achieving it. Any skilled performance, even opening a door or writing one's name, involves hundreds of input-output sensation-nerve-muscle coordinations. The learner first visualizes the general task and consciously selects particular movements to be made. As he proceeds with the task, he plans the details and executes the steps with reference to the goal to be achieved. As the act is repeated, the subtasks may appear in different forms; eventually, as the learner integrates separate movements into a smoothly coordinated pattern, the subtasks drop out.

These steps can be illustrated in the skill performance of driving a car. The beginning driver gives a great deal of his attention individually to the clutch, brake, accelerator, speedometer, steering wheel, where he is in relation to the edge of the road, the locations of other cars around him and the presumed intentions of their drivers, traffic lights, street signs, pedestrians, and countless other stimuli. So preoccupied is the beginner with these subtasks that he is unable to carry on a conversation with his passenger. Repetitions of the act of driving bring about a consolidation and habituation of the subtasks and responses. No longer does he have to consciously think about shifting, steering, or braking. As a result of habituation, the movements occur automatically. At this point, the maturing driver is likely to be carrying on an animated conversation with his passenger and is probably little aware of making the many individual movements and adjustments required in driving the car.

Use of cues.   A skilled performer can be distinguished from one with less skill by his manner of utilizing cues. Cues are stimuli, originating both internally and externally, which guide an individual's responses in performing a skill. The beginner is more dependent than the expert on direct visual cues. The beginning typist or pianist must look at the keyboard to use only muscle cues in "feeling" the location on the keyboard of a letter or note. The experienced performer requires fewer cues and is able to take advantage of equivalent cues. The symphony orchestra violinist reads music in phrases rather than in separate notes. He also recognizes the equivalence of the term *allegro* in the musical score to the quick tempo of the conductor's beat, to the "sound" in his mind of the music played at a quick tempo, and to the "feel" in his muscles of playing the music at an allegro tempo.

A skilled performer also makes finer and more precise cue discriminations than one who is less skilled. The fine musician can discriminate between two tones that sound the same to most persons in the audience. The center fielder, anticipating the direction of a possible fly ball, responds to cues in the batter's movements even before the ball is hit.

As mastery of a skill increases, cue discriminations become more automatic and the number of cues required for performing the skill decreases. The many direct visual cues required by the beginning driver mentioned above drop out as his experience increases and his skill improves.

Feedback and correction.　　When he feels his car drifting to the left or right—perhaps because of road conditions, wind, or the condition of the tires or brakes—the driver moves the steering wheel slightly to compensate. The driver's sense that his car is drifting is an example of the process of *feedback;* his movement of the steering wheel is an example of *correction,* a response to feedback. Feedback and correction are interrelated processes that occur throughout a skilled performance. An experienced typist, pianist, high jumper, golfer, or lathe operator continuously evaluates his performance from feedback received through his sense of timing or the "feel" of his muscles and corrects his performance accordingly.

The phases of a skill performance thus correspond to the model of behavior proposed by Miller, Galanter, and Pribram.[2] They suggest that behavior can be described in terms of what they call TOTE units. TOTE is an acronym for Test-Operate-Test-Exit. The initial *test* consists of the learner's concept of the task or problem facing him. The task may involve a skilled performance (such as driving a car or shaping a piece of wood on a lathe) or it may involve a cognitive process (such as discovering the concept or principle needed to explain a phenomenon). *Operate* stands for the learner's response to the initial test—turning the steering wheel, guiding the lathe, or testing a hypothesis relative to a concept or principle. The next *test* involves a comparison of the results obtained by the operation process and the criteria of the goal of the process—arriving at a destination, making a table leg, explaining a phenomenon. This step involves the processes of feedback and correction described above. Often, many test-operate-test-operate-test units are required before the goal is achieved. When the criteria of the goal have been met, the test-operate sequence terminates, a step that is called *exit.*

The selection of particular TOTE units to be employed in the performance of a psychomotor skill implies the existence of a plan. *Plan* is a central construct of the theory of Miller and his associates and is defined as any hierarchical process in the organism that can control the order in which a sequence of operations is to be performed. A plan is for the organism essentially the same as a program is for a computer.

Coordination of movements.　　The performance of a skill usually requires a series of many simple movements involving the coordination of

---

[2] George A. Miller, Eugene Galanter, and Karl H. Pribram, *Plans and the Structure of Behavior* (New York: Holt, Rinehart and Winston, 1960).

many muscles. In the early stages of learning a skill, each movement tends to be performed as a separate act. The beginning driver is likely to focus in turn on releasing the brake, shifting the gear, letting out the clutch, and pressing lightly on the accelerator. The beginning typist concentrates on hitting the correct individual keys. The resulting performances are usually a series of jerky movements.

With practice, these separate movements become integrated into one smooth, rhythmic movement. This integration is what is meant by the term *motor coordination.* In such a coordination of movements, some responses are subordinated, others are blended together, and a few are emphasized. In a well-coordinated skill performance, these responses are carefully timed, each separate act occurring at the proper moment and in the proper sequence. The skilled typist and pianist respond not to separate letters or notes but to phrases or sequences of phrases. Coordination of responses permits the typist or pianist to incorporate longer or more complex sequences into the continuous rhythmical movements of a skilled performance.

Speed and accuracy.   As a skilled performance comes to reflect more and more the operation of the processes described above, the performer's speed and accuracy usually increase. Indeed, speed and accuracy are the characteristics that most clearly distinguish the highly skilled performance from the less skilled performance. The typist, for example, with increased skill, is able to type more words per minute and make fewer errors doing it.

Acquiring and Improving Skill Performance

The quality of a skill performance is influenced by several kinds of variables. Frequent mention has been made of the wide differences that exist between learners in such factors as strength, size, maturity, coordination, cultural background, and motivation. Considerable attention has been given to these *learner variables* in previous chapters. The performance of a given skill can also be analyzed in relation to the levels of strength, speed, reaction time, perceptual acuity, manual dexterity, and motor control required for the performance of that skill. These components can be referred to as *skill variables.* Guilford[3] has devised a matrix portraying the influence of variables of this kind (see Table 18–1). He has identified strength, impulsion, speed, static precision, dynamic precision, coordination, and flexibility as psychomotor factors. A psychomotor ability involves the movement or manipulation of some part of the body in relation to a psychomotor factor. Many psychomotor skills involve the integration of several psychomotor abilities. Weight lifting, for example, would require

---

[3] J. P. Guilford, "A System of Psychomotor Abilities," *American Journal of Psychology,* 71 (1958), 165.

Table 18–1.   Matrix of Psychomotor Abilities

Part of Body Involved	Strength	Impulsion	Speed	Static Precision	Dynamic Precision	Coordination	Flexibility
Gross body	General strength	General reaction time		Static balance	Dynamic balance	Gross bodily coordination	
Trunk	Trunk strength						Trunk flexibility
Limbs	Limb strength	Limb thrust	Arm speed	Arm steadiness	Arm aiming		Leg flexibility
Hand					Hand aiming	Hand dexterity	
Finger		Tapping	Finger speed			Finger dexterity	

Source: J. P. Guilford, "A System of Psychomotor Abilities," *American Journal of Psychology*, 71 (1958), 165. Used by permission.

not only gross general strength, trunk strength, and limb strength, but also gross static balance and gross bodily coordination. Throwing a baseball would utilize limb thrust, arm aiming, arm speed, trunk and leg flexibility, and gross bodily coordination. Those who teach motor skills may find it useful to analyze specific skills (such as typing, operating a lathe, shooting a basketball) in relation to the matrix of psychomotor abilities shown in Table 18–1.

Instruction and guidance.   The learning of a psychomotor skill does not necessarily depend upon receiving instruction from an outside source. Many simple motor skills can be mastered through practice undertaken on one's own. Some artists, musicians, and athletes possessing unusual aptitudes for skill performance can even develop their special abilities with little or no instruction. However, most skills are more quickly and efficiently learned with the help of external instructions.[4]

Guidance is a critical variable that can substantially influence the ease and speed with which a skill is learned. In early studies by Koch[5] and Ludgate,[6] an adequate amount of guidance provided early in the learning of a maze resulted in fewer errors than guidance introduced later in the

[4] Bryant J. Cratty, *Movement Behavior and Motor Learning* (Philadelphia: Lea and Febiger, 1964), p. 252.

[5] Helen L. Koch, "The Influence of Mechanical Guidance upon Maze Learning," *Psychological Monographs*, 5 (1923).

[6] K. E. Ludgate, "The Effect of Manual Guidance upon Maze Learning," *Psychological Monographs*, 1 (1923).

training. Cratty[7] suggests that pretask guidance should be mainly concerned with communicating knowledge of spatial relationships, the speed of movement desired, or the force required for performance of the skill. Both visual demonstration and manual guidance may be helpful at this stage, but they should be appropriate to the student's level of comprehension.

The teacher should guard against giving the student too much guidance or verbal instruction. Too much infcrmation at one time may make it difficult for the student to integrate new responses into patterns he has already learned. Too much focus on specific elements of a skill may impede the student's gaining a feeling for the whole skill. Cratty suggests that verbal instructions are most effective if given before the beginning of a skill performance or during its initial stages. Instructions given during the performance of the task should not interfere with the learner's movement patterns. At this point, visual demonstrations or a small amount of manual guidance may be superior to verbal instructions. Visual cues in the form of films or demonstrations tend to be superior to movement cues in learning such skills as golf, tennis, or baseball.

Speed versus accuracy.   Although both speed and accuracy are characteristics of a skilled performance, it is obvious that for such skills as painting, sculpturing, ceramics, and woodworking, accuracy may be more important than speed. In other skills, such as handwriting, typewriting, or drafting, both speed and accuracy are important.

Solley[8] studied the effects of instructions emphasizing speed, accuracy, or both speed and accuracy on the performance of three groups trying to hit a target. During an initial training period, each group was given different instructions on speed and accuracy. After that period, all three groups were instructed to place equal emphasis on accuracy and speed. It was found that the initial training period had a pronounced effect on later performance. Subjects whose training emphasized speed increased in accuracy while maintaining speed. Subjects whose training emphasized accuracy decreased in accuracy as soon as they increased their speed. Solley concluded that in motor skills where speed is a significant factor in ultimate performance, the initial emphasis should be on speed, with accuracy secondary. In skills where both speed and accuracy are required, the initial training should emphasize both.

Knowledge of results.   Knowledge of a skill performance is a prerequisite for improving the performance. As we mentioned earlier, information relating to the adequacy or correctness of a performance is sometimes called *feedback*. Knowledge of results also functions as *reinforcement*, since those movements associated with correct performance tend to be

---

[7] Cratty, pp. 252–264.

[8] W. H. Solley, "The Effects of Verbal Instruction of Speed and Accuracy upon the Learning of a Motor Skill," *Research Quarterly,* 23 (1952), 231–240.

repeated. Such knowledge can be communicated through the verbal comments of an instructor or observer, through the visual confirmation of accuracy, speed, or some other success criterion, or through the feel of a successfully completed movement. Knowledge of results will enable some learners to correct and improve performance through self-instruction; for other learners, further visual demonstrations, manual guidance, or verbal instruction may be needed.

The importance of knowledge of results in improving psychomotor skill performance has been demonstrated in several studies. The effectiveness of such feedback is improved when it is immediate rather than delayed.[9] The effectiveness of feedback is also improved if it is given continuously and frequently.[10] There is some evidence suggesting that students improve in their performance of a skill even when the feedback calling attention to correct performance is slightly disagreeable. Jones[11] asked two groups of adolescents to operate a punchboard maze. To learn the maze, the students had to make choices involving both correct and incorrect responses. For one group an agreeable stimulus consisting of a pattern of lights was flashed on a board for every correct response; for the other group a disagreeable vibration in the stylus used to perform the task signaled a correct response. Jones found no differences in performance between the two groups and concluded that information relating to the correctness of a response may be reinforcing even if it is given in an unpleasant manner.

Effective practice.   Practice of a skill should be conducted under conditions that approximate as closely as possible those under which the skill is to be performed. One learns what he does. Practicing typing actual sentences is more consistent with the criterion goal to be achieved than is practicing typing nonsense syllables. Similarly, studying English words is more efficacious in improving one's English vocabularly than studying Latin.

The superiority of practicing a skill under conditions approximating those of performance was demonstrated by Gates and Taylor.[12] One group of children traced letter forms on transparent paper placed over the forms, while another group practiced writing by copying a model. The tracing group improved their ability to trace letters, but when they were later tested for their ability to write, their writing was much poorer than those who practiced actual writing.

[9] Joel G. Greenspoon and Sally Foreman, "Effect of Delay of Knowledge of Results on Learning a Motor Task," *Journal of Experimental Psychology*, 51 (1956), 226–228.

[10] G. F. Arps, "Work with Knowledge of Results versus Work without Knowledge of Results," *Psychological Monographs*, 28 (1920), 125.

[11] Harold E. Jones, "Trial and Error Learning with Differential Cues," *Journal of Experimental Psychology*, 35 (1945), 31–45.

[12] Arthur I. Gates and Grace A. Taylor, "The Acquisition of Motor Control in Writing by Preschool Children," *Teachers College Record*, 24 (1923), 459–468.

Massed versus distributed practice.   Most studies show that the learning of psychomotor skills occurs more rapidly when practice sessions are well spaced. Spaced practice of motor skills is especially recommended for elementary school children, who vary considerably in physical maturity, energy levels, attention span, and interest. Many motor skills, such as handwriting, baseball, or playing a musical instrument, require the coordination and integration of both physical movements and cognitive processes. This suggests a further need for spaced practice.

Doré and Hilgard[13] showed that scores in pursuit rotor learning at the end of each successive minute within three-minute massed practice trials showed decreases that approximated progressive work decrements characteristic of work curves. Figure 18–1 shows that one group practiced pursuit rotor learning for one minute and rested for three minutes (*distributed practice*), while the other group practiced for three minutes and rested for one minute (*massed practice*). The gain from practice shows as recovery over the one-minute rests, but the massed practice group shows no performance advantage even though it had three times as much practice as the other group.

The findings of a later study by Whitley[14] confirm the results of previous studies which reported higher *performance* of psychomotor skills under distributed practice than under massed practice, but the Whitley study differs from others in finding no differences in the *learning* of the two groups. Sixty college men (30 in each group) were given 35 trials in either distributed practice or massed practice in the performance of a paced contour foot-tracking task that provides both visual and auditory feedback indicating to the subject when he is on target. While performance (as measured by amount of time on target) was significantly higher under conditions of distributed practice, the groups did not differ significantly in amount learned (as measured by the difference in average scores between the first three and the last three trials). Thus, learning of a psychomotor task does occur in massed practice even though performance is likely to be impaired by muscle or mental fatigue that interferes with motor coordination.

Appropriate practice units.   For simple performances, such as stroking a golf ball or broad jumping—performances involving the integration of several responses into one continuous movement—practicing the skill as a whole is probably superior to practicing the skill in parts. However, in complex performances, such as playing the piano, swimming, playing tennis, or playing shortstop, breaking the total performance down into separate skills or components, each of which may logically constitute a whole, appears to be more advantageous. As the smaller wholes are mastered, practice should refocus on larger, more comprehensive units of the skill.

[13] L. R. Doré and E. R. Hilgard, "Spaced Practice and the Maturation Hypothesis," *Journal of Psychology*, 4 (1937), 245–259.

[14] J. D. Whitley, "Effects of Practice Distribution on Learning of a Fine Motor Skill," *Research Quarterly*, 41 (December 1970), 576–583.

Figure 18–1.   Distributed practice in pursuit learning. Group *A* practiced one minute and rested three minutes, while Group *B* practiced three minutes and rested one minute. Scores at each minute within the three-minute trials show progressive work decrement.

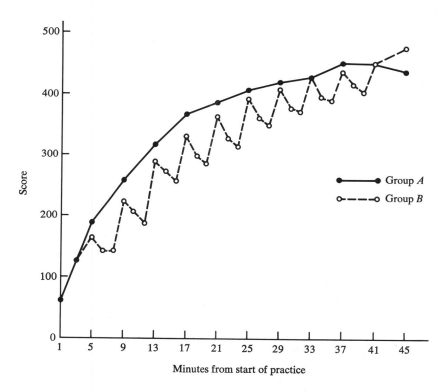

Source: L. R. Doré and Ernest R. Hilgard, "Spaced Practice and the Maturation Hypothesis," *Journal of Psychology*, 4 (1937), 245–259. Used by permission.

Overlearning.   Some psychologists suggest that a skill is more likely to be retained if practice of the skill is continued beyond the point when it was first performed correctly—a phenomenon known as *overlearning*. How much overlearning is needed for the retention of a skill? Melnick[15] had four groups of 20 subjects each practice balancing on a stabilometer (balancing oneself while standing on a freely moving horizontal board) until the learning criterion of balancing for 28 seconds of a 30-second trial was achieved. The four groups received zero, 50, 100, or 200 percent overlearning practice (for example, the 200 percent group was required to

[15] M. J. Melnick, "Effects of Overlearning on the Retention of a Gross Motor Skill," *Research Quarterly*, 42 (March 1971), 60–69.

practice twice as long a time as was required to reach the criterion). One half of the subjects in each of the four groups returned after one week to take the test for retention, while the other half returned after one month.

The results showed that immediate recall of the skill after one week and after one month was facilitated by overlearning, 50 percent overlearning proving in most instances as effective as 100 percent and 200 percent overlearning. The subjects who received 200 percent additional practice, however, had significantly better retention than the subjects with zero percent overlearning after the one-month interval.

Instructional Strategies

The teacher can use verbal instructions, visual demonstrations, and manual guidance in introducing a psychomotor skill to students and in helping students to improve their performances of this skill. By using knowledge of results, praise, encouragement, and evaluational procedures, the teacher can also influence students' progress in skill performance.

Although some teaching strategies may be expected to be superior to others, observations show that teachers using quite different approaches can obtain equally good results in helping students to improve their skill performances. It may be useful to analyze the strategies Mr. Haynes used in teaching his ninth grade woodworking class to use the power jig saw:

Yesterday, in the last part of the period, I had introduced my ninth grade class in wood shop to the proper way of operating the power jig saw and had demonstrated its use by cutting out a figure of a horse and rider. Today I reviewed briefly the steps required for inserting jig saw blades and in operating the machine. Then, while the class worked on their figures and designs for cutouts, I allowed two boys at a time to take turns inserting the correct blade and to get the feel of the saw by cutting spontaneous designs on scrap wood.

Later, during the latter half of the double period, several of the boys were ready to use the jig saw to cut out their figures and designs. Joe and Henry, two boys who have had previous experience with power tools, proceeded to cut out their designs on the jig saw with no need of correction or help from me. For these boys my verbal instructions appeared to be sufficient in enabling them to perform the skill. Ned Frost did not get very far with his cutting before the blade bent. I recalled from working with Ned previously that he has difficulty conceptualizing verbal instructions in concrete terms. I showed him on the machine how the improper adjustment of the tension sleeve had caused the blade to bend. When some of the other boys encountered minor mishaps, my asking, "What do you think went wrong?" enabled them to find their error.

Later in the period, as I watched Ed Conroy start to cut out his design, I noticed that he was rather tense as he placed both hands on the face of his material and tried to wiggle it through. I went over to where he was working with the jig saw, asked him to grasp the ends of the board, placed my hands on his and guided the board as the blade cut along the line. I took my hand away, and he relaxed noticeably as he continued and completed his cutting.

Several points related to the strategies of teaching a psychomotor skill are revealed in this excerpt. Mr. Haynes provided both verbal instructions and visual demonstrations of how to insert blades and operate a jig saw. He also provided students with the opportunity to practice the skill. Each boy practiced inserting the blade, and each had brief opportunities to get the feel of cutting with the jig saw using scrap material before cutting out the design for his project.

Mr. Haynes modified his teaching strategy to fit the needs and abilities of each boy. For some boys, verbal instructions were sufficient for preparing them to operate the jig saw; for Ned, however, a visual demonstration was needed, and for Ed, manual guidance was helpful. The boys gained knowledge of results through immediate feedback on the difficulties encountered operating the saw. When the machine was not working properly or the cut turned out to be imperfect, Mr. Haynes encouraged independent evaluation by asking the boy to analyze what he thought had gone wrong. Mr. Haynes was also quick to reinforce correct performance by praising a student not only for a good product but also for demonstrating good form in operating the saw and for finding the cause of any error himself.

Affective Learning

Affective learning consists of responses (expressed as positive or negative feelings) acquired as one evaluates the meaning of an idea, object, person, or event in terms of the maintenance and enhancement of his view of himself and the world. Affective learning is of particular interest to us because people are likely to respond to ideas, objects, persons, and events as much by what they think and feel about them as by what they know about them. Thus, affective learning—in the form of tastes, preferences, attitudes, and values—exerts a strong influence on behavior. Since attitudes and values are probably the most representative affective outcomes of learning, we shall focus our discussion on the nature and acquisition of attitudes and values.

Attitudes

An *attitude* is a predisposition to react favorably or unfavorably toward ideas, objects, persons, events, or situations. We can think of an attitude as a kind of mental *set* which leads one to respond to ideas, persons, and objects in terms of previously acquired feelings and thoughts. The object toward which one is thus predisposed to respond in a certain way is called an *attitude object*. It may be a physical object, a person, a group of people, an institution, an idea, or a particular characteristic of any of these.

Defining an attitude as a predisposition to respond favorably or unfavorably toward some object suggests that attitudes, like motives, provide *direction* to anticipated behavior. An attitude, however, is not the same as a motive. It may be recalled that a motive is an energy change and performs an energizing function in pushing the organism in the direction of the desired goal response. An attitude prepares an individual to be motivated in particular ways, but does not energize him.

It should be emphasized that attitudes, as well as feelings and emotions, are not innate but learned. Attitudes are the valuative meanings acquired and generalized from an individual's experiences with a particular idea, person, or object. The concepts upon which attitudes are based can, in varying degrees, be accurate or inaccurate, valid or invalid; and an individual's responses to those concepts can themselves be accurate or inaccurate, valid or invalid. One may have acquired a concept of the relationship between heavy smoking and the incidence of lung cancer yet maintain a favorable attitude toward smoking. This type of situation may point to a conflict in attitudes, a topic we shall discuss later.

Measurement of attitudes.   We can gain information about a person's attitudes through inference from direct observation of his behavior. Observing that a student joins enthusiastically into all school activities, makes positive comments about his school, and expresses disappointment if forced to miss school because of illness, we can infer that the student's attitude toward school is positive. We may wish, however, to ascertain the student's predispositions to respond favorably or unfavorably to a much larger sample of phenomena. For this, direct observation alone is not enough, and we usually turn to the use of attitude scales.

Attitude scales seek tc assess the degree of a subject's favorable or unfavorable response toward each of several items. Typically, an attitude scale samples a person's attitudes within a limited subject or area. Individual scales, for example, have been developed to elicit attitudes toward teaching, children, students' classroom behavior, child-rearing practices, authority, conformity, and minority groups. An attitude scale for measuring authoritarianism which has been widely used in research is the *California F Scale*, developed by Adorno and his associates.[16] Although high scores on this scale presumably identify the authoritarian personality, one who is extremely conservative politically, it appears that the scale may relate to a complex of other variables as well. One variable that seems to be related

---

[16] T. W. Adorno et al., *The Authoritarian Personality* (New York: Harper & Row, 1950).

to authoritarianism is what Rokeach[17] describes as open-mindedness versus closed-mindedness as revealed in one's attitudes and behavior. More recent studies suggest that authoritarianism and closed-mindedness are probably not isolated traits but are combinations of other characteristics. A so-called liberal intellectual, for example, may be open-minded with respect to most social and political issues and closed-minded with respect to most economic issues.

Figure 18–2 presents part of an attitude questionnaire that seeks to elicit from college students or adults their attitudes toward children. To be useful, an attitude scale, like any other measuring instrument, must give consistent results when administered on successive occasions and must measure the quality it claims to measure. It must, in other words, be reliable and valid. One who constructs an attitude scale seeks to eliminate ambiguous statements, so that each item in the scale will, as nearly as possible, convey the same meaning to all respondents. A test is considered reliable when an individual's responses to items in it do not change substantially when the test is administered to him on successive occasions. A test is considered valid if its results agree with other evidences of the individual's responses toward the attitude object. A positive response toward reading revealed in an attitude scale can be checked for validation against information on the proportion of the individual's leisure time spent in reading, the frequency of his trips to the library, and the amount of time he spends talking about books or articles he has read. We should remember, however, that inferences of an individual's attitudes, to be valid, must be drawn from a broad sampling of his behavior in a variety of situations.

Attitude formation and change.   Allport[18] has identified four ways in which attitudes are formed. One way is through the *integration of numerous specific responses* of a similar type into a generalized response pattern. An example of attitudes formed through the integration of responses is the strong, positive feelings that one develops toward a tried and true friend through countless experiences of shared interests, concern, empathy, support, and affection, or, on the other hand, in the uniformly unpleasant, disappointing, or dissatisfying experiences one may have had in dealing with a particular business firm.

A second way attitudes are formed, according to Allport, is through the *differentiations* one makes in the original matrix of attitudes he has acquired. One acquires attitudes by differentiation when, for example, his feelings and actions toward another cultural group change as the result of a commonality of feeling and empathy which develop from a close association with one or more individuals of that group.

The third way is through a *traumatic experience.* An example of an attitude formed by a single traumatic experience is the generalized feeling

[17] M. Rokeach, *The Open and Closed Mind* (New York: Basic Books, 1960).

[18] Gordon W. Allport, "Attitudes," in Carl Murchison, ed., *Handbook of Social Psychology* (Worcester, Mass.: Clark University Press, 1935), pp. 810–812.

Figure 18–2.   Excerpts from a Scale Eliciting Attitudes toward Children

Attitude Questionnaire

Listed below are a number of statements of opinion or of behavior that might or might not apply to you. You will probably find yourself agreeing with some items and disagreeing with others. We are interested in the extent to which you agree or disagree.

Mark each statement in the left margin according to how much you agree or disagree with it. Please mark every one. Write in 1, 2, 3, 4, 5, or 6 depending on how you feel in each case.

> 1 - I disagree very much
> 2 - I disagree pretty much
> 3 - I disagree a little
> 4 - I agree a little
> 5 - I agree pretty much
> 6 - I agree very much

There is no set of answers to these statements that is right for everyone: your answers will reflect your own point of view, which is the important thing.

_____Children should be seen and not heard.

_____Young people should be free to decide whether some mores and values of their parents are still relevant.

_____Self-discipline and respect for authority are essential in developing a well-integrated personality.

_____The authority of one's conscience is a more trustworthy guide to behavior than the authority of parents or teachers.

_____Children are usually the best judges of what is good for them.

_____Schools have no right to tell students how they should wear their hair.

_____Children should have enough respect for their teachers to sit quietly and do what they say.

_____Disobedience should be understood not punished.

_____Children ought to be allowed to study whatever interests them.

_____A child who is too obedient makes me uncomfortable.

Source: Sandra Scarr, "How to Reduce Authoritarianism among Teachers," *Journal of Educational Research,* 63 (April 1970), 367–372. Selective items used by permission of Sandra Scarr.

of distrust of everyone that one would feel after abandonment or rejection by family or friends.

The fourth way in which attitudes are formed is through *identification* with parents, teachers, or peers. The acquisition of ready-made attitudes through identification with others frequently occurs unconsciously and probably is related to the needs to be loved and to belong. The learning of prejudice frequently involves attitudes that are acquired through identification with parents, peers, and others. Trager and Yarrow[19] conclude that prejudices can be communicated to children by parents who place restrictions on their children's friendships or encourage friendships only with particular children.

Educators as well as society in general are especially interested in the ways attitudes can be changed. McGuire[20] describes several ways of effecting attitude change. Verbal communication is a powerful means for influencing attitude change. The effectiveness of the message seems to depend upon its source: Who expressed the attitude? The statement of a public figure can be expected to exert a greater influence on public opinion than that of a little-known citizen, but the power of the statement in shaping attitudes seems to depend upon the speaker's *credibility, attractiveness,* and *power.* Physicians and scientists tend to be accorded high credibility for statements which relate to their areas of expertise; high credibility for their pronouncements on political issues and foreign policy, for which they have no special competence or knowledge, may be unwarranted. The attractiveness of the source of attitude statements depends upon the degree of similarity and familiarity of the source and the persons to whom the statements are addressed. We are more likely to be receptive to opinions of persons familiar to us or persons perceived to be very much like ourselves than to those of unfamiliar or dissimilar persons. The power of the source of attitude statements may be manifested in the role and status of the source: parent, teacher, employer, or group. Each of these exerts power through being in a position to dispense rewards and punishments to enforce compliance with behavior and policies that are consistent with the attitudes and opinions of the power source.

The mass media, especially TV, are presumed to be effective channels for shaping attitudes. Millions of dollars are spent in trying to influence the buying preferences of millions of consumers and to create positive attitudes in voters toward a particular political candidate. Studies show that while a TV blitz may increase the sales of a product, it may be ineffective in changing attitudes of voters sufficiently to elect a political candidate. One can demonstrate, however, that the mass media are effective in disseminating information. Studies of *Sesame Street* show clearly that

[19] Helen G. Trager and Marian R. Yarrow, *They Learn What They Live* (New York: Harper & Row, 1952), pp. 347–352.

[20] W. J. McGuire, "The Nature of Attitudes and Attitude Change," in G. Lindsey and E. Aronson, eds., *The Handbook of Social Psychology*, Vol. 3 (Reading, Mass.: Addison-Wesley, 1969), pp. 136–314.

children learn from mere exposure to television.[21] Where attitude change is dependent upon information presented to the viewer, information communicated by television may thus effect changes in attitudes.

Conflicts in attitudes.   An individual acquires some kind of valuative meaning from every experience and, through time, becomes predisposed favorably or unfavorably toward a myriad of objects, persons, ideas, and events. Often, the meanings of his experiences produce in him two strongly held but incompatible attitudes. The child is in conflict, for instance, when events prevent him from maintaining positive attitudes toward parents and teachers and equally positive attitudes toward peers, justice, and fair play. An adult frequently faces conflicts in attitudes with respect to the demands and expectations of his sex role or his job. A bright, energetic woman with high achievement motivation may avoid competing with men for position and power out of a fear of being viewed as unfeminine. The American may find that his strong positive attitudes toward freedom and individuality conflict with his positive attitude toward conformity. His belief in competition and free enterprise may conflict with his equally strong belief in brotherly love and adherence to the golden rule. His positive attitude toward equality of opportunity for all people may conflict with his attitudes toward home and community.

In resolving such conflicts, the individual may seek to maintain those attitudes toward objects, people, or ideas that are most important to him, or he may seek to compromise his attitudes to make them compatible with one another. A politician frequently does this in order to satisfy the disparate elements of his constituency. He may come out in favor of a controversial law provided certain safeguards are built into the law to protect the interests of those of his constituents who oppose it.

Two theories have been advanced to explain and predict the behavior of persons in conflict. The first of these, propsed by Dollard and Miller,[22] is presented in Figure 18–3. In the figure, points of conflict are shown as the intersections of gradients representing tendencies to approach and to avoid a goal. As a person approaches a goal toward which he has conflicting attitudes, his feelings of avoidance become stronger. When these feelings are strong enough, the person is likely to terminate his approach and withdraw to a point where his feelings of approach and avoidance balance each other, the point in the figure where the gradients of approach and avoidance intersect. The person is likely to remain at this point of conflict until his attitudes change.

The second explanation of conflict is Festinger's[23] theory of *cognitive dissonance.* According to Festinger, a person experiences conflict when he

[21] Samuel Ball and G. A. Bogatz, *The First Year of* Sesame Street: *An Evaluation* (Princeton, N. J.: Educational Testing Service, 1970).

[22] John Dollard and Neal E. Miller, *Personality and Psychotherapy* (New York: McGraw-Hill Book Co., 1950), pp. 350–360.

[23] Leon Festinger, *Theory of Cognitive Dissonance* (Stanford, Calif.: Stanford University Press, 1962).

Figure 18–3.   How Increasing the Strength of Approach in an Approach-Avoidance Conflict Increases the Amount of Conflict

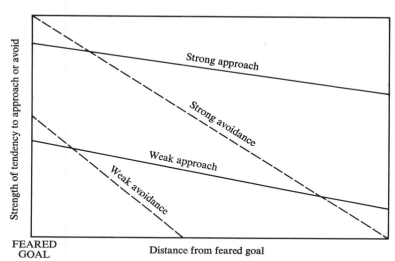

Source: John Dollard and Neal E. Miller, *Personality and Psychotherapy* (New York: McGraw-Hill Book Co., 1950), p. 361. Used by permission.

perceives that alternative choices facing him are incompatible. Having to choose one alternative and reject the other produces cognitive dissonance. The amount of dissonance that exists after a decision has been made is a direct function of the number of things about the person's behavior, beliefs, or attitudes that a person knows are inconsistent with the choice he has made. To reduce this dissonance, according to Festinger's theory, the person reevaluates his attitudes, modifying them to fit the choice he has made. Perhaps a college student, after a careful analysis, has written a term paper very critical of a theory of motivation, not realizing that his professor identifies strongly with the theory. After receiving a grade of *C* on the paper and reading the professor's critical comments, the student experiences dissonance. He reduces this dissonance by adopting a more positive attitude toward the theory or by adopting a negative attitude toward the professor, whichever better enables him to maintain his self-concept.

Studies of attitudes.   A number of studies have found that attitudes expressed by children and youth reflect changes associated with development. Piaget,[24] for example, suggests that it is possible to distinguish three broad stages in children's development of an attitude toward the applica-

[24] Jean Piaget, *The Moral Judgment of the Child* (New York: Free Press, 1965).

tion of justice. During the first stage, children under the age of seven believe that "just" is what is commanded by an adult. During the second stage, when children are between the ages of seven and 11, equality in the application of justice seems to outweigh every other consideration. Finally, during the third stage, when children are 11 or 12, attitudes toward equality are modified by the notion of equity. In this last stage the child no longer thinks of equal rights of individuals except as they relate to a particular situation.

Benton[25] investigated that part of Piaget's theory as it relates to sex differences in attitudes expressed by preadolescents during stage 3. In this study the attitudes and bargaining behavior of preadolescent boys and girls with respect to the division of rewards following differential performance in reading was examined. Same-sex pairs of friends, nonfriends, and neutrals were constituted, and one member of each pair (the choice determined randomly) was informed that he had passed the reading test. Passing the test meant that the successful one could choose between a more or a less desirable toy to play with, the other member getting the toy the successful member did not choose. The results of this study showed that preadolescent boys, more often than preadolescent girls, when successful in reading and paired with a friend or a nonfriend, chose the more desirable toy in favoring themselves over their peers. Girls, however, both those who passed and those who failed the reading test, when paired with a friend or a neutral, indicated a preference for an equal division of preferred toys. They found the possibility of an unequal allocation of toys upsetting, and only after prolonged bargaining efforts to reach a settlement would they reluctantly agree to an equity solution (where one would receive the preferred toy). These results, which show preadolescent boys in stage 3 and preadolescent girls in stage 2 of Piaget's theory of attitude formation regarding distributive justice, probably reflect peer group and socialization differences within each sex.

There appears to be a growing acceptance of each other by blacks and whites with further desegregation and lowering of racial barriers. Green,[26] however, found that whites' acceptance of blacks was related to the particular situation in which the two races interacted rather than reflecting a generalized attitude toward blacks. Twenty-two moderately antiblack white college students and 22 moderately equalitarian white college students, grouped in terms of their scores on a behavioral and attitude measure, were shown 32 sketches of persons in various poses, 16 of which contained all-white subjects and 16 of which portrayed interracial situations. The 44 subjects were asked to indicate which pictures they would pose in with respect to four degrees of intimacy (from equality in a public

[25] A. A. Benton, "Productivity, Distributive Justice, and Bargaining among Children," *Journal of Personal and Social Psychology*, 18 (April 1971), 68–78.

[26] J. A. Green, "Attitudinal and Situational Determinants of Intended Behavior toward Blacks," *Journal of Personality and Social Psychology*, 22 (April 1972), 13–17.

situation to a fairly close heterosexual relationship) and four expected uses of the photographs (from a Peace Corps brochure used in a foreign country to use in a *Life* magazine article).

The results of this study revealed that as the degree of intimacy increased, the number of rejections of interracial sketches increased. At the lowest degree of exposure (Peace Corps brochure), there was little difference among mean rejection scores on different degrees of intimacy. As predicted, moderately equalitarian subjects were more willing to pose with blacks than were moderately antiblack subjects. This study shows that moderate racial attitudes are related to behavior; the subjects, regardless of racial attitudes, were less willing to pose with blacks as the degree of intimacy increased.

A number of studies have investigated the influence of college attendance on the formation of attitudes. Jacob[27] found that college experiences exert little influence on students' standards of behavior, quality of judgment, sense of responsibility, keenness of understanding, or guiding beliefs. The values of American college students were found to be remarkably homogeneous, considering the variety of their backgrounds and their relatively unrestricted opportunities for thought and personal development. Students in this study appeared to be contented, were unabashedly self-centered, and aspired to material gratifications for themselves and their families.

In a study of one large midwestern university, Lehmann, Sinha, and Harnett[28] found that over the four-year period, students became less stereotyped and dogmatic in their beliefs and more "outer directed" in their value orientations. Women underwent a more marked change in their attitudes and values than did their male classmates. Students who dropped out of college manifested in some instances the same type of behavior as students who remained until graduation. Lehmann and his associates concluded that college acts as a catalyst to speed up changes that would occur anyway as the individual matures.

It would appear from the studies cited above that attendance at college has some effect in shaping students' attitudes and values, but that the effect is varied and in some cases indeterminate. Neither the quality of teaching nor the method of instruction appears to influence to any great extent the attitudes and values students form. For those students whose attitudes and values do change in college, the impetus does not seem to come from the formal educational process. Rather, it seems to come from the distinctive climate of a few institutions, from the influence and personal magnetism of a sensitive teacher, or from a students' significant personal experiences.

[27] Philip E. Jacob, *Changing Values in College* (New York: Harper & Row, 1957).

[28] Irvin J. Lehmann, Birenda K. Sinha, and Rodney T. Harnett, "Changes in Attitudes and Values Associated with College Attendance," *Journal of Educational Psychology*, 57 (April 1966), 89–98.

Values

A *value* is a preference for something cherished or desired; it is linked to one's satisfaction of needs, his realization of goals, and the maintenance and enhancement of his self-concept. Raths, Harmin, and Simon[29] suggest that the process of valuing involves the activities of *choosing, prizing,* and *acting:*

1. *Choosing freely.*
2. *Choosing from among alternatives.*
3. *Choosing after thoughtful consideration of the consequences of each alternative.*
4. *Prizing and cherishing.*
5. *Affirming.*
6. *Acting upon choices.*
7. *Repeating (action manifesting a value is likely to occur again and again in a variety of situations).*

Values are organized in a hierarchy and are manifested in the consistency of one's behavior. Values, like attitudes, orient and prepare the individual to respond to his environment in predetermined ways. Although tastes, attitudes, and values all connote preferences, values differ from tastes and attitudes in the stronger commitment and involvement of the individual which his values evoke.

The learning of values.   Values are learned in the same way that attitudes are learned. A principal way values are learned is through identification with significant others. The child comes to perceive situations in the same way that the model—a parent, uncle, teacher, coach, or athletic hero—perceives them. The child experiences some of the same feelings of empathy with the model and adopts many of the same goals, attitudes, and values. Although the model may seek to inculcate in the child certain beliefs and values, the child often acquires values unconsciously through the process of identification.

The importance of the teacher as a model in influencing students' forming of values is revealed in Battle's[30] study of personal values and

---

[29] Louis E. Raths, Merrill Harmin, and Sidney B. Simon, *Values and Teaching* (Columbus, Ohio: Merrill Publishing Co., 1966).

[30] H. J. Battle, "Relation between Personal Values and Scholastic Achievement," *Journal of Experimental Education,* 20 (September 1957), 27–41.

scholastic achievement. He investigated the influence of values on pupils and teachers in the determination of school marks in a public high school. A test containing value statements for 10 classes of values was administered to a sample of high school teachers and their pupils. The study found that among pupils of similar aptitude, age, and sex, those who received high marks tended to have value patterns more closely related to those considered ideal by the teachers who determined the marks than they were to the value patterns of those who received low marks. Battle concluded that the degree of similarity between the teacher's ideal and the pupil's value pattern is directly related to the teacher's evaluation of the pupil's achievement.

Although values are formed through interactions with significant others, the process of valuing is a very personal experience. It is the individual himself who freely chooses from among alternatives, prizes and affirms what he has chosen, and acts upon his choices. Raths and his co-workers[31] suggest that the teacher has a vital role in helping children and youth *clarify their values*. The value clarificaton strategy is one in which the teacher responds to a student's value statement with a nonjudgmental comment (usually a question). The purpose is to encourage the student to reflect upon what he has chosen, what he prizes, or what he has done. The teacher's question, serving as a gentle prod, puts responsibility on the student to look at his behavior or the ideas he has expressed. The question does not lead to an extended discussion; the class activity moves on, and the student can ponder the idea then or later. If the student is to choose freely, the teacher must accept the student's choosing not to consider the position he has taken. Essential to a value clarification strategy is the establishment of an open, permissive atmosphere. Students must feel psychologically safe to speak their minds without fear of harsh judgment or ridicule by peers or teacher. The use of value clarification responses by the teacher is revealed in the following anecdote.

> *Today, at the beginning of class, my eighth grade social studies class began commenting on a newspaper article which reported that some poor families had allegedly received welfare payments for which they were ineligible. Henry broke in and said heatedly, "People who are too lazy to work should not sponge off the rest of us!"*
>
> *"Are you saying," I asked, "that the government should never help people in need?"*
>
> *"Well, ah, maybe if they deserve it, it might be all right," Henry replied.*
>
> *Karen broke in, "People have a right to the basic needs of life—food, shelter, clothing, transportation—if the economic system or poor health prevents them from working."*
>
> *I asked, "How long have you felt this way?"*

[31] Raths, Harmin, and Simon, *Values and Teaching*.

> *Karen answered, "Ever since I saw the movie* Sounder, *the story of a poor black family in the South."*
> *"This is a topic we may wish to discuss further at a later date,"*
> *I said as we prepared to leave on our field trip.*

In this episode the teacher avoids moralizing, criticizing, or evaluating either student's statement. The teacher's response to each student's value statement places responsibility on the student to look at his own behavior and his own ideas. The teacher's questions should be ones to which only the student knows the answer, and they should be asked in a nonjudgmental manner:

1.   *Reflect back on what the student has said and add, "Is that what you mean?"*

2.   *Reflect back on what the student has said with distortions and add, "Is that what you mean?"*

3.   *"How long have you felt that way?"*

4.   *"Should everyone believe that?"*

5.   *"Could you give me some examples of that?"*

In employing a strategy of value clarification, the teacher need not remain neutral or refrain from stating his own values and beliefs. If his students are not accustomed to critical thinking and taking an independent position on issues, the teacher should withhold his beliefs and values until the students feel free to assume a position independent of others. If the students are free to express their views independently, the teacher, by stating his own views and values, demonstrates that issues can be discussed openly. He can also help students to clarify their beliefs and values by marking value statements in themes and other written work with symbols which ask the student, "Do you believe this?" or "Do you want to change this?"

Teachers report that a value clarification procedure is much more effective in helping students discover what they really believe and value than merely giving the students warmth and acceptance. Although some studies have produced mixed results, other studies using a value clarification procedure show that students exposed to it did develop more consistent attitudes and personal purposes than in classes that did not employ this procedure. One study, by James Raths,[32] examined the relationship between pupils' values and scholastic underachievement. He hypothesized that underachievement is related in part to the student's failure to acquire and to

---

[32] James D. Raths, "Underachievement and a Search for Values," *Journal of Educational Sociology*, 14 (May 1961), 423–424.

clarify a set of values. Raths predicted that as attitudes are clarified and values develop, underachieving students will find new purpose in their schoolwork and their achievement will increase. Several short individual conferences were held with a small experimental group of underachievers over the period of a semester for the purpose of helping these students clarify their attitudes, beliefs, interests, purposes, aspirations, and values. In these conferences, the adult provided empathic support by listening and reacting to the student's discussions of topics of interest to him. After one semester, the experimental group registered a greater significant change toward higher class rank and grade point average than did a matched control group who had no conferences.

Values are also learned and modified through the processes of identification, differentiation, and integration, as shown in the following anecdotes from the case records of Tab, age six, Skippy, age 10, Doris, age 14, and Margaret Anne, age 18.

> March 18.   *Tab was walking with a few other students and me. As we walked by the flag pole he stopped short and jerked my hand. "I've got a good idea," he said. "We're first ones out, and while we wait for the others let's sing to the flag." The flags were beautiful flying against the blue sky and white clouds. The others agreed so they pledged allegiance to the flag and sang "America." "That was really fun," said Tab.*

> December 2.   *We were making plans for a presentation of Christmas carols and songs to be given before the PTA by the upper grades.*
>
> *In the discussion, we listed three types of songs: the carols, songs dealing with Christmas customs, and songs of the Jewish Hanukkah. My class had presented the Hanukkah the previous year, so I stated that I thought it was now some other class's turn to do it and that the eighth grade had volunteered. In the voting I noticed that the Gentile children all voted to present a carol and the Jewish children didn't vote. I asked them what the trouble was.*

> Skippy: *You didn't give us a chance to vote. You didn't mention Hanukkah.*

> Teacher: *Yes, I did. I told you the eighth grade was doing it.*

> Skippy: *But we want to.*

> Teacher: *But you did it last year. Can't you see it would be fairer to give someone else the opportunity?*

> Skippy: *Not if we want to do it more. There are more Jewish kids in this room than in the eighth grade.*

A Christian child: *Yes, but if you have Hanukkah every year, when do we get a chance? Christmas belongs to us, not to you.*

Skippy: *Yeah, that's the way it always goes. You always get everything, and we always lose out.*

Feeling that the discussion was too heated, I dropped it here and changed the subject.

April 8.   *Doris was supposed to bring me her report card during the sixth period. She came in smiling. Her hair was beautifully arranged in a long pageboy style. I complimented her on how nice it looked. She said, "I can't stand my hair if it is out of place. I like to work with it. I have five different shades of rinse I use on it. I like the bronze rinse best, but it costs the most."*

Doris discussed with me something of her personal concerns. "There are three high school boys I like, one in particular, but none of them will look at me. I'll have a problem when it comes to finding a husband. I'll have to find one who is a member of the church. Mama wouldn't mind too much if he weren't a member, but it would break Daddy's heart if I married somebody outside the church."

December 10.   *Margaret Anne was in my classroom this evening discussing things with other senior boys and girls. Margaret Anne said, "Well, the Student Council is going to be respected if I have to see to it myself. Most of the members sit at the meetings and never say anything. We had a boy up for going through the furnace room all the time, and they wouldn't say anything. Then I told him that we had told him several times not to go through, and I asked him why he continued. He said that he didn't see why he couldn't because the teachers did all the time. When I told him that there were only about twelve or thirteen teachers who did compared to three or four hundred pupils, he just looked at me."*

One of the girls asked, "What did you do to him?"

Margaret Anne said, "I told him to write a two-hundred-word essay entitled 'Why I should not go through the furnace room.'"

Another student asked, "And suppose he doesn't do it?"

Margaret Anne answered, "Then I'll write it myself and make him copy it. At least he'll know why he shouldn't and will learn to respect the Student Council."

Values and behavior.   The influence on behavior of a strong value orientation is strikingly shown in a study by Deutsch.[33] Deutsch studied the influence of varying types of orientation—cooperative, individualistic, and

---

[33] Morton Deutsch, "Conflict and Its Resolution," paper presented at the convention of the American Psychological Association, Chicago, September 5, 1965.

competitive—on individual behavior in an interpersonal conflict situation. In one study, a group of adolescents was invited to play "chicken" in the laboratory using a trucking game. In the laboratory game, each of two players was paid a fee for taking his truck from a starting point to a destination; from the fee was deducted the cost of the trip, which was determined by the amount of time it took to complete the trip. The players had to drive their trucks in opposite directions on the same road, and a large section of the road was only one lane wide. The players could see the positions of both trucks at all times. If they arrived at the narrow section of the road at the same time, the players had to decide whether to go on or "chicken out." If he chose, each player could lock his truck in forward gear, committing himself irreversibly to an attempt to get through the narrow section. This commitment was immediately made known to the other player through a signaling device. If the truck collided, the trial was ended and each player was charged money for the time spent since the beginning of the trial. The subjects played the game for 20 trials.

In one experiment, the subjects were divided into two groups and each group was given a different set of instructions—"chicken" instructions or "problem-solving" instructions. Under "chicken" instructions, subjects were told that the game separated people into two groups, "those who give in under pressure and those who do not." Under "problem-solving" instructions, subjects were told that the game separated people into two other groups, "those who can arrive at a solution to a problem that will bring maximum benefits to both players and those who cannot work out the solution." Both groups were told, "It's important for you to earn as much money as you can and to lose as little as possible in the game." The subjects played for real money in amounts that were not insignificant to them.

The results of the study are striking. The "chicken" instructions resulted in substantial mutual loss for nine of 10 pairs of subjects, with the modal pair having more than 10 collisions in 20 trials. The "problem-solving" instructions, however, resulted in substantial mutual gain for all but three pairs of subjects, with the modal pair having less than four collisions in 20 trials. Deutsch concludes from this and other studies that both cooperative and competitive situations tend to be self-confirming and self-perpetuating; each tends to persist even if a change occurs in the originating conditions. The communication patterns, attitudes, perceptions, task orientations, and outcomes evoked by a given process tend to elicit the very same process that evoked them.

Summary

Optimum self-development and psychological health depend upon the full development and integration of all of man's powers. Thus, one's effective functioning as a person requires the blending of affective, cognitive, and psychomotor components of behavior into a harmonious, integrated whole.

586   Learning and the Educative Process

The term *psychomotor* refers to a class of responses which involve the action and coordination of muscles in the movement of the body or any of its parts. A skilled psychomotor performance is characterized by (1) an accurate conception of the task, (2) efficient use of cues, (3) feedback and correction, (4) coordination of movements, and (5) speed and accuracy. Teachers can assist a student in acquiring and improving a skill with verbal instructions, visual demonstrations, and manual guidance. Verbal instructions appear to be most effective if given before skill performance or during the initial stages of performance. During later stages, visual demonstrations or minimal manual guidance may be superior to verbal instructions.

In the learning of psychomotor skills which require speed in performance, the initial emphasis should be on speed, with accuracy secondary. In the learning of skills which require both speed and accuracy, the initial emphasis should be on both.

Immediate knowledge of results, providing feedback and reinforcement, is important in helping a student to improve a skill performance. Effective practice is also important and should be conducted under conditions as close as possible to those under which the skill is to be performed. The performance of most psychomotor skills is more rapid when practice sessions are well spaced. In the case of a relatively simple skill, it is usually advantageous to practice the whole skill at once. In the case of a more complex skill, it is usually advantageous to divide the total performance into separate skills or components, each of which can be practiced by itself.

A skill is more likely to be retained if practice of the skill is continued beyond the point at which it was first performed correctly—a phenomenon known as *overlearning*. Fifty percent overlearning is as effective as 100 percent or 200 percent to recall a skill after one week or one month; 200 percent overlearning gives significantly better results than zero overlearning after one month.

Affective learning, another important category of learning outcomes, is the acquisition of valuative meanings for ideas, objects, persons, and events. Affective learnings are manifested in tastes, preferences, attitudes, and values.

An *attitude* is a predisposition to react favorably or unfavorably toward an idea, object, person, event, or situation. The object toward which one is thus predisposed is called an *attitude object*. Information about a person's attitudes can be gained by making inferences from his behavior, but an attitude scale is more frequently used to sample a person's attitudes on a specific subject.

Attitudes are learned (1) through the integration of numerous specific responses, (2) through differentiations made in an original matrix of attitudes, (3) through dramatic experience or trauma, and (4) through imitation and identification. The acquisition of ready-made attitudes through identification with parents, teachers, or peers contributes to the satisfaction of one's needs to be loved, to belong, to play roles, and to deal competently with the world.

Verbal communication is a powerful means of effecting attitude change, but its effectiveness depends upon the credibility, attractiveness, and power of the source. The mass media, and especially TV, can be effective in changing attitudes if the basis for attitude change is information communicated by the mass media. In the case of a conflict between attitudes, the individual resolves the conflict by maintaining the attitude most important to him or by modifying his attitudes so as to make them compatible with each other. This second method is an illustration of Festinger's theory of *cognitive dissonance*.

Studies of attitude change among children and youth reveal that attitude change is associated with development, as suggested by Piaget. There is evidence that whites, regardless of their racial attitudes, are progressively less willing to respond positively to interacting with blacks as the degree of intimacy with blacks increases. College appears to produce a homogeneity of values among students. The attitudes and values of college students are modified, if at all, not in formal classroom experiences but in personally significant experiences with unusual professors or peers.

A *value* is a preference for something cherished or desired. The process of valuing involves the activities of choosing, prizing, and acting upon choices made. Values differ from tastes and attitudes in the stronger commitment and involvement of the individual which his values evoke. A principal way values are learned is through identification with a significant other who serves as a model. Students can be helped to form values through a value clarification process in which the teacher asks nonjudgmental questions which seek to encourage the student to reflect on his value statement or action. Laboratory studies show that strong value orientations tend to persist even if changes occur in the situation in which they were first acquired.

Study Questions

1. You have been observing students performing a variety of psychomotor skills: writing a theme, playing the piano, and driving a golf ball. How would you ascertain in each case the degree to which a student's errors in performing are due to correctable factors, such as use of cues or feedback, and the degree to which his errors are due to limitations of inherited body structure and coordination?

2. A student learning a psychomotor skill often becomes very dependent on the instructor for information about, for instance, what he should do to correct his mistakes. As an instructor, what steps would you take in trying to lessen the student's dependence on you?

3. What reasons can you suggest to account for the greater emphasis which schools appear to place on cognitive learning as compared to affective learning of attitudes and values? What dangers do you see in this trend?

4. Attitudes contributing to prejudice and discrimination are reflected in the racial conflicts and social unrest of the contemporary world.

For the grade level and subject you expect to teach, what learning experiences would you plan that might encourage students to examine the attitudes they hold toward other peoples, cultures, religions, and political systems?

5.   Many would say that teachers should refrain from indoctrinating students with their values and points of view. The value clarification procedure suggested by Raths and others seeks to have students choose freely, reflect, prize, and act on their choices and beliefs. If teachers carefully avoid making value statements, is there a danger that students will come to believe that values should not be revealed or talked about? Will teachers who are unwilling to express their personal views to students come to be viewed by students as phonies? Discuss.

Suggested Readings

International Association for Childhood Education. *Feelings and Learning.* Washington, D. C.: Association for Childhood Education, 1965. Contains photographs documenting the key experiences in the affective life of the young child and papers by Anna Freud, Lois Murphy, and others discussing the various aspects of the young child's emotional development and its relation to learning.

Cratty, Bryant J. *Movement Behavior and Motor Learning.* Philadelphia: Lea and Febiger, 1964. Presents fundamental concepts and principles of human movement and motor performance. Chapter 12 examines the problems of retention, whole versus part learning, and mass versus distributed practice. Chapter 13 discusses strategies teachers can employ to guide psychomotor learning.

Festinger, Leon. *A Theory of Cognitive Dissonance.* Stanford, Calif.: Stanford University Press, 1962. Proposes and discusses a theory of cognitive dissonance. Hypothesizes that the individual experiencing dissonance is motivated to reduce dissonance and achieve consonance and to avoid situations which might increase dissonance.

Raths, Louis E., Merrill Harmin, and Sidney B. Simon. *Values and Teaching.* Columbus, Ohio: Merrill Publishing Co., 1966. Describes a procedure through which teachers can help students clarify what they value. By asking the student thought-provoking, nonthreatening questions, the teacher encourages the student to make choices, to prize and affirm, and to act in accordance with his choices. Suggested value-clarifying questions, teacher-student dialogues, and results of research or value-clarifying procedures are described.

Part Five

Facilitating Development and Learning

Organizing the Classroom for Learning

19

Our most pressing educational problem is not how to increase the efficiency of the schools and colleges; it is how to create and maintain a humane society.

Charles E. Silberman

In spite of man's long experience with the act of teaching and in spite of the considerable study given to teaching in recent years, we still do not have a clear understanding of what good teaching is or how to foster it. There appear to be as many approaches to effective teaching as there are good teachers. This lack of a precise definition of good teaching has caused some educators to deemphasize the teaching aspect and to emphasize the learner and the learning aspects of the teaching-learning activity. These educators contend that the important thing is not what the teacher does but what happens to the learner. A somewhat extreme statement of this view is made by Rogers:

My experience has been that I cannot teach another person how to teach. . . . I have come to feel that the only learning which significantly influences behavior is self-discovered, self-appropriated learning. Such self-discovered learning, truth that has been personally appropriated and assimilated in experience, cannot be directly communicated to another. . . . Such experience would imply that we would do away with teaching. People would get together if they wished to learn.[1]

Many will sympathize with Rogers' concern for the learner. Nevertheless, it is clear that much of what students learn is greatly influenced by what teachers do in their efforts to foster learning: Learning in school is an interpersonal experience.

[1] Carl R. Rogers, *On Becoming a Person* (Boston: Houghton Mifflin Co., 1961), pp. 276–277.

Teaching, as it is presently conceived, is not simply a matter of applying principles, procedures, or formulae to learning situations or problems. Teaching is still much more of an art than a science or technology. Teachers, however, as well as artists, utilize scientifically validated generalizations in the proper performance of their skills.

The milieu in which teaching takes place is continuously changing and is influenced by a great many variables, both known and unknown. In such a fluid and complex situation, the teacher must deal with many alternatives. He begins with a plan, but he cannot possibly foresee the modifications and redirections that may be required by the exigencies of the teaching situation. Hence, the tentative, spontaneous, and intuitive responses that teachers make in guiding learning are more like those of an artist than those of a technician. For teaching, "there is no complete catalog of recipes to combine certain ingredients under certain conditions to obtain certain effects. If there were, teaching would be a technology, and we could train teachers to apply purely technical skills to prearranged objectives."[2]

It would seem, then, that at present we cannot hope to provide a prescription detailing what a teacher should do to effect learning in students. On the other hand, most educators agree on some of the criteria of good teaching and some of the characteristics of poor teaching. Moreover, the increasing body of research into teaching methods, procedures, roles, and behavior contributes to our increased understanding of these complex activities. While we cannot specify precisely the effects of certain particular teaching methods, we can predict that certain methods are *more likely* to lead to certain outcomes than to certain other outcomes.

Teaching is here defined as *any interpersonal influence aimed at changing the ways in which persons can or will behave.*[3] This admittedly broad definition makes teachers of parents, ministers, peer group members, youth leaders, psychotherapists, and friends. In this book, however, we are concerned only with the activities of the assigned teacher in the classroom.

A Model of Teacher Behavior

The model of teacher behavior presented here was proposed by Macdonald and Zaret[4] for studying the relative flexibility or rigidity of teacher behavior in verbal interactions with learners. Macdonald and Zaret use the terms *openness* and *closedness* to designate the end points of a continuum

---

[2] Thomas E. Clayton, *Teaching and Learning* (Englewood Cliffs, N.J.: Prentice-Hall, 1965), p. 6.

[3] N. L. Gage, "Paradigm for Research on Teaching," in N. L. Gage, ed., *Handbook of Research on Teaching* (Chicago: Rand McNally and Co., 1963), p. 96.

[4] James B. Macdonald and Esther Zaret, "Report of a Study of Openness in Classroom Interaction" (Milwaukee: College of Education, University of Wisconsin, 1967). Mimeographed.

of teacher expectations and classroom behavior. The open teacher is one who exhibits maximum awareness and acceptance of the learner and his capabilities, needs, and aspirations. The closed teacher is characterized by perceptual rigidity, which limits his awareness and acceptance of the learner and the learner's capabilities, needs, and aspirations. Macdonald and Zaret hypothesize that the open teacher is more likely to make decisions that will encourage the student to explore and to consider a variety of responses in promoting his own development and learning.

Macdonald and Zaret's model of teacher behavior is shown in Figure 19–1. The *evaluation* or information-processing phase of the model encom-

Figure 19–1. Conceptual Framework of Teacher Behavior and Its Relationship to Learner Responses

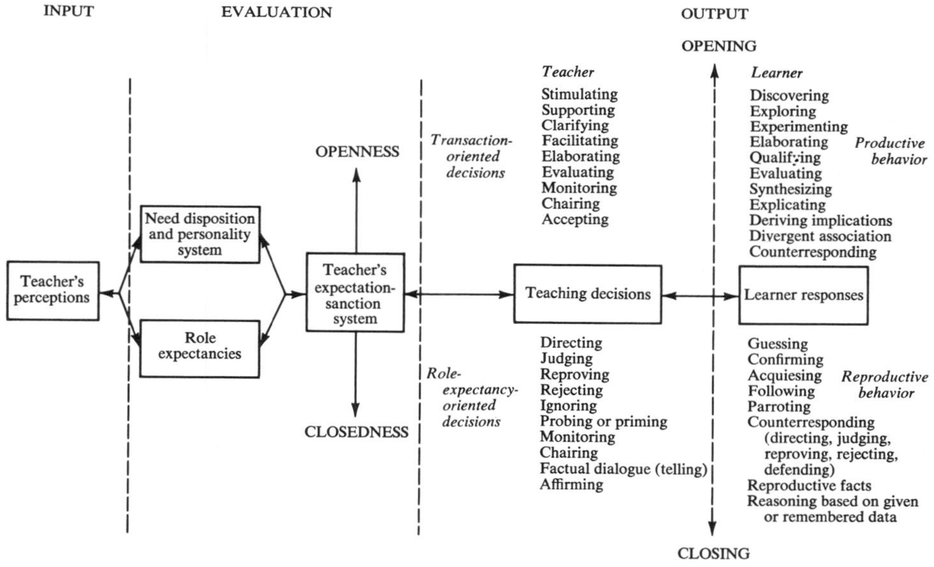

INPUT   EVALUATION   OUTPUT

                                                            OPENING

                                              Teacher   *Learner*
                                              Stimulating   Discovering
                                              Supporting   Exploring
                                              Clarifying   Experimenting
                OPENNESS   *Transaction-* Facilitating   Elaborating   *Productive*
                              oriented   Elaborating   Qualifying   *behavior*
                              decisions   Evaluating   Evaluating
                                              Monitoring   Synthesizing
                                              Chairing   Explicating
                                              Accepting   Deriving implications
   Need disposition   Divergent association
   and personality   Counterresponding
   system

Teacher's   Teacher's   Teaching decisions   Learner responses
perceptions   expectation-
                 sanction
                 system

   Role   Directing   Guessing
   expectancies   Judging   Confirming
                              Role-   Reproving   Acquiescing   *Reproductive*
                              expectancy-   Rejecting   Following   *behavior*
                              oriented   Ignoring   Parroting
                CLOSEDNESS   *decisions*   Probing or priming   Counterresponding
                                              Monitoring   (directing, judging,
                                              Chairing   reproving, rejecting,
                                              Factual dialogue (telling)   defending)
                                              Affirming   Reproductive facts
                                                                       Reasoning based on given
                                                                         or remembered data

                                                            CLOSING

Source: James B. Macdonald and Esther Zaret, "Report of a Study of Openness in Classroom Interaction" (Milwaukee: College of Education, University of Wisconsin, 1967). Mimeographed. Used by permission.

passes the psychological, cognitive, and affective processes discussed in earlier chapters. Factors in the evaluation phase are the teacher's motivations, perceptions, beliefs, goals, attitudes, values, and self-concept. The teacher who is open perceives fewer discrepancies between his observations of students and his expectations of what students should be like. He is more likely to accept students as they are rather than to respond to them in terms of preconceived notions. The fewer discrepancies between his perceptions and his expectations mean that the open teacher is less threatened, and hence has less need to distort what he perceives. The teacher whose psychological-cognitive-affective system is more closed experiences many more conflicts between his perceptions and his expectations of students and the learning situation. He adjusts to the increase in threat produced by these discrepancies by distorting what he perceives so that it is more consistent with his expectations and beliefs about students and their learning.

The open or closed quality of a teacher's expectations and beliefs is reflected in his teaching output, his decisions and behaviors affecting students. Open teacher behaviors and decisions are *transaction oriented*—that is, they function to facilitate and expand learning. They encourage students to respond with open, *productive behavior* of their own, behavior that is manifested in efforts to explore, to extend, and to elaborate the concepts and skills acquired in the classroom. The closed teacher's behaviors and decisions, on the other hand, are *role-expectancy oriented*—that is, they function to direct, to judge, or to reprove in eliciting specific, prescribed, conforming, *reproductive behavior* from students (acquiescing, following, parroting what has been given them by teacher or textbook).

Organizing for Learning

We shall here examine studies of the teacher's role in (1) establishing a climate favorable for learning, (2) facilitating the learning of students, and (3) influencing behavior change.

Establishing a Favorable Climate

There is some disagreement among educators over the kind of classroom atmosphere that is most conducive to learning. Some educators maintain that optimal learning will not occur if the pupil feels so safe and contented that he is not stimulated or challenged to seek new experiences and to change. This book has suggested, however, that optimal pupil development and learning will occur in social-emotional climates in which the pupil feels valued and accepted and has a sense of belonging.

One line of evidence favoring the establishment of a relatively nonthreatening, psychologically safe climate for learning is to be found in the studies of anxiety and learning. The results of these studies are not unequivocal, but they do suggest that high anxiety is associated with low achievement. Among elementary school children, high-anxiety subjects make significantly more errors in a complex learning task than do low-anxiety subjects.[5] Anxiety is negatively correlated with intelligence and school

---

[5] A. Castaneda, B. McCandless, and D. Palermo, "The Relationship of Anxiety in Children to Performance in a Complex Learning Task," *Child Development*, 27 (1956), 333–337.

achievement; that is, in general, children who register high anxiety tend to score lower on IQ and achievement tests.[6]

Further evidence of the relationship between climate and learning is found in a classic study of Lewin, Lippitt, and White,[7] who investigated the effects of authoritarian, democratic, and laissez-faire social climates and leadership roles on individual and group behavior. Four groups of 11-year-old boys (with five boys in each group) were organized into clubs whose major activity was making papier mâché masks and various club insignias. Each club met for three six-week periods under three successive leaders, one of whom employed a democratic, another an autocratic, and the third a laissez-faire leadership style. Under the *authoritarian* leader all determination of policy was made by the leader. Under the *democratic* leader all policies were a matter of group discussion and decision, encouraged and assisted by the leader. Under *laissez-faire* leadership complete freedom was permitted for group or individual decision, with a minimum of leader participation. Descriptions of group and individual behavior and interviews with children, parents, and teachers were analyzed to ascertain the effects of these varying leadership styles on the work and interpersonal behavior of the boys in each group.

A major finding of this study was that different styles of leadership produce differences in social climate and differing group and individual behavior. Under authoritarian leadership, the boys became frustrated. They reacted with greater hostility, aggression, and a nearly unanimous dislike of their leader. More scapegoats emerged in authoritarian groups, and aggression increased when the leader left the room. Under democratic leadership, in contrast, the boys were responsive, spontaneous, friendly to one another, and more generous in their praise of one another's work. They continued working when the leader left the room and showed higher levels of frustration tolerance and less aggression and hostility. Under laissez-faire leadership, group members became dissatisfied with their lack of efficiency and accomplishment. In addition to confusion and uncertainty, there emerged in the laissez-faire situation a vicious circle involving frustration, which led to aggression, which led, in turn, to mutual frustration.

An important implication of this study is that the teacher or leader is the single most significant variable influencing the social-emotional climate of the group or classroom. Leadership styles, not individual leaders themselves, are the primary factors to which children react. This clear demonstration of the influence of the leader on group life and the accomplishments and interpersonal relationships of the group has important consequences for education. As McDonald[8] has cautioned, however, we

---

[6] S. B. Sarason et al., *Anxiety in Elementary School Children* (New York: John Wiley, 1960).

[7] K. Lewin, R. L. Lippitt, and R. K. White, "Patterns of Aggressive Behavior in Experimentally Created 'Social Climates,'" *Journal of Social Psychology*, 10 (1939), 271–299.

[8] Frederick J. McDonald, *Educational Psychology*, 2nd ed. (Belmont, Calif.: Wadsworth Publishing Co., 1965), p. 523.

should not overgeneralize the results of this study. The terms *democracy* and *autocracy* mean different things to different people, and different children may give quite different interpretations to a teacher's behavior.

The influence of contrasting types of teacher control on pupil behavior has also been studied by Anderson.[9] Two types of teacher control were identified, "dominative" and "socially integrative." The teacher was considered dominative when the rigidity of his responses stifled differences in others, reduced the interplay of individual differences, and hence made understanding more difficult. The dominating teacher sets the goals of the learning experience and directs the activities of pupils toward reaching these goals. The socially integrative teacher is generally spontaneous and flexible, attempts to bring out differences in others and to find common purposes among these differences, and encourages self-direction of pupils toward achievement of goals. The principal findings of this study indicate that the teacher's classroom personality and pattern of behavior influence the behavior of the children under him. Kindergarten and primary grade teachers who used dominative techniques with children produced aggressive and antagonistic behavior in the children. Children expressed their aggression and antagonism not only toward the teacher but also toward peers, and a vicious circle of dominative behavior was created. In contrast, teachers who used socially integrative behaviors facilitated the adoption of integrative, cooperative, and self-directive behaviors by children. Thus, tendencies toward the dominative and uncooperative behavior so inimical to the need satisfactions of both teacher and pupils were minimized.

Evidence from numerous later studies[10] underscores the importance of the teacher's role and behavior in establishing a social-emotional climate conducive to learning. Climates that induce high anxiety generally produce lower academic performance. Studies of classroom groups reveal that the teacher is the most important variable in determining the climate of a learning situation. Positive, learner-centered climates are associated with greater productivity, increased learning, and warmer, more positive attitudes than are less positive, teacher-centered climates.

Facilitating the Learning of Students

The following description of the learning experience, based upon generalizations that have emerged from educational method and to a lesser extent from learning theory, presents characteristics and qualities which many educators hope or expect to see exemplified in classroom learning.

---

[9] H. H. Anderson, "Domination and Socially Integrative Behavior," in R. G. Barker, J. S. Kounin, and H. F. Wright, eds., *Child Behavior and Development* (New York: McGraw-Hill Book Co., 1943), pp. 459–483.

[10] See Ned A. Flanders, "Personal-Social Anxiety as a Function in Experimental Learning Situations," *Journal of Educational Research*, 45 (1951), 100–110; Hugh V. Perkins, "The Effects of Climate and Curriculum on Group Learning," *Journal of Educational Research*, 44 (December 1950), 269–286; and R. Schmuck, "Some Aspects of Classroom Social Climate," *Psychology in the Schools*, 3 (January 1966), 59–65.

Not all of the characteristics are found in every learning experience, and some educators may hold somewhat different views of classroom learning. The description, then, is general and somewhat idealized but substantially accurate.

1. Learning occurs when there is a change in the learner as the result of practice, training, or experience. This is an often used definition of learning which points to the teacher's major goal—to bring about change in the learner. Implicit in this definition is the concept of learning as an active process. The learner must respond, either overtly or covertly, in exploring, relating, testing, and refining the concepts, skills, and feelings that emerge from his experience. Moreover, learning is an active response of the total organism—not just the brain, hands, or body. The learner therefore must be seen as an organized, unified whole. Learning must also be organized in relation to clearly defined objects—objectives that reflect the needs of students as well as the needs of society. Learning experiences should provide for the uniqueness of each learner and allow him to be active in a variety of ways. Though pupils do learn by listening passively to a lecture or viewing a film, more active response—discussing, searching, exploring, testing, evaluating, and synthesizing—bring out learning of greater depth and breadth.

2. Learning is most likely to occur when pupils are ready and able to engage in activities and experiences that are relevant to that particular learning. Chapter 16 described several dimensions of readiness—maturity, intelligence, intellectual development, and experience—and discussed the influence of each dimension on the learning process. When the learner's readiness is not assessed and taken into consideration, neither practice nor the efforts of the teacher are likely to be effectual. In addition to the dimensions of readiness already mentioned, an optimal learning experience would also be attuned to the pupil's psychological readiness for learning. Learning tends to take place more readily if the pupil perceives learning activities as useful and important to him. This implies that the teacher should know a great deal about individual pupils and should continuously explore with his pupils the relevance for their own lives of what they are learning.

3. Objectives and goals define the behavioral changes sought and direct the activities of teacher and pupils in the learning experience. Objectives and goals can be implicit or explicit. Although the teacher's objectives and goals frequently dominate classroom learning, the learner is likely to be more actively involved and his learning more significant if he shares in selecting and setting the goals of learning, in planning ways to achieve them, and in measuring his own progress toward them. Before he can share the goal-setting and plan-learning experiences cooperatively with students, the teacher may have to modify his perceptions of his own role and of his students' capacities for responsible self-direction. He must perceive that students need not depend on the teacher in order to learn, that talents and resources lie not only with the teacher but with the total group, and that students can, if given the chance, organize and pursue meaningful learning activities responsibly and independently. In organizing the classroom for learning, the teacher should check periodically to make certain that pupils' choices and decisions are playing a part in goal setting, planning, and evaluation.

4. The motivations of the learner influence his responses to learning situations and the kinds and qualities of behavior change that emerge from these situations.   The individual's motivations relate to the satisfaction or dissatisfaction of specific needs. For certain tasks, high motivation may be less effective than a moderate level of drive. Strong motivation, for example, can improve performance of relatively simple tasks involving few cues, but is likely to produce lower performance of more complex tasks involving many cues. As noted earlier, motivation that arouses anxiety tends to distract the learner and to result in undesirable learning.

The emphasis that schools place on grades and other rewards (incentives characteristic of extrinsic motivation) is lamented by many who feel that learning that increases one's capabilities and competence is its own reward (incentives characteristic of intrinsic motivation). Both intrinsic and extrinsic motives, however, influence all human behavior. Organizing the classroom so as to maximize intrinsic and minimize extrinsic motives in learning is seen by many as one of the most important tasks of the teacher.

5. Self factors play a decisive role in learning.   The individual behaves according to the way he perceives himself and his world. Especially important in influencing his responses to the learning situation is his self-concept as a learner. Successful students reveal in their behavior the self-images "I am able to learn" and "I like school."

The learning experience is greatly influenced by the level of aspiration set by the learner in response to his self-concept. Pupils need help and practice in setting goals for themselves. By providing adequate feedback and evaluation, a teacher can help students to modify their aspirations so that the goals are neither so low as to elicit little effort nor so high as to invite failure. In considering the many self factors that influence the learning experience, the sensitive teacher will be especially responsive to individual differences among learners and to the personal history of each learner.

6. Knowledge of success promotes learning.   It has frequently been stated that behavior is purposeful. We have noted that the learner's responses in learning situations appear to relate to the satisfactions of his needs. Logic and empirical evidence suggest that the coping, striving, problem-solving behaviors characteristic of learning do not persist indefinitely in the absence of feedback. Knowledge of results, therefore, plays a significant role in all learning theories.

Learning is effective when the learner is able to see and to analyze the results of his own performance and to ascertain progress in the learning task. Thus, in organizing a classroom for learning, the teacher can aid the learner by describing and demonstrating good performance and by inform-ing the learner of his mistakes, his degree of improvement, or his success-ful performance. It is especially important that the slow or retarded learner be made aware that he is able to spell correctly or to recognize two more words today than he was able to recognize yesterday.

7. *Failure can be used to build toward success in learning, but too many failures tend to discourage and to block learning.* Most of us have had some experience with intense or repeated failure and are well aware of the effects of repeated failure in diminishing motivation and level of perform-ance. In pointing to the adverse effects of too much failure, we are not suggesting that children be protected from any experience of failure whatso-ever. Such a situation would be unrealistic and would deny children the opportunity to learn from failure. Children need help and experience in analyzing their failures—in seeing what their mistakes are, why they are making them, and how they can avoid them in the future. Therefore, the social-emotional climate of the classroom should permit and encourage students to risk possible failure—although in a culture and an age that puts a high premium on getting the right answer, such a climate may not be easy to establish.

8. *Some learnings are enhanced through first-hand, concrete experiences, while others can be achieved as effectively through vicarious experiences.* Children learn most easily and readily those things that relate to their own concrete experiences and thus have personal meaning and significance for them: a visit to city hall, talks with a city official about problems of govern-ment, opportunities to make their own forecasts from weather maps and data from a classroom weather station. To depend on first-hand or concrete experience at all times, however, would be foolish or impossible. The accu-mulated wisdom of a culture is communicated to succeeding generations through established customs and traditions and through literature and art forms. Students are able to identify themselves with people, events, and ideas beyond face-to-face contacts, and eventually to show concern for prob-lems larger than those they can solve at first hand, problems they can learn about only through second- and third-hand sources, such as books and the mass media.

9. *Learning is enhanced when several rather than few sensory media are employed.* One acquires meanings from experience through each of the senses: sight, hearing, smell, taste, and touch. However, the great stress that is placed in school upon verbal, symbolic, and cognitive learning has re-sulted in a disproportionately high reliance on visual and auditory media. Children also need opportunities to experience and to learn through touch-ing, tasting, and smelling.

Persons vary in their sensitivity to various kinds of sensory stimuli. Some children are tactually oriented; others are kinesthetically or spatially oriented. An individual student's perferred mode of experiencing is often revealed in his learning behavior. Some students can learn how a radio works by reading about it, others by seeing a film, others through learning to diagram circuits. Thus, many modes of experiencing and responding should be made available to students in their learning.

10.   Learning is facilitated when students acquire increased self-understanding and self-direction.   This generalization again emphasizes the very considerable contributions that pupils themselves make to their own learning. One of the purposes of education is to help pupils become independent, self-directive individuals, fully able to cope effectively with the life problems they encounter. Effective self-direction depends on a measure of self-understanding. Self-understanding is promoted in a climate of acceptance, in which the individual is encouraged to accept himself and his feelings, to examine the meanings of his experience, to evaluate objectively and realistically his own behavior, and to plan courses of action that promote growth and self-enhancement.

Teacher Influence and Behavior Change

The notion, emerging from earlier studies, that the teacher or leader is a significant variable influencing group climate and learning has stimulated numerous investigations of teacher influence and behavior change. From a series of investigations by Flanders[11] there has emerged an observation procedure for studying how the spontaneous behavior of a teacher affects learning in the classroom. Using this procedure, a classroom observer classifies verbal statements into one of 10 categories (see Table 19–1). Seven categories apply to teacher statements, two to student statements, and one to silence or confusion. This system—the classifying of verbal behavior during a particular period of classroom activity—is called *interaction analysis.*[12] The procedure produces a series of numbers representing a sequence of teacher-student interactions. For example, in the categorization sequence 4–8, 3–5, the teacher asks a question, the student answers the teacher's question, and the teacher builds on the student's answer and then adds further facts or opinions of his own. Each pair of categorizations (4–8, 8–3, 3–5) is tallied on a cell matrix. By means of this matrix, statements that a teacher makes as an immediate response to students can be isolated and compared with statements that trigger student participation.

One of the results of Flanders' research is "the rule of two thirds," which says that, generally, about two thirds of classroom time is spent in talking; that the chances are two out of three that the person talking is the teacher; and that the teacher spends two thirds of his "talking" time ex-

[11] Ned A. Flanders, *Teacher Influence, Pupil Attitudes, and Achievement*, Report of Cooperative Research Project No. 397 (Washington, D. C.: Office of Education, U. S. Department of Health, Education, and Welfare, 1960).

[12] For a further explanation of interaction analysis procedure, see Edmund J. Amidon and Peggy Amidon, *Interaction Analysis Training Kit—Lever 1* (Minneapolis: Association for Productive Teaching, 1967).

Table 19–1.   Categories for Interaction Analysis

Teacher talk

Indirect influence

1.* *Accepts feeling:* Accepts and clarifies the feeling tone of the students in a nonthreatening manner. Feelings may be positive or negative. Predicting or recalling feelings included.

2. *Praises or encourages:* Praises or encourages student action or behavior. Jokes that release tension, not at the expense of another individual, nodding head or saying "um hm?" or "go on" are included.

3. *Accepts or uses ideas of student:* Clarifying, building, or developing ideas suggested by a student. As teacher brings more of his own ideas into play, shift to category 5.

4. *Asks questions:* Asking a question about content or procedure with the intent that a student answer.

Direct influence

5. *Lecturing:* Giving facts or opinions about content or procedure; expressing his own ideas, asking rhetorical questions.

6. *Giving directions:* Directions, commands, or orders with which a student is expected to comply.

7. *Criticizing or justifying authority:* Statements intended to change student behavior from nonacceptable to acceptable pattern; bawling someone out; stating why the teacher is doing what he is doing; extreme self-reference.

Student talk

8. *Response:* Talk by students in response to teacher. Teacher initiates the contact or solicits student statement.

9. *Initiation:* Talk by students which they initiate. If "calling on" student is only to indicate who may talk next, observer must decide whether student wanted to talk. If he did, use this category.

---

10. *Silence or confusion:* Pauses, short periods of silence and periods of confusion in which communication cannot be understood by the observer.

Source: Ned A. Flanders, "Interaction Analysis in the Classroom: A Manual for Observers" (Minneapolis: College of Education, University of Minnesota, 1959). Mimeographed. Used by permission.

* There is *no* scale implied by these numbers. Each number is classificatory; it designates a particular kind of communication event. To write these numbers down during observation is to enumerate, not to judge a position on a scale.

pressing facts or his own opinions, giving directions, or criticizing students. Flanders also found, however, that in classrooms where there is greater freedom for intellectual curiosity, more expression of ideas, more positive feelings, and higher achievement, the rule of two thirds becomes "the rule of one half"; in such classrooms, the teacher spends more time asking questions, clarifying, praising, encouraging, and developing student ideas and opinions.

Of particular interest in Flanders' research is his investigation of the ratio of a teacher's *indirect influence* (statements in categories 1–4 of Table 19–1) to his *direct influence* (statements in categories 5–7), which Flanders refers to as the *I/D ratio*. Although indirect patterns were found, on the whole, to stimulate more achievement regardless of student ability, direct teacher influence was found to increase learning when the student perceived clearly and accepted the learning goal.

Another variable used by Flanders to differentiate superior from less superior patterns of teacher influence was *teacher flexibility*, the teacher's tendency or ability to use a different pattern of influence in different phases of the instructional process. In superior classrooms, marked by greater teacher flexibility, pupils seem to depend less upon the teacher and to concentrate more energy on the learning task and less energy on finding out how to please the teacher.[13] Investigations of teacher behavior and role have continued, leading to the development of numerous sophisticated scales and instruments designed to measure and assess various dimensions of teacher role and influence on pupil behavior.[14]

Flanders' interaction analysis enables the teacher to assess his effectiveness in helping the class achieve specific learning objectives. It provides few clues, however, to the effectiveness of the teacher's verbal interaction in facilitating the learning of the individual student. Good and Brophy[15] argue that a clearer picture of the relationships between teacher behavior variables and student performance measures might be obtained if the individual student rather than the group were used as a unit of analysis in studies of teacher behavior and role.

Since the teacher frequently serves as an instructional leader in working with students, studies of leadership training and style may provide further data which would be helpful to our understanding of teacher influence and behavior change. Fiedler[16] has reviewed numerous studies of leadership effectiveness in industry, government, and the armed services and found that leaders with greater training and experience performed no better in their leadership roles than leaders with little or no training and experience. He concluded that most leaders learn to become leaders on the job without any specific preparation for leadership. Instead of relying on training and experience for developing effective leadership, Fiedler proposes a *contingency model of leadership* which postulates that effective group performance depends upon the proper match between (1) the leader's style of

---

[13] Ned A. Flanders, "Teacher and Classroom Influences on Individual Learning," in A. H. Passow, ed., *Nurturing Individual Potential* (Washington, D. C.: Association for Supervision and Curriculum Development, N.E.A., 1963), pp. 57–65.

[14] See Anita Simon and E. G. Boyer, eds., *Mirrors for Behavior: An Anthology of Observation Instruments*, Vols. 1–14 (Philadelphia: Research for Better Schools, 1970).

[15] T. L. Good and J. E. Brophy, "Analyzing Classroom Interaction: A More Powerful Alternative," *Educational Technology*, 11 (October 1971), 36–41.

[16] Fred E. Fiedler, *A Theory of Leadership Effectiveness* (New York: McGraw-Hill Book Co., 1967); see also Fred E. Fiedler, "The Trouble with Leadership Training Is That It Doesn't Train Leaders," *Psychology Today*, 6 (February 1973), 23–30, 92.

interacting with his subordinates and (2) the degree to which the situation gives control and influence to the leader. According to this model, leaders can be classified either as relatively relationship motivated (interested in good personal relationships with his co-workers) or as relatively task motivated (interested in performing the task well). The task variable may be highly favorable to the leader (he is liked, he has position and power, and he has been given a narrowly defined task to do), or it may be unfavorable (the leader is disliked, he has little power, and the task is vaguely defined). The critical problem is to determine which kind of leadership each group situation calls for. Results of studies completed thus far show that task-motivated leaders perform better in situations that are favorable to them and also in situations that are very unfavorable. The relationship-motivated leader seems to perform best when his power is neither great nor little and success of the task depends upon the group members' contributing their ideas. It makes little sense, therefore, to speak of a good leader or a poor leader. There are only leaders who perform well in one situation and not well in other situations.

Teachers appear to fit one or the other of these leadership styles, relationship motivated or task motivated. Many teachers probably try to incorporate both of these qualities into their teaching, but pupils tend to perceive the teacher as more oriented toward one quality than the other. Similarly, school subjects can be viewed as more or less structured, some with precise, observable behavioral objectives and others with objectives which are vague and less observable. It appears, then, that Fiedler's contingency model of leadership may have important implications for our understanding of teacher influence and behavior change. We would hypothesize that effective teaching is dependent upon achieving a closer match between the leadership style of the teacher and the learning task as well as the specific needs and backgrounds of the students. This would seem to be a fertile hypothesis meriting further exploration and research.

Encouraging Self-Directing Learning

Two quite different teaching methodologies, each with its corresponding view of the learner, are described in Flanders' studies of teacher influence. One type of teacher, the "direct influence" type, spends most of his class time lecturing, giving directions, and criticizing—in general treating the student as relatively passive. In contrast, teachers using the "indirect influence" approach reflect a view of the learner as actively influencing the learning situation. One type of learning that involves the learner's active participation and the teacher's use of indirect influence is *discovery learning*. It may be recalled from Chapter 15[17] that the learner is more likely to

[17] See pp. 485–486, 488–489.

acquire a sound grasp and understanding of facts, concepts, and principles if he has discovered them for himself than if he has read about them or has the material explained to him. Concepts, principles, and solutions acquired by discovery are more likely to be remembered, to be transferred to other situations, and to relate to the personal interests and goals of the learner. We shall examine next the ways in which discovery and self-directed learning have been implemented in programs of open education and career education.

Open Education

Learning by discovery is an important characteristic of *open education*, a program of preschool and elementary education which features a free, informal, highly individualized, child-centered learning experience. The historical roots of open education can be found in the educational philosophy of John Dewey and progressive education in America during the 1930s. The influence of progressive education in America waned after 1940, but the idea of a freer, individualized, child-centered education became the cornerstone of British preschool and primary education after World War II. The practices of British primary schools which adopted this philosophy have exerted a continuing influence on elementary education in the United States during the past decade.

Respect for and trust in the child are probably the most fundamental principles of open education. This type of education is based on the assumption that all children want to learn and will learn if the emphasis is on learning and not on teaching. Open education differs from traditional education in its emphasis on each child's thinking processes instead of rote skill acquisition, and on freedom and responsibility rather than on conformity and following directions.[18]

An observer in an open school classroom in Britain enrolling eight- and nine-year-olds observed the following learning activities in progress.

Two girls *at back table making chart on heartbeats—from sparrow to hibernating frogs (fastest to slowest)—includes teachers' and children's heartbeats—girls are in process of inking in the chart with colored ink.*

Reading corner, girl *writing about gerbils (has their cage in front of her while she's writing; she pokes them for me to see when I walk by),* girl *writing about birth (class has just seen sex education film),* girl *writing creative story,* boy *reading* The Silver Sword (*boy*

---

[18] E. B. Nyquist, "Open Education—Its Philosophy, Historical Perspectives, and Implications," *The Science Teacher*, 38 (September 1971), 25–28.

completely oblivious to rest of class, forgets to go to lunch when class dismissed, has to be touched by teacher to go).

Center table, newt (kind of water lizard) in fish tank, one boy sketching it, one boy observing it and recording observations of its movements, one boy writing about it from information in resource book in front of him.

Girl at solitary desk writing about Japan, using two resource books.

Three boys working with dry cell battery at one desk—teacher working with them.

Two boys working from same math card (probabilities and squares)—one boy working from math book—all at own desks in four-desk group.

Two girls completing maps of Japan for own books on Japan —two boys and two girls working on writing and illustrations for own books on Japan—one girl copying Japanese painting from book, using fabric and sewing rather than painting—one boy copying different Japanese painting same way—all at long group of desks at back of room.

Two girls writing about birth—one girl drawing a fetus, copying from a resource book—all at own desks in four-desk group.

On one bulletin board children's compositions and drawings about pregnancy and birth.

On other bulletin board children's Japanese ghost stories—children told me teacher had read them Japanese ghost stories in conjunction with classwork on Japan, then urged [them] to write own Japanese-style ghost stories.[19]

From this description it is evident that open education provides a format in which children are free to learn at their own pace and in their own way. Open education puts learning where it belongs—squarely on the learner. For the child, it is working on things in which he is interested, being free, feeling respected and worthwhile, and having jobs to do and purposes that are meaningful. Part of feeling good about oneself is being able to exercise control over his own life. The learning of skills and development of understandings in subject areas, when integrated around self-selected projects and activities, help one to feel successful and are a part of his sense of fulfillment.[20]

A close examination of open education reveals that it is consistent with current psychological theory. The relationship between open education and Piaget's theory of intellectual development is particularly evident. Piaget has shown that the child is the principal agent in his own education

[19] V. R. Rogers, "Open Schools on the British Model," *Educational Leadership*, 29 (February 1972), 401. Used with permission.

[20] Nyquist, pp. 25–28.

and mental development; the crucial factor in Piaget's theory is the child's own activity in assimilating his experiences and accommodating to them. In the process the child is forming mental images or structures which correspond to his experiences, and he is continually modifying these structures as a result of new experiences. The self-directed learning of open education is instrumental in the child's development of these cognitive structures.

We recall, too, that in Piaget's theory of intellectual development more than maturation is involved. The increasing complexity and adaptability of the child's thought depend upon his opportunities to think about something, to have appropriate new experiences. Though the child carries on his learning by himself with one or two others, it does not occur in isolation. The teacher plays an active but quite different role in open education than in the traditional classroom. In open education the teacher serves as a facilitator of learning, providing an inviting environment, encouragement, guidance, and assistance. He works with individuals and small groups helping to set goals and achieve them, raising questions, intervening when necessary, observing the children, and assessing progress. Children's growth is evaluated on an individual basis in terms of strengths and weaknesses that permits diagnosis and planning.

A unique feature of open education as practiced in the British primary schools is the family or vertical grouping of students. Several age groups (five-, six-, and seven-year olds, for example) are placed together in one classroom. In a multiage group the younger students are stimulated by the older students, whose involvement in reading, writing, and math enable them to serve as models for the younger ones.

The British primary school has been studied extensively by American educators, with the result that increasing numbers of schools in the United States are organized around the open education concept. The architectural design of some schools features open classrooms without walls in order to facilitate an informal, open education such as that described above. Needless to say, however, an open education is not dependent on particular physical facilities, nor do open classrooms guarantee open education. Open education centers in the way adults, especially teachers and principals, feel about and respond to children and to their needs for development and learning.

How effective is open education? Unfortunately, we have no definitive answer. The outcomes of open education are often expressed in the unique accomplishments of individual students—results which cannot be expressed in terms of gains in standardized achievement test scores. Characteristically, evaluations of open education take the form of anecdotal descriptions (such as those presented earlier in this section) which show the children independently involved in a variety of learning activities.[21] These descriptions generally show the children as happy, involved, self-directive, and

---

[21] For evaluative descriptions of open education learning, see Charles E. Silberman, *Crisis in the Classroom: The Remaking of American Education* (New York: Random House, 1970), pp. 275–322; and Lillian Weber, *The English Infant School and Informal Education* (Englewood Cliffs, N. J.: Prentice-Hall, 1971), pp. 17–144.

confident of themselves and their work. In short, it appears that along with their respect for and trust in the child and his capabilities, adherents of open education believe deeply that the assumptions underlying this kind of education are sound and supportable now. Of central importance is their belief in the capabilities of the child to be self-directive and actively involved in his own development and learning.

Ideally, open education should start with the young child and provide a model for his learning over his entire career. The success of a program of open education would seem to depend upon the involvement of parents, teachers, and administrators in personal support of teachers, in-service training of teachers, tolerance of flexibility, and patience toward pupil involvement in informal learning. Open education is not a panacea for the problems facing American education, but it does seem to offer unusual opportunities for personal growth and fulfillment by both pupils and teachers.

Career Education

Further opportunities for discovery and self-directive learning by students are being offered by programs of career education or career development. *Career education* is a program of education experiences, curricula, instruction, and counseling which seeks to prepare each individual for a life of economic independence, personal fulfillment, and an appreciation for the dignity of work. Career education is a lifelong, systematic way of acquainting students with the world of work in their elementary and junior high school years and preparing them in high school and in college to enter into and advance in a career of their own choosing. For adults, career education is a way to reenter formal education and upgrade their skills or acquire new ones for a different career. Such programs embrace all occupations and professions and can include any individual, whether in or out of school.[22]

This renewed interest in career education is a reflection of the concern that 2.5 million young people leave high school or college each year without a real career goal, much less the preparation to reach it. Equally disturbing is the large number of adults, earlier products of our education system, who spend all or at least part of their working life in an occupation that engages neither their interest nor their talents. By 1980, 101 million Americans are expected to be in the national labor force, one sixth more than the 86 million in 1970. At present 80 percent of our youth do not graduate from college, and the unemployment rate among high school graduates, with or without some college, is more than three times as high as that of vocational education graduates.[23] Thus, the task of career education is to

[22] R. M. Worthington, "A Home-Community-Based Career Education Model," *Educational Leadership*, 30 (December 1972), 213–214.

[23] "Equipping Students for the World of Work," *Nation's Schools*, 88 (December 1971), 35.

equip students for a world of work whose needs and job opportunities are continuously shifting.

The broad outline of a comprehensive program of career education that is being developed by the U. S. Office of Education for implementation in our public schools is shown in Figure 19–2. Attitude building, career ori-

Figure 19–2.   Suggested Career Education Experiences by Grade Level

Grades 1-6	Grades 7-8	Grades 9-10	Grades 11-12		
Student develops self-awareness and understanding of his interests and abilities.					Job
Student develops attitudes about the personal, social, and economic significance of work.					
Occupational awareness	*Occupational orientation and exploration*	*Occupational exploration in depth, beginning specialization*	*Specialization*	100 percent placement	Non baccalaureate program
Student is informed about occupations through a series of clusters representing the entire world of work.	Student explores several clusters of his choice.	Student selects one cluster to explore in greater depth. Develops entry-level skill. May change cluster if desired.	Student specializes in one cluster. Takes prerequisites for further education and/or intensive skill training for job entry.		Baccalaureate program

Source: A. L. Hardwick, "Career Education—A Model for Implementation," *Business Education Forum*, 25 (May 1971), 3–5. Used by permission.

entation, and vocational guidance as well as exploratory activities would begin in the elementary grades to create motivation to work. Specific skill orientation would start in the middle grades to acquaint students with machines, tools, and equipment. Since there are more than 23,000 active job titles in the United States today, these jobs have been grouped into 15 occupational clusters, such as business and office occupations, public service occupations, and health occupations. Many schools are using the cluster framework in orienting students toward careers. Simple job cluster skills are introduced in junior high school. As the student progresses through high school and the post-high school programs of his choice, he can choose among specific skills training, job cluster skills training, pretechnical and prevocational education, advanced vocational and technical education, and college preparatory education. Upgrading and retraining through continued educational programs would be available throughout adulthood.

Career education is a means of personalizing education for every student through developing a curriculum that is meaningful, realistic, and viable for him. It seeks to involve the student in his own learning through helping him acquire the skills needed for making a livelihood for himself and his future family no matter at what level of the education system he leaves.

Discipline and Classroom Control

In organizing the classroom for learning, the teacher will want to give some thought to how he will respond to situations which involve discipline and classroom control. Whether he will be able to maintain classroom control is a question which arouses uncertainty and anxiety in the first-year teacher. Because nearly every interpersonal encounter is extremely complex, it is not possible to offer a prescription or formula which will ensure success in handling every discipline problem that is likely to arise. Yet there is a body of substantiated principles of human behavior available which each teacher can apply in his own way in dealing with particular situations involving students with specific needs and problems.

In a very real sense nearly all of the concepts and principles of development and learning encountered thus far contribute to our understanding of behavior which calls for correction and discipline. In Chapter 3, we noted that human behavior has direction and purpose. Behavior is the organism's response to some inner disequilibrium, tension, or need—a state of arousal we have called motivation. When motivated, the individual responds to need by directing energy toward a goal associated with satisfaction of the need. Frequently, a discipline problem arises when the ways students use to satisfy their needs conflict with the needs of the teacher or other classmates. The student may seek to satisfy his physiological needs for activity or release of tension caused by hunger, illness, or fatigue by restlessness, inattention, or walking around the classroom. Such behavior may pose a threat to the planned learning experience and maintenance of classroom control—important elements in the teacher's need to feel adequate in his role as a teacher. Similarly, the student may respond to threats to his needs for affection, belonging, and approval by calling out in class, disturbing others, demanding help from the teacher, disobeying, or showing disrespect for the teacher. Low academic achievement and failure to make the team or gain acceptance of peers are common threats to the student's needs for achievement, competence, and self-esteem. As noted in Chapter 9, the frustration stemming from unmet needs frequently leads to aggression toward others. The student may vent his frustration by physical or verbal aggression toward the teacher or his peers or by open defiance of the teacher.

The teacher's effectiveness in handling situations involving discipline depends upon his understanding the causes of the student's misbehavior. Especially important is that the teacher *accept the feelings* the student is expressing through his misbehavior. A teacher who responds to a student's outburst by going to him and saying softly, "We all feel angry with those who hurt us," is more likely to calm him than he would by scolding, threats, or expulsion from the classroom. Often, however, the teacher must take corrective action immediately, before he has had an opportunity to ascertain the causes of the student's misbehavior. For example, the teacher may need to step in to break up a fight or to prevent injury to the student or to others. In general, action by the teacher which is firm but calming, sympathetic, nonpunitive, and expeditious is more likely to be effective in resolving conflict and getting the class back to the learning activity than action that is tough and punitive. Later, after tempers have cooled, it is often useful to have a conference with the students involved in an effort to resolve the issues that caused the conflict.

Research consistently shows that it is not possible to describe effective teaching in terms of a specific set of teacher behaviors. A variety of teaching styles have been found to be effective in promoting learning. Although every teacher tends to develop his own unique teaching style, including his patterns of relating to students and maintaining classroom control, there are some general principles which have proven effective in evoking positive responses from students.

1. A favorable climate for learning is based upon the establishment of mutual respect between teacher and pupils.   The teacher's attitude toward students crucially affects his relationships with them and the maintenance of classroom control. The teacher who genuinely likes students, accepts them, and appears confident that they will accept and respond to him quickly earns the respect of the class. He recognizes that students are likely to test him and that many of the negative feelings students express relate to causes outside the classroom situation. The understanding teacher acts on the principle that behavior is caused. Many pupils' misbehaviors are the result of conflicts at home or with peers or are normal symptoms of the particular growth period the student is passing through. A teacher who accepts the student's angry feelings, expresses concern, and redirects the student's attention back to the learning activity frequently finds that the misbehavior quickly disappears. To establish a relationship of mutual respect with students, the teacher has to feel positive about himself and his abilities—qualities which each of us can attain with the help of family, friends, teachers, and colleagues. In short, the teacher views students as real people with whom he will be engaged in productive interaction and learning. If the teacher has been successful in gaining the mutual respect of his students, he is likely to be seen by them as a sympathetic, concerned, friendly adult instead of as the stereotype of a suspicious, unfriendly, punitive policeman.

2. Since students early seek to ascertain the limits of the classroom setting, the teacher may wish to establish some class rules.   Most of us are more likely to be effective and to gain satisfaction from an experience if we know what to expect and know what will be expected of us. Pupils entering a classroom for the first time are no different. What the teacher expects of students can be communicated by a few simple rules. A few rules are likely to prove more satisfactory than many rules, since students will find it easier to remember and to comply if few rather than many rules are presented. Beyond some rules established by the school administration or board of education, the rules selected by the teacher—often with suggestions from the class—should focus on creating a classroom situation that respects the rights of all and is conducive to learning. It will probably be necessary for the teacher to monitor the students' general compliance with the rules until adherence to them has become automatic.

3. *Be well prepared for the class, and begin the class promptly.* Experienced teachers have found that misbehavior is more frequent during times when the learning goals and tasks have not been clearly set forth or are not understood by the students. The start of the period should be the signal for beginning the learning activity or lesson. Delays in starting class often lead to pupils' continuing their talking, running around the room, or being out in the hall—activities which are inimical to productive learning.

Kounin,[24] in his studies of discipline and group management, found that the teacher can do much to prevent misbehavior from occurring. Misbehavior tended to be minimal in classrooms where the learning activities were varied and challenging and where the teacher maintained tempo and momentum during the learning tasks and during transition periods between tasks. In addition, teachers with better classroom control were able to cope with two events simultaneously. These teachers knew what was going on at all times and maintained the group's focus on the learning activity without getting sidetracked by the behavior or the problems of a single student. Kounin's research confirms what many teachers have always known, that the most effective classroom control centers in developing a learning environment and school program which minimize the opportunities for misbehavior to occur.

4. *The teacher should develop and use a variety of ways of handling misbehavior.* Differences in the causes of misbehavior, in the needs of students, and in the circumstances of a given situation mean that the teacher who has few ways of dealing with misbehavior is likely to be less effective in resolving conflicts than the teacher who has a large repertoire of ways. However, methods of control which are successful for some teachers are often ineffective when used by other teachers. The ways of handling discipline which a teacher adopts should be consistent with his philosophy of education, his personality, and his beliefs about children and youth and their development. A teacher who seeks to establish a feeling of mutual respect with students is unlikely to resort to corporal punishment, sarcasm,

---

[24] Jacob S. Kounin, *Discipline and Group Management in Classrooms* (New York: Holt, Rinehart and Winston, 1970), pp. 140–145.

and ridicule, since these methods destroy a sense of valuing and respect. The *use of threats of punishment is likely to be counterproductive* and should be avoided unless the teacher is prepared to carry out the threats. Sometimes punishment is necessary, but in using it the teacher may run the risk of aggravating the conflict instead of resolving it.

Some types of teacher responses seem to be more effective than others in reducing misbehavior in various situations. *Minor infractions of rules can at times be overlooked.* A goal of the teacher is to create and maintain an environment where maximum time and energies of students and teacher are devoted to learning activities. Remedial action by the teacher is warranted if opportunities for learning are adversely affected by misbehavior.

Students are more likely to remain alert and attentive if the *teacher moves around the class,* encouraging and helping students rather than remaining in one place for the whole period. *Helping a student* who is having difficulty with an assignment is likely to reduce the student's frustration and forestall misbehavior. Some emotionally charged situations can be defused by *an anecdote, a joke, or a humorous remark.* Some teachers have worked out an arrangement with fellow teachers ahead of time whereby one teacher can send a student to another classroom for a short time so that he can settle down. Note that this is not a punishment but a response to the student's needs.

In general, it is wise to deal as expeditiously as possible with situations that interfere with the learning activity. For this reason, the teacher should avoid arguing with a student or taking class time to discuss a conflict situation. *Suggest a conference for reconciling differences later, after tempers have cooled.* After resolving a conflict between teacher and student, *the teacher should make a special effort to reestablish rapport with the student.* The teacher, by showing a willingness to forget past differences, does much through his friendly smile and easy manner to reestablish a feeling of mutual trust and respect.

The teacher should *avoid any conflict's becoming a contest between himself and the student.* If it becomes a contest, the teacher has lost, for the student has succeeded in taking the teacher's and the class's attention away from the learning activity. If the conflict continues, it may be increasingly difficult to redirect the class's attention back to the learning tasks at hand; conflict and interruption interfere with the rhythm and continuity of the learning experience.

Finally, the teacher is likely to grow in his own self-respect and in the respect of his students if he strives to *handle most behavior problems himself* without appeal to outside authority.

5.   *How the teacher handles a student's misbehavior frequently influences the behavior of other students in the class.*   Kounin[25] refers to this influence of the teacher on other members of the class as the "ripple effect."

---

[25] Kounin, pp. 140–145.

Through a series of studies, Kounin investigated the ripple effect in classrooms from kindergarten through college. He found that kindergarten teachers who were *clear* and *firm* in their correction of a child increased the conformity of children who were not involved. Firmness was particularly effective in decreasing misbehavior among deviancy-prone kindergarten children. The *roughness* of the kindergarten teacher manifested in her angry looks, threats, or punishments produced few ripple effects and appeared to be counterproductive. A display of emotion by the teacher did not result in improved behavior of the children who witnessed the misbehavior; it merely upset them.

Among elementary school children in a camp setting and among students entering high school, how the leader or teacher handled misbehavior produced little or no ripple effects. In the case of high school students, however, the student's motivation toward learning the subject seemed to make a difference in whether he was influenced by the teacher's mode of disciplining another student. If the student was highly motivated to learn that subject, the teacher's discipline resulted in a greater inclination for that student to behave well in that class. If, however, his motivation was low, the teacher's action had little impact on the student's behavior.

College students appeared to be only marginally influenced by how the instructor handled a contrived situation of a student's coming late to class. Students who observed a strong response by the instructor (bawling out the student) felt the class was less relaxed than did students in another class who witnessed the same instructor making a more friendly, helpful response in noting the student's tardiness. Many students dismissed the incident by hypothesizing that the instructor may have had an argument with his wife or gotten caught in a traffic jam that morning.

6. *The teacher, however, should recognize when a situation is beyond his control and should call for outside help when the situation demands it.* One should not infer that the suggestions offered thus far will resolve all problems of discipline that are likely to arise. No such conclusion is warranted, for obviously no method of handling discipline is foolproof. Some students are very difficult to handle even for the skilled and experienced teacher. In nearly every classroom there will be some students who reveal symptoms of emotional disturbance. Some of these students will respond positively to the procedures described above, but others will not. Conferences with parents, guidance counselor, and principal, referral to psychological services for testing and therapy, or recommendation for placement in a special class may be indicated. The teacher should seek outside help in handling students when the usual methods of classroom control have failed or when there is injury or threat of injury to teacher or students.

7. *The ultimate goal of discipline, as well as of education in general, is the attainment of self-discipline and self-direction by students themselves.* Interpersonal conflict is both a deterrent to and an opportunity for further development and learning. Unresolved conflicts impede growth, while the changes in attitudes and skills acquired in resolving conflicts are in them-

selves evidences of increased growth and self-development. Achieving a measure of independence is the mark of a mature person. Individuals demonstrate their independence when they respond in terms of a personally validated set of values and beliefs and not solely in terms of controls established by others. Self-discipline and self-direction are marks of mature, independent human beings.

Summary

In spite of man's long experience with the act of teaching, we still do not have a clear understanding of what good teaching is or how to foster it. Teaching takes place in a milieu that is continuously changing and is influenced by a great many variables, both known and unknown. Teaching in a broad sense is any *interpersonal influence aimed at changing the ways in which persons can or will behave.*

A model of teacher behavior proposed by Macdonald and Zaret hypothesizes that the more open a teacher is to experience, the more likely he is to make effective, spontaneous decisions in direct response to the learner. Such decisions will expand opportunities for variations in the learner's productive behavior.

A first step in organizing for learning is the establishment of a favorable climate for learning. Studies of anxiety and learning show that classroom climates that induce high anxiety in students are less facilitative of high academic performance than are climates characterized by low anxiety. Studies reveal that the teacher is the most important variable determining the climate in learning situations.

A descriptive model for facilitating the learning of students emphasizes the view of learning as change involving the active response of the learner, the important role of readiness in facilitating learning, the need for goals for defining behavioral changes and guiding learning activities, and the central role of self factors, especially motivation, in learning. The model also stresses the importance of knowledge of success in promoting learning, the positive and negative effects of failure in promoting learning, the need for both concrete and vicarious experience, the facilitative effects of the use of many sensory media, and the contributions students can make in increasing their own learning.

Studies of teacher influence and behavior change reveal that the teacher's use of indirect influence is associated with greater student achievement and decreased student dependence on the teacher.

Self-directed learning is a principal feature of *open education*, a program of preschool and elementary education which features a free, informal, highly individualized, child-centered learning experience. Further opportunities for discovery and self-directive learning are provided in *career education*, a program extending from elementary school to beyond high school that is designed to assist students in their choice of and preparation for a career.

An important asset to the teacher in organizing the classroom for learning is his understanding and skills in handling problems of discipline and classroom control. A key to effective discipline is the establishment of mutual respect between teacher and pupils. Especially important is that the teacher accept the feelings that the student is expressing through his misbehavior. The ultimate goal of discipline, as well as of education in general, is the attainment of self-discipline and self-direction by students themselves.

Study Questions

1.   Carl Rogers writes, "It seems to me that anything that can be taught to another is relatively inconsequential and has little or no significant influence on behavior." What do you believe Rogers means by this statement? Discuss.

2.   Focus for a moment on the grade level or subject you plan to teach. Describe some learning experiences through which your students might satisfy their needs for belongingness, independence, and self-esteem.

3.   We see a great many students who make an active response in the learning situation only after the teacher asks, says, or assigns something. Some students do not make any overt response at all. What kind of learning environment or teaching strategies do you think are needed to trigger continuous self-initiated learning activities and self-directed learning?

4.   In what ways would you expect children enrolled for six years in an open education elementary school to be different from children enrolled for six years in a traditional elementary school program? Discuss the strengths and weaknesses of each program for preparing individuals to cope effectively in a rapidly changing world.

5.   Would you expect a classroom with no discipline problems to be a more favorable environment for learning than a classroom where some conflicts arise and then are resolved? Discuss.

Suggested Readings

Flanders, Ned A. *Analyzing Teaching Behavior*. Reading, Mass.: Addison-Wesley Publishing Co., 1970. An introduction to techniques for analyzing classroom behavior using Flander's technique of interaction analysis. Describes systems for coding spontaneous verbal communication, arranging the data, and analyzing the results to study patterns of teaching and learning. Shows how a teacher can carry on a study of his own classroom interaction.

Kounin, Jacob S. *Discipline and Group Management in Classrooms*. New York: Holt, Rinehart and Winston, 1970. Describes a series of experiments investigating the influence of the teacher's techniques for handling misbehavior on the behavior of other students in the classroom. The teacher's influence on other students is greatest in kindergarten, where her clarity and firmness in correcting misbehavior lead to increased conformity by other children in the class. Describes the qualities of classroom management which facilitate learning and lessen the incidence of misbehavior and the teacher's need to deal with it.

Rogers, Carl R. *Freedom to Learn*. Columbus, Ohio: Merrill Publishing Co., 1969. An eminent psychotherapist and founder of client-centered therapy speaks to teachers in describing learning in which students and teacher are free to discover and explore the personal meanings of their experiences. Proposes a person-oriented education that would, if adopted, revolutionize contemporary education.

Silberman, Charles E. *Crisis in the Classroom: The Remaking of American Education*. New York: Vantage Books, 1970. A report of an intensive study of American public education during the late 1960s. Points out that the mindlessness characteristic of much of American education destroys spontaneity of learning and prevents our thinking deeply about the purposes and consequences of education. Chapter 6 describes the philosophy and program of open education as practiced in the English primary schools, and Chapter 7 describes open education programs that have been developed in the United States.

Weber, Lillian. *The English Infant School and Informal Education*. Englewood Cliffs, N. J.: Prentice-Hall, 1971. Describes the program of informal open education that has been developed in many primary schools in England since World War II. The book is a detailed report of personal observations by an American educator who studied English primary education in particular schools over a period of several months during periodic visits to Britain.

Films

Effective Learning in the Elementary School, 16 mm, sound, black and white, 20 min. Bloomington: Audiovisual Center, Indiana University. A fifth grade teacher relates some of her own experiences in trying to make learning more effective. She says that in her class teacher and pupil work together on reading, writing, arithmetic, social studies, and creative arts, but that motivation for work is strengthened through unit projects which provide opportunities for developing other important skills.

Instructional Methods and Patterns of Organization

20

We have yet to create the best school of which we are capable. To close the gap between reality and our best visions is a great task of human engineering, the mission that challenges every educator who wants to make good schools better.

John I. Goodlad and Robert H. Anderson

In the preceding chapter we described some of the ways in which the teacher can implement his models of the teaching-learning experience in order to establish a social and emotional climate conducive to learning. After such a climate has been established, further choices must be made of instructional methods and patterns of organization to be employed in carrying learning forward.

Instructional Methods

In this discussion we shall consider only the general instructional methods teachers use in facilitating classroom learning. Instructional methods in special subjects (such as typewriting, shorthand, industrial arts, home economics, music, art, physical education, speech, dramatics, foreign languages, and laboratory sciences) will not concern us here. We shall focus instead on those methods of instruction common to most subjects, with special emphasis on academic subjects.

Lecture versus Discussion Methods

The lecture method of teaching dates from antiquity and is based upon a conception of education in which a knowledgeable scholar or teacher communicates what he knows to less mature, less knowledgeable pupils. In institutions where the primary goal of education is perceived to be the transmitting of knowledge, the lecture method is still popular and widely used. One of the major propositions presented in the model of the learning experience in the preceding chapter, however, was that learning as a change in behavior is most likely to occur when it involves an active, overt response on the part of the learner. Since students usually have few opportunities to make active responses during lectures, they receive little feedback with which to test and to explore the meanings they perceive in the ideas presented by the lecturer. Lack of feedback does not appear to hinder the student in acquiring knowledge if he is motivated and if the material is not too difficult. Research evidence shows, however, that when the development of concepts or problem-solving skills is the major learning goal, active participation on the part of the learner is more effective than passive listening or observing.[1]

Many studies have compared the relative effectiveness of the lecture method with other methods of teaching. Most studies show few significant differences between comparable groups taught by lecture and discussion methods when knowledge of specific facts is the criterion used to assess effectiveness of instruction. However, discussion and problem-solving methods have proved to be superior in contributing to the understanding of concepts,[2] in promoting problem-solving skills and scientific attitudes,[3] and in increasing positive attitudes of teachers toward teaching and children.[4]

Many colleges and universities have endeavored to obtain the advantages of both the lecture and discussion methods by incorporating both into the same course. This pattern has been especially prevalent where lecture sections are quite large. Courses which combine lecture and discussion or recitation appear to elicit more favorable student attitudes than those in which lecturing predominates. Evidence is conflicting, however, as to whether lectures supplemented with separate small discussion classes are any better in teaching facts and principles than is a combination of lecturing and discussion during the same class session. When learning objectives include both the acquisition of information and the development of concepts, the combination of lecture and discussion methods offers important advantages. McKeachie[5] points out that the lecture can effectively present new research findings, whereas discussion can give students opportunities to analyze studies, discover relationships, and develop generalizations. Participating actively in discussion can assist students not

---

[1] W. J. McKeachie, "Research on Teaching at the College and University Level," in N. L. Gage, ed., *Handbook of Research on Teaching* (Chicago: Rand McNally & Co., 1963), p. 1,126.

[2] C. S. Hirschman, "An Investigation of the Small Group Discussion Classroom Method on Criteria of Understanding, Pleasantness, and Self-Confidence Induced" (unpublished master's thesis, University of Pittsburgh, 1952).

[3] J. D. Barnard, "The Lecture-Demonstration versus the Problem-Solving Method of Teaching a College Science Course," *Science Education*, 26 (1942), 121–132.

[4] J. E. Casey and B. E. Weaver, "An Evaluation of Lecture Method and Small Group Method of Teaching in Terms of Knowledge of Content, Teacher Attitudes, and Social Status," *Journal of Colorado-Wyoming Academy of Science*, 4 (1956), 54.

[5] McKeachie, p. 1,127.

only in learning generalizations but also in developing skill in critical thinking.

A recent review by Costin[6] of more than 90 studies which investigated the relative effectiveness of lecture versus other methods of instruction revealed that lecturing cannot automatically be presumed to be less desirable than discussion. There is some evidence that high-ability students acquire more facts and principles when the emphasis on lecturing is increased, while low-ability students gain more from an increase in discussion. As noted above, however, discussion methods appear to be clearly superior to the lecture in stimulating critical thinking and in enabling students to interpret data, develop generalizations, and apply them to new situations. Discussion methods also appear to be superior in influencing long-term goals and subsequent behavior.

Group discussion, however, can be an effective method of learning only if the teacher and pupils learn needed group skills for playing the roles required for group problem solving. An important skill is the ability to establish an effective climate for discussion. Basic to achieving an open, frank exchange of views is a feeling of mutual trust and personal regard between each member and the leader of the group. Each participant must feel sufficiently secure to state or accept disagreement or criticism without being unduly threatened. Once this climate has been established, the first task in the initial stages of group discussion often is to examine and clarify the purposes of the meeting or the discussion. Even in a well-structured classroom learning activity, the purposes of the discussion may not be entirely clear.

If class discussions are to be productive, they must be kept relevant to the problem or topic. This is a responsibility of both the leader and the group members. Effective group discussion also requires the development of a high degree of sensitivity among group members to the feelings and ideas of others. It is important to hear not only what the other person is saying but what he is trying to say. Productive group discussions also require that group members distinguish between opinions and facts, between inferences and facts, and between judgments and facts.

Whether in discussions or in lectures, communication among teacher and students is a vital element in the achievement of any objective. The various types of communication observable in learning situations are shown in Figure 20–1. Frequently the teacher is a *lecturer* or information giver in demonstrating a stitch in sewing, the operation of a machine in shop, the use of lab equipment in chemistry, or how to serve in tennis. The *tutorial* mode of communication may be employed by the teacher in providing individual help to a student on seat work, projects, or papers or helping a child who is having difficulty in reading. A *group discussion with a designated leader* is a useful mode of communication in reading and discussing a story in the reading circle, in group or committee work for

---

[6] Frank Costin, "Lecturing versus Other Methods of Teaching: A Review of Research," *British Journal of Educational Technology*, 1 (1972), 4–31.

Figure 20–1.   Various Types of Communicative Relationships between Teachers and Students

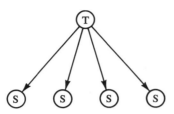

1. Lecturer. The situation calls for one-way communication with students in the class.

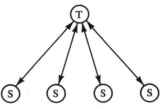

2. Tutorial. The teacher seeks to promote two-way communication with students in the class.

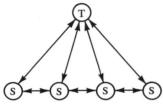

3. Group discussion with a designated leader. The teacher or leader maintains two-way communication and encourages communication among students or group members.

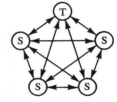

4. Group discussion without a designated leader. The teacher becomes a co-participant in the group and encourages two-way communication among all members of the group, including himself.

Source: Adapted from H. C. Lindgren, *Educational Psychology in the Classroom*, 4th ed. (New York: John Wiley, 1972), p. 258. Used by permission.

planning a party or a project, or in conducting a class meeting or student council meeting. In any of these, a student rather than the teacher may be in the role of leader. Finally, a *group discussion* format *without a designated leader* may be used in brainstorming sessions which seek to elicit maximum participation of all group members and to facilitate critical thinking and problem-solving by the total group. It is clear, then, that the effective teacher has a variety of instructional methods and modes of communicating with the class, any of which may be introduced and changed in accordance with the needs of the particular learning activity.

Student-Centered versus Teacher-Centered Teaching

Because the discussion method involves student participation, we tend to associate this method with student-centered teaching. However, group discussions can be dominated by the teacher, and lectures may be so informal that student participation predominates. Therefore, it seems more useful and accurate to define the dimension of *learner centeredness* versus *teacher centeredness* in terms of the degree to which students and teacher share in the responsibility for identifying learning goals and for planning, carrying out, and evaluating learning activities. (Some of the variables which distinguish learner-centered classrooms from teacher-centered classrooms are shown in Table 20–1.)

Table 20–1. Characteristics of Teacher-Centered and Learner-Centered Teaching

Student Centered	Instructor Centered
Goals	
Determined by group.	Determined by instructor.
Emphasis upon affective and attitudinal changes.	Emphasis upon intellectual changes.
Attempts to develop group cohesiveness.	No attempt to develop group cohesiveness.
Classroom activities	
Much student participation.	Much instructor participation.
Student-student interaction.	Instructor-student interaction.
Instructor accepts erroneous or irrelevant student contributions.	Instructor corrects, criticizes, or rejects erroneous or irrelevant student contributions.
Group decides upon own activities.	Instructor determines activities.
Discussion of students' personal experiences encouraged.	Discussion kept on course materials.
Deemphasis of tests and grades.	Traditional use of tests and grades.
Students share responsibility for evaluation.	
Instructor interprets feelings and ideas of class member when necessary for class progress.	Instructor avoids interpretation of feelings.
Reaction reports.	No reaction reports.

Source: W. J. McKeachie, "Research on Teaching at the College and University Level," in N. L. Gage, ed., *Handbook of Research on Teaching* (Chicago: Rand McNally & Co., 1963), p. 1,134. Used by permission.

Some researchers have found, however, that the designations of student centered and teacher centered may not be as sharply defined as many had supposed. Earlier, Anderson[7] concluded from his review of studies investigating the effects of authoritarian and democratic leader-

[7] R. C. Anderson, "Learning in Discussion: A Résumé of the Authoritarian-Democratic Studies," *Harvard Educational Review*, 29 (1959), 201–215.

ship (and their semantic equivalents, student centered and teacher centered) on learning that the authoritarian-democratic construct is a grossly oversimplified dimension which is inadequate for measuring leadership effectiveness. The results of a more recent study by Costin[8] tend to confirm Anderson's findings. The responses of college students to statements of teacher classroom behavior which were thought to relate to teacher-centered or student-centered teaching yielded four factors: (1) student involvement, (2) teacher support, (3) negative affect, and (4) teacher control. The low correlations between factors 1 and 2 and 3 and 4, each pair of which is presumed to relate to teacher centeredness or student centeredness, suggest that these and similar terms have not been adequately conceptualized or defined.

In spite of difficulties in the conceptualization of student centeredness or teacher centeredness, most teachers and their students (though they may not agree) tend to see the teaching behavior and style of a given teacher as fitting one or the other category, student centered or teacher centered. Students who favor a student-centered experience may be unable to influence the teacher to decide not to conduct the class in a teacher-centered manner, but their resistance to learning in such a class (characteristically expressed as disinterest, apathy, boredom, withdrawal, or failure to study or to complete assignments) may provide the teacher with feedback about their needs, interests, and concerns. On the other hand, the teacher may find it difficult to organize a learner-centered class if the students seek to remain dependent on him or if they fail to accept the teacher's invitation to share in the identification of goals and in the planning, carrying out, and evaluating of learning activities.

Several of the propositions that were part of the model of the learning experience presented in the preceding chapter provide support for student-centered approaches to learning. Those that refer to change in the learner, to the importance of his motivations and self-structure, and to the facilitation of learning through increased self-understanding and greater self-direction appear to be particularly relevant to the goals of student-centered learning.

McKeachie[9] points out that teaching methods described as "student centered," "nondirective," "group centered," or "democratic" often vary widely, but that all have as their inspiration the desire to break away from the traditional instructor-dominated classroom and to encourage greater student participation and responsibility. The results of student-centered teaching may not be all positive, however. In its more extreme forms, student-centered teaching may result in lower achievement of such learning goals as knowledge of facts. Feedback and organization and structure are important to the learning process. If the teacher's role as information giver is reduced, his opportunities for providing feedback and for organizing and

---

[8] Frank Costin, "Empirical Test of the 'Teacher-Centered' versus 'Student-Centered' Dichotomy," *Journal of Educational Psychology*, 62 (October 1971), 410–412.

[9] McKeachie, p. 1,134.

structuring content are sharply curtailed; thus, much of the burden for providing these functions falls on group members. In some groups, members may be capable of performing these functions, but in other groups they may not.

If student-centered teaching reduces students' dependence on the instructor and thus diminishes his influence as a prestige figure, it could possibly also reduce his ability to effect attitudinal changes in students. McKeachie[10] suggests, however, that this may be more than compensated for by increased recognition of group members as sources of influence. If, for example, a student's participation in group discussions earns him recognition and praise, his motivation should increase. This prediction was substantiated by Thistlethwaite,[11] who found that National Merit Scholars felt that one of the outstanding characteristics of teachers who contributed most to their desire to learn was "allowing time for classroom discussion." Other characteristics mentioned included "modifying course content to meet students' needs and interests," "treating students as colleagues," "taking a personal interest in students," and "providing evaluations reassuring the student of his creative or productive potentialities."

Studies investigating teacher-centered and student-centered methods of teaching have found in general that members of student-centered classes do not score higher on achievement tests emphasizing facts and information than do students in teacher-centered classes. However, learners in student-centered classes do express greater satisfaction with the course, register more positive attitudes toward the subject area, make greater gains in personal adjustment, and select more frequently the subject as their vocational choice.

One way teachers can facilitate student learning in learner-centered classrooms is through the types of questions they ask. Many of the questions which teachers ask students require only low-level memory responses of factual information. Learning is more likely to involve the students themselves if they are asked *higher level questions which stimulate evaluation and productive thinking.* Sanders[12] urges that teachers make increasing use of questions which evoke responses that relate to higher level educational objectives of the cognitive domain: translation, interpretation, application, analysis, synthesis, and evaluation. The following teacher questions are illustrative of the ways students can be encouraged to use higher level cognitive processes.

    1.   *What thought is being expressed in this cartoon? What in your own words is the meaning of* manifest destiny? (*translation*)

---

[10] McKeachie, pp, 1,134–1,135.

[11] Donald L. Thistlethwaite, *College Press and Changes in Study Plans of Talented Students* (Evanston, Ill.: National Merit Scholarship Corp., 1960).

[12] Norris M. Sanders, *Classroom Questions: What Kinds?* (New York: Harper & Row, 1966).

2. *Use data in the population tables and graphs to answer the question "What was the rate of population increase in the United States between 1960 and 1970?" (interpretation)*

3. *Why did the science experiment turn out that way? (analysis)*

4. *What hypotheses can you suggest that would explain why nations in the tropics seldom develop an industrialized civilization? (synthesis)*

5. *Assuming resources were limited, what principles would you use for recommending the best ways of helping people get out of poverty—increasing the quality of educational resources provided the poor or guaranteeing a job to every able person willing to work? (evaluation)*

Teacher questions which stimulate higher level cognitive processes in students may increase the effectiveness of learner-centered education, but some criticize this approach because it puts the teacher in the role of the inquirer instead of the student. Our instructional strategies should instead foster inquiring and problem-solving skills in students. One way of bringing the student back to the center of the educational stage is to *provide opportunities for every child to become a teacher.* Tutoring programs for helping disadvantaged students improve in school performance have shown that the tutors often make greater gains in achievement than the children being tutored. Mobilization for Youth, a New York City anti-poverty program, found that over a five-month period in which older children tutored younger children with learning difficulties, those tutored gained 6.0 months while the tutors gained 3.4 years in reading achievement.[13] Thus, the best way to learn something is to teach it to someone else.

Many teachers fail to recognize that there are some things that students can learn better from one another than they can from adults or from books. A student may have more empathy for the student who is experiencing difficulty in learning than will the teacher. Moreover, many students accept correction more readily from a peer than they do from an adult. The student who is corrected by a classmate is likely to be less defensive because the classmate is not an authority figure. Thelen[14] suggests that learning through helping each other has advantages over the traditional system of learning through competing with each other. Learning from each other makes the acquisition of knowledge and skills valuable, not in the service of competition for grades but as the means for personally significant interaction with others.

Another way of making learner-centered education more effective is

---

[13] Alan Gartner, Mary C. Kohler, and Frank Riessman, *Children Teach Children: Learning by Teaching* (New York: Harper & Row, 1971), pp. 10–11, 37–41.

[14] Herbert A. Thelen, "The Humane Person Defined," paper presented at the Secondary Education Conference, St. Louis, November 1967.

through the use of academic games. The word *game* in this context does not imply play—though the game may be fun—but instead designates a problem-solving simulated situation in which a winner is identified. Most simulation games deal with political, social, or economic issues, but recently games have been developed for science classes. One game which confronts students with a problem involving the interrelationship between science and society is *A Pollution Game*,[15] which is an integral part of a seventh grade life science program.

A Pollution Game *is designed to simulate some of the frustrating technological and social problems that beset people attempting to ameliorate air and water pollution. Students must develop collaborative strategies to minimize pollution from their businesses while at the same time remaining financially solvent. In the game, as in real life, the participants win the pollution game if they survive or lose it if the quality of the environment is seriously neglected.*

Educational games appear to utilize important principles of learning and teaching. Games require the active participation of students, they provide immediate feedback, and they are goal directed (winning). Most games require physical movement as well as interaction among players. They provide opportunities for participation and learning for other than the class leaders, and they require the student to use the higher cognitive processes of synthesis, application, and analysis.[16]

Role Playing

Role playing is a valuable teaching technique, for it enables the player to become totally involved in the situation being enacted. A role-playing procedure called *sociodrama* has proved particularly useful for exploring feelings in an educational setting. Sociodrama is used to try out and evaluate several possible solutions to a problem facing a group. Consider the following problem:

School boundaries have recently been changed in this district, and now about 200 students from lower class homes have been re-

---

[15] *A Pollution Game*, a component of the ERC Life Science program for grade seven (Cleveland, Ohio 44113: Educational Research Council of America, Rockefeller Building).

[16] A. K. Gordon, *Six Booklets on Academic Games* (Chicago: Science Research Associates, 1968).

assigned to Jefferson High School, which heretofore had served pre-dominantly middle class communities. Fights, ugly words, and bad feelings have developed between lower class and middle class students. Feelings became intense this week when the results of school-wide elections revealed that no lower class student was elected as a cheerleader or class officer—even though several had campaigned and worked hard in the elections.

Students might be selected to play the parts of lower class and middle class students engaged in heated discussion in the homeroom after the announcement of the election results. The following are steps that can be used for obtaining full benefit from such a role-playing experience.

1. *First comes a general discussion about the situation. This is called the warm-up. Factors are brought out just enough to give the players a sense of knowing the problem. The stage is set with whatever props are necessary to make the playing easier and more definite—table, chair, books, etc.*

2. *Second is the enactment of the situation. The teacher watches this enactment and cuts the playing at any moment that seems productive for the purpose at hand.*

3. *The third step is interviewing the players to see how they felt as they were playing and what their interpretations are of what they were doing. This leads into group discussion of the consequences of the solution offered in the enactment.*

4. *Finally comes the reenactment, with interviewing and discussion following. In role playing we are not seeking to establish an answer as the right one. We find that many satisfactory solutions are possible to nearly every situation involving people and that each solution carries with it negative and positive connotations. Our purpose is to examine these negative and positive elements in the light of our individual and group feelings to find solutions that are tolerable to us—ones which we wish to live.*[17]

Solutions are discussed not as abstract situations but rather in terms of their meaning for the persons concerned. Especially important are the

[17] Condensed from Howard Lane and Mary Beauchamp, *Human Relations in Teaching: The Dynamics of Helping Children Grow*, copyright 1955, pp. 274, 276–278. Used by permission of Prentice-Hall, Inc., Englewood Cliffs, New Jersey.

opportunities to explore feelings and to look at the long-term consequences of each solution. Another use of role playing is in helping individuals to gain insight into their own feelings, values, and motivations. It is essential that the actors be free to act out the situation as they really feel it and that the teacher is careful to give no judgments on the feelings or values expressed.

The teacher's function is to help the group members draw out of their role playing as many ideas and learnings as they are able to assimilate. Sociodrama enables one to bring out vividly the differences between the perceptions of persons involved in an event; it also enables the individual to gain added insight into his own motivations and values.

It is important in role playing that the teacher structure situations and remain in control so that no one is harmed. The teacher is cautioned not to ask persons with serious emotional problems to play roles which would arouse feelings or criticisms too difficult for them to handle. The following are examples of situations which can be played out in sociodrama.

1. *Roosevelt Senior High School was desegregated by court order beginning in September. Because of neighborhood housing patterns, desegregation involved busing in 450 black students from a previously all-black high school. Total enrollment at Roosevelt is 1,500. The first month of desegregation went fairly smoothly, but early in October 100 blacks staged a protest demonstration and listed a number of grievances: no black was elected cheerleader, blacks are punished more severely than whites for breaking school rules, and no black history and black literature courses have been offered as promised. Begin by having blacks play the roles of blacks and whites who face one another in a confrontation. Then have the whites play both black and white roles in a confrontation situation. Have players reverse roles.*

2. *Several members of Miss Brown's ninth grade class were noisy and disrespectful during a school assembly. Mr. Abbott, the principal, commented over the public address system about the poor behavior of some students. Miss Brown gave a heavy homework assignment that evening. The next day only three students handed in homework papers. Work out several solutions to the problem in structured sociodrama.*

3. *After recess I found Clara crying. She said, "The girls have started a good club and asked three boys to be in it. I want to be in it, but they won't let me." One girl answered, "Miss H., Clara is crying to be in our club, but we can't let her be in. She can't get along with anybody." Play the situation with Clara playing her own role, and then reverse roles.*

Patterns of Organization

Grouping for Learning

Whenever children have been assembled to be taught, their teachers have found it expedient to classify them in some manner for instruction. The traditional method of grouping has been by chronological age, with promotions to a higher grade contingent upon successful completion of work for a particular grade. The percentage of failures under this system has been high. In our large cities during the period from 1850 to 1891, the percentage of students who failed to be promoted ranged from 17 to 46 percent.[18]

After 1900, public school enrollment increased sharply and a need arose for multiple classes for the same grade or subject. The criterion most often applied to divide students into classes was some measure of actual or potential ability. In using such a criterion, it was assumed that grouping children into the able, the average, and the less able can be done accurately and easily, and that the ablest group, thus "set free," will rise to unprecedented heights.[19] Educational practices based on these assumptions led to widespread use of so-called homogeneous or ability grouping, which has persisted to the present. Reading ability or achievement test scores have tended to replace IQ scores as the principal basis for grouping pupils homogeneously. Various other measures, however, such as physical maturity, social maturity, and organismic age, have also been used.

In recent years, studies of homogeneous grouping have brought the whole concept into question. Wilhelms and Westby-Gibson[20] have pointed out that if a group of children are divided into levels by any criterion or combination of criteria whatever, the total variability within each group is reduced only by about 20 percent. After these groups have been formed, they will still be markedly heterogeneous because of the tremendous range of individual differences which remain for all but the variable chosen as the basis for the division. The group cannot be homogeneous, because the individuals in it are not homogeneous within themselves. This suggests that any presumed homogeneity of instructional groups is an illusion, and that the concept itself is a misnomer.

There appears to be little support for other claims that have been made for ability grouping. After reviewing the research, Eash[21] concluded

[18] Douglas E. Lawson, "Analysis of Historic and Philosophic Considerations for Homogeneous Grouping," *Educational Administration and Supervision*, 43 (May 1957), 257–270.

[19] Lawson, pp. 257–270.

[20] F. T. Wilhelms and D. Westby-Gibson, "Grouping: Research Offers Leads," *Educational Leadership*, 18 (April 1961), 410–413.

[21] Maurice J. Eash, "Grouping: What Have We Learned?" *Educational Leadership*, 18 (April 1961), 429–434.

that ability grouping does not in itself produce improved achievement in children. Improved achievement appears to be related to more complex factors, such as curriculum adaptation, teaching methods, materials, and the ability of the teacher to relate to children. Miriam Goldberg and her associates,[22] for example, found that gains in achievement among fifth and sixth grade pupils were influenced more strongly by teachers and group differences in individual classrooms than by the presence or absence of gifted pupils, the range of ability in the class, or even the intellectual ability of the pupils.

Husen and Sevsen[23] found that under ability grouping, average and lower ability students appear to suffer from the deprivation of intellectual stimulation that occurs when brighter children are removed from the class. On the other hand, the achievement of more able children appears not to be adversely affected when they remain in a class with average and lower ability students, at least through elementary school. It appears, too, that children from higher socioeconomic classes placed in higher ability groups do not necessarily benefit from the increased emphasis upon academic work, at least through elementary and beginning junior high school.

Since teachers continue to teach students in groups, some type of grouping procedure will be used in organizing for instruction. Evidence supporting any method of grouping is meager, so tradition is likely to govern the choice of the method of grouping. However, a variety of grouping innovations have been proposed, and these apply not only to the classification of pupils but also to the assignment of teachers and the choice of instructional procedures. One such innovation has been suggested by Thelen,[24] who has proposed a concept of "teachable grouping" in which students are assigned to a particular teacher's class because they possess the same or similar characteristics as students with whom (in the teacher's judgment) the teacher has been most successful in the past. Thelen investigated the concept of teachable grouping by comparing the achievement performance, attitudes toward learning, and personality characteristics of students who appeared to be "getting a great deal out of class" and students who seemed to be getting very little out of the same class. An intensive study of the classes of 13 teachers of academic subjects in grades eight to 11 revealed that "teachable" students gained no more on achievement tests and tended to like the teacher only slightly more than did control (less teachable) students. However, teachable students did tend to like one another better and to express a higher level of satisfaction with class activities and with the course as a whole than did the control group. Teachable students were also judged to be more psychologically mature—they were more work oriented, freer in expressing emotion, more secure in the face of hostility,

[22] Miriam L. Goldberg, A. Harry Passow, and Joseph Justman, *The Effects of Ability Grouping* (New York: Teachers College Press, Columbia University, 1966).

[23] Tortsen Husen and Nils Eric Sevsen, "Pedagogic Milieu and Development of Intellectual Skills," *The School Review*, 68 (Spring 1960), 36–51.

[24] Herbert A. Thelen, *Classroom Grouping for Teachability* (New York: John Wiley, 1967).

more autonomous, more cooperative, and better able to work with others in a group situation. Although the efficacy of teachable groups for increasing student achievement was not demonstrated by Thelen's research, the concept is an attractive one and should be tested by further research.

Horizontal and Vertical Organization

The appearance of many different types of grouping has made it necessary to distinguish between different meanings and uses of the term. Goodlad and Rehage[25] point out that schools exhibit both vertical and horizontal patterns of organization. The *vertical organization* of the school serves to classify students upwardly from admission to graduation. The division of students into grade levels (first, second, third) has been the traditional pattern of vertical organization. *Multigrading* and *nongrading* are alternative patterns. In a multigraded school, students in a classroom are permitted to work in several grades at once, depending on their progress in each subject. In a nongraded school, grade designations are entirely removed from some or all classes.

The *horizontal organization* of the school divides the student body among available teachers. Homogeneous and heterogeneous groupings of students into classes are the best-known examples of horizontal organization. Team teaching is a newer pattern of horizontal organization. Schools utilizing team teaching may be either graded or nongraded.

Nongraded programs.   Nongrading is a pattern of vertical school organization which, its adherents believe, would give teachers more time to study the progress of individual pupils before making a decision on retention or promotion. A nongraded program, in which a decision on promotion or retention is delayed two or three years, increases the probability that most children will complete the primary program in the normal period of time. The nongraded program seeks to increase the opportunities for each child to develop his capacities to the fullest, to provide for the continuous development of all children, and to reduce the incidence of the frustration that accompanies failure. Moreover, by increasing opportunities for success, the nongraded program reduces the feelings of frustration which accompany failure.

In most cases, only the primary grades are organized on a nongraded basis. A few schools, however, are experimenting with nongrading in the intermediate grades. Nongrading appears to have had its greatest influence on the program and patterns of grouping in reading. Characteristically, the reading experiences of the primary years are organized into eight to 10 sequential steps or levels through which the child moves at his own rate. The number of reading levels in each classroom is limited, thereby reducing

[25] John I. Goodlad and Kenneth Rehage, "Unscrambling the Vocabulary of School Organization," *The NEA Journal*, 51 (November 1962), 34–36.

the range of reading abilities found in many classrooms. Overlapping levels between classes permit pupils to move up or down easily. A unique feature of the nongraded plan is the flexibility it allows in moving a child from group to group or from one classroom to another at any time his growth warrants such a change.[26]

Numerous studies have attempted to assess the effectiveness of nongraded programs in comparison with the traditional graded programs in elementary schools. McLoughlin,[27] in his review of 42 of these studies, found little evidence of one program's being superior in those areas of achievement that were studied. In half of the studies, there were no substantial differences in general reading performance of children from graded and nongraded classes, and in the remaining studies children from nongraded classes appeared to have a slight advantage over those from graded programs. In total arithmetic achievement, children from graded classes appeared to have a slight edge. The findings for language arts and total achievement scores for children in the two programs were inconclusive.

Regardless of how adjustment is measured, there is little evidence that the nongraded school improves it. Nongrading thus appears to make little difference in either the scholastic performance of children or their adjustment at any level of the school program. This is true for children currently in nongraded programs as well as those who had been in a nongraded program at the primary level and moved on to intermediate classes.

Teachers seem to like the nongraded school because it allows them to personalize learning and provide instruction more in harmony with the child's development and readiness for learning. Nevertheless, in over 70 percent of the measures used in teacher appraisals of graded and nongraded programs, no significant differences in teacher satisfaction were found. The teachers stated that both kinds of programs permitted them to understand children and to help them progress at a rate commensurate with their abilities.

The studies also reveal that the overall similarities in instructional practices in graded and nongraded classes are greater than the differences. In both settings teachers organize their classes in much the same way and use approximately the same instructional materials. They evaluate students in the same way and are equally knowledgeable about differences among their students. McLoughlin concludes that until some of the ambiguity about nongrading is removed and meaningful distinctions are made between the two programs, educators are likely to perpetuate graded schools in the misguided belief that they are operating nongraded schools.

Team teaching. The phrase *team teaching* has been used to describe a number of different arrangements for the assigning of teachers and the grouping of pupils. Examples of team teaching vary from simple *coordinate teaching,* in which two teachers are assigned to a large class and are equally

---

[26] See Hugh V. Perkins, "Nongraded Programs: What Progress?" *Educational Leadership*, 19 (December 1961), 166–169.

[27] W. P. McLoughlin, "The Effectiveness of the Nongraded School," *International Review of Education*, 18 (1972), 194–211.

responsible for instruction, to a hierarchy of teachers—for instance, team leader, senior teacher, auxiliary teacher, intern teacher, teacher's aide, and clerk. Where there are persons performing a variety of specific instructional tasks, as in this case, the term *differentiated staffing* is also used.

Implicit in the concept of team teaching is the belief that the wider range of competencies and skills provided by two or more teachers is superior to the narrower range provided by a single teacher. Today's tremendous increase in knowledge, the emphasis upon more mathematics, more science and more language, and the stress on the education of the gifted have caused educators to question whether one teacher can teach all subjects to all children with equal effectiveness and skill.

In team teaching, the strengths of several teachers are pooled so as to increase the quality of the instructional program. Team teaching is expected to redound to the benefit of the individual pupil, since a team of teachers and specialists conferring and planning together have opportunities to plan experiences in relation to the individual pupil's needs. Moreover, the flexibility of scheduling and grouping under team teaching permits a teacher to achieve closer contacts with individual pupils. Finally, advocates of team teaching note that by encouraging teachers to work together and to develop special competencies and leadership abilities, team teaching increases the professional status of teaching.

Team teaching is a major feature of Trump's[28] plan for the utilization of staff and the reorganization of the secondary school. This experimental plan, now being implemented in a number of secondary schools, is organized around three kinds of activities: large-group instruction, individual study, and small-group discussion. The organization of instruction provided for by Trump's plan is shown in Table 20–2. Emphasis is upon flexibility, with the size of groups and length of class periods varying from day to day. Some aspects of learning are presented by specially qualified teachers to relatively large groups of students. This frees other teachers to work with other students individually or in small discussion groups. Under the plan, a student is expected to assume more individual responsibility for learning than he would be expected to assume in a traditional classroom.

Trump's plan calls for students to engage in individual study activities singly or in groups of two or three. Conferences between students and instructors are held whenever necessary to clarify goals, content, or personal problems. Students read, listen to records and tapes, gather data, analyze, think, and solve problems in projects which require them to assume increased responsibility for their own direction.

Studies comparing team teaching with instruction in self-contained classrooms have found few differences in pupil achievement or pupil attitudes toward school. Rhodes,[29] in a study of a random sample of pupils

[28] J. Lloyd Trump, *Images of the Future* (Washington D. C.: National Association of Secondary School Principals, N.E.A., 1959).

[29] Fen Rhodes, "Team Teaching Compared with Traditional Instruction in Grades Kindergarten through Six," *Journal of Educational Psychology*, 62 (April 1971), 110–116.

Table 20–2. Plan of Organization of Instruction under the Trump Plan

	Large-Group Instruction	Small-Group Discussion	Individual Study
Activity	Introduction Motivation Explanation Planning Group study Enrichment Generalization Evaluation	Group examination of terms and concepts and solutions of problems	Read
			Listen to records and tapes
		Reach areas of agreement and disagreement	View, question, analyze, think
		Improve interpersonal relations	Experiment, examine, investigate, consider evidence
			Write, create, memorize, record, make
			Visit
			Self-appraise
Place	Auditorium, little theater, cafeteria, study hall, classrooms joined via television or remodeling, other large room	Conference room, classroom	Library, laboratories, workshops, project and material centers, museums, inside and outside the school plant
School time	About 40 percent	About 20 percent	About 40 percent

Source: J. Lloyd Trump, *Images of the Future* (Washington D. C.: National Association of Secondary School Principals, N.E.A., 1959). Used by permission.

from a school utilizing team teaching and a school organized into self-contained classrooms, found that in no case was team teaching superior to traditional classroom instruction. Moreover, team teaching was worse in average reading gain and, to some extent, in the degree of improvement of pupil attitudes. Teachers of team-taught classes were significantly more positive than teachers in the control school, but within the school using teaming there were no differences in teacher attitudes. Parents of team-taught children were found to be no more or less favorable in their opinion of school effectiveness than parents of children attending the control school.

Great care must be exercised in the forming of teams to ensure that the competencies of team members complement one another and that their personalities and ways of working are reasonably harmonious. It is obvious that some teachers who perform well in self-contained classrooms may be ineffective when teamed with other teachers. The greatest advantage of team teaching is that it permits the pooling of staff resources for developing a more extensive instructional program than could be produced by teachers working individually. However, Drummond[30] questions many of the educational advantages claimed for team teaching. Large group meetings, for example, by limiting the interactions between students and a superior teacher, may result in the individual student's learning less than he would in a regular classroom. Moreover, some of the advantages of team teaching, such as increased flexibility of grouping and self-direction of learners, can also be obtained by other patterns of organization.

Grouping by sex.   According to Waetjen and Grambs,[31] differences in sex roles make for differences in school learning. Girls, for instance, generally receive higher grades and fewer failures than boys, and achieve greater language development and verbal fluency. Boys, on the other hand, tend to score higher in quantitative skills and transfer.

Because boys and girls differ in the ways they learn, it has been hypothesized that the learning of each sex can be increased if boys and girls are segregated into classes adapted to the learning modes and patterns of each. In a test of this hypothesis, Fisher and Waetjen[32] conducted a study to ascertain whether boys and girls in eighth grade sex-segregated classes achieve at higher levels in English and have more adequate self-concepts than pupils in mixed classes. The findings of this study, however, show that students in sex-segregated classes do not register greater gains in English achievement, nor do they report more adequate self-concepts than students in mixed classes. On the contrary, pupils in the mixed classes tested by Fisher and Waetjen scored higher on four comparisons of English achievement.

Sex is a variable which educators should take into consideration when organizing and planning for learning. Further research is needed to point the direction to ways to adapt classroom procedures to utilize more effectively the learning advantages related to the learner's sex.

Grouping within the Classroom

Grouping students within a classroom is a problem that faces nearly every teacher. Although the teacher may desire to teach the class as one group, the number of students and the individual differences among them suggest the desirability of organizing the class into smaller subgroups. Some kinds of learning, such as problem solving, may be more effectively

[30] Harold D. Drummond, "Team Teaching: An Assessment," *Educational Leadership*, 19 (December 1961), 160–165.

[31] Walter B. Waetjen and Jean D. Grambs, "Sex Differences: A Case of Educational Evasion?" *Teachers College Record*, 65 (December 1963), 261–271.

[32] John K. Fisher and Walter B. Waetjen, "An Investigation of the Relationship between Separation by Sex of Eighth Grade Boys and Girls and English Achievement and Self-Concept," *Journal of Educational Research*, 59 (May–June 1966), 409–412.

achieved in small-group study than in individual or large-group study. Small groups are more likely to elicit the active responses and involvement of learners than are large groups. Through this involvement, students learn to set goals, to plan, and to work cooperatively. In small groups, students have opportunities to acquire the social and work skills needed to become concerned, responsible citizens.

A variety of suggestions have been made for grouping students in specific subject fields. Schmid[33] found that fifth grade children in groups they chose for themselves registered larger gains in arithmetic than did peers in groups formed by the teacher. In addition, children working in groups of their own choice were more responsive than children working in teacher-formed groups. Wilhelms and Westby-Gibson[34] suggest that in forming groups in social studies, it is advantageous to have a diversity of interests, points of view, and talents represented in each group. In free reading and recreational activities, however, it is probably best to encourage the formation of spontaneous, informal groups around shared interests or friendships.

Gordon[35] suggests the following principles to guide teachers in grouping students for learning:

1. *The grouping should recognize the purposes of the individual child.*

2. *Heterogeneous groupings give children opportunities for learning to live and work with a variety of other people.*

3. *The number of children in the basic classroom group should be small enough for face-to-face encounters.*

4. *Children should remain in the same group long enough to develop a stake in one another's welfare and growth.*

5. *Each child should have the opportunity to share what he has with peers and to be challenged by peers.*

Ideal or best ways for grouping students may be an illusion. In organizing for learning, each teacher should be guided by his understanding of individual students and by his and the class's educational objectives.

[33] John A. Schmid, "A Study of the Uses of Sociometric Techniques for Forming Instructional Groups for Number Work in the Fifth Grade" (unpublished doctor's dissertation, University of Maryland, 1960).

[34] Wilhelms and Westby-Gibson, pp. 429–434.

[35] Julia W. Gordon, "Grouping and Human Values," *School Life,* 45 (July 1963), 10–15.

Summary

After a climate of learning has been established, further choices must be made of instructional methods and patterns of organization. While lecturing is a traditional and familiar method of instruction, most studies show few significant differences between comparable groups taught by lecture and discussion methods when knowledge of specific facts is the criterion used to assess effectiveness of instruction. Discussion methods appear to be superior to the lecture in stimulating critical thinking, in encouraging the interpretation of data and the drawing of inferences, and in influencing long-term goals and future behavior. If a group is viewed as made up of persons with information, talents, and skills to contribute to the group endeavor, then effective modes of communication will be seen as those that encourage two-way communication among all members of the group, including the teacher or leader.

A variable that differentiates learning experiences and teaching methods into two rather distinct types is the amount of direct influence and control which a teacher exerts on classroom activity. The dimensions of *learner centeredness* and *teacher centeredness* are reflected in the degree to which the student and the teacher share in the responsibility for identifying learning goals and for planning, carrying out, and evaluating learning activities.

Research investigating student-centered versus teacher-centered teaching reveals that members of student-centered classes generally do not score higher on achievement tests emphasizing facts and information than do students in teacher-centered classes. However, learners in student-centered classes do appear to show greater satisfaction with the course, more positive attitudes toward the subject area, and greater gains in personal adjustment. Students in these classes are also more likely to select the subject field as their vocational choice. Other ways that teachers can facilitate learner-centered learning are through asking questions which stimulate students' cognitive processes of evaluation and productive thinking, providing opportunities for students to teach other students, and introducing pupils to simulated educational games.

Since school learning is largely a group experience, one of the responsibilities of the school or teacher in organizing for learning is to determine the bases on which children are to be grouped for instruction. Although ability grouping is the pattern of most schools, there is little evidence that this method is the most satisfactory one.

Several innovations in grouping students have been tried. The nongraded program, which seeks to implement a continuous program of learning for children of varying abilities and rates of maturation, appears to be sound, but the great promise it holds has not yet been realized. The organization of nongraded programs has so far tended to focus more attention on structured materials and techniques and less attention on the child's needs and interests.

Team teaching, an innovation found in both elementary and secondary schools, seeks to make available to pupils the varied competencies and skills of two or more teachers. While pooling the strengths of several teachers may increase the quality of the instructional program, the emphasis team teaching places upon organization, scheduling, and team assignments may also cause the needs of the individual student to be overlooked.

There is considerable evidence that boys and girls differ in the ways they perceive and the ways they learn. Sex is yet another variable which educators should take into consideration when organizing for learning.

Grouping students within a classroom is a problem that faces nearly every teacher. Probably the most important criterion for effective learning is flexibility. There appears to be no best way of grouping students for learning. In organizing for learning, each teacher should be guided by his understanding of individual students and by his and the class's educational objectives.

Study Questions

1. What do you believe determines the teacher's choice of instructional methods—lecture versus discussion, teacher centered versus learner centered, role playing, or what? What methods were used by the most effective teachers you have known?

2. Although the evidence is conflicting, there appears to be a greater range of pupil gains associated with student-centered than with teacher-centered teaching. How would one reconcile these results with the observation that most teachers are probably more teacher centered than learner centered? Discuss.

3. Identify problems or situations in your own teaching which might be meaningfully and profitably explored by your class through role playing or socio-drama.

4. Research findings appear to cast considerable doubt upon the efficacy of ability grouping in promoting learning, yet this pattern tends to be widely used in our public schools. How would you account for this seeming discrepancy between research and practice? Discuss.

5. What weight will you give to what variables in grouping students within your class? Describe the procedures you expect to use in grouping your students. How will you evaluate the effectiveness of these procedures?

Suggested Readings

Gage, Nathaniel L., ed. *Handbook of Research on Teaching.* Chicago: Rand McNally & Co., 1963. A series of comprehensive papers which report the findings of thousands of studies that have investigated the many facets and dimensions of teaching. Examines extensively the conceptual and methodological problems involved in conducting research on teaching.

Goodlad, John I., and Robert H. Anderson. *The Nongraded Elementary School.* Revised Edition. New York: Harcourt Brace Jovanovich, 1963. The authors challenge the efficacy of the graded school structure. Evidence is presented which suggests that the realities of child development require that schools break away from the rigorous ordering of children's abilities and achievements.

Hillson, Maurie. *Change and Innovation in Elementary School Organization.* New York: Holt, Rinehart and Winston, 1965. A series of readings discussing new patterns of grouping and organization of the elementary school. The selections consider ability, homogeneous, departmentalized, and multi-grade patterns of grouping, as well as team teaching and non-graded patterns of organization.

Trump, J. Lloyd. *Images of the Future.* Washington, D. C.: National Association of Secondary School Principals, N.E.A., 1959. Describes an experimental program which features three major kinds of grouping: large-group instruction, individual study, and small-group discussion. Emphasis upon self-directed learning and flexibility.

Films

Experiment in Excellence, Part 1, 16 mm, sound, black and white, 27 min; Part 2, 16 mm, sound, black and white, 27 min. Syracuse, N. Y.: Film Library, Syracuse University. Presents some of the modern educational techniques that have been adopted by schools throughout the country: speed reading, advanced placement programs, language laboratories, and team teaching. Particular emphasis is given to the role of the teacher in providing individual attention to each student.

Ways of Learning, 16 mm, sound, black and white, 11 min. Syracuse, N. Y.: Film Library, Syracuse University. Describes the teaching procedures used in a beginning-level general education course taught at Antioch College. Shows the use of new teaching-learning procedures designed to develop self-directed learning.

Evaluating Development and Learning

21

Evaluation is the process of making meaning out of experience. No one could learn from his experiences except by utilizing the feedback from these experiences and converting it into meaning for the future.

Rodney A. Clark and Walcott H. Beatty

In this chapter we shall be concerned with the processes of measuring and evaluating the development and learning of students in school. In the larger perspective of human experience, however, we continuously evaluate ourselves and are evaluated by others without the use of formal tests. We are judged on how well we do our jobs and on the adequacy of our performances as husbands, wives, fathers, mothers, presidents of clubs, responsible citizens, and a host of other roles and activities. Thus, the processes of evaluation, like those of learning, appear to be coextensive with life itself.

Evaluation is a topic that arouses both positive and negative feelings in many of us. No matter how adequate we may be, someone's evaluation of our behavior in a given situation may find us lacking. On the other hand, evaluations in which our performance is judged adequate, competent, or successful provide feedback that serves as a powerful stimulus for further successful behavior. Experiencing this ambivalence of feelings, a great many persons resignedly accept testing and evaluation as necessary evils. This is unfortunate, because evaluation processes are essential tools for making progress in achieving our most important goals. Without the use of reliable, valid measuring instruments and evaluation procedures, progress toward any of the outcomes of learning described in previous chapters would likely be haphazard and uncertain.

Evaluation is the process through which teacher and pupils judge the extent to which the goals of education are being achieved. Most educational goals relate to certain expected changes in student behavior, changes which are taken as evidence of the student's development and learning. Much classroom learning, therefore, is evaluated through the teacher's informal observations. The first grade teacher notes the children who recognize words that were introduced the day before and the children who are able to use cues in learning a new word. Similarly, learning is revealed in the history student's analysis of a current political crisis in relation to past events in history; in the science student's testing of alternative hypotheses before offering a tentative conclusion; and in the typing student's improved rhythm, increase in speed, and decrease in errors.

These everyday observations reveal to the teacher which aspects of a performance need correction and improvement and which do not require further attention. Unplanned or casual evaluations, however, are often erroneous or incomplete. Isolated behaviors of a student may not be typical, or they may constitute too small a sample to reflect accurately what the student has learned. Therefore, systematic, planned measurements of behavior change are needed if evaluation is to fulfill its role in promoting learning.

Evaluation is a process of judging performances in relation to given criteria. Evaluation has three aspects: "(1) a judgment of what, in general, constitutes a desirable behavior change; (2) a means of measuring whether the behavior change has occurred and, if so, to what degree; and (3) a judgment of the 'acceptability' of a particular behavior change."[1]

What it is that constitutes a desirable behavior change is specified by the learning objectives the teacher has chosen. A learning objective may be the correct spelling of a specified number of words of a particular level of difficulty, the solving of quadratic equations, a particular number of errorless words typed per minute, or the demonstration of correct procedure in the use of a power lathe in wood shop.

Measuring whether and to what degree a behavior has occurred involves the assigning of value to a student's performance in relation to some yardstick or criterion. The means used for assessing change is frequently a test, but it may be a rating scale, a composition, a report, an interview, a conference, or observations of students' overt behaviors in various situations. Some of these means will yield more reliable data for evaluating student learning than others. The task of estimating the reliability and validity of evaluation devices will be discussed later in the chapter.

A judgment of the "acceptability" of a particular performance is made by the teacher or pupil with reference to the behavior criterion or standard whose achievement is a goal of the learning activity. The criterion or standard may be correctly spelling all the words on the third grade list or solving two-factor multiplication problems. More frequently, however, the standard is a percentage of correct responses, say 70 percent, which is designated as the passing grade or minimum level of acceptability.

To determine how "acceptable" the student's performance is, the teacher makes a judgment based on his criteria of acceptable degrees or amounts of change in student behavior. A fifth grade student's score on a standardized achievement test in reading comprehension may meet the criterion of acceptability generally expected of a seventh grade student, while the score of a classmate corresponds to the acceptable level or norm

---

[1] Frederick J. McDonald, *Educational Psychology*, 2nd ed. (Belmont, Calif.: Wadsworth Publishing Co., 1965), p. 581.

of the average fourth grade student. Some learning tasks (such as recognizing printed words, doing simple number problems, or typing errorless words) may be evaluated in relation to a single inflexible standard. More frequently, however, a criterion of acceptable performance takes into consideration the maturity and capacity of the learner. It would be unrealistic to apply the same standards to first grade children as to sixth grade children, or to apply the same standards to mentally retarded children as to children of normal intelligence.

The reader may have noted the distinctions we have made in our use of the terms *measurement* and *evaluation*. A further clarification of these terms may be useful, since these concepts are frequently confused and misused. Evaluation is more inclusive than measurement; but in order for evaluation to be useful and effective, it should be based upon measurement of some sort. Measurement is concerned with the collection of data upon which evaluative judgments can be made. *Measurement* can be defined as the process of assigning numbers to the individual members of a set of objects or persons for the purpose of differentiating the degree to which they possess the characteristic being measured.[2] The task of measurement includes (1) the developing or obtaining of an instrument or device which adequately measures the behavior represented by the criterion, (2) the administration of such an instrument, and (3) the scoring of responses obtained by the instrument. Tests are the most familiar and most frequently used of measuring instruments; for evaluating some learning objectives, however, other measurement procedures may be more appropriate. Measurement, in essence, is the act of discriminating between the performances of two or more persons. Evaluation is the rendering of judgments about pupil progress in terms of a criterion of desirable behavior. According to Lindgren,[3] anything that a teacher does to determine how well an educational program is succeeding is evaluation.

The major purpose of evaluation is to promote the development and learning of students. Both student and teacher have a stake in ascertaining whether the desired behavior changes have occurred during or after the learning activity. The student seeks some kind of confirmation that his responses and his understanding of concepts or content are appropriate, acceptable, or correct. Only through some kind of feedback in the form of confirmation or lack of confirmation will he have the evidence that he needs to judge whether he is more likely to achieve the desired behavior criterion by maintaining or by modifying his present behavior.

Evaluation also provides the teacher with feedback. The teacher wishes to ascertain whether his present methods, materials, and approaches are effective in influencing the desired behavior changes in his students. Since feedback concerning the student's progress in learning is of vital

---

[2] Robert E. Ebel, *Measuring Educational Achievement* (Englewood Cliffs, N. J.: Prentice-Hall, 1965), pp. 454–455.

[3] Henry C. Lindgren, *Educational Psychology in the Classroom*, 4th ed. (New York: John Wiley, 1972), p. 320.

interest to both student and teacher, the learning goals of the class should be explicit and clearly understood by pupils as well as teacher.

In providing confirmation of the student's acceptable or correct responses, evaluation provides reinforcement to the learner in the form of reward or satisfaction. We recall from Chapter 15 that the learner tends to repeat those responses which were reinforced on previous occasions: These reinforced responses become strengthened and "learned." In the absence of evaluation and feedback, the learner is likely to become anxious and confused. Either he will give up and not respond in the learning situation, or he will modify his behavior in seeking a situation which will provide some kind of feedback.

Finally, systematic evaluation of pupil's achievements enables the school to report the educational progress of students to parents and serves as a basis for making educational decisions. A student's school marks and achievement test scores furnish one basis for determining whether he should be admitted to specific courses, programs, or curricula, or to a specific college or university; they may also determine in part his acceptability for certain kinds of employment. The most important kind of evaluation, however, is that which facilitates and improves learning performance. Good teaching and effective learning do not occur without careful evaluation. Thus, teaching, learning, and evaluation are interrelated parts of the total educational process.

Formulating Learning Objectives

The first step in evaluation is a question: What is to be evaluated? What kinds of changes in pupil behavior are we looking for? It is essential that learning objectives be identified and clarified in order that the behaviors and activities of teacher and pupils can have direction and purpose. All teaching is predicated on at least an implicit set of learning objectives. If objectives are unstated or vague or are not communicated to students, or if the objectives bear little relationship to learning activities, then learning outcomes may be quite different from those that were planned for, desired behavior changes may not occur, and educational purposes are likely to be thwarted.

Evaluation procedures should be consistent with the stated objectives of the learning activity. This principle implies that the method of measurement employed must assess the attainment of a stated behavioral objective and should yield data on the entire range of stated objectives.[4] A set of educational objectives for a school system, course, or unit of work is a matter of choice, and the educational objectives that are chosen reflect the

[4] McDonald, p. 585.

value judgments of the community, school sytem, school, teacher, or some combination of these. Hopefully, too, a statement of objectives will reflect the developmental needs, interest, and concerns of students.

Statements of objectives may suffer from inadequacies and limitations in a number of ways. First, many teachers, in stating objectives, may not distinguish between *immediate* and *ultimate* objectives.[5] Such objectives as "educating pupils for good citizenship" or "educating for life adjustment" suggest behavior changes which can be assessed only at some future time, after schooling has been completed. Although immediate objectives should contribute to the later achievement of ultimate objectives, only immediate objectives are amenable to current assessment. We can evaluate a student's knowledge of the steps through which a bill becomes a law, but we cannot evaluate whether he will, as a good citizen, exercise his right to vote and be informed on national and local issues 10 years from now.

Other shortcomings of many statements of objectives are that they focus on too narrow a range of behaviors or are too general and vague. Frequently, teachers will state that their objectives are to teach certain arithmetic concepts and skills or to communicate specific principles of science. The difficulty with such objectives is that they identify an area of subject matter content to be presented but do not specify the behavior changes that students are expected to demonstrate.

A further shortcoming of many statements of objectives is the frequent discrepancy between their highly generalized but impressive goals and the virtual absence of classroom activities related to these goals. Achieving the ability to think critically and to communicate these thoughts clearly to others is a laudable objective, but it means little if no specific behavior changes or planned learning experiences relate to it.

Partial lists of behavioral objectives which have been developed for various subjects and grade levels follow. The first of these lists is for kindergarten.[6]

Communicating

1.   *Naming objects and experiences*

    a. *The child can name objects common to his environment.*
    b. *The child can talk about the experience in which he has been involved.*
    c. *The child can classify objects and shows increased specificity in description.*

[5] McDonald, p. 585.

[6] Louise M. Berman, *Toward New Programs for Young Children: Program and Research Possibilities*, No. 1 (College Park: University Nursery Kindergarten, University of Maryland, 1970).

2.   *Communicating with others*

   a. *The child can repeat back in his own words what another has said.*
   b. *The child can respond appropriately to the meaning of a statement of another person.*
   c. *From his own experience the child can respond to another person in such a way that he takes the other person beyond his original thinking.*

3.   *Nonverbal communication*

   a. *The child uses gestures, facial expressions, or other forms of nonverbal communication when he does not yet have the words to say what he wishes.*
   b. *The child uses words in addition to nonverbal communication.*
   c. *The child can differentiate between various forms of nonverbal communication.*

   An evaluation procedure designed to state and to assess the achievement of learning objectives in terms of particular behavior changes and learning experiences has been developed for elementary school science by the Commission on Science Education of the American Association for the Advancement of Science. This procedure begins with the selection and definition of "action words," which denote observable activities. To *know*, to *understand* and to *appreciate* seem to connote learning, but they are not as easily translated into observable performances as are the action words that follow:[7]

   1.   Identifying. *The individual selects (by pointing to, touching, or picking up) the correct object of a class, in response to its class name. For example: Upon being asked, "Which animal is the frog?" when presented with a set of small animals, the child is expected to pick up, clearly point to, or touch the frog . . .*

   2.   Distinguishing. *Identifying objects or events which are potentially confusable (square, rectangle), or when two contrasting identifications (such as right and left) are involved.*

   3.   Constructing. *Generating a construction or drawing which identifies a designated object or set of conditions. Example: Beginning with a line segment, the request is made, "Complete this figure so that it represents a triangle."*

---

[7] Commission on Science Education, American Association for the Advancement of Science, *An Evaluation Model and Its Application: Science—A Process Approach* (Washington, D. C.: American Association for the Advancement of Science, 1965), pp. 4–5. Used by permission.

4.   Naming. *Supplying the correct name (orally or in written form) for a class of objects or events. Example: "What is this three-dimensional object called?" Response: "A cone."*

5.   Ordering. *Arranging two or more objects or events in proper order in accordance with a stated category. For example: "Arrange these moving objects in order of their speeds."*

6.   Describing. *Generating and naming all of the necessary categories of objects, object properties, or even properties that are relevant to the description of a designated situation. Example: "Describe this object." The child's decription is considered sufficiently complete when there is a probability of approximately 1 that any other individual is able to use the description to identify the object or event.*

7.   Stating a rule. *Makes a verbal statement (not necessarily in technical terms) which conveys a rule or principle, including the names of the proper classes of objects or events in their correct order. Example: "What is the test for determining whether this surface is flat?" The acceptable response requires the mention of the application of a straightedge, in various directions, to determine if the surface touches all along the edge in each position.*

8.   Applying a rule. Using a learned principle or rule to derive an *answer to a question. The question is stated in such a way that the individual must employ a rational process to arrive at the answer. Such a process may be simple, as "Property A is true, property B is true, therefore property C must be true."*

9.   Demonstrating. *Performing the operations necessary to the application of a rule or principle. Example: "Show how you would tell whether this surface is flat." The answer requires that the individual use a straightedge to determine if the surface touches the edge at all points and in various directions.*

10.   Interpreting. *The child should be able to identify objects or events in terms of their consequences. There will be a set of rules or principles always connected with this behavior.*

The following is a partial list of behavioral objectives for a course in eighth grade mathematics.[8]

Number Systems

1.   *Recognize and apply the addition and multiplication properties of the rational number system.*

---

[8] *Guidelines to Mathematics, 6–8*, Bulletin No. 186 (Madison: Wisconsin Department of Public Instruction, undated), p. 15.

2.   *Recognize and apply the multiplication properties of the system of integers.*
3.   *Define subtraction in terms of addition in the systems of integers and rational numbers. (Example:* a − b *means* a + (−b)*).*

Ratio and Proportion

Use proportions to solve problems involving similar triangles.

Computation

1.   *Add, subtract, multiply, and divide integers and rational numbers.*
2.   *Approximate square roots of positive integers.*
3.   *Express repeating decimals in fractional form.*
4.   *Compute the mean of a set of rational numbers.*
5.   *Compute products and quotients if numbers expressed in exponential notation (including scientific notation). Examples:*

$$3^7 \times 3^5 = 3^{12}; \; a^5 \div a^2 = a^3$$
$$(3 \times 10^2)(2.3 \times 10^3) = 6.9 \times 10^5$$

6.   *Perform a series of operations in proper order when grouping symbols are omitted, i.e., multiplications and divisions are performed first, in left to right order, then additions and subtractions are performed in left to right order.*

Since many persons, including educators, tend to view curriculum in terms of content (information, concepts, and skills to be taught and learned), it may be useful to show that a clearly formulated objective has two dimensions, a behavioral aspect and a content aspect. The interrelating of content and behavior aspects in formulating objectives for a hypothetical high school course in biology is shown in Table 21–1. The headings of the columns list nine kinds of behavior aimed for in this particular course. In the left-hand column are listed the topics or units of contents with respect to which the behavioral changes listed across the top are sought. An X marking the intersection of a behavioral column and a content row indicates that a behavioral aspect applies in this particular area of content. Thus, a student in this course is expected to develop an understanding of important facts and principles for every one of the content aspects, but he is expected to develop social attitudes only in connection with heredity and genetics, viruses and disease, vertebrates, biology of man, and ecological relationships.

Mastery Learning

Much of school learning is evaluated by the teacher's judging a pupil's performance on a test or other measure in relation to the performances of

Table 21-1. The Interrelationships between Behavioral Objectives and Content for a High School Course in Biology

	Understands Important Facts and Principles	Knowledge of Classifications and Categories	Ability to Interpret Data	Ability to Apply Principles	Ability to Analyze Relationships	Ability to Plan and Carry Out Problem-Solving Experiment	Ability to Interpret and Evaluate Scientific Study Results	Development of Broad and Mature Interests	Development of Social Attitudes
The nature of life Chemical basis of life, the cell	X		X	X	X	X	X	X	
The continuity of life Heredity and genetics	X		X	X	X	X	X	X	X
Microbiology Viruses, bacteria, disease	X	X	X	X	X	X	X	X	X
Multicellular plants Root, stem, leaf; structure and function	X	X	X	X	X	X	X	X	
Invertebrates Sponges, worms, mollusks, insects	X	X	X	X	X	X	X	X	
Vertebrates Fishes, amphibians, reptiles, birds, mammals	X	X	X	X	X	X	X	X	X
Biology of man Body framework, nutrition, circulation	X		X	X	X		X	X	X
Ecological relationships Environmental interrelationships in plant and animal life	X	X	X	X	X	X	X	X	X

Source: Content derived from J. H. Otto and Albert Towle, *Modern Biology* (New York: Holt, Rinehart and Winston, 1963). Objectives derived from Benjamin S. Bloom, ed., *Taxonomy of Educational Objectives. Handbook I. Cognitive Domain* (New York: David McKay Co., 1956). Used by permission.

other pupils in the class or course. Characteristically, the distribution of the pupils' scores forms a normal, bell-shaped curve[9] or some variation thereof. In a normally distributed set of scores, the scores of most pupils will cluster at or on either side of the mean and will likely earn them an average grade, such as a *C*. The number of pupils receiving scores below the mean will tail off toward one end of the distribution curve; these pupils will receive a below average grade (perhaps a *D* or an *F*). Correspondingly, the pupils receiving scores above the mean will also tail off in number in the other direction, and they will receive an above average grade (perhaps a *B* or an *A*). Bloom[10] points out that the procedure of evaluating the individual's performance by comparing it to others in the class results in wasting the abilities and potential of a great many students. By distributing marks according to a normal curve, teachers seem to expect and to guarantee that a portion of the class will do poorly, either just get by or fail. We recall from earlier chapters the debilitating effects which school failure has on a student's motivation and self-concept.

Bloom offers the concept of *mastery learning* as an alternative method of evaluating students' performances. In a mastery learning type of evaluation, the student's performance is judged on the basis of whether he meets or fails to meet the criterion level specified for a given learning objective. For example, the student either does or does not correctly identify different kinds of cells under the microscope. Or he does or does not write a two-page essay which contains fewer than six errors in spelling and punctuation. In mastery learning the student is presented with a series of learning objectives which students taking this course should be able to achieve. Criterion scores are established on measures used to evaluate each learning objective, and the student's performance is marked "mastery" or "nonmastery" in terms of whether or not it met the criterion. How the student performs in relation to classmates is irrelevant in mastery learning; his performance is judged only in relation to the criterion.

To use a mastery learning strategy, the teacher must break a topic or a course down into a series of individual units, each of which can be achieved in a relatively brief period—say from two days to two weeks. A criterion performance level is defined for each learning objective, and students who meet or surpass this level are judged to have mastered that objective or task. Employing a mastery learning strategy need not interfere with the teacher's preferred mode or style of teaching. Presumably, the learning activities selected by the teacher will in any case be those that facilitate students' achieving a mastery level of performance. To implement a mastery learning strategy, the teacher need only construct brief diagnostic-progress tests to determine which of the unit tasks the student has or has not mastered and what he has to do to complete his unit learning. These

---

[9] See a graphic representation of the normal curve on p. 672.

[10] Benjamin S. Bloom, "Learning for Mastery," in Benjamin S. Bloom, J. Thomas Hastings, and George F. Madaus, eds., *Handbook on Formative and Summative Evaluation of Student Learning* (New York: McGraw-Hill Book Co., 1971), pp. 43–57.

tests, often referred to as criterion-referenced measures, will be described later in the chapter. For students who have thoroughly mastered the unit, these tests should reinforce their learning and assure them that their learning approach and study habits are adequate. For students who do not achieve mastery on the first try, these tests should identify particular learning difficulties—concepts, skills, and processes which need additional work.

The advantages of a mastery learning strategy are that it identifies specifically for both teacher and student the concepts and skills to be learned in a given course. In addition, the evaluation process focuses upon the progress of the individual student in relation to the goals of the course— rather than in relation to the performance of his classmates. Finally, successful mastery of a unit of learning provides the student with positive recognition of his competence and success and contributes to the development of the positive self-image that is so important for his continuing development and learning.

Alternatives to Behavioral Objectives

In spite of the logic supporting the use of behavioral objectives and their widespread use in education, many critics contend that it is not possible to formulate meaningful behavioral objectives for important outcomes in some subject areas. Some find it difficult to define behaviorally affective outcomes of learning (such as attitudes, values, and interests). In subjects such as art, music, dramatics, and creative writing, the *process* (of self-expression and creativity) is often a more important learning objective than the *product* (which is easier to define behaviorally and easier to evaluate).

Still other critics, who conceive of education as freeing the individual for personal growth and self-fulfillment, question the whole notion of a standard set of behavioral objectives that should be required of all students. In the view of these critics, behavioral objectives may serve as a deterrent to important learnings. Some of the most significant learning experiences which teachers and pupils plan for, such as going on a field trip, putting on a play, or putting out a class newspaper, appear to bear little relationship to preestablished behavioral objectives. Finally, since behavioral objectives are specific, there is a strong likelihood that children may be engaged in fairly narrow, repetitious, often boring tasks that may be required to achieve these objectives. In short, behavioral objectives are the goals of the teacher and the school; seldom are they the learning goals of students.

Raths[11] suggests that instead of choosing activities designed to bring about specific behavioral changes in students, teachers might select learning activities for inclusion in the curriculum in terms of other educational criteria, such as enabling children to make informed choices, to engage in

---

[11] James D. Raths, "Teaching without Specific Objectives," *Educational Leadership*, 28 (April 1971), 714–720.

inquiry into new ideas, to accomplish activities successfully in terms of different levels of ability, and to work on things that are relevant to the purposes of students themselves. Perhaps we should limit our use of behavioral objectives to outcomes where they are particularly appropriate and to those things we all need to know or know how to do in order to get along in society, such as learning to read, to compute, to communicate, and to relate to others.

Thus, while the formation of learning objectives is the first step in the process of evaluating development and learning, many feel that if objectives which cannot be behaviorally defined are excluded, unfortunate constraints could be placed on personal growth and the development of individuality.

Requirements of an Evaluation Procedure

Before an evaluative judgment can be made about a quality or level of performance, some kind of measurement must be carried out. The measurement process, as we noted earlier, enables us to ascertain whether the expected behavior change has occurred and, if it has, to what extent. Some evidences of learning are revealed by direct observations of behavior. We might, for instance, ascertain a child's reading skill by hearing or watching him read; or we might determine a student's skill in tennis, typing, or playing the violin by watching him or listening to him perform. Other types of behavior may not relate directly to a given objective, but an inference can be drawn from a student's behavior which does relate to the objective. For instance, we can make inferences about a student's interest in science from his frequent selection of books on science and his frequent mention of scientific events, inventions, and discoveries.

Other evidences of learning are revealed most clearly on a test or other measuring device. Since a measuring device samples only a portion of the *population of behaviors* (all the possible ways in which one might demonstrate behavior change) which constitute a body of content, the sample must be representative of the behaviors associated with that unit or course. For a measuring instrument to be representative, it must be comprehensive. A comprehensive test of American history would include items on colonial history as well as items on the Civil War and twentieth-century history. The test would seek to elicit student responses revealing an understanding of social history as well as political and economic history. While a test should be comprehensive, it should also seek to measure only those behavior changes which students have had the opportunity of learning in connection with a particular unit, course, or learning activity. One cannot construct a valid measuring instrument if he lacks detailed information about the learning activity he is seeking to evaluate. Finally, ease of administration and scoring are practical factors which influence the choice and use of a particular measuring instrument or procedure.

Reliability

Every measurement procedure must be reliable; that is, the results obtained by successive administrations of a test or procedure to the same subjects must be consistent. An educational achievement test can be considered reliable if the students of a particular class, without further study, place in about the same rank-order position on a second administration of the test as they did in the first administration. Thus, reliability is a measure of how accurately or how consistently a test or other procedure measures what it purports to measure.

No measuring instrument, not even a yardstick, is perfect—largely because of what we call *errors of measurement*. Errors of measurement can result from a faulty measuring instrument, or from the anxiety or fatigue of those being measured, or from less than optimal conditions of administration. A measuring instrument may be unreliable if some of the items in it are ambiguous or if the number of items it contains is not sufficient to provide an adequate assessment of the learning that has occurred in a given area. A test item is ambiguous if students consistently misinterpret what it asks for. A measuring instrument is also likely to be unreliable if it measures only a small proportion of the course content or expected learning outcomes. Thus, a student's performance on a 100-item test of biological science is a more reliable measure of what he has learned than is his performance on a 10-item test on the same content. The longer test provides a more complete sampling of what the student has been expected to learn; hence, the reliability of a test can be increased by lengthening it. Again, it is essential that the additional items be representative of content area and relevant to the learning activity being evaluated.

Validity

In asking how valid a test is, we are asking whether the test measures what we want it to measure. Does this test really measure the student's knowledge and understanding of American history, or is it a test of how well he can memorize a body of facts? Is this other test a measure of arithmetic reasoning, or does it measure mental aptitude? The problem of validity is somewhat more elusive than that of reliability and is more difficult to demonstrate. Because of the difficulties in determining validity, many teachers assume that their tests and other measuring devices are valid without taking the effort to find out whether or not their assumption is tenable.

If one were able to show that the items of his test do match the course content and instructional objectives, he would then be able to claim that his test has *content* or *face validity*. This is essentially what a teacher does when he prepares a test blueprint, a detailed description of the learning objectives and of the course content relating to these objectives. Thus, a teacher's own test will probably have validity if he has made a wise and thoughtful analysis of course objectives and if he has exercised care, skill, and ingenuity in building test items to match the blueprint.

A biology teacher who finds that the scores of his students on a teacher-made biology examination have a correlation of .75 with the scores these same students made on a standardized biology test on similar material has demonstrated that his teacher-made test has *concurrent validity*. A demonstration of concurrent validity involves comparing or correlating the results of a new measuring instrument with an instrument whose validity has already been determined. Demonstrations of *construct* and *predictive validity* involve more extensive procedures and are undertaken when one is developing a standardized test or a measuring instrument for research purposes. An instrument has construct validity when those who score high on it also score high on traits or abilities related to the qualities being measured. A science test has construct validity if students who score high on it are observed to use an analytical approach in the solution of problems more frequently than students who score low on the test. A high school biology test has predictive validity if those who score high on it also do well in biology in college.

Construction of Classroom Tests

Most teachers do not give sufficient time and care to the construction of classroom tests. Developing a good test is something of an art. It is not something that happens as the result of the teacher's jotting down questions as he leafs through the textbook. Constructing a valid test is a deliberate and time-consuming process and requires thoughtful reflection. Stanley,[12] recognizing that a satisfactory test is extremely difficult to construct, suggests that several teachers might do well to work together on a test.

The primary function of a test, as of any evaluation procedure, is to ascertain to what extent pupils have achieved the objectives of instruction. If a test is to measure pupil achievement in all of the learning objectives, it must be carefully designed and planned to include items or questions relating to each objective. Particularly, the relative importance of an objective must be reflected in the number of items allotted to it or the number of points which can be earned on that part of the test. If a teacher writes objective test items as they occur to him without regard to course objectives or the scope of course content, the course is likely to be out of balance—overrepresenting some objectives or topics and underrepresenting others.

Lack of balance in a test often results because it is easier to write

---

[12] Julian C. Stanley, *Measurement in Today's Schools* (Englewood Cliffs, N. J.: Prentice-Hall, 1964), p. 171.

Table 21–2.   Test Blueprint for Evaluating Achievement of Objectives of a High School Course in Biology

Weighting	Learning Objectives in Terms of Behavior	Content
30%	1. Understands important facts and principles.	protoplasm · DNA · pericardium Golgi body · meiosis · neuron homeostasis · mutation · myxedema photosynthesis · cilia · corpus luteum ATP · epithelial tissue · progesterone
10%	2. Knows and uses appropriate classification systems.	Identifying, distinguishing between, and ordering exemplars of various forms of plant and animal life: phylum, division, class, order, genus, and species.
10%	3. Demonstrates ability to interpret data.	Data are presented showing relationships among eight families in which feeble-mindedness appears. Student responds to statements with (1) true, (2) insufficient evidence, or (3) false. Example: Where both parents were feeble-minded, all children who lived beyond infancy were feeble-minded.
20%	4. Applies principles in solving problems.	Examples: 1. If the DNA amino acid code consisted of two bases instead of three, how many amino acids could be coded? 2. Why is it easier to digest sour milk than fresh milk? 3. How would you design an experiment to prove whether or not the eye really sees an image upside down while the brain interprets it oppositely?
10%	5. Analyzes relationships between phenomena and events.	Analyze the relationships between: 1. Different forms of energy. 2. Plants and animals. 3. Function and structure of organs. 4. Systems of the human body. 5. Climate, soil, water, forests, and wildlife.
10%	6. Synthesizes various data in formulating hypotheses and deriving statements of relationships.	Can derive and elaborate concepts and generalizations concerning fundamental life processes: reproduction, growth, differentiation, integration, metablism, hierarchy of control and function, anabolism, catabolism.
10%	7. Interprets and evaluates critically results of a scientific study.	Example: Two bean plants were planted in each of six three-inch pots. Three pots contained clay and were placed in a cupboard. Three pots containing sandy soil were placed in a window. All pots were watered regularly and uniformly. After three weeks the bean plants grown in the window had sturdy stalks and large green leaves. The bean plants grown in the cupboard had spindly stems and small yellow leaves. The investigator concluded that light is necessary for the normal growth of bean seedlings.

Total time for test—50 minutes.
Total number of test items—50.
40% of items to be drawn from textbook and readings.
40% of items drawn from lectures and class discussions.
20% of items drawn from laboratory work and demonstrations.

items that test recall and recognition of facts than it is to develop items that call for an understanding of generalizations or an application of principles. Moreover, it is easier to develop items or questions on some topics than it is on others. This is likely to lead to a preponderance of items or questions on the more testable topics or objectives. By failing to test some learning objectives or by testing others with disproportionate emphasis, a test falls short of its purpose. What students find emphasized on tests they will tend to emphasize in their study and preparation. Thus, the kind of test a teacher uses may cause students to emphasize in their study the recognition or recall of facts—learning objectives quite different from those the teacher may think he is emphasizing, namely, the evaluation of evidence and the application of principles.

As suggested, the first step in planning a test is to state and to define the learning objectives in terms of behavior. The second step is to outline the content to be covered by the test. (These two steps are incorporated in Table 21–2.) The third step is to relate the statement of objectives and the course content in developing a *test blueprint*.[13] In a test blueprint, test content is elaborated in detail. The blueprint contains only those objectives that can be measured either wholly or in part by paper-and-pencil test. To complete the blueprint, the test maker must decide on the relative emphasis to be given to each learning objective and content area. He may indicate relative emphasis by assigning a percentage to each objective. Each percentage serves as a guide to the number of items allotted that particular objective or topic on an objective test or the weight of the scoring of answers to essay questions. A test blueprint also contains the number of items on the test, the total time for the test, and the proportion of test items to be drawn from class lectures, discussion, laboratory sessions, and the textbook or other readings. A test blueprint for measuring the objectives of a high school course in biology in relation to course content is shown in Table 21–2. Objectives 8 and 9 in Table 21–1 (objectives relating to the development of interests and social attitudes) are not included in the blueprint in Table 21–2, since these are not readily measured by achievement tests.

Developing a test blueprint undoubtedly takes some time, but it does help to ensure some kind of evaluation of each learning objective and area of course content. The analysis required by the test blueprint clarifies the objectives of the unit or course, guides in the preparation of a sound test, and aids in the teaching of the unit itself.

Developing Objective Tests

The two kinds of tests now in general use are the *essay* test and the *objective test*. An essay test requires the student to plan his own answer

---

[13] For a further discussion of the test blueprint, see Robert L. Thorndike and Elizabeth Hagen, *Measurement and Evaluation in Psychology and Education*, 3rd ed. (New York: John Wiley, 1969), pp. 40–50.

and express it in his own words. An objective test usually consists of many more items than an essay test, and each item requires the testee to choose from among several designated alternatives. As we shall see, both kinds of tests have advantages and disadvantages.

Historically, the earliest type of test was probably the oral examination, in which questions were put by a teacher, an examiner, or a committee to the student, who was then marked on his ability to verbalize what he had learned. This method encouraged students to memorize facts verbatim—a sterile exercise, often performed without understanding. Performing under the scrutiny of peers as well as adults was usually an ordeal; and the amount of time required for an oral examination and the limited amount of content whose mastery could be evaluated for any one student made this a costly and inefficient method of examination. The oral examination is still used in special situations—for instance, in the evaluation of a single candidate seeking to qualify for honors at graduation, for professional certification, or for a master's or doctor's degree.

In time, written examinations took the place of oral examinations. Written examinations permit a much wider sampling of subject matter, and the student is freed from the scrutiny of teacher and pupils while he composes his answers. The chief criticism leveled at essay examinations is that teachers' marks on these examinations are unreliable. Starch and Elliott,[14] for instance, gave identical copies of an English examination paper to 142 English teachers, who were instructed to score it on the basis of 100 percent for a perfect paper. The scores assigned by the 142 teachers to the same paper ranged from 50 to 98 percent. Similar results were obtained with examination papers in geometry and in history. The unreliability of teachers' marks in scoring essay examinations led to the development of new objective examinations, consisting of a fairly large number of specific questions requiring only brief answers. The use of objective tests enables teachers to examine students over a broad area of content.

The objective test requires the individual taking the test to choose from among several designated alternatives. The principal kinds of objective examinations are (1) true-false, (2) multiple choice, (3) completion, and (4) matching.[15]

True-false items are limited to statements that are unequivocally true or demonstrably false. Because of this limitation, they measure the student's retention of specific, isolated, and often trivial facts. They appear to be best suited to test the student's recognition and definition of terms. *Completion* items ask the testee to recall and supply the best or correct answer from a limited number of possible answers. Completion tests are well suited to testing knowledge of vocabulary, names, or dates; identifica-

---

[14] D. Starch and E. C. Elliott, "Reliability of the Grading of High School Work in English," *School Review*, 20 (1912), 442–457; "Reliability of Grading Work in Mathematics," *School Review*, 21 (1913), 254–259; "Reliability of Grading Work in History," *School Review*, 21 (1913), 676–681.

[15] For specific help in writing acceptable objective test items, see Thorndike and Hagen, *Measurement and Evaluation in Psychology and Education*.

tion of concepts; and ability to solve alegbraic or numerical problems. Their chief disadvantage is that varied answers are likely to call for skill and discrimination in scoring and thus introduce subjectivity into the scoring procedure. Examples of true-false and completion items are shown in Figures 21–1 and 21–2.

A *multiple choice* item consists of two parts: (1) the stem, which presents the problem; and (2) the list of possible answers. Multiple choice items, the most flexible and most effective of all the objective items, are

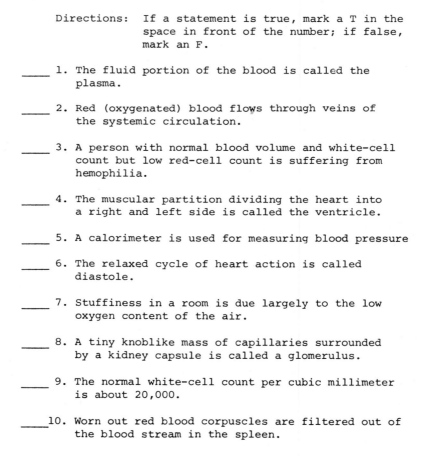

Figure 21–1.   A Portion of a True-False Test on Respiration and Circulation

Directions: If a statement is true, mark a T in the space in front of the number; if false, mark an F.

_____ 1. The fluid portion of the blood is called the plasma.

_____ 2. Red (oxygenated) blood flows through veins of the systemic circulation.

_____ 3. A person with normal blood volume and white-cell count but low red-cell count is suffering from hemophilia.

_____ 4. The muscular partition dividing the heart into a right and left side is called the ventricle.

_____ 5. A calorimeter is used for measuring blood pressure

_____ 6. The relaxed cycle of heart action is called diastole.

_____ 7. Stuffiness in a room is due largely to the low oxygen content of the air.

_____ 8. A tiny knoblike mass of capillaries surrounded by a kidney capsule is called a glomerulus.

_____ 9. The normal white-cell count per cubic millimeter is about 20,000.

_____10. Worn out red blood corpuscles are filtered out of the blood stream in the spleen.

Source: J. H. Otto, Sam S. Blanc, and E. H. Crider, *Series A, Tests in Biology* (New York: Holt, Rinehart and Winston, 1960). Used by permission.

Figure 21-2.   Examples of Completion Items in Tests in Biology

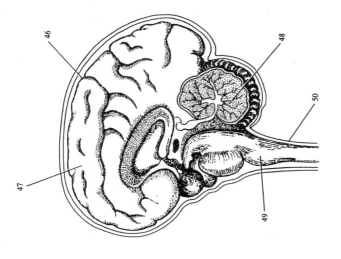

Directions: After each of the following statements,
write the word that completes the statement.

1. Chromosomes appear, shorten, and thicken
   during the stage of mitosis known as _____

2. Another name for reduction division is _____

3. Characteristics which are present but
   which do not appear in hybrids are
   termed _____

4. Genes operate independently of other
   genes. This fact illustrates Mendel's
   Law of _____

Directions: This drawing is a cross section
of the human brain. Write the
names of the numbered parts in
the corresponding spaces below.

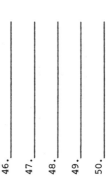

46. _____

47. _____

48. _____

49. _____

50. _____

Source: J. H. Otto, Sam S. Blanc, and E. H. Crider, *Series A, Tests in Biology*
(New York: Holt, Rinehart and Winston, 1960). Used by permission.

particularly useful for measuring information, vocabulary, understanding, application of principles, and the interpretation of data. For examples of multiple choice items, see Figure 21–3.

A *matching* test, actually a type of multiple choice test, measures the student's ability to recall relationships between pairs of items. Instead of a simple problem or stem, several problems are listed in one column, and a list of possible answers in another column. The testee must match items in the two columns. Matching items are often used in history tests, to measure the student's ability to relate names and events. Figure 21–4 shows that

Figure 21–3.   A Series of Matching Items on Foods and Digestion

Directions: Match the terms on the left with the definitions on the right, using letter answers.

A. Amino acid   1. The roof of the mouth   _____

B. Colon   2. The large intestine   _____

C. Esophagus   3. Fingerlike projections
                        from the wall of the
D. Palate   small intestine   _____

E. Peristalsis   4. The sphincter valve at
                        the lower end of the
F. Pylorus   stomach   _____

G. Villi   5. The end product of
                        protein digestion   _____

H. Mesentery
                     6. A fanlike membrane which
                        anchors the loops of
                        intestine   _____

                     7. Rhythmic contractions of
                        the smooth muscle layers
                        of digestive organs   _____

                     8. The region of the alimentary
                        canal extending from pharynx
                        to stomach.   _____

Source: J. H. Otto, Sam S. Blanc, and E. H. Crider, *Series A, Tests in Biology* (New York: Holt, Rinehart and Winston, 1960). Used by permission.

Figure 21–4. Examples of Multiple-Choice Items in Tests in Biology

> Directions: Select the best choice to complete the
> following statements. Write its letter
> in the space at the right.

1. The function of the sensory neurons is to carry impulses
   from the skin and sense organs to the
   > A. muscles
   > B. brain
   > C. brain and spinal cord
   > D. motor neurons   _____

2. Acetylcholine is a chemical substance which causes
   > A. muscles to contract
   > B. blindness
   > C. deafness
   > D. color blindness   _____

3. The cerebral cortex controls
   > A. involuntary actions
   > B. voluntary actions
   > C. the sympathetic system
   > D. the parasympathetic system   _____

When on Thursday, February 8, 1951, a Chicagoan,
Mrs. Dorothy Mae Stevens, was found unconscious in a
passageway after a night of exposure to subzero weather,
"she was literally frozen stiff." Her temperature had
dropped to an unprecedented 64 degrees (Fahrenheit).
Twenty hours after her arrival at Michael Reese Hospital
her temperature had risen to 98.2 degrees. Early Friday
it was 101 and later 100.

4. At a body temperature of 64 degrees
   > A. the blood carries more oxygen to the cells than
   >   normally because more gases dissolve in fluids at
   >   low temperatures rather than at high temperatures
   > B. the blood vessels of the skin are dilated because
   >   the vasoconstrictor muscles are related
   > C. the heart beats more rapidly because the cold
   >   stimulates the heart center in the medulla
   > D. most activities slow down because all chemical
   >   activities decrease as the temperature falls _____

5. The immediate cause of Mrs. Stevens' unconsciousness
   was probably due to
   > A. lack of a sufficient amount of oxygen to the
   >   brain cells
   > B. lowering of the external temperature
   > C. slow pulse rate
   > D. decrease in muscle tone
   > E. low breathing rate   _____

Source: Items 1, 2, and 3 are from J. H. Otto, Sam S. Blanc, and E. H.
Crider, *Series A, Tests in Biology* (New York: Holt, Rinehart and Winston, 1960).
Items 4 and 5 are from Benjamin S. Bloom, *Taxonomy of Learning Objectives.
Handbook 1. Cognitive Domain* (New York: David McKay Co., 1956). Used by
permission.

matching items can be adapted to test the student's ability to identify correctly a series of related organs, parts, or concepts in biology.

Scoring of objective tests consists of placing a key beside the answers marked by the student and counting the number of correct responses. Since (except for completion items) there is only one correct answer, error and bias on the part of the grader are eliminated. Moreover, the ease of scoring makes the objective test attractive to teachers. Although this kind of examination is relatively time consuming and difficult to prepare, the items can be used again and again. And, as noted earlier, an objective test does permit a much broader sampling of content in a given subject. Students are able to respond to 50 multiple choice items or 100 true-false items during an hour's examination, whereas only six to eight essay questions could be answered in this time.

A chief criticism of objective examinations is that they emphasize isolated, often trivial, bits of information and thus measure the student's ability to recognize the right answer but not his understanding of the material or his ability to recall or reproduce the right answer. In spite of this criticism, students who make high scores on objective tests also do well on essay examinations.[16] Thus, the two kinds of tests appear to measure the same kinds of competencies.

A further criticism of objetcive examinations is that they fail to measure the abilities of students to organize their ideas, to think through problems, to analyze relationships, and to apply principles. This criticism may be valid for true-false, completion, and matching items, but multiple choice tests are flexible enough to test almost any objective that can be measured by a paper-and-pencil test.

There does appear to be some basis for the belief that a teacher communicates his objectives through the kinds of tests he gives and that students prepare for objective tests and for essay tests in different ways. Unless the teacher using objective tests includes items that measure such objectives as analysis of relationships, application of principles, and interpretation of data, his tests will reflect only informational goals. Students will focus on learning specific bits of information in that course. The limitations of strict information learning are all the more distressing when we recall the high incidence of forgetting of facts that occurs during the six weeks following the completion of a course.

Essay Tests

As noted earlier, an essay examination asks the student to write extended answers to a relatively few questions. The essay examination has the following advantages: (1) It permits the student to organize his own

[16] Lindgren, p. 331.

answer and to express his individuality in the answers he writes on the test. (2) It requires the student to produce rather than merely to recognize the right answer. (3) If questions are well prepared, it can bring out the examinee's ability to select important facts and ideas, relate them to one another, and organize them into a coherent whole.

Thorndike and Hagen[17] offer several suggestions for the construction of good essay tests. Before starting to write an essay question, the teacher should have in mind the mental processes he wishes the students to use in answering the question. If the teacher is measuring pupils' abilities to comprehend, analyze, apply, interpret, evaluate, interrelate, contrast, or to think divergently, then he should begin an essay question with such words or phrases as *compare, contrast, give reasons for, present arguments for or against, explain how or why,* or *what if.* Questions beginning with *what, who, when,* and *list* should be avoided, since they generally elicit only specific bits of information. Imperatives such as *discuss* also should be avoided because they do not pinpoint clearly the task the examinee is expected to carry out in answering the question.

The following essay questions seek to measure the attainment of learning objectives (presented earlier in the chapter) for a high school course in biology.

1. *Self-preservation is a basic instinct of all vertebrates. Compare it with species preservation and give illustrations of each.*

2. *Trace a nerve impulse through a reflex action starting with a nerve ending in the skin and ending with a muscle response. Explain how reflex actions are often safeguards against serious injury.*

3. *Distinguish between an* addiction (*such as occurs with the use of drugs and alcohol) and a* habit (*such as, for example, the tobacco habit*).

4. *Explain the changes in chromosome number which occur during meiosis and fertilization, and tell why these changes are necessary in preserving the proper number of chromosomes in the organism.*[18]

Because of the potential low reliability of teachers' scoring of essay examinations, special care should be taken by the teacher to ensure that his evaluations of answers to essay questions are as objective as possible. The following suggestions[19] may help the scorer maintain some uniformity

[17] Thorndike and Hagen, pp. 57–63.

[18] Otto, Blanc, and Crider, *Series A, Tests in Biology.*

[19] Thorndike and Hagen, p. 56.

and consistency in his scoring of different answers to the same question.

First, the scorer should know exactly what factors are being measured by the test. If more than one quality is being measured, each should be evaluated separately. For example, a literature test might be given one score for the facts presented and another score for the organization and quality of written expression. Next, the scorer should prepare a model answer, showing the points that should be included in a satisfactory answer and specifying the maximum credit for each item or subitem. This model provides a common frame of reference for evaluating each paper. After the preliminary model has been prepared, it should be checked against a sample of student responses to the question to ascertain whether it is consistent with the students' interpretations of and answers to the question. The model and scoring scheme should then be modified so that it can serve as an adequate yardstick.

By reading all answers to one question before going on to the next question, the scorer can maintain a more uniform standard of evaluation, since he can compare one student's answer with another's. Moreover, this procedure lessens the contamination of the scorer's judgment with what the student wrote on a previous question.

Finally, the less the scorer knows about the person who wrote the answer, the more objectively he can grade what has been written.

Two types of procedures are generally used for scoring essay examinations. The first is to sort all answers to a single question into five piles on the basis of their quality (superior, good, fair, poor, inferior). Then, each paper is given a numerical score based on some type of equal-interval scale, such as 5, 4, 3, 2, 1 or 15, 12, 9, 6, 3. In this manner, each paper is scored for all questions, and an overall score is computed. Another method is to construct a scale based on samples of responses representing degrees of correctness. Each pupil's answer to a question is then compared with the scale samples, and a scale value is assigned to the answer in terms of its degree of correctness as compared with the scale.

While both teachers and students will have their preferences for administering or taking an essay or an objective examination, we cannot state that one type is superior to the other. Each type has its strengths and weaknesses. Neither the essay test nor the objective test is satisfactory as a sole measure of academic achievement. Whether to administer an essay examination or an objective examination is likely to be determined by the particular learning objectives sought, the type of concept, skill, or content matter being assessed, and the characteristics and needs of the students being tested. If learning objectives direct learners to interpret and to interrelate ideas and to integrate a number of facts and concepts, such as might be required in the study of history or literature, then an essay examination would probably be the best vehicle for measuring the attainment of these objectives. If ability to organize one's ideas and to express them well in written English is not a goal of a particular learning activity, then an objective examination might be a more valid measure of what a class has learned in mathematics, science, business law, or electronics. Table 21–3 lists the strengths and weaknesses of essay and objective examinations.

Table 21–3. Comparison of Essay and Objective Examinations

	Essay	Objective
Abilities measured	Requires the student to express himself in his own words, using information from his own background and knowledge.	Requires the student to select correct answers from given options, or to supply an answer limited to one word or phrase.
	Can tap high levels of reasoning, such as required in inference, organization of ideas, and comparison and contrast.	Can also tap high levels of reasoning, such as required in inference, organization of ideas, and comparison and contrast.
	Does not measure purely factual information efficiently.	Measures knowledge of facts efficiently.
Scope	Covers only a limited field of knowledge in any one test. Essay questions take so long to answer that relatively few can be answered in a given period. Also, the student who is especially fluent can often avoid discussing points of which he is unsure.	Covers a broad field of knowledge in one test. Since objective questions can be answered quickly, one test can contain many questions. A broad coverage helps provide reliable measurement.
Incentive to pupils	Encourages pupils to learn how to organize their own ideas and express them effectively.	Encourages pupils to build a broad background of knowledge and abilities.
Ease of preparation	Requires writing only a few questions for a test. Tasks must be clearly defined, general enough to offer some leeway, specific enough to set limits.	Requires writing many questions for a test. Wording must avoid ambiguities and giveaways.
Scoring	Usually very time consuming to score.	Can be scored quickly.
	Permits teachers to comment directly on the reasoning processes of individual pupils. However, an answer may be scored differently by different teachers or by the same teacher at different times.	Answer generally scored only right or wrong, but scoring is very accurate and consistent.

Source: *Making the Classroom Test: A Guide for Teachers*, Evaluation and Advisory Service Series, No. 4. © First edition, copyright 1959 by Educational Testing Service. Second edition, 1961. Reproduced by permission.

Criterion-Referenced Measures

Early in this chapter a strategy of mastery learning was described in which the teacher breaks down a subject or course into specific, well-defined learning objectives. Each of these objectives is defined in terms of a criterion level of performance which a student must attain to achieve mastery for that objective or task. The measures which a teacher needs to assess students' mastery of specific objectives are called *criterion-refer-enced measures.*

Criterion-referenced measures have some of the same characteristics as the objective and essay tests which we have just discussed. Like objective and essay tests, criterion-referenced measures should be reliable and valid. The construction of test items for a criterion-referenced measure will differ from that for an achievement test, since our goal in the former is to find out what a student can do, not how he stands in comparison with others; we are interested in a standard of performance—mastery—rather than in variability of performance. Hence, in constructing test items for a criterion-referenced measure, the teacher must make sure that each item represents the class of behaviors delimited by the criterion.[20] The following are items that might be included in a criterion-referenced test in biology.

1.   *Name in proper sequence the chemical changes in the digestion of food that occurs in the stomach.*

2.   *Prepare a tissue slide and correctly identify under the microscope the different kinds of cells observable on that slide.*

3.   *Describe correctly the changes that occur in the human cardiovascular system when a weakened heart can no longer pump aerated blood sufficient for the needs of tissues in all parts of the body.*

4.   *Describe correctly in sequence the steps through which information coded into the structure of the DNA molecule is translated into a hereditary trait.*

The interpretation of a criterion-referenced test is that the student has either met the criterion (achieved mastery) or he has not met it. The criterion level need not be set at 100 percent. For some tasks 80 percent or 90 percent correct responses might be selected as representing mastery.

Other Evaluation Procedures

Observation of Behavior

The teacher observes and describes pupil behavior in written anecdotes and case records primarily to increase his own understanding of the pupil's development and learning. He can use these same recorded behavioral data for evaluating a pupil's progress with respect to a range of learning objectives.

---

[20] W. J. Popham and T. R. Husak, "Implications of Criterion-Referenced Measurement," *Journal of Educational Measurement,* 6 (Spring 1969), 1–9.

Although behavioral data on pupils are useful to educators in many ways, the difficulties of obtaining adequate, reliable samples of pupils' behavior have imposed limitations on their use. As noted in Chapter 2, anecdotal descriptions often contain opinions, generalizations, and interpretations instead of facts about the student's behavior. The following entry is illustrative.

> *Tom is a large, overage boy in my sixth grade class. He is loud and boisterous and frequently bothers others, so that they cannot complete their work. He seldom completes his assignments, but instead wastes his time drawing racing cars and diagramming radio and television circuits. On the playground he is aggressive, plays roughly with other children, and is something of a bully.*

This generalized description of Tom and his behavior is of only limited help in evaluating his development and learning. It tells us more about the values, biases, and expectations of the person who wrote the description than it tells us about Tom. For information obtained by observation to be valid, it must first of all be specific, factual, and descriptive. Second, a representative sample of a student's behavior must be obtained by observations of him in a variety of situations. We cannot assume that the way Tom behaves in arithmetic is the way he is all the time. We need to observe Tom in reading, in the lunchroom, on the playground, and before and after school if we are to obtain a balanced picture of what he is really like.

In the following anecdotal description of the behavior of Clare, a first grader, we note first that the teacher has described objectively and completely Clare's behavior during one period, the reading period, on a specific day. The second entry presents a more generalized description of Clare's behavior, based on observations and descriptions of Clare in many specific situations.

> *March 6.   Clare's reading group is the fastest one of four. This year I am giving the children many easy books before they are introduced to a hard-back book. The vocabularies are similar in most of the preprimers. Since we have been introducing the second and third of a series of preprimers, Clare has been more interested in reading.*

> *March 27.   Clare is in the most mature reading group. The group has about 10 children in it. This group has read 10 preprimers from the Ginn and Scott-Foresman series. Clare frequently makes comments about the stories and helps others whether they need help or not. She often asks to be the first one to read. When given her turn, she reads with head cocked to one side. She reads well— smoothly, with understanding and humor, but methodically. She al-*

ways tries to sit next to the teacher. When it is necessary to ask her to be quiet or to listen, she usually complies temporarily with a smile on her face.

Observations of classroom behavior frequently yield evidences of pupils' behavior change not revealed in paper-and-pencil tests. As indicated earlier, a teacher should continuously check his initial inferences of behavior change by further observations of the pupil. This is necessary to ensure that one's observations of pupil behavior are reliable and also to pick up changes in the pupil's behavior as soon as they occur. Table 21–4 presents a list of categories of student behaviors and learning activities which can assist one in observing pupils' classroom behavior.

Table 21–4.　Observation Categories of Student Behavior and Learning Activities

Student Behavior

LISWAT	Interested in ongoing work: listening and watching—passive.
REWR	Reading or writing; working in assigned area—active.
HIAC	High activity or involvement: reciting or using large muscles—positive feeling.
WOA	Intent on work in another curricular area: school activity not assigned to be done right then.
WNA	Intent on work of nonacademic type: preparing for work assignment, cleaning out desk, etc.
SWP	Social, work-oriented—*peer:* discussing some aspect of schoolwork with classmate.
SWT	Social, work-oriented—*teacher:* discussing some phase of work with teacher.
SF	Social, friendly: talking to peer on subject unrelated to schoolwork.
WDL	Withdrawal: detached, out of contact with people, ideas, classroom situation; daydreaming.

Learning Activities

DISC	Large-group discussion: entire class discusses an issue or evaluates an oral report.
REC	Class recitation: teacher questions, student answers—entire class or portion of it participating.
IND	Individual work or project: student is working alone on task that is not a common assignment.
SEAT	Seat work, reading or writing, common assignment.
GRP	Small-group or committee work: student is part of group or committee working on assignment.
REP	Oral reports—individual or group: student is orally reporting on book, current events, or research.

Source: Hugh V. Perkins, "A Procedure for Assessing the Classroom Behavior of Students and Teachers," *American Educational Research Journal*, 1 (November 1964), 251. Reproduced by permission.

Projects and Papers

Projects and papers give clear indications of a pupil's achievement of learning objectives. Through such activities, the student can demonstrate his individual abilities and talents, and he often acquires more knowledge and information than is called for on a test. The science fairs held in many junior and senior high schools provide ample opportunity for students to acquire a broad range of knowledge and skills by working on science projects.

Projects provide opportunities for students with limited reading and language skills to have a meaningful learning experience and to demonstrate some of the skills and concepts they have learned. Mature students and those with reading and language skills can demonstrate considerable ability in independent research papers if they are working on something that is interesting and important to them and if they are given freedom to choose and to develop their own subject. Thus, teachers would do well to involve students actively in the initiating, carrying out, and evaluating of projects and papers.

Standardized Achievement Tests

Standardized tests are tests that have been constructed to measure specific kinds and qualities of behavior for which available norms show the average or expected performance of persons at each age or grade level. The standardized tests most familiar to teachers and students are those that measure intelligence or intellectual aptitude and school achievement, but other standardized measures have been developed to assess interests, special aptitudes, personality, personal and social adjustment, and self-concept.[21]

Since qualities of behavior such as intelligence and scholastic achievement are multidimensional, a standardized test of intelligence or achievement frequently consists of a battery of several tests. An intelligence battery may have individual tests of vocabulary, analogies, spatial relationships, arithmetic reasoning, quantitative concepts, and nonverbal performance; an achievement battery may have separate scales for reading, langauge arts, and arithmetic, and possibly social studies, science, map reading, and study skills as well.

Most standardized tests appear in published form, but this is no guarantee of their quality. Judgments on the quality of a given test can be

[21] For a discussion of these tests, see L. J. Cronbach, *Essentials of Psychological Testing*, 3rd ed. (New York: Harper & Row, 1970); and A. Anastasi, *Psychological Testing*, 3rd ed. (New York: Macmillan Co., 1968).

made by analyzing the information about its reliability and validity reported in the *Mental Measurements Yearbooks* edited by O. K. Buros (Gryphon Press, Highland Park, New Jersey). Unless one has had courses in educational measurements or statistics, he may wish to seek the assistance of a counselor or psychometrist in interpreting the information contained in the Buros reference.

The major value of a standardized test is that its results can be used to assess the performances of a specific individual, a class, a school, or a school district in relation to another comparable group. One may wish to compare the school achievement of a particular sixth grade class or all the sixth grade classes in a school district with that of sixth-grade children in classrooms or districts in other parts of the city, county, state, or country. Such data are useful in evaluating school programs, but they should be interpreted carefully, since groups that seem very similar may in fact be incomparable.

Characteristically, standardized tests have been administered to large samples of subjects, and performance *norms* have been developed through analyses of the scores obtained from these several samples. The samples of subjects selected constitute comparison groups. For example, the authors of a standardized achievement battery for a junior high school would have the battery administered to groups of seventh, eighth, and ninth grade students in large and small schools; in middle class and lower class communities; in rural, urban, and suburban areas; and in different regions of the country. If these several samples of students collectively can be presumed to be representative of seventh, eighth, and ninth grade students in the United States, then the average scores for each grade and each subscale of the battery would serve as the basis for deriving the *national norms* for this test.

Generally, the raw scores for each grade and subscale are converted to percentile scores ranging from 1 to 99. A percentile score indicates the percentage of students in the relative *comparison group* who scored above and below the student receiving that percentile score. Thus, an eighth grade student whose performance on a subscale or a total test battery yields a percentile score of 75 has scored higher than 75 percent of the eighth graders in the comparison group on that measure and lower than 25 percent of the comparison group.

Achievement test batteries developed for students in grades one to 12 often report norms in *grade equivalents*. A student whose score on a reading test yields a grade equivalent of 6 has performed as well as an average sixth grade student.

A comparison between a student's achievement test score and the norms for that test indicates this student's *relative performance* when matched against the performance of the comparison group. Educators should exercise caution in interpreting achievement test scores. Norms do not represent ideal performances, nor do they represent what students ought to know. Moreover, norms that are based on the average performance (in arithmetic or language usage, for example) of a diverse population in all parts of the United States are likely to be inadequate for judging the degree to which the learning objectives of a specific teacher and specific class have been achieved.

Standardized tests differ from teacher-made tests in that the former usually prescribe a set of specific controlled conditions under which they are to be administered. These conditions are generally set forth in the test manual which accompanies each test. Included in the manual is a statement of directions for taking the test that is read to examinees. If it is a timed test, the time limits for each part of the test are specified. Observance of these time limits by the test administrator ensures that all students have an equal opportunity to perform the tasks called for on the test. Directions read by the test administrator may urge persons taking the test to answer only when they are sure they are right, or may inform them that they will not be penalized for guessing. Thus, the prescribed set of conditions sought in the administration and scoring of a standardized test is a control to ensure comparable performances by all persons taking the test.

Standardized achievement test batteries are generally administered at specified grade levels, together with a standardized group intelligence test, as part of the school's overall testing program. No particular standardized achievement test will measure all of a teacher's learning objectives for his particular class; however, the results do provide information on the achievement of learning goals common to like classes or courses—at least in the elementary grades. As students progress up the educational ladder, there is less and less agreement concerning the skills, concepts, and information that should comprise a common core of learnings. Moreover, as students become older, the range of individual differences in their aptitudes and interests becomes wider and more varied. Consequently, achievement test batteries appear to be less useful for evaluating the effectiveness of specific learning activities in secondary schools than they are in elementary schools.[22]

Reporting Pupil Progress

School Marks

After the task of measurement—whether by pupil recitation, teacher-made test, teacher observation, or standardized test—has been completed, the job of making and reporting judgments of pupils' performance in relation to a criterion performance still must be done. After evaluations of pupil behaviors have been made, some report of these evaluations should be given to the pupils themselves if the evaluations are to influence their subsequent performances in these learning activities.

Few would question the necessity of evaluation and feedback in im-

[22] Lindgren, pp. 336–337.

proving learning, but that part of the evaluation process which involves the giving of a mark to stand for the student's achievement is frequently disturbing to teachers, parents, and pupils alike. Few issues in education have been so fraught with strong feelings, divergent points of view, and controversy as has been the problem of assigning school marks. Although school marks are only symbols of pupil achievement, often of low reliability at best, high marks are avidly sought and prized as evidence of one's intellectual attainments and as evidence predicting success in an achievement-oriented, highly competitive culture. Few will doubt that a high grade point average is an important prerequisite for admission to a prestige college, university, graduate school, or professional school; for receiving a favorable job opportunity; and for winning approval from family and friends. In view of the continuing interest in and emphasis upon school marks, a further study of this aspect of the evaluation procedure is indicated.

After a test or other measuring device has been scored, it is necessary to evaluate the learner's status or change in behavior as represented by this score. This involves the classifying of scores made by the pupils into various levels or categories of acceptability or unacceptability of performance. Thus, each student's raw score is translated into a percentage score or placed in a category to indicate his position in relation to others in the group with whom he is being compared. The teacher might designate 70 percent as the minimum score for a passing grade, or he might categorize scores and distribute grades according to some kind of a frequency curve. He might decide that the three papers with the lowest scores will receive a grade of *F*, or he might decide to give no paper an *F* grade. In any case, the teacher should inform his students of the criteria he has used to arrive at grades and of the meaning of the grading symbols.

The teacher's labeling of categories of acceptable and unacceptable performance by assigning percent scores or letter marks is, of course, arbitrary. This arbitrariness is largely the result of a lack of clearly defined, generally acepted, and scrupulously observed definitions of what various marks should mean and a lack of relevant, objective evidence to use as a basis for assigning marks.

Perhaps the most perplexing problem that confronts the teacher-evaluator is the question "What does a mark represent?" Presumably, it represents an estimate of the kinds of achievement or behavior change that have occurred in relation to the objectives of the unit, course, or learning activity. We use the term *estimate* because no test or other measuring device can be expected to measure everything a person knows about American history, English literature, or algebra.

First of all, the teacher-evaluator must decide, "Does this mark represent some level of absolute achievement (that is, my concept of what any student at this level of development should know or perform); or does it represent this student's achievement relative to achievements of other comparable students?" A school mark presumably represents the student's achievement relative to the achievements of comparable students; but the other criterion too frequently influences a teacher's marking practice. In addition, unless neatness, effort, the development of strong motivation, or positive attitudes and values is included among the learning objectives to be achieved, the assigning of a mark should not be influenced by these factors. Yet most teachers, either consciously or unconsciously, are probably influenced in some degree by these and other nonrelevant factors in their assignment of grades. Battle[23] found that students with the highest achievement as measured by school marks had attitudes and values more like those of the teachers awarding these marks than did the average student. Students with low achievement, on the other hand, had attitudes and values markedly unlike those of their teachers.

Some studies show that the sex of the teacher and the sex and IQ of the student influence the assigning of school marks. For example, in a class in beginning algebra, Carter[24] found that teachers gave girls significantly higher marks than boys, that women teachers in general gave higher marks than did men teachers, and that teachers' marks reflect not only student achievement but also student intelligence. This tendency for irrelevant factors to influence grades helps to explain the low reliability of teachers' marks.

Can the process of grading be made less arbitrary? It is possible to assign school marks according to a normal curve which reflects the spread or distribution of scores in a group. Figure 21–5 shows a normal curve of distribution and the relations of various derived scores to the normal curve and to one another. The *standard deviation* is a measure of variability, dispersion, or spread of a set of scores. In a normal distribution, 68.26 percent of all the scores lie within one standard deviation of the mean. The *percentile equivalent* is a number indicating the percentage of scores in the whole distribution which fall below the point at which a particular given score lies. A *quartile* is one of three points which divide a distribution of scores into four parts of equal frequency. Q_1 refers to the first quartile and corresponds to the twenty-fifth percentile; Md refers to the median or fiftieth percentile; and Q_3 refers to the third quartile or seventy-fifth percentile. The terms *z-scores* and *T-scores* refer to two *standard scores* (scores, derived from raw scores, that can be expressed on a uniform standard scale without seriously altering their relationship to other scores in the distribution). *CEEB* and *AGCT* refer to two standardized measures, the College Entrance Examination Board and the Army General Classification Test. The *stanine* scores, normally distributed standard scores ranging from 1 to 9, can serve as a model for assigning marks according to the normal curve of distribution. Here again, however, the teacher must decide how wide each band should be for each grade. Should a grade of *A* be assigned to stanine scores 8 and 9 and a grade of *F* to stanine scores 1 and 2? How wide should the *B*, *C*, and *D* bands be?

In practice, the distribution curve of a teacher's grades for a class seldom follows the normal symmetrical curve exactly, since most classes are perceived to vary somewhat from the theoretically normal group. Indeed, there is a tendency for teachers to assign overall a greater proportion of

    [23] H. J. Battle, "Relation between Personal Values and Scholastic Achievement," *Journal of Experimental Education*, 26 (1957), 27–41.

    [24] R. S. Carter, "How Invalid Are Marks Assigned by Teachers?" *Journal of Educational Psychology*, 43 (April 1952), 218–228.

Figure 21–5.　　The Normal Curve of Distribution, Percentiles, and Standard Scores

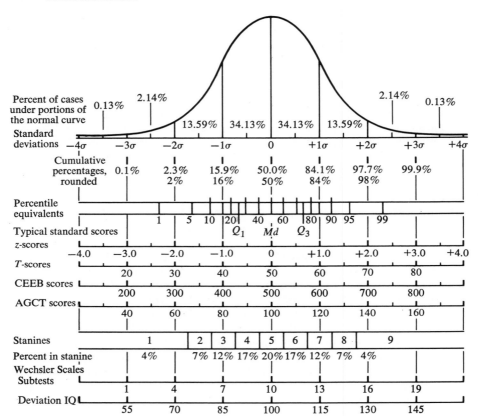

Source: Reproduced by permission of The Psychological Corporation, New York, New York.

A and *B* grades than *D* and *F* grades. Thus, the average grade on a five-point scale is usually not a *C* but somewhere between a *B* and a *C*.

In spite of the limitations of school marks, they remain probably the best single predictor of success in college, since the characteristics that enable a person to receive high grades at lower educational levels are presumed to contribute to academic achievement at higher levels.

Improving Marking Practices

There is strong dissatisfaction among some educators with current practices of marking and reporting student progress in academic achievement. The most frequent criticism is that no one really knows what a letter grade of *B* or *C* actually means. Compressing into a single letter mark an evaluation of a person's performance over several months or several years commits a gross injustice in failing to represent adequately the uniqueness, variability, and complexity of human behavior.

One approach to improving marking practices which some teachers use is giving students the option of *contracting for the grade* which they wish to earn in the course. A contract is a signed agreement and commitment between the student and teacher. It consists of specific tasks which the student must complete in order to achieve the grade he desires. A well-written contract includes behavioral objectives for each activity, criteria for acceptable performance, methods of evaluation, and methods which can be used in reaching the objectives.[25] The standard of performance and the amount of work required for each grade (*A, B, C*) is specified in the contract. It focuses on individualizing instruction, independent study, and cooperative planning between student and teacher.[26] Thus, the student becomes an active participant in his learning and the philosophy of individual and shared responsibility for mutually acceptable goals is implemented.

The initial reaction of most students is one of bewildered but cautious acceptance. Some students object to signing a contract because they prefer to put themselves in the hands of the teacher or because they feel that they might be unable to keep the commitments. As the semester progresses, some students change their level of aspiration as a result of a more realistic perception of the demands made upon them. Dash[27] reports that student response to contract grading is positive and that students tend to receive higher grades under a contract system than under traditional evaluative procedures. The success of the procedure from the teacher's viewpoint seems to depend upon (1) breaking down topics into tasks which can be evaluated upon completion and (2) stating instructional objectives and activities in unambiguous behavioral terms.

In an effort to reduce the pressure on students for grades, some schools have experimented with the use of two grade classifications, "pass" and "fail," in place of the familiar five-mark grading system. Such a marking system does appear to reduce the pressure on students to strive for high grades, but it also reduces some students' motivation to perform as well as they might if recognition were given for superior performance. Moreover, the pass-fail system of marking provides even less information on the individual student's progress in learning than does the five-mark grading system. Recently, however, some colleges and universities have introduced the pass-fail system for one elective course each semester or year in an effort to

[25] T. T. Haddock, "Individualized Instruction through Student Contracts," *Arizona Teacher*, 55 (May 1967), 10–11, 28.

[26] K. Nagle, "Contract for Individual Projects," *Business Education Forum*, 24 (April 1970), 19–20.

[27] E. F. Dash, "Contract for Grades," *The Clearing House*, 45 (December 1970), 231–235.

encourage students to explore new fields of study without fear of receiving
a poor grade.

More descriptive forms of reporting students' progress have been
used for some years in many elementary schools. The chief advantages to be
noted in the report form shown in Figure 21–6 are the identification and listing of the various individual competencies and skills under reading, language, social studies, science, and mathematics, and the spaces provided for
the teacher to write brief descriptions of the student's progress in school.
Another type of report of student progress takes the form of a letter from
the teacher to the parent, in which the teacher is free to comment on many
phases of the child's development and learning.

Another reporting practice used widely in the elementary school is
the parent-teacher conference.[28] This and the teacher's visit to the home provide unusual opportunities for teacher and parent to communicate to each
other information useful in assessing the child's development and learning.
In conducting a teacher-parent conference, the teacher should strive first to
put the parent at ease and to develop a rapport with the parent. This may
be facilitated by encouraging the parent to discuss the child. Although all
the information the teacher reports may not be positive, he should be positive in his acceptance of the child and his potentialities for growth. Information on the child's progress in learning should be presented frankly and
should be accompanied by the teacher's ideas about how to help the child
improve. The teacher may also wish to encourage the parent to offer suggestions for helping the child and to invite the parent to visit the classroom. It
is desirable to conclude on a constructive, pleasant, or positive note—with a
statement of encouragement or reassurance or a plan for cooperative action.

A cooperative evaluation program has been tried in the three junior
high schools of one school district.[29] The ultimate purpose of this program,
whose development is still in progress, is to replace course grades and report cards with measures of status and growth in the four, five, or six most
widely recognized objectives of each field of study. These schools will continue to use report cards in their present form until parents, after receiving
better and fuller information from the new reports, question the continued
use of the traditional report card.

An evaluation committee serves as the coordinating body for administering this cooperative evaluation program in all three schools. The specific functions of this committee are to direct the program, to appoint advisers to small groups of 20 to 30 students, to receive reports of all
"measures for the record" (newly developed evidences of achievement, such

[28] A useful handbook on conducting parent-teacher conferences is Katherine E.
D'Evelyn, *Individual Parent-Teacher Conferences* (New York: Bureau of Publications,
Teachers College, Columbia University, 1945).

[29] Frances R. Link and Paul B. Diederich, "A Cooperative Evaluation Program,"
in Fred T. Wilhelms, ed., *Evaluation as Feedback and Guide* (Washington D. C.: Association for Supervision and Curriculum Development, N.E.A., 1967), pp. 121–180. Material
taken from this reference is used by permission of the Association for Supervision and
Curriculum Development and the authors. Copyright © 1967 by the Association for Supervision and Curriculum Development.

Figure 21-6. Report Card Containing a Statement of School Purposes, Individual Competencies and Skills Covered by Each Academic Subject, and Space for the Teacher to Write Descriptions of the Student's Progress

PUPIL

SCHOOL   GRADE   TEACHER   YEAR

Aims and Purposes of Our School

In our school we strive to:
- understand the child as an individual
- provide the child with opportunities to learn basic skills
- help the child develop an incentive to learn
- develop self-discipline
- encourage individual intellectual growth and curiosity
- assist the child in his social and emotional adjustment
- promote the child's physical health
- help the child develop a sense of values

To bring about these aims and purposes, we provide developmental experiences in the following areas:

LANGUAGE ARTS reading, oral language, written language, creative writing, handwriting, spelling literature, foreign language

MATHEMATICS number facts, number language, processes, problem solving

SCIENCE natural and physical phenomena

MUSIC singing, rhythms, creative activities, listening

ARTS fine dramatic, crafts

PHYSICAL EDUCATION individual skills and games, health

ACHIEVEMENT

A check (√) indicates your child's achievement in relation to Grade Level expectancies.

Skill in using instructional materials	READING			MATHEMATICS			SPELLING		
	1	2	3	1	2	3	1	2	3
Above Grade Level									
On Grade Level									
Below Grade Level									

ATTENDANCE RECORD

	End of Year
Days Tardy	
Days Absent	
Days Present	

CONFERENCE REPORT

Scheduled   Date

Held   Yes ☐ No ☐

PLACEMENT

(To Be Completed at the End of the School Year)

Your child has been assigned to grade _____ for the coming school year.

_____ TEACHER

_____ PRINCIPAL

Pupil Progress Report Grades 1, 2, & 3

Board of Education of Prince George's County, Maryland

The following symbols indicate your child's progress in terms of his ability:

VG – Very Good   S – Satisfactory   NI – Needs to Improve   U – Unsatisfactory

KNOWLEDGE AND SKILLS

	CONF	REPORTING PERIODS		
		1	2	3
LANGUAGE ARTS				
Reading				
Ready for reading				
Reads with understanding				
Retains basic vocabulary				
Works out new words				
Reads well to others				
Shows wide interest in reading				
Language				
Hears and distinguishes differences in sounds				
Speaks distinctly				
Expresses ideas well orally				
Expresses ideas well in written work				
Uses correct English				
Writes creatively				
Handwriting				
Forms letters correctly				
Spaces letters and words correctly				
Joins letters and slanting letters correctly in cursive writing				
Spelling				
Spells assigned words correctly				
Uses correct spelling in written work				
SOCIAL STUDIES AND SCIENCE				
Assumes responsibility				
Takes part in group discussions				
Helps the group to plan				
Helps carry out the plan				
Shows interest				
Shows growth in acquiring information				
Shows an understanding of science around us				
MATHEMATICS				
Is developing an understanding of the number system				
Is learning and using number facts correctly				
Works accurately				
Uses reasoning in problem solving				
Shows understanding of numbers in everyday living				
ART				
MUSIC				
PHYSICAL EDUCATION				
WORK HABITS				
SOCIAL ATTITUDES				

TEACHER'S COMMENTS

FIRST REPORTING PERIOD

SECOND REPORTING PERIOD

THIRD REPORTING PERIOD

Parent's comments may be made on the reverse side of this form. If comments are written by parents, please detach this section and return in the child's envelope to the school.

Source: Reproduced by permission of the Board of Education of Prince George's County, Maryland.

as reports and projects), to file these measures in the record folders of these students, and to transmit copies to parents at least three times a year, with interpretive comments whenever they are needed. Initially, the evaluation committee identified and accepted six learning goals: writing competence, independent reading, critical thinking, interests, work habits, and acceptance by peers.

Presently, advisers are usually members of teaching teams in which most of the new "measures of record" have been tried out. Later, students will be assigned advisers of their own choice. The plan is to involve all teachers as advisers. The principal function of the adviser is to know how each student in his advisory group is getting along in all courses and activities. His information comes from official detailed reports on each "measure for the record" prepared by each academic department. These are sent to the advisers of students concerned, not directly to the parents. Ultimately, only the adviser will report directly to parents and then only to the parents of the 20 to 30 students in his advisory group.

A "report for the record" is usually limited to a single page, so that it can be duplicated and copies made available to the teacher making the report, the student, the adviser, the parents, and the guidance counselor. These reports usually include a statement of the objectives measured, a description of the measuring device or procedure (sometimes with sample items), the reliability and standard error of the scores if these have been computed, distributions of the scores of the groups tested, and some indication of the position of the student in these distributions in the form of a numerical score or letter symbol referring to the quality of his performance in a particular area.

To achieve greater objectivity in teachers' scoring of papers, the pupils' names are withheld, and each paper is scored independently by two or more teachers.

This cooperative evaluation program appears to offer an alternative to present methods of evaluation that fail to report student performance adequately. In comparison to a letter symbol, the "measure of record" offers more valid, complete, and useful information to student, parent, employer, and college admissions officer on the student's strengths and weaknesses in the various phases of a particular subject or field. Such a program appears to point the direction in which future effort to improve evaluation procedures should move.

Testing and Contemporary Culture

Many persons lament the increasing use of tests and the widespread emphasis placed on test results in our contemporary culture. So strong is the negative feeling toward tests in some that it has resulted in a kind of cultural bias toward testing in all its forms. There is a feeling on the part of many that our present tests do not measure real growth and change in behavior. Rather than to reject test data altogether, however, a constructive course would be to improve the quality of tests and to develop a variety of procedures or instruments yielding data on the same learning objective, whose results can then be verified to obtain a more valid picture of student performance.

In a culture as complex as ours, judgments must continuously be made of people's potentialities or their competencies for playing needed roles in the culture. Many of those who decry the emphasis upon tests and testing have little to suggest in the way of alternative procedures. In the absence of alternatives, there is a tendency to fall back on subjective judgments, which are likely to be more subject to error than a mediocre test.

Our previous discussion has emphasized the shortcomings and limitations of tests. However, when interpreted cautiously and viewed in conjunction with other types of relevant data, test data can provide important information upon which to make judgments in assessing student achievement. One is less likely to make unwarranted interpretations of test results if he remembers that a test is composed of a limited number of samples selected from a large number of possible behaviors relating to a given learning objective. For a valid assessment of a student's achievement, the teacher must continue to obtain samples of the student's behavior on that learning dimension until a fairly consistent picture of his performance emerges.

Finally, measurement and evaluation are too often viewed as adjuncts to learning rather than integral parts of the teaching-learning process. A cardinal principle is that *evaluation should be continuous*. Plans for evaluating behavior change should be made at the same time that learning objectives are agreed upon and refined and curriculum content and materials are developed. Too often, evaluation procedures are developed hastily after the course is well underway. The improvement of learning and instruction depends on one's obtaining reliable, valid information on student behavior changes. We cannot teach well and students will not learn effectively if data on learning performance are faulty or lacking.

Accountability

Many of the difficulties and frustrations that the American people encounter in trying to solve pressing social problems are reflected in criticisms of their schools. So great is America's faith in its schools for providing the education needed for America to maintain its preeminence in the world that any setback in national life results in questions being asked about the effectiveness of our schools. In contrast to the accountability practiced in business and industry, school boards and administrators have been unable to provide a satisfactory answer to the question "How much pupil achievement (in reading, arithmetic, or any other subject) does the education dollar purchase?" With the squeeze on school budgets brought on in part by taxpayers' resistance to paying higher taxes, the frequent posing of this question and the efforts to answer it have become known as *accountability in education.*

The term *accountability* embodies the notion that school systems and schools, or more precisely the professional educators who operate them, should be responsible for what children learn.[30] In recent years several approaches have been proposed and tried out in response to the issues raised by accountability. One approach has been the introduction of output-oriented management methods into schools. These methods include the regular, comprehensive evaluation of new and ongoing programs, comparative evaluations of school performance, and the external educational audit such as that which is now required in certain federally funded programs. In addition, performance incentives for school personnel have been introduced in the form of pay schedules based on measured performance of pupils and differentiated staffing as a basis of both pay and promotion.

A second approach in responding to the issues of the school's accountability for pupil achievement is performance contracting. *Performance contracting* is an arrangement whereby a private organization or business firm acting as a contractor signs an agreement with a school board that it will improve pupils' performance in basic skills by certain amounts. The contractor is paid according to his success in bringing students' performance up to specific levels. If he succeeds he makes a profit. If he fails, he is not paid. This approach has taken the education covered by the contract out of the hands of professional educators. The marked success of some of the early projects in performance contracting have had to be reevaluated when it was learned that part of this success was allegedly due to using in their teaching items later found in the performance tests, a phenomenon known as "teaching for the tests."

A third approach to accountability in education is the movement toward *decentralization* and *community control* in large city school systems. Under this approach it is believed that increased accountability for the operation and effectiveness of the school's teaching-learning activities can be achieved when authority and responsibility in large school systems are shifted from a central administration and school board to local administrators, principals, and in some cases local school boards.

A fourth approach to accountability in education, the most radical one, is the sanctioning and establishment of *alternative schools.* Under this plan private schools would compete with existing public schools for students. Parents would be given "education vouchers" redeemable from public funds which they would use to pay for the education of their children at whatever school—public or private—they chose for their children.

Each of these approaches has been tried out in only a limited way, and none thus far has provided an adequate answer to the issue of accountability in education. The problem is enormously complex, since the child's achievement is influenced by many variables besides the quality of teaching

---

[30] S. M. Barro, "An Approach to Developing Accountability Measures for the Public Schools," *Phi Delta Kappan,* 52 (December 1970), 196–205.

he receives. Barro[31] has proposed a statistical model for accountability in education which would seek to identify the amount of contribution to pupil performance by each of the agents in the educational process. The basic technique is multiple regression analysis of the relationship between pupil performance and various pupil, teacher, and school characteristics. The task involves isolating that part of pupil achievement which the teacher cannot control or be responsible for—pupil characteristics, other classroom variables, and school characteristics. This procedure would be expected to yield a figure representing the proportion of a pupil's achievement attributable to being in a particular teacher's class.

We can expect further efforts to improve accountability in education as the schools seek to compete for public support with other programs having high national priority.

Summary

Testing and evaluation engender ambivalent feelings in many persons in contemporary society. Evaluation provides feedback that serves as a powerful stimulus for continuing adequate behavior or improving inadequate behavior. Without reliable, valid measuring instruments and evaluation procedures, progress toward achieving any of the outcomes of learning would likely be haphazard and uncertain.

Evaluation is a process of judging performances in relation to given criteria. It includes (1) a judgment of what, in general, constitutes a desirable behavior change; (2) a means of measuring whether the behavior change has occurred and, if so, to what degree; and (3) a judgment of the acceptability of a particular behavior change.

Evaluation is more inclusive than measurement, but for evaluation to be valid, it should be based upon measurement of some sort. *Measurement,* in essence, is the act of discriminating between the performances of two or more persons. Tests are familiar measuring instruments, but other kinds of devices for measuring specific kinds of performance or behavior change can also be used.

Identifying the goals to be achieved during a proposed learning activity is the teacher's first step in organizing for learning. Many learning objectives are difficult to measure and evaluate because of a failure to distinguish between *immediate* and *ultimate* objectives, because they focus on too narrow a range of behaviors, or because they are too general or vague. Learning objectives are of little effect if planned experiences have little or no relationship to these objectives.

If learning involves a change in behavior, it would seem to be appropriate to assess the achievement of learning objectives in terms of reliably

---

[31] Barro, pp. 196–205.

observable behavior. In describing the instructional objectives of an elementary school science curriculum, action words, such as *identifying, distinguishing, constructing, naming, ordering, describing, demonstrating,* and *interpreting* can be used. When curriculum is viewed in terms of content—information, concepts, skills to be taught and learned—a clearly formulated objective is seen to have two aspects: a behavioral aspect and a content aspect. The use of behavioral objectives is particularly relevant in *mastery learning,* a type of instruction in which the student's performance is judged on whether it meets or fails to meet the criterion level specified for a given learning objective. It has been pointed out, however, that some important learning objectives are difficult to define in behavioral terms. Exclusive reliance on behavioral objectives could, it is felt, place unfortunate constraints on personal growth and the development of individuality.

The essential requirements of an evaluation procedure are that it be reliable and that it be valid. Reliability is a measure of how accurately or how consistently a test or other procedure measures what it is supposed to measure. In asking how valid a test is, we are asking whether the test measures what we want it to measure.

The primary function of a test, as of any evaluation procedure, is to ascertain to what extent pupils have achieved the objectives of instruction. If a test is to measure pupil achievement in all the learning objectives, it must be carefully designed to include items or questions relating to each objective. An important step in planning a test is to relate the statement of objectives and course content in developing a *test blueprint.* In the test blueprint, the test maker indicates the relative emphasis that is to be given in the test to each learning objective and content area.

The unreliability of teachers' marks in scoring essay examinations led to the development of new objective examinations consisting of a fairly large number of specific questions requiring only brief answers. The objective test requires the individual taking the test to choose from among designated alternatives. The principal kinds of objective examinations are (1) *true-false,* (2) *multiple choice,* (3) *completion,* and (4) *matching.* Although choice-type objective examinations have been criticized for their failure to measure students' abilities or organize ideas, to think through problems, to analyze relationships, and to apply principles, proponents contend that multiple choice tests can be used to test almost any objective that can be measured by a paper-and-pencil test.

The chief advantage of the essay examination is that it provides the student with an opportunity to organize his own answer. Because of the potential low reliability of teachers' scoring of essay examinations, special care should be taken to ensure that evaluation of answers to essay questions is as objective as possible. Both objective and essay tests have their strengths and weaknesses. However, *criterion-referenced measures* can be used to assess students' mastery of specific objectives such as those employed in mastery learning. The teacher's choice of which type to use should take into account the learning objectives to be evaluated, the nature of the course content, and the characteristics and abilities of the students being evaluated.

Other evaluation procedures include observations of students' behavior, projects and papers, and standardized tests. Observations of classroom behavior frequently yield evidence of pupil behavior change not revealed in paper-and-pencil tests, but, to be valid, the teacher's descriptions of observed classroom behavior must be objective and complete. Projects and papers have the potential of arousing strong student interest and involvement in an activity which permits the student to demonstrate his individual interests and talents. The major value of a standardized test is that its results can be used to assess the performances of a specific individual, class, school, or school district in relation to other, comparable groups of students.

After a test or other measuring device has been scored, it is necessary to evaluate the learner's status or change in behavior as represented by this score. This involves the classifying of scores made by pupils into various levels or categories of acceptability or unacceptability. This is essentially the task of assigning school marks.

Considerable dissatisfaction has been expressed with current practices of marking and reporting student progress. The chief criticism is that a single letter grade is grossly inadequate for representing the uniqueness, variability, and complexity of human behavior. Contract grading, report cards which provide space for descriptive comments and identify important learning objectives in each curriculum area, parent-teacher conferences, and cooperative evaluation programs in which descriptive evaluations are made of each student with respect to important learning objectives are promising alternatives to traditional systems of grading.

Study Questions

1. What are some of the specific objectives, stated in terms of observable behavior, that you would develop for the subject and grade you will teach? Are some of these behaviors more fundamental than others? If so, arrange the behavioral objectives you have identified into a hierarchy.

2. How would you organize and/or modify these behavioral objectives in implementing a mastery learning procedure in your classroom? What problems would be likely to be encountered in reporting to parents the child's progress under mastery learning? What solutions would you offer for these problems?

3. What factors would you consider in deciding whether to administer an objective examination, an essay examination, or some other form of evaluation?

4. In the subject or grade you will teach, should one evaluate Frank Abell's performance in relation to the performances of the rest of the class, or should Frank be evaluated in relation to his capacities, aptitudes, and his level of knowledge and skill in the subject when he began this course? Defend your answer.

5.   What distinctions, if any, would you make between the terms *evaluation* and *grading*?

6.   We are reminded that evaluation should be an integral part of the planning and preparation of every learning activity. Also, for a very long time we have been told that evaluation should be continuous. What explanations would you offer for teachers' tendencies to treat evaluation as something apart from the learning activity (as evidenced by the fact that planning for evaluation often occurs long after the learning activity has gotten underway)?

Suggested Readings

Bloom, Benjamin S., ed. *Taxonomy of Educational Objectives. Handbook I. Cognitive Domain.* New York: David McKay Co., 1956; David R. Krathwohl, Benjamin S. Bloom, and Bertram B. Masia. *Taxonomy of Educational Objectives. Handbook II. Affective Domain.* New York: David McKay Co., 1964. These references identify the range of educational objectives relative to the cognitive and affective domains of learning. Clear distinctions are made between various kinds and levels of cognitive and affective learning. Included are examples of statements of objectives in each domain together with test items designed to provide evidence of the achievement of each objective.

Ebel, Robert L. *Measuring Educational Achievement.* Englewood Cliffs, N. J.: Prentice-Hall, 1965. Introduces and discusses concepts, principles, and procedures for assisting teachers to prepare better tests of educational achievement. Various types of tests and the methods teachers can use to evaluate their own tests are discussed.

Gronlund, Norman E. *Measurement and Evaluation in Teaching.* Second Edition. New York: Macmillan Co., 1971. Describes principles and procedures of evaluation that are essential to good teaching. Discusses the topics which relate to three fundamental steps in evaluation: (1) identifying and defining instructional objectives in behavioral terms, (2) constructing or selecting the evaluation instruments that most effectively appraise these specific learning outcomes, and (3) using the results to improve learning.

Thorndike, Robert L., and Elizabeth Hagen. *Measurement and Evaluation in Psychology and Education.* Third Edition. New York: John Wiley, 1969. A comprehensive and widely used text on educational measurement written primarily for persons who will use and interpret tests. Chapters 3 and 4 offer guidance to teachers in the planning, preparation, and evaluation of teacher-made tests.

Wilhelms, Fred T., ed. *Evaluation as Feedback and Guide.* Washington, D. C.: Association for Supervision and Curriculum Development, N.E.A., 1967. Evaluation is seen as an important factor in curriculum improvement because it influences motivation and thus influences instructional programs. This yearbook suggests that current evaluation procedures fall far short of fulfilling their task of facilitating learning through the improvement of instruction. The plea is for evaluation that will enable the student not only to appraise himself validly, but will enable him to take greater responsibility for his own learning.

Students Who Need Special Help

22

No matter how close to psychopathic our children may sometimes look, we haven't found one of them yet who didn't have lots of potential areas of value appeal lying within him.

Fritz Redl

Children with marked physical or intellectual handicaps which prevent them from making satisfactory progress in a regular school program have come to be referred to as exceptional children. In general, an *exceptional child* is one who deviates intellectually, physically, socially, or emotionally so markedly from what is considered to be normal that he requires special instruction and services.[1] Exceptional children are both those with physical or intellectual handicaps and those with unusual physical or intellectual gifts. Table 22–1 presents estimates of the incidence in the United States of various types of handicapped exceptional children requiring special education services. In Table 22–1, the category *mentally retarded* includes "educable" children (IQs of 55 to 80) and "trainable" children (IQs below 55). The category *major learning disabilities* comprises children who have some type of cerebral dysfunction (such as brain damage).

It is beyond the scope of this book to discuss every type of exceptional child in depth. In this chapter we shall focus on three types of exceptional children: the culturally disadvantaged child; the emotionally disturbed child; and the high-ability underachiever.

The Culturally Disadvantaged Student

Who Are the Culturally Disadvantaged?

The term *disadvantaged*[2] by definition implies unfavorable circumstances—influences that are detrimental and harmful. As used by social

[1] William M. Cruickshank and G. Orville Johnson, *Education of Exceptional Children and Youth* (Englewood Cliffs, N. J.: Prentice-Hall, 1958), p. 3.

[2] The term *culturally deprived* has also been used to refer to the poor, but this term has lost favor, since every social group has a culture and many of the ethnic poor

Table 22–1.   Estimated Number of Children Needing Special Education Services, 1974–1975

Handicap	Number	Percentage of Total School Population
Visually handicapped	49,900	.1
Deaf	37,425	.075
Hard of hearing	249,500	.5
Speech handicapped	1,746,500	3.5
Crippled and other health disorders	249,500	.5
Emotionally disturbed	998,000	2.0
Mentally retarded	1,147,700	2.3
Major learning disabilities	499,000	1.0
Total	4,977,525	9.975

Source: *Projections of Educational Statistics to 1980–1981* (Washington, D. C.: U. S. Department of Health, Education, and Welfare, 1971). Based on an estimated 49.9 million children in elementary schools in the United States in 1974–1975.

scientists, the term refers to sizable minorities of peoples in the United States who are denied the opportunities available to most Americans for achieving the basic human goals of physical comfort and survival, self-worth, self-esteem, and relatedness to others. While one may be disadvantaged due to physical or intellectual limitations, the major cause of one's being disadvantaged in our society is poverty. In the culture of the poor, populated largely but not exclusively by ethnic minorities, the advantages enjoyed by those in the majority culture are absent. Although we tend to think of the disadvantaged as residing in the black ghettos of our large cities, the disadvantaged are to be found also in small towns, in the rural slums of backwoods Appalachia, in the shotgun shacks of cotton hands in Mississippi, in the Spanish barrios of El Paso, on American Indian reservations, and in the migrant worker camps of New Jersey and California. Indeed, because of decades of discrimination and apathy on the part of the more affluent, pockets of poverty can be found in almost every geographical section of this nation.

It is difficult to estimate the number of children who come from homes which are classified as disadvantaged. A conservative estimate by Havighurst[3] is that about 15 percent of Americans are disadvantaged. Of

have a rich and elaborate culture. The cult of the ghetto, for example, has its own language, mores, and means of survival. In short, it is people who are deprived, not the culture.

[3] Robert J. Havighurst, "Minority Subcultures and the Law of Effect," in Frances F. Korton, Stuart W. Cook, and John I. Lacey, eds., *Psychology and Problems of Society* (Washington, D. C.: American Psychological Association, 1970).

these, about 20 million are English-speaking Caucasians, 8 million are blacks, 3 million are Spanish-speaking, and a half million are American Indians. Thus, in absolute numbers more whites are disadvantaged than blacks, but proportionately more blacks (35 percent blacks versus 10 percent whites) are classified as disadvantaged.

Persons disadvantaged by poverty not only are deprived of the basic physical needs for food, clothing, and shelter, but also receive the least and poorest public services for health, education, and roads. The disparities between rich and poor are particularly evident in their schools and equality of educational opportunity. Not only do the poorest communities have inadequate school facilities, equipment, curricula, educational standards, and quality of teaching compared to those of the more affluent communities in the same school district, but great disparities are also evident in the amount of money spend per child on education in more affluent and poorer school districts. These differences help to explain the frequently reported finding that academic achievement varies directly with socioeconomic status.[4]

Inequality of educational opportunity tends to sustain the culture of poverty by denying the disadvantaged the opportunity to acquire the level and quality of education needed to break out of poverty. Moreover, the inadequate resources of the home are unable to provide the disadvantaged child with the proper sensory stimulation and experiences so important for later cognitive development. Piaget[5] and Hunt[6] both emphasize the importance of early sensory stimulation and social experience for later linguistic and mathematical learning and development of logical thinking.

The culturally disadvantaged, therefore, are those whose poverty both limits their chances for achieving minimal physical comfort and well-being and restricts the opportunities for experience and education that would enable their children to escape from the bonds of poverty.

Characteristics of the Disadvantaged

Differences among the disadvantaged are as great as those found in other social groups. Disadvantaged children differ in their motives, goals, behavior patterns, zeal for education, and predisposition toward delinquency. In short, if we are to understand a particular child, we must view him as a unique individual. We should avoid ascribing to him qualities that may be characteristic only of the group as a whole. Yet, as noted in Chapter 6, there are notable differences between disadvantaged and middle

---

[4] Patricia Sexton, *Education and Income* (New York: Viking Press, 1961).

[5] Jean Piaget, *Origins of Intelligence in Children* (New York: W. W. Norton & Co., 1963).

[6] J. McVicker Hunt, *Intelligence and Experience* (New York: Ronald Press, 1961).

class children which have important implications for their development and learning.

For the disadvantaged child, life in an overcrowded slum apartment or rural tenant house offers a minimal range of stimuli. The lower class home has few if any pictures on the wall and few toys or utensils to play with. In view of the meager resources available for food and basic necessities, few resources are likely to be spent for introducing variations in color and form into a drab home. The sparsity of objects and lack of diversity of utensils, furniture, and equipment in the home provide the disadvantaged child with few opportunities to manipulate and organize the visual properties of his environment. Lacking appropriate stimuli and individualized training (which a hard-pressed, tired working mother or disinterested baby-sitter is unlikely to provide), the slum child is handicapped in his efforts perceptually to organize and discriminate between the shadings and nuances of his environment. His playthings are likely to consist of a ball, broomstick, broken doll, and discarded kitchen pot, objects which lack the different shapes, colors, and sizes which the middle class child finds in brightly colored, multishaped blocks or the variety of cooking utensils available to him. Since success in reading depends upon the child's having the requisite form discrimination, visual spatial organization, and auditory discrimination, the limited stimulation and inadequate training which the disadvantaged child experiences during the preschool years ill prepares him for reading and academic learning in school.[7] There is considerable evidence that these deficits are difficult for the slum child to overcome.

While the language of the ghetto, rich in varied syntax and idiom, serves the disadvantaged child well for communicating with parents and peers, it is often a handicap in the performance of academic tasks in the traditional school. It will be recalled from Chapter 16 that Bernstein,[8] in his study of linguistic behavior in lower and middle class subjects, found that the language of lower class children tends to be "restricted" in form.[9] Language in restricted form serves to communicate signals and directions and to confine thinking to a low level of repetitiveness. The language of the middle and upper classes, on the other hand, is described as "elaborated" and serves to communicate ideas, relationships, feelings, and subjective states. The elaborative style of communication is more individualized and specific and provides a wide range of linguistic and behavioral alternatives in interpersonal interaction.

If the acquisition of language is a prerequisite for concept formation and problem solving, language deficiencies among disadvantaged children would appear to handicap them in acquiring the cognitive development that

---

[7] Martin Deutsch, "The Disadvantaged Child and the Learning Process," in A. H. Passow, ed., *Education in Depressed Areas* (New York: Bureau of Publications, Teachers College, Columbia University, 1963), pp. 163–179.

[8] Basil Bernstein, "Social Class and Linguistic Development," in A. H. Halsey, Jean Floud, and C. Arnold Anderson, eds., *Education, Economy, and Society* (New York: Free Press, 1961).

[9] See pp. 512–513.

is so important for academic learning. Several studies seem to confirm this. Deutsch[10] found that disadvantaged children are relatively proficient on motor tasks, on tasks which require a short attention span, and on tasks which involve concrete objects. They are apt to be poor, however, in abstract conceptualization and in the categorizing of visual stimuli. The Ausubels[11] found that when the acquisition of certain formal language forms is delayed, disadvantaged children and youth experience difficulty in making the transition from concrete to abstract modes of thought. The language patterns and concrete modes of thought of lower class children appear to limit reading achievement more than arithmetic achievement. The arithmetic scores of a group of black children aged seven to 10 in Prince Edward County, Virginia, who had been deprived of formal education for four years were higher than their reading scores.[12] These studies seem to support the observation that disadvantaged children tend to depend more on concrete than on symbolic experiences in learning concepts. Their perceptual styles and their linguistic modes appear to be either inadequate for or irrelevant to the academic demands of the traditional school.

Many have observed that lower class children appear to be less highly motivated for academic and vocational achievement than do their middle and upper class peers. Moreover, symbolic rewards and postponement of gratification seem to have limited value in motivating the child toward academic achievement. The low achievement motivation of lower class children reflects in part these children's perceptions of the limited opportunities and rewards available to them.

Important differences can be noted also between middle class and lower class children in their attitudes toward school and learning as well as their attitudes toward self and others. Lower class children and their parents tend to view education primarily in terms of its job market value, and their goal is achieving the minimum level of education needed for employment. In contrast to the popular stereotype, many lower class parents value education for their children, viewing education as a means of their children's escaping from poverty; but when the school, by its poor instruction and inadequate facilities, frustrates these aspirations of lower class parents, their attitudes toward the school become negative. Some evidence of self-deprecation and negative self-concepts on the part of lower class children has been noted by several writers,[13] but the evidence is equivocal. Moreover,

---

[10] Deutsch, pp. 163–179; also Martin Deutsch, *Minority Group and Class Status as Related to Social and Personality Factors in Scholastic Achievement*, Society for Applied Anthropology Monograph No. 2 (Ithaca, N. Y.: Cornell University, 1960).

[11] David P. Ausubel and Pearl Ausubel, "Ego Development among Segregated Negro Children," in Passow, *Education in Depressed Areas*, pp. 109–141.

[12] Edmund W. Gordon, "Educational Achievement in the Prince Edward County Free School" (New York: Ferkauf Graduate School of Education, Yeshiva University, 1965). Mimeographed.

[13] Regina Goff, "Some Educational Implications of the Influence of Rejection in Aspiration Levels of Minority Group Children," *Journal of Experimental Education*, 23 (December 1954), 179–183; R. M. Dreger and K. S. Miller, "Comparative Psychological

other studies[14] show little evidence of depressed self-concepts among disadvantaged children. Even where it is present, however, negative self-concept may not have an unfavorable influence on achievement, since positive or negative feelings of self-worth may operate respectively to depress or accelerate achievement.[15]

Teaching the Disadvantaged

Several first-hand accounts of teaching in ghetto schools[16] provide a general picture of the experiences encountered by the middle class teacher working with lower class children. Described are the disrepair of the buildings, the lack of proper books and equipment, the inadequate facilities, the frustrations of the teacher in trying to cope with hyperactive, apathetic, or unresponsive children, and the efforts of the children themselves to cover up their felt inadequacies for dealing with the requirements of the typical school program. While these accounts may not be representative of the school experiences of disadvantaged children, they do reflect the frustrations of teachers and children in ghetto schools in trying to achieve meaningful learning in the face of inadequate materials and facilities and inflexible school policies.

We noted earlier the language deficits and the preference for concrete thought that handicap disadvantaged children in achieving the level of academic performance expected of them in school. Several studies confirm the observation that disadvantaged children make progressively lower scores in IQ and have a slower rate of achievement in reading during successive years at school. Goldberg[17] found that the mean IQ scores of in-migrant Puerto Rican and black children in New York City were lower than those of these groups who were born in New York, but in-migrant and indigenous groups of both cultures experienced a loss in mean IQ of three to six points between the third and sixth grades. The mean IQs of other New York City children were initially higher and increased between the third and sixth grades. Similar trends were noted in mean reading achievement, with Puerto Rican and black children starting at or near grade level in reading

---

Studies of Negroes and Whites in the United States," *Psychological Bulletin,* 57 (September 1960), 361–402; S. Keller, "The Social World of the Urban Slum Child," *American Journal of Orthopsychiatry,* 33 (October 1963), 823–831.

[14] Gordon, "Educational Achievement in the Prince Edward County Free School"; also James S. Coleman et al., *Equality of Educational Opportunity,* OE 38001 (Washington, D. C.: U. S. Government Printing Office, 1966), p. 218.

[15] E. W. Gordon, "The Determination of Educatability," in Jerome Hellmuth, ed., *Disadvantaged Child,* Vol. 3 (New York: Brunner Mazel, 1970), 249–267.

[16] See Jonathan Kozol, *Death at an Early Age* (Boston: Houghton Mifflin Co., 1967); Herbert Kohl, *36 Children* (New York: New American Library, 1967); Sunny Decker, *An Empty Spoon* (New York: Harper & Row, 1969).

[17] Miriam Goldberg, "Factors Affecting Educational Attainment in Depressed Urban Areas," in Passow, *Education in Depressed Areas,* pp. 68–100.

in the third grade but falling behind (one year below grade level for blacks and two years below grade level for Puerto Ricans) when retested in the sixth grade. Similarly, a study of in-migrating blacks in Philadelphia revealed a steady improvement in IQ scores as length of residence in Philadelphia increased.[18]

These data and the observed lower achievement and apathy of many disadvantaged children have created the unfortunate impression in the minds of many middle class teachers, white and black, that lower class children in general cannot learn what the school is supposed to teach. Disadvantaged children often do perform poorly in a traditional academic curriculum for reasons that have already been noted. Many teachers in ghetto schools lack sensitivity and insight into the differences in needs and backgrounds of disadvantaged children compared to middle class children. Moreover, academic retardation, slow progress in school learning, and the disruptive behavior of some disadvantaged students frustrate and threaten the self-esteem of these teachers. They rationalize their lack of success with these children by concluding either that they cannot teach or that these children cannot learn. In any event, the natural inclination of these teachers is to escape from the ghetto school and its problems as soon as possible.

If the feeling that disadvantaged children cannot learn becomes fixed in teachers' minds, teachers are likely to respond to these children in terms of the "self-fulfilling prophecy." That is, teachers respond to these children as if they are unable to learn, and the children in turn come to believe they cannot learn and proceed to behave in a manner that confirms the teachers' expectations. In short, when teachers expect less, students learn less. This phenomenon was strikingly demonstrated in a study by Rosenthal and Jacobson,[19] who administered an IQ test at the beginning of the year to all six grades of an elementary school and then told the teachers that certain pupils were "late bloomers" and were expected to make an academic spurt during this year at school. Without informing the teachers or children, however, the selection of "late bloomers" was made randomly—that is, their selection bore no relationship to their test scores. When all the children were tested at the end of the school year, the "late bloomers" had made gains in IQ which exceeded the gains of other children in their classroom groups. The difference was particularly evident in the first and second grades, where about one half of the "late bloomers" gained 20 or more IQ points; only about one fifth of their classmates made similar gains. While the Rosenthal and Jacobson study has been criticized on methodological grounds,[20] other studies as well as personal observation leads us to suspect that teachers do treat children differently in accordance with their expectations and that children respond in ways that reinforce teachers' expecta-

[18] Everett S. Lee, "Negro Intelligence and Selective Migration: A Philadelphia Test of the Klineberg Hypothesis," *American Sociological Review*, 16 (1951), 227–233.

[19] Robert Rosenthal and Lenore Jacobson, *Pygmalion in the Classroom* (New York: Holt, Rinehart and Winston, 1968).

[20] See Robert E. Snow, "Unfinished Pygmalion," *Contemporary Psychology*, 14 (April 1969), 197–199.

tions. Brophy and Good,[21] after asking first grade teachers to rank the children in their classes according to their perceptions of each child's achievement, noted that teachers reinforced the correct answers of highs rather than lows, did more rephrasing of questions for highs, and gave them more hints. Wilkerson[22] reports on the enthusiasm generated in a fourth grade class of a ghetto school studying the history of black Americans. These fourth graders became excited about the story of John Brown's raid on Harpers Ferry and decided to plan their scheduled assembly program around this event. In the presentation, which was a big success, the principal was especially impressed with the performance of the black child who played John Brown. The principal seemed particularly nonplussed, however, when the teacher remarked with a deliberate touch of irony: "Oh, yes, he has an IQ of 80."

It seems likely, however, that the self-fulfilling expectations which teachers have of some students is not a universal phenomenon. It is probably more prevalent in some teachers than in others, and it likely has more adverse effects on the attitudes, achievement, and self-concepts of some students than others. Moreover, the effects of teacher expectations on student performance may be more crucial at certain times of the school year than at others. Teacher expectations probably exert a stronger influence on the teacher's responses to some children early in the school year, before the teacher has had an opportunity to observe and get to know students. It is clear that much more research is needed so that we can learn when and how teacher expectations become self-fulfilling and how a teacher can be helped to avoid or to correct his misperceptions of students.[23]

To be an effective teacher of disadvantaged children requires, first of all, that one genuinely accept these children and their cultural differences. Although many of these children enter school with language patterns which handicap their school achievement, it is important that the teacher believe in the children and treat them as being able to learn. A middle class teacher can increase his effectiveness in teaching lower class children by extending his knowledge of the language and culture of the lower class community. Some teachers in ghetto schools have increased their understanding of the children and community by planned visits to their pupils' homes and attendance at important cultural events and community celebrations. Finally, it is evident that major curriculum changes must be instituted in teaching these children. Curriculum content in ghetto classes should focus on topics that relate to the real life experiences of these children and should utilize concrete modes of thinking. Kozol,[24] for example, found that his fourth

[21] Jere E. Brophy and Thomas L. Good, "Teachers' Communication of Differential Expectations for Children's Classroom Performance: Some Behavior Data," *Journal of Educational Psychology*, 61 (October 1970), 365–374.

[22] Doxey A. Wilkerson, "Compensatory Education," in Sheldon Marcus and Harry N. Rivlin, eds., *Conflicts in Urban Education* (New York: Basic Books, 1970), pp. 19–39.

[23] Jere E. Brophy and Thomas L. Good, "Teacher Expectations: Beyond the Pygmalion Controversy," *Phi Delta Kappan*, 54 (December 1972), 276–278.

[24] Kozol, p. 189.

grade class in a ghetto school of Boston gained understanding and meaning from reading Langston Hughes' "Ballad of the Landlord." Fantini and Weinstein[25] report that role playing the meaning of such terms as *cool* and *jiving*, interpreting a passage written in "hip" language, discussing differences in skin color, and discussing practical uses of money are activities which elicit enthusiastic responses from disadvantaged children.

Programs for the Disadvantaged

A recognition of the language and experiential handicaps of disadvantaged children and their adverse influence on children's school achievement has led to the development of numerous intervention programs designed to raise the academic performance of these children. One approach, represented by the Harlem Youth project in New York City and the Banneker project in St. Louis, seeks to assist children already in slum schools to improve their performance. In Harlem crash programs in remedial reading were instituted, and extensive programs of cultural enrichment featuring trips to zoos, theaters, parks, and concerts were carried out. In the Banneker project the goal was to change the attitudes of teachers and parents as well as the attitudes and self-concepts of children themselves into believing that they can learn and succeed in school.[26]

In an effort to ascertain, if possible, the root causes of lower academic performance of disadvantaged children and youth, the federal government in 1965 conducted a massive study of equality of educational opportunity in the United States. Under the direction of James S. Coleman, a task force of researchers administered achievement tests and self-report questionnaires to approximately 600,000 children in grades one, three, six, nine, and 12 in about 4,000 schools which, while representative of public schools nationally, nevertheless had high enrollments of various groups of disadvantaged children.

The report[27] (known as the Coleman report) revealed that socioeconomic background is more important as a predictor of academic performance than is race. The higher the educational level of the parents (a rough indicator of social class status), the higher the achievement is likely to be of children of all backgrounds—white and black, rich and poor, urban and rural. The Coleman report shows that while the physical quality of the schools varies, it does not vary as much as was expected and does not have an appreciable effect on the achievement of children in these schools. The report does show, however, that minority group children score higher in

[25] Mario D. Fantini and Gerald Weinstein, *The Disadvantaged: Challenge to Education* (New York: Harper & Row, 1968), pp. 375–416.

[26] Kenneth B. Clark, *Dark Ghetto: Dilemmas of Social Power* (New York: Harper Torchbooks, 1965).

[27] James S. Coleman et al., *Equality of Educational Opportunity*.

academic performance when placed in racially integrated schools. The important factor contributing to high academic achievement of disadvantaged students is contact with peers from middle class families.

Further analyses of the Coleman study data have been made, and one study, by Jencks and his co-workers,[28] has aroused considerable comment and controversy. The main thrust of Jencks's argument is that the schools have failed to reduce differences among various socioeconomic, cultural, and racial groups in school achievement, and that this in large part has contributed to inequalities of adult incomes. Prior to the Coleman report and the enactment of massive federal aid-to-education programs in the mid-1960s, many people believed that the main reason poor children do not escape from poverty is that they do not acquire the basic cognitive skills which would enable them to get and keep a well-paid job. Hence, the solution seemed to lie in educational reform that would enable poor children to gain cognitive skills and put them on a more equal footing with middle class children. The findings of the Coleman report and the Jencks study seemed to invalidate these assumptions and the educational strategy derived from them. From these studies it was concluded: (1) The quality of the schools attended by black and white children in America is more nearly equal than anyone had supposed. (2) The gap between the achievement of black and white children becomes wider rather than narrower over 12 years at school. (3) Therefore, there is no reason to suppose that increasing the flow of resources into the schools will reduce differences in achievement, let alone eliminate inequalities in incomes among different social groups. Jencks concluded that only through noneducational policies of narrowing the gaps between family incomes is equality among individuals and groups likely to be achieved.

Jencks's conclusions have been challenged on many fronts.[29] Although he conceded that schools do have a role in the social development of children, the message that many draw from Jencks's conclusions is that much of what happens in school is not very important. Many question Jencks' contention that education should bear the major responsibility for bringing about greater equality among individuals and groups. To contend that schools should reduce inequalities in educational opportunities does not mean that education per se can or should make all people equal. Individual differences and inequalities among people can in some degree be reduced, but they cannot be eliminated. The purposes of education far transcend the inequality issue. Education is necessary and justifiable because it provides each individual, regardless of his station in life, with more opportunities for self-enhancement and fulfillment than he would have if educa-

---

[28] Christopher Jencks et al., *Inequality: A Reassessment of the Effect of Family and Schooling in America* (New York: Basic Books, 1972).

[29] See Philip W. Jackson, "After Apple Picking," *Harvard Educational Review*, 43 (February 1973), 51–60; Alice M. Rivlin, "Forensic Social Science," *Harvard Educational Review*, 43 (February 1973), 61–75; R. Edmonds, "A Black Response to Christopher Jencks's Inequality and Certain Other Issues," *Harvard Educational Review*, 43 (February 1973), 76–86; and Kenneth B. Clark, "Social Policy, Power, and Social Science Research," *Harvard Educational Review*, 43 (February 1973), 113–121.

tion were not available. In short, education is important to the individual and to society, regardless of the person's rank vis-à-vis others.

Although some early intervention programs in schools resulted in marked changes in attitudes and achievement, the greatest hope for increasing the academic performance of disadvantaged children appeared to center in an intensive program of language and developmental experiences for these children during the preschool years. A major response to this need was the introduction of the national Head Start program in 1965. The central focus of Head Start has been on preschool education, but the Child Development Centers sponsored by the program have been responsible for a comprehensive intervention program which also includes health services to children, social services to families, psychological services, nutritional services, and a parent participation program. The educational program, at first limited to the summer months and later extended to the academic year, emphasizes speaking, listening, the development of vocabulary, experiences for developing various sensory modalities, motor activities, and the broadening of cultural experiences through field trips and the like. The low adult-child ratio in Head Start classes provides many opportunities for an intensive, enriching experience.

Since no prescribed preschool program was required for Head Start projects, different models of programs were encouraged, tried out, and evaluated. Four of the better-known programs will be described: (1) the Institute of Developmental Studies approach of Martin Deutsch, (2) the Bereiter and Engelmann academically oriented preschool for disadvantaged children, (3) the Gray and Klaus Demonstration and Research Center in Early Education, and (4) the Montessori approach.

The approach of an early preschool intervention program at the Institute for Developmental Studies, New York City, developed by Martin Deutsch,[30] is based upon the developmental theories of Piaget, Hunt, Bruner, and Montessori. Sensorimotor, perceptual, and ideational aspects of experience in this program emphasize contact with concrete materials to foster the development of verbal labeling and perceptual discrimination. Language training is a part of every classroom activity. The child is called by his name at every opportunity, all classroom equipment is verbally labeled by the child, and the child is encouraged to use names in referring to people and objects. The teacher encourages the child to move from monosyllabic responses to more complex polysyllabic ones by requiring the child to describe the activities he would like to participate in. Children's self-concepts are enhanced by providing children with white and black dolls, telling stories of black children, and having each child view himself in a full-length mirror.

Bereiter and Engelmann[31] contend that disadvantaged children are handicapped because they have not had the formal experiences which pre-

---

[30] Martin Deutsch, *The Disadvantaged Child* (New York: Basic Books, 1967).

[31] Carl Bereiter and Siegfried Engelmann, *Teaching Disadvantaged Children in the Preschool* (Englewood Cliffs, N. J.: Prentice-Hall, 1966).

pare them for successful academic achievement at school. Their program consists of formal classroom experiences for four-year-old children which are designed to start the child at a low level of presumed initial knowledge and increase it rapidly and efficiently to the level of his first grade classmates. Small intensive classes in language, arithmetic, and reading are conducted daily. Language instruction centers on learning rules of language and logic, arithmetic instruction emphasizes counting and simple equations, and reading instruction emphasizes visual and auditory discrimination and recognition of words. Pattern drills are used, with children shouting the answers in unison. Positive reinforcement is used extensively. During two years' participation in this program, children made average gains of 1.5 to 2.5 years in language, arithmetic, and reading.

The Early Training Program of Gray and Klaus[32] at the George Peabody College for Teachers, Nashville, focuses on improving attitudes toward achievement and aptitudes for achievement. The program emphasizes extensive use of reinforcement. Much of the reinforcement is verbal, is focused on specific aspects of performance so the child will know what is expected of him, and is directed toward getting the child to explore and experiment. A major goal of the program is developing the child's need for achievement (*nAch*), accomplished by encouraging children to better their performances at home in games learned at school. Delay of gratification is encouraged by giving children many opportunities to choose between immediate and delayed rewards, to observe the consequences of delayed rewards, and to be reinforced immediately whenever delayed rewards are selected. Children exposed to these treatments showed immediate gains in IQ, which were maintained fairly well through the program. The IQs of the control group, on the other hand, declined during the same period. In subsequent testing, children in the experimental group maintained their higher mean IQ levels, but growth in IQ was at a slower rate. Improvement in performance, it will be noted, was due to changes effected in the child's motivational patterns instead of learning academic skills per se.

The Montessori approach is a structured program developed initially in 1907 by Maria Montessori,[33] an Italian educator, for preschool children from the slums of Rome. This approach uses didactic materials, gymnastics, and exercises aimed at enhancing language development, improving skills of perception and concentration, and refining manual skills. Montessori believed that children are capable of acquiring language, reading, and arithmetic skills before the age of six. Practice is given in developing the necessary skills and coordination for writing, which in turn provides the necessary training for reading. Her concept of sensitive periods which indicate a readiness for learning stresses the importance of offering training in various areas of learning at the earliest possible age.

[32] Susan W. Gray and R. A. Klaus, "The Early Training Project: A Seventh Year Report," *Child Development*, 41 (December 1970), 909–924.

[33] Maria Montessori, *The Montessori Method* (New York: Schocken, 1964).

The curriculum seeks to achieve a balance between manual and physical activity, between the concrete and the abstract, and between direct and vicarious experiences. Emphasis is upon discovery and self-education, upon process rather than the product of learning. Tasks of the Montessori school are designed to educate the senses, offer practice in observation, emphasize vocabulary work, encourage interest in science, and provide practice in numbers and calculation. The teacher must be adept at anticipating the child's needs. Repetition is a major element of the program, and the goal is perfection. The teacher guides the child toward this goal but does not show disapproval of what the child does incorrectly. Didactic material used in the classroom, some of which is breakable, provides continuous feedback to the child, thus assuring him opportunities for self-education. Although this program contrasts sharply with the other preschool programs which have been described, adherents to the Montessori method have established numerous Montessori schools in the United States and other countries.

Compensatory Education: Success or Failure?

In an effort to help disadvantaged children overcome the language and experience handicaps in making normal progress in school, numerous large-scale federally funded programs (such as Head Start, Follow Through, and Upward Bound) were initiated during the period 1965–1970. Although controlled studies of some of these projects show remarkable achievement gains by disadvantaged children and youth during the period of treatment, these gains are seldom maintained in follow-up testing. In the Westinghouse–Ohio University study,[34] for example, an evaluation of the achievement of children in first, second, and third grades who had had Head Start experience revealed that neither summer nor full-year Head Start programs had any significant long-term effects on the children's cognitive growth. In a few full-year Head Start centers, Head Start children's advantage in achievement over non-Head Start children persisted only to the end of first grade.[35] The report of the impact of Head Start concluded by recommending that more effective programs, procedures, and techniques be developed for remedying the effects of poverty on disadvantaged children.

Supporters of compensatory education, such as Wilkerson,[36] maintain that an adequate program of compensatory education has yet to be developed. The lack of success of many early programs has been attributed to

[34] Westinghouse Learning Corporation/Ohio University, *The Impact of Head Start* (Springfield, Va.: Clearinghouse for Federal Scientific and Technical Information, U. S. Department of Commerce, June 12, 1969).

[35] M. S. Smith and J. Bissell, "Report Analysis: The Impact of Head Start," *Harvard Educational Review*, 40 (February 1970), 51–104.

[36] Wilkerson, "Compensatory Education," in Marcus and Rivlin, *Conflicts in Urban Education*, pp. 19–39.

persistent stereotypes which suggest that academic retardation and failure result from the inability of poor children to make normal academic progress. Some have suggested that the ineffectiveness of compensatory education may be due in part to its failure to develop innovative methods and materials for disadvantaged children. In spite of well-documented differences in background between lower and middle class children, pupils from the ghetto still are exposed to methods, materials, and experiences which have little relevance for the children or the ghetto community from which they come. The task still before us is one of making boards of education and school personnel accountable for the outcomes of education and move with increased vigor toward providing a more humane, viable, and relevant education for all our children.

The Emotionally Disturbed Student

Symptoms of Emotional Disturbance

Of the many kinds of students who need special help, the emotionally disturbed child is one whom the teacher in a regular classroom frequently finds most difficult to understand. There are several reasons for this. First, emotional disturbance may be revealed in a variety of behaviors, many of which appear to be quite different from other symptoms of disturbance. For example, extreme submissiveness, withdrawal, and a compulsiveness for achieving perfection are frequently as much symptoms of emotional maladjustment as the more familiar evidences of antisocial behavior—persistent attention seeking, aggression toward others or toward self, rigid or grossly distorted perceptions and delusions, bizarre behaviors, self-hate, and fantasy. Second, some types of emotional disturbance in students may go unrecognized because of unresolved emotional conflicts which the teacher still carries within himself. The teacher with a strong dependency tie to a parent, for example, may not recognize the student's strong dependence on the teacher as a symptom of potential maladjustment.

The teacher's task of identifying and helping the emotionally disturbed student is further complicated by the fact that *disturbing* behavior (such as disrupting and attention seeking) does not in itself mean that the individual is emotionally disturbed. Aggressive or attention-seeking behavior may be a quite normal response to a stressful situation of limited duration or to changes in physical maturity. For example, the child who has a new sibling or who is not allowed by his peers to join in a game may respond with aggression, name calling, or regression to an earlier pattern of behavior. Scornful remarks, teasing, and uncontrollable giggling are a few of the quite normal but disturbing behaviors characteristic of each sex's response to members of the opposite sex during preadolescence.

How, then, can one distinguish between emotionally disturbed and relatively healthy children, both of whom behave at times in similar ways? Several criteria have been suggested to assist teachers in spotting the child who may be emotionally disturbed. Single or infrequent instances of aggression, giggling, or impertinence can be dealt with by a frown, a disapproving comment, humor, or temporary isolation from the group—whatever teacher response has in the past proven efficacious for eliminating the disturbing behavior for this student or group of students. Most children engage in disturbing antics at one time or another, but if appropriate action by the teacher causes the disturbing behavior to subside, it is unlikely to be considered a serious problem.

More serious or more significant disturbing behaviors may be manifested in one or a combination of ways.[37] *Repetitious behavior* is a symptom of deeper underlying tensions. Continued aggressiveness, distractions, or daydreaming require further psychological study and understanding. A serious *single disturbance* may reflect a severe maladjustment in the child or deeper disorder within the group. A severe temper tantrum or sharp drop-off in academic performance indicates a need for further study. Finally, a child may engage in a *succession of different disturbances* which may appear to be unrelated. For example, a child may be very tense and hyperactive on one day, continuously hitting and pushing other children the next day, and moody and withdrawn the following day. Each of these disturbing behaviors mirrors the same complex problem or frustration. A clinically oriented teacher may be able to assist a child manifesting the first two types of emotional disturbance, but a child exhibiting the third type of disturbance should be referred for professional help to a psychological clinic or trained therapist.

In addition to the characteristics and symptoms already cited, nearly all emotionally disturbed persons experience a high degree of anxiety. The sources and manifestations of this anxiety vary with each type of emotional disturbance. The neurotic child's anxiety centers in his psychic fear of the disaster he feels will follow if he is forced to give up his neurotic behavior pattern. The anxiety of the psychotic child, on the other hand, frequently relates to his confusion of identity, perceptual distortions, inability to separate real and unreal, and fear of survival in the face of a wide assortment of dangers he perceives around him. Many emotionally disturbed children also experience difficulty in controlling their instinctual drives and impulses. The inability of these children to delay gratification, to tolerate frustration of immediate desires, or to hold back their urges in favor of long-term goals contributes to their difficulties in learning situations.

Because the emotionally disturbed person must expend energy in coping with anxiety and controlling his impulses, he experiences a moderate to marked reduction in behavioral freedom which in turn reduces his

---

[37] Charlotte Buhler, Faith Smitter, and Sybil Richardson, *Childhood Problems and the Teacher* (New York: Holt, Rinehart and Winston, 1952).

ability to function effectively in learning or in working with others. This loss of freedom affecting the child's educative and social experiences may be manifested in any one or more of five patterns of behavior: [38]

1. *An inability to learn which cannot be adequately explained by intellectual, sensory, neurophysiological, or general health factors.*

2. *An inability to build or to maintain satisfactory interpersonal relationships with peers and teachers.*

3. *Inappropriate or immature types of behavior or feelings under normal conditions.*

4. *A general pervasive mood of unhappiness or depression.*

5. *A tendency to develop physical symptoms, such as speech problems, pains, or fears, associated with personal or school problems.*

After the teacher has distinguished between children who are normal but disturbing and children who are emotionally disturbed, he is faced with the need to learn more about the emotionally disturbed student he wishes to help.

Studying the Emotionally Disturbed

Disturbed behavior, like normal behavior, has many causes; hence, many of the principles of behavior introduced in earlier chapters also apply to the emotionally disturbed student. A major difference between normal and disturbed behavior is that the latter often appears to be more irrational. For this reason, the causes of disturbed behavior are often more difficult to unravel.

When seeking to identify causes of behavior, the teacher is cautioned to avoid the assumption that one has explained behavior if he has given it a label or described its symptoms. Subjective labels—"attention seeking," "mischievousness," "laziness," "belligerence," or "boredom"— provide little insight into disturbed behavior and offer little help in explaining its causes. Instead of citing symptoms, we should ask, "What are the possible reasons this child behaves in this manner?" *By labeling a behavior, one does not explain it.*

---

[38] Eli M. Bower and Nadine M. Lambert, "In-School Screening of Children with Emotional Handicaps," in Nicholas J. Long, William C. Morse, and Ruth G. Newman, eds., *Conflict in the Classroom* (Belmont, Calif.: Wadsworth Publishing Co., 1965), pp. 128–129.

Symptoms, however, do provide useful clues for understanding behavior. After the student's symptoms have been identified, teachers should evaluate the symptoms and test their relevance to assumed or known causes. By failing to evaluate symptoms, educators may, for instance, blame the home situation for chronic misbehavior that in fact is more closely related to the difficulty of academic work or to a lack of acceptance or understanding by teacher and peers. A key to interpreting and evaluating a behavioral symptom is the frequency and persistence with which a behavior pattern is used and its apparent effectiveness in enabling the individual to avoid or to cope with real or potential sources of threat.

Finally, prerequisite to understanding the emotionally disturbed child (as well as all human beings) is the accumulation, sifting, and analysis of a great deal of information about the child's past experiences and his present situation with respect to organic, interpersonal, cultural, and self factors. Because many of the real causes of behavior may be obscure, it is especially important that accurate, complete information be obtained. If one has adequate information, he is less likely to resort to oversimplified categorizations or labels. Collecting and having available valid information about an emotionally disturbed child is required if the teacher is to help him.

Helping the Emotionally Disturbed

Educators, parents, and community agencies have long recognized that existing psychological clinics, private therapists, and residential institutions can care for only a very small proportion of the severely maladjusted children and youth in this country. Since the school cannot depend upon clinics, professionals, and community agencies for treating the increasing number of emotionally disturbed children and youth, the school must develop its own programs and facilities for children who are unable to profit from learning activities in regular classrooms.

Cohen and LaVietes[39] suggest a number of ways of helping disturbed children through selective programing and modification of curriculum content. First of all, they point out, disturbed children have vague and distorted perceptions of time and often become anxious under pressure of time limits. Thus, the teacher's timing in the introduction and termination of activities, his use of time allotments and schedules, and his flexibility in adapting these to changing group needs influence the effectiveness of the learning situation and the child's ability to function in the group. Because of the brief attention spans, intolerance of frustration, and extreme emotional patterns of emotionally handicapped children, pacing and sequencing

---

[39] Rosalyn S. Cohen and Ruth LaVietes, "Clinical Principles in Curriculum Selection," in Jerome Hellmuth, ed., *Educational Therapy*, Vol. 1 (Seattle: Seattle Seguin School, 1966), pp. 139–154. Material describing curricula and programs for the emotionally disturbed is used with permission.

of activities are essential for their effective learning. For example, introducing a quiet, structured activity such as handwriting after an active lunch period helps to reduce tension and anxiety in the classroom. Sudden or abrupt transitions from one activity to another is another source of tension for these children. Tension may arise from the child's inability to detach himself from what he is doing, his fear of the unfamiliar, or the effects of frequent changes in activity. Providing simple, nonchallenging, repetitive activities such as singing or coloring books and maintaining emotional contact with children prevents disorganization and makes the transitions between learning activities smoother.

The use of repetition and the maintenance of routines are especially important for stabilizing the world of the disturbed child. Routines, such as following a schedule or returning things to their assigned places, enable the child to order his world and provide him an opportunity to become comfortable with his environment.

High sensitivity to intense auditory or visual stimulation is characteristic of children who are emotionally disturbed. Thus, by endeavoring to control sensory input, the teacher is able to minimize distractions that could arouse impulsive behavior. At the same time, emotionally disturbed children tend to show strong preferences for specific sensory modalities and to distort many sensory experiences. By gradually exposing the child to other modalities, the teacher may help to minimize such a child's sensory distortions.

Some emotionally disturbed children cannot distinguish between fantasy and reality or become preoccupied with one particular fantasy for long periods. Curriculum materials which help such children to distinguish between fantasy and reality serve to minimize the limiting effects of perceptual distortion and inadequate cognitive functioning. Moreover, since the styles of thinking of disturbed children are either overly abstract or overly concrete, the teacher should become acquainted with each child's style of thinking and its limitations and help the child to acquire a more effective style.

Since emotionally disturbed children often lack a sense of curiosity, they sometimes have difficulty comprehending things unrelated to their past experience and distinguishing between the possible and the impossible. Science activities most likely to be stabilizing to the emotionally disturbed child are those related to the child's immediate life experience and containing constructive rather than destructive elements and ideas. The study of weather and the seasons, for example, may be more appropriate for the disturbed child than studies of lightning, earthquakes, and volcanoes. Art, music, dramatic play, and physical education also have potential for assisting seriously disturbed children to clarify their feelings, but, again, content and activities must be carefully planned to prevent overstimulation and anxiety-arousing associations.

The principles summarized above may appear to be most relevant to the task of working with groups or classes of emotionally disturbed students. Yet, for the teacher in a regular classroom who may have only one or two such students, these principles contain important suggestions. How might a regular classroom teacher work with a student whose emotional problems complicate his adjustment and hinder his learning in school? One approach is revealed in excerpts from the case of Herb Hendricks:

Herb Hendricks is 15 and in the seventh grade. Herb's height is 63 inches, and he weighs 100 pounds. He is of slight build and is exceedingly energetic. His eyes are dark brown and very expressive, as is his entire countenance. He has an older sister and a younger brother. His father is a mechanic, but his mother does not work outside the home.

At age six, Herb contracted polio and was hospitalized for several months. His record shows that during a medical examination he was irritable, nervous, talked all the time, and had no goals. Last year, the medical record stated that Herb has a typical behavior problem and recommended that he attend a mental hygiene clinic. This has been complied with. Last year, results on the Otis Mental Ability Test revealed Herb had an IQ of 104 and his achievement was at grade level for all subjects except reading and language, which were above grade level.

This description, written by a former teacher, is found in the cumulative record: "Herb has real ability, but he is careless and irresponsible. He contracted polio several years ago. There are no physical handicaps as a result, but he is terrifically spoiled and his mother is under the impression that it has left him with several nondescript ailments. He has had little discipline at home, and this naturally shows up in his school life. He is easily led into mischief and is prone to carry even a casual joke too far."

Last year Herb encountered a great deal of difficulty in adjusting satisfactorily to junior high school. Finally, he became disturbed to the extent that it became advisable for him to discontinue his formal education. Previously, I taught Herb in the sixth grade and discovered his challenging and interesting individuality. My principal motive in selecting him for study is my sincere hope that by careful observation it will be possible to assist in enabling him to become a more intelligent and responsible citizen.

Herb returned to school this year and was placed in section 7C. It seems he formed several acquaintances in the group which were not too desirable. As a result of this, the progress of the entire section was retarded due to the personal attention which they required. At the conclusion of five weeks of school, his homeroom teacher suggested that he be transferred to 7A in hopes that he would react more favorably with new associates.

October 21.   This evening the 7A section was dismissed and several of the boys and girls remained after school to talk with me.

After conversing with them for approximately 15 minutes, I suddenly noticed that Herb was still sitting in his seat. No one was near him, and he looked terribly dejected. I ventured no comment, and finally he came up to my desk with measured steps. Very abruptly he stated, "Did you know that I missed my bus?"

"No, I didn't realize that," I responded. "Have you a reason for remaining?"

"Yes, I want to talk to you," he said. He then inquired, "Did you know they were getting up a petition to get me kicked out of this section?"

I had overheard some discussion of this. I asked, "Why do you think they are doing this? When you entered this room we decided that you were going to begin a new record."

Herb remained perfectly motionless, and I saw tears creeping into his eyes. Suddenly he burst out, "Well, I did make up my mind to do that, but I don't know, I went back to my classes and every teacher seemed to have her eyes on me. No matter what happened I was always blamed for it, so I decided that if they were looking for trouble, I would give it to them."

After a few moments silence I continued, "Do you think perhaps it would be a good idea for your mother to come to school and meet all of your teachers?"

He smiled and replied, "Yes, tomorrow."

October 23.   The question was raised in our faculty meeting as to how profitable Herb's continuance in school was. The viewpoint of the specialized instructors was that the progress of the entire class was impeded by his insistence upon becoming the constant center of attention. They expressed the feeling that what he was acquiring was too minor to warrant the deducted time from the group. I suggested a conference in two weeks with Mrs. Hendricks and each of his instructors.

October 27.   Mrs. Hendricks came to school this afternoon. Herb was enthusiastic as he ushered her into the room. He waited downstairs while we conversed. Mrs. Hendricks asked, "Don't you believe Herb is settling down better this year?"

I responded, "Yes, but more improvement is desirable."

Proceeding to tell me about his visit to the mental health clinic, she said, "Herb told me there wasn't anything wrong with him, but he thought someone should examine the doctor because he asked him such dumb questions." After this statement Mrs. Hendricks laughed heartily and continued, "You know, I wish Herb wouldn't mix with that awful gang over our way. It was just by luck that he wasn't with them when they broke into all those places." Just at this moment one of Herb's teachers came up the hall and I invited her in to confer with Mrs. Hendricks. The instructor related numerous incidents in which Herb had been exceedingly arrogant and defiant.

Mrs. Hendricks said, "I know Herb is quite emotional and high-strung because he is that way at home."

Herb came back to the room and his mother inquired, "When shall I contact you again?"

"Every two weeks," Herb said. Then he put his arm around her and said, "Don't you think my Mom is cute? Dad sure is lucky!"

October 28.   We decided this morning to elect the person most suitable for our announcer in the Thanksgiving Assembly. Herb spoke to me several days ago and desired some part in the program. The class enumerated the necessary qualities for this position, and I particularly emphasized the requirement of a voice which would carry in the auditorium. This is difinitely one of Herb's assets, and the class recognized it by electing him with a great majority. When he was informed that he would be our announcer, his eyes sparkled and he smiled broadly as he slid into his seat.

November 12.   Mrs. Hendricks came to school today. After exchanging casual greetings, she immediately inquired, "Have you heard any of those tales about Herb?"

I responded, "He spoke to me about an incident yesterday evening, but other than that I know nothing about it."

Quickly, she continued, "Well, I am going to speak to the principal about the matter. Everyone will think that I don't care what becomes of him. Whenever he isn't home by nine o'clock I begin calling about the neighborhood for him." Mrs. Hendricks proceeded down to the office and met me later in the cafeteria for lunch. She informed me that Herb was encountering special difficulty with several faculty members, so I suggested that she meet with them and discuss the problem. Approximately a half hour later, Mrs. Hendricks returned to my room practically in tears. She was so upset that she requested smoking privileges three times and was of course refused. Apparently Mrs. Hendricks did not use much psychology in conversing with the instructors. She informed one of them that Herb referred to her as his enemy number one. The expression which she used to describe the teacher's reaction to this statement was she "blew her top" and declared that "the feeling was mutual." I then said, "I will go down and take the math class so that you can meet with this faculty member also."

November 19.   We had a practice this morning for our Thanksgiving Assembly. I was quite discouraged yesterday with Herb's performance, but before going home he faithfully reassured me of vast improvement today. The curtains opened and all eyes were anxiously awaiting the arrival of Herb. Members of the chorus turned around and looked at me, but I ventured no comment. Finally, Herb came swaggering out on the stage swinging his arms and click-

ing his heels together. He continued to walk up to the very edge of the stage and as he spoke he balanced himself there like Humpty Dumpty. As he returned backstage, he waved gaily to one of his friends sitting down in the chorus. During the rehearsal of the play, I saw his mischievous eyes peering through the window curtains and his head ducking around the corner of the supposedly closed door.

When we returned to the classroom, one of the pupils raised his hand and said, "I think we should elect another announcer." Herb looked up and was obviously quite startled. I inquired, "All of those in favor of electing another announcer please raise your right hands." Practically the entire class affirmed this. We proceeded with our election. I particularly noticed that Herb cast his vote, but that his eyes were stormy and his lips were firmly compressed.

The patterns revealed in these excerpts continued throughout the year that Herb was studied by Miss Preston. Herb continued behaving in ways that brought him into conflict with teachers, principal, and peers. He disrupted play rehearsals and classes with his antics on numerous occasions and was suspended from school after he and two of his friends were truant and were picked up by the police hitchhiking to Baltimore. His mother continued to come to school periodically to confer with his teachers, but there is little evidence that her perceptions and attitudes or those of the teachers changed as the result of these conferences. Miss Preston made two visits to Herb's home, where she was warmly received by Herb and his parents. The parents were aware of Herb's difficulties, but took little positive action to help him to improve. Instead, they expressed the hope that he would outgrow his problems. Miss Preston maintained her calm, nonjudgmental acceptance of Herb while using every opportunity to help him examine his feelings and analyze the effects of his behavior on others. Her acceptance of Herb as a person resulted in a temporary reduction of antisocial behavior. Before long, however, the disturbing behavior recurred.

Yet there are several positive factors which suggest a favorable prognosis for Herb. He has a normal IQ and his achievement is at grade level. He appears to feel secure in his family and with Miss Preston, and Miss Preston has made some progress in enlisting aid in helping him from other teachers.

One might expect that frequent conferences between Herb's mother and his teachers would lead to greater understanding of Herb and a positive change in his behavior. However, Mrs. Hendricks continued to indulge Herb and continued to be unable to comprehend the seriousness of his problem. By reason of this kind of lack of understanding, it is of the utmost importance that the parent receive professional counseling at the same time as the child.

It appears that a small special class under a teacher skilled in working with maladjusted students might permit Herb to make greater progress in development and learning than he would in a regular schedule of junior high school classes. Newman[40] describes an experimental program of re-education for a group of six boys, ages eight to 10, who were far more seriously disturbed and hyperaggressive than Herb. This study sought to ascertain whether severely disturbed, hyperaggressive children of normal intelligence and with no perceptible organic damage can learn more effective patterns of psychological adjustment. The first task of the reeducation program was to help the boys unlearn the damaging experiences and responses of their past. The teachers, in attempting to be as accepting and permissive as possible, said to the boys, "This is not your old school; it is different. We like you here; we will help you if you will let us. No matter what you do, you will not be expelled." The activities of the experimental school program included block building, games, cutting out pictures, and puppetry, as well as reading, writing, and arithmetic. If a boy was unable to continue an activity during class, a new activity was started, and he was given individual help. He was not removed from the class so long as his disruptiveness did not break up the school activity. To satisfy the boys' needs for individual attention, their need for skills, and their need not to expose their scholastic inadequacies before peers, individual tutoring was used. Evaluations of the boys' daily classroom behavior revealed that during the two-year period of reeducation, five of the six boys developed more positive self-pictures, greater ability to cope with fears and to postpone gratification of infantile needs, and more positive relationships with adults and peers. Thus, the primary goal of teaching this type of severely disturbed, hyperaggressive student—that is, altering his perceptions of himself, his environment, and the people in his environment—was achieved.

Helping Teachers of the Emotionally Disturbed

A variety of programs have been developed to assist teachers in working with emotionally disturbed students and to promote mental health in the regular classroom. Newman and her associates[41] describe a comprehensive program of "technical assistance" which provides on-the-spot help for teachers who are baffled, frustrated, and discouraged in their efforts to help one or more emotionally disturbed children. Consultants providing technical assistance can be called into a school or classroom to help with a problem involving a specific child or group of children. For instance, a consultant was called in to help a teacher who lost her temper when Billy

---

[40] Ruth G. Newman, "Changes in Learning Patterns of Hyperaggressive Children," in Long, Morse, and Newman, *Conflict in the Classroom*, pp. 446–453; Ruth G. Newman, "A Study of the Difficulties of Hyperaggressive, Emotionally Disturbed Children in Adjusting to School and in Deriving Satisfying Learning Experiences from School" (unpublished doctor's dissertation, University of Maryland, 1957).

[41] Ruth G. Newman et al., "Technical Assistance," report of the Washington School of Psychiatry, Washington, D. C., 1964. Summary used by permission.

interrupted her lesson for the fourth time by bursting out with loud cat-
calls. Her loss of control was unbecoming, and she felt that she had
alienated other students in the class. She was filled with chagrin and self-
loathing. The consultant, after breaking through the teacher's defensive-
ness, communicated to her the following facts:

1.   *Losing one's temper might have been a mistake in that instance,
     but it was a very human mistake.*

2.   *Nothing was gained for Billy or herself in doing so and some-
     thing might have been temporarily lost in her relationship with
     the class.*

3.   *Billy needs limits.*

4.   *The time to tackle Billy was the second catcall, not the fourth,
     before Billy got out of bounds completely and before the
     teacher had reached her level of frustration.*

5.   *Records and reports of Billy's behavior with other teachers
     point to the possibility that Billy did this because he wanted
     attention and because he was conveying a message that the
     work was too hard for him at that given moment. Rather than
     be called on and appear dumb to his classmates, he was break-
     ing up the class.*

The teacher gave the consultant important information about Billy.
The consultant, in turn, supported the teacher's observations and efforts to
deal with the situation and helped the teacher gain insight into other
methods and materials that could be used to influence Billy's behavior and
improve his opportunities for achievement. After a careful review of the
situation, teacher and consultant together planned ways the teacher could
help Billy and reestablish rapport with the class.

Morse[42] offers another plan for helping teachers who have emotionally disturbed children in their classrooms. He suggests that each
school include on its staff a "crisis teacher" who would work with pupils
whose behavior exhausts the teacher and prevents other students from
learning. Thus, the crisis teacher is a resource immediately available when
a deterioration in classroom deportment and learning occurs. He is available not only to teachers but also to individual pupils. His work with individual pupils may involve tutoring, an informal talk, a diversionary activity,
or an intensive life space interview. What the crisis teacher does is what
any teacher would want to do were it possible to act on the basis of the
needs of the individual child rather than the large-group learning process.

[42] William C. Morse, " 'The Crisis Teacher,' Public School Provision for the Disturbed Pupil," *The University of Michigan School of Education Bulletin,* 37 (April 1962),
101–104.

Morse emphasizes that the crisis teacher can be effective only to the degree that the entire staff of the school is concerned about understanding and helping the deviant child.

The Underachiever

The problem of high-ability students who do not achieve at levels commensurate with their potential has been for many years the focus of considerable concern on the part of educators. For more than half a century, periodic assessments of intellectual aptitude and school achievement by standardized measures of large populations of students have provided data useful in effecting improvements in individual and group learning and in modifying educational programs. These assessments have often shown, however, a wide disparity between intelligence scores and achievement measures for a great number of students, students who have become known as underachievers. In general, an *underachiever* can be defined as a student whose academic performance, judged by either grades or achievement test scores, is markedly below his measured or demonstrated aptitude for academic achievement.[43]

The phenomenon of underachievement, especially among high-ability students, is particularly baffling to teachers and parents because it seems so illogical that students with high measured ability should not necessarily perform at least moderately well in school. The finding that many students do not perform academically in a manner commensurate with their mental abilities lends further support to the proposition that academic performance, like human behavior in general, is the product of many varied and complex forces. This conclusion was expressed by Bowman: "The characteristics that distinguish the underachiever are not superficial ones; they involve the deepest roots of a personality."[44]

Family Backgrounds of Achievers and Underachievers

The importance of family and cultural factors in behavior and development noted in earlier chapters leads one to expect that unfavorable family and cultural factors are related to underachievement. Research tends to confirm this. Families of underachieving students are generally lower in socioeconomic status than are families of achievers. High-achieving

[43] Leonard M. Miller, ed., *Guidance for the Underachiever with Superior Ability*, OE-25021 (Washington, D. C.: Office of Education, U. S. Department of Health, Education, and Welfare, 1961), p. 15.

[44] Paul H. Bowman, "Factors Related to Scholastic Underachievement" (Quincy, Ill.: Quincy Youth Development Project, undated). Mimeographed.

students, more frequently than low-achieving students, name their fathers as having been an important influence in their lives. The high achiever, in contrast to the underachiever, is more frequently the first-born or an only child. Mothers of high achievers, in contrast to mothers of low achievers, place a higher value on imagination, hold higher educational expectations for their children, and perceive their children as more independent and responsible.[45]

Social, ethnic, and religious family differences are also related to differences in children's achievement motivation and academic performance. Strodtbeck,[46] who investigated the influence of family interaction and values on achievement, motivations, and self-perceptions of Jewish and Italian adolescent boys, found that the Jewish family's values encourage higher achievement than do the Italian family's values. In families of both cultures, where a strong father dominates the son, the son may feel that he faces forces beyond his control. He may give up and not try to achieve.

Achievers' and Underachievers' Perceptions of Parents

One might expect that achieving students would perceive themselves as more accepted and valued by parents, while underachieving students would perceive themselves as less valued, but the evidence on this point is neither consistent nor conclusive. Morrow and Wilson[47] found that high achievers more often than underachievers described their parents as approving, trusting, affectionate, and encouraging (but not pressuring), and described themselves as accepting their parents' standards. Both achievers and underachievers in Morrow and Wilson's study, however, expressed considerable respect and affection for their parents, described their parents' relationships as relatively harmonious, and stated that they were neither seriously overprotected nor excessively pressured to achieve.

A somewhat different view of parents was expressed by students in a study by Williams.[48] High achievers reported that their parents exerted strong pressures on them to perform well academically, to maintain strict standards, and to obtain needed help from parents and siblings. Although parents did punish them by withholding privileges, these children felt that

---

[45] J. V. Pierce, *Educational Motivation Patterns of Superior Students Who Do and Do Not Achieve in High School*, Cooperative Research Project No. 208 (Washington, D. C.: Office of Education, U. S. Department of Health, Education, and Welfare, 1960).

[46] Fred L. Strodtbeck, "Family Interaction, Values, and Achievement," in D. C. McClelland et al., eds., *Talent and Society* (Princeton, N. J.: D. Van Nostrand Co., 1958), pp. 135–195.

[47] William R. Morrow and Robert C. Wilson, "Family Relations of Bright High Achieving and Underachieving High School Boys," *Child Development*, 32 (September 1961), 501–509.

[48] B. B. Williams, "Identifying Factors Relating to Success in School" (Rochester, N. Y.: West Irondequoit Central School, April 20, 1962). Mimeographed.

their parents trusted and had faith in them and encouraged them to be independent and responsible. In contrast, underachievers perceived in their relationships with their parents a lack of firmness and strictness and reported unfavorable parental comparisons with successful siblings. Underachievers also reported conflict with parents over school matters, a feeling of a lack of praise and support from parents, and little feeling of independence.

Sex Differences in Achievement

Underachievement in one's sex group is a very different phenomenon for boys than for girls. Haggard[49] found that boys develop greater proficiency in abstract reasoning and using linguistic symbol systems, while girls seem to develop greater facility in use of the tangible, rule-bound skills associated with spelling and language. Research on problem solving, however, shows that while, in general, males are superior to females in problem solving, the more appropriate the problem is to the subject's sex role, the more the sex differences are diminished.[50]

The general superiority of girls over boys in academic achievement during elementary school and high school, especially in language, has been attributed to a variety of reasons. It has been suggested that girls' earlier physical maturation is one advantage. Pierce[51] suggests, however, that differing cultural expectations for boys and girls may provide a more comprehensive explanation for sex differences in achievement. In middle class culture, girls are required to be more conforming than boys, and, by conforming in social behavior and school tasks, girls achieve earlier and more readily. Furthermore, the fact that most teachers are women, especially in the elementary school, means that girls can identify more readily than boys with the teacher and her values.

Differences in Motivation and Cognitive Style

Some studies have found a close relationship between achievement motivation and scholastic achievement, while other studies have found low correlations between these variables. In interviews with students, Williams[52] found that high achievers held high internalized standards and goals for

---

[49] Ernest A. Haggard, "Socialization, Personality, and Academic Achievement in Gifted Children," *The School Review*, 65 (1957), 388–414.

[50] G. A. Milton, "Sex Differences in Problem Solving as a Function of Role Appropriateness in the Problem Content," *Psychological Reports*, 5 (1959), 705–708.

[51] Pierce, *Educational Motivation Patterns of Superior Students*.

[52] Williams, p. 16.

school success and tremendous inner pressure to compete and to succeed coupled with strong feelings of guilt when they did not do their homework. All the students interviewed agreed that the inner pressure stemmed from their parents. Underachievers, on the other hand, reported difficulty in accepting increased responsibility for their own learning, a loss of closeness to the teacher when changing teachers, and a lack of inner goal, occupation orientation, and serious intention of going to college. Many enjoyed reading, but not school-assigned reading. Other studies[53] have found that high-achieving and overachieving boys express a greater need for the value of achievement than do high- and overachieving girls and underachieving boys and girls. Another study[54] found that high achievers in high school regard college as preparation for graduate school and a professional career, while underachievers view college as direct vocational preparation.

Overachievers and underachievers also differ in their cognitive styles and their approaches to learning tasks. Overachievers, in contrast to under-achievers, are more empirical and excel in tasks where rote memory is useful or required. The relationships they see between objects and events are based on frequency of occurrence rather than on common attributes. Instead of formal analysis, they rely on past experiences in approaching new problems. Underachievers, on the other hand, are more analytic and more abstract in their cognitive activity, more prone to dig under the surface of a problem, and more likely to organize events in terms of formal characteristics.[55]

Differences in Self-Perceptions and Adjustment

Achievers and underachievers reveal markedly different perceptions of themselves and the school situation. Underachievers report that they are unable to do well in the classroom if their teacher does not organize well, dislikes them, ignores them, or if the teacher himself is disinterested in the subject. They are embarrassed in front of teachers, concerned about their reputations, and anxious whenever new material is not covered in class and they have to learn it for themselves at home. Achievers, on the other hand, report that they keep studying and trying even though the teacher is boring, has discipline problems, or is disinterested in his subject. They report that getting good grades is not always related to what is learned.[56] Achievers are

[53] J. V. Pierce, *Sex Differences in Achievement Motivation*, Cooperative Research Report No. 1097 (Washington, D. C.: Office of Education, U. S. Department of Health, Education, and Welfare, 1962); Jerome S. Bruner and A. J. Caron, "Cognition, Anxiety, and Achievement in the Preadolescent," paper read at the American Psychological Convention, 1959.

[54] E. Frankel, "A Comparative Study of Achieving and Underachieving High School Boys of High Intellectual Ability," *Journal of Educational Research*, 53 (1960), 172–180.

[55] Bruner and Caron, "Cognition, Anxiety, and Achievement in the Preadolescent."

[56] Williams, p. 15.

somewhat more stable and confident than underachievers, and they score higher on tests of creativity.[57]

Studies of self-concept and achievement reported in Chapter 8 reveal that underachievers generally have less adequate self-concepts than do achievers. Underachieving boys, in particular, view themselves as inadequate, passive, reckless, mischievous, restless, and powerless to improve or change the situation. Raph, Goldberg, and Passow[58] found that high and low achievers do not differ significantly in self-estimates with respect to personal and social abilities and characteristics. They do, however, differ significantly on school-related or task-oriented items—suggesting that underachieving youths appraise realistically the discrepancy between their ability and their performance. There is also a tendency for high school underachievers to evaluate themselves as "pretty average" or "about like others." Seeing themselves as having higher ability holds little attraction, for this seems to promise only the dubious reward of higher expectations, which they feel themselves unable to fulfill, regardless of the effort they expend.

These studies also show that underachievers repeatedly identify a particular teacher as the cause of their failure. In addition to blaming teachers, however, underachievers also blame themselves. They say, for example, "If I just studied more . . . if I weren't so lazy . . . if I applied myself, I could do it." When asked for their reasons for not applying themselves, underachievers seem to be at a loss: "I keep on telling myself I'm going to try to do my best. But when the time comes, well, I get in trouble, and I can't help it. I don't know." It appears that irrational factors are operative and that some underachievers are unable to function effectively even when they try.

The studies reviewed above present a highly generalized and incomplete picture of the underachiever. What is an underachiever really like? Consider the case of Jeff, as seen through the eyes of his teacher:

> *Jeff is 11 years old and is repeating the fifth grade. His IQ in the second grade on the California Test of Mental Maturity was 105 and on another form of the same test in the fourth grade his IQ was 99. Results of the California and Stanford Achievement tests show him to be from one to two grade levels below fifth grade in most subjects. His father is a polisher in a local industrial plant, and his mother is a paint sprayer. Both of his parents have a high school education. He has two older sisters, one entering eighth grade and the other a sophomore in high school.*
>
> *Last year's teacher made the following entry in Jeff's perma-*

---

[57] Department of Special Services Staff, Champaign, Illinois, "Factors Associated with Underachievement and Overachievement of Intellectually Gifted Children," *Exceptional Children*, 28 (1961), 167–175.

[58] Jane B. Raph, Miriam L. Goldberg, and A. H. Passow, *Bright Underachievers* (New York: Teachers College Press, Columbia University, 1966), pp. 181–183.

nent record: "Jeff is an extremely nervous boy. He cannot force himself to be still and always has his mind on something other than his studies. Though he always appears cheerful, I feel that he is extremely unhappy. He has often indicated that the other children do not like him, yet he goes out of his way to be a good sport. He has an exceptional sense of humor for his age and has a good mind. He daydreams frequently, at which times he appears sad. His feelings are easily hurt and he cries easily. Both parents are extremely concerned, and both work, and Jeff, seeking companionship, has gotten into several theft and vandalism problems after school."

September 30.   *In my month's observation I have found him looking out of the window much of the time, even though his seat is on the opposite side of the room from the windows. I have had to remind him to watch his book when we are checking spelling or reading workbooks. Often I ask his opinion on a subject being discussed, then see him search his books to find what we are talking about. He has several times been kept after school because of disobeying one rule or another, usually for talking boisterously or not finishing work. He chews gum whenever he can get by with it.*

October 12.   *I was giving the individualized oral reading test furnished by the* Weekly Reader *magazine to all class members. When Jeff read to me, he read fairly well. When I questioned him about the main ideas he remembered all that he had read. I praised him for his performance and he just sat still in his seat, with slightly flushed face showing that he had heard me.*

November 2.   *Today we were studying our* Weekly Reader *and one of the news items was about water skiing. Jeff paid close attention to this item although he had been looking out of the window up to this time. He volunteered the information that his father was an expert water skier. He said he goes to Cherokee Lake and can really do a lot of tricks on his skis. I remembered now how his first grade teacher had told of how much he talked about his father and of how proud he seemed to be of his father.*

November 21.   *This morning I mentioned to Jeff that tonight was PTA and the night for the conference with his parents. He quickly said, "Miss Terrell, they won't come. They never come to PTA." I suggested that he remind them of the date anyway.*
     Jeff's parents came tonight, even arriving 10 minutes early for their conference. I showed them his achievement record and told them I was sure he knew more than the achievement scores reflected, but I thought it possible that Jeff had not kept his mind on the test when taking it. I pointed out that in his oral reading to me and consequent answering of questions he registered very good understanding and had a good memory for facts. His mother said she had asked

him to read to her at home and he had little trouble with the words, and she, too, thought he understood what he was reading. We discussed his dreaminess, and the parents said that had been his trouble in other years.

His mother said Jeff was much interested in science and liked to read about that. She said he seemed to like our changing classes as we do in the subject block system this year. She said that practice would get the youngsters ready for later years in junior high. Both parents thanked me for letting them come in the evening, as they said last year they had taken off work to come in the daytime and it was more convenient this way. They did not remain for the PTA meeting.

December 1.   *In English we were studying outlining to give good reports orally. We had the beginning of an outline in our books which was to be finished. As I checked around the room, I noticed that Jeff was including items not in the story in the book. I asked him where he got those items. He said, "Well, they show in the picture!" I checked and found that he was quite right.*

December 5.   *Jeff's grades for the past six weeks in my room were as follows: Reading D, Writing C⁻, Spelling C, English D⁺. The social studies teacher gave me grades for him of C in geography and D in history. The math-science teacher has not yet reported. In the last six weeks he dropped one letter in reading, spelling, and almost two grades in English. He remained the same in writing and geography and came up one letter in history. His English grade was low because of his not learning a poem, making a book report, or correcting wrong assignments. The requirements were heavier than last time.*

December 9.   *When Jeff received his grade card, he asked me why he had gotten a D in reading. I had already explained his grades to him before, but he must not have remembered about the D. I got out my grade book and showed him that all of his* Weekly Reader *quizzes had been F, his workbook was unsatisfactory, and his seatwork exercise totals had given him an average score of 56 percent. Then I explained that I had raised the grade, really, because I knew that his oral work was better than F and I had given him the benefit of what he knew generally. He had a serious expression on his face all the time I was talking. When I finished, he nodded, but turned away very slowly. He did not question his English grade, but I had also explained that to him earlier in the week.*

I asked him to keep at his work steadily, not letting himself get lost in thought. I told him it was my belief that he forgot to keep at his work, then realized he was not getting done and would hurry through his workbook pages just to get done and did not really try hard. He nodded slightly and went out of the room.

March 16.   *Lately I have had a struggle with Jeff when I have insisted that he keep his desk free of notes to girls. Mrs. R., a sixth grade teacher, related that some of the mothers of girls in our rooms are taking them by car to the theater and leaving them there, not realizing that inside the girls meet several boys who sit with them, hold hands, kiss them, cuddle up to them, and so on. These boys are from their school class, and Jeff is one of them.*

By accident, someone on Jeff's telephone line lifted the receiver and heard a conversation Jeff had with Genevieve, one of his girl friends.

Jeff: *Do you love me?*

Genevieve: *Yes.*

Jeff: *Do you love me a whole lot?*

Genevieve: *Yes, sure.*

Jeff: *Tonight my folks are going away, and I want you to come over. Then you can really show me if you love me or not.*

Jeff went on to say, "Oh, the things we can do!" Mrs. R. said the whole conversation was very suggestive.

These excerpts describe an underachiever who probably does not have high ability. It appears that Jeff has a long history of daydreaming and not completing his work. His parents appear cooperative, but not deeply concerned. We can make hypotheses about Jeff's poor school performance, but the record reveals few clues pointing to the likely causes for Jeff's low achievement.

Helping the Underachiever

Unfortunately, little research has been devoted to the development and evaluation of programs designed to help underachievers increase their scholastic performance. One of the few extensive programs for under-achievers was carried out in one New York City high school and is reported by Raph, Goldberg, and Passow.[59] Initially, one tenth grade class of gifted underachieving boys was assigned to the same teacher for home-room and for social studies. It was hypothesized that if these students could share one another's problems and could at the same time become closely identified with and receive support from a teacher, their general

[59] Raph, Goldberg, and Passow, pp. 136–179.

attitudes and performances would improve. Although some students did improve, the average marks earned by underachievers in this class were not significantly different from the average marks earned by matched underachievers in the regular school program.

In the eleventh grade, this special class was assigned to a social studies teacher who had been successful in working with honor students. This teacher, expecting high-quality performance, was unable to accept the erratic, tardy, and often slipshod work of these students. School marks dropped precipitously, and resistance to the teacher was expressed in poor work and disturbing class behavior. The special class was placed with a different teacher in the second semester, a teacher who allowed more leeway in performance standards, showed interest in individual problems of students, and taught much-needed study skills. Although individual students showed improvements in school marks, at the end of two years the average marks received by members of this special group did not differ significantly from those of the underachieving control group. This experience seems to suggest that grouping underachievers together in a class may not be wise, since underachieving classmates tend to give one another negative support.

Placing other groups of underachievers in a special geometry class and in group guidance and study skill classes also resulted in no significant improvement in school marks. It appears that for many underachieving students underachievement becomes a deeply rooted way of life, unamenable to change through school efforts. If this is so, then perhaps preventive programs, administered early in elementary school, would be more efficacious than curative programs, administered in later grades.

A similar approach to helping underachieving gifted pupils was used by Smith.[60] An eighth grade class in arithmetic was organized so that three class sessions a week were devoted to subject matter and two class sessions a week were conducted as seminars. Through seminar discussions, efforts were made to help students develop more adequate self-concepts. By the end of the year, 11 of the 16 students had shown some academic improvement, with seven of these maintaining their level of progress through the ninth grade. Those improving in achievement were found to have replaced negative self-attitudes with positive ones.

The influence of a supportive adult in reducing underachievement by listening and reacting to a student's discussions of topics of personal interest was demonstrated by Raths[61] in a study cited in Chapter 18. In face-to-face conferences, a nonteaching adult, by providing empathic support, endeavored to help an underachiever clarify his attitudes, beliefs, interests, purposes, and aspirations. After one semester, the group of underachievers receiving this treatment registered a significant change toward higher rank in class and grade point average; a control group of underachievers did not.

---

[60] M. C. Smith, "Motivating the Underachieving Gifted Pupil in Junior High School," *Journal of Secondary Education*, 36 (1961), 79–82.

[61] James D. Raths, "Underachievement and a Search for Values," *Journal of Educational Sociology*, 34 (May 1961), 423–424.

Will underachievers make greater progress if placed in a class of equally bright but achieving students (homogeneous grouping), or will they make greater progress in a classroom where there are varying levels of achievement (heterogeneous grouping)? Karnes and her associates,[62] in studying this problem in grades two to five, hypothesized that gifted underachievers placed in homogeneous classes with high achievers would be stimulated to raise their level of achievement, would become more creative, and would perceive their peers and parents as being more accepting of of them than would underachieving intellectually gifted children in heterogeneous classes. Karnes and her associates found that underachievers in homogeneous classes make greater gains in achievement, score higher on a test of creativity, and express a greater acceptance and valuing of their parents than do underachieving gifted children placed in heterogeneous classes.

Summary

Nearly every teacher has seen in his classroom some students with physical, emotional, or mental handicaps that cause them to make little progress in school. These children have come to be referred to as exceptional children. An *exceptional child* is one who deviates intellectually, physically, socially, or emotionally so markedly from what is considered to be normal growth and development that he requires a special class or supplementary instruction and services. Three types of exceptional children who arouse the concern of most teachers are the culturally disadvantaged child, the emotionally disturbed child, and the underachiever.

The culturally disadvantaged child is one whose poverty both limits his chances for achieving minimal physical comfort and well-being and restricts his opportunities for the education that would enable him to escape from the bonds of poverty. The limited stimulation and inadequate training which the disadvantaged child experiences during the preschool years ill prepare him for reading and academic learning in school. Disadvantaged children tend to depend more on concrete than on symbolic experiences in learning concepts. At the same time, their perceptual styles and linguistic modes appear to be either inadequate for or irrelevant to the academic demands of the traditional school.

The observed lower achievement and apathy of many disadvantaged children have created the unfortunate impression in the minds of many middle class teachers that lower class children in general cannot learn. If teachers respond to these children as if they are unable to learn, the children will come to believe they cannot learn and proceed to behave in a

---

[62] M. B. Karnes et al., "The Efficacy of Two Organizational Plans for Underachieving Intellectually Gifted Children," *Exceptional Children*, 30 (May 1963), 438–446.

manner that confirms "self-fulfilling prophecy." To be an effective teacher of disadvantaged children requires that one genuinely accept these children and their cultural differences. It is evident, too, that curriculum content in ghetto classes should focus on topics that relate to the real life experiences of these children and utilize concrete modes of thinking.

A recognition of the language and experiential handicaps of disadvantaged children has led to the development of numerous programs designed to raise their academic performance. For the most part, Head Start and similar programs have focused on providing intensive language and developmental experiences during the preschool years. Although controlled studies of some projects in compensatory education show remarkable achievement gains by disadvantaged children during the period of treatment, these gains are seldom maintained in follow-up testing. The disappointing results appear to reflect continued stereotyped beliefs that disadvantaged children are incapable of making normal academic progress. Some of the ineffectiveness of compensatory education may be due to a lack of innovative methods and materials for these children.

Of all the many kinds of students who need special help, the emotionally disturbed child is one whom the teacher in a regular classroom frequently finds most difficult to understand and to help. Disturbing behavior may be repetitious behavior, such as continual aggressiveness, distractions, or daydreaming; a serious single disturbance, such as a severe temper tantrum or sharp decline in academic performance; or a succession of different disturbances that may appear to be unrelated.

Many of the principles of behavior that increase our understanding of normal students are also useful in the study of the emotionally disturbed. When seeking to identify causes of behavior, the teacher is cautioned to avoid the assumption that one has explained behavior if he has given it a label or described its symptoms. Teachers are advised to weigh symptoms and to consider their relations to their assumed or known causes. Collecting reliable information about an emotionally disturbed student is a necessary first step toward helping him.

Characteristic of nearly all categories of emotional disturbance is high anxiety. Since a child's anxiety must be reduced before the child can make progress in mastering academic skills, the teacher must recognize manifestations of anxiety and modify the situation so as to reduce that anxiety. The anxieties of emotionally disturbed children may be reduced through selective programming and modification of curriculum content. A therapeutic curriculum for emotionally disturbed children should emphasize meaningful emotional content useful in explaining human action, should clarify emotional distortions, should define and classify emotions in terms of appropriateness or inappropriateness, and should teach the meaning of facial expressions and gestures.

Among the programs that have been developed to assist teachers in working with emotionally disturbed students are those that provide on-the-spot help to teachers of emotionally disturbed children or provide a "crisis teacher" in a school to work directly with these children when problems arise.

The problem of why many high-ability students do not achieve at levels commensurate with their potential has been for many years the focus of considerable concern on the part of educators. In general, an *under-achiever* can be defined as a student whose academic performance, judged by either grades or achievement test scores, is markedly below his measured or demonstrated aptitude for academic achievement.

Family, social class, and cultural factors appear to be related to underachievement. Moreover, underachievement among males appears to be a distinctly different phenomenon from underachievement among females. In cognitive activity, the underachiever tends to be more analytic, more abstract, and more likely to dig under the surface of a problem, while overachievers are more empirical and excel in tasks that require a good memory. The self-concepts of male underachievers reveal that they see themselves as inadequate, mischievous, argumentative, and restless. Often, they feel alienated from society and family and do not accept the ideals, goals, and values of the dominant culture. Underachieving girls tend to be ambivalent in their feelings toward themselves. The poorer personal adjustment of underachievers is reflected in their antisocial tendencies, their poorer family relations, their complaining, their hostility, their dissatisfaction, and their strong urge to escape the pressures of school.

Few researchers have focused on helping the underachiever to improve his academic performance. Helping underachievers to clarify their attitudes, beliefs, and aspirations through empathic support appears to hold considerable promise for helping the underachiever to improve his academic performance. Placing gifted underachievers in classes with high achievers seems to result in the underachievers raising their academic performance. Several studies have noted, however, that placing underachievers together in one class or group may not be wise, since underachieving classmates tend to give one another negative support and block the progress of the group.

Study Questions

1. What learning experiences would you plan for disadvantaged students in your class who seem unable to handle the regular curriculum?

2. The "self-fulfilling prophecy" relates to the expectations which teachers have of students' academic performance. Should we as teachers avoid having any expectations or goals concerning our students' school achievement? Discuss.

3. Describe the range of behaviors revealed by emotionally disturbed students at the maturity level you plan to teach. What are some of the ways in which you would try to help these students?

4. Which of the special programs for helping teachers understand and work with emotionally disturbed students that you have learned about

appear best suited for helping you and the emotionally disturbed students whom you plan to teach? Discuss.

5.   What explanations would you offer for the seemingly limited understanding of the causes of underachievement that research studies have provided? What hypotheses would you offer to explain this phenomenon?

6.   Should a student have a right to be an underachiever if he chooses, or should we deny him that right? Discuss.

Suggested Readings

Fantini, Mario D., and Gerald Weinstein. *The Disadvantaged: Challenge to Education.* New York: Harper & Row, 1968. Views the problems of the disadvantaged in the larger context of the total educational establishment and society. Contends that only through understanding the problems of the disadvantaged can we come to an understanding of the educational problems confronting all children in America. Presents many excellent examples of curriculum innovations that can be used in facilitating the learning of the disadvantaged.

Long, Nicholas J., William C. Morse, and Ruth G. Newman, eds. *Conflict in the Classroom.* Belmont, Calif.: Wadsworth Publishing Co., 1965. A book of readings discussing methods of identifying, helping, teaching, and treating emotionally disturbed children in the classroom. Chapters 4 and 5 describe several types of school programs being used to help these students.

Passow, A. H., ed. *Education in Depressed Areas.* New York: Bureau of Publications, Teachers College, Columbia University, 1963. A series of papers analyzing the unique development, the nature of existing and required instructional procedures, the characteristics of personnel and material resources, and other aspects of the problems faced by schools in depressed urban areas.

Raph, Jane B., Miriam L. Goldberg, and A. H. Passow. *Bright Underachievers.* New York: Teachers College Press, Columbia University, 1966. Reviews studies of underachievement and reports the findings of two extensive studies of underachievement conducted by the Horace Mann-Lincoln Institute of Teachers College, Columbia University.

Films

The Exceptional Child: The Socially Maladjusted Child, 16 mm, sound, black and white, 29 min. Bloomington: Audiovisual Center, Indiana University. Discusses the problems of the socially maladjusted child and explains the causes and factors related to the development of maladjustment. Interviews with a delinquent boy and the parent of a socially maladjusted youngster are shown.

Problem of Pupil Adjustment: The Dropout, 16 mm, sound, black and white, 20 min. Bloomington: Audiovisual Center, Indiana University. Examines the reasons the school failed to meet the needs of Steve Martin, who dropped out of school as soon as the law permitted. Emphasizes the importance of a life adjustment program in the school and of relating class subjects to the interests of the students.

Problem of Pupil Adjustment: The Stay-In, 16 mm, sound, black and white, 19 min. Bloomington: Audiovisual Center, Indiana University. Shows how a school which concentrates on meeting the needs of students can reduce the number of dropouts.

Teaching and the Educative Process　　23

The degree to which I can create relationships which facilitate the growth of others as separate persons is a measure of the growth I have achieved in myself.

Carl R. Rogers

Creating the conditions that facilitate optimum development and learning calls for effective teaching. There is little agreement, however, on the criteria that should be used for judging effective teaching or on how the effectiveness of teaching can be measured. By examining briefly some of the approaches that have been used to define and measure teaching effectiveness, we may be able to gain a clearer understanding of the problem.

If the goal of the educative process is to bring about certain desired changes in pupils, an obvious way of assessing a teacher's effectiveness is to measure the extent to which these changes actually occur under the teacher's tutelage. Judging teacher effectiveness in this manner is not as simple as it appears; difficulties arise in measuring pupil growth and in determining precisely how much of the change can be directly attributed to the teacher. It is difficult to obtain comparable measures of pupil growth for pupils who differ in aptitudes, initial level of learning, and rate of intellectual development. The difficulty of determining precisely what changes can be attributed to the teacher relates to our inability to distinguish between what the present learning situation and what past learning situations have each contributed to a student's present performance.

Another approach to the problem of judging teacher effectiveness has been to identify, according to some external criterion, a group of "effective" teachers and a contrasting group of "ineffective" teachers. The external criterion chosen might be the gain students have made on a standardized achievement test or the independence and flexibility students demonstrate in solving problems. A large number of teacher characteristics studies have been conducted for the purpose of discovering which traits or combinations of traits are closely associated with the chosen criterion of teacher effectiveness. Finding that certain traits are highly correlated with the criterion would permit one to predict that an individual possessing these traits would become an effective teacher. However, the results of most of these studies have been disappointing. For a host of variables (including intelligence, mastery of subject matter, age, experience, cultural background, socioeconomic status, sex, marital status, teaching attitude, teaching aptitude, job interest, voice quality, and special abilities), little or no relationship has been found with teaching effectiveness.

The view that effective teaching is a matter of acquiring certain competencies is also open to question. Combs[1] points out that we can seldom prescribe what a beginner should do by examining what an expert does. Some methods used by the expert can only be used because he is an expert. An experienced teacher, for example, may have learned to deal with classroom disturbances by ignoring them, but the beginning teacher dare not ignore them. Moreover, the development of long lists of competencies has the discouraging effect of setting impossible goals of excellence. The fallacy of using particular competencies as a measure of good teaching, irrespective of personalities, situations, or purposes, is evident when we realize that by such a criterion some of the people who taught us most would be classified as poor teachers! The difficulties in defining and assessing effective teaching have been summarized by Ellena, Stevenson, and Webb: "There appears to be no such single person as the universally effective teacher. Teaching is a complex of professions, each widely differing in requirements and activities. Teaching is as complex as the educational process in the modern world."[2]

The relatively fruitless efforts that have been expended in attempts to identify characteristics of effective teaching have led to a new and quite different concept of teaching. This new conception of teaching centers in *what the teacher is*, his personal sense of being and becoming, rather than in what the teacher does. This does not reflect a view of the teacher as passive. Rather, it reflects a view of the teacher's activity as a response to the personal meanings that emerge from his analysis and understanding of his students' needs, perceptions, and self-concepts, as well as his own needs, perceptions, and self-concept. According to this view, what the teacher does in the teaching-learning encounter is done in response not to some prescription of effective teaching but to the personal meanings of the encounter with students.

A Model of Effective Teaching

Our model of effective teaching consists of a series of propositions presented as guidelines for facilitating optimum development and learning.

[1] Arthur W. Combs, *The Professional Education of Teachers* (Boston: Allyn & Bacon, 1965), pp. 4–6.

[2] William J. Ellena, Margaret Stevenson, and Harold V. Webb, *Who's a Good Teacher?* (Washington, D. C.: American Association of School Administrators, Department of Classroom Teachers of the N.E.A., National School Board Association, 1961), p. 36.

23

The model of effective teaching is admittedly global and utopian. In our view, effective teaching should not be judged by the number of students who achieved a given criterion score on an achievement test. Our concern is with broader and more fundamental changes in behavior. In our view, teaching should be judged effective to the degree that both students and teacher are observed during and following a learning experience to be self-involved and actively engaged in the search for the meaning and relevance of ideas and problems that perplex them. In short, learning is effective to the degree that it stimulates students and teacher to engage in self-initiated searches for increased understanding. This type of behavior is most characteristic of what has been variously described as the self-actualizing person,[3] the fully functioning person,[4] or the adequate personality.[5] This is an individual who is experiencing self-fulfillment, who is becoming that which he is capable of being.

1. The effective teacher is involved and concerned with people.   Involvement with and concern for others is the hallmark of a real human being in the full meaning of the term. The teacher's involvement and concern are centered in his students and in their development and learning. What a teacher is and does must, of necessity, relate to those whom he seeks to guide and help. Too many teachers view their task as teaching subjects or skills rather than as helping people to grow and to learn. While effective teaching certainly calls for much more than being involved and concerned, optimum learning of students is unlikely to occur when these qualities are lacking in the teacher-pupil relationship.

Kelley describes the stake which the fully functioning person has in others: "He has a selfish interest in those around him and has responsibility in some degree for that quality."[6] The concepts of involvement and concern are expressed in a question by Rogers: "How can I promote a relationship which this person may use for his own personal growth?"[7] Combs describes the adequate personality as having a strong identification with others: "Warmth and humanity come easily to these people as a logical outgrowth of their feeling of oneness with their fellows."[8]

The introductions to two case records reveal something of the involvement and concern which two teachers felt for two students:

When John was given written assignments to do in school, he would write only one or two sentences. They were so poorly written

[3] A. H. Maslow, *Motivation and Personality* (New York: Harper & Row, 1954).

[4] Carl R. Rogers, *On Becoming a Person* (Boston: Houghton Mifflin Co., 1961).

[5] Arthur W. Combs and Donald Snygg, *Individual Behavior* (New York: Harper & Row, 1959).

[6] Earl C. Kelley, "The Fully Functioning Self," in Arthur W. Combs, ed., *Perceiving, Behaving, Becoming* (Washington, D. C.: Association for Supervision and Curriculum Development, N.E.A., 1962), p. 18.

[7] Rogers, p. 32.

[8] Combs, *Perceiving, Behaving, Becoming*, pp. 54–55.

that they were not legible compared to the work of his peer group. This peer group did not accept him. I thought this would be a good opportunity to try to help John to overcome his writing difficulty and also help him to be accepted by his peer group.

I selected the child designated in this study by his nickname, Skippy, as the most normal child in my room. I also had a personal desire to attain a more sympathetic understanding of children of the Jewish faith, who now form about 50 percent of my class membership.

2. The effective teacher is accepting and empathic in relating to others. A teacher can hardly be involved with and concerned about his students without at the same time experiencing an acceptance of and empathy for them. Indeed, the teacher's involvement and concern are expressed in his acceptance of students as worthwhile, valued individuals, each possessing potentialities for growth and fulfillment.

The focus of the teaching-learning experience is upon what happens to people. Of primary interest and concern are the changes in pupils' development and learning that emerge from the teaching-learning activity. Effective teaching, however, also enhances the growth of the teacher. Few would doubt that teachers learn much from their students, but this learning does not occur automatically. Learning from students is most likely to occur when the teacher is open, perceptive, and sensitive to the feelings as well as the words of students. Involvement, concern, acceptance, and empathy between teacher and pupils are realized only when there is free, open communication between them.

The learning of the teacher from his pupils can take many forms. Frequently, teaching provides opportunities to achieve insights into how people learn or fail to learn. Students' comments, questions, and illustrations will often illuminate meaning and significance in concepts the teacher may not have thought of or considered. If given freedom, encouragement, and opportunities to interact, students will raise significant issues that may never have occurred to the teacher.

The qualities of acceptance and empathy are discussed by Rogers:

When I can accept another person, which means specifically accepting the feelings and attitudes and beliefs that are a real and vital part of him, then I am assisting him to become a person. . . . If I can provide a certain type of relationship, the other person will discover within himself the capacity to use that relationship for growth, and change and personal development will occur.[9]

---

[9] Rogers, pp. 21, 33.

A teacher's acceptance and empathy toward children can be revealed in a variety of ways, as the following excerpts show.

February 9.   During our sharing periods the past two weeks, the children have shared their hobbies with other members of the class. When John's turn came, he went up in front of the room and said, "Class, I want you to see my new dinosaur model. It is a trachodon, and it was a vegetarian. Trachodon *means 'rough-toothed.' They spent most of their time in water. They had about two thousand teeth. Their worst and greatest enemy was tyrannosaurus rex. These creatures died out by the end of the crustacean period." John pranced back and forth in front of the class as he talked on for more than 20 minutes about the trachodon.*

Finally, Beth cut in, "Don't you know about anything else? I'm sick of hearing about dinosaurs."

John's smile faded; he stuck out his lip and said, "Well, they're important to me."

Mrs. W. volunteered, "Most of us have hobbies or activities which seem almost as important to us as eating. Frank likes baseball, Frances is thrilled with every new addition to her collection of foreign dolls, and for John it is dinosaurs. We have learned a lot today from John about dinosaurs, and we will be counting on John to give us more information about dinosaurs when we begin to study about them in two weeks." John's face broke into a smile as he took his seat.

February 23.   Barbara came to me this morning and said, "Mrs. C., I'm in the best group in arithmetic. Don't you think I'm doing all right?" I told her I thought she was doing very well with our new work in fractions. "Why, then," she asked, "did you call my father and tell him I was failing and would have to do a lot of practicing?" (I was caught!)

I said, "Barbara, some practicing is good for all of us, but I'm afraid your father misunderstood. I'll arrange a conference with him and we'll talk it over." (I have not even talked to the father. I get no response to requests for conferences.)

February 17.   Ben is a 13-year-old slow learner attending a rural school in a mining community. A photographer's representative gave me a sample package of six small photos and one enlargement of a girl with braided hair. Ben said, "Please, Mrs. K., give me one of them."

I said, "Ben, you don't know this girl."

He said, "That doesn't make any difference."

Davy said, "I bet Ben wants it because she looks something like Carol." He turned around and said, "Ben, is that the reason?"

Ben said, "Yes, she has pretty braids like Carol has." I asked what he would do with it. He said he wanted it to put in his room to make it pretty.

Davy said, "Don't give them to Ben. Give them to Stover, Lynn, Barry, and me." (Davy is always trying to strive for recognition from these boys. He rejected Ben on choice of work partners in the sociometric test.)

Ben gave me a hurt look. I said, "Ben, whom would you like me to give them to?"

He said, "I don't care, but I would like to have just one."

I said, "All right, you make your choice, since I have six small ones and one large one."

He gave a big grin and said, "Gee, thanks, I'll take the big one and tack it on the wall in my room where I sleep." I gave the smaller pictures to Davy and the boys he had chosen.

3. The effective teacher accepts and understands himself.   The involvement, concern, acceptance, and empathy of the teacher for others, especially his students, are dependent upon the continuing personal growth of the teacher himself. Acceptance of others is not a quality that suddenly appears fully developed. A number of studies have shown that acceptance of others is achieved to the degree that one accepts himself. In analyzing client statements made during therapy, Sheerer[10] found that there was a substantial and significant positive relationship between expressed attitudes of acceptance of self and expressed acceptance of others.

Self-acceptance and self-understanding are of primary importance in the individual's full development of his potentialities. Fromm points out that concern for others and concern for self are neither alternatives nor opposites. Self-love does not imply selfishness. The ability to love productively springs from a love of self. If one can love only others, he cannot love at all. Fromm concludes, "Just as one has to know another person and his real needs in order to love him, one has to know one's own self in order to understand what the interests of the self are and how they can be served."[11]

Rogers,[12] in his description of a growth-facilitating therapeutic relationship, states that when the therapist is open, genuine, warm, positive, acceptant, and empathic in his relationship with his client, then the client, finding someone else listening acceptantly to his feelings, little by little becomes able to listen to himself. As he expresses more and more hidden and shameful aspects of self, the therapist shows a consistent and unconditional positive regard for him and his feelings. Gradually, the client begins to take the same attitude toward himself; he begins to accept himself as he is and

---

[10] Elizabeth T. Sheerer, "An Analysis of the Relationship between Acceptance for Self and Acceptance and Respect for Others," *Journal of Consulting Psychology*, 13 (June 1949), 169–175.

[11] Erich Fromm, *Man for Himself* (New York: Holt, Rinehart and Winston, 1947), p. 134.

[12] Rogers, pp. 61–63.

is therefore ready to move forward in the process of becoming. The quality of reciprocal self-acceptance achieved in such a therapeutic relationship holds considerable promise for interpersonal relationships in the classroom. As teachers genuinely come to accept themselves, they have a greater readiness to accept students. Self-acceptance in the one has the effect of encouraging reciprocal self-acceptance in the other.

The emphasis that Combs places on self-acceptance in the development of the adequate personality also has implications for effective teaching. The primary quality of the adequate personality is a positive view of self. An individual with an adequate personality sees himself as liked, wanted, accepted, able, and as having dignity, integrity, worth, and importance. It is important that a student preparing to become a teacher feel that "It is all right to be me," and that "This self with which I begin can become a good teacher."[13]

Rogers[14] has indicated that self-acceptance tends to free the individual from guilt and anxiety, which distort his feelings about and perceptions of himself. When one accepts himself, he is able to view himself and his world with increased openness and objectivity, qualities essential to self-understanding.

In the following excerpts the teachers of John and Skippy each demonstrate qualities of self-acceptance and self-understanding:

October 31.   *On Saturday evening, October 29, I helped seat people at the church supper. Today, before school started, John said, "Mrs. W., you sure seated a lot of people Saturday night. You must have enjoyed doing it because you kept on smiling."*

I said, "Yes, I did enjoy seeing a lot of people that I hadn't seen for a long time."

He said with a big grin, "I sure had fun."

November 15.   *Skippy was lingering around my desk, obviously with something to say. So finally I asked, "What is it, Skippy? The thing to do is to say it and get it over with and it won't trouble you."*

Skippy blurted out, "Miss Denham, you weren't fair this morning." (He looked as if it had been an effort to say it.)

Teacher: *"In what way?"*

Skippy: *"You don't like Jackie, and this morning you let it show. You were meaner to him than you are to any of the rest of us."*

Teacher: *"How, Skippy? I simply told him to stay in his seat."*

---

[13] Combs, *The Professional Education of Teachers*, p. 100.
[14] Rogers, pp. 183–198.

Skippy: *"Oh, it wasn't what you said. It was the way you said it. You weren't friends."*

(This is an embarrassingly accurate observation. The child in question is the whiney, immature type I find difficult to sympathize with.)

Because of his marked progress in reading during the fall semester, Skippy was transferred to the higher, A section of fifth grade. On February 17, Miss Denham saw Skippy and asked him how he liked the A section.

Skippy: *"Not so well. I can do the work so far and the kids are nice, but I liked the B section better. You know, those kids have it tough."*

Teacher: *"How?"*

Skippy: *"Well, A kids are brighter and can do more. No matter how hard they try the B kids can't 'cause they're dumber. Why are some kids dumber than others?"*

Teacher: *"Lots of reasons. Environment, homes, heredity, opportunity, illness, handicaps."*

Skippy: *"Why didn't God make everyone equal?"*

Teacher: *"Probably because he realized it would be uninteresting if we were all alike, don't you think?"*

Skippy: *"That isn't what I meant. Why are some kids dumb and why are you deaf?"*

Teacher: *"I don't know that exact answer, but I do know I'm not deaf because God wanted it that way. I had an ear disease that medical men didn't know enough to prevent or control. As they learn more about it, that form of deafness will disappear, and that is the reason it is so important to be eager to learn. Sometimes we help scientists by money contributions to have freedom to learn, and their knowledge removes our inequalities. Make sense?"*

Skippy: *"Un-huh, but it's tough on the guys who have the inequalities."*

4. An effective teacher is well informed.   Doing an effective job of teaching is a demanding and difficult task. To be effective, a teacher needs to acquire both depth and breadth of knowledge about the subject, content, and skills he is communicating, the learners whom he is helping and guiding, and the learning process.

Many would agree that learning involves much more than merely acquiring information. In an earlier discussion of perception, we noted that knowledge does not exist in its own right before learning begins. Rather, knowledge is unique to the individual, is subjectively held, and is a product of experience. Kelley points out that "we can of course learn from others, but we can only learn those parts of what others can offer which we can fit into our experience and purposes."[15]

Learning, as Combs has suggested, is the acquisition of personal meanings from the data of one's experience: "Any piece of information will have its effect upon behavior in the degree to which an individual discovers its personal meaning."[16] Content, then, must be meaningful to the teacher as well as his students, but a fact, concept, or principle can be expected to mean something quite different for each. Instead of collecting facts, teachers need skills for discovering meaning in facts and for helping students to discover their own meanings in facts.[17]

The teacher can help students to discover personal meanings in facts, concepts, and experiences by helping them to accept and clarify their feelings about events and concepts they encounter. If this is done, learning is likely to be related to the fulfillment of students' purposes rather than the teacher's purposes.

It is probably more difficult now than ever before for the teacher or any professional person to remain knowledgeable and well informed. We are witnessing an explosion of knowledge of awesome proportions. The consequences of this knowledge explosion are profound. One of the most significant of these is the growing tendency to view the human being as an *information processor* rather than as a collector or storer of knowledge. In a world in which it is becoming virtually impossible to know everything, even in one's limited field of interest, the importance of education in helping learners to clarify personal meanings and to become skilled processors of data is clearly evident. Knowledge in the form of facts and information is no longer the mark of an educated man. Rather, the educated person is now one who is continuously developing new processing skills required to cope with the problems posed by an increasingly complex world.

A second implication of the knowledge exposition is that if teachers and others are to continue to be well informed, they must become *lifelong learners*. A teacher may be fairly well informed in his major field when he completes an undergraduate or graduate program, but he will not remain well informed unless he continues to study and to grow. It is imperative

[15] Earl C. Kelley, *Education for What Is Real* (New York: Harper & Row, 1947), p. 62.

[16] Arthur W. Combs, "Personality Theory and Its Implications for Curriculum Development," in Alexander Frazier, ed., *Learning More about Learning* (Washington, D. C.: Association for Supervision and Curriculum Development, N.E.A., 1959), p. 10.

[17] Combs, *The Professional Education of Teachers*, pp. 44–47.

that the teacher keep abreast of developments in the subject fields he teaches and in the field of education.

One of the ways in which teachers can further their knowledge of their profession is through participation in such projects as child study programs. Evaluations of one child-study program have revealed that teachers participating in this type of professional study increase their knowledge of children and youth and that they utilize classroom practices that are more frequently associated with better rather than poorer teaching.[18] Lehman[19] found that among the teachers of one school system who participated in a child and youth study program, 73 percent of those teaching in junior high school and 63 percent of those teaching in elementary school were rated higher by their principals in the spring than they had been in the fall. Other factors undoubtedly contributed to these gains, but it can be presumed that participation in child and youth study was a contributing factor.

Greene[20] found from analyses of their case records on children that teachers participating in a three-year child study program became increasingly more positive in their ways of handling children and showed steady and significant decreases in their use of negative methods of handling children. Teachers who used more positive methods stimulated positive respones from children, whereas teachers who used more negative methods stimulated negative responses. Other studies have shown that during three years of participation in a program of child study, teachers increased in their ability to analyze and to draw sound conclusions from case study data and revealed greater sensitivity to and use of human development principles.[21]

5. *The effective teacher is one who gives of himself in helping others to grow, to learn, and to become.*   This proposition seems to express the essence of what it means to be a teacher. Rogers[22] offers several clues to how a teacher can help a learner to grow, to learn, and to become. Rogers specifies the attributes of a true helper: genuineness and transparency on the part of the helper, warm acceptance and personal valuing of the one being helped, and an ability to see the world and the self of the other person as the other sees them. A person experiencing a relationship based on these qualities can be expected to become more integrated and more effective, more similar to the person he would like to be, more self-directing and self-confident, more understanding and acceptant of others, and better able to cope with problems of life in a more adequate and comfortable manner.

---

[18] Richard M. Brandt and Hugh V. Perkins, "Research Evaluating a Child Study Program," *Monographs of the Society for Research in Child Development*, 21 (1956), 62.

[19] Inez W. Lehman, "Evaluation of the Individual Child Study Groups in Long Beach, California" (unpublished master's thesis, Stanford University, 1952).

[20] John D. Greene, "Changes in Curriculum Practices of Teachers Who Participated in Child Study" (unpublished doctor's dissertation, University of Maryland, 1952).

[21] Brandt and Perkins, pp. 35–38, 68–76.

[22] Rogers, pp. 37–38.

A helping relationship between a teacher and students can mainfest itself through many different responses and activities. The following are some general patterns of helping relationships:

1. *Children are free to express what they feel and seem secure in their knowledge that the teacher likes them as they are.*

2. *Goals are clearly defined; structure is understood and accepted by the group.*

3. *Within appropriate limits, children are given responsibility and freedom to work.*

4. *Less teacher domination; more faith that children can find answers satisfying to them.*

5. *Less teacher talk; more listening to children, allowing them to use the teacher and the group as a sounding board when ideas are explored.*

6. *Less questioning for the right answer, more open-ended questions with room for differences and exploration of many answers.*

7. *More acceptance of mistakes. The very process of becoming involves the challenge of new experiences, of trying the unknown, all of which necessarily results in some mistakes being made.*

8. *The teacher communicates clearly to children that learning is self-learning. Faith is demonstrated that all children want to become, and pupils show satisfaction as they become aware of their growth.*[23]

A teacher who possesses a fair measure of the qualities which we have enumerated has numerous opportunities for helping a student to develop, to learn, and to become. One teacher with the qualities necessary to establish a helping relationship is Mrs. W., who is portrayed in the following excerpts.

December 5.   *The class was in line to get dressed for the physical education period. John was sitting at his desk, and his P.E. clothes were in his hands. I asked, "John, aren't you going to dress for P.E. today?"*

He put his head down and said in a low, defeated-like voice, "I

[23] Combs, *Preceiving, Behaving, Becoming*, p. 237.

don't want to dress for P.E. I can't do the things the other kids can do anyway. Could I please be excused from dressing?"

I said in a kindly and encouraging voice, "John, you may be excused but please try *to do what the class does.* You can if you try. *Nearly everyone has some things in life that are hard for them to do. I had trouble learning to roller skate when I was a little girl. I always say, 'Practice makes perfect.' " The class said, "Come on, John. We will help you."*

He lifted his head and said with a big smile, "I'll try real hard." The rest of the children dressed, and all went to P.E. class.

December 16. We were writing stories about our pets. The participation and results were very good. Each child had his story ready to correct by the middle of the period. John brought his story on dinosaurs to me, smiled, and said, "When I try I can really accomplish things that I want to do and have it ready on time." His story was good, and no corrections had to be made.

I patted him on the back and said, "John, I am really proud of the job you have done. Please keep that effort alive!"

He smiled and said, "OK."

March 6. After school we were talking about the short unit we had planned on dinosaurs. I said, "John, since your hobby is the study of dinosaurs, I would like for you to take charge. We have planned and formed our questions. But you don't always complete your other assignments."

He jumped up like a jack-in-the-box and in a very loud voice said, "Completing the assignments is no problem—I'll get them done! If I take charge, will you call me 'Professor'? I am so excited!"

The following excerpt illustrates the helping relationship of Miss Denham with Skippy, one of her fifth grade students:

January 24. Skippy asked me for a conference to discuss the poor test grades he had received recently. He asked me to write a note to his parents explaining the situation, as Skippy's father has been very critical of his low marks. In the note, I explained Skippy's request for the note, that I felt that he did not need a tutor because he was capable of doing the work and a tutor might make him weaker because he would rely on outside help, that his low grades were due to a phase of poor conduct which I felt was already past, that Skippy had made nearly a year's progress in reading in a half year by standard measurements and I thought that should be considered good.

Skippy read the note and asked, "Will you please change that to Mr. Roth? Dad gets mad because teachers always send everything to Mom."

I changed my greeting from Dear Mrs. Roth to Dear Mr. and Mrs. Roth.

Skippy: *"You see, Dad always shows up when things go wrong, gets the wrong idea, and raises Cain. I go to Maine to camp every year and it's grand there. The very day Mom and Dad came to see me one of the kids hit me in the face with a hard ball and I had a couple of teeth out and some stitches in my lip when Dad saw me. He nearly had a fit and wanted to bring me right home. I had an awful hard time showing him it was just an accident and the camp does take care of us."*

Teacher: *"He wants you to be just about perfect, doesn't he?"*

Skippy: *"I guess thats' it."*

Teacher: *"I wonder if you can realize that might be one of your troubles, Skippy. You are trying so hard to please your dad on tests that maybe you guess rather than think. I really think you could read better than your reading score indicated, but you tried to read too fast and made too many mistakes."*

Skippy: *"Maybe. I'm always scared."*

Teacher: *"Couldn't you face the fact that you are trying to do your best on tests and let it go at that?"*

Skippy: *"I can try. There's one thing more. Could you please let me take that spelling test over and not tell Dad?"*

Teacher (*at this point wisdom deserted me and I decided in favor of the golden rule*): *"Yes."*

Skippy: *"Gee, thanks. You're a pal."*

The model of the effective teacher presented above has focused more on what the teacher is than upon specific characteristics of what he does. We do not wish to leave the impression that our effective teacher is a superman or superwoman. Effective teachers can be found in nearly every school. Many, indeed, are superior persons, and most have developed capacities for continuous self-growth. As one studies the chapters of this book in seeking an understanding of the ways in which the processes of human development and learning influence the becoming of children and youth, the sensitive, growing teacher cannot help reflecting on how these same processes, motivational, physical, cultural, and psychological, have shaped his own life. It is true that our personalities have been formed by many influences, both favorable and unfavorable, and that over some of these influences we had little control.

Summary

The relatively fruitless efforts that have been made to identify the characteristics of effective teaching have led to the development of a conception of teaching centering in what a teacher *is,* his personal sense of being and becoming, rather than on what a teacher *does.* This concept of effective teaching is expressed in the teacher's unique responses to the personal meanings of his encounter with students.

We propose a model of effective teaching consisting of five propositions that define dimensions of the process of facilitating optimum development and learning. The guidelines or criteria embodied in the propositions of the model define the effective teacher's role in the teaching-learning activity. The five propositions of the model are as follows:

1.   *The effective teacher is involved and concerned with people.*

2.   *The effective teacher is accepting and empathic in relating to others.*

3.   *The effective teacher accepts and understands himself.*

4.   *The effective teacher is well informed.*

5.   *The effective teacher is one who gives of himself in helping others to grow, to learn, and to become.*

Education is predicated on the belief that people can change. An understanding of human development and learning offers a key to the continual growth and becoming of both students and teacher.

Study Questions

1.   Some educators have suggested that a major task of preservice teacher education is to help prospective teachers develop a view of teaching that is not confined to the view they acquired as students. What are some of the reasons that students' attitudes toward teaching are often more strongly influenced by what they have experienced as students than by what has been communicated in professional courses in teacher education?

2.   Write out a brief description of one of the best teachers you have ever had. In what ways are the qualities of your best teacher similar to or different from those of the effective teacher presented in this chapter?

3.   What kinds of experiences should prospective teachers have to enable them to develop the qualities suggested by the model of effective teaching? Discuss.

4.   Are all persons capable of achieving a measure of self-understanding? What factors or experiences would likely contribute to self-understanding, and what ones might be expected to limit one's understanding of himself? Discuss.

Suggested Readings

Ashton-Warner, Sylvia. *Teacher*. New York: Bantam Books, 1963. Story of a gifted teacher's methods and experiences teaching the Maori children of New Zealand. Describes learning as an organic experience serving to bridge one culture to another. Affirms that learning based upon the child's intrinsic interests produces dramatic effects in personal fulfillment.

Combs, Arthur W., ed. *Perceiving, Behaving, Becoming*. Washington, D.C.: Association for Supervision and Curriculum Development, N.E.A., 1962. Contains papers by Kelley, Maslow, Rogers, and Combs describing the qualities of the fully functioning, self-actualizing, truly adequate personality. The implications of the concept of the adequate personality for teaching and learning are discussed.

Combs, Arthur W. *The Professional Education of Teachers*. Boston: Allyn & Bacon, 1965. Discusses the implications for teaching of perceptual psychology—which is deeply concerned with people, values, perceptions, and man's eternal search for being and becoming—and the problem of improving teacher education.

Rogers, Carl R. *Freedom to Learn*. Columbus, Ohio: Merrill Publishing Co., 1969. An eminent psychotherapist and founder of client-centered therapy speaks to teachers in describing learning in which students and teacher are free to discover and explore the personal meanings of their experiences. Proposes a person-oriented education that would, if adopted, revolutionize education.

Films

Guiding the growth of Children, 16 mm, sound, black and white, 18 min. Bloomington: Audiovisual Center, Indiana University. Shows through the personal experiences of a fifth grade teacher that guiding the growth of the student as an individual is the most important part of the teacher's job.

If These Were Your Children, Part 1, 16 mm, sound, black and white, 28 min.; Part 2, 16 mm, sound, black and white, 21 min. New York: Metropolitan Life Insurance Co., 1 Madison Ave. Shows how a concerned, accepting, and knowledgeable teacher provides a stimulating, growth-facilitating environment enhancing the development and learning of a second grade class. Specific problems of development and individual differences among children are highlighted.

Case Index

Author Index

Subject Index